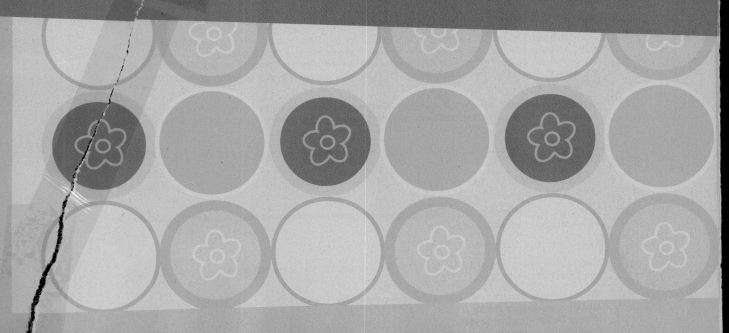

# BLOSSOM

## THE COMPLETE NEW TESTAMENT

**NELSON BIBLES**
A Division of Thomas Nelson Publishers
*Since 1798*

www.thomasnelson.com

**NCV**™
NEW CENTURY VERSION®

# Blossom: The Complete New Testament

# TABLE OF CONTENTS

# Letter from the Editors

You could use many different words to describe the Bible.

The Bible is like a flashlight or a lighthouse. When the world feels like a dark place or you feel lost, the Bible makes things seem brighter, and it shows you the right way to go.

The Bible is like a telescope. A telescope makes far-away stars and planets seem really close. When God seems really far away, the Bible helps us see him more clearly.

The Bible is like a mirror. When you read it, you see yourself in it. It teaches you things about yourself—good things and things you have to change.

The Bible is like bread and water. When your soul is hungry and thirsty, reading God's Word fills you up.

The Bible is like a sword. When you know the truth in the Bible, you have a weapon that you can use to fight against the temptation to do wrong things.

The Bible is like a friend. When you're all alone, reading your Bible makes you feel like God is right there with you, talking to you. (He is!)

The Bible is like a novel, an encyclopedia, a poem, and a letter all rolled into one. The Bible tells many stories of God and his people; it gives important information that we need in our lives; it contains beautiful poetry; and God tells us about his love from the first page to the last. In fact, the Bible is a little like a magazine, too, because it has so many different types of "articles" to read.

Here are some other types of articles you'll find in your Blossom BibleZine: Dig Deeper explains different Bible verses in a way that makes sense for your life today. Read It/Do It gives easy-to-follow ideas on how to live out what the Bible teaches. You'll also find many of God's Promises explained. The Q&A boxes have helpful answers to questions girls your age are asking. Check out Be Your Best and Cool! for great advice and quirky facts that can help you grow as a Christian. Read about what other tween girls are doing for God in the Shine Your Light articles. The monthly Calendars will give you lots to look forward to, and the Quizzes will help you get to know yourself better.

There are a few other neat features in Blossom, but we'll let you discover the rest yourself. We know you're going to want to read all the great articles, but don't forget to read the most important part of this book: the black-and-white words of the New Testament! The rest won't help you much if you're not digging into God's Word. Keep a notebook handy to write down things you want to remember and to do some of the suggested exercises.

Our prayer is that as you read your Bible, you will blossom into the wonderful girl God made you to be!

—The Editors of Blossom

# A Note about the NEW CENTURY VERSION

God never intended the Bible to be too difficult for his people. To make sure God's message was clear, the authors of the Bible recorded God's Word in familiar everyday language. These books brought a message that the original readers could understand. These first readers knew that God spoke through these books. Down through the centuries, many people wanted a Bible so badly that they copied different Bible books by hand!

Today, now that the Bible is readily available, many Christians do not regularly read it. Many feel that the Bible is too hard to understand or irrelevant to life.

The *New Century Version* captures the clear and simple message that the very first readers understood. This version presents the Bible as God intended it: clear and dynamic.

A team of scholars from the World Bible Translation Center worked together with twenty-one other experienced Bible scholars from all over the world to translate the text directly from the best available Greek and Hebrew texts. You can trust that this Bible accurately presents God's Word as it came to us in the original languages.

Translators kept sentences short and simple. They avoided difficult words and worked to make the text easier to read. They used modern terms for places and measurements. And they put figures of speech and idiomatic expressions ("he was gathered to his people") in language that even children understand ("he died").

Following the tradition of other English versions, the *New Century Version* indicates the divine name, *Yahweh*, by putting LORD, and sometimes GOD, in capital letters. This distinguishes it from *Adonai*, another Hebrew word that is translated Lord.

We acknowledge the infallibility of God's Word and yet our own frailty. We pray that God will use this Bible to help you understand his rich truth for yourself. To God be the glory.

# Prayers & Reflection

## Prayer of Salvation

Dear God, thank you for loving me and for making a way for me to be with you in heaven. I know that I am a sinner and that I can never be perfect. Please forgive me for my sins and come into my life. I believe that you are the Lord and Father of all. I believe that your Son, Jesus Christ, died on the cross for my sins, was raised from the dead, and lives today with you in heaven. Lord, please help me to stay strong in my faith as I face many important decisions and major temptations during my teenage years. I want my life to show how much I love you every day. I give my life and my heart to you. Amen.

*If you have just prayed the Prayer of Salvation, we would love to hear from you.*
*Please log on to www.myfaithandlife.com and click on "Share Your Story."*
*Welcome to the family of God!*

## Prayer of Dedication to God

Dear Lord, today I pray that you will open my ears, my eyes, and my heart to what you want to teach me. I want to know you, Father. As I read the Bible today, please teach me something new about who you are and about how I can love you more. I pray that you will take my life and mold me into the girl you want me to be. Lord, I want to obey you every day and to show your love to my friends and family. Please help me to be kind, humble, wise, patient, and gentle. I give this day and our time together to you—I'm excited to spend time with you. In your holy name. Amen.

## Time of Reflection

What praises and prayer requests are you talking with God about today? What do you hope to learn from your time with God as you read through *Blossom*? Sometimes it helps to get things down on paper, so feel free to use this next section to record your thoughts.

_____

_____

_____

_____

_____

_____

# THE COMPLETE NEW TESTAMENT

# MATTHEW

**D**o you ever feel like you don't belong? Matthew really didn't fit in! He was a Jew who collected taxes for the Roman government. Since the Romans ruled the Jews at that time, the Jews saw tax collectors as enemy agents!

But when Jesus invited Matthew to follow him, Matthew dropped what he was doing to go with Jesus. Imagine—the teacher *everyone* was talking about wanted to be with him! Matthew's life was changed forever. Later he wrote this book so other people could know and follow Jesus.

Matthew's readers were probably Jews who had been reading the Old Testament all their lives. Matthew was careful to point out the Old Testament prophecies about Jesus' life. When you read Matthew's book, look for statements like this: "So what God had said through the prophet Jeremiah came true" (Matthew 2:17).

Some other highlights from Matthew are:

➜ Matthew 5—7 (sometimes called *The Sermon on the Mount*): This collection of Jesus' teachings gives us guidelines for living.

➜ Matthew 5:3—10 (also called the *Beatitudes*): These promises describe the good things we can expect, even if we have hard times now.

➜ Matthew 28:19—20 (some people call this the *Great Commission*): Matthew knew that most of the people who read his book would be Jews, but he also wanted non-Jewish people to hear the Good News. His book contains Jesus' final instructions for his followers. Jesus told them to tell people all over the world about him.

# MATTHEW TELLS ABOUT JESUS, THE KING OF THE JEWS

## THINGS TO TALK WiTH GOD ABOUT . . .

### The Family History of Jesus

1 This is the family history of Jesus Christ. He came from the family of David, and David came from the family of Abraham.

[2] Abraham was the father[n] of Isaac.
Isaac was the father of Jacob.
Jacob was the father of Judah and his brothers.
[3] Judah was the father of Perez and Zerah.
(Their mother was Tamar.)
Perez was the father of Hezron.
Hezron was the father of Ram.
[4] Ram was the father of Amminadab.
Amminadab was the father of Nahshon.
Nahshon was the father of Salmon.
[5] Salmon was the father of Boaz.
(Boaz's mother was Rahab.)
Boaz was the father of Obed.
(Obed's mother was Ruth.)
Obed was the father of Jesse.
[6] Jesse was the father of King David.
David was the father of Solomon.
(Solomon's mother had been Uriah's wife.)
[7] Solomon was the father of Rehoboam.

Rehoboam was the father of Abijah.
Abijah was the father of Asa.[n]
[8] Asa was the father of Jehoshaphat.
Jehoshaphat was the father of Jehoram.
Jehoram was the ancestor of Uzziah.
[9] Uzziah was the father of Jotham.
Jotham was the father of Ahaz.
Ahaz was the father of Hezekiah.
[10] Hezekiah was the father of Manasseh.

speakout!

What things worry you the most?

Going in deep water worries me because I don't know how to swim well. —Katie, 10

## Bible Bios
Miriam (Exodus 2:1–10; Numbers 12:1–15)

We first see Miriam's wisdom and loyalty in the way she quickly came up with a plan to protect her baby brother, Moses, from the Egyptians. Later, as a grown woman, she used the talents God had given her to lead the Hebrew women in praising God (Exodus 15:20–21). But Miriam became jealous. She felt people listened to Moses more than to her. She convinced her other brother, Aaron, to speak badly about Moses with her. God was furious about this! He gave them a serious warning and then Miriam discovered she had a terrible skin disease called leprosy. Her brothers begged God to forgive her and, after seven days, he did heal her. Don't let jealousy ruin your life! Use the special gifts God gave you . . . without comparing yourself to others.

1:2 **father** *"Father" in Jewish lists of ancestors can sometimes mean grandfather or more distant relative.* 1:7 **Asa** *Some Greek copies read "Asaph," another name for Asa (see 1 Chronicles 3:10).*

Manasseh was the father of Amon.
Amon was the father of Josiah.
[11] Josiah was the grandfather of
Jehoiachin[n] and his brothers.
(This was at the time that the
people were taken to Babylon.)
[12] After they were taken to Babylon:
Jehoiachin was the father of
Shealtiel.
Shealtiel was the grandfather of
Zerubbabel.
[13] Zerubbabel was the father of Abiud.

Abiud was the father of Eliakim.
Eliakim was the father of Azor.
[14] Azor was the father of Zadok.
Zadok was the father of Akim.
Akim was the father of Eliud.
[15] Eliud was the father of Eleazar.
Eleazar was the father of Matthan.
Matthan was the father of Jacob.
[16] Jacob was the father of Joseph.
Joseph was the husband of Mary,
and Mary was the mother of
Jesus.
Jesus is called the Christ.

[17] So there were fourteen generations from Abraham to David. And there were fourteen generations from David until the people were taken to Babylon. And there were fourteen generations from the time when the people were taken to Babylon until Christ was born.

## The Birth of Jesus Christ

[18] This is how the birth of Jesus Christ came about. His mother Mary was engaged[n] to marry Joseph, but before they married, she learned she was pregnant by the power of the Holy Spirit. [19] Because Mary's husband, Joseph, was a good man, he did not want to disgrace her in public, so he planned to divorce her secretly.

[20] While Joseph thought about these things, an angel of the Lord came to him in a dream. The angel said, "Joseph, descendant of David, don't be afraid to take Mary as your wife, because the baby in her is from the Holy Spirit. [21] She will give birth to a son, and you will name him Jesus,[n] because he will save his people from their sins."

[22] All this happened to bring about what the Lord had said through the prophet: [23] "The virgin will be pregnant. She will have a son, and they will name him Immanuel,"[n] which means "God is with us."

[24] When Joseph woke up, he did what the Lord's angel had told him to do. Joseph took Mary as his wife, [25] but he did not have sexual relations with her until she gave birth to the son. And Joseph named him Jesus.

## Wise Men Come to Visit Jesus

2 Jesus was born in the town of Bethlehem in Judea during the time when Herod was king. When Jesus was born, some wise men from the east came to Jerusalem. [2] They asked, "Where is the baby who was born to be the king of the Jews? We saw his star in the east and have come to worship him."

[3] When King Herod heard this, he was troubled, as were all the people in Jerusalem. [4] Herod called a meeting of all the leading priests and teachers of the law and asked them where the Christ would be born. [5] They answered, "In the town of Bethlehem in Judea. The prophet wrote about this in the Scriptures:

## dig deeper

### Matthew 4:1–4

You know that little voice. The one that wants you to spread gossip or to lie to your parents about your homework. The voice that reminds you that you're too tired to read your Bible or tells you it's okay to talk back to your teachers. You're not imagining things! The "voice" of temptation belongs to the devil; and he's just as real as any other character in the Bible.

It's not a sin to be tempted; if it was, then Jesus would have sinned! At the very beginning of Jesus' ministry on earth, the Holy Spirit led Jesus to go into the desert for forty days (Matthew 4:1–4). During that time, Jesus didn't have any food. So when the devil showed up to try to trap Jesus into sinning, it must have been very tempting!

Yet Jesus did not sin. In fact, he responded correctly to temptation by saying the truth out loud. He remembered what God had said and he didn't even consider discussing the possibility of turning against his Father.

When you're tempted to sin, remember Jesus' example. He didn't give the devil a chance. Instead, he stood up for the truth he knew from the Bible. You don't have to give in to sin!

1:11 Jehoiachin The Greek reads "Jeconiah," another name for Jehoiachin (see 2 Kings 24:6 and 1 Chronicles 3:16). 1:18 engaged For the Jewish people an engagement was a lasting agreement, which could only be broken by a divorce. If a bride-to-be was unfaithful, it was considered adultery, and she could be put to death. 1:21 Jesus The name "Jesus" means "salvation." 1:23 "The virgin ... Immanuel" Quotation from Isaiah 7:14.

[6]"But you, Bethlehem, in the
    land of Judah,
  are not just an insignificant village
    in Judah.
  A ruler will come from you
    who will be like a shepherd for my
    people Israel.' "          *Micah 5:2*
[7]Then Herod had a secret meeting with the wise men and learned from them the exact time they first saw the star. [8]He sent the wise men to Bethlehem, saying, "Look carefully for the child. When you find him, come tell me so I can worship him too."

[9]After the wise men heard the king, they left. The star that they had seen in the east went before them until it stopped above the place where the child was. [10]When the wise men saw the star, they were filled with joy. [11]They came to the house where the child was and saw him with his mother, Mary, and they bowed down and worshiped him. They opened their gifts and gave him treasures of gold, frankincense, and myrrh. [12]But God warned the wise men in a dream not to go back to Herod, so they returned to their own country by a different way.

## Jesus' Parents Take Him to Egypt

[13]After they left, an angel of the Lord came to Joseph in a dream and said, "Get up! Take the child and his mother and escape to Egypt, because Herod is starting to look for the child so he can kill him. Stay in Egypt until I tell you to return."

[14]So Joseph got up and left for Egypt during the night with the child and his mother. [15]And Joseph stayed in Egypt until Herod died. This happened to bring about what the Lord had said through the prophet: "I called my son out of Egypt."[n]

## Herod Kills the Baby Boys

[16]When Herod saw that the wise men had tricked him, he was furious. So he gave an order to kill all the baby boys in Bethlehem and in the surrounding area who were two years old or younger. This was in keeping with the time he learned from the wise men. [17]So what God had said through the prophet Jeremiah came true:

[18]"A voice was heard in Ramah
    of painful crying and deep
    sadness:
  Rachel crying for her children.
  She refused to be comforted,
    because her children are dead."
                      *Jeremiah 31:15*

## Joseph and Mary Return

[19]After Herod died, an angel of the Lord spoke to Joseph in a dream while he was in Egypt. [20]The angel said, "Get up! Take the child and his mother and go to the land of Israel, because the people who were trying to kill the child are now dead."

[21]So Joseph took the child and his mother and went to Israel. [22]But he heard that Archelaus was now king in Judea since his father Herod had died. So Joseph was afraid to go there. After being warned in a dream, he went to the area of Galilee, [23]to a town called Nazareth, and lived there. And so what God had said through the prophets came true: "He will be called a Nazarene."[n]

## The Work of John the Baptist

**3** About that time John the Baptist began preaching in the desert area of Judea. [2]John said, "Change your hearts and lives because the kingdom of heaven is near." [3]John the Baptist is the one Isaiah the prophet was talking about when he said:

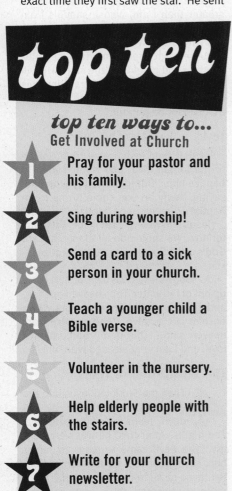

## top ten

### top ten ways to...
### Get Involved at Church

**1** Pray for your pastor and his family.

**2** Sing during worship!

**3** Send a card to a sick person in your church.

**4** Teach a younger child a Bible verse.

**5** Volunteer in the nursery.

**6** Help elderly people with the stairs.

**7** Write for your church newsletter.

**8** Help in the kitchen after a church supper.

**9** Straighten up the chairs.

**10** Show up every week!

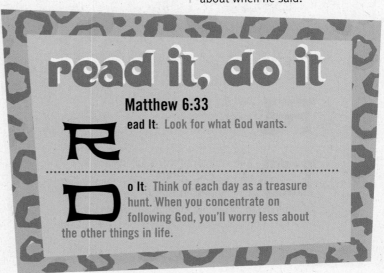

# read it, do it

**Matthew 6:33**

**R**ead It: Look for what God wants.

**D**o It: Think of each day as a treasure hunt. When you concentrate on following God, you'll worry less about the other things in life.

2:15 **"I called . . . Egypt."** *Quotation from Hosea 11:1.*   2:23 **Nazarene** *A person from the town of Nazareth. Matthew may be referring to Isaiah 11:1, where the Hebrew word translated "branch" sounds like "Nazarene."*

# Bible Basics

Sometimes called the Word of God or the Scriptures, the Bible is God's message to us. Think of it as a long letter from God that tells the story of his love for all people—including you! In one Book, we can read history, prophecy, poetry, love stories, letters, proverbs (wise sayings), and laws. The Bible has two main parts with many smaller parts: the Old Testament has thirty-nine books and the New Testament has twenty-seven. Together, these sixty-six books describe all the exciting things God has done from the beginning of the world until the first century A.D. But do you know the best part? The stories and lessons in the Bible still apply to our lives today!

"This is a voice of one
who calls out in the desert:
'Prepare the way for the Lord.
Make the road straight for him.' "
*Isaiah 40:3*

[4] John's clothes were made from camel's hair, and he wore a leather belt around his waist. For food, he ate locusts and wild honey. [5] Many people came from Jerusalem and Judea and all the area around the Jordan River to hear John. [6] They confessed their sins, and he baptized them in the Jordan River.

[7] Many of the Pharisees and Sadducees came to the place where John was baptizing people. When John saw them, he said, "You are snakes! Who warned you to run away from God's coming punishment? [8] Do the things that show you really have changed your hearts and lives.

[9] And don't think you can say to yourselves, 'Abraham is our father.' I tell you that God could make children for Abraham from these rocks. [10] The ax is now ready to cut down the trees, and every tree that does not produce good fruit will be cut down and thrown into the fire.[n]

[11] "I baptize you with water to show that your hearts and lives have changed. But there is one coming after me who is greater than I am, whose sandals I am not good enough to carry. He will baptize you with the Holy Spirit and fire. [12] He will come ready to clean the grain, separating the good grain from the chaff. He will put the good part of the grain into his barn, but he will burn the chaff with a fire that cannot be put out."[n]

## Jesus Is Baptized by John

[13] At that time Jesus came from Galilee to the Jordan River and wanted John to baptize him. [14] But John tried to stop him, saying, "Why do you come to me to be baptized? I need to be baptized by you!"

[15] Jesus answered, "Let it be this way for now. We should do all things that are God's will." So John agreed to baptize Jesus.

[16] As soon as Jesus was baptized, he came up out of the water. Then heaven opened, and he saw God's Spirit coming down on him like a dove. [17] And a voice from heaven said, "This is my Son, whom I love, and I am very pleased with him."

## The Temptation of Jesus

4 Then the Spirit led Jesus into the desert to be tempted by the devil. [2] Jesus fasted for forty days and nights. After this, he was very hungry. [3] The devil came to Jesus to tempt him, saying, "If you are the Son of God, tell these rocks to become bread."

[4] Jesus answered, "It is written in the Scriptures, 'A person lives not on bread alone, but by everything God says.' "[n]

[5] Then the devil led Jesus to the holy city of Jerusalem and put him on a high place of the Temple. [6] The devil said, "If you are the Son of God, jump down, because it is written in the Scriptures:

'He has put his angels in charge
of you.
They will catch you in their hands
so that you will not hit your foot
on a rock.' " *Psalm 91:11–12*

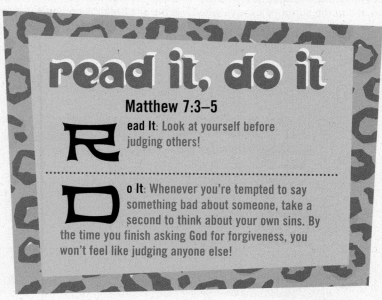

## read it, do it

### Matthew 7:3–5

**Read It**: Look at yourself before judging others!

**Do It**: Whenever you're tempted to say something bad about someone, take a second to think about your own sins. By the time you finish asking God for forgiveness, you won't feel like judging anyone else!

**3:10 The ax . . . fire.** *This means that God is ready to punish his people who do not obey him.* **3:12 He will . . . out.** *This means that Jesus will come to separate good people from bad people, saving the good and punishing the bad.* **4:4 'A person . . . says.'** *Quotation from Deuteronomy 8:3.*

# January

start here

**1** New Year's Day—Write down five dreams you have for this year. Tell God about them!

**2**

**3** Write thank-you cards for special Christmas gifts you received, especially from far-away relatives.

**4**

**5**

**6** Pull out a dictionary and learn 5 new interesting words.

**7**

**8**

**9** Pray for your city's police and fire departments.

**10** Memorize Philippians 4:8.

**11**

**12**

**13** Pray for a person of influence: Today is Orlando Bloom's birthday.

**14**

**15** Ask your mom or dad to tell you something they love about you. Then give them a big hug.

**16** Martin Luther King Day (USA)—Find out who he was and what he did.

**17**

**18**

**19** If there's snow outside, make a snow angel! (If not, make paper snowflakes.)

**20**

**21**

**22** Think of someone at your church that you don't know very well and pray for him or her.

**23**

**24**

**25** Pray for a person of influence: Today is Alicia Keys's birthday.

**26**

**27** Offer to take the trash out this week (and do it!).

**28** Pray for a person of influence: Today is Elijah Wood's birthday.

**29**

**30** Draw a funny cartoon about your best friend and give it to her the next time you see her!

**31** Pray for a person of influence: Today is Justin Timberlake's birthday.

Roxie says, "Make a list!"

[7]Jesus answered him, "It also says in the Scriptures, 'Do not test the Lord your God.' "[n]

[8]Then the devil led Jesus to the top of a very high mountain and showed him all the kingdoms of the world and all their splendor. [9]The devil said, "If you will bow down and worship me, I will give you all these things."

[10]Jesus said to the devil, "Go away from me, Satan! It is written in the Scriptures, 'You must worship the Lord your God and serve only him.' "[n]

[11]So the devil left Jesus, and angels came and took care of him.

## Jesus Begins Work in Galilee

[12]When Jesus heard that John had been put in prison, he went back to Galilee. [13]He left Nazareth and went to live in Capernaum, a town near Lake Galilee, in the area near Zebulun and Naphtali. [14]Jesus did this to bring about what the prophet Isaiah had said:

[15]"Land of Zebulun and land of
     Naphtali
  along the sea,
  beyond the Jordan River.
     This is Galilee where the non-
     Jewish people live.
[16]These people who live in darkness
     will see a great light.
  They live in a place covered with the
     shadows of death,
  but a light will shine on them."

*Isaiah 9:1–2*

## Jesus Chooses Some Followers

[17]From that time Jesus began to preach, saying, "Change your hearts and lives, because the kingdom of heaven is near."

[18]As Jesus was walking by Lake Galilee, he saw two brothers, Simon (called Peter) and his brother Andrew. They were throwing a net into the lake because they were fishermen. [19]Jesus said, "Come follow me, and I will make you fish for people." [20]So Simon and Andrew immediately left their nets and followed him.

[21]As Jesus continued walking by Lake Galilee, he saw two other brothers, James and John, the sons of Zebedee. They were in a boat with their father Zebedee, mending their nets. Jesus told them to come with him. [22]Immediately they left the boat and their father, and they followed Jesus.

## Jesus Teaches and Heals People

[23]Jesus went everywhere in Galilee, teaching in the synagogues, preaching the Good News about the kingdom of heaven, and healing all the people's diseases and sicknesses. [24]The news about Jesus spread all over Syria, and people brought all the sick to him. They were suffering from different kinds of diseases. Some were in great pain, some had demons, some were epileptics,[n] and some were paralyzed. Jesus healed all of them. [25]Many people from Galilee, the Ten Towns,[n] Jerusalem, Judea, and the land across the Jordan River followed him.

## Jesus Teaches the People

5 When Jesus saw the crowds, he went up on a hill and sat down. His followers came to him, [2]and he began to teach them, saying:

[3]"They are blessed who realize their
     spiritual poverty,
  for the kingdom of heaven belongs
     to them.
[4]They are blessed who grieve,
  for God will comfort them.
[5]They are blessed who are humble,
  for the whole earth will be theirs.
[6]They are blessed who hunger and
     thirst after justice,
  for they will be satisfied.
[7]They are blessed who show mercy to
     others,
  for God will show mercy to them.
[8]They are blessed whose thoughts
     are pure,
  for they will see God.
[9]They are blessed who work for peace,
  for they will be called God's
     children.
[10]They are blessed who are persecuted
     for doing good,
  for the kingdom of heaven belongs
     to them.
[11]"People will insult you and hurt you. They will lie and say all kinds of evil

## read it, do it

### Matthew 7:12

**R** ead It: Treat others the way you want to be treated.

**D** o It: Respect your sister's or mom's privacy. If you don't like people going through your stuff or reading your diary, don't do it to others!

**4:7** '**Do . . . God.**' *Quotation from Deuteronomy 6:16.* **4:10** '**You . . . him.**' *Quotation from Deuteronomy 6:13.* **4:24 epileptics** *People with a disease that causes them sometimes to lose control of their bodies and maybe faint, shake strongly, or not be able to move.* **4:25 Ten Towns** *In Greek, called "Decapolis." It was an area east of Lake Galilee that once had ten main towns.*

# dig deeper

## Matthew 5:44

Like most tweens, you can probably think of one or two people who always seem to be mean to you. No matter what you do, they're determined to make your life miserable. Wouldn't it be nice, just once, to get revenge? Well God has a different idea. He says in Matthew 5:44, "But I say to you, love your enemies. Pray for those who hurt you."

What?! You're probably thinking, If they don't care about me, why should I care about them? This was a strange idea to the people in Jesus' time, too. They liked the idea of revenge a whole lot bet-ter. But Jesus wanted to change things, because he loves all people, no matter who they are or what they've done.

It's not easy to love an "enemy." But because God loves us so much, we can share his love with others—even those who are mean to us. Praying for our enemies also helps us learn to care about them. We never know what hurt or loneliness they might be hiding underneath their cruel behavior. Ask God to bless them and to help them accept his love! Loving your enemies is not the easy thing to do, but it's God's way of letting us share his love in a hurting world!

---

ever refuses to obey any command and teaches other people not to obey that command will be the least important in the kingdom of heaven. But whoever obeys the commands and teaches other people to obey them will be great in the kingdom of heaven. [20]I tell you that if you are no more obedient than the teachers of the law and the Pharisees, you will never enter the kingdom of heaven.

### Jesus Teaches About Anger

[21]"You have heard that it was said to our people long ago, 'You must not murder anyone.'[n] Anyone who murders another will be judged.' [22]But I tell you, if you are angry with a brother or sister,[n] you will be judged. If you say bad things to a brother or sister, you will be judged by the council. And if you call someone a fool, you will be in danger of the fire of hell.

[23]"So when you offer your gift to God at the altar, and you remember that your brother or sister has something against you, [24]leave your gift there at the altar. Go and make peace with that person, and then come and offer your gift.

[25]"If your enemy is taking you to court, become friends quickly, before you go to court. Otherwise, your enemy might turn you over to the judge, and the judge

## Q & A

**Q** Did all the stuff in the Bible really happen?

---

things about you because you follow me. But when they do, you will be blessed. [12]Rejoice and be glad, because you have a great reward waiting for you in heaven. People did the same evil things to the prophets who lived before you.

### You Are Like Salt and Light

[13]"You are the salt of the earth. But if the salt loses its salty taste, it cannot be made salty again. It is good for nothing, except to be thrown out and walked on.

[14]"You are the light that gives light to the world. A city that is built on a hill cannot be hidden. [15]And people don't hide a light under a bowl. They put it on a lamp-stand so the light shines for all the people in the house. [16]In the same way, you should be a light for other people. Live so that they will see the good things you do and will praise your Father in heaven.

### The Importance of the Law

[17]"Don't think that I have come to destroy the law of Moses or the teaching of the prophets. I have not come to destroy them but to bring about what they said. [18]I tell you the truth, nothing will disappear from the law until heaven and earth are gone. Not even the smallest letter or the smallest part of a letter will be lost until everything has happened. [19]Who-

**A** Yes! Scientists have found evidence for many of the Bible stories. We also have original copies of different parts of the Bible, which were written not long after the events happened. If these reports were not true, people would have destroyed these writings or made sure there was proof that the stories were false. Best of all, God uses the Bible to change people's lives, so we can be sure that this amazing book can be trusted!

---

5:21 'You . . . anyone.' *Quotation from Exodus 20:13; Deuteronomy 5:17.*  5:22 **sister** *Some Greek copies continue, "without a reason."*

# Relationships

Grandparents come in all shapes, sizes, and personalities. Maybe you only see them on holidays, or maybe they live next door. Maybe they bring you fancy presents, or maybe they always forget your name. No matter what, grandparents deserve special respect. Show them consideration by greeting them, offering to help when you visit, and asking about their lives. Listening to their stories might help you understand or appreciate them more. Proverbs 17:6 tells us that grandparents are proud of their grandchildren—you are a treasure and a reward. Treat them in a way that makes them feel truly rewarded!

might give you to a guard to put you in jail. [26]I tell you the truth, you will not leave there until you have paid everything you owe.

## Jesus Teaches About Sexual Sin

[27]"You have heard that it was said, 'You must not be guilty of adultery.'[n] [28]But I tell you that if anyone looks at a woman and wants to sin sexually with her, in his mind he has already done that sin with the woman. [29]If your right eye causes you to sin, take it out and throw it away. It is better to lose one part of your body than to have your whole body thrown into hell. [30]If your right hand causes you to sin, cut it off and throw it away. It is better to lose one part of your body than for your whole body to go into hell.

## Jesus Teaches About Divorce

[31]"It was also said, 'Anyone who divorces his wife must give her a written divorce paper.'[n] [32]But I tell you that anyone who divorces his wife forces her to be guilty of adultery. The only reason for a man to divorce his wife is if she has sexual re-

lations with another man. And anyone who marries that divorced woman is guilty of adultery.

## Make Promises Carefully

[33]"You have heard that it was said to our people long ago, 'Don't break your promises, but keep the promises you make to the Lord.'[n] [34]But I tell you, never swear an oath. Don't swear an oath using the name of heaven, because heaven is God's throne. [35]Don't swear an oath using the name of the earth, because the earth belongs to God. Don't swear an oath using the name of Jerusalem, be-cause that is the city of the great King. [36]Don't even swear by your own head, because you cannot make one hair on your head become white or black. [37]Say only yes if you mean yes, and no if you mean no. If you say more than yes or no, it is from the Evil One.

## Don't Fight Back

[38]"You have heard that it was said, 'An eye for an eye, and a tooth for a tooth.'[n]

## cool

### Useful Salt

Besides making your fries tastier, how many things is salt used for? Researchers have discovered about fourteen thousand uses. Salt can melt icy roads, clean things, treat wounds, put out grease fires, remove odors from shoes, and do lots more. What a handy mineral God made for us!

*You* can be just as useful. Jesus called Christians the "salt of the earth" (Matthew 5:13). With God's help, you can add flavor to people's lives, help them when they're hurt, warm their cold hearts, and many other things. Ask God to use you today!

[39]But I tell you, don't stand up against an evil person. If someone slaps you on the right cheek, turn to him the other cheek also. [40]If someone wants to sue you in court and take your shirt, let him have your coat also. [41]If someone forces you to go

**5:27** '**You . . . adultery.**' *Quotation from Exodus 20:14; Deuteronomy 5:18.* **5:31** '**Anyone . . . divorce paper.**' *Quotation from Deuteronomy 24:1.* **5:33** '**Don't . . . Lord.**' *This refers to Leviticus 19:12; Numbers 30:2; Deuteronomy 23:21.* **5:38** '**An eye . . . tooth.**' *Quotation from Exodus 21:24; Leviticus 24:20; Deuteronomy 19:21.*

with him one mile, go with him two miles. [42]If a person asks you for something, give it to him. Don't refuse to give to someone who wants to borrow from you.

## Love All People

[43]"You have heard that it was said, 'Love your neighbor[n] and hate your enemies.' [44]But I say to you, love your enemies. Pray for those who hurt you.[n] [45]If you do this, you will be true children of your Father in heaven. He causes the sun to rise on good people and on evil people, and he sends rain to those who do right and to those who do wrong. [46]If you love only the people who love you, you will get no reward. Even the tax collectors do that. [47]And if you are nice only to your friends, you are no better than other people. Even those who don't know God are nice to their friends. [48]So you must be perfect, just as your Father in heaven is perfect.

## Jesus Teaches About Giving

**6** "Be careful! When you do good things, don't do them in front of people to be seen by them. If you do that, you will have no reward from your Father in heaven.

[2]"When you give to the poor, don't be like the hypocrites. They blow trumpets in the synagogues and on the streets so that people will see them and honor them. I tell you the truth, those hypocrites already have their full reward. [3]So when you give to the poor, don't let anyone know what you are doing. [4]Your giving should be done in secret. Your Father can see what is done in secret, and he will reward you.

## Jesus Teaches About Prayer

[5]"When you pray, don't be like the hypocrites. They love to stand in the synagogues and on the street corners and pray so people will see them. I tell you the truth, they already have their full reward. [6]When you pray, you should go into your room and close the door and pray to your Father who cannot be seen. Your Father can see what is done in secret, and he will reward you.

[7]"And when you pray, don't be like those people who don't know God. They continue saying things that mean noth-

ing, thinking that God will hear them because of their many words. [8]Don't be like them, because your Father knows the things you need before you ask him. [9]So when you pray, you should pray like this:

'Our Father in heaven,
  may your name always be kept holy.
[10]May your kingdom come
  and what you want be done,
    here on earth as it is in heaven.
[11]Give us the food we need for each
    day.
[12]Forgive us for our sins,
  just as we have forgiven those who
    sinned against us.
[13]And do not cause us to be tempted,
  but save us from the Evil One.' [The
    kingdom, the power, and the
    glory are yours forever. Amen.][n]
[14]Yes, if you forgive others for their sins, your Father in heaven will also forgive you for your sins. [15]But if you don't forgive others, your Father in heaven will not forgive your sins.

## god's promises

### Matthew 6:6

How many different ways can you think of to pray? Some people close their eyes and bow their heads to thank God for the food they're about to eat. Others talk to God in their heads while riding the bus to school. Some people pray in front of huge groups of people while others prefer to pray in a small group. Many people pray when they lie in bed at night.

In Matthew 6:6, Jesus said that when we pray, we should go to our room and close the door! Did he mean that God only hears those prayers? Was he saying that we shouldn't pray anywhere else or that we should only pray in secret? Not quite.

Actually, Jesus' words remind us that prayer is a special conversation we have with God. We shouldn't pray to make other people think we're holy or good. And we shouldn't pray only when we're at church or with our families! We can have really special and private conversations with God when we're all alone.

When we talk to God honestly and with a humble heart—just as if no one else is in the room to hear us—he answers our prayers and blesses us!

*We can have really special conversations with God when we're all alone.*

---

**5:43** **'Love your neighbor'** *Quotation from Leviticus 19:18.* **5:44** **you** *Some Greek copies continue, "Bless those who curse you, do good to those who hate you." Compare Luke 6:28.* **6:13** **The . . . Amen.** *Some Greek copies do not contain the bracketed text.*

## Jesus Teaches About Worship

[16]"When you fast,[n] don't put on a sad face like the hypocrites. They make their faces look sad to show people they are fasting. I tell you the truth, those hypocrites already have their full reward. [17]So when you fast, comb your hair and wash your face. [18]Then people will not know that you are fasting, but your Father, whom you cannot see, will see you. Your Father sees what is done in secret, and he will reward you.

## God Is More Important than Money

[19]"Don't store treasures for yourselves here on earth where moths and rust will destroy them and thieves can break in and steal them. [20]But store your treasures in heaven where they cannot be destroyed by moths or rust and where thieves cannot break in and steal them. [21]Your heart will be where your treasure is.

[22]"The eye is a light for the body. If your eyes are good, your whole body will be full of light. [23]But if your eyes are evil, your whole body will be full of darkness. And if the only light you have is really darkness, then you have the worst darkness.

[24]"No one can serve two masters. The person will hate one master and love the other, or will follow one master and refuse to follow the other. You cannot serve both God and worldly riches.

## Don't Worry

[25]"So I tell you, don't worry about the food or drink you need to live, or about the clothes you need for your body. Life is more than food, and the body is more than clothes. [26]Look at the birds in the air. They don't plant or harvest or store food in barns, but your heavenly Father feeds them. And you know that you are worth much more than the birds. [27]You cannot add any time to your life by worrying about it.

[28]"And why do you worry about clothes? Look at how the lilies in the field grow. They don't work or make clothes for themselves. [29]But I tell you that even Solomon with his riches was not dressed as beautifully as one of these flowers. [30]God clothes the grass in the field, which is alive today but tomorrow is thrown into the fire. So you can be even more sure that God will clothe you. Don't have so little faith! [31]Don't worry and say, 'What will we eat?' or 'What will we drink?' or 'What will we wear?' [32]The people who don't know God keep trying to get these things, and your Father in heaven knows you need them. [33]Seek first God's kingdom and what God wants. Then all your other needs will be met as well. [34]So don't worry about tomorrow, because tomorrow will have its own worries. Each day has enough trouble of its own.

## Be Careful About Judging Others

7 "Don't judge others, or you will be judged. [2]You will be judged in the same way that you judge others, and the amount you give to others will be given to you.

[3]"Why do you notice the little piece of dust in your friend's eye, but you don't notice the big piece of wood in your own eye? [4]How can you say to your friend, 'Let me take that little piece of dust out of your eye'? Look at yourself! You still have that big piece of wood in your own eye. [5]You hypocrite! First, take the wood out of your own eye. Then you will see clearly to take the dust out of your friend's eye.

[6]"Don't give holy things to dogs, and don't throw your pearls before pigs. Pigs will only trample on them, and dogs will turn to attack you.

## Ask God for What You Need

[7]"Ask, and God will give to you. Search, and you will find. Knock, and the door will open for you. [8]Yes, everyone who asks will receive. Everyone who searches will find. And everyone who knocks will have the door opened.

[9]"If your children ask for bread, which of you would give them a stone? [10]Or if your children ask for a fish, would you give them a snake? [11]Even though you are bad, you know how to give good gifts to your children. How much more your heavenly Father will give good things to those who ask him!

## STARTING HIGH SCHOOL

Walking down the halls of a high school is enough to frighten most people! Changing classes five to seven times a day can be hard to figure out, and you're probably not looking forward to final exams. But Matthew 6:34 tells us not to worry about anything! Everyone understands that it takes time to adjust. There will be teachers and older students who can answer questions and help you feel calm. If you don't know anyone at your high school, don't be concerned about being lonely—you'll meet many new people! And you won't be bored; there will be lots of opportunities to try new things.

---

**did you know?**

70% of preteens think it's important to be involved in politics.

—Trends & Tudes. Harris Interactive. October 2004.

---

## Be YOUR BEST!

Check a mirror before going out. If you can see bra straps, panty lines, or anything else that should be hidden, you're showing too much! We know they're there, but we don't need to see them. Similarly, don't spill your guts to *everyone,* but trust God with your most private things.

---

**6:16 fast** *The people would give up eating for a special time of prayer and worship to God. It was also done to show sadness and disappointment.*

# ASK, AND GOD WILL GIVE TO YOU. SEARCH, AND YOU WILL FIND. KNOCK, AND THE DOOR WILL OPEN FOR YOU.

## The Most Important Rule

12"Do to others what you want them to do to you. This is the meaning of the law of Moses and the teaching of the prophets.

## The Way to Heaven Is Hard

13"Enter through the narrow gate. The gate is wide and the road is wide that leads to hell, and many people enter through that gate. 14But the gate is small and the road is narrow that leads to true life. Only a few people find that road.

## People Know You by Your Actions

15"Be careful of false prophets. They come to you looking gentle like sheep, but they are really dangerous like wolves. 16You will know these people by what they do. Grapes don't come from thornbushes, and figs don't come from thorny weeds. 17In the same way, every good tree produces good fruit, but a bad tree produces bad fruit. 18A good tree cannot produce bad fruit, and a bad tree cannot produce good fruit. 19Every tree that does not produce good fruit is cut down and thrown into the fire. 20In the same way, you will know these false prophets by what they do.

21"Not all those who say 'You are our Lord' will enter the kingdom of heaven. The only people who will enter the kingdom of heaven are those who do what my Father in heaven wants. 22On the last day many people will say to me, 'Lord, Lord, we spoke for you, and through you we forced out demons and did many miracles.' 23Then I will tell them clearly, 'Get away from me, you who do evil. I never knew you.'

## Two Kinds of People

24"Everyone who hears my words and obeys them is like a wise man who built his house on rock. 25It rained hard, the floods came, and the winds blew and hit that house. But it did not fall, because it was built on rock. 26Everyone who hears my words and does not obey them is like a foolish man who built his house on sand. 27It rained hard, the floods came, and the winds blew and hit that house, and it fell with a big crash."

28When Jesus finished saying these things, the people were amazed at his teaching, 29because he did not teach like their teachers of the law. He taught like a person who had authority.

## Jesus Heals a Sick Man

8 When Jesus came down from the hill, great crowds followed him. 2Then a man with a skin disease came to Jesus. The man bowed down before him and said, "Lord, you can heal me if you will."

3Jesus reached out his hand and touched the man and said, "I will. Be healed!" And immediately the man was healed from his disease. 4Then Jesus said to him, "Don't tell anyone about this. But

**dig deeper**

### Matthew 9:13

When you see rich kids who seem to get everything they want, are you tempted to feel jealous? Do you secretly wish you had their parents? Believe it or not, a lot of those kids might be happier if they had your parents!

Many young people say they would prefer to have less stuff and spend more time with their parents. The problem is that some parents try to buy their kids' love. They work long hours to make lots of money to buy more and more stuff for their children. But because they're working so much, they don't see their kids much. Think about it: would you give up all the hugs and kisses and loving words from your parents for more stuff? It might seem fun for a while, but you'd end up feeling pretty lonely and sad.

This helps us understand what Jesus meant when he said, "I want kindness more than I want animal sacrifices" (Matthew 9:13). He wants you to love and obey him more than he wants you to just sit in church or give your offering. He wants you to worship him and spend time with him. He doesn't want your "stuff" as much as he wants you!

go and show yourself to the priest[n] and offer the gift Moses commanded[n] for people who are made well. This will show the people what I have done."

30% of girls often think about how their parents get along.

—Taylor KidsPulse 2004 Report. Taylor Research & Consulting Group. http://www.thetaylorgroup.com/get_download.cfm

**did you know?**

## Jesus Heals a Soldier's Servant

[5]When Jesus entered the city of Capernaum, an army officer came to him, begging for help. [6]The officer said, "Lord, my servant is at home in bed. He can't move his body and is in much pain."

[7]Jesus said to the officer, "I will go and heal him."

[8]The officer answered, "Lord, I am not worthy for you to come into my house. You only need to command it, and my servant will be healed. [9]I, too, am a man under the authority of others, and I have soldiers under my command. I tell one soldier, 'Go,' and he goes. I tell another soldier, 'Come,' and he comes. I say to my servant, 'Do this,' and my servant does it."

[10]When Jesus heard this, he was amazed. He said to those who were following him, "I tell you the truth, this is the greatest faith I have found, even in Israel. [11]Many people will come from the east and from the west and will sit and eat with Abraham, Isaac, and Jacob in the kingdom of heaven. [12]But those people who should be in the kingdom will be thrown outside into the darkness, where people will cry and grind their teeth with pain."

[13]Then Jesus said to the officer, "Go home. Your servant will be healed just as you believed he would." And his servant was healed that same hour.

## Jesus Heals Many People

[14]When Jesus went to Peter's house, he saw that Peter's mother-in-law was sick in bed with a fever. [15]Jesus touched her hand, and the fever left her. Then she stood up and began to serve Jesus.

[16]That evening people brought to Jesus many who had demons. Jesus spoke and the demons left them, and he healed all the sick. [17]He did these things to bring about what Isaiah the prophet had said:

"He took our suffering on him
and carried our diseases."

*Isaiah 53:4*

# Christian Girls Around the World

## Nessa: *Australia*

Nessa is only twelve years old, but she has already lived in five different countries . . . on four continents! It's been exciting for her to experience England (where she was born and has relatives), Malaysia, Vietnam, Canada, and Australia. Although her family just moved back to Canada, Australia is still fresh in her mind.

There are many unusual animals in Australia. You probably already thought of kangaroos and koalas. But there are also wallabies, platypuses, possums, dingoes, and Tasmanian devils! Nessa's favorite creatures were the interesting birds that are different from anywhere else.

Compared to most kids, Nessa knows a lot about other cultures (her mom is from Iran and her dad is from Singapore) so it is easy for her and her older sister to adjust whenever the family moves. In Australia, even though she's shy, Nessa was able to make friends quickly and enjoyed going to church with them.

Preteens in Australia seem to have two favorite hobbies: sports and shopping! Many of the kids play soccer (it's called football there) and, on weekends, they spend their time shopping—especially the teenagers. Nessa says that girls in Australia are very concerned about fashion and appearance.

Most people in Australia call themselves Christians, but only some of them go to church. Nessa's friends never reacted badly when she said she was a Christian, and they always enjoyed going to church with her when she invited them. Many of the kids don't get to attend church because their parents don't go.

When Nessa was four years old, her mother became a Christian, and Nessa put her faith in Jesus, too! Her Sunday School teachers helped her grow in her faith. Now Nessa prays a lot and reads her Bible to stay strong in her faith. What she sometimes finds difficult is that, as a Christian, she's not supposed to be mean when someone else is mean to her. But remembering the Bible verses she's learned always helps her.

Whenever a school teacher or someone else says something that goes against what she's learned in the Bible, Nessa is patient. She says that she believes in God and "that's it!" No one can change her mind about that!

---

8:4 **show . . . priest** *The Law of Moses said a priest must say when a Jewish person with a skin disease was well.*  8:4 **Moses commanded** *Read about this in Leviticus 14:1–32.*

# Q&A

**Q** My friend wants to borrow ten dollars from me. I'm not sure if I should let her have it. What does the Bible say?

**A** Matthew 5:42 and Luke 6:34–35 tell us to let people—even our enemies—borrow from us if they need something, without expecting to get paid back. As a tween, though, you should always check with your parents for situations you're not sure about. If they agree your friend really needs the money, consider giving it as a gift. Don't throw your money around, but remember that God will bless you for being kind to others.

## People Want to Follow Jesus

[18]When Jesus saw the crowd around him, he told his followers to go to the other side of the lake. [19]Then a teacher of the law came to Jesus and said, "Teacher, I will follow you any place you go."

[20]Jesus said to him, "The foxes have holes to live in, and the birds have nests, but the Son of Man has no place to rest his head."

[21]Another man, one of Jesus' followers, said to him, "Lord, first let me go and bury my father."

[22]But Jesus told him, "Follow me, and let the people who are dead bury their own dead."

## Jesus Calms a Storm

[23]Jesus got into a boat, and his followers went with him. [24]A great storm arose on the lake so that waves covered the boat, but Jesus was sleeping. [25]His followers went to him and woke him, saying, "Lord, save us! We will drown!"

[26]Jesus answered, "Why are you afraid? You don't have enough faith." Then Jesus got up and gave a command to the wind and the waves, and it became completely calm.

[27]The men were amazed and said, "What kind of man is this? Even the wind and the waves obey him!"

## Jesus Heals Two Men with Demons

[28]When Jesus arrived at the other side of the lake in the area of the Gadarene[n] people, two men who had demons in them met him. These men lived in the burial caves and were so dangerous that people could not use the road by those caves. [29]They shouted, "What do you want with us, Son of God? Did you come here to torture us before the right time?"

[30]Near that place there was a large herd of pigs feeding. [31]The demons begged Jesus, "If you make us leave these men, please send us into that herd of pigs."

[32]Jesus said to them, "Go!" So the demons left the men and went into the pigs. Then the whole herd rushed down the hill into the lake and were drowned. [33]The herdsmen ran away and went into town, where they told about all of this and what had happened to the men who had demons. [34]Then the whole town went out to see Jesus. When they saw him, they begged him to leave their area.

## Jesus Heals a Paralyzed Man

**9** Jesus got into a boat and went back across the lake to his own town. [2]Some people brought to Jesus a man who was paralyzed and lying on a mat. When Jesus saw the faith of these people, he said to the paralyzed man, "Be encouraged, young man. Your sins are forgiven."

## STAND UP, TAKE YOUR MAT, AND GO HOME.

[3]Some of the teachers of the law said to themselves, "This man speaks as if he were God. That is blasphemy!"[n]

[4]Knowing their thoughts, Jesus said, "Why are you thinking evil thoughts? [5]Which is easier: to say, 'Your sins are forgiven,' or to tell him, 'Stand up and walk'? [6]But I will prove to you that the Son of Man has authority on earth to forgive sins." Then Jesus said to the paralyzed man, "Stand up, take your mat, and go home." [7]And the man stood up and went home. [8]When the people saw this, they were amazed and praised God for giving power like this to human beings.

## Jesus Chooses Matthew

[9]When Jesus was leaving, he saw a man named Matthew sitting in the tax collector's booth. Jesus said to him, "Follow me," and he stood up and followed Jesus.

[10]As Jesus was having dinner at Matthew's house, many tax collectors and "sinners" came and ate with Jesus and his followers. [11]When the Pharisees saw this, they asked Jesus' followers, "Why does your teacher eat with tax collectors and sinners?"

[12]When Jesus heard them, he said, "It is not the healthy people who need a doctor, but the sick. [13]Go and learn what this

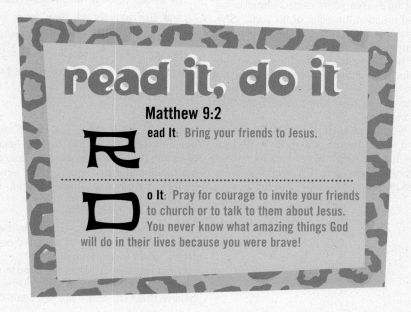

# read it, do it

**Matthew 9:2**

**R**ead It: Bring your friends to Jesus.

**D**o It: Pray for courage to invite your friends to church or to talk to them about Jesus. You never know what amazing things God will do in their lives because you were brave!

**8:28 Gadarene** *From Gadara, an area southeast of Lake Galilee. The exact location is uncertain and some Greek copies read "Gergesene"; others read "Gerasene."* **9:3 blasphemy** *Saying things against God or not showing respect for God.*

means: 'I want kindness more than I want animal sacrifices.'[n] I did not come to invite good people but to invite sinners."

## Jesus' Followers Are Criticized

[14]Then the followers of John[n] came to Jesus and said, "Why do we and the Pharisees often fast[n] for a certain time, but your followers don't?"

[15]Jesus answered, "The friends of the bridegroom are not sad while he is with them. But the time will come when the bridegroom will be taken from them, and then they will fast.

[16]"No one sews a patch of unshrunk cloth over a hole in an old coat. If he does, the patch will shrink and pull away from the coat, making the hole worse. [17]Also, people never pour new wine into old leather bags. Otherwise, the bags will break, the wine will spill, and the wine bags will be ruined. But people always pour new wine into new wine bags. Then both will continue to be good."

## Jesus Gives Life to a Dead Girl and Heals a Sick Woman

[18]While Jesus was saying these things, a leader of the synagogue came to him. He bowed down before Jesus and said, "My daughter has just died. But if you come and lay your hand on her, she will live again." [19]So Jesus and his followers stood up and went with the leader.

[20]Then a woman who had been bleeding for twelve years came behind Jesus and touched the edge of his coat. [21]She was thinking, "If I can just touch his clothes, I will be healed."

[22]Jesus turned and saw the woman and said, "Be encouraged, dear woman. You are made well because you believed." And the woman was healed from that moment on.

[23]Jesus continued along with the leader and went into his house. There he saw the funeral musicians and many people crying. [24]Jesus said, "Go away. The girl is not dead, only asleep." But the people

> I DID NOT COME TO INVITE GOOD PEOPLE BUT TO INVITE SINNERS.

# dig deeper

## Matthew 11:28–29

You know what it feels like to carry a heavy load. Your backpack may feel like a heavy load as you walk home from school or lug it to your class. Maybe you've felt the emotional burden of dealing with bad news or difficult circumstances in your life.

In Jesus' time, the rabbis (teachers) placed "loads" on their students by asking them to follow many rules and live exactly as they were instructed. Jesus tells his followers in Matthew 11:28–29 that he is no ordinary teacher. He is the Son of God! And he promises to help you with your burdens. He says, "Come to me, all of you who are tired and have heavy loads, and I will give you rest. Accept my teachings and learn from me, because I am gentle and humble in spirit, and you will find rest for your lives."

Jesus does not ask us to do anything that he is not willing to help us do. You can find real rest in Jesus by giving him your heavy "load" of worry and doubt. You don't have to live the Christian life on your own! In fact, it was never meant to be lived that way. Ask Jesus to teach you and to give you the rest that he promises.

laughed at him. [25]After the crowd had been thrown out of the house, Jesus went into the girl's room and took hold of her hand, and she stood up. [26]The news about this spread all around the area.

## Jesus Heals More People

[27]When Jesus was leaving there, two blind men followed him. They cried out, "Have mercy on us, Son of David!"

[28]After Jesus went inside, the blind men went with him. He asked the men, "Do you believe that I can make you see again?"

They answered, "Yes, Lord."

[29]Then Jesus touched their eyes and said, "Because you believe I can make you see again, it will happen." [30]Then the men were able to see. But Jesus warned them strongly, saying, "Don't tell anyone about this." [31]But the blind men left and spread the news about Jesus all around that area.

[32]When the two men were leaving, some people brought another man to Jesus. This man could not talk because he had a demon in him. [33]After Jesus forced the demon to leave the man, he was able

---

**9:13 'I want . . . sacrifices.'** *Quotation from Hosea 6:6.* **9:14 John** *John the Baptist, who preached to people about Christ's coming (Matthew 3, Luke 3).* **9:14 fast** *The people would give up eating for a special time of prayer and worship to God. It was also done to show sadness and disappointment.*

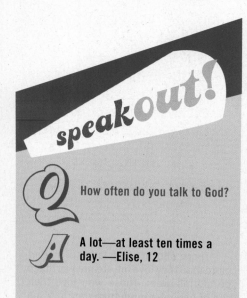

## speak out!

**Q** How often do you talk to God?

**A** A lot—at least ten times a day. —Elise, 12

to speak. The crowd was amazed and said, "We have never seen anything like this in Israel."

[34]But the Pharisees said, "The prince of demons is the one that gives him power to force demons out."

[35]Jesus traveled through all the towns and villages, teaching in their synagogues, preaching the Good News about the kingdom, and healing all kinds of diseases and sicknesses. [36]When he saw the crowds, he felt sorry for them because they were hurting and helpless, like sheep without a shepherd. [37]Jesus said to his followers, "There are many people to harvest but only a few workers to help harvest them. [38]Pray to the Lord, who owns the harvest, that he will send more workers to gather his harvest."[n]

### Jesus Sends Out His Apostles

**10** Jesus called his twelve followers together and gave them authority to drive out evil spirits and to heal every kind of disease and sickness. [2]These are the names of the twelve apostles: Simon (also called Peter) and his brother Andrew; James son of Zebedee, and his brother John; [3]Philip and Bartholomew; Thomas and Matthew, the tax collector; James son of Alphaeus, and Thaddaeus; [4]Simon the Zealot and Judas Iscariot, who turned against Jesus.

[5]Jesus sent out these twelve men with the following order: "Don't go to the non-Jewish people or to any town where the Samaritans live. [6]But go to the people of Israel, who are like lost sheep. [7]When you go, preach this: 'The kingdom of heaven is near.' [8]Heal the sick, raise the dead to life again, heal those who have skin diseases, and force demons out of people. I give you these powers freely, so help other people freely. [9]Don't carry any money with you—gold or silver or copper. [10]Don't carry a bag or extra clothes or sandals or a walking stick. Workers should be given what they need.

[11]"When you enter a city or town, find some worthy person there and stay in that home until you leave. [12]When you enter that home, say, 'Peace be with you.' [13]If the people there welcome you, let your peace stay there. But if they don't welcome you, take back the peace you wished for them. [14]And if a home or town refuses to welcome you or listen to you, leave that place and shake its dust off your feet.[n] [15]I tell you the truth, on the Judgment Day it will be better for the towns of Sodom and Gomorrah[n] than for the people of that town.

### Jesus Warns His Apostles

[16]"Listen, I am sending you out like sheep among wolves. So be as clever as snakes and as innocent as doves. [17]Be careful of people, because they will arrest you and take you to court and whip you in their synagogues. [18]Because of me you will be taken to stand before

## Shine Your Light

The summer she was eleven years old, Sarah's hands got a good workout scooping ice cream cones for the senior citizens at an assisted living center. She learned a lot about strong arm muscles and being friends with people older than her.

Every Thursday night, Sarah put on a big smile as she handed out double-scoop cones. After dishing up seconds and thirds, Sarah sat and talked with the older men and women.

Sarah loved to hear about what these people did for fun when they were her age. One of the women that Sarah became friends with, Ruth, liked to do lots of the same things Sarah did! As preteens, both Ruth and Sarah liked to run, sing at church, and play on the beach.

Through Ruth and the other seniors at the assisted living center, Sarah felt God's love. Each time she was given a hug or a birthday card, she could see how much these people cared for her.

Is there a senior center in your neighborhood? See if they have a time you could hang out with some of the adults. You'll be surprised at how much they'll love having you around!

---

9:37–38 **"There are . . . harvest."** *As a farmer sends workers to harvest the grain, Jesus sends his followers to bring people to God.*   10:14 **shake . . . feet** *A warning. It showed that they had rejected these people.*   10:15 **Sodom and Gomorrah** *Two cities that God destroyed because the people were so evil.*

governors and kings, and you will tell them and the non-Jewish people about me. ¹⁹When you are arrested, don't worry about what to say or how to say it. At that time you will be given the things to say. ²⁰It will not really be you speaking but the Spirit of your Father speaking through you.

²¹"Brothers will give their own brothers to be killed, and fathers will give their own children to be killed. Children will fight against their own parents and have them put to death. ²²All people will hate you because you follow me, but those people who keep their faith until the end will be saved. ²³When you are treated badly in one city, run to another city. I tell you the truth, you will not finish going through all the cities of Israel before the Son of Man comes.

²⁴"A student is not better than his teacher, and a servant is not better than his master. ²⁵A student should be satisfied to become like his teacher; a servant should be satisfied to become like his master. If the head of the family is called Beelzebul, then the other members of the family will be called worse names!

## Fear God, Not People

²⁶"So don't be afraid of those people, because everything that is hidden will be shown. Everything that is secret will be made known. ²⁷I tell you these things in the dark, but I want you to tell them in the light. What you hear whispered in your ear you should shout from the housetops. ²⁸Don't be afraid of people, who can kill the body but cannot kill the soul. The only one you should fear is the one who can destroy the soul and the body in hell. ²⁹Two sparrows cost only a penny, but not even one of them can die without your Father's knowing it. ³⁰God even knows how many hairs are on your head. ³¹So don't be afraid. You are worth much more than many sparrows.

## Tell People About Your Faith

³²"All those who stand before others and say they believe in me, I will before my Father in heaven that they belong to me. ³³But all who stand before others and say they do not believe in me, I will say before my Father in heaven that they do not belong to me.

³⁴"Don't think that I came to bring peace to the earth. I did not come to bring peace, but a sword. ³⁵I have come so that

'a son will be against his father,
   a daughter will be against her
      mother,
   a daughter-in-law will be against her
      mother-in-law.
³⁶ A person's enemies will be
      members of his own family.'
                              *Micah 7:6*

ALL THOSE WHO STAND BEFORE OTHERS AND SAY THEY BELIEVE IN ME, I WILL SAY BEFORE MY FATHER IN HEAVEN THAT THEY BELONG TO ME.

³⁷"Those who love their father or mother more than they love me are not worthy to be my followers. Those who love their son or daughter more than they love me are not worthy to be my followers. ³⁸Whoever is not willing to carry the cross and follow me is not worthy of me. ³⁹Those who try to hold on to their lives will give up true life. Those who give up their lives for me will hold on to true life. ⁴⁰Whoever accepts you also accepts me, and whoever accepts me also accepts the One who sent me. ⁴¹Whoever meets a prophet and accepts him will receive the reward of a prophet. And whoever accepts a good person because that person is good will receive the reward of a good person. ⁴²Those who give one of these little ones a cup of cold water because they are my followers will truly get their reward."

## Jesus and John the Baptist

**11** After Jesus finished telling these things to his twelve followers, he left there and went to the towns in Galilee to teach and preach.

²John the Baptist was in prison, but he heard about what the Christ was doing. So John sent some of his followers to Jesus. ³They asked him, "Are you the One who is to come, or should we wait for someone else?"

⁴Jesus answered them, "Go tell John what you hear and see: ⁵The blind can see, the crippled can walk, and people with skin diseases are healed. The deaf can hear, the dead are raised to life, and the Good News is preached to the poor. ⁶Those who do not stumble in their faith because of me are blessed."

⁷As John's followers were leaving, Jesus began talking to the people about John. Jesus said, "What did you go out into

## top ten ways to...
**Share God's Love with Strangers**

**1** Smile at them.

**2** Share your cookies with a girl you don't know at school.

**3** Give someone your seat on the bus.

**4** Buy a flower and give it to the first lady you see.

**5** Volunteer at a senior's home.

**6** Collect trash from someone's lawn.

**7** Give your mailman a New Testament.

**8** Welcome new kids at your church.

**9** Say hello to cafeteria workers.

**10** Hold the door open for people.

# HOW MUCH DO YOU WORRY?

In Matthew 6:25–34, Jesus told his followers that they didn't have to worry about things like food or clothes because God gives us everything we need! How much do you worry?

1. **Your teacher says there's a math test next Friday on the last two chapters you learned. You:**
   a. Feel sick. You're sure you're going to fail no matter what.
   b. Get nervous. You're not sure if you can be ready in time.
   c. Start planning how you're going to study each day.
   d. Think, "I'll review everything on Thursday night."

2. **When you find out your grandmother is in the hospital because she fell, you:**
   a. Start crying and yelling, "I don't want her to die!"
   b. Have trouble sleeping at night because you're not sure if she's okay.
   c. Pray for her and take her some flowers.
   d. Continue playing your video game.

3. **When you think about becoming a teenager, you:**
   a. Know it's going to be the most miserable, horrible, awful time in your life.
   b. Worry that it will be difficult a lot of the time.
   c. Know that God will be there with you the whole time.
   d. Think, "Ha! It's going to be nothing!"

4. **Your best friend hasn't called you for two days. You:**
   a. Are sure she's got a new best friend and send her a long e-mail saying how upset you are.
   b. Wonder if you said something wrong and start feeling bad.
   c. Try calling her. When there's no answer, you pray for her and decide to wait a few more days.
   d. Hardly notice.

## How much do you worry?

If you answered mostly **As**, you're in panic mode! Slow down and breathe. Your wild imagination makes you worry way too much. In Matthew 11:28, Jesus said: "Come to me, all of you who are tired and have heavy loads, and I will give you rest." Ask God to take away your heavy load of worry. He wants you to rest in him and trust him!

If you answered mostly **Bs**, you're a little worried. You care about people and situations, which is great, but at some point you have to trust God with those worries. First Peter 5:7 says, "Give all your worries to him, because he cares about you." Pray that God will help you to keep caring…without worrying.

If you answered mostly **Cs**, you are trusting God. When a situation is serious, you don't panic or let it trouble you. Keep going to God with your concerns and asking him to show you what to do. After you've done what you can, know that you can trust him with the rest.

If you answered mostly **Ds**, you're too confident. Ask yourself if you care enough about the people around you. What about your future? Pray that God will help you pay more attention to what's going on around you. He can turn your confidence into a good thing and use it to encourage others!

WE PLAYED MUSIC FOR YOU, BUT YOU DID NOT DANCE; WE SANG A SAD SONG, BUT YOU DID NOT CRY.

the desert to see? A reed[n] blown by the wind? [8]What did you go out to see? A man dressed in fine clothes? No, those who wear fine clothes live in kings' palaces. [9]So why did you go out? To see a prophet? Yes, and I tell you, John is more than a prophet. [10]This was written about him:

'I will send my messenger ahead of you,
who will prepare the way for you.'
*Malachi 3:1*

[11]I tell you the truth, John the Baptist is greater than any other person ever born, but even the least important person in the kingdom of heaven is greater than John. [12]Since the time John the Baptist came until now, the kingdom of heaven has been going forward in strength, and people have been trying to take it by force. [13]All the prophets and the law of Moses told about what would happen until the time John came. [14]And if you will believe what they said, you will believe that John is Elijah, whom they said would come. [15]Let those with ears use them and listen!

[16]"What can I say about the people of this time? What are they like? They are like children sitting in the marketplace, who call out to each other,

[17]'We played music for you, but you
did not dance;
we sang a sad song, but you did
not cry.'

[18]John came and did not eat or drink like other people. So people say, 'He has a demon.' [19]The Son of Man came, eating and drinking, and people say, 'Look at him! He eats too much and drinks too much wine, and he is a friend of tax collectors and sinners.' But wisdom is proved to be right by what she does."

## Jesus Warns Unbelievers

[20]Then Jesus criticized the cities where he did most of his miracles, because the people did not change their lives and stop sinning. [21]He said, "How terrible for you, Korazin! How terrible for you, Bethsaida! If the same miracles I did in you had happened in Tyre and Sidon,[n] those people would have changed their lives a long time ago. They would have worn rough cloth and put ashes on themselves to show they had changed. [22]But I tell you, on the Judgment Day it will be better for Tyre and Sidon than for you. [23]And you, Capernaum,[n] will you be lifted up to heaven? No, you will be thrown down to the depths. If the miracles I did in you had happened in Sodom,[n] its people would have stopped sinning, and it would still be a city today. [24]But I tell you, on the Judgment Day it will be better for Sodom than for you."

## Jesus Offers Rest to People

[25]At that time Jesus said, "I praise you, Father, Lord of heaven and earth, because you have hidden these things from the people who are wise and smart. But you have shown them to those who are like little children. [26]Yes, Father, this is what you really wanted.

[27]"My Father has given me all things. No one knows the Son, except the Father. And no one knows the Father, except the Son and those whom the Son chooses to tell.

[28]"Come to me, all of you who are tired and have heavy loads, and I will give you rest. [29]Accept my teachings and learn from me, because I am gentle and humble in spirit, and you will find rest for your lives. [30]The burden that I ask you to accept is easy; the load I give you to carry is light."

## Jesus Is Lord of the Sabbath

**12** At that time Jesus was walking through some fields of grain on a Sabbath day. His followers were hungry, so they began to pick the grain and eat it. [2]When the Pharisees saw this, they said to Jesus, "Look! Your followers are doing what is unlawful to do on the Sabbath day."

[3]Jesus answered, "Have you not read what David did when he and the people with him were hungry? [4]He went into God's house, and he and those with him ate the holy bread, which was lawful only for priests to eat. [5]And have you not read

## Baptism

**B**aptism is a symbol of having our sins washed away because of Jesus' death on the cross. John the Baptist was a prophet God sent to tell people that Jesus was coming and to warn them to stop sinning. He baptized people when they chose to give up their evil ways and obey God. In baptism, people may be dunked under water or have just a few drops of water sprinkled on their heads. Baptism shows we are forgiven by Jesus and ready to start a new life serving him. It is a way to publicly show people that you believe in Jesus!

11:7 **reed** It means that John was not ordinary or weak like grass blown by the wind. 11:21 **Tyre and Sidon** Towns where wicked people lived. 11:21, 23 **Korazin . . . Bethsaida . . . Capernaum** Towns by Lake Galilee where Jesus preached to the people. 11:23 **Sodom** A city that God destroyed because the people were so evil.

in the law of Moses that on every Sabbath day the priests in the Temple break this law about the Sabbath day? But the priests are not wrong for doing that. [6]I tell you that there is something here that is greater than the Temple. [7]The Scripture says, 'I want kindness more than I want animal sacrifices.'[n] You don't really know what those words mean. If you understood them, you would not judge those who have done nothing wrong.

[8]"So the Son of Man is Lord of the Sabbath day."

## Jesus Heals a Man's Hand

[9]Jesus left there and went into their synagogue, [10]where there was a man with a crippled hand. They were looking for a reason to accuse Jesus, so they asked him, "Is it right to heal on the Sabbath day?"[n]

[11]Jesus answered, "If any of you has a sheep, and it falls into a ditch on the Sabbath day, you will help it out of the ditch. [12]Surely a human being is more important than a sheep. So it is lawful to do good things on the Sabbath day."

[13]Then Jesus said to the man with the crippled hand, "Hold out your hand." The man held out his hand, and it became well again, like the other hand. [14]But the Pharisees left and made plans to kill Jesus.

## Jesus Is God's Chosen Servant

[15]Jesus knew what the Pharisees were doing, so he left that place. Many people followed him, and he healed all who were sick. [16]But Jesus warned the people not to tell who he was. [17]He did these things to bring about what Isaiah the prophet had said:

[18]"Here is my servant whom I have chosen.
I love him, and I am pleased with him.
I will put my Spirit upon him,
and he will tell of my justice to all people.
[19]He will not argue or cry out;
no one will hear his voice in the streets.
[20]He will not break a crushed blade of grass
or put out even a weak flame
until he makes justice win the victory.
[21]In him will the non-Jewish people find hope." _Isaiah 42:1–4_

## Jesus' Power Is from God

[22]Then some people brought to Jesus a man who was blind and could not talk, because he had a demon. Jesus healed the man so that he could talk and see. [23]All the people were amazed and said, "Perhaps this man is the Son of David!"

[24]When the Pharisees heard this, they said, "Jesus uses the power of Beelzebul, the ruler of demons, to force demons out of people."

[25]Jesus knew what the Pharisees were thinking, so he said to them, "Every

## god's promises

### Matthew 15:4

"Your room better be clean before we leave!" "No more television until your homework is done." "Eat your vegetables!" Does it seem like your mom or dad is always making you do stuff you don't like to do?

Obeying our parents is a pretty tough job sometimes. We don't always want to do the things they tell us to do—in fact, we often want to do the exact opposite. God knew that it would not always be easy to obey our parents. He even gave us a special promise to encourage us. God promises that honoring our parents helps us have a long and happy life.

"Honor your father and mother" is one of the Ten Commandments that God gave to the Israelites a long time ago. Jesus rebuked people who made excuses for not honoring their parents. Honoring your parents means making your best effort to do what they ask you to do and treating them with respect.

If you have a difficult time obeying your parents, ask God to help you. When you try hard to obey your parents, you might be surprised at what happens. You'll probably get along better with them, and you'll definitely know that you are pleasing God.

_God promises that honoring our parents helps us have a long and happy life._

> GOOD PEOPLE HAVE GOOD THINGS IN THEIR HEARTS, AND SO THEY SAY GOOD THINGS. BUT EVIL PEOPLE HAVE EVIL IN THEIR HEARTS, SO THEY SAY EVIL THINGS.

kingdom that is divided against itself will be destroyed. And any city or family that is divided against itself will not continue. <sup>26</sup>And if Satan forces out himself, then Satan is divided against himself, and his kingdom will not continue. <sup>27</sup>You say that I use the power of Beelzebul to force out demons. If that is true, then what power do your people use to force out demons? So they will be your judges. <sup>28</sup>But if I use the power of God's Spirit to force out demons, then the kingdom of God has come to you.

<sup>29</sup>"If anyone wants to enter a strong person's house and steal his things, he must first tie up the strong person. Then he can steal the things from the house.

<sup>30</sup>"Whoever is not with me is against me. Whoever does not work with me is working against me. <sup>31</sup>So I tell you, people can be forgiven for every sin and everything they say against God. But whoever speaks against the Holy Spirit will not be forgiven. <sup>32</sup>Anyone who speaks against the Son of Man can be forgiven, but anyone who speaks against the Holy Spirit will not be forgiven, now or in the future.

### People Know You by Your Words

<sup>33</sup>"If you want good fruit, you must make the tree good. If your tree is not good, it will have bad fruit. A tree is known by the kind of fruit it produces. <sup>34</sup>You snakes! You are evil people, so how can you say anything good? The mouth speaks the things that are in the heart. <sup>35</sup>Good people have good things in their hearts, and so they say good things. But evil people have evil in their hearts, so they say evil things. <sup>36</sup>And I tell you that on the Judgment Day people will be responsible for every careless thing they have said. <sup>37</sup>The words you have said will be used to

judge you. Some of your words will prove you right, but some of your words will prove you guilty."

### The People Ask for a Miracle

<sup>38</sup>Then some of the Pharisees and teachers of the law answered Jesus, saying, "Teacher, we want to see you work a miracle as a sign."

<sup>39</sup>Jesus answered, "Evil and sinful people are the ones who want to see a miracle for a sign. But no sign will be given to them, except the sign of the prophet Jonah. <sup>40</sup>Jonah was in the stomach of the big fish for three days and three nights. In the same way, the Son of Man will be in the grave three days and three nights. <sup>41</sup>On the Judgment Day the people from Nineveh[n] will stand up with you people who live now, and they will show that you are guilty. When Jonah preached to them, they were sorry and changed their lives. And I tell you that someone greater than Jonah is here. <sup>42</sup>On the Judgment Day, the Queen of the South[n] will stand up with you people who live today. She will show that you are guilty, because she came from far away to listen to Solomon's wise teaching. And I tell you that someone greater than Solomon is here.

# Shine Your Light

**W**eekends are a great time to relax and have fun. No school means you have the whole day to play, right? Actually, a group of preteen girls who like to serve decided to spend part of their weekends volunteering at a church "soup kitchen."

After church one Sunday each month, they took gallon containers of soup and loaves of bread and rode to a downtown church. With help from several adults, they served hundreds of homeless people a lunch of hot soup and bread.

The girls were really happy to see the grateful smiles of the men and women who came to enjoy the hot meal. They also found out that serving others can be a lot of fun! Jesus said that he didn't come to be served, but to serve others (Mark 10:45). He looked for people others rejected or people who didn't have a lot of money and helped them.

You can help others just like Jesus did. If you attend a church, ask the pastor about where you can serve. You can also pray and ask God to show you how to be his servant. He wants to give you the joy that comes from helping others!

**12:41 Nineveh** *The city where Jonah preached to warn the people. Read Jonah 3.* **12:42 Queen of the South** *The Queen of Sheba. She traveled a thousand miles to learn God's wisdom from Solomon. Read 1 Kings 10:1–13.*

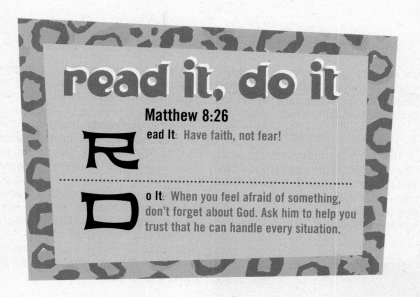

## read it, do it

### Matthew 8:26

**R**ead It: Have faith, not fear!

**D**o It: When you feel afraid of something, don't forget about God. Ask him to help you trust that he can handle every situation.

Otherwise they might really
understand
what they see with their eyes
and hear with their ears.
They might really understand
in their minds
and come back to me and be
healed.' *Isaiah 6:9–10*

[16]But you are blessed, because you see with your eyes and hear with your ears. [17]I tell you the truth, many prophets and good people wanted to see the things that you now see, but they did not see them. And they wanted to hear the things that you now hear, but they did not hear them.

## Jesus Explains the Seed Story

[18]"So listen to the meaning of that story about the farmer. [19]What is the seed that fell by the road? That seed is like the person who hears the message about the kingdom but does not understand it. The Evil One comes and takes away what was planted in that person's heart. [20]And what is the seed that fell on rocky ground? That seed is like the person who hears the teaching and quickly accepts it with joy. [21]But he does not let the teaching go deep into his life, so he keeps it only a

## People Today Are Full of Evil

[43]"When an evil spirit comes out of a person, it travels through dry places, looking for a place to rest, but it doesn't find it. [44]So the spirit says, 'I will go back to the house I left.' When the spirit comes back, it finds the house still empty, swept clean, and made neat. [45]Then the evil spirit goes out and brings seven other spirits even more evil than it is, and they go in and live there. So the person has even more trouble than before. It is the same way with the evil people who live today."

## Jesus' True Family

[46]While Jesus was talking to the people, his mother and brothers stood outside, trying to find a way to talk to him. [47]Someone told Jesus, "Your mother and brothers are standing outside, and they want to talk to you."[n]

[48]He answered, "Who is my mother? Who are my brothers?" [49]Then he pointed to his followers and said, "Here are my mother and my brothers. [50]My true brother and sister and mother are those who do what my Father in heaven wants."

## A Story About Planting Seed

**13** That same day Jesus went out of the house and sat by the lake. [2]Large crowds gathered around him, so he got into a boat and sat down, while the people stood on the shore. [3]Then Jesus used stories to teach them many things. He said: "A farmer went out to plant his seed. [4]While he was planting, some seed fell by the road, and the birds came and ate it all up. [5]Some seed fell on rocky ground, where there wasn't much dirt. That seed grew very fast, because the ground was not deep. [6]But when the sun rose, the plants dried up, because they did not have deep roots. [7]Some other seed fell among thorny weeds, which grew and choked the good plants. [8]Some other seed fell on good ground where it grew and produced a crop. Some plants made a hundred times more, some made sixty times more, and some made thirty times more. [9]Let those with ears use them and listen."

## Why Jesus Used Stories to Teach

[10]The followers came to Jesus and asked, "Why do you use stories to teach the people?"

[11]Jesus answered, "You have been chosen to know the secrets about the kingdom of heaven, but others cannot know these secrets. [12]Those who have understanding will be given more, and they will have all they need. But those who do not have understanding, even what they have will be taken away from them. [13]This is why I use stories to teach the people: They see, but they don't really see. They hear, but they don't really hear or understand. [14]So they show that the things Isaiah said about them are true:

'You will listen and listen, but you
will not understand.
You will look and look, but you will
not learn.
[15]For the minds of these people
have become stubborn.
They do not hear with their ears,
and they have closed their eyes.

# Q & A

**Q** Is it okay to talk to people online if my parents don't know them?

**A** You should talk to your parents about what their rules are. They probably want to know who you're chatting with, and you need to respect that. Being online for a long time isn't the best idea, especially if strangers or kids you don't know very well can start chatting with you. Some kids have been hurt or even killed by a stranger they started chatting with online. Your parents want to protect you, so respect them if they want to see who you talk to and what you say.

12:47 **Someone . . . you."** *Some Greek copies do not have verse 47.*

short time. When trouble or persecution comes because of the teaching he accepted, he quickly gives up. [22]And what is the seed that fell among the thorny weeds? That seed is like the person who hears the teaching but lets worries about this life and the temptation of wealth stop that teaching from growing. So the teaching does not produce fruit[n] in that person's life. [23]But what is the seed that fell on the good ground? That seed is like the person who hears the teaching and understands it. That person grows and produces fruit, sometimes a hundred times more, sometimes sixty times more, and sometimes thirty times more."

## A Story About Wheat and Weeds

[24]Then Jesus told them another story: "The kingdom of heaven is like a man who planted good seed in his field. [25]That night, when everyone was asleep, his enemy came and planted weeds among the wheat and then left. [26]Later, the wheat sprouted and the heads of grain grew, but the weeds also grew. [27]Then the man's servants came to him and said, 'You planted good seed in your field. Where did the weeds come from?' [28]The man answered, 'An enemy planted weeds.' The servants asked, 'Do you want us to pull up the weeds?' [29]The man answered, 'No, because when you pull up the weeds, you might also pull up the wheat. [30]Let the weeds and the wheat grow together until the harvest time. At harvest time I will tell the workers, "First gather the weeds and tie them together to be burned. Then gather the wheat and bring it to my barn." ' "

## Stories of Mustard Seed and Yeast

[31]Then Jesus told another story: "The kingdom of heaven is like a mustard seed that a man planted in his field. [32]That seed is the smallest of all seeds, but when it grows, it is one of the largest garden plants. It becomes big enough for the wild birds to come and build nests in its branches."

[33]Then Jesus told another story: "The kingdom of heaven is like yeast that a woman took and hid in a large tub of flour until it made all the dough rise."

[34]Jesus used stories to tell all these things to the people; he always used stories to teach them. [35]This is as the prophet said:
"I will speak using stories;
  I will tell things that have been
    secret since the world was
    made."      *Psalm 78:2*

## Jesus Explains About the Weeds

[36]Then Jesus left the crowd and went into the house. His followers came to him and said, "Explain to us the meaning of the story about the weeds in the field."

[37]Jesus answered, "The man who planted the good seed in the field is the Son of Man. [38]The field is the world, and the good seed are all of God's children who belong to the kingdom. The weeds are those people who belong to the Evil One. [39]And the enemy who planted the bad seed is the devil. The harvest time is the end of the age, and the workers who gather are God's angels.

[40]"Just as the weeds are pulled up and burned in the fire, so it will be at the end of the age. [41]The Son of Man will send out

## dig deeper

### Matthew 18:1-7

Do you spend a lot of time wishing you were grown up? Do you sometimes feel like adults—and maybe even God—don't think you're important because you're still young? Guess what? In God's eyes, kids are the top of the class!

In Matthew 18:1-7, Jesus surprised his followers. When they asked, "Who is the greatest in the kingdom of heaven?" he didn't pick any of them! Instead, Jesus called to a little child to stand in front of all those grown men. He told them, "You must change and become like little children. Otherwise, you will never enter the kingdom of heaven. The greatest person in the kingdom of heaven is the one who makes himself humble like this little child." Wow!

Kids, even almost-teenagers, need someone to take care of them. They have to trust their parents and other adults to love and care for them. God wants you—and everyone—to trust him as the perfect Father who will love you forever. Whether you're going on eleven or going on seventy, trust is the only way to get into heaven. No matter what great things you do as you grow older, always be a "child" in your heart by trusting God for everything!

---

13:22 **produce fruit** *To produce fruit means to have in your life the good things God wants.*

## Bible Bios

### Peter
#### (Matthew 14:25–33)

The New Testament says a lot about Peter, a faithful follower who shared the message about Jesus with many people. Early in his relationship with Jesus, though, he didn't always have the strongest faith. One day, while fishing on a big lake with some other followers, he saw Jesus walking toward him . . . on the water! So cool. Peter wanted to try it, too. So he asked Jesus to let him walk on the water.

When Jesus said, "Come," Peter got out and started walking toward Jesus. It worked! Well . . . until he nervously looked around and saw the waves. As soon as he took his eyes off Jesus, he started to sink. Of course, Jesus rescued him, but he reminded Peter not to doubt anymore.

Whatever *you* go through in life, keep your eyes on Jesus, and you'll be just fine!

his angels, and they will gather out of his kingdom all who cause sin and all who do evil. ⁴²The angels will throw them into the blazing furnace, where the people will cry and grind their teeth with pain. ⁴³Then the good people will shine like the sun in the kingdom of their Father. Let those with ears use them and listen.

### Stories of a Treasure and a Pearl

⁴⁴"The kingdom of heaven is like a treasure hidden in a field. One day a man found the treasure, and then he hid it in the field again. He was so happy that he went and sold everything he owned to buy that field.

⁴⁵"Also, the kingdom of heaven is like a man looking for fine pearls. ⁴⁶When he found a very valuable pearl, he went and sold everything he had and bought it.

### A Story of a Fishing Net

⁴⁷"Also, the kingdom of heaven is like a net that was put into the lake and caught many different kinds of fish. ⁴⁸When it was full, the fishermen pulled the net to the shore. They sat down and put all the good fish in baskets and threw away the bad fish. ⁴⁹It will be this way at the end of the age. The angels will come and separate the evil people from the good people. ⁵⁰The angels will throw the evil people into the blazing furnace, where people will cry and grind their teeth with pain."

⁵¹Jesus asked his followers, "Do you understand all these things?"

They answered, "Yes, we understand."

⁵²Then Jesus said to them, "So every teacher of the law who has been taught about the kingdom of heaven is like the owner of a house. He brings out both new things and old things he has saved."

### Jesus Goes to His Hometown

⁵³When Jesus finished teaching with these stories, he left there. ⁵⁴He went to his hometown and taught the people in the synagogue, and they were amazed. They said, "Where did this man get this wisdom and this power to do miracles? ⁵⁵He is just the son of a carpenter. His mother is Mary, and his brothers are James, Joseph, Simon, and Judas. ⁵⁶And all his sisters are here with us. Where then does this man get all these things?" ⁵⁷So the people were upset with Jesus.

But Jesus said to them, "A prophet is honored everywhere except in his hometown and in his own home."

⁵⁸So he did not do many miracles there because they had no faith.

### How John the Baptist Was Killed

**14** At that time Herod, the ruler of Galilee, heard the reports about Jesus. ²So he said to his servants, "Jesus is John the Baptist, who has risen from the dead. That is why he can work these miracles."

³Sometime before this, Herod had arrested John, tied him up, and put him into prison. Herod did this because of Herodias, who had been the wife of Philip, Herod's brother. ⁴John had been telling Herod, "It is not lawful for you to be married to Herodias." ⁵Herod wanted to kill John, but he was afraid of the people, because they believed John was a prophet.

⁶On Herod's birthday, the daughter of Herodias danced for Herod and his guests, and she pleased him. ⁷So he promised with an oath to give her anything she wanted. ⁸Herodias told her daughter what to ask for, so she said to Herod, "Give me the head of John the Baptist here on a platter." ⁹Although King Herod was very sad, he had made a promise, and his dinner guests had heard him. So Herod ordered that what she asked for be done. ¹⁰He sent soldiers to the prison to cut off John's head. ¹¹And they brought it on a platter and gave it to the girl, and she took it to her mother. ¹²John's followers came and got his body and buried it. Then they went and told Jesus.

### More than Five Thousand Fed

¹³When Jesus heard what had happened to John, he left in a boat and went to a lonely place by himself. But the crowds heard about it and followed him on foot

## Q & A

**Q** I'm really different from the rest of my family. How can I get along with them?

**A** Try to focus more on the things you have in common and enjoying those things together. Also, remember that differences aren't bad . . . they can make a family very interesting! Don't try to be someone you're not and respect your parents, brothers, and sisters the way they are. And hopefully they will do the same for you (Matthew 7:12).

from the towns. ¹⁴When he arrived, he saw a great crowd waiting. He felt sorry for them and healed those who were sick.

¹⁵When it was evening, his followers came to him and said, "No one lives in this place, and it is already late. Send the people away so they can go to the towns and buy food for themselves."

¹⁶But Jesus answered, "They don't need to go away. You give them something to eat."

¹⁷They said to him, "But we have only five loaves of bread and two fish."

¹⁸Jesus said, "Bring the bread and the fish to me." ¹⁹Then he told the people to sit down on the grass. He took the five loaves and the two fish and, looking to heaven, he thanked God for the food. Jesus divided the bread and gave it to his followers, who gave it to the people. ²⁰All the people ate and were satisfied. Then the followers filled twelve baskets with the leftover pieces of food. ²¹There were about five thousand men there who ate, not counting women and children.

## Jesus Walks on the Water

²²Immediately Jesus told his followers to get into the boat and go ahead of him across the lake. He stayed there to send the people home. ²³After he had sent them away, he went by himself up into the hills to pray. It was late, and Jesus was there alone. ²⁴By this time, the boat was already far away from land. It was being hit by waves, because the wind was blowing against it.

> PETER SAID, "LORD, IF IT IS REALLY YOU, THEN COMMAND ME TO COME TO YOU ON THE WATER."

²⁵Between three and six o'clock in the morning, Jesus came to them, walking on the water. ²⁶When his followers saw him walking on the water, they were afraid. They said, "It's a ghost!" and cried out in fear.

²⁷But Jesus quickly spoke to them, "Have courage! It is I. Do not be afraid."

²⁸Peter said, "Lord, if it is really you, then command me to come to you on the water."

²⁹Jesus said, "Come."

And Peter left the boat and walked on the water to Jesus. ³⁰But when Peter saw the wind and the waves, he became afraid and began to sink. He shouted, "Lord, save me!"

³¹Immediately Jesus reached out his hand and caught Peter. Jesus said, "Your faith is small. Why did you doubt?"

³²After they got into the boat, the wind became calm. ³³Then those who were in the boat worshiped Jesus and said, "Truly you are the Son of God!"

³⁴When they had crossed the lake, they came to shore at Gennesaret. ³⁵When the people there recognized Jesus, they told people all around there that Jesus had come, and they brought all their sick to him. ³⁶They begged Jesus to let them

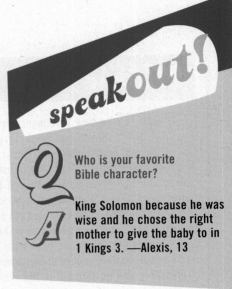

touch just the edge of his coat, and all who touched it were healed.

## Obey God's Law

**15** Then some Pharisees and teachers of the law came to Jesus from Jerusalem. They asked him, ²"Why don't your followers obey the unwritten laws which have been handed down to us? They don't wash their hands before they eat."

³Jesus answered, "And why do you refuse to obey God's command so that you can follow your own teachings? ⁴God said, 'Honor your father and your mother,'ⁿ and 'Anyone who says cruel things to his father or mother must be put to death.'ⁿ ⁵But you say a person can tell his father or mother, 'I have something I could use to help you, but I have given it to God already.' ⁶You teach that person not to honor his father or his mother. You rejected what God said for the sake of your own rules. ⁷You are hypocrites! Isaiah was right when he said about you:

⁸'These people show honor to me
    with words,
  but their hearts are far from me.
⁹Their worship of me is worthless.
  The things they teach are nothing
    but human rules.' "

*Isaiah 29:13*

¹⁰After Jesus called the crowd to him, he said, "Listen and understand what I am saying. ¹¹It is not what people put into their mouths that makes them unclean. It is what comes out of their mouths that makes them unclean."

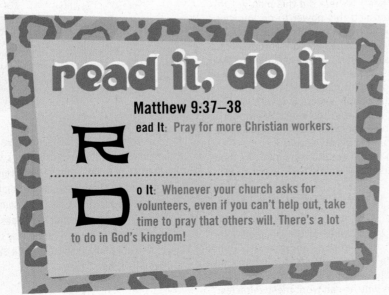

# read it, do it

## Matthew 9:37–38

**R**ead It: Pray for more Christian workers.

**D**o It: Whenever your church asks for volunteers, even if you can't help out, take time to pray that others will. There's a lot to do in God's kingdom!

---

15:4 'Honor . . . mother.' *Quotation from Exodus 20:12; Deuteronomy 5:16.*   15:4 'Anyone . . . death.' *Quotation from Exodus 21:17.*

¹²Then his followers came to him and asked, "Do you know that the Pharisees are angry because of what you said?"

¹³Jesus answered, "Every plant that my Father in heaven has not planted himself will be pulled up by the roots. ¹⁴Stay away from the Pharisees; they are blind leaders.ⁿ And if a blind person leads a blind person, both will fall into a ditch."

¹⁵Peter said, "Explain the example to us."

¹⁶Jesus said, "Do you still not understand? ¹⁷Surely you know that all the food that enters the mouth goes into the stomach and then goes out of the body. ¹⁸But what people say with their mouths comes from the way they think; these are the things that make people unclean. ¹⁹Out of the mind come evil thoughts, murder, adultery, sexual sins, stealing, lying, and speaking evil of others. ²⁰These things make people unclean; eating with unwashed hands does not make them unclean."

## Jesus Helps a Non-Jewish Woman

²¹Jesus left that place and went to the area of Tyre and Sidon. ²²A Canaanite

### COOL

#### Beyond Bleach

White socks . . . what a pain to clean! No matter how often you wash them, they always end up looking greyish. Bleach can often help. Bleach attacks dirt with oxygen, breaking it up into smaller bits that are easily washed away. Pretty cool!

One day Jesus' followers saw the whitest clothing anyone has ever seen! Jesus stood on a mountain talking with Elijah and Moses when "his clothes became white as light" (Matthew 17:2)—whiter than any person could make them. Jesus' majesty glowed from the inside out! Not even bleach can do that!

## THEN HIS FOLLOWERS FILLED SEVEN BASKETS WITH THE LEFTOVER PIECES OF FOOD.

woman from that area came to Jesus and cried out, "Lord, Son of David, have mercy on me! My daughter has a demon, and she is suffering very much."

²³But Jesus did not answer the woman. So his followers came to Jesus and begged him, "Tell the woman to go away. She is following us and shouting."

²⁴Jesus answered, "God sent me only to the lost sheep, the people of Israel."

²⁵Then the woman came to Jesus again and bowed before him and said, "Lord, help me!"

²⁶Jesus answered, "It is not right to take the children's bread and give it to the dogs."

²⁷The woman said, "Yes, Lord, but even the dogs eat the crumbs that fall from their masters' table."

²⁸Then Jesus answered, "Woman, you have great faith! I will do what you asked." And at that moment the woman's daughter was healed.

## Jesus Heals Many People

²⁹After leaving there, Jesus went along the shore of Lake Galilee. He went up on a hill and sat there. ³⁰Great crowds came to Jesus, bringing with them the lame, the blind, the crippled, those who could not speak, and many others. They put them at Jesus' feet, and he healed them. ³¹The crowd was amazed when they saw that people who could not speak before were now able to speak. The crippled were made strong. The lame could walk, and the blind could see. And they praised the God of Israel for this.

## More than Four Thousand Fed

³²Jesus called his followers to him and said, "I feel sorry for these people, because they have already been with me three days, and they have nothing to eat. I don't want to send them away hungry. They might faint while going home."

³³His followers asked him, "How can we get enough bread to feed all these people? We are far away from any town."

³⁴Jesus asked, "How many loaves of bread do you have?"

They answered, "Seven, and a few small fish."

³⁵Jesus told the people to sit on the ground. ³⁶He took the seven loaves of bread and the fish and gave thanks to God. Then he divided the food and gave it to his followers, and they gave it to the people. ³⁷All the people ate and were satisfied. Then his followers filled seven baskets with the leftover pieces of food. ³⁸There were about four thousand men there who ate, besides women and children. ³⁹After sending the people home, Jesus got into the boat and went to the area of Magadan.

## The Leaders Ask for a Miracle

**16** The Pharisees and Sadducees came to Jesus, wanting to trick him. So they asked him to show them a miracle from God.

²Jesus answered,ⁿ "At sunset you say we will have good weather, because the sky is red. ³And in the morning you say that it will be a rainy day, because the sky is dark and red. You see these signs in the sky and know what they mean. In the same way, you see the things that I am doing now, but you don't know their meaning. ⁴Evil and sinful people ask for a

### Q&A

**Q** Is there really a hell?

**A** Revelation 21:8, Matthew 13:41—42, Mark 9:48 (and many other verses) describe hell. Yes, it's real; the punishment for sin is spiritual death in hell. But God made an escape route! By believing in Jesus' death and resurrection and asking him to forgive our sins, we become right with God. If you've done that, don't be afraid of hell. Your future is in heaven!

15:14 **leaders** *Some Greek copies continue, "of blind people."* 16:2–3 **answered** *Some Greek copies do not have the rest of verse 2 and verse 3.*

miracle as a sign, but they will not be given any sign, except the sign of Jonah."[n] Then Jesus left them and went away.

## Guard Against Wrong Teachings

[5]Jesus' followers went across the lake, but they had forgotten to bring bread. [6]Jesus said to them, "Be careful! Beware of the yeast of the Pharisees and the Sadducees."

[7]His followers discussed the meaning of this, saying, "He said this because we forgot to bring bread."

[8]Knowing what they were talking about, Jesus asked them, "Why are you talking about not having bread? Your faith is small. [9]Do you still not understand? Remember the five loaves of bread that fed the five thousand? And remember that you filled many baskets with the leftovers? [10]Or the seven loaves of bread that

# dig deeper

### Matthew 19:16–22

Do you know the game "Simon Says?" A leader gives out instructions such as "touch your nose" or "jump up and down," but you're only supposed to follow them if she first says, "Simon says . . ." If you make a mistake, you're out! It's fun to compete with a big group and see who can stay in the game the longest. But, after a while, it gets a bit tiring and confusing and, at some point, even the best player makes a mistake and is out. No matter how many times she got it right, one mistake means it's over for her!

It's a lot like following God's rules. Some people try hard to obey them. Like the rich young man of Matthew 19:16–22, they might succeed at keeping most of the rules. But the Bible says that a person who fails to obey one command is guilty of breaking all of them. So don't think, "Well, I never murdered anyone," because you've probably loved money too much, right?

Does it seem hopeless? It's not! Because God knew you would never be able to keep all his rules, he made a way for you to be forgiven. Thank him right now for sending Jesus to save you from the punishment for breaking God's laws!

# Q & A

**Q** I'm sick of living on a farm! I want to move to the city but I can't. What can I do about how I feel?

**A** This isn't easy to do, but God wants us to appreciate and be satisfied with what we have. Colossians 3:15 says, "Always be thankful." Living in the city can get tiring after a while, too, because there's more noise, traffic, pollution, and people! Ask your parents if you can all take a short trip to the city sometime for a change of scenery. In the meantime, try to be grateful. Only you can control how you feel!

fed the four thousand and the many baskets you filled then also? [11]I was not talking to you about bread. Why don't you understand that? I am telling you to beware of the yeast of the Pharisees and the Sadducees." [12]Then the followers understood that Jesus was not telling them to beware of the yeast used in bread but to beware of the teaching of the Pharisees and the Sadducees.

## Peter Says Jesus Is the Christ

[13]When Jesus came to the area of Caesarea Philippi, he asked his followers, "Who do people say the Son of Man is?"

[14]They answered, "Some say you are John the Baptist. Others say you are Elijah, and still others say you are Jeremiah or one of the prophets."

[15]Then Jesus asked them, "And who do you say I am?"

[16]Simon Peter answered, "You are the Christ, the Son of the living God."

[17]Jesus answered, "You are blessed, Simon son of Jonah, because no person taught you that. My Father in heaven showed you who I am. [18]So I tell you, you are Peter.[n] On this rock I will build my church, and the power of death will not be able to defeat it. [19]I will give you the

**16:4 sign of Jonah** *Jonah's three days in the fish are like Jesus' three days in the tomb. The story about Jonah is in the Book of Jonah.* **16:18 Peter** *The Greek name "Peter," like the Aramaic name "Cephas," means "rock."*

28

keys of the kingdom of heaven; the things you don't allow on earth will be the things that God does not allow, and the things you allow on earth will be the things that God allows." 20Then Jesus warned his followers not to tell anyone he was the Christ.

## Jesus Says that He Must Die

21From that time on Jesus began telling his followers that he must go to Jerusalem, where the Jewish elders, the leading priests, and the teachers of the law would make him suffer many things. He told them he must be killed and then be raised from the dead on the third day.

22Peter took Jesus aside and told him not to talk like that. He said, "God save you from those things, Lord! Those things will never happen to you!"

23Then Jesus said to Peter, "Go away from me, Satan![n] You are not helping me! You don't care about the things of God, but only about the things people think are important."

24Then Jesus said to his followers, "If people want to follow me, they must give up the things they want. They must be willing even to give up their lives to follow me. 25Those who want to save their lives will give up true life, and those who give up their lives for me will have true life. 26It is worthless to have the whole world if they lose their souls. They could never pay enough to buy back their souls. 27The Son of Man will come again

> IF PEOPLE WANT TO FOLLOW ME, THEY MUST GIVE UP THE THINGS THEY WANT. THEY MUST BE WILLING EVEN TO GIVE UP THEIR LIVES TO FOLLOW ME.

with his Father's glory and with his angels. At that time, he will reward them for what they have done. 28I tell you the truth, some people standing here will see the Son of Man coming with his kingdom before they die."

## Jesus Talks with Moses and Elijah

**17** Six days later, Jesus took Peter, James, and John, the brother of James, up on a high mountain by themselves. 2While they watched, Jesus' appearance was changed; his face became bright like the sun, and his

clothes became white as light. 3Then Moses and Elijah[n] appeared to them, talking with Jesus.

4Peter said to Jesus, "Lord, it is good that we are here. If you want, I will put up three tents here—one for you, one for Moses, and one for Elijah."

5While Peter was talking, a bright cloud covered them. A voice came from the cloud and said, "This is my Son, whom I love, and I am very pleased with him. Listen to him!"

6When his followers heard the voice, they were so frightened they fell to the ground. 7But Jesus went to them and touched them and said, "Stand up. Don't be afraid." 8When they looked up, they saw Jesus was now alone.

9As they were coming down the mountain, Jesus commanded them not to tell anyone about what they had seen until the Son of Man had risen from the dead.

10Then his followers asked him, "Why do the teachers of the law say that Elijah must come first?"

11Jesus answered, "They are right to say that Elijah is coming and that he will make everything the way it should be. 12But I tell you that Elijah has already come, and they did not recognize him. They did to him whatever they wanted to do. It will be the same with the Son of Man; those same people will make the Son of Man suffer." 13Then the followers

understood that Jesus was talking about John the Baptist.

## Jesus Heals a Sick Boy

14When Jesus and his followers came back to the crowd, a man came to Jesus and bowed before him. 15The man said, "Lord, have mercy on my son. He has epilepsy[n] and is suffering very much, because he often falls into the fire or into the water. 16I brought him to your followers, but they could not cure him."

17Jesus answered, "You people have no faith, and your lives are all wrong. How long must I put up with you? How long must I continue to be patient with you? Bring the boy here." 18Jesus commanded the demon inside the boy. Then the demon came out, and the boy was healed from that time on.

19The followers came to Jesus when he was alone and asked, "Why couldn't we force the demon out?"

20Jesus answered, "Because your faith is too small. I tell you the truth, if your faith is as big as a mustard seed, you can say to this mountain, 'Move from here to there,' and it will move. All things will be possible for you. [21That kind of spirit comes out only if you use prayer and fasting.]"[n]

# Q&A

Q  Is drinking wine or beer a sin?

A  Some people believe it is a sin, but the Bible doesn't exactly say that. What it does say, very clearly, is that getting drunk or becoming addicted to something (like drugs or cigarettes) is sinful. Ephesians 5:18 says, "Do not be drunk with wine, which will ruin you, but be filled with the Spirit." Many people can't control how much they drink, so when you're of legal drinking age, you may decide it's better not to start at all!

16:23 **Satan** Name for the devil, meaning "the enemy." Jesus means that Peter was talking like Satan.  17:3 **Moses and Elijah** Two of the most important Jewish leaders in the past. God had given Moses the Law, and Elijah was an important prophet.  17:15 **epilepsy** A disease that causes a person sometimes to lose control of his body and maybe faint, shake strongly, or not be able to move.  17:21 **That . . . fasting.** Some Greek copies do not contain the bracketed text.

# Q & A

**Q** Why is baptism important?

**A** You could compare it to a wedding. A couple could get married privately in front of a judge, but when they do it in front of others, they're showing everyone that they've made a commitment to each other. Baptism shows people that you're a Christian and are now following Jesus. Also, when you're dipped in or sprinkled with water, it's like saying the old you has died and the new you, with God's Spirit living inside you, has come to life (see Romans 6:4)!

## Jesus Talks About His Death

²²While Jesus' followers were gathering in Galilee, he said to them, "The Son of Man will be handed over to people, ²³and they will kill him. But on the third day he will be raised from the dead." And the followers were filled with sadness.

## Jesus Talks About Paying Taxes

²⁴When Jesus and his followers came to Capernaum, the men who collected the Temple tax came to Peter. They asked, "Does your teacher pay the Temple tax?"

²⁵Peter answered, "Yes, Jesus pays the tax."

Peter went into the house, but before he could speak, Jesus said to him, "What do you think? The kings of the earth collect different kinds of taxes. But who pays the taxes—the king's children or others?"

²⁶Peter answered, "Other people pay the taxes."

Jesus said to Peter, "Then the children of the king don't have to pay taxes. ²⁷But we don't want to upset these tax collectors. So go to the lake and fish. After you catch the first fish, open its mouth and you will find a coin. Take that coin and give it to the tax collectors for you and me."

## Who Is the Greatest?

**18** At that time the followers came to Jesus and asked, "Who is greatest in the kingdom of heaven?"

²Jesus called a little child to him and stood the child before his followers. ³Then he said, "I tell you the truth, you must change and become like little children. Otherwise, you will never enter the kingdom of heaven. ⁴The greatest person in the kingdom of heaven is the one who makes himself humble like this child.

⁵"Whoever accepts a child in my name accepts me. ⁶If one of these little children believes in me, and someone causes that child to sin, it would be better for that person to have a large stone tied around the neck and be drowned in the sea. ⁷How terrible for the people of the world because of the things that cause them to sin. Such things will happen, but how terrible for the one who causes them to happen! ⁸If your hand or your foot causes you to sin, cut it off and throw it away. It is better for you to lose part of your body and live forever than to have two hands and two feet and be thrown into the fire that burns forever. ⁹If your eye causes you to sin, take it out and throw it away. It is better for you to have only one eye and live forever than to have two eyes and be thrown into the fire of hell.

## A Lost Sheep

¹⁰"Be careful. Don't think these little children are worth nothing. I tell you that they have angels in heaven who are always with my Father in heaven. [¹¹The Son of Man came to save lost people.]ⁿ

¹²"If a man has a hundred sheep but one of the sheep gets lost, he will leave the other ninety-nine on the hill and go to look for the lost sheep. ¹³I tell you the truth, if he finds it he is happier about that one sheep than about the ninety-nine that were never lost. ¹⁴In the same

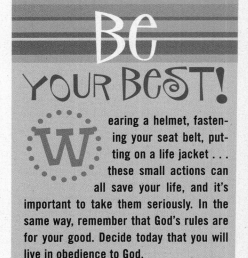

# Be YOUR BEST!

**W** earing a helmet, fastening your seat belt, putting on a life jacket . . . these small actions can all save your life, and it's important to take them seriously. In the same way, remember that God's rules are for your good. Decide today that you will live in obedience to God.

# read it, do it

## Matthew 23:12

**R** ead It: Stay humble!

**D** o It: See how many days you can go without boasting about yourself. It should get easier every day! Pray that God will help you have a humble heart and not a proud one.

---

18:11 **The . . . people.** *Some Greek copies do not contain the bracketed text.*

## god's promises

### Matthew 21:22

There's a joke that says, "If you want a puppy, start by asking your parents for a horse." But that's called manipulation, and God doesn't like it. (Manipulation means trying to control a situation in a dishonest or mean way.) And you probably won't feel good knowing that a person did something for you because you made them or tricked them into it.

The more you love your parents and respect their wishes, the more success you will have in getting what you ask for. That's different from manipulation. When you love someone, you don't ask for things that would make them unhappy. You trust that they will give you the very best they have for you.

In this verse, Jesus promises that Christians can have whatever they ask God for. That doesn't mean he'll send you new shoes every week or free tickets to a concert. He didn't promise to answer selfish prayers. When you love God, you want the same things he wants, so your prayer requests always please him. Especially when you trust him to answer in the very best way.

What's the best thing you can ask for? Anything that helps you or other people know and love God better. You better believe God will answer that prayer!

*You better believe God will answer that prayer!*

## An Unforgiving Servant

²¹Then Peter came to Jesus and asked, "Lord, when my fellow believer sins against me, how many times must I forgive him? Should I forgive him as many as seven times?"

²²Jesus answered, "I tell you, you must forgive him more than seven times. You must forgive him even if he wrongs you seventy times seven.

²³"The kingdom of heaven is like a king who decided to collect the money his servants owed him. ²⁴When the king began to collect his money, a servant who owed him several million dollars was brought to him. ²⁵But the servant did not have enough money to pay his master, the king. So the master ordered that everything the servant owned should be sold, even the servant's wife and children. Then the money would be used to pay the king what the servant owed.

²⁶"But the servant fell on his knees and begged, 'Be patient with me, and I will pay you everything I owe.' ²⁷The master felt sorry for his servant and told him he did not have to pay it back. Then he let the servant go free.

²⁸"Later, that same servant found another servant who owed him a few dollars. The servant grabbed him around the neck and said, 'Pay me the money you owe me!'

²⁹"The other servant fell on his knees and begged him, 'Be patient with me, and I will pay you everything I owe.'

³⁰"But the first servant refused to be patient. He threw the other servant into prison until he could pay everything he owed. ³¹When the other servants saw what had happened, they were very sorry. So they went and told their master all that had happened.

³²"Then the master called his servant in and said, 'You evil servant! Because you begged me to forget what you owed, I told you that you did not have to pay anything. ³³You should have showed mercy to that other servant, just as I showed mercy to you.' ³⁴The master was

way, your Father in heaven does not want any of these little children to be lost.

### When a Person Sins Against You

¹⁵"If your fellow believer sins against you,ⁿ go and tell him in private what he did wrong. If he listens to you, you have helped that person to be your brother or sister again. ¹⁶But if he refuses to listen, go to him again and take one or two other people with you. 'Every case may be proved by two or three witnesses.'ⁿ ¹⁷If he refuses to listen to them, tell the church.

If he refuses to listen to the church, then treat him like a person who does not believe in God or like a tax collector.

¹⁸"I tell you the truth, the things you don't allow on earth will be the things God does not allow. And the things you allow on earth will be the things that God allows.

¹⁹"Also, I tell you that if two of you on earth agree about something and pray for it, it will be done for you by my Father in heaven. ²⁰This is true because if two or three people come together in my name, I am there with them."

### . . . GOD HAS JOINED THE TWO TOGETHER, SO NO ONE SHOULD SEPARATE THEM.

18:15 **against you** *Some Greek copies do not have "against you."*   18:16 **'Every . . . witnesses.'** *Quotation from Deuteronomy 19:15.*

# Relationships

If you are not used to being around handicapped people, it can seem a bit awkward or even scary to be with them. When Jesus encountered two blind men on the side of the road, the Bible says he had compassion on them. Rather than laughing or pointing at them, he listened to them—and healed their eyes (Matthew 20:29–34)! We should have compassion like Jesus did. We can't heal wounds or make disabilities disappear, but we can treat handicapped people with the same gentleness that Jesus displayed.

very angry and put the servant in prison to be punished until he could pay everything he owed.

35"This king did what my heavenly Father will do to you if you do not forgive your brother or sister from your heart."

## Jesus Teaches About Divorce

**19** After Jesus said all these things, he left Galilee and went into the area of Judea on the other side of the Jordan River. 2Large crowds followed him, and he healed them there.

3Some Pharisees came to Jesus and tried to trick him. They asked, "Is it right for a man to divorce his wife for any reason he chooses?"

4Jesus answered, "Surely you have read in the Scriptures: When God made the world, 'he made them male and female.'[n] 5And God said, 'So a man will leave his father and mother and be united with his wife, and the two will become one body.'[n] 6So there are not two, but one. God has joined the two together, so no one should separate them."

7The Pharisees asked, "Why then did Moses give a command for a man to divorce his wife by giving her divorce papers?"

8Jesus answered, "Moses allowed you to divorce your wives because you refused to accept God's teaching, but divorce was not allowed in the beginning. 9I tell you that anyone who divorces his wife and marries another woman is guilty of adultery.[n] The only reason for a man to divorce his wife is if his wife has sexual relations with another man."

10The followers said to him, "If that is the only reason a man can divorce his wife, it is better not to marry."

11Jesus answered, "Not everyone can accept this teaching, but God has made some able to accept it. 12There are different reasons why some men cannot marry. Some men were born without the ability to become fathers. Others were made that way later in life by other people. And some men have given up marriage because of the kingdom of heaven. But the person who can marry should accept this teaching about marriage."[n]

## Jesus Welcomes Children

13Then the people brought their little children to Jesus so he could put his hands on them[n] and pray for them. His followers told them to stop, 14but Jesus said, "Let the little children come to me. Don't stop them, because the kingdom of heaven belongs to people who are like these children." 15After Jesus put his hands on the children, he left there.

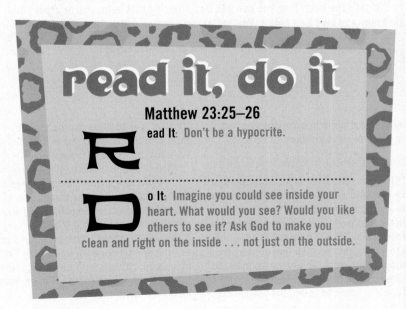

# read it, do it

## Matthew 23:25–26

**R**ead It: Don't be a hypocrite.

**D**o It: Imagine you could see inside your heart. What would you see? Would you like others to see it? Ask God to make you clean and right on the inside . . . not just on the outside.

**19:4** 'he made . . . female' *Quotation from Genesis 1:27 or 5:2.* **19:5** 'So . . . body.' *Quotation from Genesis 2:24.* **19:9** adultery *Some Greek copies continue, "And anyone who marries a divorced woman is guilty of adultery." Compare Matthew 5:32.* **19:12** **But . . . marriage.** *This may also mean, "The person who can accept this teaching about not marrying should accept it."* **19:13** **put his hands on them** *Showing that Jesus gave special blessings to these children.*

## dig deeper

### Matthew 24:9–12

Imagine you read this in a magazine: "There has never been so much evil in the world. Most people have stopped loving others. Millions of people have stopped loving God, too. They have given up on Jesus Christ, tossed out the Bible, and quit going to church. Instead, they have embraced the lies of false prophets."

Whoa! That would never happen, right? Here's a surprise: that's what Jesus said people would be like at the end of history. How did he know? After all, people have been sinful since the be-ginning of time. Jesus warned that people would continue to do a lot of the evil things they were doing at that time. He warned us that things would not get better as the decades and centuries went by. People would become even more re-bellious against God.

Read the first paragraph again. Since Jesus warned us, we shouldn't be surprised no matter who falls away and no matter how hateful they become. De-cide today that you will love God with all your heart, soul, strength, and mind. And that you will never stop loving oth-ers. No matter what happens, stay true to the end!

### A Rich Young Man's Question

[16]A man came to Jesus and asked, "Teacher, what good thing must I do to have life forever?"

[17]Jesus answered, "Why do you ask me about what is good? Only God is good. But if you want to have life forever, obey the commands."

[18]The man asked, "Which commands?" Jesus answered, " 'You must not mur-der anyone; you must not be guilty of adultery; you must not steal; you must not tell lies about your neighbor; [19]honor your father and mother;[n] and love your neighbor as you love yourself.' "[n]

[20]The young man said, "I have obeyed all these things. What else do I need to do?"

[21]Jesus answered, "If you want to be perfect, then go and sell your posses-sions and give the money to the poor. If you do this, you will have treasure in heaven. Then come and follow me."

[22]But when the young man heard this, he left sorrowfully, because he was rich.

[23]Then Jesus said to his followers, "I tell you the truth, it will be hard for a rich person to enter the kingdom of heaven. [24]Yes, I tell you that it is easier for a camel to go through the eye of a needle than for a rich person to enter the kingdom of God."

[25]When Jesus' followers heard this, they were very surprised and asked, "Then who can be saved?"

[26]Jesus looked at them and said, "For people this is impossible, but for God all things are possible."

[27]Peter said to Jesus, "Look, we have left everything and followed you. So what will we have?"

[28]Jesus said to them, "I tell you the truth, when the age to come has arrived, the Son of Man will sit on his great throne. All of you who followed me will also sit on twelve thrones, judging the twelve tribes of Israel. [29]And all those who have left houses, brothers, sisters, father, mother,[n] children, or farms to follow me will get much more than they left, and they will have life forever. [30]Many who are first now will be last in the future. And many who are last now will be first in the future.

### A Story About Workers

**20** "The kingdom of heav-en is like a person who owned some land. One morning, he went out very early to hire some people to work in his vineyard. [2]The man agreed to pay the workers one coin[n] for working that day. Then he sent them into the vineyard to work. [3]About nine o'clock the man went to the market-place and saw some other people stand-ing there, doing nothing. [4]So he said to them, 'If you go and work in my vineyard, I will pay you what your work is worth.' [5]So they went to work in the vineyard. The man went out again about twelve o'clock and three o'clock and did the same thing. [6]About five o'clock the man went to the marketplace again and saw others standing there. He asked them, 'Why did you stand here all day doing

### . . . FOR GOD ALL THINGS ARE POSSIBLE.

**19:19 'You . . . mother.'** Quotation from Exodus 20:12–16; Deuteronomy 5:16–20. **19:19 'love . . . yourself'** Quotation from Leviticus 19:18. **19:29 mother** Some Greek copies continue, "or wife." **20:2 coin** A Roman denarius. One coin was the average pay for one day's work.

# Q&A

**Q** My parents are letting me go on a short mission trip to Mexico. How can I get ready?

**A** Ask lots of people to pray for you, especially at your church. (You pray, too!) Then, do some research on Mexico so you'll know some things about the culture before you get there. Check your packing list with your team leader to make sure you've got whatever you need. Then . . . go and have a great time serving God!

nothing?' [7]They answered, 'No one gave us a job.' The man said to them, 'Then you can go and work in my vineyard.'

[8]"At the end of the day, the owner of the vineyard said to the boss of all the workers, 'Call the workers and pay them. Start with the last people I hired and end with those I hired first.'

[9]"When the workers who were hired at five o'clock came to get their pay, each received one coin. [10]When the workers who were hired first came to get their pay, they thought they would be paid more than the others. But each one of them also received one coin. [11]When they got their coin, they complained to the man who owned the land. [12]They said, 'Those people were hired last and worked only one hour. But you paid them the same as you paid us who worked hard all day in the hot sun.' [13]But the man who owned the vineyard said to one of those workers, 'Friend, I am being fair to you. You agreed to work for one coin. [14]So take your pay and go. I want to give the man who was hired last the same pay that I gave you. [15]I can do what I want with my own money. Are you jealous because I am good to those people?'

[16]"So those who are last now will someday be first, and those who are first now will someday be last."

## Jesus Talks About His Own Death

[17]While Jesus was going to Jerusalem, he took his twelve followers aside privately and said to them, [18]"Look, we are going to Jerusalem. The Son of Man will be turned over to the leading priests and the teachers of the law, and they will say that he must die. [19]They will give the Son of Man to the non-Jewish people to laugh at him and beat him with whips and crucify him. But on the third day, he will be raised to life again."

## A Mother Asks Jesus a Favor

[20]Then the wife of Zebedee came to Jesus with her sons. She bowed before him and asked him to do something for her.

[21]Jesus asked, "What do you want?"

She said, "Promise that one of my sons will sit at your right side and the other will sit at your left side in your kingdom."

[22]But Jesus said, "You don't understand what you are asking. Can you drink the cup that I am about to drink?"[n]

The sons answered, "Yes, we can."

[23]Jesus said to them, "You will drink from my cup. But I cannot choose who will sit at my right or my left; those places belong to those for whom my Father has prepared them."

[24]When the other ten followers heard this, they were angry with the two brothers. [25]Jesus called all the followers together and said, "You know that the rulers of the non-Jewish people love to show their power over the people. And their important leaders love to use all their authority. [26]But it should not be that way among you. Whoever wants to become great among you must serve the rest of you like a servant. [27]Whoever wants to become first among you must serve the rest of you like a slave. [28]In the same way, the Son of Man did not come to be served. He came to serve others and to give his life as a ransom for many people."

## Jesus Heals Two Blind Men

[29]When Jesus and his followers were leaving Jericho, a great many people followed him. [30]Two blind men sitting by the road heard that Jesus was going by, so they shouted, "Lord, Son of David, have mercy on us!"

[31]The people warned the blind men to be quiet, but they shouted even more, "Lord, Son of David, have mercy on us!"

[32]Jesus stopped and said to the blind men, "What do you want me to do for you?"

[33]They answered, "Lord, we want to see."

[34]Jesus felt sorry for the blind men and touched their eyes, and at once they could see. Then they followed Jesus.

## Jesus Enters Jerusalem as a King

**21** As Jesus and his followers were coming closer to Jerusalem, they stopped at Bethphage at the hill called the Mount of Olives. From there Jesus sent two of his followers [2]and said to them, "Go to the town you can see there. When you enter it, you will quickly find a donkey tied there with its colt. Untie them and bring them to me. [3]If anyone asks you why you are taking the donkeys, say that the Master needs them, and he will send them at once."

[4]This was to bring about what the prophet had said:

[5]"Tell the people of Jerusalem,
 'Your king is coming to you.
He is gentle and riding on a donkey,
 on the colt of a donkey.' "
 *Isaiah 62:11; Zechariah 9:9*

[6]The followers went and did what Jesus told them to do. [7]They brought the donkey and the colt to Jesus and laid their coats on them, and Jesus sat on them. [8]Many people spread their coats on the road. Others cut branches from

## speakout!

**Q** What do you do when you're worried?

**A** I read my Bible because it calms me. —Hannah, 10

---

**20:22 drink . . . drink** *Jesus used the idea of drinking from a cup to ask if they could accept the same terrible things that would happen to him.*

# BibLe BasicS

**B**ible study. Devotions. Time with God. What do all these mean? Studying the Bible is not just following a set of rules to "discover" what the Bible says and then be done. Instead, it's more like an adventure! The Bible has so much to say for your life today, and it is fresh each time you read it. Studying the Bible could be reading through a book to look for common themes. It could be getting together with friends to discuss what you think God is saying in a passage. Or you could ask someone at church to explain a verse. Studying the Bible always includes asking God to show himself to you. It can't be complete unless it changes your life!

the tree, only leaves. So Jesus said to the tree, "You will never again have fruit." The tree immediately dried up.

[20] When his followers saw this, they were amazed. They asked, "How did the fig tree dry up so quickly?"

[21] Jesus answered, "I tell you the truth, if you have faith and do not doubt, you will be able to do what I did to this tree and even more. You will be able to say to this mountain, 'Go, fall into the sea.' And if you have faith, it will happen. [22] If you believe, you will get anything you ask for in prayer."

## Leaders Doubt Jesus' Authority

[23] Jesus went to the Temple, and while he was teaching there, the leading priests and the elders of the people came to him. They said, "What authority do you have to do these things? Who gave you this authority?"

[24] Jesus answered, "I also will ask you a question. If you answer me, then I will tell you what authority I have to do these things. [25] Tell me: When John baptized people, did that come from God or just from other people?"

the trees and spread them on the road. [9] The people were walking ahead of Jesus and behind him, shouting,

"Praise[n] to the Son of David!
God bless the One who comes in the name of the Lord!
*Psalm 118:26*
Praise to God in heaven!"

[10] When Jesus entered Jerusalem, all the city was filled with excitement. The people asked, "Who is this man?"

a house for prayer.'[n] But you are changing it into a 'hideout for robbers.'"[n]

[14] The blind and crippled people came to Jesus in the Temple, and he healed them. [15] The leading priests and the teachers of the law saw that Jesus was doing wonderful things and that the children were praising him in the Temple, saying, "Praise[n] to the Son of David." All these things made the priests and the teachers of the law very angry.

[11] The crowd said, "This man is Jesus, the prophet from the town of Nazareth in Galilee."

## Jesus Goes to the Temple

[12] Jesus went into the Temple and threw out all the people who were buying and selling there. He turned over the tables of those who were exchanging different kinds of money, and he upset the benches of those who were selling doves. [13] Jesus said to all the people there, "It is written in the Scriptures, 'My Temple will be called

[16] They asked Jesus, "Do you hear the things these children are saying?"

Jesus answered, "Yes. Haven't you read in the Scriptures, 'You have taught children and babies to sing praises'?"[n]

[17] Then Jesus left and went out of the city to Bethany, where he spent the night.

## The Power of Faith

[18] Early the next morning, as Jesus was going back to the city, he became hungry. [19] Seeing a fig tree beside the road, Jesus went to it, but there were no figs on

# cool

## Heart and Soul

**T**here's a two-part tune that many people can pick out on the piano even if they've never taken lessons and can't read music. You probably know it . . . maybe you even play it with a friend sometimes. But a lot of people can't name the song! It's "Heart and Soul" by Frank Loesser. (Look it up to see if that's the one you know.)

A verse in the Bible talks about "heart and soul," too! In Matthew 22:37, Jesus said to love God "with all your heart, all your soul, and all your mind." Practice that one!

**21:9, 15 Praise** *Literally, "Hosanna," a Hebrew word used at first in praying to God for help. At this time it was probably a shout of joy used in praising God or his Messiah.* **21:13 'My Temple . . . prayer.'** *Quotation from Isaiah 56:7.* **21:13 'hideout for robbers'** *Quotation from Jeremiah 7:11.* **21:16 'You . . . praises.'** *Quotation from the Septuagint (Greek) version of Psalm 8:2.*

They argued about Jesus' question, saying, "If we answer, 'John's baptism was from God,' Jesus will say, 'Then why didn't you believe him?' [26]But if we say, 'It was from people,' we are afraid of what the crowd will do because they all believe that John was a prophet."

[27]So they answered Jesus, "We don't know."

Jesus said to them, "Then I won't tell you what authority I have to do these things.

## A Story About Two Sons

[28]"Tell me what you think about this: A man had two sons. He went to the first son and said, 'Son, go and work today in my vineyard.' [29]The son answered, 'I will not go.' But later the son changed his mind and went. [30]Then the father went to the other son and said, 'Son, go and work today in my vineyard.' The son answered, 'Yes, sir, I will go and work,' but he did not go. [31]Which of the two sons obeyed his father?"

The priests and leaders answered, "The first son."

## Thunder and Lightning

Electricity likes to travel between positive and negative "charges." When clouds develop a strong *negative* electrical charge, they react with the *positive* charge of the earth. Then . . . KAPOW! In about a second, the lightning bolt heats the air around it to five times the temperature of the sun! The air then expands faster than the speed of sound, causing us to hear crashing thunder.

If you think that's cool, check this out! Matthew 24:27 says that when Jesus comes back, "He will be seen by everyone, like lightning flashing from the east to the west."

## THE STONE THAT THE BUILDERS REJECTED BECAME THE CORNERSTONE.

Jesus said to them, "I tell you the truth, the tax collectors and the prostitutes will enter the kingdom of God before you do. [32]John came to show you the right way to live. You did not believe him, but the tax collectors and prostitutes believed him. Even after seeing this, you still refused to change your ways and believe him.

## A Story About God's Son

[33]"Listen to this story: There was a man who owned a vineyard. He put a wall around it and dug a hole for a winepress and built a tower. Then he leased the land to some farmers and left for a trip. [34]When it was time for the grapes to be picked, he sent his servants to the farmers to get his share of the grapes. [35]But the farmers grabbed the servants, beat one, killed another, and then killed a third servant with stones. [36]So the man sent some other servants to the farmers, even more than he sent the first time. But the farmers did the same thing to the servants that they had done before. [37]So the man decided to send his son to the farmers. He said, 'They will respect my son.' [38]But when the farmers saw the son, they said to each other, 'This son will inherit the vineyard. If we kill him, it will be ours!' [39]Then the farmers grabbed the son, threw him out of the vineyard, and killed him. [40]So what will the owner of the vineyard do to these farmers when he comes?"

[41]The priests and leaders said, "He will surely kill those evil men. Then he will lease the vineyard to some other farmers who will give him his share of the crop at harvest time."

[42]Jesus said to them, "Surely you have read this in the Scriptures:

'The stone that the builders rejected
   became the cornerstone.
The Lord did this,
   and it is wonderful to us.'
                    *Psalm 118:22–23*

[43]"So I tell you that the kingdom of God will be taken away from you and given to people who do the things God wants in his kingdom. [44]The person who falls on this stone will be broken, and on whomever that stone falls, that person will be crushed."[n]

[45]When the leading priests and the Pharisees heard these stories, they knew Jesus was talking about them. [46]They wanted to arrest him, but they were afraid of the people, because the people believed that Jesus was a prophet.

## A Story About a Wedding Feast

**22** Jesus again used stories to teach them. He said, [2]"The kingdom of heaven is like a king who prepared a wedding feast for his son. [3]The king invited some people to the feast. When the feast was ready, the king sent his servants to tell the people, but they refused to come.

[4]"Then the king sent other servants, saying, 'Tell those who have been invited that my feast is ready. I have killed my best bulls and calves for the dinner, and everything is ready. Come to the wedding feast.'

[5]"But the people refused to listen to the servants and left to do other things. One went to work in his field, and another went to his business. [6]Some of the other people grabbed the servants, beat them, and killed them. [7]The king was furious and sent his army to kill the murderers and burn their city.

[8]"After that, the king said to his servants, 'The wedding feast is ready. I invited those people, but they were not worthy to come. [9]So go to the street corners and invite everyone you find to come to my feast.' [10]So the servants went into the streets and gathered all the people they could find, both good and bad. And the wedding hall was filled with guests.

[11]"When the king came in to see the guests, he saw a man who was not dressed for a wedding. [12]The king said, 'Friend, how were you allowed to come in here? You are not dressed for a wedding.' But the man said nothing. [13]So the king told some servants, 'Tie this man's hands and feet. Throw him out into the darkness, where people will cry and grind their teeth with pain.'

[14]"Yes, many are invited, but only a few are chosen."

## Is It Right to Pay Taxes or Not?

[15]Then the Pharisees left that place and made plans to trap Jesus in saying some-

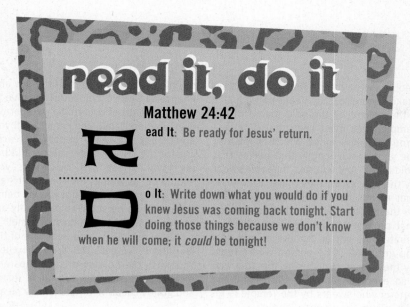

## read it, do it

### Matthew 24:42

**R**ead It: Be ready for Jesus' return.

**D**o It: Write down what you would do if you knew Jesus was coming back tonight. Start doing those things because we don't know when he will come; it *could* be tonight!

---

³⁵One Pharisee, who was an expert on the law of Moses, asked Jesus this question to test him: ³⁶"Teacher, which command in the law is the most important?" ³⁷Jesus answered, " 'Love the Lord your God with all your heart, all your soul, and all your mind.'ⁿ ³⁸This is the first and most important command. ³⁹And the second command is like the first: 'Love your neighbor as you love yourself.'ⁿ ⁴⁰All the law and the writings of the prophets depend on these two commands."

### Jesus Questions the Pharisees

⁴¹While the Pharisees were together, Jesus asked them, ⁴²"What do you think about the Christ? Whose son is he?"

They answered, "The Christ is the Son of David."

⁴³Then Jesus said to them, "Then why did David call him 'Lord'? David, speaking by the power of the Holy Spirit, said,

⁴⁴'The Lord said to my Lord,
  "Sit by me at my right side,
   until I put your enemies under your
      control." '          *Psalm 110:1*
⁴⁵David calls the Christ 'Lord,' so how can the Christ be his son?"

⁴⁶None of the Pharisees could answer Jesus' question, and after that day no one was brave enough to ask him any more questions.

### Jesus Accuses Some Leaders

**23** Then Jesus said to the crowds and to his followers, ²"The teachers of the law and the Pharisees have the authority to tell you what the law of Moses says. ³So you should obey and follow whatever they tell you, but their lives are not good examples for you to follow. They tell you to do things, but they themselves don't do them. ⁴They make strict rules and try to force people to obey them, but they are unwilling to help those who struggle under the weight of their rules.

⁵"They do good things so that other people will see them. They enlarge the little boxesⁿ holding Scriptures that they wear, and they make their special prayer

thing wrong. ¹⁶They sent some of their own followers and some people from the group called Herodians.ⁿ They said, "Teacher, we know that you are an honest man and that you teach the truth about God's way. You are not afraid of what other people think about you, because you pay no attention to who they are. ¹⁷So tell us what you think. Is it right to pay taxes to Caesar or not?"

¹⁸But knowing that these leaders were trying to trick him, Jesus said, "You hypocrites! Why are you trying to trap me? ¹⁹Show me a coin used for paying the tax." So the men showed him a coin.ⁿ ²⁰Then Jesus asked, "Whose image and name are on the coin?"

²¹The men answered, "Caesar's."

dies without having children, his brother must marry the widow and have children for him. ²⁵Once there were seven brothers among us. The first one married and died. Since he had no children, his brother married the widow. ²⁶Then the second brother also died. The same thing happened to the third brother and all the other brothers. ²⁷Finally, the woman died. ²⁸Since all seven men had married her, when people rise from the dead, whose wife will she be?"

²⁹Jesus answered, "You don't understand, because you don't know what the Scriptures say, and you don't know about the power of God. ³⁰When people rise from the dead, they will not marry, nor

Then Jesus said to them, "Give to Caesar the things that are Caesar's, and give to God the things that are God's."

²²When the men heard what Jesus said, they were amazed and left him and went away.

### Some Sadducees Try to Trick Jesus

²³That same day some Sadducees came to Jesus and asked him a question. (Sadducees believed that people would not rise from the dead.) ²⁴They said, "Teacher, Moses said if a married man

will they be given to someone to marry. They will be like the angels in heaven. ³¹Surely you have read what God said to you about rising from the dead. ³²God said, 'I am the God of Abraham, the God of Isaac, and the God of Jacob.'ⁿ God is the God of the living, not the dead."

³³When the people heard this, they were amazed at Jesus' teaching.

### The Most Important Command

³⁴When the Pharisees learned that the Sadducees could not argue with Jesus' answers to them, the Pharisees met together.

**GOD IS THE GOD OF THE LIVING, NOT THE DEAD.**

**22:16 Herodians** *A political group that followed Herod and his family.* **22:19 coin** *A Roman denarius. One coin was the average pay for one day's work.* **22:32 'I am . . . Jacob.'** *Quotation from Exodus 3:6.* **22:37 'Love . . . mind.'** *Quotation from Deuteronomy 6:5.* **22:39 'Love . . . yourself.'** *Quotation from Leviticus 19:18.* **23:5 boxes** *Small leather boxes containing four important Scriptures. Some Jews tied these to their foreheads and left arms, probably to show they were very religious.*

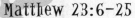

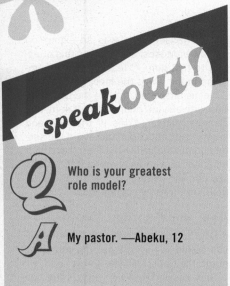

## speakout!

**Q** Who is your greatest role model?

**A** My pastor. —Abeku, 12

clothes very long. ⁶Those Pharisees and teachers of the law love to have the most important seats at feasts and in the synagogues. ⁷They love people to greet them with respect in the marketplaces, and they love to have people call them 'Teacher.'

⁸"But you must not be called 'Teacher,' because you have only one Teacher, and you are all brothers and sisters together. ⁹And don't call any person on earth 'Father,' because you have one Father, who is in heaven. ¹⁰And you should not be called 'Master,' because you have only one Master, the Christ. ¹¹Whoever is your servant is the greatest among you. ¹²Whoever makes himself great will be made humble. Whoever makes himself humble will be made great.

¹³"How terrible for you, teachers of the law and Pharisees! You are hypocrites! You close the door for people to enter the kingdom of heaven. You yourselves don't enter, and you stop others who are trying to enter. [¹⁴How terrible for you, teachers of the law and Pharisees. You are hypocrites. You take away widows' houses, and you say long prayers so that people will notice you. So you will have a worse punishment.]ⁿ

¹⁵"How terrible for you, teachers of the law and Pharisees! You are hypocrites! You travel across land and sea to find one person who will change to your ways. When you find that person, you make him more fit for hell than you are.

¹⁶"How terrible for you! You guide the people, but you are blind. You say, 'If

people swear by the Temple when they make a promise, that means nothing. But if they swear by the gold that is in the Temple, they must keep that promise.' ¹⁷You are blind fools! Which is greater: the gold or the Temple that makes that gold holy? ¹⁸And you say, 'If people swear by the altar when they make a promise, that means nothing. But if they swear by the gift on the altar, they must keep that promise.' ¹⁹You are blind! Which is greater: the gift or the altar that makes the gift holy? ²⁰The person who swears by the altar is really using the altar and also everything on the altar. ²¹And the person who swears by the Temple is really using the Temple and also everything in the Temple. ²²The person who swears by heaven is also using God's throne and the One who sits on that throne.

²³"How terrible for you, teachers of the law and Pharisees! You are hypocrites! You give to God one-tenth of everything you earn—even your mint, dill, and cumin.ⁿ But you don't obey the really important teachings of the law—justice, mercy, and being loyal. These are the things you should do, as well as those other things. ²⁴You guide the people, but you are blind! You are like a person who picks a fly out of a drink and then swallows a camel!ⁿ

²⁵"How terrible for you, teachers of the law and Pharisees! You are hypocrites! You wash the outside of your cups and dishes, but inside they are full of things you got by cheating others and by pleas-

## Shine Your Light

**D**on't you love that wonderful, warm feeling you get when you wrap up in a blanket on a cold winter day? Well, one young girl does, and here's what she did to give others that gift, too!

Wendy, from Salem, Oregon, first started crocheting when she was nine. She wanted to find a way to use her new skill to help others. When she learned about an organization that used crocheted and knitted squares to make afghans (blankets) for homeless people, she knew that she could help.

Along with crocheting squares, Wendy started asking for help from her friends and family. Working together, they were able to make dozens of squares in a short time, and those squares were made into warm blankets for people in need.

We all have skills and talents that we can use to help others. And when we work together, we can accomplish great things! Ask some of your friends what their skills and talents are. Maybe you could even start a club and work together on a project that would help someone in need. Jesus said that whenever we help others, we are really doing it for him (Matthew 25:40).

---

**23:14 How . . . punishment.** *Some Greek copies do not contain the bracketed text.* **23:23 mint, dill, and cumin** *Small plants grown in gardens and used for spices. Only very religious people would be careful enough to give a tenth of these plants.* **23:24 You . . . camel!** *Meaning, "You worry about the smallest mistakes but commit the biggest sin."*

# Q & A

**Q** Ever since I became a Christian, my twin sister has started treating me weird. Why won't she talk to me like she used to?

**A** If the two of you have shared all your activities and interests until now, she probably feels suddenly disconnected from you. You have a relationship with Jesus, and she might feel left out. Give her time to deal with her feelings while you pray for her and show her more love than ever. Don't push your new faith onto her, but be ready to patiently talk about it if she has questions.

ing only yourselves. [26]Pharisees, you are blind! First make the inside of the cup clean, and then the outside of the cup can be truly clean.

[27]"How terrible for you, teachers of the law and Pharisees! You are hypocrites! You are like tombs that are painted white. Outside, those tombs look fine, but inside, they are full of the bones of dead people and all kinds of unclean things. [28]It is the same with you. People look at you and think you are good, but on the

inside you are full of hypocrisy and evil.

[29]"How terrible for you, teachers of the law and Pharisees! You are hypocrites! You build tombs for the prophets, and you show honor to the graves of those who lived good lives. [30]You say, 'If we had lived during the time of our ancestors, we would not have helped them kill the prophets.' [31]But you give proof that you are descendants of those who murdered the prophets. [32]And you will complete the sin that your ancestors started.

[33]"You are snakes! A family of poisonous snakes! How are you going to escape

God's judgment? [34]So I tell you this: I am sending to you prophets and wise men and teachers. Some of them you will kill and crucify. Some of them you will beat in your synagogues and chase from town to town. [35]So you will be guilty for the death of all the good people who have been killed on earth—from the murder of that good man Abel to the murder of Zechariah[n] son of Berakiah, whom you murdered between the Temple and the altar. [36]I tell you the truth, all of these things will happen to you people who are living now.

## Jesus Feels Sorry for Jerusalem

[37]"Jerusalem, Jerusalem! You kill the prophets and stone to death those who are sent to you. Many times I wanted to gather your people as a hen gathers her chicks under her wings, but you did not let me. [38]Now your house will be left completely empty. [39]I tell you, you will not see me again until that time when you will say, 'God bless the One who comes in the name of the Lord.' "[n]

## The Temple Will Be Destroyed

**24** As Jesus left the Temple and was walking away, his followers came up to show him the Temple's buildings. [2]Jesus asked, "Do you see all these buildings? I tell you the truth, not one stone will be left on another. Every stone will be thrown down to the ground."

[3]Later, as Jesus was sitting on the Mount of Olives, his followers came to be alone with him. They said, "Tell us, when will these things happen? And what will be the sign that it is time for you to come again and for this age to end?"

[4]Jesus answered, "Be careful that no one fools you. [5]Many will come in my name, saying, 'I am the Christ,' and they will fool many people. [6]You will hear about wars and stories of wars that are coming, but don't be afraid. These things

must happen before the end comes. [7]Nations will fight against other nations; kingdoms will fight against other kingdoms. There will be times when there is no food for people to eat, and there will be earthquakes in different places. [8]These things are like the first pains when something new is about to be born.

[9]"Then people will arrest you, hand you over to be hurt, and kill you. They will hate you because you believe in me. [10]At that time, many will lose their faith, and they will turn against each other and hate each other. [11]Many false prophets will come and cause many people to believe lies. [12]There will be more and more evil in the world, so most people will stop showing their love for each other. [13]But those people who keep their faith until the end will be saved. [14]The Good News about God's kingdom will be preached in all the world, to every nation. Then the end will come.

[15]"Daniel the prophet spoke about 'a blasphemous object that brings destruction.'[n] You will see this standing in the holy place." (You who read this should understand what it means.) [16]"At that time, the people in Judea should run away to the mountains. [17]If people are on the roofs[n] of their houses, they must not go down to get anything out of their houses. [18]If people are in the fields, they must not go back to get their coats. [19]At that time, how terrible it will be for women who are pregnant or have nursing babies! [20]Pray that it will not be winter or a Sabbath day when these things happen and you have to run away, [21]because at that time there will be much trouble. There will be more trouble than there has ever been since the beginning of the world until now, and nothing as bad will ever happen again. [22]God has decided to make that terrible time short. Otherwise, no one would go on living. But God will make that time short to help the people he has chosen. [23]At that time, someone might say to you, 'Look, there is the Christ!' Or another person might say, 'There he is!' But don't believe them. [24]False Christs and false prophets will come and perform great wonders and miracles. They will try to fool even the people God has chosen, if that is possible. [25]Now I have warned you about this before it happens.

[26]"If people tell you, 'The Christ is in the desert,' don't go there. If they say, 'The

23:35 **Abel . . . Zechariah** *In the order of the books of the Hebrew Old Testament, the first and last men to be murdered.* 23:39 **'God . . . Lord.'** *Quotation from Psalm 118:26.* 24:15 **'a blasphemous object that brings destruction'** *Mentioned in Daniel 9:27; 12:11 (see also Daniel 11:31).* 24:17 **roofs** *In Bible times houses were built with flat roofs. The roof was used for drying things such as flax and fruit. And it was used as an extra room, as a place for worship, and as a cool place to sleep in the summer.*

Christ is in the inner room,' don't believe it. 27When the Son of Man comes, he will be seen by everyone, like lightning flashing from the east to the west. 28Wherever the dead body is, there the vultures will gather.

29"Soon after the trouble of those days,

'the sun will grow dark,
   and the moon will not give its light.
The stars will fall from the sky.
   And the powers of the heavens
   will be shaken.'

*Isaiah 13:10; 34:4*

30"At that time, the sign of the Son of Man will appear in the sky. Then all the peoples of the world will cry. They will see the Son of Man coming on clouds in the sky with great power and glory. 31He will use a loud trumpet to send his angels all around the earth, and they will gather his chosen people from every part of the world.

32"Learn a lesson from the fig tree: When its branches become green and soft and new leaves appear, you know summer is near. 33In the same way, when you see all these things happening, you will know that the time is near, ready to come. 34I tell you the truth, all these things will happen while the people of this time are still living. 35Earth and sky will be destroyed, but the words I have said will never be destroyed.

## When Will Jesus Come Again?

36"No one knows when that day or time will be, not the angels in heaven, not even the Son.*n* Only the Father knows. 37When the Son of Man comes, it will be like what happened during Noah's time. 38In those days before the flood, people were eating and drinking, marrying and giving their children to be married, until the day Noah entered the boat. 39They knew nothing about what was happening until the flood came and destroyed them. It will be the same when the Son of Man comes. 40Two men will be in the field. One will be taken, and the other will be left. 41Two women will be grinding grain with a mill.*n* One will be taken, and the other will be left.

42"So always be ready, because you don't know the day your Lord will come. 43Remember this: If the owner of the house knew what time of night a thief

## dig deeper

### Matthew 26:69–75

**Picture this:** At the mall, you bump into some girls you know. You're all chatting when you notice a lady from your church handing out pamphlets and trying to talk with people about Jesus. One of the girls asks you: "You go to church, don't you? Do you have to do stuff like that, too, Church Girl?" The other girls giggle.

How embarrassing! You notice the lady looking in your direction and waving. Do you pretend you didn't see her? Do you ignore the question and change subjects? Do you wave back and quietly say, "Yeah, I go to church but I'm not really into that stuff"?

One of Jesus' closest followers, Peter, found himself in a similar situation in Matthew 26:69–75. After Jesus was arrested, Peter followed . . . but from way behind. While he waited to see what would happen to Jesus, he hung around some strangers and warmed himself by their campfire. He was asked three times if he knew Jesus, and three times he said he didn't! Peter was scared to tell the truth.

Afterward he cried a lot. He was ashamed that, instead of sticking up for Jesus, he had tried to protect himself. Jesus did forgive him later, but Peter learned a good lesson! Ask God to give you the courage to tell people how much you love Jesus!

was coming, the owner would watch and not let the thief break in. 44So you also must be ready, because the Son of Man will come at a time you don't expect him.

45"Who is the wise and loyal servant that the master trusts to give the other servants their food at the right time? 46When the master comes and finds the servant doing his work, the servant will be blessed. 47I tell you the truth, the master will choose that servant to take care of everything he owns. 48But suppose that evil servant thinks to himself, 'My master will not come back soon,' 49and he begins to beat the other servants and eat and get drunk with others like him? 50The master will come when that servant is not ready and is not expecting him. 51Then the master will cut him in pieces and send him away to be with the hypocrites, where people will cry and grind their teeth with pain.

**24:36 not even the Son** *Some Greek copies do not have this phrase.* **24:41 mill** *Two large, round, flat rocks used for grinding grain to make flour.*

## Be YOUR BeST!

**P**ut that sunscreen on! Doctors keep advising us to protect ourselves from the sun's harmful UV rays. You don't *see* the "enemy" but it's there! As a Christian, you also need to ask God to protect you from temptation's power. Think of the Holy Spirit as your spiritual sunscreen!

## A Story About Ten Bridesmaids

**25** "At that time the kingdom of heaven will be like ten bridesmaids who took their lamps and went to wait for the bridegroom. [2]Five of them were foolish and five were wise. [3]The five foolish bridesmaids took their lamps, but they did not take more oil for the lamps to burn. [4]The wise bridesmaids took their lamps and more oil in jars. [5]Because the bridegroom was late, they became sleepy and went to sleep.

[6]"At midnight someone cried out, 'The bridegroom is coming! Come and meet him!' [7]Then all the bridesmaids woke up and got their lamps ready. [8]But the foolish ones said to the wise, 'Give us some of your oil, because our lamps are going out.' [9]The wise bridesmaids answered, 'No, the oil we have might not be enough for all of us. Go to the people who sell oil and buy some for yourselves.'

[10]"So while the five foolish bridesmaids went to buy oil, the bridegroom came. The bridesmaids who were ready went in with the bridegroom to the wedding feast. Then the door was closed and locked.

[11]"Later the others came back and said, 'Sir, sir, open the door to let us in.' [12]But the bridegroom answered, 'I tell you the truth, I don't want to know you.'

[13]"So always be ready, because you don't know the day or the hour the Son of Man will come.

## A Story About Three Servants

[14]"The kingdom of heaven is like a man who was going to another place for a visit. Before he left, he called for his servants and told them to take care of his things while he was gone. [15]He gave one servant five bags of gold, another servant two bags of gold, and a third servant one bag of gold, to each one as much as he could handle. Then he left. [16]The servant who got five bags went quickly to invest the money and earned five more bags. [17]In the same way, the servant who had two bags invested them and earned two more. [18]But the servant who got one bag went out and dug a hole in the ground and hid the master's money.

[19]"After a long time the master came home and asked the servants what they did with his money. [20]The servant who was given five bags of gold brought five more bags to the master and said, 'Master, you trusted me to care for five bags of gold, so I used your five bags to earn five more.' [21]The master answered, 'You did well. You are a good and loyal servant. Because you were loyal with small things, I will let you care for much greater things. Come and share my joy with me.'

[22]"Then the servant who had been given two bags of gold came to the master and said, 'Master, you gave me two bags of gold to care for, so I used your two bags to earn two more.' [23]The master answered, 'You did well. You are a good and loyal servant. Because you were loyal with small things, I will let you care for much greater things. Come and share my joy with me.'

[24]"Then the servant who had been given one bag of gold came to the master and said, 'Master, I knew that you were a hard man. You harvest things you did not plant. You gather crops where you did not sow any seed. [25]So I was afraid and went and hid your money in the ground. Here is your bag of gold.' [26]The master answered, 'You are a wicked and lazy servant! You say you knew that I harvest things I did not plant and that I gather crops where I did not sow any seed. [27]So you should have put my gold in the bank. Then, when I came home, I would have received my gold back with interest.'

[28]"So the master told his other servants, 'Take the bag of gold from that servant and give it to the servant who has ten bags of gold. [29]Those who have much will get more, and they will have much more than they need. But those who do not have much will have everything taken away from them.' [30]Then the master said, 'Throw that useless servant outside, into the darkness where people will cry and grind their teeth with pain.'

## The King Will Judge All People

[31]"The Son of Man will come again in his great glory, with all his angels. He will be King and sit on his great throne. [32]All the nations of the world will be gathered before him, and he will separate them into two groups as a shepherd separates the sheep from the goats. [33]The Son of Man will put the sheep on his right and the goats on his left.

[34]"Then the King will say to the people on his right, 'Come, my Father has given you his blessing. Receive the kingdom God has prepared for you since the world was made. [35]I was hungry, and you gave me food. I was thirsty, and you gave me

> ## I TELL YOU THE TRUTH, ANYTHING YOU DID FOR EVEN THE LEAST OF MY PEOPLE HERE, YOU ALSO DID FOR ME.

something to drink. I was alone and away from home, and you invited me into your house. [36]I was without clothes, and you gave me something to wear. I was sick, and you cared for me. I was in prison, and you visited me.'

[37]"Then the good people will answer, 'Lord, when did we see you hungry and give you food, or thirsty and give you something to drink? [38]When did we see you alone and away from home and invite you into our house? When did we see you without clothes and give you something to wear? [39]When did we see you sick or in prison and care for you?'

[40]"Then the King will answer, 'I tell you the truth, anything you did for even the least of my people here, you also did for me.'

[41]"Then the King will say to those on his left, 'Go away from me. You will be punished. Go into the fire that burns forever

that was prepared for the devil and his angels. [42]I was hungry, and you gave me nothing to eat. I was thirsty, and you gave me nothing to drink. [43]I was alone and away from home, and you did not invite me into your house. I was without clothes, and you gave me nothing to wear. I was sick and in prison, and you did not care for me.'

[44]"Then those people will answer, 'Lord, when did we see you hungry or thirsty or alone and away from home or without clothes or sick or in prison? When did we see these things and not help you?'

[45]"Then the King will answer, 'I tell you the truth, anything you refused to do for even the least of my people here, you refused to do for me.'

[46]"These people will go off to be punished forever, but the good people will go to live forever."

## The Plan to Kill Jesus

**26** After Jesus finished saying all these things, he told his followers, [2]"You know that the day after tomorrow is the day of the Passover Feast. On that day the Son of Man will be given to his enemies to be crucified."

[3]Then the leading priests and the elders had a meeting at the palace of the high priest, named Caiaphas. [4]At the meeting, they planned to set a trap to arrest Jesus and kill him. [5]But they said, "We must not do it during the feast, because the people might cause a riot."

## Perfume for Jesus' Burial

[6]Jesus was in Bethany at the house of Simon, who had a skin disease. [7]While Jesus was there, a woman approached him with an alabaster jar filled with expensive perfume. She poured this perfume on Jesus' head while he was eating.

[8]His followers were upset when they saw the woman do this. They asked, "Why waste that perfume? [9]It could have been sold for a great deal of money and the money given to the poor."

[10]Knowing what had happened, Jesus said, "Why are you troubling this woman? She did an excellent thing for me. [11]You will always have the poor with you, but you will not always have me. [12]This woman poured perfume on my body to prepare me for burial. [13]I tell you the truth, wherever the Good News is preached in all the

world, what this woman has done will be told, and people will remember her."

## Judas Becomes an Enemy of Jesus

[14]Then one of the twelve apostles, Judas Iscariot, went to talk to the leading priests. [15]He said, "What will you pay me for giving Jesus to you?" And they gave him thirty silver coins. [16]After that, Judas watched for the best time to turn Jesus in.

## Jesus Eats the Passover Meal

[17]On the first day of the Feast of Unleavened Bread, the followers came to Jesus. They said, "Where do you want us to prepare for you to eat the Passover meal?"

[18]Jesus answered, "Go into the city to a certain man and tell him, 'The Teacher says: "The chosen time is near. I will have the Passover with my followers at your house."'" [19]The followers did what Jesus told them to do, and they prepared the Passover meal.

[20]In the evening Jesus was sitting at the table with his twelve followers. [21]As they were eating, Jesus said, "I tell you the truth, one of you will turn against me."

[22]This made the followers very sad. Each one began to say to Jesus, "Surely, Lord, I am not the one who will turn against you, am I?"

[23]Jesus answered, "The man who has dipped his hand with me into the bowl is the one who will turn against me. [24]The Son of Man will die, just as the Scriptures say. But how terrible it will be for the person who hands the Son of Man over to be killed. It would be better for him if he had never been born."

[25]Then Judas, who would give Jesus to his enemies, said to Jesus, "Teacher, surely I am not the one, am I?"

Jesus answered, "Yes, it is you."

## The Lord's Supper

[26]While they were eating, Jesus took some bread and thanked God for it and broke it. Then he gave it to his followers and said, "Take this bread and eat it; this is my body."

[27]Then Jesus took a cup and thanked God for it and gave it to the followers. He said, "Every one of you drink this. [28]This is my blood which is the new[n] agreement that God makes with his people. This blood is poured out for many to forgive their sins. [29]I tell you this: I will not drink of this fruit of the vine[n] again until that day when I drink it new with you in my Father's kingdom."

[30]After singing a hymn, they went out to the Mount of Olives.

## Jesus' Followers Will Leave Him

[31]Jesus told his followers, "Tonight you will all stumble in your faith on account of me, because it is written in the Scriptures:

'I will kill the shepherd,
and the sheep will scatter.'
*Zechariah 13:7*

[32]But after I rise from the dead, I will go ahead of you into Galilee."

[33]Peter said, "Everyone else may stumble in their faith because of you, but I will not."

[34]Jesus said, "I tell you the truth, tonight before the rooster crows you will say three times that you don't know me."

[35]But Peter said, "I will never say that I don't know you! I will even die with you!" And all the other followers said the same thing.

## Jesus Prays Alone

[36]Then Jesus went with his followers to a place called Gethsemane. He said to them, "Sit here while I go over there and pray." [37]He took Peter and the two sons

**26:28 new** *Some Greek copies do not have this word. Compare Luke 22:20.* **26:29 fruit of the vine** *Product of the grapevine; this may also be translated "wine."*

<sup>45</sup>Then Jesus went back to his followers and said, "Are you still sleeping and resting? The time has come for the Son of Man to be handed over to sinful people. <sup>46</sup>Get up, we must go. Look, here comes the man who has turned against me."

## Jesus Is Arrested

<sup>47</sup>While Jesus was still speaking, Judas, one of the twelve apostles, came up. With him were many people carrying swords and clubs who had been sent from the leading priests and the Jewish elders of the people. <sup>48</sup>Judas had planned to give them a signal, saying, "The man I kiss is Jesus. Arrest him." <sup>49</sup>At once Judas went to Jesus and said, "Greetings, Teacher!" and kissed him.

<sup>50</sup>Jesus answered, "Friend, do what you came to do."

Then the people came and grabbed Jesus and arrested him. <sup>51</sup>When that happened, one of Jesus' followers reached for his sword and pulled it out. He struck the servant of the high priest and cut off his ear.

<sup>52</sup>Jesus said to the man, "Put your sword back in its place. All who use swords will be killed with swords. <sup>53</sup>Surely you know I could ask my Father, and he would give me more than twelve armies of angels. <sup>54</sup>But it must happen this way to bring about what the Scriptures say."

<sup>55</sup>Then Jesus said to the crowd, "You came to get me with swords and clubs as if I were a criminal. Every day I sat in the Temple teaching, and you did not arrest me there. <sup>56</sup>But all these things have happened so that it will come about as the prophets wrote." Then all of Jesus' followers left him and ran away.

## Jesus Before the Leaders

<sup>57</sup>Those people who arrested Jesus led him to the house of Caiaphas, the high priest, where the teachers of the law and the elders were gathered. <sup>58</sup>Peter followed far behind to the courtyard of the

## god's promises

Matthew 28:18–20

Your best friend is moving away. What do you say? You both cry a little and promise to e-mail every day and call on Sundays and come and visit during summer vacation. You wonder who will help you with your math homework and who will sit by you at lunch.

Jesus was going away. He had come back to life from the dead and had spent forty days with his friends and followers. But now he was going back to heaven where he came from. Jesus wasn't dying again—he had his eternal, resurrected body—but he still was leaving. What did he say to his followers?

Jesus promised that he would give them all the authority they needed to tell others about him. Jesus promised that he would never really leave them. Though they couldn't see him, his Spirit would come and be with them—and with every other believer—until the very end of the world. After Jesus had risen up into the sky, past the clouds, God gave his followers one last promise: Jesus will come back again!

You've never seen Jesus, but his promise is for you, too. He is your best friend, and he is with you always. And someday—you will see him when he returns!

**Jesus promised that he will never really leave us!**

of Zebedee with him, and he began to be very sad and troubled. <sup>38</sup>He said to them, "My heart is full of sorrow, to the point of death. Stay here and watch with me."

<sup>39</sup>After walking a little farther away from them, Jesus fell to the ground and prayed, "My Father, if it is possible, do not give me this cup<sup>n</sup> of suffering. But do what you want, not what I want." <sup>40</sup>Then Jesus went back to his followers and found them asleep. He said to Peter, "You men could not stay awake with me for one hour?

<sup>41</sup>Stay awake and pray for strength against temptation. The spirit wants to do what is right, but the body is weak."

<sup>42</sup>Then Jesus went away a second time and prayed, "My Father, if it is not possible for this painful thing to be taken from me, and if I must do it, I pray that what you want will be done."

<sup>43</sup>Then he went back to his followers, and again he found them asleep, because their eyes were heavy. <sup>44</sup>So Jesus left them and went away and prayed a third time, saying the same thing.

"MY FATHER, IF IT IS POSSIBLE, DO NOT GIVE ME THIS CUP OF SUFFERING. BUT DO WHAT YOU WANT, NOT WHAT I WANT."

26:39 cup *Jesus is talking about the terrible things that will happen to him. Accepting these things will be very hard, like drinking a cup of something bitter.*

high priest's house, and he sat down with the guards to see what would happen to Jesus.

59The leading priests and the whole Jewish council tried to find something false against Jesus so they could kill him. 60Many people came and told lies about him, but the council could find no real reason to kill him. Then two people came and said, 61"This man said, 'I can destroy the Temple of God and build it again in three days.'"

62Then the high priest stood up and said to Jesus, "Aren't you going to answer? Don't you have something to say about their charges against you?" 63But Jesus said nothing.

Again the high priest said to Jesus, "I command you by the power of the living God: Tell us if you are the Christ, the Son of God."

64Jesus answered, "Those are your words. But I tell you, in the future you will see the Son of Man sitting at the right hand

of God, the Powerful One, and coming on clouds in the sky."

65When the high priest heard this, he tore his clothes and said, "This man has said things that are against God! We don't need any more witnesses; you all heard him say these things against God. 66What do you think?"

The people answered, "He should die."

67Then the people there spat in Jesus' face and beat him with their fists. Others slapped him. 68They said, "Prove to us that you are a prophet, you Christ! Tell us who hit you!"

## Peter Says He Doesn't Know Jesus

69At that time, as Peter was sitting in the courtyard, a servant girl came to him and said, "You also were with Jesus of Galilee."

70But Peter said to all the people there that he was never with Jesus. He said, "I don't know what you are talking about."

71When he left the courtyard and was at the gate, another girl saw him. She said to the people there, "This man was with Jesus of Nazareth."

72Again, Peter said he was never with him, saying, "I swear I don't know this man Jesus!"

73A short time later, some people standing there went to Peter and said, "Surely you are one of those who followed Jesus. The way you talk shows it."

74Then Peter began to place a curse on himself and swear, "I don't know the man." At once, a rooster crowed. 75And Peter remembered what Jesus had told him: "Before the rooster crows, you will say three times that you don't know me." Then Peter went outside and cried painfully.

## Jesus Is Taken to Pilate

**27** Early the next morning, all the leading priests and elders of the people decided that Jesus should die. 2They tied him, led him away, and turned him over to Pilate, the governor.

## Judas Kills Himself

3Judas, the one who had given Jesus to his enemies, saw that they had decided to kill Jesus. Then he was very sorry for what he had done. So he took the thirty silver coins back to the priests and the

leaders, 4saying, "I sinned; I handed over to you an innocent man."

The leaders answered, "What is that to us? That's your problem, not ours."

5So Judas threw the money into the Temple. Then he went off and hanged himself.

6The leading priests picked up the silver coins in the Temple and said, "Our law does not allow us to keep this money with the Temple money, because it has paid for a man's death." 7So they decided to use the coins to buy Potter's Field as a place to bury strangers who died in Jerusalem. 8That is why that field is still called the Field of Blood. 9So what Jeremiah the prophet had said came true: "They took thirty silver coins. That is how little the Israelites thought he was worth. 10They used those thirty silver coins to buy the potter's field, as the Lord commanded me."[n]

## Pilate Questions Jesus

11Jesus stood before Pilate the governor, and Pilate asked him, "Are you the king of the Jews?"

Jesus answered, "Those are your words."

12When the leading priests and the elders accused Jesus, he said nothing.

13So Pilate said to Jesus, "Don't you hear them accusing you of all these things?"

14But Jesus said nothing in answer to Pilate, and Pilate was very surprised at this.

## Pilate Tries to Free Jesus

15Every year at the time of Passover the governor would free one prisoner whom the people chose. 16At that time there was a man in prison, named Barabbas,[n] who was known to be very bad. 17When the people gathered at Pilate's house, Pilate said, "Whom do you want me to set free: Barabbas[n] or Jesus who is called the Christ?" 18Pilate knew that they turned Jesus in to him because they were jealous.

19While Pilate was sitting there on the judge's seat, his wife sent this message to him: "Don't do anything to that man, because he is innocent. Today I had a dream about him, and it troubled me very much."

20But the leading priests and elders convinced the crowd to ask for Barabbas to be freed and for Jesus to be killed.

21Pilate said, "I have Barabbas and Jesus. Which do you want me to set free for you?"

## Get It

## Evangelism

Evangelism means telling other people how much Jesus loves us and about the amazing way he saves us from our sins. Jesus' last words to his followers are called the "Great Commission" (Matthew 28:19–20). These words are meant for us, too, and they tell us to teach people all over the world about Jesus' love and help them learn to follow him. Some people, called missionaries, go to other countries to evangelize. But you can share the Good News about Jesus right where you are by telling your friends, family, neighbors, and other people you meet about what Jesus has done for you!

27:9–10 "They . . . commanded me." *See Zechariah 11:12–13 and Jeremiah 32:6–9.* 27:16–17 **Barabbas** *Some Greek copies read "Jesus Barabbas."*

WHEN THE ARMY OFFICER AND THE SOLDIERS GUARDING JESUS SAW THIS EARTHQUAKE AND EVERYTHING ELSE THAT HAPPENED, THEY WERE VERY FRIGHTENED AND SAID, "HE REALLY WAS THE SON OF GOD!"

The people answered, "Barabbas."

[22] Pilate asked, "So what should I do with Jesus, the one called the Christ?"

They all answered, "Crucify him!"

[23] Pilate asked, "Why? What wrong has he done?"

But they shouted louder, "Crucify him!"

[24] When Pilate saw that he could do nothing about this and that a riot was starting, he took some water and washed his hands[n] in front of the crowd. Then he said, "I am not guilty of this man's death. You are the ones who are causing it!"

[25] All the people answered, "We and our children will be responsible for his death."

[26] Then he set Barabbas free. But Jesus was beaten with whips and handed over to the soldiers to be crucified.

[27] The governor's soldiers took Jesus into the governor's palace, and they all gathered around him. [28] They took off his clothes and put a red robe on him. [29] Using thorny branches, they made a crown, put it on his head, and put a stick in his right hand. Then the soldiers bowed before Jesus and made fun of him, saying, "Hail, King of the Jews!" [30] They spat on Jesus. Then they took his stick and began to beat him on the head. [31] After they finished, the soldiers took off the robe and put his own clothes on him again. Then they led him away to be crucified.

## Jesus Is Crucified

[32] As the soldiers were going out of the city with Jesus, they forced a man from Cyrene, named Simon, to carry the cross for Jesus. [33] They all came to the place called Golgotha, which means the Place of the Skull. [34] The soldiers gave Jesus wine mixed with gall[n] to drink. He tasted the wine but refused to drink it. [35] When the soldiers had crucified him, they threw lots to decide who would get his clothes.[n] [36] The soldiers sat there and continued watching him. [37] They put a sign above Jesus' head with a charge against him. It said: THIS IS JESUS, THE KING OF THE JEWS. [38] Two robbers were crucified beside Jesus, one on the right and the other on the left. [39] People walked by and insulted Jesus and shook their heads, [40] saying, "You said you could destroy the Temple and build it again in three days. So save yourself! Come down from that cross if you are really the Son of God!"

[41] The leading priests, the teachers of the law, and the Jewish elders were also making fun of Jesus. [42] They said, "He saved others, but he can't save himself! He says he is the king of Israel! If he is the king, let him come down now from the cross. Then we will believe in him. [43] He trusts in God, so let God save him now, if God really wants him. He himself said, 'I am the Son of God.'" [44] And in the same way, the robbers who were being crucified beside Jesus also insulted him.

## Jesus Dies

[45] At noon the whole country became dark, and the darkness lasted for three hours. [46] About three o'clock Jesus cried out in a loud voice, "Eli, Eli, lama sabachthani?" This means, "My God, my God, why have you abandoned me?"

[47] Some of the people standing there who heard this said, "He is calling Elijah."

[48] Quickly one of them ran and got a sponge and filled it with vinegar and tied it to a stick and gave it to Jesus to drink. [49] But the others said, "Don't bother him. We want to see if Elijah will come to save him."

[50] But Jesus cried out again in a loud voice and died.

[51] Then the curtain in the Temple[n] was torn into two pieces, from the top to the bottom. Also, the earth shook and rocks broke apart. [52] The graves opened, and many of God's people who had died were raised from the dead. [53] They came out of the graves after Jesus was raised from the dead and went into the holy city, where they appeared to many people.

[54] When the army officer and the soldiers guarding Jesus saw this earthquake and everything else that happened, they were very frightened and said, "He really was the Son of God!"

[55] Many women who had followed Jesus from Galilee to help him were standing at a distance from the cross, watching. [56] Mary Magdalene, and Mary the mother of James and Joseph, and the mother of James and John were there.

## Jesus Is Buried

[57] That evening a rich man named Joseph, a follower of Jesus from the town of Arimathea, came to Jerusalem. [58] Joseph went to Pilate and asked to have Jesus' body. So Pilate gave orders for the soldiers to give it to Joseph. [59] Then Joseph took the body and wrapped it in a clean linen cloth. [60] He put Jesus' body in a new tomb that he had cut out of a wall of rock, and he rolled a very large stone to block the entrance of the tomb. Then Joseph went away. [61] Mary Magdalene and the other woman named Mary were sitting near the tomb.

## The Tomb of Jesus Is Guarded

[62] The next day, the day after Preparation Day, the leading priests and the Pharisees went to Pilate. [63] They said, "Sir, we remember that while that liar was still alive he said, 'After three days I will rise from the dead.' [64] So give the order for the tomb to be guarded closely till the third day. Otherwise, his followers might come and steal the body and tell people that

# Q&A

**Q** I'm spending the summer at my grandparents' cottage. There's no TV or computer! How can I keep from dying of boredom?

**A** Some kids can only dream of a vacation like this! Explore outdoors, read books, write letters, or do artwork. Ask your grandma to teach you how to cook or bake some yummy things. Play board games with your grandpa. Ask to hear funny stories about your parents. Your grandparents won't be around forever, so enjoy this time with them!

27:24 washed his hands He did this as a sign to show that he wanted no part in what the people did. 27:34 gall Probably a drink of wine mixed with drugs to help a person feel less pain. 27:35 clothes Some Greek copies continue, "So what God said through the prophet came true, 'They divided my clothes among them, and they threw lots for my clothing.'" See Psalm 22:18. 27:51 curtain in the Temple A curtain divided the Most Holy Place from the other part of the Temple. That was the special building in Jerusalem where God commanded the Jewish people to worship him.

he has risen from the dead. That lie would be even worse than the first one." ⁶⁵Pilate said, "Take some soldiers and go guard the tomb the best way you know." ⁶⁶So they all went to the tomb and made it safe from thieves by sealing the stone in the entrance and putting soldiers there to guard it.

## Jesus Rises from the Dead

**28** The day after the Sabbath day was the first day of the week. At dawn on the first day, Mary Magdalene and another woman named Mary went to look at the tomb.

²At that time there was a strong earthquake. An angel of the Lord came down from heaven, went to the tomb, and rolled the stone away from the entrance. Then he sat on the stone. ³He was shining as bright as lightning, and his clothes were white as snow. ⁴The soldiers guarding the tomb shook with fear because of the angel, and they became like dead men.

⁵The angel said to the women, "Don't be afraid. I know that you are looking for Jesus, who has been crucified. ⁶He is not here. He has risen from the dead as he said he would. Come and see the place where his body was. ⁷And go quickly and tell his followers, 'Jesus has risen from the dead. He is going into Galilee ahead of you, and you will see him there.'" Then the angel said, "Now I have told you."

⁸The women left the tomb quickly. They were afraid, but they were also very happy. They ran to tell Jesus' followers what had happened. ⁹Suddenly, Jesus met them and said, "Greetings." The women came up to him, took hold of his feet, and worshiped him. ¹⁰Then Jesus said to them, "Don't be afraid. Go and tell my followers to go on to Galilee, and they will see me there."

## The Soldiers Report to the Leaders

¹¹While the women went to tell Jesus' followers, some of the soldiers who had been guarding the tomb went into the city to tell the leading priests everything that had happened. ¹²Then the priests met with the elders and made a plan. They paid the soldiers a large amount of money ¹³and said to them, "Tell the people that Jesus' followers came during the night and stole the body while you were

# dig deeper

## Mark 4:30–32

The shortest boy in your first grade class is now a head taller than all his classmates. Your toughest subject in school becomes the one you get your highest grade in. The girl you thought was mean and selfish turns out to be a very caring and loyal friend. We call situations like this—where the outcome surprises you because of the facts you knew at the start—ironies.

Jesus gave his followers a cool example of an irony . . . and taught an important lesson through it! He explained how a tiny mustard seed grows up to become a really large tree—much bigger than you would expect when you looked at the seed. "It produces large branches, and the wild birds can make nests in its shade," he said (Mark 4:32).

Jesus compared God's kingdom to that little mustard seed. Jesus' birth in a stable and his simple life with twelve average followers didn't impress too many people at first. One day, though, everyone who ever lived will realize God's greatness and power. Because of Jesus, everyone who trusts in him can have eternal life in heaven!

asleep. ¹⁴If the governor hears about this, we will satisfy him and save you from trouble." ¹⁵So the soldiers kept the money and did as they were told. And that story is still spread among the people even today.

## Jesus Talks to His Followers

¹⁶The eleven followers went to Galilee to the mountain where Jesus had told them to go. ¹⁷On the mountain they saw Jesus and worshiped him, but some of them did not believe it was really Jesus. ¹⁸Then Jesus came to them and said, "All power in heaven and on earth is given to me. ¹⁹So go and make followers of all people in the world. Baptize them in the name of the Father and the Son and the Holy Spirit. ²⁰Teach them to obey everything that I have taught you, and I will be with you always, even until the end of this age."

notes

# MARK

**M**ark made a big mistake. At least, the apostle Paul thought so. Mark went home halfway through a mission trip (Acts 13:13). But later Mark went on to be a valuable worker in the early church (2 Timothy 4:11) and to write this book about Jesus' life. He probably never met Jesus, but he heard all about him from people who had, like the apostle Peter.

Being a Christian isn't easy. Mark may have found that leaving home and traveling with Paul was harder than he expected. He has a lot to say about suffering in his book.

You've probably experienced some hard things in life already—maybe a death in your family, maybe divorce, or maybe the challenge of losing friends and having to make new ones.

Mark was probably writing to Christians in Rome. The government there was giving Christians a hard time and even killing some of them! Mark wanted them to know they weren't alone. Jesus suffered too—far more than we ever will. Mark writes about difficulties, but he also gives us the good news: Jesus experienced death on a cross so we could experience eternal life with God!

# MARK TELLS ABOUT JESUS, THE SUFFERING MESSIAH

## THINGS TO TALK WITH GOD ABOUT . . .

_____

_____

_____

_____

_____

_____

_____

### John Prepares for Jesus

**1** This is the beginning of the Good News about Jesus Christ, the Son of God,[n] [2]as the prophet Isaiah wrote:

"I will send my messenger ahead of you,
who will prepare your way."

*Malachi 3:1*

[3]"This is a voice of one
who calls out in the desert:
'Prepare the way for the Lord.
Make the road straight for him.'"

*Isaiah 40:3*

[4]John was baptizing people in the desert and preaching a baptism of changed hearts and lives for the forgiveness of sins. [5]All the people from Judea and Jerusalem were going out to him. They confessed their sins and were baptized by him in the Jordan River. [6]John wore clothes made from camel's hair, had a leather belt around his waist, and ate locusts and wild honey. [7]This is what John preached to the people: "There is one coming after me who is greater than I; I am not good enough even to kneel down and untie his sandals. [8]I baptize you with water, but he will baptize you with the Holy Spirit."

### Jesus Is Baptized

[9]At that time Jesus came from the town of Nazareth in Galilee and was baptized by John in the Jordan River. [10]Immediately, as Jesus was coming up out of the water, he saw heaven open. The Holy Spirit came down on him like a dove, [11]and a voice came from heaven: "You are my Son, whom I love, and I am very pleased with you."

[12]Then the Spirit sent Jesus into the desert. [13]He was in the desert forty days and was tempted by Satan. He was with the wild animals, and the angels came and took care of him.

### Jesus Chooses Some Followers

[14]After John was put in prison, Jesus went into Galilee, preaching the Good News from God. [15]He said, "The right time has come. The kingdom of God is near. Change your hearts and lives and believe the Good News!"

[16]When Jesus was walking by Lake Galilee, he saw Simon[n] and his brother Andrew throwing a net into the lake because they were fishermen. [17]Jesus said to them, "Come follow me, and I will make you fish for people." [18]So Simon and Andrew immediately left their nets and followed him.

[19]Going a little farther, Jesus saw two more brothers, James and John, the sons of Zebedee. They were in a boat, mending their nets. [20]Jesus immediately called them, and they left their father in the boat with the hired workers and followed Jesus.

### Jesus Forces Out an Evil Spirit

[21]Jesus and his followers went to Capernaum. On the Sabbath day he went to the synagogue and began to teach. [22]The people were amazed at his teaching, because he taught like a person who had authority, not like their teachers of the law. [23]Just then, a man was there in the synagogue who had an evil spirit in him. He shouted, [24]"Jesus of Nazareth! What do you want with us? Did you come to destroy us? I know who you are—God's Holy One!"

[25]Jesus commanded the evil spirit, "Be quiet! Come out of the man!" [26]The evil spirit shook the man violently, gave a loud cry, and then came out of him.

[27]The people were so amazed they asked each other, "What is happening here? This man is teaching something new, and with authority. He even gives commands to evil spirits, and they obey him." [28]And the news about Jesus spread quickly everywhere in the area of Galilee.

### Jesus Heals Many People

[29]As soon as Jesus and his followers left the synagogue, they went with James and John to the home of Simon[n] and Andrew. [30]Simon's mother-in-law was sick in bed with a fever, and the people told Jesus about her. [31]So Jesus went to her bed,

## cool

### Lava Lamps

**E**ver seen a cool lamp with strange globs floating around in a dim light? A lava lamp is a glass container sitting on a heat source. A liquid plus some translucent wax (meaning the light can go through it) fill up the container. As the heat melts the wax, it gets lighter and slowly floats up but, near the top, it starts to cool off so it sinks down again.

People like to show off their lava lamps because they're so cool! As Christians, we should also let people see the light of Jesus in our lives (Matthew 5:15)!

**1:1 the Son of God** *Some Greek copies do not have this phrase.* **1:16, 29 Simon** *Simon's other name was Peter.*

took her hand, and helped her up. The fever left her, and she began serving them.

[32]That evening, after the sun went down, the people brought to Jesus all who were sick and had demons in them. [33]The whole town gathered at the door. [34]Jesus healed many who had different kinds of sicknesses, and he forced many demons to leave people. But he would not allow the demons to speak, because they knew who he was.

[41]Jesus felt sorry for the man, so he reached out his hand and touched him and said, "I will. Be healed!" [42]Immediately the disease left the man, and he was healed.

[43]Jesus told the man to go away at once, but he warned him strongly, [44]"Don't tell anyone about this. But go and show yourself to the priest. And offer the gift Moses commanded for people who are made well.[n] This will show

teaching them God's message. [3]Four people came, carrying a paralyzed man. [4]Since they could not get to Jesus because of the crowd, they dug a hole in the roof right above where he was speaking. When they got through, they lowered the mat with the paralyzed man on it. [5]When Jesus saw the faith of these people, he said to the paralyzed man, "Young man, your sins are forgiven."

[6]Some of the teachers of the law were sitting there, thinking to themselves, [7]"Why does this man say things like that? He is speaking as if he were God. Only God can forgive sins."

[8]Jesus knew immediately what these teachers of the law were thinking. So he said to them, "Why are you thinking these things? [9]Which is easier: to tell this paralyzed man, 'Your sins are forgiven,' or to tell him, 'Stand up. Take your mat and walk'? [10]But I will prove to you that the Son of Man has authority on earth to forgive sins." So Jesus said to the paralyzed man, [11]"I tell you, stand up, take your mat, and go home." [12]Immediately the paralyzed man stood up, took his mat, and walked out while everyone was watching him.

The people were amazed and praised God. They said, "We have never seen anything like this!"

**The average kid spends 70 minutes per day on the phone.**

**did you know?**

—IFOP-Canada Market Research 2002 Tweens Survey

[35]Early the next morning, while it was still dark, Jesus woke and left the house. He went to a lonely place, where he prayed. [36]Simon and his friends went to look for Jesus. [37]When they found him, they said, "Everyone is looking for you!"

[38]Jesus answered, "We should go to other towns around here so I can preach there too. That is the reason I came." [39]So he went everywhere in Galilee, preaching in the synagogues and forcing out demons.

### Jesus Heals a Sick Man

[40]A man with a skin disease came to Jesus. He fell to his knees and begged Jesus, "You can heal me if you will."

the people what I have done." [45]The man left there, but he began to tell everyone that Jesus had healed him, and so he spread the news about Jesus. As a result, Jesus could not enter a town if people saw him. He stayed in places where nobody lived, but people came to him from everywhere.

### Jesus Heals a Paralyzed Man

**2** A few days later, when Jesus came back to Capernaum, the news spread that he was at home. [2]Many people gathered together so that there was no room in the house, not even outside the door. And Jesus was

[13]Jesus went to the lake again. The whole crowd followed him there, and he taught them. [14]While he was walking along, he saw a man named Levi son of Alphaeus, sitting in the tax collector's booth. Jesus said to him, "Follow me," and he stood up and followed Jesus.

[15]Later, as Jesus was having dinner at Levi's house, many tax collectors and "sinners" were eating there with Jesus and his followers. Many people like this followed Jesus. [16]When the teachers of the law who were Pharisees saw Jesus eating with the tax collectors and "sinners," they asked his followers, "Why does he eat with tax collectors and sinners?"

[17]Jesus heard this and said to them, "It is not the healthy people who need a doctor, but the sick. I did not come to invite good people but to invite sinners."

### Jesus' Followers Are Criticized

[18]Now the followers of John[n] and the Pharisees often fasted[n] for a certain time. Some people came to Jesus and

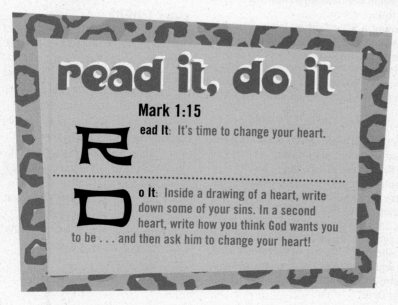

## read it, do it

### Mark 1:15

**R**ead It: It's time to change your heart.

**D**o It: Inside a drawing of a heart, write down some of your sins. In a second heart, write how you think God wants you to be . . . and then ask him to change your heart!

**1:44 Moses . . . well** *Read about this in Leviticus 14:1–32.* **2:18 John** *John the Baptist, who preached to the Jewish people about Christ's coming (Mark 1:4–8).* **2:18 fasted** *The people would give up eating for a special time of prayer and worship to God. It was also done to show sadness and disappointment.*

## I DID NOT COME TO INVITE GOOD PEOPLE BUT TO INVITE SINNERS.

said, "Why do John's followers and the followers of the Pharisees often fast, but your followers don't?"

¹⁹Jesus answered, "The friends of the bridegroom do not fast while the bridegroom is still with them. As long as the bridegroom is with them, they cannot fast. ²⁰But the time will come when the bridegroom will be taken from them, and then they will fast.

²¹"No one sews a patch of unshrunk cloth over a hole in an old coat. Otherwise, the patch will shrink and pull away—the new patch will pull away from the old coat. Then the hole will be worse. ²²Also, no one ever pours new wine into old leather bags. Otherwise, the new wine will break the bags, and the wine will be ruined along with the bags. But new wine should be put into new leather bags."

### Jesus Is Lord of the Sabbath

²³One Sabbath day, as Jesus was walking through some fields of grain, his followers began to pick some grain to eat. ²⁴The Pharisees said to Jesus, "Why are your followers doing what is not lawful on the Sabbath day?"

²⁵Jesus answered, "Have you never read what David did when he and those with him were hungry and needed food? ²⁶During the time of Abiathar the high priest, David went into God's house and ate the holy bread, which is lawful only for priests to eat. And David also gave some of the bread to those who were with him."

²⁷Then Jesus said to the Pharisees, "The Sabbath day was made to help people; they were not made to be ruled by the Sabbath day. ²⁸So then, the Son of Man is Lord even of the Sabbath day."

### Jesus Heals a Man's Hand

**3** Another time when Jesus went into a synagogue, a man with a crippled hand was there. ²Some people watched Jesus closely to see if he would heal the man on the Sabbath day so they could accuse him.

³Jesus said to the man with the crippled hand, "Stand up here in the middle of everyone."

⁴Then Jesus asked the people, "Which is lawful on the Sabbath day: to do good or to do evil, to save a life or to kill?" But they said nothing to answer him.

⁵Jesus was angry as he looked at the people, and he felt very sad because they were stubborn. Then he said to the man, "Hold out your hand." The man held out his hand and it was healed. ⁶Then the Pharisees left and began making plans with the Herodians[n] about a way to kill Jesus.

### Many People Follow Jesus

⁷Jesus left with his followers for the lake, and a large crowd from Galilee followed him. ⁸Also many people came from Judea, from Jerusalem, from Idumea,

## god's promises

### Mark 7:24–30

Have you ever needed God's help with something big but were afraid to ask? We often have situations in our lives that seem too huge for us to handle. Even the small issues can be scary!

In Mark 7:24–30, we learn about a woman whose daughter was possessed by a demon. She knew she needed God's help to heal her daughter; he was the only one who had the power to do such a big thing. When the woman came and asked Jesus to help her daughter, he made the young girl better immediately!

The woman had absolute faith in Jesus' power and showed this when she asked him for help. Traveling all the way to see him also showed how bold her faith was. Jesus rewarded the woman's faith. When we believe God can and will do big things, he takes care of us, too! We can't visit Jesus like the woman did, but we can pray in faith that God hears and answers us.

Sometimes we can't see God's answer to our prayers for help right away, but when we have faith in his power, God promises to take care of us in the way he knows is best.

*When we believe God can and will do big things, he takes care of us.*

**3:6 Herodians** *A political group that followed Herod and his family.*

from the lands across the Jordan River, and from the area of Tyre and Sidon. When they heard what Jesus was doing, many people came to him. [9]When Jesus saw the crowds, he told his followers to get a boat ready for him to keep people from crowding against him. [10]He had healed many people, so all the sick were pushing toward him to touch him. [11]When evil spirits saw Jesus, they fell down before him and shouted, "You are the Son of God!" [12]But Jesus strongly warned them not to tell who he was.

## Jesus Chooses His Twelve Apostles

[13]Then Jesus went up on a mountain and called to him those he wanted, and they came to him. [14]Jesus chose twelve and called them apostles.[n] He wanted them to be with him, and he wanted to send them out to preach [15]and to have the authority to force demons out of people. [16]These are the twelve men he chose: Simon (Jesus named him Peter), [17]James and John, the sons of Zebedee (Jesus named them Boanerges, which means "Sons of Thunder"), [18]Andrew, Philip,

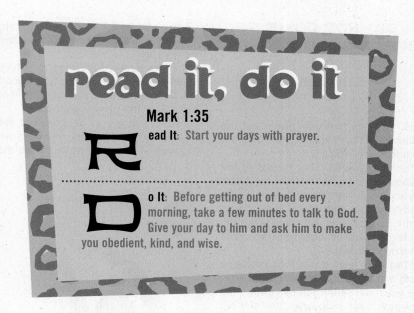

## cool

### Hairy Stuff

Try this: sit down with your best friend one day and try counting the hairs on her head. You'll probably give up somewhere after number 136!

Did you know that we've got about 110,000 hairs on our heads? (More if you're blonde and less if you're a red-head.) What's even more amazing is that God knows *exactly* how many hairs are on your head. You're so special to him that he even cares about a little detail like that!

Bartholomew, Matthew, Thomas, James the son of Alphaeus, Thaddaeus, Simon the Zealot, [19]and Judas Iscariot, who later turned against Jesus.

## Some People Say Jesus Has a Devil

[20]Then Jesus went home, but again a crowd gathered. There were so many people that Jesus and his followers could not eat. [21]When his family heard this, they went to get him because they thought he was out of his mind. [22]But the teachers of the law from Jerusalem were saying, "Beelzebul is living inside him! He uses power from the ruler of demons to force demons out of people."

[23]So Jesus called the people together and taught them with stories. He said, "Satan will not force himself out of people. [24]A kingdom that is divided cannot continue, [25]and a family that is divided cannot continue. [26]And if Satan is against himself and fights against his own people, he cannot continue; that is the end of Satan. [27]No one can enter a strong person's house and steal his things unless he first ties up the strong person. Then he can steal things from the house. [28]I tell you the truth, all sins that people do and all the things people say against God can be forgiven. [29]But anyone who speaks against the Holy Spirit will never be forgiven; he is guilty of a sin that continues forever."

[30]Jesus said this because the teachers of the law said that he had an evil spirit inside him.

## Jesus' True Family

[31]Then Jesus' mother and brothers arrived. Standing outside, they sent someone in to tell him to come out. [32]Many people were sitting around Jesus, and they said to him, "Your mother and brothers[n] are waiting for you outside."

[33]Jesus asked, "Who are my mother and my brothers?" [34]Then he looked at those sitting around him and said, "Here are my mother and my brothers! [35]My true brother and sister and mother are those who do what God wants."

## A Story About Planting Seed

**4** Again Jesus began teaching by the lake. A great crowd gathered around him, so he sat down in a boat near the shore. All the people stayed on the shore close to the water. [2]Jesus taught them many things, using stories. He said, [3]"Listen! A farmer went out to plant his seed. [4]While he was planting, some seed fell by the road, and the birds came and ate it up. [5]Some seed fell on rocky ground where there wasn't much dirt. That seed grew very fast, because the ground was not deep. [6]But when the sun rose, the plants dried up because they did not have deep roots. [7]Some other seed fell among thorny weeds, which grew and choked the good

---

**3:14 and called them apostles** *Some Greek copies do not have this phrase.*   **3:32 brothers** *Some Greek copies continue, "and sisters."*

plants. So those plants did not produce a crop. [8]Some other seed fell on good ground and began to grow. It got taller and produced a crop. Some plants made thirty times more, some made sixty times more, and some made a hundred times more."

[9]Then Jesus said, "Let those with ears use them and listen!"

## Jesus Tells Why He Used Stories

[10]Later, when Jesus was alone, the twelve apostles and others around him asked him about the stories.

[11]Jesus said, "You can know the secret about the kingdom of God. But to other people I tell everything by using stories [12]so that:

'They will look and look, but they will not learn.
    They will listen and listen, but they will not understand.
If they did learn and understand,
    they would come back to me and be forgiven.'"        *Isaiah 6:9–10*

## Jesus Explains the Seed Story

[13]Then Jesus said to his followers, "Don't you understand this story? If you don't, how will you understand any story? [14]The farmer is like a person who plants God's message in people. [15]Sometimes the teaching falls on the road. This is like the people who hear the teaching of God, but Satan quickly comes and takes away the teaching that was planted in them. [16]Others are like the seed planted on rocky ground. They hear the teaching and quickly accept it with joy. [17]But since they don't allow the teaching to go deep into their lives, they keep it only a short time. When trouble or persecution comes because of the teaching they accepted, they quickly give up. [18]Others are like the seed planted among the thorny weeds. They hear the teaching, [19]but the worries of this life, the temptation of wealth, and many other evil desires keep the teaching from growing and producing fruit[n] in their lives. [20]Others are like the seed planted in the good ground. They hear the teaching and accept it. Then they grow and produce fruit—sometimes thirty times more, sometimes sixty times more, and sometimes a hundred times more."

## Use What You Have

[21]Then Jesus said to them, "Do you hide a lamp under a bowl or under a bed? No! You put the lamp on a lampstand. [22]Everything that is hidden will be made clear and every secret thing will be made known. [23]Let those with ears use them and listen!

[24]"Think carefully about what you hear. The way you give to others is the way God will give to you, but God will give you even more. [25]Those who have understanding will be given more. But those who do not

> ## I DID NOT COME TO INVITE GOOD PEOPLE BUT TO INVITE SINNERS.

# Q&A

**Q** Can a Christian become a movie star? I would love to be rich and famous like my favorite actress.

**A** Money and popularity are not sins, but they shouldn't be our goals in life (1 Timothy 6:10 and Mark 8:36). Luke 16:13 says it's impossible to serve God and riches at the same time. Movie stars face many temptations because of the type of life they have. But there are Christian movie stars, and you could use your position as a celebrity to share Jesus with others. Just ask God to help you make goals that match his plans, and remember to put him *first* in your life.

# Relationships

**H** ow did Jesus treat young kids? The same way we should— with love. When his disciples told some children to stay away from Jesus because he was an important man, Jesus became upset! He said, "Let the little children come to me. Don't stop them, because the kingdom of God belongs to people who are like these children" (Mark 10:14). Jesus saw that the kids had soft hearts toward God. Like Jesus, you can welcome little children to follow after Jesus. Start by setting an example with your own life!

**4:19 producing fruit** *To produce fruit means to have in your life the good things God wants.*

have understanding, even what they have will be taken away from them."

## Jesus Uses a Story About Seed

26Then Jesus said, "The kingdom of God is like someone who plants seed in the ground. 27Night and day, whether the person is asleep or awake, the seed still grows, but the person does not know how it grows. 28By itself the earth produces grain. First the plant grows; then the head, and then all the grain in the head. 29When the grain is ready, the farmer cuts it, because this is the harvest time."

## A Story About Mustard Seed

30Then Jesus said, "How can I show you what the kingdom of God is like? What story can I use to explain it? 31The kingdom of God is like a mustard seed, the smallest seed you plant in the ground. 32But when planted, this seed grows and becomes the largest of all garden plants. It produces large branches, and the wild birds can make nests in its shade."

33Jesus used many stories like these to teach the crowd God's message—as much as they could understand. 34He always used stories to teach them. But when he and his followers were alone, Jesus explained everything to them.

# Q&A

**Q** Can I copy one of my CDs to give to my best friend?

**A** Music and books have copyrights. That means it's illegal to give out (or sell) copies of something without permission. Many people disobey copyright laws because they figure the artists or authors have enough money. But it's still stealing. Instead of giving her a copy, why not just lend her yours? If she really likes it, she should buy her own copy.

## ■ Bible Bios — The Bleeding Woman
### (Mark 5:24–34)

The Bible tells us about a woman (we don't know her name) who suffered for twelve years from a mysterious disease doctors couldn't cure. You'd think she'd feel discouraged and upset. Actually, she had great faith that God could heal her!

One day, as Jesus was on his way to heal a young girl, this woman walked behind him and touched his robe, believing it was enough to heal her body. Maybe she felt too ashamed to talk to Jesus directly . . . but she had enough faith to go to him. And her faith was rewarded! Her sickness left her immediately. Jesus knew what she had done. When he turned to speak to her, her private faith became public. Everyone around her witnessed Jesus' power. You, too, can trust that God has enough love and power to help you!

## Jesus Calms a Storm

35That evening, Jesus said to his followers, "Let's go across the lake." 36Leaving the crowd behind, they took him in the boat just as he was. There were also other boats with them. 37A very strong wind came up on the lake. The waves came over the sides and into the boat so that it was already full of water. 38Jesus was at the back of the boat, sleeping with his head on a cushion. His followers woke him and said, "Teacher, don't you care that we are drowning!"

39Jesus stood up and commanded the wind and said to the waves, "Quiet! Be still!" Then the wind stopped, and it became completely calm.

40Jesus said to his followers, "Why are you afraid? Do you still have no faith?"

41The followers were very afraid and asked each other, "Who is this? Even the wind and the waves obey him!"

## A Man with Demons Inside Him

5 Jesus and his followers went to the other side of the lake to the area of the Gerasene[n] people. 2When Jesus got out of the boat, instantly a man with an evil spirit came to him from the burial caves. 3This man lived in the caves, and no one could tie him up, not even with a chain. 4Many times people had used chains to tie the man's hands and feet, but he always broke them off. No one was strong enough to control him. 5Day and night he would wander around the burial caves and on the hills, screaming and cutting himself with stones. 6While Jesus was still far away, the man saw him, ran to him, and fell down before him.

7The man shouted in a loud voice, "What do you want with me, Jesus, Son of the Most High God? I command you in God's name not to torture me!" 8He said this because Jesus was saying to him, "You evil spirit, come out of the man."

9Then Jesus asked him, "What is your name?"

He answered, "My name is Legion,"[n] because we are many spirits." 10He begged Jesus again and again not to send them out of that area.

11A large herd of pigs was feeding on a hill near there. 12The demons begged Jesus, "Send us into the pigs; let us go into them." 13So Jesus allowed them to do this. The evil spirits left the man and went into the pigs. Then the herd of pigs—about two thousand of them—rushed down the hill into the lake and were drowned.

14The herdsmen ran away and went to the town and to the countryside, telling everyone about this. So people went out to see what had happened. 15They came to Jesus and saw the man who used to have the many evil spirits, sitting, clothed, and in his right mind. And they were frightened. 16The people who saw this told the others what had happened to the man who had the demons living in him, and they told about the

**5:1 Gerasene** *From Gerasa, an area southeast of Lake Galilee. The exact location is uncertain and some Greek copies read "Gergesene"; others read "Gadarene."* **5:9 Legion** *Means very many. A legion was about five thousand men in the Roman army.*

54

Mark

pigs. [17]Then the people began to beg Jesus to leave their area.

[18]As Jesus was getting back into the boat, the man who was freed from the demons begged to go with him. [19]But Jesus would not let him. He said, "Go home to your family and tell them how much the Lord has done for you and how he has had mercy on you." [20]So the man left and began to tell the people in the Ten Towns[n] about what Jesus had done for him. And everyone was amazed.

## Jesus Gives Life to a Dead Girl and Heals a Sick Woman

[21]When Jesus went in the boat back to the other side of the lake, a large crowd gathered around him there. [22]A leader of the synagogue, named Jairus, came there, saw Jesus, and fell at his feet. [23]He begged Jesus, saying again and again, "My daughter is dying. Please come and put your hands on her so she will be healed and will live." [24]So Jesus went with him.

A large crowd followed Jesus and pushed very close around him. [25]Among them was a woman who had been bleeding for twelve years. [26]She had suffered very much from many doctors and had spent all the money she had, but instead of improving, she was getting worse. [27]When the woman heard about Jesus, she came up behind him in the crowd and touched his coat. [28]She thought, "If I can just touch his clothes, I will be healed." [29]Instantly her bleeding stopped, and she felt in her body that she was healed from her disease.

[30]At once Jesus felt power go out from him. So he turned around in the crowd and asked, "Who touched my clothes?"

[31]His followers said, "Look at how many people are pushing against you! And you ask, 'Who touched me?'"

[32]But Jesus continued looking around to see who had touched him. [33]The woman, knowing that she was healed, came and fell at Jesus' feet. Shaking with fear, she told him the whole truth. [34]Jesus said to her, "Dear woman, you are made well because you believed. Go in peace; be healed of your disease."

[35]While Jesus was still speaking, some people came from the house of the synagogue leader. They said, "Your daughter is dead. There is no need to bother the teacher anymore."

[36]But Jesus paid no attention to what they said. He told the synagogue leader, "Don't be afraid; just believe."

[37]Jesus let only Peter, James, and John the brother of James go with him. [38]When they came to the house of the synagogue leader, Jesus found many people there making lots of noise and crying loudly. [39]Jesus entered the house and said to them, "Why are you crying and making so much noise? The child is not dead, only asleep." [40]But they laughed at him. So, after throwing them out of the house, Jesus took the child's father and mother and his three followers into the room where the child was. [41]Taking hold of the girl's hand, he said to her, "Talitha, koum!" (This means, "Young girl, I tell you to stand up!") [42]At once the girl stood right up and began walking. (She was twelve years old.) Everyone was completely amazed. [43]Jesus gave them strict orders not to tell people about this. Then he told them to give the girl something to eat.

## Jesus Goes to His Hometown

6 Jesus left there and went to his hometown, and his followers went with him. [2]On the Sabbath day he taught in the synagogue. Many people heard him and were amazed, saying, "Where did this man get these teachings? What is this wisdom that has been given to him? And where did he get the power to do miracles? [3]He is just the carpenter, the son of Mary and the brother of James, Joseph, Judas, and Simon. And his sisters are here with us." So the people were upset with Jesus.

# top ten

## top ten ways to...
### Be a Good Friend

1. Listen carefully to what she says.
2. Hide cheery notes in your friend's bag or locker.
3. Pray for her every day.
4. Be nice to her parents.
5. Dedicate a song to her on the radio.
6. Forgive her when she makes a mistake.
7. Apologize when you make a mistake!
8. Give her a list of things you appreciate about her.
9. Sit with her quietly when she's sad.
10. Remind her how special she is to God.

# Q & A

**Q** Is it wrong for Christians to do yoga?

**A** There is a religious background to yoga that many people don't know about (or don't take seriously), and it's *not* Christian! Yoga teaches that humans can become gods or part of God through the meditation exercises and that "salvation" means solving all the world's problems. The Bible teaches that we can only be saved through Jesus (John 14:6). Yoga exercises might be OK for your body, but be sure to guard your mind and soul.

5:20 **Ten Towns** In Greek, called "Decapolis." It was an area east of Lake Galilee that once had ten main towns.

## dig deeper

### Mark 8:34–35

"Outwit, outplay, outlast." Being a survivor on a TV reality show means doing whatever it takes to win. Even if it means lying or letting other people get hurt. You might help someone else out for a while, but you're always thinking about what's best for you.

Being a follower of Jesus means doing just the opposite. Jesus said, "If people want to follow me, they must give up the things they want. They must be willing even to give up their lives" (Mark 8:34). Then Jesus told them the secret. People who try to win in life by putting themselves first actually end up losing. The people who are willing to *not* get everything they want, to be last, even to die, just because they love Jesus, are the ones who end up having true life. True life is knowing God and living with him forever someday.

Jesus isn't talking about giving up your dreams or not doing your best in school or with your family and friends. Jesus wants you to know that, even when you give up your right to be first, when you sacrifice your time to help someone out, when you're willing to forgive someone who hurt you, you're not losing anything at all. If you're doing it because you love him—you're the winner!

---

preached that people should change their hearts and lives. [13]They forced many demons out and put olive oil on many sick people and healed them.

## How John the Baptist Was Killed

[14]King Herod heard about Jesus, because he was now well known. Some people said,[n] "He is John the Baptist, who has risen from the dead. That is why he can work these miracles."

[15]Others said, "He is Elijah."[n]

Other people said, "Jesus is a prophet, like the prophets who lived long ago."

[16]When Herod heard this, he said, "I killed John by cutting off his head. Now he has risen from the dead!"

[17]Herod himself had ordered his soldiers to arrest John and put him in prison in order to please his wife, Herodias. She had been the wife of Philip, Herod's brother, but then Herod had married her. [18]John had been telling Herod, "It is not lawful for you to be married to your brother's wife." [19]So Herodias hated John and wanted to kill him. But she couldn't, [20]because Herod was afraid of John and protected him. He knew John was a good and holy man. Also, though John's preaching always bothered him, he enjoyed listening to John.

[21]Then the perfect time came for Herodias to cause John's death. On Herod's birthday, he gave a dinner party for the most important government leaders, the commanders of his army, and the most important people in Galilee. [22]When the daughter of Herodias[n] came in and danced, she pleased Herod and the people eating with him.

So King Herod said to the girl, "Ask me for anything you want, and I will give it to you." [23]He promised her, "Anything you ask for I will give to you—up to half of my kingdom."

[24]The girl went to her mother and asked, "What should I ask for?"

Her mother answered, "Ask for the head of John the Baptist."

[25]At once the girl went back to the king and said to him, "I want the head of John the Baptist right now on a platter."

### "HAVE COURAGE! IT IS I. DO NOT BE AFRAID."

---

[4]Jesus said to them, "A prophet is honored everywhere except in his hometown and with his own people and in his own home." [5]So Jesus was not able to work any miracles there except to heal a few sick people by putting his hands on them. [6]He was amazed at how many people had no faith.

Then Jesus went to other villages in that area and taught. [7]He called his twelve followers together and got ready to send them out two by two and gave them authority over evil spirits. [8]This is what Jesus commanded them: "Take nothing for your trip except a walking stick. Take no bread, no bag, and no money in your pockets. [9]Wear sandals, but take only the clothes you are wearing. [10]When you enter a house, stay there until you leave that town. [11]If the people in a certain place refuse to welcome you or listen to you, leave that place. Shake its dust off your feet[n] as a warning to them."[n]

[12]So the followers went out and

6:11 Shake . . . feet A warning. It showed that they were rejecting these people. 6:11 them Some Greek copies continue, "I tell you the truth, on the Judgment Day it will be better for the towns of Sodom and Gomorrah than for the people of that town." See Matthew 10:15. 6:14 Some people said Some Greek copies read "He said." 6:15 Elijah A great prophet who spoke for God and who lived hundreds of years before Christ. See 1 Kings 17. 6:22 When . . . Herodias Some Greek copies read "When his daughter Herodias."

56

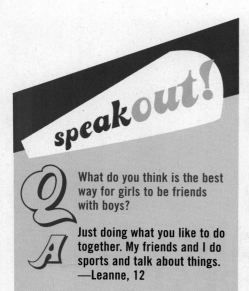

²⁶Although the king was very sad, he had made a promise, and his dinner guests had heard it. So he did not want to refuse what she asked. ²⁷Immediately the king sent a soldier to bring John's head. The soldier went and cut off John's head in the prison ²⁸and brought it back on a platter. He gave it to the girl, and the

girl gave it to her mother. ²⁹When John's followers heard this, they came and got John's body and put it in a tomb.

## More than Five Thousand Fed

³⁰The apostles gathered around Jesus and told him about all the things they had done and taught. ³¹Crowds of people were coming and going so that Jesus and his followers did not even have time to eat. He said to them, "Come away by yourselves, and we will go to a lonely place to get some rest."

³²So they went in a boat by themselves to a lonely place. ³³But many people saw them leave and recognized them. So from all the towns they ran to the place where Jesus was going, and they got there before him. ³⁴When he arrived, he saw a great crowd waiting. He felt sorry for them, because they were like sheep without a shepherd. So he began to teach them many things.

³⁵When it was late in the day, his followers came to him and said, "No one lives in this place, and it is already very late. ³⁶Send the people away so they can go to the countryside and towns around here to buy themselves something to eat."

³⁷But Jesus answered, "You give them something to eat."

They said to him, "We would all have to work a month to earn enough money to buy that much bread!"

³⁸Jesus asked them, "How many loaves of bread do you have? Go and see."

When they found out, they said, "Five loaves and two fish."

³⁹Then Jesus told his followers to have the people sit in groups on the green grass. ⁴⁰So they sat in groups of fifty or a hundred. ⁴¹Jesus took the five loaves and two fish and, looking up to heaven, he thanked God for the food. He divided the bread and gave it to his followers for them to give to the people. Then he divided the two fish among them all. ⁴²All the people ate and were satisfied. ⁴³The followers filled twelve baskets with the leftover pieces of bread and fish. ⁴⁴There were five thousand men who ate.

## Jesus Walks on the Water

⁴⁵Immediately Jesus told his followers to get into the boat and go ahead of him to Bethsaida across the lake. He stayed there to send the people home. ⁴⁶After sending them away, he went into the hills to pray.

⁴⁷That night, the boat was in the middle of the lake, and Jesus was alone on the land. ⁴⁸He saw his followers struggling hard to row the boat, because the wind was blowing against them. Between three and six o'clock in the morning, Jesus came to them, walking on the water, and he wanted to walk past the boat. ⁴⁹But when they saw him walking on the water, they thought he was a ghost and cried out. ⁵⁰They all saw him and were afraid. But quickly Jesus spoke to them and said, "Have courage! It is I. Do not be afraid." ⁵¹Then he got into the boat with them, and the wind became calm. The followers were greatly amazed. ⁵²They did not understand about the miracle of the five loaves, because their minds were closed.

⁵³When they had crossed the lake, they came to shore at Gennesaret and tied the boat there. ⁵⁴When they got out of the boat, people immediately recognized Jesus. ⁵⁵They ran everywhere in that area and began to bring sick people on mats wherever they heard he was. ⁵⁶And everywhere he went—into towns, cities, or countryside—the people brought the sick to the marketplaces. They begged him to let them touch just the edge of his coat, and all who touched it were healed.

## Obey God's Law

**7** When some Pharisees and some teachers of the law came from Jerusalem, they gathered around Jesus. ²They saw that some of Jesus' followers ate food with hands that were not clean, that is, they hadn't washed them. ³(The Pharisees and all the Jews never eat before washing their hands in the way required by their unwritten laws. ⁴And when they buy something in the market, they never eat it until they wash themselves in a special way. They also follow many other unwritten laws, such as the washing of cups, pitchers, and pots.ⁿ)

⁵The Pharisees and the teachers of the law said to Jesus, "Why don't your followers obey the unwritten laws which have been handed down to us? Why do your followers eat their food with hands that are not clean?"

⁶Jesus answered, "Isaiah was right when he spoke about you hypocrites. He wrote,

'These people show honor to me with words,
    but their hearts are far from me.
⁷Their worship of me is worthless.
    The things they teach are nothing
        but human rules.' *Isaiah 29:13*
⁸You have stopped following the commands of God, and you follow only human teachings."ⁿ

⁹Then Jesus said to them, "You cleverly ignore the commands of God so you can follow your own teachings. ¹⁰Moses said, 'Honor your father and your mother,'ⁿ

**7:4 pots** *Some Greek copies continue, "and dining couches."* **7:8 teachings** *Some Greek copies continue, "You wash pitchers and jugs and do many other such things."* **7:10 'Honor . . . mother.'** *Quotation from Exodus 20:12; Deuteronomy 5:16.* **7:10 'Anyone . . . death.'** *Quotation from Exodus 21:17.*

and 'Anyone who says cruel things to his father or mother must be put to death.'[n] [11]But you say a person can tell his father or mother, 'I have something I could use to help you, but it is Corban—a gift to God.' [12]You no longer let that person use that money for his father or his mother. [13]By your own rules, which you teach people, you are rejecting what God said. And you do many things like that."

[14]After Jesus called the crowd to him again, he said, "Every person should listen to me and understand what I am saying. [15]There is nothing people put into their bodies that makes them unclean. People are made unclean by the things that come out of them. [[16]Let those with ears use them and listen.]"[n]

[17]When Jesus left the people and went into the house, his followers asked him about this story. [18]Jesus said, "Do you still not understand? Surely you know that nothing that enters someone from the outside can make that person unclean. [19]It does not go into the mind, but into the stomach. Then it goes out of the body." (When Jesus said this, he meant that no longer was any food unclean for people to eat.)

[20]And Jesus said, "The things that come out of people are the things that make them unclean. [21]All these evil things begin inside people, in the mind: evil thoughts, sexual sins, stealing, murder, adultery, [22]greed, evil actions, lying, doing sinful things, jealousy, speaking evil of others, pride, and foolish living. [23]All these evil things come from inside and make people unclean."

## Jesus Helps a Non-Jewish Woman

[24]Jesus left that place and went to the area around Tyre.[n] When he went into a house, he did not want anyone to know he was there, but he could not stay hidden. [25]A woman whose daughter had an evil spirit in her heard that he was there. So she quickly came to Jesus and fell at his feet. [26]She was Greek, born in Phoenicia, in Syria. She begged Jesus to force the demon out of her daughter.

[27]Jesus told the woman, "It is not right to take the children's bread and give it to the dogs. First let the children eat all they want."

[28]But she answered, "Yes, Lord, but even the dogs under the table can eat the children's crumbs."

## dig deeper

### Mark 9:43-48

Imagine this: Your sister gets on your nerves so you kick her doll across the room. Your mom finds out and tells you to cut off the foot you kicked it with.

Sound crazy? Mark 9:43 says, "If your hand causes you to sin, cut it off." Does that mean God really wants us to cut off the parts of our bodies that we sin with? No . . . because sin doesn't start in your foot or your hand or your ear. Sin starts in your heart, when you are selfish and disobedient and hateful. You could cut your tongue off to not say mean things, but you could still hate someone in your mind. You could cut off your hand not to steal, but you could find another way to do it. You could sit in an empty room all day and commit lots of sins in your head!

So what did Jesus mean? He was using an extreme example to make a point: it would be better to lose a part of your body than to go on sinning with it. Basically, he was telling us to get rid of the things in our lives that tempt us to sin, such as bad habits, inappropriate items, or harmful relationships. If anything keeps you far from God, you should cut it off!

[29]Then Jesus said, "Because of your answer, you may go. The demon has left your daughter."

[30]The woman went home and found her daughter lying in bed; the demon was gone.

## Jesus Heals a Deaf Man

[31]Then Jesus left the area around Tyre and went through Sidon to Lake Galilee, to the area of the Ten Towns.[n] [32]While he was there, some people brought a man to him who was deaf and could not talk plainly. The people begged Jesus to put his hand on the man to heal him.

[33]Jesus led the man away from the crowd, by himself. He put his fingers in the man's ears and then spit and touched the man's tongue. [34]Looking up to heaven, he sighed and said to the man, "Ephphatha!" (This means, "Be opened.") [35]Instantly the man was able to hear and to use his tongue so that he spoke clearly.

[36]Jesus commanded the people not to tell anyone about what happened. But the more he commanded them, the more

**7:16 Let . . . listen.** *Some Greek copies do not contain the bracketed text.* **7:24 Tyre** *Some Greek copies continue, "and Sidon."* **7:31 Ten Towns** *In Greek, called "Decapolis." It was an area east of Lake Galilee that once had ten main towns.*

# Q & A

**Q** Is there any sin God won't forgive? I'm worried.

**A** God will never refuse to forgive you—check out 1 John 1:9. The only condition is that you must first forgive others who have done wrong to you. Mark 11:26 says, "But if you don't forgive other people, then your Father in heaven will not forgive your sins." As long as you're truly sorry, there's no need to worry!

they told about it. [37]They were completely amazed and said, "Jesus does everything well. He makes the deaf hear! And those who can't talk he makes able to speak."

## More than Four Thousand People Fed

**8** Another time there was a great crowd with Jesus that had nothing to eat. So Jesus called his followers and said, [2]"I feel sorry for these people, because they have already been with me for three days, and they have nothing to eat. [3]If I send them home hungry, they will faint on the way. Some of them live a long way from here."

[4]Jesus' followers answered, "How can we get enough bread to feed all these people? We are far away from any town."

[5]Jesus asked, "How many loaves of bread do you have?"

They answered, "Seven."

[6]Jesus told the people to sit on the ground. Then he took the seven loaves, gave thanks to God, and divided the bread. He gave the pieces to his followers to give to the people, and they did so. [7]The followers also had a few small fish. After Jesus gave thanks for the fish, he told his followers to give them to the people also. [8]All the people ate and were satisfied. Then his followers filled seven baskets with the leftover pieces of food. [9]There were about four thousand people

who ate. After they had eaten, Jesus sent them home. [10]Then right away he got into a boat with his followers and went to the area of Dalmanutha.

## The Leaders Ask for a Miracle

[11]The Pharisees came to Jesus and began to ask him questions. Hoping to trap him, they asked Jesus for a miracle from God. [12]Jesus sighed deeply and said, "Why do you people ask for a miracle as a sign? I tell you the truth, no sign will be given to you." [13]Then Jesus left the Pharisees and went in the boat to the other side of the lake.

## Guard Against Wrong Teachings

[14]His followers had only one loaf of bread with them in the boat; they had forgotten to bring more. [15]Jesus warned them, "Be careful! Beware of the yeast of the Pharisees and the yeast of Herod."

[16]His followers discussed the meaning of this, saying, "He said this because we have no bread."

[17]Knowing what they were talking about, Jesus asked them, "Why are you talking about not having bread? Do you still not see or understand? Are your minds closed? [18]You have eyes, but you don't really see. You have ears, but you don't really listen. Remember when [19]I divided five loaves of bread for the five thousand? How many baskets did you fill with leftover pieces of food?"

They answered, "Twelve."

[20]"And when I divided seven loaves of bread for the four thousand, how many baskets did you fill with leftover pieces of food?"

They answered, "Seven."

[21]Then Jesus said to them, "Don't you understand yet?"

## Jesus Heals a Blind Man

[22]Jesus and his followers came to Bethsaida. There some people brought a blind man to Jesus and begged him to touch the man. [23]So Jesus took the blind man's hand and led him out of the village. Then he spit on the man's eyes and put his hands on the man and asked, "Can you see now?"

[24]The man looked up and said, "Yes, I see people, but they look like trees walking around."

[25]Again Jesus put his hands on the man's eyes. Then the man opened his eyes wide and they were healed, and he was able to see everything clearly. [26]Jesus told him to go home, saying, "Don't go into the town."[n]

**8:26 town** Some Greek copies continue, "Don't even go and tell anyone in the town."

# Bible Basics

The people who first received the books that make up our Bible could tell that these messages were from God. For one thing, the messages matched what they already knew about him. We know from the gospels that Jesus referred to the Old Testament as God's Word. We also know that much of the New Testament was accepted as Scripture soon after Jesus lived. The writers of the New Testament books had been with Jesus or were closely connected with Jesus' followers. The first Christians knew that all these men could be trusted. The Bible has always been seen as God's Word; we can still trust it today!

# Relationships

**B**eing a "big sister" can mean getting to stay up later and going to the mall with your friends . . . and it can mean doing dishes, laundry, and mowing the lawn! Colossians 3:23–24 says that whenever you serve others—even those in your family— you should work as if you're serving the Lord. Remember, your family is a team. If your job seems too hard and you need extra encouragement, then tell your parents. They probably appreciate you more than you know. And remember, Jesus knows exactly how you feel. He was a big brother, too!

## Peter Says Jesus Is the Christ

27Jesus and his followers went to the towns around Caesarea Philippi. While they were traveling, Jesus asked them, "Who do people say I am?"

28They answered, "Some say you are John the Baptist. Others say you are Elijah,[n] and others say you are one of the prophets."

29Then Jesus asked, "But who do you say I am?"

Peter answered, "You are the Christ."

30Jesus warned his followers not to tell anyone who he was.

31Then Jesus began to teach them that the Son of Man must suffer many things and that he would be rejected by the Jewish elders, the leading priests, and the teachers of the law. He told them that the Son of Man must be killed and then rise from the dead after three days. 32Jesus told them plainly what would happen. Then Peter took Jesus aside and began to tell him not to talk like that. 33But Jesus turned and looked at his followers. Then he told Peter not to talk that way. He said, "Go away from me, Satan![n] You don't care about the things of God, but only about things people think are important."

34Then Jesus called the crowd to him, along with his followers. He said, "If people want to follow me, they must give up the things they want. They must be willing even to give up their lives to follow me. 35Those who want to save their lives will give up true life. But those who give up their lives for me and for the Good News will have true life. 36It is worthless to have the whole world if they lose their souls. 37They could never pay enough to buy back their souls. 38The people who live now are living in a sinful and evil time. If people are ashamed of me and my teaching, the Son of Man will be ashamed of them when he comes with his Father's glory and with the holy angels."

9Then Jesus said to the people, "I tell you the truth, some people standing here will see the kingdom of God come with power before they die."

## Jesus Talks with Moses and Elijah

2Six days later, Jesus took Peter, James, and John up on a high mountain by themselves. While they watched, Jesus' appearance was changed. 3His clothes became shining white, whiter than any person could make them. 4Then Elijah and Moses[n] appeared to them, talking with Jesus.

5Peter said to Jesus, "Teacher, it is good that we are here. Let us make three tents—one for you, one for Moses, and one for Elijah." 6Peter did not know what to say, because he and the others were so frightened.

7Then a cloud came and covered them, and a voice came from the cloud, saying, "This is my Son, whom I love. Listen to him!"

8Suddenly Peter, James, and John looked around, but they saw only Jesus there alone with them.

9As they were coming down the mountain, Jesus commanded them not to tell anyone about what they had seen until the Son of Man had risen from the dead. 10So the followers obeyed Jesus, but they discussed what he meant about rising from the dead.

# Q&A

**Q** Is it possible to become perfect and stop sinning?

**A** First Corinthians 15:34 tells us to stop sinning and, in Leviticus 11:45, God said: "You must be holy because I am holy." So *holiness* and not sinning are possible. God wouldn't ask us to do something we can't. But it's obviously very hard, so we need to ask for the Holy Spirit's help. *Perfect* means there's nothing wrong with us . . . and that won't happen until we get to heaven!

**8:28 Elijah** *A man who spoke for God and who lived hundreds of years before Christ. See 1 Kings 17.* **8:33 Satan** *Name for the devil meaning "the enemy." Jesus means that Peter was talking like Satan.*
**9:4 Elijah and Moses** *Two of the most important Jewish leaders in the past. God had given Moses the Law, and Elijah was an important prophet.*

# February

start here

**1** Help your brother or sister clean his or her room.

**2** Pray for a person of influence: Today is Shakira's birthday.

**3**

**4** Look at yourself in the mirror and say, "You are a work of art!" Then thank God for creating you with love and care.

**5** Give the rest of your family a chance to use the phone today!

**6**

**7** Pray for a person of influence: Today is Ashton Kutcher's birthday.

**8**

**9** Give your sister or best friend a really warm hug!

**10** Clean up underneath your bed. (Yuck! What is that??)

**11** Pray for a person of influence: Today is Jennifer Aniston's birthday.

**12**

**13** President's Day (USA)—Pray for the president of the United States.

**14** Valentine's Day—Cheer up a single adult you know by giving her a valentine.

**15**

**16** Turn off your music and lie on your bed quietly for 15 minutes. Think about God and what he might want to say to you.

**17**

**18**

**19** Read 1 Corinthians 13:4–7.

**20**

**21** Pray for a person of influence: Today is Jennifer Love Hewitt's birthday.

**22** Pray for a person of influence: Today is Drew Barrymore's birthday.

**23**

**24**

**25**

**26**

**27** Write down your top five pet peeves. Ask God to give you patience with those things.

**28** Try styling your hair a different way today. Ask someone you trust for her honest opinion.

**29**

**30**

Maggie says, "Make a list!"

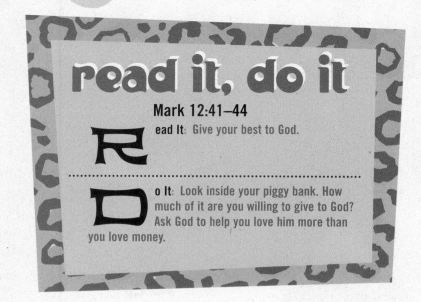

## read it, do it

### Mark 12:41–44

**R**ead It: Give your best to God.

**D**o It: Look inside your piggy bank. How much of it are you willing to give to God? Ask God to help you love him more than you love money.

---

[11]Then they asked Jesus, "Why do the teachers of the law say that Elijah must come first?"

[12]Jesus answered, "They are right to say that Elijah must come first and make everything the way it should be. But why does the Scripture say that the Son of Man will suffer much and that people will treat him as if he were nothing? [13]I tell you that Elijah has already come. And people did to him whatever they wanted to do, just as the Scriptures said it would happen."

### Jesus Heals a Sick Boy

[14]When Jesus, Peter, James, and John came back to the other followers, they saw a great crowd around them and the teachers of the law arguing with them. [15]But as soon as the crowd saw Jesus, the people were surprised and ran to welcome him.

[16]Jesus asked, "What are you arguing about?"

[17]A man answered, "Teacher, I brought my son to you. He has an evil spirit in him that stops him from talking. [18]When the spirit attacks him, it throws him on the ground. Then my son foams at the mouth, grinds his teeth, and becomes very stiff. I asked your followers to force

**"I DO BELIEVE! HELP ME TO BELIEVE MORE!"**

the evil spirit out, but they couldn't."

[19]Jesus answered, "You people have no faith. How long must I stay with you? How long must I put up with you? Bring the boy to me."

[20]So the followers brought him to Jesus. As soon as the evil spirit saw Jesus, it made the boy lose control of himself, and he fell down and rolled on the ground, foaming at the mouth.

[21]Jesus asked the boy's father, "How long has this been happening?"

The father answered, "Since he was very young. [22]The spirit often throws him into a fire or into water to kill him. If you can do anything for him, please have pity on us and help us."

[23]Jesus said to the father, "You said, 'If you can!' All things are possible for the one who believes."

[24]Immediately the father cried out, "I do believe! Help me to believe more!"

[25]When Jesus saw that a crowd was quickly gathering, he ordered the evil spirit, saying, "You spirit that makes people unable to hear or speak, I command you to come out of this boy and never enter him again!"

[26]The evil spirit screamed and caused the boy to fall on the ground again. Then the spirit came out. The boy looked as if he were dead, and many people said, "He is dead!" [27]But Jesus took hold of the boy's hand and helped him to stand up.

[28]When Jesus went into the house, his followers began asking him privately, "Why couldn't we force that evil spirit out?"

[29]Jesus answered, "That kind of spirit can only be forced out by prayer."[n]

### Jesus Talks About His Death

[30]Then Jesus and his followers left that place and went through Galilee. He didn't want anyone to know where he was, [31]because he was teaching his followers. He said to them, "The Son of Man will be handed over to people, and they will kill him. After three days, he will rise from the dead." [32]But the followers did not understand what Jesus meant, and they were afraid to ask him.

### Who Is the Greatest?

[33]Jesus and his followers went to Capernaum. When they went into a house there, he asked them, "What were you arguing about on the road?" [34]But the followers did not answer, because their argument on the road was about which one of them was the greatest.

[35]Jesus sat down and called the twelve apostles to him. He said, "Whoever wants to be the most important must be last of all and servant of all."

[36]Then Jesus took a small child and had him stand among them. Taking the child in his arms, he said, [37]"Whoever accepts a child like this in my name accepts me.

## Q&A

**Q** While I was on the Internet, I accidentally saw some "dirty" pictures. I can't stop thinking about what I saw. What should I do?

**A** It seems hard to avoid Web sites, magazines, or movies with not-so-good pictures or stories. For many people, looking at them can become a terrible habit that's very hard to break. Ask God to help you stop thinking about it, and then do your best to fill your mind with good things (see Philippians 4:8). The devil will try to tempt you to sin . . . but God will help you if you ask!

**9:29 prayer** *Some Greek copies continue, "and fasting."*

> "WHOEVER WANTS TO BE THE MOST IMPORTANT MUST BE LAST OF ALL AND SERVANT OF ALL."

And whoever accepts me accepts the One who sent me."

## Anyone Not Against Us Is for Us

[38]Then John said, "Teacher, we saw someone using your name to force demons out of a person. We told him to stop, because he does not belong to our group."

[39]But Jesus said, "Don't stop him, because anyone who uses my name to do powerful things will not easily say evil things about me. [40]Whoever is not against us is with us. [41]I tell you the truth, whoever gives you a drink of water because you belong to the Christ will truly get his reward.

[42]"If one of these little children believes in me, and someone causes that child to sin, it would be better for that person to have a large stone tied around his neck and be drowned in the sea. [43]If your hand causes you to sin, cut it off. It is better for you to lose part of your body and live forever than to have two hands and go to hell, where the fire never goes out. [[44]In hell the worm does not die; the fire is never put out.][n] [45]If your foot causes you to sin, cut it off. It is better for you to lose part of your body and to live forever than to have two feet and be thrown into hell. [[46]In hell the worm does not die; the fire is never put out.][n] [47]If your eye causes you to sin, take it out. It is better for you to enter the kingdom of God with only one eye than to have two eyes and be thrown into hell. [48]In hell the worm does not die; the fire is never put out. [49]Every person will be salted with fire.

[50]"Salt is good, but if the salt loses its salty taste, you cannot make it salty again. So, be full of salt, and have peace with each other."

## Jesus Teaches About Divorce

**10** Then Jesus left that place and went into the area of Judea and across the Jordan River. Again, crowds came to him, and he taught them as he usually did.

[2]Some Pharisees came to Jesus and tried to trick him. They asked, "Is it right for a man to divorce his wife?"

[3]Jesus answered, "What did Moses command you to do?"

[4]They said, "Moses allowed a man to write out divorce papers and send her away."[n]

[5]Jesus said, "Moses wrote that command for you because you were stubborn. [6]But when God made the world, 'he made them male and female.'[n] [7]So a man will leave his father and mother and be united with his wife,[n] [8]and the two will become one body.'[n] So there are not two, but one. [9]God has joined the two together, so no one should separate them."

[10]Later, in the house, his followers asked Jesus again about the question of divorce. [11]He answered, "Anyone who divorces his wife and marries another woman is guilty of adultery against her.

## god's promises

### Mark 10:13–16

Have you ever wanted to enter a contest or call in an answer to a radio station, only to find out that you had to be "age eighteen or older?" Sure, you need to be an adult to vote or drive or buy a house—but win a contest? That feels unfair, doesn't it?

Thankfully, God's promises are not reserved for people age eighteen or older. In fact, Jesus promises that the kingdom of God belongs to the young. Not just the young in years (or *you* might get too old for it!), but the young in heart. He's not talking about people who like to play volleyball and video games. God's promise of his kingdom is for those who come to him with open arms and trusting hearts, just like those little children did that day.

Some people think you need to wait until you're an adult to make a decision to trust Jesus as your Lord and Savior. But you're never too young to come into God's kingdom. Jesus doesn't want you to wait. His kingdom is open to you. You come in as more than just a royal subject—you're God's royal child. But only if you believe.

*You're never too young to come into God's kingdom!*

9:44, 46 **In . . . out.** *Some Greek copies do not contain the bracketed text.* 10:4 **"Moses . . . away."** *Quotation from Deuteronomy 24:1.* 10:6 **'he made . . . female'** *Quotation from Genesis 1:27.* 10:7 **and . . . wife** *Some Greek copies do not have this phrase.* 10:7–8 **'So . . . body.'** *Quotation from Genesis 2:24.*

[12]And the woman who divorces her husband and marries another man is also guilty of adultery."

## Jesus Accepts Children

[13]Some people brought their little children to Jesus so he could touch them, but his followers told them to stop. [14]When Jesus saw this, he was upset and said to them, "Let the little children come to me. Don't stop them, because the kingdom of God belongs to people who are like these children. [15]I tell you the truth, you must accept the kingdom of God as if you were a little child, or you will never enter it." [16]Then Jesus took the children in his arms, put his hands on them, and blessed them.

## A Rich Young Man's Question

[17]As Jesus started to leave, a man ran to him and fell on his knees before Jesus. The man asked, "Good teacher, what must I do to have life forever?"

[18]Jesus answered, "Why do you call me good? Only God is good. [19]You know the commands: 'You must not murder anyone. You must not be guilty of adultery. You must not steal. You must not tell lies about your neighbor. You must not cheat. Honor your father and mother.' "[n]

[20]The man said, "Teacher, I have obeyed all these things since I was a boy."

[21]Jesus, looking at the man, loved him and said, "There is one more thing you need to do. Go and sell everything you have, and give the money to the poor, and you will have treasure in heaven. Then come and follow me."

[22]He was very sad to hear Jesus say this, and he left sorrowfully, because he was rich.

[23]Then Jesus looked at his followers and said, "How hard it will be for the rich to enter the kingdom of God!"

[24]The followers were amazed at what Jesus said. But he said again, "My children, it is very hard[n] to enter the kingdom of God! [25]It is easier for a camel to go through the eye of a needle than for a rich person to enter the kingdom of God."

[26]The followers were even more surprised and said to each other, "Then who can be saved?"

[27]Jesus looked at them and said, "For people this is impossible, but for God all things are possible."

[28]Peter said to Jesus, "Look, we have left everything and followed you."

[29]Jesus said, "I tell you the truth, all those who have left houses, brothers, sisters, mother, father, children, or farms for me and for the Good News [30]will get

**93% of kids feel their parents love them.**
—Sonna, Linda, Ph.D. *The Everything Tween Book*. Avon, Massachusetts: Adams Media Corporation, 2003.

**did you know?**

more than they left. Here in this world they will have a hundred times more homes, brothers, sisters, mothers, children, and fields. And with those things, they will also suffer for their belief. But in this age they will have life forever. [31]Many who are first now will be last in the future. And many who are last now will be first in the future."

## Jesus Talks About His Death

[32]As Jesus and the people with him were on the road to Jerusalem, he was leading the way. His followers were amazed, but others in the crowd who followed were afraid. Again Jesus took the twelve apostles aside and began to tell them what was about to happen in Jerusalem. [33]He said, "Look, we are going to Jerusalem. The Son of Man will be turned over to the leading priests and the teachers of the law. They will say that he must die, and they will turn him over to the non-Jewish people, [34]who will laugh at him and spit on him. They will beat him with whips and crucify him. But on the third day, he will rise to life again."

## Two Followers Ask Jesus a Favor

[35]Then James and John, sons of Zebedee, came to Jesus and said, "Teacher, we want to ask you to do something for us."

[36]Jesus asked, "What do you want me to do for you?"

[37]They answered, "Let one of us sit at your right side and one of us sit at your left side in your glory in your kingdom."

[38]Jesus said, "You don't understand what you are asking. Can you drink the cup that I must drink? And can you be baptized with the same kind of baptism that I must go through?"[n]

[39]They answered, "Yes, we can."

Jesus said to them, "You will drink the same cup that I will drink, and you will be baptized with the same baptism that I must go through. [40]But I cannot choose who will sit at my right or my left; those places belong to those for whom they have been prepared."

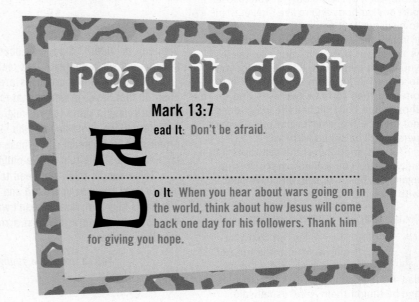

# read it, do it

## Mark 13:7

**R**ead It: Don't be afraid.

**D**o It: When you hear about wars going on in the world, think about how Jesus will come back one day for his followers. Thank him for giving you hope.

---

**10:19 'You . . . mother.'** *Quotation from Exodus 20:12–16; Deuteronomy 5:16–20.* **10:24 hard** *Some Greek copies continue, "for those who trust in riches."* **10:38 Can you . . . through?** *Jesus was asking if they could suffer the same terrible things that would happen to him.*

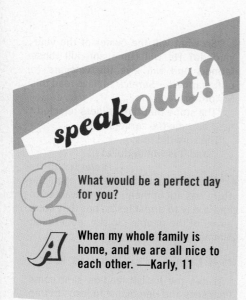

## speakout!

**Q** What would be a perfect day for you?

**A** When my whole family is home, and we are all nice to each other. —Karly, 11

⁴¹When the other ten followers heard this, they began to be angry with James and John.

⁴²Jesus called them together and said, "The other nations have rulers. You know that those rulers love to show their power over the people, and their important leaders love to use all their authority. ⁴³But it should not be that way among you. Whoever wants to become great among you must serve the rest of you like a servant. ⁴⁴Whoever wants to become the first among you must serve all of you like a slave. ⁴⁵In the same way, the Son of Man did not come to be served. He came to serve others and to give his life as a ransom for many people."

### Jesus Heals a Blind Man

⁴⁶Then they came to the town of Jericho. As Jesus was leaving there with his followers and a great many people, a blind beggar named Bartimaeus son of Timaeus was sitting by the road. ⁴⁷When he heard that Jesus from Nazareth was walking by, he began to shout, "Jesus, Son of David, have mercy on me!"

⁴⁸Many people warned the blind man to be quiet, but he shouted even more, "Son of David, have mercy on me!"

⁴⁹Jesus stopped and said, "Tell the man to come here."

So they called the blind man, saying, "Cheer up! Get to your feet. Jesus is calling you." ⁵⁰The blind man jumped up, left his coat there, and went to Jesus.

⁵¹Jesus asked him, "What do you want me to do for you?"

The blind man answered, "Teacher, I want to see."

⁵²Jesus said, "Go, you are healed because you believed." At once the man could see, and he followed Jesus on the road.

### Jesus Enters Jerusalem as a King

**11** As Jesus and his followers were coming closer to Jerusalem, they came to the towns of Bethphage and Bethany near the Mount of Olives. From there Jesus sent two of his followers ²and said to them, "Go to the town you can see there. When you enter it, you will quickly find a colt tied, which no one has ever ridden. Untie it and bring it here to me. ³If anyone asks you why you are doing this, tell him its Master needs the colt, and he will send it at once."

⁴The followers went into the town, found a colt tied in the street near the door of a house, and untied it. ⁵Some people were standing there and asked, "What are you doing? Why are you untying that colt?" ⁶The followers answered the way Jesus told them to answer, and the people let them take the colt.

⁷They brought the colt to Jesus and put their coats on it, and Jesus sat on it. ⁸Many people spread their coats on the road. Others cut branches in the fields and spread them on the road. ⁹The people were walking ahead of Jesus and behind him, shouting,

"Praise God!
God bless the One who comes in
 the name of the Lord!
                                        *Psalm 118:26*
¹⁰God bless the kingdom of our father
 David!
 That kingdom is coming!
Praiseⁿ to God in heaven!"

¹¹Jesus entered Jerusalem and went into the Temple. After he had looked at everything, since it was already late, he went out to Bethany with the twelve apostles.

¹²The next day as Jesus was leaving Bethany, he became hungry. ¹³Seeing a fig tree in leaf from far away, he went to see if it had any figs on it. But he found no figs, only leaves, because it was not the right season for figs. ¹⁴So Jesus said to the tree, "May no one ever eat fruit from you again." And Jesus' followers heard him say this.

### Jesus Goes to the Temple

¹⁵When Jesus returned to Jerusalem, he went into the Temple and began to throw out those who were buying and selling there. He turned over the tables of those who were exchanging different kinds of money, and he upset the benches of those who were selling doves. ¹⁶Jesus refused to allow anyone to carry goods through the Temple courts. ¹⁷Then he taught the people, saying, "It is written in the Scriptures, 'My Temple will be called a house for prayer for people from all nations.'ⁿ But you are changing God's house into a 'hideout for robbers.'"ⁿ

¹⁸The leading priests and the teachers of the law heard all this and began trying to find a way to kill Jesus. They were afraid of him, because all the people were amazed at his teaching. ¹⁹That evening, Jesus and his followersⁿ left the city.

### The Power of Faith

²⁰The next morning as Jesus was passing by with his followers, they saw the fig tree dry and dead, even to the roots. ²¹Peter remembered the tree and said to Jesus, "Teacher, look! The fig tree you cursed is dry and dead!"

## Q & A

**Q** Is it OK to give someone a gift that someone else gave me but I don't want?

**A** This isn't a question of sinning. It's more about being grateful, polite . . . and wise! Keep it for a while and try to learn to like it. You *could* give it to someone else one day, if you haven't used it, but make sure it's to someone the gift-giver doesn't know at all and that you really think the other person will like it.

11:10 **Praise** Literally, "Hosanna," a Hebrew word used at first in praying to God for help, but at this time it was probably a shout of joy used in praising God or his Messiah. 11:17 **'My Temple . . . nations.'** Quotation from Isaiah 56:7. 11:17 **'hideout for robbers'** Quotation from Jeremiah 7:11. 11:19 **his followers** Some Greek copies mention only Jesus here.

# BE YOUR BEST!

**I**t can be tempting to pick at scabs from scratches or pimples, but don't do it! Small wounds and scars just need time to heal. If someone has hurt your feelings, forgive them and ask God to help you be patient as your heart slowly heals. Give it time . . . it *will* go away.

²²Jesus answered, "Have faith in God. ²³I tell you the truth, you can say to this mountain, 'Go, fall into the sea.' And if you have no doubts in your mind and believe that what you say will happen, God will do it for you. ²⁴So I tell you to believe that you have received the things you ask for in prayer, and God will give them to you. ²⁵When you are praying, if you are angry with someone, forgive him so that your Father in heaven will also forgive your sins. [²⁶But if you don't forgive other people, then your Father in heaven will not forgive your sins.]"ⁿ

## Leaders Doubt Jesus' Authority

²⁷Jesus and his followers went again to Jerusalem. As Jesus was walking in the Temple, the leading priests, the teachers of the law, and the elders came to him. ²⁸They said to him, "What authority do you have to do these things? Who gave you this authority?"

²⁹Jesus answered, "I will ask you one question. If you answer me, I will tell you what authority I have to do these things. ³⁰Tell me: When John baptized people, was that authority from God or just from other people?"

³¹They argued about Jesus' question, saying, "If we answer, 'John's baptism was from God,' Jesus will say, 'Then why didn't you believe him?' ³²But if we say, 'It

was from other people,' the crowd will be against us." (These leaders were afraid of the people, because all the people believed that John was a prophet.)

³³So they answered Jesus, "We don't know."

Jesus said to them, "Then I won't tell you what authority I have to do these things."

## A Story About God's Son

**12** Jesus began to use stories to teach the people. He said, "A man planted a vineyard. He put a wall around it and dug a hole for a winepress and built a tower. Then he leased the land to some farmers and left for a trip. ²When it was time for the grapes to be picked, he sent a servant to the farmers to get his share of the grapes. ³But the farmers grabbed the servant and beat him and sent him away empty-handed. ⁴Then the man sent another servant. They hit him on the head and showed no respect for him. ⁵So the man sent another servant, whom they killed. The man sent many other servants; the farmers beat some of them and killed others.

⁶"The man had one person left to send, his son whom he loved. He sent him last of all, saying, 'They will respect my son.'

⁷"But the farmers said to each other, 'This son will inherit the vineyard. If we kill him, it will be ours.' ⁸So they took the son, killed him, and threw him out of the vineyard.

⁹"So what will the owner of the vineyard do? He will come and kill those farmers and will give the vineyard to other farmers. ¹⁰Surely you have read this Scripture:

'The stone that the builders rejected
　became the cornerstone.
¹¹The Lord did this,
　and it is wonderful to us.' "
*Psalm 118:22–23*

¹²The Jewish leaders knew that the story was about them. So they wanted to find a way to arrest Jesus, but they were afraid of the people. So the leaders left him and went away.

## Is It Right to Pay Taxes or Not?

¹³Later, the Jewish leaders sent some Pharisees and Herodiansⁿ to Jesus to trap him in saying something wrong. ¹⁴They came to him and said, "Teacher, we know that you are an honest man. You are not afraid of what other people think about you, because you pay no attention to who they are. And you teach the truth about God's way. Tell us: Is it right to pay taxes to Caesar or not? ¹⁵Should we pay them, or not?"

But knowing what these men were really trying to do, Jesus said to them, "Why are you trying to trap me? Bring me a coin to look at." ¹⁶They gave Jesus a coin, and he asked, "Whose image and name are on the coin?"

They answered, "Caesar's."

¹⁷Then Jesus said to them, "Give to Caesar the things that are Caesar's, and give

## ■ Bible Bios

### The Poor Widow
### (Mark 12:41–44)

**W**e don't know the name of the poor widow who came into the Temple to put her two coins into the offering box. We *do* know that even though she had almost nothing in life, she still worshiped God and showed her love for him by giving everything she had. Jesus noticed what she did. He told his followers that her offering was far greater than the big amounts of money the rich people put into the box. He knew that she was giving up everything, while the rich people just gave a small part of all that they had. The widow could have kept her coins—no one expected her to give them. But she gave out of love for God. She gave cheerfully . . . and Jesus admired her for it!

Would *you* give up something important for God?

**11:26 But . . . sins.** *Some Greek copies do not contain the bracketed text.* **12:13 Herodians** *A political group that followed Herod and his family.*

## god's promises

Mark 11:24

Think about your mornings. Do you run around hysterically, trying on fifteen outfits and a bunch of shoes to get the right look? During the rest of the day, do you worry about homework, friends, money, and what people think? All that worrying uses up a lot of energy! God has a better way for us to use our energy. In Mark 11:24 Jesus tells us that we can ask God for anything!

Many kids around the world worry about having enough food and clothes. They can ask God to provide their basic needs each day. Other kids might have enough money, but they need to ask God for help with their family or getting along with their friends.

God has promised to answer your prayers! That doesn't mean he'll make you rich or give you lots of choices every day. It *does* mean you don't have to worry because he listens to you and answers your prayers in just the right way. He just asks that you really believe that he will. Show God that you believe him—use your energy to pray instead of worrying! Whether you have a lot or a little, you can feel secure in knowing that God is looking out for all of your needs.

*God has promised to answer your prayers!*

---

tures say, and don't you know about the power of God? [25]When people rise from the dead, they will not marry, nor will they be given to someone to marry. They will be like the angels in heaven. [26]Surely you have read what God said about people rising from the dead. In the book in which Moses wrote about the burning bush,[n] it says that God told Moses, 'I am the God of Abraham, the God of Isaac, and the God of Jacob.'[n] [27]God is the God of the living, not the dead. You Sadducees are wrong!"

### The Most Important Command

[28]One of the teachers of the law came and heard Jesus arguing with the Sadducees. Seeing that Jesus gave good answers to their questions, he asked Jesus, "Which of the commands is most important?"

[29]Jesus answered, "The most important command is this: 'Listen, people of Israel! The Lord our God is the only Lord. [30]Love the Lord your God with all your heart, all your soul, all your mind, and all your strength.'[n] [31]The second command is this: 'Love your neighbor as you love yourself.'[n] There are no commands more important than these."

[32]The man answered, "That was a good answer, Teacher. You were right when you said God is the only Lord and there is no other God besides him. [33]One must love God with all his heart, all his mind, and all his strength. And one must love his neighbor as he loves himself. These commands are more important than all the animals and sacrifices we offer to God."

[34]When Jesus saw that the man answered him wisely, Jesus said to him, "You are close to the kingdom of God." And after that, no one was brave enough to ask Jesus any more questions.

[35]As Jesus was teaching in the Temple, he asked, "Why do the teachers of the law say that the Christ is the son of David? [36]David himself, speaking by the Holy Spirit, said:

'The Lord said to my Lord,
  "Sit by me at my right side,
    until I put your enemies under your
      control." '          *Psalm 110:1*

[37]David himself calls the Christ 'Lord,' so how can the Christ be his son?" The large crowd listened to Jesus with pleasure.

[38]Jesus continued teaching and said, "Beware of the teachers of the law. They like to walk around wearing fancy clothes,

---

to God the things that are God's." The men were amazed at what Jesus said.

### Some Sadducees Try to Trick Jesus

[18]Then some Sadducees came to Jesus and asked him a question. (Sadducees believed that people would not rise from the dead.) [19]They said, "Teacher, Moses wrote that if a man's brother dies, leaving a wife but no children, then that man must marry the widow and have children

for his brother. [20]Once there were seven brothers. The first brother married and died, leaving no children. [21]So the second brother married the widow, but he also died and had no children. The same thing happened with the third brother. [22]All seven brothers married her and died, and none of the brothers had any children. Finally the woman died too. [23]Since all seven brothers had married her, when people rise from the dead, whose wife will she be?"

[24]Jesus answered, "Why don't you understand? Don't you know what the Scrip-

---

**12:26 burning bush** *Read Exodus 3:1–12 in the Old Testament.*   **12:26 'I am . . . Jacob.'** *Quotation from Exodus 3:6.*   **12:29–30 'Listen . . . strength.'** *Quotation from Deuteronomy 6:4–5.*
**12:31 'Love . . . yourself.'** *Quotation from Leviticus 19:18.*

# cool

## Strange Laws

It's hard to know how many of the "strange laws" listed on the Internet are true, but some will make you giggle. For example: in North Carolina, it's against the law for dogs and cats to fight. In Miami, it's illegal to imitate an animal. And in West Virginia, only babies can ride in a baby stroller.

Well, here's a law that's not strange or silly. Jesus called it the greatest commandment: "Love the Lord your God with all your heart, all your soul, all your mind, and all your strength" (Mark 12:30).

and they love for people to greet them with respect in the marketplaces. [39]They love to have the most important seats in the synagogues and at feasts. [40]But they cheat widows and steal their houses and then try to make themselves look good by saying long prayers. They will receive a greater punishment."

**did you know?**
49% of students ask questions in class when they don't understand the teacher.
—Trends & Tudes. Harris Interactive. January 2003.
http://harrisinteractive.com/news/newsletters/k12news/HI_Trends&TudesNews2003_V2_iss1.pdf

## True Giving

[41]Jesus sat near the Temple money box and watched the people put in their money. Many rich people gave large sums of money. [42]Then a poor widow came and put in two small copper coins, which were only worth a few cents.

[43]Calling his followers to him, Jesus said, "I tell you the truth, this poor widow gave more than all those rich people.

[44]They gave only what they did not need. This woman is very poor, but she gave all she had; she gave all she had to live on."

## The Temple Will Be Destroyed

**13** As Jesus was leaving the Temple, one of his followers said to him, "Look, Teacher! How beautiful the buildings are! How big the stones are!"

[2]Jesus said, "Do you see all these great buildings? Not one stone will be left on another. Every stone will be thrown down to the ground."

[3]Later, as Jesus was sitting on the Mount of Olives, opposite the Temple, he was alone with Peter, James, John, and Andrew. They asked Jesus, [4]"Tell us, when will these things happen? And what will be the sign that they are going to happen?"

[5]Jesus began to answer them, "Be careful that no one fools you. [6]Many people will come in my name, saying, 'I am the One,' and they will fool many people. [7]When you hear about wars and stories of wars that are coming, don't be afraid. These things must happen before the end comes. [8]Nations will fight against other nations, and kingdoms against other kingdoms. There will be earthquakes in different places, and there will be times when there is no food for people to eat. These things are like the first pains when something new is about to be born.

[9]"You must be careful. People will arrest you and take you to court and beat you in their synagogues. You will be forced to stand before kings and governors, to tell them about me. This will happen to you because you follow me. [10]But before these things happen, the Good News must be told to all people. [11]When you are arrested and judged, don't worry ahead of time about what you should say. Say whatever is given you to say at that time, because it will not really be you speaking; it will be the Holy Spirit.

## Q & A

**Q** My parents fight a lot, and I think it's because of me. How can I tell if they still love me?

**A** Try talking to them about it. Couples fight for different reasons; it's probably not about you. Tell your parents how you feel. Give them a chance to explain the problem and to tell you that they *do* love you. Don't forget to pray for your parents and to show them how much *you* love *them!* Be the best daughter you can be. That's all you can do!

[12]"Brothers will give their own brothers to be killed, and fathers will give their own children to be killed. Children will fight against their own parents and cause them to be put to death. [13]All people will hate you because you follow me, but those people who keep their faith until the end will be saved.

[14]"You will see 'a blasphemous object that brings destruction'[n] standing where it should not be." (You who read this should understand what it means.) "At that time, the people in Judea should run away to the mountains. [15]If people are on the roofs[n] of their houses, they must not go down or go inside to get anything out of their houses. [16]If people are in the fields, they must not go back to get their coats. [17]At that time, how terrible it will be for women who are pregnant or have nursing babies! [18]Pray that these things will not happen in winter, [19]because those days will be full of trouble. There will be more trouble than there has ever been since the beginning, when God made the world, until now, and nothing as bad will ever happen again. [20]God has decided to make that terrible time short. Otherwise, no one would go on living. But God will make that time short to help the people he has chosen. [21]At that time, someone might say to you, 'Look, there is the Christ!' Or another person might

**13:14** 'a blasphemous object that brings destruction' *Mentioned in Daniel 9:27; 12:11 (cf. Daniel 11:31).* **13:15 roofs** *In Bible times houses were built with flat roofs. The roof was used for drying things such as flax and fruit. And it was used as an extra room, as a place for worship, and as a cool place to sleep in the summer.*

# WHAT KIND OF SEED ARE YOU?

Read Matthew 13:1–23 and then check to see which kind of seed you are!

**1.** Your Sunday school teacher or youth pastor gives a great talk about loving your enemies. You...

  **a.** Shake your head and think, "I'm sure that's not what God really meant."

  **b.** Decide to try it out but give up when your friends don't understand.

  **c.** Tell yourself you're going to try it out. By the time you're heading home, you've forgotten everything.

  **d.** Pray that God will help you love your enemies. When someone bugs you, you do your best to be kind to her.

**2.** Your favorite part of church is...

  **a.** Going home.

  **b.** Visiting after the service.

  **c.** The choir or worship band.

  **d.** The sermon.

**3.** When people ask if you go to church, you say:

  **a.** "Yeah, but only because my parents make me go."

  **b.** "Uh, yes, but I'm not a religious nut or anything."

  **c.** "I go...if I don't have soccer practice or a babysitting job."

  **d.** "Of course I do! It's the best part of my week."

**4.** You're watching your favorite TV show when your little brother asks for help with something. You:

  **a.** Yell, "No! Can't you see I'm busy?" and turn up the volume.

  **b.** Start whining about how unfair it is that you always have to help out at home and how you never get time for yourself.

  **c.** Drag your feet and keep your eye on the TV so you can still see what's going on.

  **d.** Feel disappointed about missing your show but turn off the TV and go to help with a cheerful attitude.

## What kind of seed are you?

**If you answered mostly As,** you are like the seed that fell along the path. You need to take time to understand the Bible in order to follow God. Get into a good church, study the Bible regularly, and commit to praying. God will help you understand more if you ask him.

**If you answered mostly Bs,** you are like the seed that fell on rocky places. You believe in Jesus but worry more about what people think than about what God thinks. You might give up when people give you a hard time because of your faith. Ask God to give you deeper faith so you can persevere as a Christian.

**If you answered mostly Cs,** you are like the seed that fell among the thorns. Perhaps you accepted Jesus as your Savior at one time. But you've given your time and attention to other things in your life and haven't been growing as a Christian. Ask Jesus to help you "weed out" the things in your life that can "choke" your relationship with him.

**If you answered mostly Ds,** you are like the seed that fell on good soil. You believed God's Word, accepted Jesus as your Savior, and are growing as a Christian by living a life that pleases God. Keep up the good work!

say, 'There he is!' But don't believe them. ²²False Christs and false prophets will come and perform great wonders and miracles. They will try to fool even the people God has chosen, if that is possible. ²³So be careful. I have warned you about all this before it happens.

²⁴"During the days after this trouble comes,

'the sun will grow dark,
and the moon will not give its light.
²⁵The stars will fall from the sky.
And the powers of the heavens will be shaken.' *Isaiah 13:10; 34:4*

²⁶"Then people will see the Son of Man coming in clouds with great power and glory. ²⁷Then he will send his angels all around the earth to gather his chosen people from every part of the earth and from every part of heaven.

²⁸"Learn a lesson from the fig tree: When its branches become green and soft and new leaves appear, you know summer is near. ²⁹In the same way, when you see these things happening, you will know that the time is near, ready to come. ³⁰I tell you the truth, all these things will happen while the people of this time are still living. ³¹Earth and sky will be destroyed, but the words I have said will never be destroyed.

³²"No one knows when that day or time will be, not the angels in heaven, not even the Son. Only the Father knows. ³³Be careful! Always be ready,ⁿ because you don't know when that time will be. ³⁴It is like a man who goes on a trip. He leaves his house and lets his servants take care of it, giving each one a special job to do. The man tells the servant guarding the door always to be watchful. ³⁵So always be ready, because you don't know when the owner of the house will come back. It might be in the evening, or at midnight, or in the morning while it is still dark, or when the sun rises. ³⁶Always be ready. Otherwise he might come back suddenly and find you sleeping. ³⁷I tell you this, and I say this to everyone: 'Be ready!'"

EARTH AND SKY WILL BE DESTROYED, BUT THE WORDS I HAVE SAID WILL NEVER BE DESTROYED.

13:33 **ready** *Some Greek copies continue, "and pray."*

# dig deeper

## Mark 15:37–39

The four Gospels (Matthew, Mark, Luke, and John) give us a good picture of everything that happened before, during, and after Jesus' death on the cross. As you read these stories, you can't help but feel sad for the way Jesus was treated. After three years of healing people's bodies and souls, it all ended with him being unfairly accused, arrested, and killed.

Even though he was God, Jesus still suffered and experienced pain: "Then Jesus cried out in a loud voice and died" (Mark 15:37). Something so amazing happened next that an army officer standing near the cross said, "This man really was the Son of God!" (Mark 15:39). He knew that something miraculous had happened.

The Temple (where Jewish people went to worship God) had a huge curtain that divided the main part of the building from "the Most Holy Place." God's Spirit stayed in this area and only the high priest had the right to go in there. The rest of the people could not speak to God directly; they always had to go through the high priest.

But when Jesus died, the curtain ripped apart from top to bottom . . . just like that! God was telling his people that, because of Jesus' sacrifice, we can now go to God ourselves! Do *you* have a personal relationship with God?

## The Plan to Kill Jesus

**14** It was now only two days before the Passover and the Feast of Unleavened Bread. The leading priests and teachers of the law were trying to find a trick to arrest Jesus and kill him. ²But they said, "We must not do it during the feast, because the people might cause a riot."

## A Woman with Perfume for Jesus

³Jesus was in Bethany at the house of Simon, who had a skin disease. While Jesus was eating there, a woman approached him with an alabaster jar filled with very expensive perfume, made of pure nard. She opened the jar and poured the perfume on Jesus' head.

⁴Some who were there became upset and said to each other, "Why waste that

## *Looking Ahead*

### HIGH SCHOOL TEACHERS

You may have heard stories about the difficult teachers in high school. If you're scared that teachers won't like you or will give you too much homework—relax! Your teachers aren't out to make life impossible for you; they are there to challenge you so you can grow. They want you to succeed just as much as you do. If you do your best, you'll have no problem getting along in your classes. Put away those fears before you walk into the classroom, and give your new teacher a chance! Remember that learning is important. Proverbs 15:14 says, "People with understanding want more knowledge."

perfume? [5]It was worth a full year's work. It could have been sold and the money given to the poor." And they got very angry with the woman.

[6]Jesus said, "Leave her alone. Why are you troubling her? She did an excellent thing for me. [7]You will always have the poor with you, and you can help them anytime you want. But you will not always have me. [8]This woman did the only thing she could do for me; she poured perfume on my body to prepare me for burial. [9]I tell you the truth, wherever the Good News is preached in all the world, what this woman has done will be told, and people will remember her."

### Judas Becomes an Enemy of Jesus

[10]One of the twelve apostles, Judas Iscariot, went to talk to the leading priests to offer to hand Jesus over to them. [11]These priests were pleased about this and promised to pay Judas money. So he watched for the best time to turn Jesus in.

### Jesus Eats the Passover Meal

[12]It was now the first day of the Feast of Unleavened Bread when the Passover lamb was sacrificed. Jesus' followers said to him, "Where do you want us to go and prepare for you to eat the Passover meal?"

[13]Jesus sent two of his followers and said to them, "Go into the city and a man carrying a jar of water will meet you. Follow him. [14]When he goes into a house, tell the owner of the house, 'The Teacher says: "Where is my guest room in which I can eat the Passover meal with my followers?"' [15]The owner will show you a large room upstairs that is furnished and ready. Prepare the food for us there."

[16]So the followers left and went into the city. Everything happened as Jesus had said, so they prepared the Passover meal.

[17]In the evening, Jesus went to that house with the twelve. [18]While they were all eating, Jesus said, "I tell you the truth, one of you will turn against me—one of you eating with me now."

[19]The followers were very sad to hear this. Each one began to say to Jesus, "I am not the one, am I?"

[20]Jesus answered, "It is one of the twelve—the one who dips his bread into the bowl with me. [21]The Son of Man will die, just as the Scriptures say. But how terrible it will be for the person who hands the Son of Man over to be killed. It would be better for him if he had never been born."

### The Lord's Supper

[22]While they were eating, Jesus took some bread and thanked God for it and broke it. Then he gave it to his followers and said, "Take it; this is my body."

[23]Then Jesus took a cup and thanked God for it and gave it to the followers, and they all drank from the cup.

[24]Then Jesus said, "This is my blood which is the new[n] agreement that God makes with his people. This blood is poured out for many. [25]I tell you the truth, I will not drink of this fruit of the vine[n] again until that day when I drink it new in the kingdom of God."

[26]After singing a hymn, they went out to the Mount of Olives.

### Jesus' Followers Will Leave Him

[27]Then Jesus told the followers, "You will all stumble in your faith, because it is written in the Scriptures:

'I will kill the shepherd,
　and the sheep will scatter.'

*Zechariah 13:7*

[28]But after I rise from the dead, I will go ahead of you into Galilee."

[29]Peter said, "Everyone else may stumble in their faith, but I will not."

[30]Jesus answered, "I tell you the truth, tonight before the rooster crows twice you will say three times you don't know me."

[31]But Peter insisted, "I will never say that I don't know you! I will even die with you!" And all the other followers said the same thing.

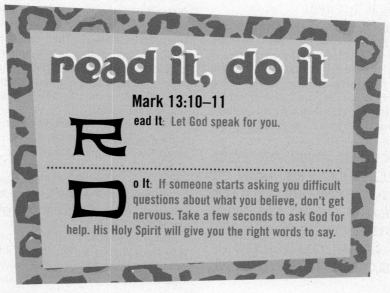

## read it, do it

### Mark 13:10–11

**Read It**: Let God speak for you.

**Do It**: If someone starts asking you difficult questions about what you believe, don't get nervous. Take a few seconds to ask God for help. His Holy Spirit will give you the right words to say.

14:24 **new** *Some Greek copies do not have this word. Compare Luke 22:20.* 14:25 **fruit of the vine** *Product of the grapevine; this may also be translated "wine."*

## Jesus Prays Alone

[32]Jesus and his followers went to a place called Gethsemane. He said to them, "Sit here while I pray." [33]Jesus took Peter, James, and John with him, and he began to be very sad and troubled. [34]He said to them, "My heart is full of sorrow, to the point of death. Stay here and watch."

[35]After walking a little farther away from them, Jesus fell to the ground and prayed that, if possible, he would not have this time of suffering. [36]He prayed, "Abba,[n] Father! You can do all things. Take away this cup[n] of suffering. But do what you want, not what I want."

[37]Then Jesus went back to his followers and found them asleep. He said to Peter, "Simon, are you sleeping? Couldn't you stay awake with me for one hour? [38]Stay awake and pray for strength against temptation. The spirit wants to do what is right, but the body is weak."

[39]Again Jesus went away and prayed the same thing. [40]Then he went back to his followers, and again he found them asleep, because their eyes were very heavy. And they did not know what to say to him.

[41]After Jesus prayed a third time, he went back to his followers and said to them, "Are you still sleeping and resting? That's enough. The time has come for the Son of Man to be handed over to sinful people. [42]Get up, we must go. Look, here comes the man who has turned against me."

## Jesus Is Arrested

[43]At once, while Jesus was still speaking, Judas, one of the twelve apostles, came up. With him were many people carrying swords and clubs who had been sent from the leading priests, the teachers of the law, and the Jewish elders.

[44]Judas had planned a signal for them, saying, "The man I kiss is Jesus. Arrest

**IN THE FUTURE YOU WILL SEE THE SON OF MAN SITTING AT THE RIGHT HAND OF GOD, THE POWERFUL ONE, AND COMING ON CLOUDS IN THE SKY.**

him and guard him while you lead him away." [45]So Judas went straight to Jesus and said, "Teacher!" and kissed him. [46]Then the people grabbed Jesus and arrested him. [47]One of his followers standing nearby pulled out his sword and struck the servant of the high priest and cut off his ear.

[48]Then Jesus said, "You came to get me with swords and clubs as if I were a criminal. [49]Every day I was with you teaching in the Temple, and you did not arrest me there. But all these things have happened to make the Scriptures come true." [50]Then all of Jesus' followers left him and ran away.

[51]A young man, wearing only a linen cloth, was following Jesus, and the people also grabbed him. [52]But the cloth he was wearing came off, and he ran away naked.

## Jesus Before the Leaders

[53]The people who arrested Jesus led him to the house of the high priest, where all the leading priests, the elders, and the teachers of the law were gathered. [54]Peter followed far behind and entered the courtyard of the high priest's house. There he sat with the guards, warming himself by the fire.

[55]The leading priests and the whole Jewish council tried to find something that Jesus had done wrong so they could kill him. But the council could find no proof of anything. [56]Many people came and told false things about him, but all said different things—none of them agreed.

[57]Then some people stood up and lied about Jesus, saying, [58]"We heard this man say, 'I will destroy this Temple that people made. And three days later, I will build another Temple not made by people.'" [59]But even the things these people said did not agree.

[60]Then the high priest stood before them and asked Jesus, "Aren't you going to answer? Don't you have something to say about their charges against you?" [61]But Jesus said nothing; he did not answer.

The high priest asked Jesus another question: "Are you the Christ, the Son of the blessed God?"

[62]Jesus answered, "I am. And in the future you will see the Son of Man sitting at the right hand of God, the Powerful One, and coming on clouds in the sky."

[63]When the high priest heard this, he tore his clothes and said, "We don't need any more witnesses! [64]You all heard him say these things against God. What do you think?"

They all said that Jesus was guilty and should die. [65]Some of the people there began to spit at Jesus. They blindfolded him and beat him with their fists and said, "Prove you are a prophet!" Then the guards led Jesus away and beat him.

## Peter Says He Doesn't Know Jesus

[66]While Peter was in the courtyard, a servant girl of the high priest came there. [67]She saw Peter warming himself at the fire and looked closely at him.

Then she said, "You also were with Jesus, that man from Nazareth."

[68]But Peter said that he was never with Jesus. He said, "I don't know or understand what you are talking about." Then Peter left and went toward the entrance of the courtyard. And the rooster crowed.[n]

[69]The servant girl saw Peter there, and again she said to the people who were standing nearby, "This man is one of those who followed Jesus." [70]Again Peter said that it was not true.

A short time later, some people were standing near Peter saying, "Surely you are one of those who followed Jesus, because you are from Galilee, too."

# Q & A

**Q** Some kids in my school say rude things to everyone all the time. They even call the teacher names to her face. What makes people so mean?

**A** Many kids have so much hurt in their hearts that they don't know what to do. It could be that they are having problems at home, or they are just plain unhappy. Most likely, their number one problem is that they don't have God. Pray for those kids whenever you hear them hurting others with their words.

**14:36 Abba** *Name that a Jewish child called his father.* **14:36 cup** *Jesus is talking about the terrible things that will happen to him. Accepting these things will be very hard, like drinking a cup of something bitter.*

[71]Then Peter began to place a curse on himself and swear, "I don't know this man you're talking about!"

[72]At once, the rooster crowed the second time. Then Peter remembered what Jesus had told him: "Before the rooster crows twice, you will say three times that you don't know me." Then Peter lost control of himself and began to cry.

## Pilate Questions Jesus

**15** Very early in the morning, the leading priests, the elders, the teachers of the law, and all the Jewish council decided what to do with Jesus. They tied him, led him away, and turned him over to Pilate, the governor.

[2]Pilate asked Jesus, "Are you the king of the Jews?"

Jesus answered, "Those are your words."

[3]The leading priests accused Jesus of many things. [4]So Pilate asked Jesus another question, "You can see that they are accusing you of many things. Aren't you going to answer?"

[5]But Jesus still said nothing, so Pilate was very surprised.

## Pilate Tries to Free Jesus

[6]Every year at the time of the Passover the governor would free one prisoner whom the people chose. [7]At that time, there was a man named Barabbas in prison who was a rebel and had committed murder during a riot. [8]The crowd came to Pilate and began to ask him to free a prisoner as he always did.

[9]So Pilate asked them, "Do you want me to free the king of the Jews?" [10]Pilate knew that the leading priests had turned Jesus in to him because they were jealous. [11]But the leading priests had persuaded the people to ask Pilate to free Barabbas, not Jesus.

[12]Then Pilate asked the crowd again, "So what should I do with this man you call the king of the Jews?"

[13]They shouted, "Crucify him!"

[14]Pilate asked, "Why? What wrong has he done?"

But they shouted even louder, "Crucify him!"

[15]Pilate wanted to please the crowd, so he freed Barabbas for them. After having Jesus beaten with whips, he handed Jesus over to the soldiers to be crucified.

[16]The soldiers took Jesus into the governor's palace (called the Praetorium) and called all the other soldiers together. [17]They put a purple robe on Jesus and used thorny branches to make a crown for his head. [18]They began to call out to him, "Hail, King of the Jews!" [19]The soldiers beat Jesus on the head many times with a stick. They spit on him and made fun of him by bowing on their knees and worshiping him. [20]After they finished, the soldiers took off the purple robe and put his own clothes on him again. Then they led him out of the palace to be crucified.

## Jesus Is Crucified

[21]A man named Simon from Cyrene, the father of Alexander and Rufus, was coming from the fields to the city. The soldiers forced Simon to carry the cross for Jesus. [22]They led Jesus to the place called Golgotha, which means the Place of the Skull. [23]The soldiers tried to give Jesus wine mixed with myrrh to drink, but he refused. [24]The soldiers crucified Jesus and divided his clothes among themselves, throwing lots to decide what each soldier would get.

[25]It was nine o'clock in the morning when they crucified Jesus. [26]There was a sign with this charge against Jesus written on it: THE KING OF THE JEWS. [27]They also put two robbers on crosses beside Jesus, one on the right, and the other on the left. [[28]And the Scripture came true that says, "They put him with criminals."][n] [29]People walked by and insulted Jesus and shook their heads, saying, "You said you could destroy the Temple and build it again in three days. [30]So save yourself! Come down from that cross!"

[31]The leading priests and the teachers of the law were also making fun of Jesus. They said to each other, "He saved other people, but he can't save himself. [32]If he is really the Christ, the king of Israel, let him come down now from the cross. When we see this, we will believe in him." The robbers who were being crucified beside Jesus also insulted him.

## Jesus Dies

[33]At noon the whole country became dark, and the darkness lasted for three hours. [34]At three o'clock Jesus cried in a loud

## BE YOUR BEST!

**B**abies can survive on just milk. But growing kids need a lot more—you need fruits, vegetables, bread, and meat! In the same way, growing Christians need more than just spiritual "milk." Dig deeper into the Bible than you have before to find the "meat" that will help you grow.

**speakout!**

If you could ask God one question (and get an answer right away), what would it be?

Why do people die when they are so young?
—Jesse, 10

**14:68** **And the rooster crowed.** Some Greek copies do not have this phrase.

**73**

WHEN THE ARMY OFFICER WHO WAS STANDING IN FRONT OF THE CROSS SAW WHAT HAPPENED WHEN JESUS DIED, HE SAID, "THIS MAN REALLY WAS THE SON OF GOD!"

voice, "Eloi, Eloi, lama sabachthani." This means, "My God, my God, why have you abandoned me?"

[35]When some of the people standing there heard this, they said, "Listen! He is calling Elijah."

[36]Someone there ran and got a sponge, filled it with vinegar, tied it to a stick, and gave it to Jesus to drink. He said, "We want to see if Elijah will come to take him down from the cross."

[37]Then Jesus cried in a loud voice and died.

[38]The curtain in the Temple[n] was torn into two pieces, from the top to the bottom. [39]When the army officer who was standing in front of the cross saw what happened when Jesus died,[n] he said, "This man really was the Son of God!"

[40]Some women were standing at a distance from the cross, watching; among them were Mary Magdalene, Salome, and Mary the mother of James and Joseph. (James was her youngest son.) [41]These women had followed Jesus in Galilee and helped him. Many other women were also there who had come with Jesus to Jerusalem.

## Jesus Is Buried

[42]This was Preparation Day. (That means the day before the Sabbath day.) That evening, [43]Joseph from Arimathea was brave enough to go to Pilate and ask for Jesus' body. Joseph, an important member of the Jewish council, was one of the people who was waiting for the kingdom of God to come. [44]Pilate was amazed that Jesus would have already died, so he called the army officer who had guarded Jesus and asked him if Jesus had already died. [45]The officer told Pilate that he was dead, so Pilate told

## dig deeper

### Mark 16:15—16

After Jesus rose from the dead, he went to see his followers. Before he went back to heaven, Jesus told his followers to spread out and tell everyone they met about the Good News: Jesus had died to take the punishment for their sins and give them eternal life! These believers—the first missionaries—didn't have to go to a special school or join an organization . . . they just had to get out there and share the special truth.

Jesus said that anyone who believes in the Good News and is baptized is saved (Mark 16:15—16). Many people believe that baptism can save someone or make them a Christian. But Jesus clearly said that it's *believing* that saves us. Look at his next words: "But anyone who does not *believe* will be punished." He didn't say "anyone who does not get *baptized.*"

God made baptism to be another step after a person becomes a Christian. Baptism shows people that God has made you a new person and that you've decided to follow Jesus from now on. God considers baptism very important. But it's not what saves you. You must *believe* in Jesus to be saved! But you also can't ignore God's instructions to be baptized. If you haven't been baptized, ask your pastor about baptism.

Joseph he could have the body. [46]Joseph bought some linen cloth, took the body down from the cross, and wrapped it in the linen. He put the body in a tomb that was cut out of a wall of rock. Then he rolled a very large stone to block the entrance of the tomb. [47]And Mary Magdalene and Mary the mother of Joseph saw the place where Jesus was laid.

### Jesus Rises from the Dead

**16** The day after the Sabbath day, Mary Magdalene, Mary the mother of James, and Salome bought some sweet-smelling spices to put on Jesus' body. [2]Very early on that day, the first day of the week, soon after sunrise, the women were on their way to the tomb. [3]They said to each

**15:28 And . . . criminals."** *Some Greek copies do not contain the bracketed text, which quotes from Isaiah 53:12.* **15:38 curtain in the Temple** *A curtain divided the Most Holy Place from the other part of the Temple. That was the special building in Jerusalem where God commanded the Jewish people to worship him.* **15:39 when Jesus died** *Some Greek copies read "when Jesus cried out and died."*

ANYONE WHO
BELIEVES AND IS
BAPTIZED WILL BE
SAVED, BUT ANYONE
WHO DOES NOT
BELIEVE WILL BE
PUNISHED.

other, "Who will roll away for us the stone that covers the entrance of the tomb?"

⁴Then the women looked and saw that the stone had already been rolled away, even though it was very large. ⁵The women entered the tomb and saw a young man wearing a white robe and sitting on the right side, and they were afraid.

⁶But the man said, "Don't be afraid. You are looking for Jesus from Nazareth, who has been crucified. He has risen from the dead; he is not here. Look, here is the place they laid him. ⁷Now go and tell his followers and Peter, 'Jesus is going into Galilee ahead of you, and you will see him there as he told you before.'"

⁸The women were confused and shaking with fear, so they left the tomb and ran away. They did not tell anyone about what happened, because they were afraid.

Verses 9–20 are not included in some of the earliest surviving Greek copies of Mark.

## Some Followers See Jesus

[⁹After Jesus rose from the dead early on the first day of the week, he showed himself first to Mary Magdalene. One time in the past, he had forced seven demons out of her. ¹⁰After Mary saw Jesus, she went and told his followers, who were very sad and were crying. ¹¹But Mary told them that Jesus was alive. She said that she had seen him, but the followers did not believe her.

¹²Later, Jesus showed himself to two of his followers while they were walking in the country, but he did not look the same as before. ¹³These followers went back to the others and told them what had happened, but again, the followers did not believe them.

## Jesus Talks to the Apostles

¹⁴Later Jesus showed himself to the eleven apostles while they were eating, and he criticized them because they had no faith. They were stubborn and refused to believe those who had seen him after he had risen from the dead.

¹⁵Jesus said to his followers, "Go everywhere in the world, and tell the Good News to everyone. ¹⁶Anyone who believes and is baptized will be saved, but anyone who does not believe will be punished. ¹⁷And those who believe will be able to do these things as proof: They will use my name to force out demons. They will speak in new languages.ⁿ ¹⁸They will pick up snakes and drink poison without being hurt. They will touch the sick, and the sick will be healed."

¹⁹After the Lord Jesus said these things to his followers, he was carried up into heaven, and he sat at the right side of God. ²⁰The followers went everywhere in the world and told the Good News to people, and the Lord helped them. The Lord proved that the Good News they told was true by giving them power to work miracles.]

16:17 languages This can also be translated "tongues."

# LUKE

**D**o you know any doctors? They have to study for a long time in order to know all about the body, how it works, and how to fix it. Doctors are often people who are interested in knowing the facts and getting things right.

Luke was a doctor. His friend Theophilus wanted to know about Jesus. So Luke studied the events of Jesus' life and wrote them down. (For the continuation of the story, see the Book of Acts.) He probably knew that many people besides Theophilus would read what he wrote about Jesus, and he was careful to get the facts straight. Luke wasn't one of Jesus' twelve followers, but he traveled with the apostle Paul and heard him teach.

These are some well-known passages from Luke's book:

→ Luke gives the most detail about *the birth of Jesus*. Many movies that show Jesus' birth get their information from chapters 1—2 of Luke's book.

→ Have you heard the great story of *The Son Who Left Home*? It's about a young man who rebels against his father. When he has spent all his money and is desperate for food, he goes crawling back home, expecting rejection. Read the end of the story in Luke 15:11—32!

→ Check out the amazing story of *Jesus on the Road to Emmaus* in Luke 24:13—35. After dying and coming back to life, Jesus meets two of his followers on the road, but they don't know who he is until after he's gone!

# LUKE TELLS ABOUT JESUS, THE SAVIOR FOR ALL PEOPLE

**Luke**

## THINGS TO TALK WITH GOD ABOUT . . .

### Luke Writes About Jesus' Life

1 Many have tried to report on the things that happened among us. ²They have written the same things that we learned from others—the people who saw those things from the beginning and served God by telling people his message. ³Since I myself have studied everything carefully from the beginning, most excellent[n] Theophilus, it seemed good for me to write it out for you. I arranged it in order, ⁴to help you know that what you have been taught is true.

**did you know?**

75% of girls like themselves the way they are.

—*Business Wire, 10/10/03,*
http://www.rab.com/newrst/article_view.cfm?id=308&type=article2

### Zechariah and Elizabeth

⁵During the time Herod ruled Judea, there was a priest named Zechariah who belonged to Abijah's group.[n] Zechariah's wife, Elizabeth, came from the family of Aaron. ⁶Zechariah and Elizabeth truly did what God said was good. They did everything the Lord commanded and were without fault in keeping his law. ⁷But they had no children, because Elizabeth could not have a baby, and both of them were very old.

⁸One day Zechariah was serving as a priest before God, because his group was on duty. ⁹According to the custom of the priests, he was chosen by lot to go into the Temple of the Lord and burn incense. ¹⁰There were a great many people outside praying at the time the incense was offered. ¹¹Then an angel of the Lord appeared to Zechariah, standing on the right side of the incense table. ¹²When he saw the angel, Zechariah was startled and frightened. ¹³But the angel said to him, "Zechariah, don't be afraid. God has heard your prayer. Your wife, Elizabeth, will give birth to a son, and you will name him John. ¹⁴He will bring you joy and gladness, and many people will be happy be- cause of his birth. ¹⁵John will be a great man for the Lord. He will never drink wine or beer, and even from birth, he will be filled with the Holy Spirit. ¹⁶He will help many people of Israel return to the Lord their God. ¹⁷He will go before the Lord in spirit and power like Elijah. He will make peace between parents and their children and will bring those who are not obeying God back to the right way of thinking, to make a people ready for the coming of the Lord."

¹⁸Zechariah said to the angel, "How can I know that what you say is true? I am an old man, and my wife is old, too."

¹⁹The angel answered him, "I am Gabriel. I stand before God, who sent me to talk to you and to tell you this good news. ²⁰Now, listen! You will not be able

# cool

## That's Deep!

The deepest spot of any ocean is in the Pacific Ocean near the Philippines. Known as "Challenger Deep," the Marianas Trench goes down almost seven miles. If you could fit the world's tallest mountain into that space, it would still be under water!

It's scary to think about water that deep . . . until you remember a special promise from God. In Micah 7:19 (in the Old Testament) we read that when God forgives our sins, he throws them "into the deepest part of the sea." That's deep! Thank God today for his awesome love and forgiveness.

> THEN MARY SAID, "MY SOUL PRAISES THE LORD; MY HEART REJOICES IN GOD MY SAVIOR . . ."

---

**1:3 excellent** *This word was used to show respect to an important person like a king or ruler.*   **1:5 Abijah's group** *The Jewish priests were divided into twenty-four groups. See 1 Chronicles 24.*

to speak until the day these things happen, because you did not believe what I told you. But they will really happen."

²¹Outside, the people were still waiting for Zechariah and were surprised that he was staying so long in the Temple. ²²When Zechariah came outside, he could not speak to them, and they knew he had seen a vision in the Temple. He could only make signs to them and remained unable to speak. ²³When his time of service at the Temple was finished, he went home.

²⁴Later, Zechariah's wife, Elizabeth, became pregnant and did not go out of her house for five months. Elizabeth said, ²⁵"Look what the Lord has done for me! My people were ashamed[n] of me, but now the Lord has taken away that shame."

### An Angel Appears to Mary

²⁶During Elizabeth's sixth month of pregnancy, God sent the angel Gabriel to Nazareth, a town in Galilee, ²⁷to a virgin. She was engaged to marry a man named Joseph from the family of David. Her name was Mary. ²⁸The angel came to her and said, "Greetings! The Lord has blessed you and is with you."

²⁹But Mary was very startled by what the angel said and wondered what this greeting might mean.

³⁰The angel said to her, "Don't be afraid, Mary; God has shown you his grace. ³¹Listen! You will become pregnant and give birth to a son, and you will name

him Jesus. ³²He will be great and will be called the Son of the Most High. The Lord God will give him the throne of King David, his ancestor. ³³He will rule over the people of Jacob forever, and his kingdom will never end."

³⁴Mary said to the angel, "How will this happen since I am a virgin?"

³⁵The angel said to Mary, "The Holy Spirit will come upon you, and the power of the Most High will cover you. For this reason the baby will be holy and will be called the Son of God. ³⁶Now Elizabeth, your relative, is also pregnant with a son though she is very old. Everyone thought she could not have a baby, but she has been pregnant for six months. ³⁷God can do anything!"

³⁸Mary said, "I am the servant of the Lord. Let this happen to me as you say!" Then the angel went away.

### Mary Visits Elizabeth

³⁹Mary got up and went quickly to a town in the hills of Judea. ⁴⁰She came to Zechariah's house and greeted Elizabeth. ⁴¹When Elizabeth heard Mary's greeting, the unborn baby inside her jumped, and Elizabeth was filled with the Holy Spirit. ⁴²She cried out in a loud voice, "God has blessed you more than any other woman, and he has blessed the baby to which you will give birth. ⁴³Why has this good thing happened to me, that the mother of my Lord comes to me? ⁴⁴When I heard your voice, the baby inside me jumped

## Prophecy

Throughout the Bible, and especially in the Old Testament, God chose men and women called prophets to tell people about things he would do. These messages were called *prophecies*. They told people how God would bless their children and grandchildren and warned about the punishments that would come if people didn't stop sinning and start obeying God again. Prophecies are messages directly from God, and they always come true. The most exciting prophecies were about Jesus, the Savior, who would come to save God's people from their sins. The Bible tells about many prophecies that really happened—just like the prophets said they would!

with joy. ⁴⁵You are blessed because you believed that what the Lord said to you would really happen."

### Mary Praises God

⁴⁶Then Mary said,
"My soul praises the Lord;
⁴⁷   my heart rejoices in God my Savior,
⁴⁸because he has shown his concern
      for his humble servant girl.
   From now on, all people will say that
      I am blessed,
⁴⁹   because the Powerful One has
         done great things for me.
   His name is holy.
⁵⁰God will show his mercy forever and
         ever
   to those who worship and serve
      him.
⁵¹He has done mighty deeds by his
         power.
   He has scattered the people who
      are proud
   and think great things about
      themselves.

### ■ Bible Bios    Elizabeth (Luke 1)

Here's proof that dreams can come true! Elizabeth (a great-aunt to Jesus) had wanted a baby for as long as she could remember, but for some reason she couldn't become pregnant. She and her husband, Zechariah, kept praying for a baby—even when they passed the normal age for having children. But God seemed silent.

It's easy to feel disappointed when you hope and pray for something and it doesn't happen. You might be tempted to quit trusting God. But not Elizabeth! She kept on praying. The Bible says she "did what God said was good." After an angel appeared to Zechariah, Elizabeth got pregnant! Her baby, known as John the Baptist, prepared people for Jesus' coming. Like Elizabeth, you can trust God with your dreams as you live for him.

1:25 **ashamed** *The Jewish people thought it was a disgrace for women not to have children.*

⁵²He has brought down rulers from
    their thrones
    and raised up the humble.
⁵³He has filled the hungry with good
    things
    and sent the rich away with
    nothing.
⁵⁴He has helped his servant, the
    people of Israel,
    remembering to show them mercy
⁵⁵as he promised to our ancestors,
    to Abraham and to his children
    forever."
⁵⁶Mary stayed with Elizabeth for about
three months and then returned home.

## The Birth of John

⁵⁷When it was time for Elizabeth to give
birth, she had a boy. ⁵⁸Her neighbors and
relatives heard how good the Lord was to
her, and they rejoiced with her.

⁵⁹When the baby was eight days old,
they came to circumcise him. They wanted
to name him Zechariah because this was
his father's name, ⁶⁰but his mother said,
"No! He will be named John."

⁶¹The people said to Elizabeth, "But no
one in your family has this name." ⁶²Then
they made signs to his father to find out
what he would like to name him.

⁶³Zechariah asked for a writing tablet
and wrote, "His name is John," and everyone was surprised. ⁶⁴Immediately Zech-

ariah could talk again, and he began
praising God. ⁶⁵All their neighbors became alarmed, and in all the mountains
of Judea people continued talking about
all these things. ⁶⁶The people who heard
about them wondered, saying, "What
will this child be?" because the Lord was
with him.

## Zechariah Praises God

⁶⁷Then Zechariah, John's father, was
filled with the Holy Spirit and prophesied:
⁶⁸"Let us praise the Lord, the God of
    Israel,
    because he has come to help his
    people and has given them
    freedom.
⁶⁹He has given us a powerful Savior
    from the family of God's servant
    David.
⁷⁰He said that he would do this
    through his holy prophets who
    lived long ago:
⁷¹He promised he would save us from
    our enemies
    and from the power of all those
    who hate us.
⁷²He said he would give mercy to our
    ancestors
    and that he would remember his
    holy promise.
⁷³God promised Abraham, our father,
⁷⁴    that he would save us from the
    power of our enemies
    so we could serve him without fear,
⁷⁵being holy and good before God as
    long as we live.

⁷⁶"Now you, child, will be called a
    prophet of the Most High God.
    You will go before the Lord to
    prepare his way.
⁷⁷You will make his people know that
    they will be saved
    by having their sins forgiven.
⁷⁸With the loving mercy of our God,
    a new day from heaven will dawn
    upon us.
⁷⁹It will shine on those who live in
    darkness,
    in the shadow of death.
    It will guide us into the path of
    peace."
⁸⁰And so the child grew up and became
strong in spirit. John lived in the desert
until the time when he came out to
preach to Israel.

## The Birth of Jesus

**2** At that time, Augustus Caesar
sent an order that all people in
the countries under Roman rule
must list their names in a register. ²This
was the first registration;ⁿ it was taken
while Quirinius was governor of Syria.
³And all went to their own towns to be
registered.

⁴So Joseph left Nazareth, a town in Galilee, and went to the town of Bethlehem
in Judea, known as the town of David. Joseph went there because he was from
the family of David. ⁵Joseph registered
with Mary, to whom he was engagedⁿ
and who was now pregnant. ⁶While they
were in Bethlehem, the time came for
Mary to have the baby, ⁷and she gave
birth to her first son. Because there were
no rooms left in the inn, she wrapped the
baby with pieces of cloth and laid him in
a feeding trough.

## Shepherds Hear About Jesus

⁸That night, some shepherds were in
the fields nearby watching their sheep.
⁹Then an angel of the Lord stood before
them. The glory of the Lord was shining
around them, and they became very
frightened. ¹⁰The angel said to them, "Do
not be afraid. I am bringing you good
news that will be a great joy to all the
people. ¹¹Today your Savior was born in
the town of David. He is Christ, the
Lord. ¹²This is how you will
know him: You will
find a baby

# Be YOUR BEST!

**W** When you want to
straighten your curly
hair (or curl your
straight hair!), it's best
to use a really hot tool to
get a smooth, shiny look. You
might go through some painful "hot"
times in your life, but you can trust God to
use them to make you shine!

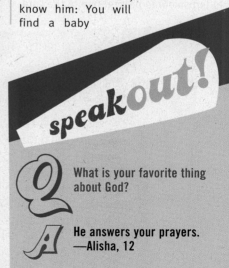

## speakout!

**Q** What is your favorite thing
about God?

**A** He answers your prayers.
—Alisha, 12

2:2 **registration** *Census. A counting of all the people and the things they own.*   2:5 **engaged** *For the Jewish people, an engagement was a lasting agreement. It could only be broken by divorce.*

wrapped in pieces of cloth and lying in a feeding box."

[13] Then a very large group of angels from heaven joined the first angel, praising God and saying:

[14] "Give glory to God in heaven,
and on earth let there be peace among the people who please God."[n]

[15] When the angels left them and went back to heaven, the shepherds said to each other, "Let's go to Bethlehem. Let's see this thing that has happened which the Lord has told us about."

[16] So the shepherds went quickly and found Mary and Joseph and the baby, who was lying in a feeding trough. [17] When they had seen him, they told what the angels had said about this child. [18] Everyone was amazed at what the shepherds said to them. [19] But Mary treasured these things and continued to think about them. [20] Then the shepherds went back to their sheep, praising God and thanking him for everything they had seen and heard. It had been just as the angel had told them.

[21] When the baby was eight days old, he was circumcised and was named Jesus, the name given by the angel before the baby began to grow inside Mary.

## Jesus Is Presented in the Temple

[22] When the time came for Mary and Joseph to do what the law of Moses taught about being made pure,[n] they took Jesus to Jerusalem to present him to the Lord.

[23] (It is written in the law of the Lord: "Every firstborn male shall be given to the Lord.")[n] [24] Mary and Joseph also went to offer a sacrifice, as the law of the Lord says: "You must sacrifice two doves or two young pigeons."[n]

## Simeon Sees Jesus

[25] In Jerusalem lived a man named Simeon who was a good man and godly. He was waiting for the time when God would take away Israel's sorrow, and the Holy Spirit was in him. [26] Simeon had been told by the Holy Spirit that he would not die before he saw the Christ promised by the Lord. [27] The Spirit led Simeon to the Temple. When Mary and Joseph brought the baby Jesus to the Temple to do what the law said they must do, [28] Simeon took the baby in his arms and thanked God:

[29] "Now, Lord, you can let me, your servant,
die in peace as you said.
[30] With my own eyes I have seen your salvation,
[31] which you prepared before all people.
[32] It is a light for the non-Jewish people to see
and an honor for your people, the Israelites."

[33] Jesus' father and mother were amazed at what Simeon had said about him. [34] Then Simeon blessed them and said to Mary, "God has chosen this child to cause the fall and rise of many in Israel.

## EVERYONE WAS AMAZED AT WHAT THE SHEPHERDS SAID TO THEM. BUT MARY TREASURED THESE THINGS AND CONTINUED TO THINK ABOUT THEM.

He will be a sign from God that many people will not accept [35] so that the thoughts of many will be made known. And the things that will happen will make your heart sad, too."

## Anna Sees Jesus

[36] There was a prophetess, Anna, from the family of Phanuel in the tribe of Asher. Anna was very old. She had once been married for seven years. [37] Then her husband died, and she was a widow for eighty-four years. Anna never left the Temple but worshiped God, going without food and praying day and night. [38] Standing there at that time, she thanked God and spoke about Jesus to all who were waiting for God to free Jerusalem.

## Joseph and Mary Return Home

[39] When Joseph and Mary had done everything the law of the Lord commanded, they went home to Nazareth, their own town in Galilee. [40] The little child grew and became strong. He was filled with wisdom, and God's goodness was upon him.

## Jesus As a Boy

[41] Every year Jesus' parents went to Jerusalem for the Passover Feast. [42] When he was twelve years old, they went to the feast as they always did. [43] After the feast days were over, they started home. The boy Jesus stayed behind in Jerusalem, but his parents did not know it. [44] Thinking that Jesus was with them in the group, they traveled for a whole day. Then they began to look for him among their family and friends. [45] When they did not find him, they went back to Jerusalem to look for him there. [46] After three days they found Jesus sitting in the Temple with the teachers, listening to them and asking

## read it, do it

### Luke 1:38

**R**ead It: Say yes to God!

**D**o It: When you pray for something and God seems to say no, thank him anyway. Trust that he knows what he's doing and keep following him!

---

2:14 **and . . . God** Some Greek copies read "and on earth let there be peace and goodwill among people." 2:22 **pure** The Law of Moses said that forty days after a Jewish woman gave birth to a son, she must be cleansed by a ceremony at the Temple. Read Leviticus 12:2–8. 2:23 **"Every . . . Lord."** Quotation from Exodus 13:2. 2:24 **"You . . . pigeons."** Quotation from Leviticus 12:8.

Luke

them questions. [47]All who heard him were amazed at his understanding and answers. [48]When Jesus' parents saw him, they were astonished. His mother said to him, "Son, why did you do this to us? Your father and I were very worried about you and have been looking for you."

[49]Jesus said to them, "Why were you looking for me? Didn't you know that I must be in my Father's house?" [50]But they did not understand the meaning of what he said.

[51]Jesus went with them to Nazareth and was obedient to them. But his mother kept in her mind all that had happened. [52]Jesus became wiser and grew physically. People liked him, and he pleased God.

## The Preaching of John

**3** It was the fifteenth year of the rule of Tiberius Caesar. These men were under Caesar: Pontius Pilate, the ruler of Judea; Herod, the ruler of Galilee; Philip, Herod's brother, the ruler of Iturea and Traconitis; and Lysanias, the ruler of Abilene. [2]Annas and Caiaphas were the high priests. At this time, the word of God came to John son of Zechariah in the desert. [3]He went all over the area around the Jordan River preaching a baptism of changed hearts and lives for the forgiveness of sins. [4]As it is written in the book of Isaiah the prophet:

"This is a voice of one
    who calls out in the desert:
'Prepare the way for the Lord.
    Make the road straight for him.
[5]Every valley should be filled in,
    and every mountain and hill should
        be made flat.
Roads with turns should be made
        straight,
    and rough roads should be made
        smooth.
[6]And all people will know about the
        salvation of God!' "
*Isaiah 40:3–5*

[7]To the crowds of people who came to be baptized by John, he said, "You are all snakes! Who warned you to run away from God's coming punishment? [8]Do the things that show you really have changed your hearts and lives. Don't begin to say to yourselves, 'Abraham is our father.' I tell you that God could make children for Abraham from these rocks. [9]The ax is now ready to cut down the trees, and every

tree that does not produce good fruit will be cut down and thrown into the fire."[n]

[10]The people asked John, "Then what should we do?"

[11]John answered, "If you have two shirts, share with the person who does not have one. If you have food, share that also."

[12]Even tax collectors came to John to be baptized. They said to him, "Teacher, what should we do?"

[13]John said to them, "Don't take more taxes from people than you have been ordered to take."

[14]The soldiers asked John, "What about us? What should we do?"

John said to them, "Don't force people to give you money, and don't lie about them. Be satisfied with the pay you get."

[15]Since the people were hoping for the Christ to come, they wondered if John might be the one.

[16]John answered everyone, "I baptize you with water, but there is one coming who is greater than I am. I am not good enough to untie his sandals. He will baptize you with the Holy Spirit and fire. [17]He will come ready to clean the grain, separating the good grain from the chaff. He will put the good part of the grain into his barn, but he will burn the chaff with a fire that cannot be put out."[n] [18]And John continued to preach the Good News, saying many other things to encourage the people.

*Shine Your Light*

Montreal, Quebec is one of the largest cities in Canada, yet the number of Christians is pretty small. One little church makes a big effort to give away tracts (pocket-sized pamphlets that explain how to become a Christian), and guess who the most eager volunteers are? A bunch of preteens just like you!

Each month, when a group from the church visits a local subway station, kids like Joshua, Abeku, Melissa, George, Alexis, Kofi, and Nicholas are there, too. As people walk through the station, the tweens cheerfully offer them a tract or a New Testament. They are involved because they love God!

The kids know that many people have believed in Jesus after reading a tract, so they're excited to help out. It's cool to think that we can love God and other people by sharing the Good News about Jesus with them. God lets us be a part of what he's doing on earth—what could be more exciting than that?

Can you think of any ways *you* can tell people in your neighborhood about Jesus? Ask God to give you opportunities to share about what he's done in your life!

3:9 **The ax . . . fire.** *This means that God is ready to punish his people who do not obey him.* 3:17 **He will . . . out.** *This means that Jesus will come to separate good people from bad people, saving the good and punishing the bad.*

[19]But John spoke against Herod, the governor, because of his sin with Herodias, the wife of Herod's brother, and because of the many other evil things Herod did. [20]So Herod did something even worse: He put John in prison.

## Jesus Is Baptized by John

[21]When all the people were being baptized by John, Jesus also was baptized. While Jesus was praying, heaven opened [22]and the Holy Spirit came down on him in the form of a dove. Then a voice came from heaven, saying, "You are my Son, whom I love, and I am very pleased with you."

## The Family History of Jesus

[23]When Jesus began his ministry, he was about thirty years old. People thought that Jesus was Joseph's son.

Joseph was the son[n] of Heli.
[24]Heli was the son of Matthat.
Matthat was the son of Levi.
Levi was the son of Melki.
Melki was the son of Jannai.
Jannai was the son of Joseph.
[25]Joseph was the son of Mattathias.
Mattathias was the son of Amos.
Amos was the son of Nahum.
Nahum was the son of Esli.
Esli was the son of Naggai.
[26]Naggai was the son of Maath.
Maath was the son of Mattathias.
Mattathias was the son of Semein.
Semein was the son of Josech.
Josech was the son of Joda.
[27]Joda was the son of Joanan.
Joanan was the son of Rhesa.
Rhesa was the son of Zerubbabel.
Zerubbabel was the grandson of Shealtiel.
Shealtiel was the son of Neri.
[28]Neri was the son of Melki.
Melki was the son of Addi.
Addi was the son of Cosam.
Cosam was the son of Elmadam.
Elmadam was the son of Er.
[29]Er was the son of Joshua.
Joshua was the son of Eliezer.
Eliezer was the son of Jorim.
Jorim was the son of Matthat.
Matthat was the son of Levi.
[30]Levi was the son of Simeon.
Simeon was the son of Judah.
Judah was the son of Joseph.
Joseph was the son of Jonam.
Jonam was the son of Eliakim.
[31]Eliakim was the son of Melea.
Melea was the son of Menna.
Menna was the son of Mattatha.
Mattatha was the son of Nathan.
Nathan was the son of David.
[32]David was the son of Jesse.
Jesse was the son of Obed.
Obed was the son of Boaz.
Boaz was the son of Salmon.[n]
Salmon was the son of Nahshon.
[33]Nahshon was the son of Amminadab.
Amminadab was the son of Admin.
Admin was the son of Arni.
Arni was the son of Hezron.
Hezron was the son of Perez.
Perez was the son of Judah.
[34]Judah was the son of Jacob.
Jacob was the son of Isaac.
Isaac was the son of Abraham.
Abraham was the son of Terah.
Terah was the son of Nahor.
[35]Nahor was the son of Serug.
Serug was the son of Reu.
Reu was the son of Peleg.
Peleg was the son of Eber.

## god's promises

Luke 6:35

Are some people easier to love than others? Maybe you love your mom because of the way she cares for you. What about your best friend? She probably makes you happy when she sticks by you, laughs at your silly jokes, and shares her last piece of gum with you. Do you have a teacher who gives you special attention? You might say you love her, too.

Well, what about the girl who always gossips about you? Or the boy who scribbled dirty words on your locker? Remember the cousin who purposely broke your favorite CD? Do you love these people, too?

Whew! Does that seem like a nearly impossible thing to do? Do you wonder why you should love them since they don't deserve it? Jesus told his followers that they should love their enemies and do good to them! He challenged people to give their enemies the things they might need, without expecting them back. Why would we do all that?

In this verse, Jesus also gave a promise. When we love unlovable people—just the way God loved us even though we have sinned—God is pleased with us and will reward us. With his help, we truly can be kind to our enemies. It's a great way to show people what God's love is like!

*When we love unlovable people, God is pleased.*

---

**3:23 son** *"Son" in Jewish lists of ancestors can sometimes mean grandson or more distant relative.* **3:32 Salmon** *Some Greek copies read "Sala."*

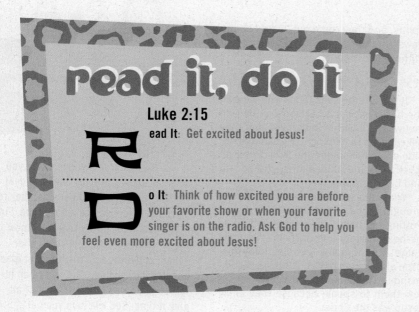

## read it, do it

Luke 2:15

**R**ead It: Get excited about Jesus!

**D**o It: Think of how excited you are before your favorite show or when your favorite singer is on the radio. Ask God to help you feel even more excited about Jesus!

Eber was the son of Shelah.
[36]Shelah was the son of Cainan.
Cainan was the son of Arphaxad.
Arphaxad was the son of Shem.
Shem was the son of Noah.
Noah was the son of Lamech.
[37]Lamech was the son of Methuselah.
Methuselah was the son of Enoch.
Enoch was the son of Jared.
Jared was the son of Mahalalel.
Mahalalel was the son of Kenan.
[38]Kenan was the son of Enosh.
Enosh was the son of Seth.
Seth was the son of Adam.
Adam was the son of God.

### Jesus Is Tempted by the Devil

**4** Jesus, filled with the Holy Spirit, returned from the Jordan River. The Spirit led Jesus into the desert [2]where the devil tempted Jesus for forty days. Jesus ate nothing during that time, and when those days were ended, he was very hungry.

[3]The devil said to Jesus, "If you are the Son of God, tell this rock to become bread."

[4]Jesus answered, "It is written in the Scriptures: 'A person does not live on bread alone.' "[n]

[5]Then the devil took Jesus and showed him all the kingdoms of the world in an instant. [6]The devil said to Jesus, "I will give you all these kingdoms and all their power and glory. It has all been given to me, and I can give it to anyone I wish. [7]If

you worship me, then it will all be yours."

[8]Jesus answered, "It is written in the Scriptures: 'You must worship the Lord your God and serve only him.' "[n]

[9]Then the devil led Jesus to Jerusalem and put him on a high place of the Temple. He said to Jesus, "If you are the Son of God, jump down. [10]It is written in the Scriptures:

'He has put his angels in charge of you
to watch over you.'        Psalm 91:11
[11]It is also written:
'They will catch you in their hands
so that you will not hit your foot on a rock.' "        Psalm 91:12

[12]Jesus answered, "But it also says in the Scriptures: 'Do not test the Lord your God.' "[n]

[13]After the devil had tempted Jesus in every way, he left him to wait until a better time.

### Jesus Teaches the People

[14]Jesus returned to Galilee in the power of the Holy Spirit, and stories about him spread all through the area. [15]He began to teach in their synagogues, and everyone praised him.

[16]Jesus traveled to Nazareth, where he had grown up. On the Sabbath day he went to the synagogue, as he always did, and stood up to read. [17]The book of Isaiah the prophet was given to him. He opened the book and found the place where this is written:

[18]"The Lord has put his Spirit in me, because he appointed me to tell the Good News to the poor. He has sent me to tell the captives they are free and to tell the blind that they can see again.        Isaiah 61:1
God sent me to free those who have been treated unfairly
        Isaiah 58:6
[19] and to announce the time when the Lord will show his kindness."
        Isaiah 61:2

[20]Jesus closed the book, gave it back to the assistant, and sat down. Everyone in the synagogue was watching Jesus closely. [21]He began to say to them, "While you heard these words just now, they were coming true!"

[22]All the people spoke well of Jesus and were amazed at the words of grace he spoke. They asked, "Isn't this Joseph's son?"

[23]Jesus said to them, "I know that you will tell me the old saying: 'Doctor, heal yourself.' You want to say, 'We heard about the things you did in Capernaum. Do those things here in your own town!' "

[24]Then Jesus said, "I tell you the truth, a prophet is not accepted in his hometown. [25]But I tell you the truth, there were many widows in Israel during the time of Elijah. It did not rain in Israel for three and one-half years, and there was no

## Q & A

**Q** I know it's a sin to take God's name in vain, but what about using other swear words?

**A** Jesus said, "People speak the things that are in their hearts" (Luke 6:45). Swear words show people what's inside your heart. A Christian who has Jesus living in her heart should watch that her words are pure. Here's a hint: if you wouldn't use the word while standing next to Jesus . . . don't use it at all! He is *always* near you.

4:4 'A person . . . alone.' *Quotation from Deuteronomy 8:3.*   4:8 'You . . . him.' *Quotation from Deuteronomy 6:13.*   4:12 'Do . . . God.' *Quotation from Deuteronomy 6:16.*

food anywhere in the whole country. [26]But Elijah was sent to none of those widows, only to a widow in Zarephath, a town in Sidon. [27]And there were many with skin diseases living in Israel during the time of the prophet Elisha. But none of them were healed, only Naaman, who was from the country of Syria."

[28]When all the people in the synagogue heard these things, they became very angry. [29]They got up, forced Jesus out of town, and took him to the edge of the cliff on which the town was built. They planned to throw him off the edge, [30]but Jesus walked through the crowd and went on his way.

## Jesus Forces Out an Evil Spirit

[31]Jesus went to Capernaum, a city in Galilee, and on the Sabbath day, he taught the people. [32]They were amazed at his teaching, because he spoke with authority. [33]In the synagogue a man who had within him an evil spirit shouted in a loud voice, [34]"Jesus of Nazareth! What do you want with us? Did you come to destroy us? I know who you are—God's Holy One!"

[35]Jesus commanded the evil spirit, "Be quiet! Come out of the man!" The evil spirit threw the man down to the ground before all the people and then left the man without hurting him.

[36]The people were amazed and said to each other, "What does this mean? With authority and power he commands evil spirits, and they come out." [37]And so the news about Jesus spread to every place in the whole area.

## Jesus Heals Many People

[38]Jesus left the synagogue and went to the home of Simon.[n] Simon's mother-in-law was sick with a high fever, and they asked Jesus to help her. [39]He came to her side and commanded the fever to leave. It left her, and immediately she got up and began serving them.

[40]When the sun went down, the people brought those who were sick to Jesus. Putting his hands on each sick person, he healed every one of them. [41]Demons came out of many people, shouting, "You are the Son of God." But Jesus commanded the demons and would not allow them to speak, because they knew Jesus was the Christ.

[42]At daybreak, Jesus went to a lonely place, but the people looked for him. When they found him, they tried to keep him from leaving. [43]But Jesus said to them, "I must preach about God's kingdom to other towns, too. This is why I was sent." [44]Then he kept on preaching in the synagogues of Judea.[n]

## Jesus' First Followers

5 One day while Jesus was standing beside Lake Galilee, many people were pressing all around him to hear the word of God. [2]Jesus saw two boats at the shore of the lake. The fishermen had left them and were washing their nets. [3]Jesus got into one of the boats, the one that belonged to Simon,[n] and asked him to push off a little from the land. Then Jesus sat down and continued to teach the people from the boat.

[4]When Jesus had finished speaking, he said to Simon, "Take the boat into deep water, and put your nets in the water to catch some fish."

[5]Simon answered, "Master, we worked hard all night trying to catch fish, and we caught nothing. But you say to put the nets in the water, so I will." [6]When the fishermen did as Jesus told them, they caught so many fish that the nets began to break. [7]They called to their partners in the other boat to come and help them. They came and filled both boats so full that they were almost sinking.

[8]When Simon Peter saw what had happened, he bowed down before Jesus and said, "Go away from me, Lord. I am a sinful man!" [9]He and the other fishermen were amazed at the many fish they caught, as were [10]James and John, the sons of Zebedee, Simon's partners.

Jesus said to Simon, "Don't be afraid. From now on you will fish for people." [11]When the men brought their boats to the shore, they left everything and followed Jesus.

## Q & A

**Q** I have to go to a new school next year, and I won't know anybody. How can I fit in?

**A** The new kids don't know anything about you, so show them a friendly and confident you! If you act shy and nervous, they're more likely to give you a hard time. Find other new kids and try to get to know them. See if you can join some after-school activities as a way to meet other people. They will see that you're an interesting person to know! Most of all, give it time. God will help you get through and make new friends.

## read it, do it

### Luke 2:20

**R**ead It: Praise God for everything.

**D**o It: After church, before you start chatting with your friends, take a minute to quietly pray and thank God for what you just learned. Encourage your friends to do the same.

4:38, 5:3 **Simon** *Simon's other name was Peter.*   4:44 **Judea** *Some Greek copies read "Galilee."*

# dig deeper

### Luke 6:46–49

Have you ever opened a cupboard or walked into a room and thought, "Why did I come here? I forgot what I'm looking for!" Most people have been in these kinds of situations because they're thinking about too many things at the same time. Our "short-term" memory sometimes doesn't work! But can you imagine looking in the mirror, walking away, and then forgetting what you look like? That's kind of extreme, isn't it?

Luke 6:46–49 tells us that it's foolish to open the Bible, read it, close it back up, and immediately forget what

God says. It's like building a house without a firm foundation. That's a disaster waiting to happen. Jesus expects us to be smarter than that!

The Bible isn't just a bunch of words. The New Testament contains God's inspired message for the followers of Jesus Christ. The first four books focus on Jesus. The fifth book, Acts, tells us about the early Christians. The next twenty-one books show how best to follow him (and what mistakes to avoid). The last book, Revelation, urges us to remain true to the end. As you read the Bible today, ask God to help you embrace it, believe it, and live it!

Judea and from Jerusalem were there. The Lord was giving Jesus the power to heal people. [18]Just then, some men were carrying on a mat a man who was paralyzed. They tried to bring him in and put him down before Jesus. [19]But because there were so many people there, they could not find a way in. So they went up on the roof and lowered the man on his mat through the ceiling into the middle of the crowd right before Jesus. [20]Seeing their faith, Jesus said, "Friend, your sins are forgiven."

[21]The Jewish teachers of the law and the Pharisees thought to themselves, "Who is this man who is speaking as if he were God? Only God can forgive sins."

[22]But Jesus knew what they were thinking and said, "Why are you thinking these things? [23]Which is easier: to say, 'Your sins are forgiven,' or to say, 'Stand up and walk'? [24]But I will prove to you that the Son of Man has authority on earth to forgive sins." So Jesus said to the paralyzed man, "I tell you, stand up, take your mat, and go home."

[25]At once the man stood up before them, picked up his mat, and went home, praising God. [26]All the people were fully amazed and began to praise God. They were filled with much respect and said, "Today we have seen amazing things!"

## Levi Follows Jesus

[27]After this, Jesus went out and saw a tax collector named Levi sitting in the tax collector's booth. Jesus said to him, "Follow me!" [28]So Levi got up, left everything, and followed him.

[29]Then Levi gave a big dinner for Jesus at his house. Many tax collectors and other people were eating there, too. [30]But the Pharisees and the men who taught the law for the Pharisees began to complain to Jesus' followers, "Why do you eat and drink with tax collectors and sinners?"

[31]Jesus answered them, "It is not the healthy people who need a doctor, but the sick. [32]I have not come to invite good people but sinners to change their hearts and lives."

## Jesus Answers a Question

[33]They said to Jesus, "John's followers often fast[n] for a certain time and pray, just as the Pharisees do. But your followers eat and drink all the time."

## Jesus Heals a Sick Man

[12]When Jesus was in one of the towns, there was a man covered with a skin disease. When he saw Jesus, he bowed before him and begged him, "Lord, you can heal me if you will."

[13]Jesus reached out his hand and touched the man and said, "I will. Be healed!" Immediately the disease disappeared. [14]Then Jesus said, "Don't tell anyone about this, but go and show yourself to the priest[n] and offer a gift for your

healing, as Moses commanded.[n] This will show the people what I have done."

[15]But the news about Jesus spread even more. Many people came to hear Jesus and to be healed of their sicknesses, [16]but Jesus often slipped away to be alone so he could pray.

## Jesus Heals a Paralyzed Man

[17]One day as Jesus was teaching the people, the Pharisees and teachers of the law from every town in Galilee and

---

**5:14 show . . . priest** *The Law of Moses said a priest must say when a Jewish person with a skin disease was well.* **5:14 Moses commanded** *Read about this in Leviticus 14:1–32.* **5:33 fast** *The people would give up eating for a special time of prayer and worship to God. It was also done to show sadness and disappointment.*

# Relationships

The new girl in your class and the immigrant family in your neighborhood have something in common. The Bible calls them aliens or strangers. Exodus 22:21 teaches us: "Do not cheat or hurt a foreigner." Hebrews 13:2 has a similar message: "Remember to welcome strangers, because some who have done this have welcomed angels without knowing it." You can follow God's command by taking care of others who are strangers. Be a friend to the new girl in school. Ask your parents if you can invite the neighbors over for a barbeque. Who knows . . . you might be "welcoming angels!"

³⁴Jesus said to them, "You cannot make the friends of the bridegroom fast while he is still with them. ³⁵But the time will come when the bridegroom will be taken away from them, and then they will fast."

³⁶Jesus told them this story: "No one takes cloth off a new coat to cover a hole in an old coat. Otherwise, he ruins the new coat, and the cloth from the new coat will not be the same as the old cloth. ³⁷Also, no one ever pours new wine into old leather bags. Otherwise, the new wine will break the bags, the wine will spill out, and the leather bags will be ruined. ³⁸New wine must be put into new leather bags. ³⁹No one after drinking old wine wants new wine, because he says, 'The old wine is better.'"

## Jesus Is Lord over the Sabbath

6 One Sabbath day Jesus was walking through some fields of grain. His followers picked the heads of grain, rubbed them in their hands, and ate them. ²Some Pharisees said, "Why do you do what is not lawful on the Sabbath day?"

³Jesus answered, "Have you not read what David did when he and those with him were hungry? ⁴He went into God's house and took and ate the holy bread, which is lawful only for priests to eat. And he gave some to the people who were with him." ⁵Then Jesus said to the

Pharisees, "The Son of Man is Lord of the Sabbath day."

## Jesus Heals a Man's Hand

⁶On another Sabbath day Jesus went into the synagogue and was teaching, and a man with a crippled right hand was there. ⁷The teachers of the law and the Pharisees were watching closely to see if Jesus would heal on the Sabbath day so they could accuse him. ⁸But he knew what they were thinking, and he said to the man with the crippled hand, "Stand up here in the middle of everyone." The man got up and stood there. ⁹Then Jesus said to them, "I ask you, which is lawful on the Sabbath day: to do good or to do evil, to save a life or to destroy it?" ¹⁰Jesus looked around at all of them and said to the man, "Hold out your hand." The man held out his hand, and it was healed.

¹¹But the Pharisees and the teachers of the law were very angry and discussed with each other what they could do to Jesus.

## Jesus Chooses His Apostles

¹²At that time Jesus went off to a mountain to pray, and he spent the night praying to God. ¹³The next morning, Jesus called his followers to him and chose twelve of them, whom he named apostles: ¹⁴Simon (Jesus named him Peter), his brother Andrew, James, John, Philip, Bartholomew, ¹⁵Matthew, Thomas, James son of Alphaeus, Simon (called the

Zealot), ¹⁶Judas son of James, and Judas Iscariot, who later turned Jesus over to his enemies.

## Jesus Teaches and Heals

¹⁷Jesus and the apostles came down from the mountain, and he stood on level ground. A large group of his followers was there, as well as many people from all around Judea, Jerusalem, and the seacoast cities of Tyre and Sidon. ¹⁸They all

# Q & A

**Q** My mom always tells me to clean my room. It's *my* room! Shouldn't I be allowed to keep it as messy as I want?

**A** Actually, it's not your room. Everything in your house belongs to your parents. They work hard to feed you, buy you clothes, give you an education, get your teeth fixed, and lots more. It's not asking much of you to keep their property clean and neat. Read Ephesians 6:1. Then ask God to change your attitude toward your parents.

## cool

### Priceless Artwork

In 2004, someone bought a ninety-nine-year-old painting by the Spanish artist Pablo Picasso for $104 million! The painting, called *Garcon a la Pipe,* became the most expensive piece of art ever sold. Before that, a Japanese businessman had bought paintings by Vincent Van Gogh and Pierre-August Renoir for about $80 million each. That's *expensive* art!

But did you know you've got *priceless* art? (That means it's so valuable you can't put a price on it.) Look outside at the awesome world God created for us. You'll never find more beautiful artwork than that . . . and it's free!

came to hear Jesus teach and to be healed of their sicknesses, and he healed those who were troubled by evil spirits. [19]All the people were trying to touch Jesus, because power was coming from him and healing them all.

[20]Jesus looked at his followers and said,

"You people who are poor are
     blessed,
   because the kingdom of God
     belongs to you.
[21]You people who are now hungry are
     blessed,
   because you will be satisfied.
 You people who are now crying are
     blessed,
   because you will laugh with joy.
[22]"People will hate you, shut you out, insult you, and say you are evil because you follow the Son of Man. But when they do, you will be blessed. [23]Be full of joy at that time, because you have a great reward in heaven. Their ancestors did the same things to the prophets.
[24]"But how terrible it will be for you
     who are rich,
   because you have had your easy
     life.
[25]How terrible it will be for you who
     are full now,
   because you will be hungry.
 How terrible it will be for you who
     are laughing now,
   because you will be sad and cry.
[26]"How terrible when everyone says only good things about you, because their ancestors said the same things about the false prophets.

### Love Your Enemies

[27]"But I say to you who are listening, love your enemies. Do good to those who hate you, [28]bless those who curse you, pray for those who are cruel to you. [29]If anyone slaps you on one cheek, offer him the other cheek, too. If someone takes your coat, do not stop him from taking your shirt. [30]Give to everyone who asks you, and when someone takes something that is yours, don't ask for it back. [31]Do to others what you would want them to do to you. [32]If you love only the people who love you, what praise should you get? Even sinners love the people who love them. [33]If you do good only to those who do good to you, what praise should you get? Even sinners do that! [34]If you lend things to people, always hoping to get something back, what praise should you get? Even sinners lend to other sinners so that they can get back the same amount! [35]But love your enemies, do good to them, and lend to them without hoping to get anything back. Then you will have a great reward, and you will be children of the Most High God, because he is kind even to people who are ungrateful and full of sin. [36]Show mercy, just as your Father shows mercy.

### Look at Yourselves

[37]"Don't judge others, and you will not be judged. Don't accuse others of being guilty, and you will not be accused of being guilty. Forgive, and you will be forgiven. [38]Give, and you will receive. You will be given much. Pressed down, shaken together, and running over, it will spill into your lap. The way you give to others is the way God will give to you."

[39]Jesus told them this story: "Can a blind person lead another blind person? No! Both of them will fall into a ditch. [40]A student is not better than the teacher, but the student who has been fully trained will be like the teacher.

[41]"Why do you notice the little piece of dust in your friend's eye, but you don't notice the big piece of wood in your own eye? [42]How can you say to your friend, 'Friend, let me take that little piece of dust out of your eye' when you cannot

## ▪ Bible Bios   Anna (Luke 2:36–38)

Baby Jesus' parents brought him to the Temple to make special sacrifices (as the religious laws required). There they met Anna, a prophetess who understood right away that the little child was the Messiah . . . the Savior of the world!

Anna's husband had died eighty-four years before this story . . . and she had been married to him for seven years. Anna must have been over one hundred years old by now! But she didn't stay home in a rocking chair thinking that she couldn't do anything anymore. Instead, she spent every day in the Temple worshiping God. She even went without food for a while so she could concentrate on praying.

After she met Jesus, Anna told many people about him! Whether you're 11 or 111, you can dedicate your life to worshiping and obeying God. He will bless you for it!

see that big piece of wood in your own eye! You hypocrite! First, take the wood out of your own eye. Then you will see clearly to take the dust out of your friend's eye.

## Two Kinds of Fruit

[43]"A good tree does not produce bad fruit, nor does a bad tree produce good fruit. [44]Each tree is known by its own fruit. People don't gather figs from thornbushes, and they don't get grapes from bushes. [45]Good people bring good things out of the good they stored in their hearts. But evil people bring evil things out of the evil they stored in their hearts. People speak the things that are in their hearts.

## Two Kinds of People

[46]"Why do you call me, 'Lord, Lord,' but do not do what I say? [47]I will show you what everyone is like who comes to me and hears my words and obeys. [48]That person is like a man building a house who dug deep and laid the foundation on rock. When the floods came, the water tried to wash the house away, but it could not shake it, because the house was built well. [49]But the one who hears my words and does not obey is like a man who built his house on the ground without a foundation. When the floods came, the house quickly fell and was completely destroyed."

## Jesus Heals a Soldier's Servant

7 When Jesus finished saying all these things to the people, he went to Capernaum. [2]There was an army officer who had a servant who was very important to him. The servant was so sick he was nearly dead. [3]When the officer heard about Jesus, he sent some Jewish elders to him to ask Jesus to come and heal his servant. [4]The men went to Jesus and begged him, saying, "This officer is worthy of your help. [5]He loves our people, and he built us a synagogue."

[6]So Jesus went with the men. He was getting near the officer's house when the officer sent friends to say, "Lord, don't trouble yourself, because I am not worthy to have you come into my house. [7]That is why I did not come to you myself. But you only need to command it, and my servant will be healed. [8]I, too, am a man under the authority of others, and I have soldiers under my command. I tell one soldier, 'Go,' and he goes. I tell another soldier, 'Come,' and he comes. I say to my servant, 'Do this,' and my servant does it."

[9]When Jesus heard this, he was amazed. Turning to the crowd that was following him, he said, "I tell you, this is the greatest faith I have found anywhere, even in Israel."

[10]Those who had been sent to Jesus went back to the house where they found the servant in good health.

## Jesus Brings a Man Back to Life

[11]Soon afterwards Jesus went to a town called Nain, and his followers and a large crowd traveled with him. [12]When he came near the town gate, he saw a funeral. A mother, who was a widow, had lost her only son. A large crowd from the town was with the mother while her son was being carried out. [13]When the Lord saw her, he felt very sorry for her and said, "Don't cry." [14]He went up and touched the coffin, and the people who were carrying it stopped. Jesus said, "Young man, I tell you, get up!" [15]And the son sat up and began to talk. Then Jesus gave him back to his mother.

[16]All the people were amazed and began praising God, saying, "A great prophet has come to us! God has come to help his people."

[17]This news about Jesus spread through all Judea and into all the places around there.

## John Asks a Question

[18]John's followers told him about all these things. He called for two of his followers [19]and sent them to the Lord to ask, "Are you the One who is to come, or should we wait for someone else?"

[20]When the men came to Jesus, they said, "John the Baptist sent us to you with this question: 'Are you the One who is to come, or should we wait for someone else?'"

[21]At that time, Jesus healed many people of their sicknesses, diseases, and evil spirits, and he gave sight to many blind people. [22]Then Jesus answered John's followers, "Go tell John what you saw and heard here. The blind can see, the crippled can walk, and people with skin diseases are healed. The deaf can hear, the dead are raised to life, and the Good News is preached to the poor. [23]Those who do not stumble in their faith because of me are blessed!"

[24]When John's followers left, Jesus began talking to the people about John: "What did you go out into the desert to see? A reed[n] blown by the wind? [25]What did you go out to see? A man dressed in fine clothes? No, people who have fine clothes and much wealth live in kings' palaces. [26]But what did you go out to

## top ten

### top ten questions to Ask Your Grandparents

**1** What was your favorite game when you were young?

**2** What hobbies did you used to have?

**3** Who was your role model?

**4** What was my mom/dad like at my age?

**5** What interesting countries have you visited?

**6** How did you meet grandma/grandpa?

**7** What's the funniest thing that ever happened to you?

**8** What's the best advice you ever received?

**9** What was your favorite job?

**10** In what ways am I like you?

---

7:24 **reed** It means that John was not ordinary or weak like grass blown by the wind.

see? A prophet? Yes, and I tell you, John is more than a prophet. [27]This was written about him:

'I will send my messenger ahead of you,
who will prepare the way for you.'

*Malachi 3:1*

[28]I tell you, John is greater than any other person ever born, but even the least important person in the kingdom of God is greater than John."

[29](When the people, including the tax collectors, heard this, they all agreed that God's teaching was good, because they had been baptized by John. [30]But the Pharisees and experts on the law refused to accept God's plan for themselves; they did not let John baptize them.)

[31]Then Jesus said, "What shall I say about the people of this time? What are they like? [32]They are like children sitting in the marketplace, calling to one another and saying,

'We played music for you, but you did not dance;
we sang a sad song, but you did not cry.'

[33]John the Baptist came and did not eat bread or drink wine, and you say, 'He has a demon in him.' [34]The Son of Man came eating and drinking, and you say, 'Look at him! He eats too much and drinks too much wine, and he is a friend of tax collectors and sinners!' [35]But wisdom is proved to be right by what it does."

### A Woman Washes Jesus' Feet

[36]One of the Pharisees asked Jesus to eat with him, so Jesus went into the Pharisee's house and sat at the table. [37]A sinful woman in the town learned that Jesus was eating at the Pharisee's house. So she brought an alabaster jar of perfume [38]and stood behind Jesus at his feet, crying. She began to wash his feet with her tears, and she dried them with her hair, kissing them many times and rubbing them with the perfume. [39]When the Pharisee who asked Jesus to come to his house saw this, he thought to himself, "If Jesus were a prophet, he would know that the woman touching him is a sinner!"

[40]Jesus said to the Pharisee, "Simon, I have something to say to you."

Simon said, "Teacher, tell me."

[41]Jesus said, "Two people owed money to the same banker. One owed five hundred coins[n] and the other owed fifty. [42]They had no money to pay what they owed, but the banker told both of them they did not have to pay him. Which person will love the banker more?"

[43]Simon, the Pharisee, answered, "I think it would be the one who owed him the most money."

Jesus said to Simon, "You are right." [44]Then Jesus turned toward the woman and said to Simon, "Do you see this woman? When I came into your house, you gave me no water for my feet, but she washed my feet with her tears and dried them with her hair. [45]You gave me no kiss of greeting, but she has been kissing my feet since I came in. [46]You did not put oil on my head, but she poured perfume on my feet. [47]I tell you that her many sins are forgiven, so she showed great love. But the person who is forgiven only a little will love only a little."

## dig deeper

### Luke 7:1–11

A man who can swivel his head and see his spine or a girl with a crocodile body—people love watching or reading about wild and bizarre things and wondering, "Is that true?"

But the man in this story wasn't looking for entertainment. He didn't need Jesus to come and perform a show or do any special effects. He just wanted his servant to be healed—and he didn't need to see it to believe it. More importantly, he believed that Jesus had so much power and authority that a command, even from far away, would drive out the sickness. Sure enough, the servant got better that very same hour. Jesus was thrilled that someone would trust him that much. So many people came to Jesus for a miracle, but they were really more interested in the show than in trusting him.

You can trust Jesus completely. When you do, he can say the same thing about you: "This is the greatest faith." Not because Jesus does a show for you or performs a miracle, but because you trust his ultimate power and authority to forgive your sins, to strengthen and guide you your whole life, and to take you to heaven someday.

**7:41 coins** *Roman denarii. One coin was the average pay for one day's work.*

[48]Then Jesus said to her, "Your sins are forgiven."

[49]The people sitting at the table began to say among themselves, "Who is this who even forgives sins?"

[50]Jesus said to the woman, "Because you believed, you are saved from your sins. Go in peace."

## The Group with Jesus

8 After this, while Jesus was traveling through some cities and small towns, he preached and told the Good News about God's kingdom. The twelve apostles were with him, [2]and also some women who had been healed of sicknesses and evil spirits: Mary, called Magdalene, from whom seven demons had gone out; [3]Joanna, the wife of Cuza (the manager of Herod's house); Susanna; and many others. These women used their own money to help Jesus and his apostles.

## A Story About Planting Seed

[4]When a great crowd was gathered, and people were coming to Jesus from every town, he told them this story:

[5]"A farmer went out to plant his seed. While he was planting, some seed fell by the road. People walked on the seed, and the birds ate it up. [6]Some seed fell on rock, and when it began to grow, it died because it had no water. [7]Some seed fell among thorny weeds, but the weeds grew up with it and choked the good plants. [8]And some seed fell on good ground and grew and made a hundred times more."

As Jesus finished the story, he called out, "Let those with ears use them and listen!"

[9]Jesus' followers asked him what this story meant.

[10]Jesus said, "You have been chosen to know the secrets about the kingdom of God. But I use stories to speak to other people so that:

'They will look, but they may not see.
They will listen, but they may not understand.' *Isaiah 6:9*

[11]"This is what the story means: The seed is God's message. [12]The seed that fell beside the road is like the people who hear God's teaching, but the devil comes and takes it away from them so they cannot believe it and be saved. [13]The seed that fell on rock is like those who hear God's teaching and accept it gladly, but they don't allow the teaching to go deep into their lives. They believe for a while, but when trouble comes, they give up. [14]The seed that fell among the thorny weeds is like those who hear God's teaching, but they let the worries, riches, and pleasures of this life keep them from growing and producing good fruit. [15]And the seed that fell on the good ground is like those who hear God's teaching with good, honest hearts and obey it and patiently produce good fruit.

## Q&A

**Q** Should I ask Jesus into my heart again after I do something wrong?

**A** If you've already asked Jesus to forgive you and be your Savior, you don't have to do that again. You don't stop becoming a Christian if you sin. But the sin does leave a stain on your relationship with Jesus, so ask for forgiveness right away. If you've been far from God for a while and are sinning a lot, you can "rededicate" yourself to him: pray for forgiveness and make a commitment to start living for him again.

## Use What You Have

[16]"No one after lighting a lamp covers it with a bowl or hides it under a bed. Instead, the person puts it on a lampstand so those who come in will see the light. [17]Everything that is hidden will become clear, and every secret thing will be made known. [18]So be careful how you listen. Those who have understanding will be given more. But those who do not have understanding, even what they think they have will be taken away from them."

## Jesus' True Family

[19]Jesus' mother and brothers came to see him, but there was such a crowd they could not get to him. [20]Someone said to Jesus, "Your mother and your brothers are standing outside, wanting to see you."

[21]Jesus answered them, "My mother and my brothers are those who listen to God's teaching and obey it!"

## Jesus Calms a Storm

[22]One day Jesus and his followers got into a boat, and he said to them, "Let's go across the lake." And so they started across. [23]While they were sailing, Jesus fell asleep. A very strong wind blew up on the lake, causing the boat to fill with water, and they were in danger.

## read it, do it

### Luke 12:23

**R** ead It: There's more to life than food and clothes.

**D** o It: For one week, skip junk food and try not to think about new clothes. Ask God to help you focus on more important things in life.

[24]The followers went to Jesus and woke him, saying, "Master! Master! We will drown!"

Jesus got up and gave a command to the wind and the waves. They stopped, and it became calm. [25]Jesus said to his followers, "Where is your faith?"

The followers were afraid and amazed and said to each other, "Who is this that commands even the wind and the water, and they obey him?"

## A Man with Demons Inside Him

[26]Jesus and his followers sailed across the lake from Galilee to the area of the Gerasene[n] people. [27]When Jesus got out on the land, a man from the town who had demons inside him came to Jesus. For a long time he had worn no clothes and had lived in the burial caves, not in a house. [28]When he saw Jesus, he cried out and fell down before him. He said with a loud voice, "What do you want with me, Jesus, Son of the Most High God? I beg

you, don't torture me!" [29]He said this because Jesus was commanding the evil spirit to come out of the man. Many times it had taken hold of him. Though he had been kept under guard and chained hand and foot, he had broken his chains and had been forced by the demon out into a lonely place.

[30]Jesus asked him, "What is your name?"

He answered, "Legion,"[n] because many demons were in him. [31]The demons begged Jesus not to send them into eternal darkness.[n] [32]A large herd of pigs was feeding on a hill, and the demons begged Jesus to allow them to go into the pigs. So Jesus allowed them to do this. [33]When the demons came out of the man, they went into the pigs, and the herd ran down the hill into the lake and was drowned.

[34]When the herdsmen saw what had happened, they ran away and told about this in the town and the countryside. [35]And people went to see what had happened. When they came to Jesus, they found the man sitting at Jesus' feet, clothed and in

his right mind, because the demons were gone. But the people were frightened. [36]The people who saw this happen told the others how Jesus had made the man well. [37]All the people of the Gerasene country asked Jesus to leave, because they were all very afraid. So Jesus got into the boat and went back to Galilee.

[38]The man whom Jesus had healed begged to go with him, but Jesus sent him away, saying, [39]"Go back home and tell people how much God has done for you." So the man went all over town telling how much Jesus had done for him.

## Jesus Gives Life to a Dead Girl and Heals a Sick Woman

[40]When Jesus got back to Galilee, a crowd welcomed him, because everyone was waiting for him. [41]A man named Jairus, a leader of the synagogue, came to Jesus and fell at his feet, begging him to come to

his house. [42]Jairus' only daughter, about twelve years old, was dying.

While Jesus was on his way to Jairus' house, the people were crowding all around him. [43]A woman was in the crowd who had been bleeding for twelve years,[n] but no one was able to heal her. [44]She came up behind Jesus and touched the edge of his coat, and instantly her bleeding stopped. [45]Then Jesus said, "Who touched me?"

When all the people said they had not touched him, Peter said, "Master, the people are all around you and are pushing against you."

[46]But Jesus said, "Someone did touch me, because I felt power go out from me." [47]When the woman saw she could not hide, she came forward, shaking, and fell down before Jesus. While all the people listened, she told why she had touched him and how she had been instantly healed. [48]Jesus said to her, "Dear woman, you are made well because you believed. Go in peace."

[49]While Jesus was still speaking, someone came from the house of the synagogue leader and said to him, "Your daughter is dead. Don't bother the teacher anymore."

[50]When Jesus heard this, he said to Jairus, "Don't be afraid. Just believe, and your daughter will be well."

[51]When Jesus went to the house, he let only Peter, John, James, and the girl's father and mother go inside with him. [52]All the people were crying and feeling sad because the girl was dead, but Jesus said, "Stop crying. She is not dead, only asleep."

[53]The people laughed at Jesus because they knew the girl was dead. [54]But Jesus took hold of her hand and called to her, "My child, stand up!" [55]Her spirit came back into her, and she stood up at once. Then Jesus ordered that she be given something to eat. [56]The girl's parents were amazed, but Jesus told them not to tell anyone what had happened.

## Jesus Sends Out the Apostles

9 Jesus called the twelve apostles together and gave them power and authority over all demons and the ability to heal sicknesses. [2]He sent the apostles out to tell about God's kingdom and to heal the sick. [3]He said to them, "Take nothing for your trip, neither a walking stick, bag, bread, money, or extra clothes. [4]When you enter a house, stay there until it is time to leave. [5]If people do not welcome you, shake the dust off of your feet[n] as you leave the town, as a warning to them."

> ## JESUS SAID, "SOMEONE DID TOUCH ME, BECAUSE I FELT POWER GO OUT FROM ME."

[6]So the apostles went out and traveled through all the towns, preaching the Good News and healing people everywhere.

## Herod Is Confused About Jesus

[7]Herod, the governor, heard about all the things that were happening and was confused, because some people said, "John the Baptist has risen from the

---

**did you know?**

70% of kids think their parents don't understand growing up today.

—Sonna, Linda, Ph.D. *The Everything Tween Book.* Avon, Massachusetts: Adams Media Corporation, 2003. p. 52

---

**8:26 Gerasene** From Gerasa, an area southeast of Lake Galilee. The exact location is uncertain and some Greek copies read "Gadarene"; others read "Gergesene." **8:30 Legion** Means very many. A legion was about five thousand men in the Roman army. **8:31 eternal darkness** Literally, "the abyss," something like a pit or a hole that has no end. **8:43 years** Some Greek copies continue, "and she had spent all the money she had on doctors." **9:5 shake . . . feet** A warning. It showed that they had rejected these people.

# March

**1**

**2** Ask your mom to play her favorite album for you. Try to make only positive comments.

**3** Learn to say "thank you" in at least one language you don't speak.

**4** Pray for someone who is hard for you to love.

**5**

**6** Pray for a person of influence: Today is Shaquille O'Neal's birthday.

**7** Read 2 Thessalonians 3:3 and thank God for his protection.

**8** Pray for a person of influence: Today is Freddie Prinze Jr.'s birthday.

**9**

**10** Make a card for your mom telling her how thankful you are for the things she does. Leave it on her pillow before bedtime.

**11**

**12**

**13** Pray for your dentist.

**14**

**15** On your way to school, ask God to use you to bless someone today.

**16**

**17** St. Patrick's Day—Look up the history behind this holiday.

**18** Pray for a person of influence: Today is Queen Latifah's birthday.

**19**

**20** Write down the names of 5 people in your life you look up to . . . and then thank God for them!

**21**

**22**

**23** Get a piggy bank or small container to start collecting pennies in.

**24**

**25** Spend an extra half hour on your homework today and think of it as a gift to yourself.

**26**

**27**

**28** Pray for a person of influence: Today is Julia Stiles's birthday.

**29**

**30**

**31** Do a secret good deed: clean all the mirrors in your house.

Charlie says, "Make a list!"

dead." [8]Others said, "Elijah has come to us." And still others said, "One of the prophets who lived long ago has risen from the dead." [9]Herod said, "I cut off John's head, so who is this man I hear such things about?" And Herod kept trying to see Jesus.

## More than Five Thousand Fed

[10]When the apostles returned, they told Jesus everything they had done. Then Jesus took them with him to a town called Bethsaida where they could be alone together. [11]But the people learned where Jesus went and followed him. He welcomed them and talked with them about God's kingdom and healed those who needed to be healed.

[12]Late in the afternoon, the twelve apostles came to Jesus and said, "Send the people away. They need to go to the towns and countryside around here and find places to sleep and something to eat, because no one lives in this place."

[13]But Jesus said to them, "You give them something to eat."

They said, "We have only five loaves of bread and two fish, unless we go buy food for all these people." [14](There were about five thousand men there.)

Jesus said to his followers, "Tell the people to sit in groups of about fifty people."

[15]So the followers did this, and all the people sat down. [16]Then Jesus took the five loaves of bread and two fish, and looking up to heaven, he thanked God for the food. Then he divided the food and gave it to the followers to give to the people. [17]They all ate and were satisfied, and what was left over was gathered up, filling twelve baskets.

## Jesus Is the Christ

[18]One time when Jesus was praying alone, his followers were with him, and he asked them, "Who do the people say I am?"

[19]They answered, "Some say you are John the Baptist. Others say you are Elijah.[n] And others say you are one of the prophets from long ago who has come back to life."

[20]Then Jesus asked, "But who do you say I am?"

Peter answered, "You are the Christ from God."

[21]Jesus warned them not to tell anyone, saying, [22]"The Son of Man must suffer

many things. He will be rejected by the Jewish elders, the leading priests, and the teachers of the law. He will be killed and after three days will be raised from the dead."

[23]Jesus said to all of them, "If people want to follow me, they must give up the things they want. They must be willing to give up their lives daily to follow me. [24]Those who want to save their lives will give up true life. But those who give up their lives for me will have true life. [25]It is worthless to have the whole world if they themselves are destroyed or lost. [26]If people are ashamed of me and my teaching, then the Son of Man will be ashamed of them when he comes in his glory and with the glory of the Father and the holy angels. [27]I tell you the truth, some people standing here will see the kingdom of God before they die."

## Jesus Talks with Moses and Elijah

[28]About eight days after Jesus said these things, he took Peter, John, and James and went up on a mountain to pray. [29]While Jesus was praying, the appearance of his face changed, and his clothes became shining white. [30]Then two men, Moses and Elijah,[n] were talking with Jesus. [31]They appeared in heavenly glory, talking about his departure which

# Q&A

**Q** My mom got pregnant with me when she wasn't married. Why does that make me feel bad?

**A** Even though you may feel unwanted, you need to know that God has always had a special plan for your life. You are not responsible for your parents' choices, so don't feel guilty! Always remember that your parents love you and that God loves you even more!

he would soon bring about in Jerusalem. [32]Peter and the others were very sleepy, but when they awoke fully, they saw the glory of Jesus and the two men standing with him. [33]When Moses and Elijah were about to leave, Peter said to Jesus, "Master, it is good that we are here. Let us make three tents—one for you, one for Moses, and one for Elijah." (Peter did not know what he was talking about.)

[34]While he was saying these things, a cloud came and covered them, and they became afraid as the cloud covered them. [35]A voice came from the cloud, saying, "This is my Son, whom I have chosen. Listen to him!"

[36]When the voice finished speaking, only Jesus was there. Peter, John, and James said nothing and told no one at that time what they had seen.

## Jesus Heals a Sick Boy

[37]The next day, when they came down from the mountain, a large crowd met Jesus. [38]A man in the crowd shouted to him, "Teacher, please come and look at my son, because he is my only child. [39]An evil spirit seizes my son, and suddenly he screams. It causes him to lose control of himself and foam at the mouth. The evil spirit keeps on hurting him and almost never leaves him. [40]I begged your followers to force the evil spirit out, but they could not do it."

[41]Jesus answered, "You people have no faith, and your lives are all wrong. How long must I stay with you and put up with you? Bring your son here."

[42]While the boy was coming, the demon threw him on the ground and made him lose control of himself. But Jesus gave a strong command to the evil spirit and healed the boy and gave him back to his father. [43]All the people were amazed at the great power of God.

## Jesus Talks About His Death

While everyone was wondering about all that Jesus did, he said to his followers, [44]"Don't forget what I tell you now: The Son of Man will be handed over to people." [45]But the followers did not understand what this meant; the meaning was hidden from them so they could not understand. But they were afraid to ask Jesus about it.

---

**9:19 Elijah** *A man who spoke for God and who lived hundreds of years before Christ. See 1 Kings 17.* **9:30 Moses and Elijah** *Two of the most important Jewish leaders in the past. God had given Moses the Law, and Elijah was an important prophet.*

## Who Is the Greatest?

⁴⁶Jesus' followers began to have an argument about which one of them was the greatest. ⁴⁷Jesus knew what they were thinking, so he took a little child and stood the child beside him. ⁴⁸Then Jesus said, "Whoever accepts this little child in my name accepts me. And whoever accepts me accepts the One who sent me, because whoever is least among you all is really the greatest."

## Anyone Not Against Us Is for Us

⁴⁹John answered, "Master, we saw someone using your name to force demons out of people. We told him to stop, because he does not belong to our group."

⁵⁰But Jesus said to him, "Don't stop him, because whoever is not against you is for you."

## A Town Rejects Jesus

⁵¹When the time was coming near for Jesus to depart, he was determined to go to Jerusalem. ⁵²He sent some messengers ahead of him, who went into a town in Samaria to make everything ready for him. ⁵³But the people there would not welcome him, because he was set on going to Jerusalem. ⁵⁴When James and John, followers of Jesus, saw this, they said, "Lord, do you want us to call fire down from heaven and destroy those people?"[n]

⁵⁵But Jesus turned and scolded them. [And Jesus said, "You don't know what kind of spirit you belong to. ⁵⁶The Son of Man did not come to destroy the souls of people but to save them."][n] Then they went to another town.

## Following Jesus

⁵⁷As they were going along the road, someone said to Jesus, "I will follow you any place you go."

⁵⁸Jesus said to them, "The foxes have holes to live in, and the birds have nests, but the Son of Man has no place to rest his head."

⁵⁹Jesus said to another man, "Follow me!"

But he said, "Lord, first let me go and bury my father."

⁶⁰But Jesus said to him, "Let the people who are dead bury their own dead. You must go and tell about the kingdom of God."

⁶¹Another man said, "I will follow you, Lord, but first let me go and say good-bye to my family."

## BE YOUR BEST!

**B**e true to your size! Clothes that are too tight or too baggy *don't* look good! Wear clothes that fit and flatter you—not just what everyone else wears. As a Christian, don't try to be someone you're not, but be thankful for the unique you God made you to be!

⁶²Jesus said, "Anyone who begins to plow a field but keeps looking back is of no use in the kingdom of God."

## Jesus Sends Out the Seventy-Two

**10** After this, the Lord chose seventy-two[n] others and sent them out in pairs ahead of him into every town and place where he planned to go. ²He said to them, "There are a great many people to harvest, but there are only a few workers. So pray to God, who owns the harvest, that he will send more workers to help gather his harvest. ³Go now, but listen! I am sending you out like sheep among wolves. ⁴Don't carry a purse, a bag, or sandals, and don't waste time talking with people on the road. ⁵Before you go into a house, say, 'Peace be with this house.' ⁶If peace-loving people live there, your blessing of peace will stay with them, but if not, then your blessing will come back to you. ⁷Stay in the same house, eating and drinking what the people there give you. A worker should be given his pay. Don't move from house to house. ⁸If you go into a town and the people welcome you, eat what they give you. ⁹Heal the sick who live there, and tell them, 'The kingdom of God is near you.' ¹⁰But if you go into a town, and the people don't welcome you, then go into the streets and say, ¹¹"Even the dirt from your town that sticks to our feet we wipe off against you."[n] But remember that the

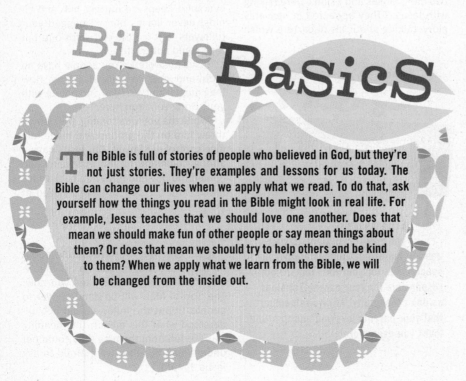

## BIBLE BASICS

**T**he Bible is full of stories of people who believed in God, but they're not just stories. They're examples and lessons for us today. The Bible can change our lives when we apply what we read. To do that, ask yourself how the things you read in the Bible might look in real life. For example, Jesus teaches that we should love one another. Does that mean we should make fun of other people or say mean things about them? Or does that mean we should try to help others and be kind to them? When we apply what we learn from the Bible, we will be changed from the inside out.

**9:54 people** *Some Greek copies continue "as Elijah did."* **9:55–56 And . . . them."** *Some Greek copies do not contain the bracketed text.* **10:1 seventy-two** *Some Greek copies read "seventy."*
**10:11 dirt . . . you** *A warning. It showed that they had rejected these people.*

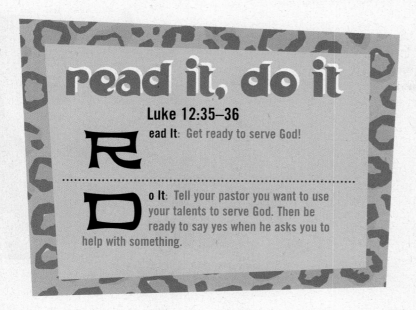

# read it, do it

### Luke 12:35–36

**R**ead It: Get ready to serve God!

**D**o It: Tell your pastor you want to use your talents to serve God. Then be ready to say yes when he asks you to help with something.

kingdom of God is near.' ¹²I tell you, on the Judgment Day it will be better for the people of Sodom[n] than for the people of that town.

## Jesus Warns Unbelievers

¹³"How terrible for you, Korazin! How terrible for you, Bethsaida! If the miracles I did in you had happened in Tyre and Sidon,[n] those people would have changed their lives long ago. They would have worn rough cloth and put ashes on themselves to show they had changed. ¹⁴But on the Judgment Day it will be better for Tyre and Sidon than for you. ¹⁵And you, Capernaum,[n] will you be lifted up to heaven? No! You will be thrown down to the depths!

¹⁶"Whoever listens to you listens to me, and whoever refuses to accept you refuses to accept me. And whoever refuses to accept me refuses to accept the One who sent me."

## Satan Falls

¹⁷When the seventy-two[n] came back, they were very happy and said, "Lord, even the demons obeyed us when we used your name!"

¹⁸Jesus said, "I saw Satan fall like lightning from heaven. ¹⁹Listen, I have given you power to walk on snakes and scorpions, power that is greater than the enemy has. So nothing will hurt you. ²⁰But you should not be happy because the spirits obey you but because your names are written in heaven."

## Jesus Prays to the Father

²¹Then Jesus rejoiced in the Holy Spirit and said, "I praise you, Father, Lord of heaven and earth, because you have hidden these things from the people who are wise and smart. But you have shown them to those who are like little children. Yes, Father, this is what you really wanted.

²²"My Father has given me all things. No one knows who the Son is, except the Father. And no one knows who the Father is, except the Son and those whom the Son chooses to tell."

²³Then Jesus turned to his followers and said privately, "You are blessed to see what you now see. ²⁴I tell you, many prophets and kings wanted to see what you now see, but they did not, and they wanted to hear what you now hear, but they did not."

## The Good Samaritan

²⁵Then an expert on the law stood up to test Jesus, saying, "Teacher, what must I do to get life forever?"

²⁶Jesus said, "What is written in the law? What do you read there?"

²⁷The man answered, "Love the Lord your God with all your heart, all your soul, all your strength, and all your mind."[n] Also, "Love your neighbor as you love yourself."[n]

²⁸Jesus said to him, "Your answer is right. Do this and you will live."

²⁹But the man, wanting to show the importance of his question, said to Jesus, "And who is my neighbor?"

³⁰Jesus answered, "As a man was going down from Jerusalem to Jericho, some robbers attacked him. They tore off his clothes, beat him, and left him lying there, almost dead. ³¹It happened that a priest was going down that road. When he saw the man, he walked by on the other side. ³²Next, a Levite[n] came there, and after he went over and looked at the man, he walked by on the other side of the road. ³³Then a Samaritan[n] traveling down the road came to where the hurt man was. When he saw the man, he felt very sorry for him. ³⁴The Samaritan went to him, poured olive oil and wine[n] on his wounds, and bandaged them. Then he put the hurt man on his own donkey and took him to an inn where he cared for him. ³⁵The next day, the Samaritan brought out two coins,[n] gave them to the innkeeper, and said, 'Take care of this man. If you spend more money on him, I will pay it back to you when I come again.'"

³⁶Then Jesus said, "Which one of these three men do you think was a neighbor to the man who was attacked by the robbers?"

³⁷The expert on the law answered, "The one who showed him mercy."

Jesus said to him, "Then go and do what he did."

## Mary and Martha

³⁸While Jesus and his followers were traveling, Jesus went into a town. A woman named Martha let Jesus stay at her house. ³⁹Martha had a sister named Mary, who was sitting

**10:12 Sodom** *City that God destroyed because the people were so evil.* **10:13 Tyre and Sidon** *Towns where wicked people lived.* **10:13, 15 Korazin, Bethsaida, Capernaum** *Towns by Lake Galilee where Jesus preached to the people.* **10:17 seventy-two** *Some Greek copies read "seventy."* **10:27 "Love . . . mind."** *Quotation from Deuteronomy 6:5.* **10:27 "Love . . . yourself."** *Quotation from Leviticus 19:18.* **10:32 Levite** *Levites were members of the tribe of Levi who helped the Jewish priests with their work in the Temple. Read 1 Chronicles 23:24–32.* **10:33 Samaritan** *Samaritans were people from Samaria. These people were part Jewish, but the Jews did not accept them as true Jews. Samaritans and Jews disliked each other.* **10:34 olive oil and wine** *Oil and wine were used like medicine to soften and clean wounds.* **10:35 coins** *Roman denarii. One coin was the average pay for one day's work.*

at Jesus' feet and listening to him teach. [40]But Martha was busy with all the work to be done. She went in and said, "Lord, don't you care that my sister has left me alone to do all the work? Tell her to help me."

[41]But the Lord answered her, "Martha, Martha, you are worried and upset about many things. [42]Only one thing is important. Mary has chosen the better thing, and it will never be taken away from her."

## Jesus Teaches About Prayer

**11** One time Jesus was praying in a certain place. When he finished, one of his followers said to him, "Lord, teach us to pray as John taught his followers."

[2]Jesus said to them, "When you pray, say:
'Father, may your name always be
kept holy.
May your kingdom come.
[3]Give us the food we need for each
day.
[4]Forgive us for our sins,
because we forgive everyone who
has done wrong to us.
And do not cause us to be
tempted.' "[n]

## Continue to Ask

[5]Then Jesus said to them, "Suppose one of you went to your friend's house at midnight and said to him, 'Friend, loan me three loaves of bread. [6]A friend of mine has come into town to visit me, but I have nothing for him to eat.' [7]Your friend inside the house answers, 'Don't bother me! The door is already locked, and my children and I are in bed. I cannot get up and give you anything.' [8]I tell you, if friendship is not enough to make him get up to give you the bread, your boldness will make him get up and give you whatever you need. [9]So I tell you, ask, and God will give to you. Search, and you will find. Knock, and the door will open for you. [10]Yes, everyone who asks will receive. The one who searches will find. And everyone who knocks will have the door opened. [11]If your children ask for[n] a fish, which of you would give them a snake instead? [12]Or, if your children ask for an egg, would you give them a scorpion? [13]Even though you are bad, you know how to give good things to your children. How much more your heavenly

## dig deeper

### Luke 10:20

The winning Olympians take the stand, the flags begin to rise behind them, and the national anthem of the winner's homeland begins to play. And if it's the music of *your* country playing, you might get tears in your eyes, just like the champion!

As Christians, we all share a true homeland, no matter where we're born here on earth. And we're looking forward to something more spectacular than a competition and more emotional than a fluttering flag. We're going to see Jesus coming again!

When Jesus comes, we'll get something better than a gold medal or a standing ovation. Jesus will give each believer a brand-new body that will never get sick or sin or die. With our new bodies, we will be able to live with God in our forever home. Without failure, without pain, and without sin.

The next time you see your country's flag, remember: when you belong to Jesus, you're a citizen of heaven. While you're living on earth, don't forget your name is written above. And every day—look up! Maybe today will be the day that Jesus returns.

Father will give the Holy Spirit to those who ask him!"

## Jesus' Power Is from God

[14]One time Jesus was sending out a demon who could not talk. When the demon came out, the man who had been unable to speak, then spoke. The people were amazed. [15]But some of them said, "Jesus uses the power of Beelzebul, the ruler of demons, to force demons out of people."

[16]Other people, wanting to test Jesus, asked him to give them a sign from heaven. [17]But knowing their thoughts, he said to them, "Every kingdom that is di-

vided against itself will be destroyed. And a family that is divided against itself will not continue. [18]So if Satan is divided against himself, his kingdom will not continue. You say that I use the power of Beelzebul to force out demons. [19]But if I use the power of Beelzebul to force out demons, what power do your people use to force demons out? So they will be your judges. [20]But if I use the power of God to force out demons, then the kingdom of God has come to you.

[21]"When a strong person with many weapons guards his own house, his possessions are safe. [22]But when someone

11:2–4 'Father . . . tempted.' *Some Greek copies include phrases from Matthew's version of this prayer (Matthew 6:9–13).* 11:11 for *Some Greek copies include the phrase "for bread, which of you would give them a stone, or if they ask for . . ."*

stronger comes and defeats him, the stronger one will take away the weapons the first man trusted and will give away the possessions.

²³"Anyone who is not with me is against me, and anyone who does not work with me is working against me.

## The Empty Person

²⁴"When an evil spirit comes out of a person, it travels through dry places, look-

ing for a place to rest. But when it finds no place, it says, 'I will go back to the house I left.' ²⁵And when it comes back, it finds that house swept clean and made neat. ²⁶Then the evil spirit goes out and brings seven other spirits more evil than it is, and they go in and live there. So the person has even more trouble than before."

## People Who Are Truly Blessed

²⁷As Jesus was saying these things, a woman in the crowd called out to Jesus, "Blessed is the mother who gave birth to you and nursed you."

²⁸But Jesus said, "No, blessed are those who hear the teaching of God and obey it."

## The People Want a Miracle

²⁹As the crowd grew larger, Jesus said, "The people who live today are evil. They want to see a miracle for a sign, but no sign will be given them, except the sign of Jonah.$^n$ ³⁰As Jonah was a sign for those people who lived in Nineveh, the Son of Man will be a sign for the people of this time. ³¹On the Judgment Day the Queen of the South$^n$ will stand up with the people who live now. She will show they are guilty, because she came from far away to listen to Solomon's wise teaching. And I tell you that someone greater than Solomon is here. ³²On the Judgment Day the people of Nineveh will stand up with the people who live now, and they will show that you are guilty. When Jonah preached to them, they were sorry and changed their lives. And I tell you that someone greater than Jonah is here.

## Be a Light for the World

³³"No one lights a lamp and puts it in a secret place or under a bowl, but on a lampstand so the people who come in can see. ³⁴Your eye is a light for the body. When your eyes are good, your whole body will be full of light. But when your eyes are evil, your whole body will be full of darkness. ³⁵So be careful not to let the light in you become darkness. ³⁶If your

whole body is full of light, and none of it is dark, then you will shine bright, as when a lamp shines on you."

## Jesus Accuses the Pharisees

³⁷After Jesus had finished speaking, a Pharisee asked Jesus to eat with him. So Jesus went in and sat at the table. ³⁸But the Pharisee was surprised when he saw that Jesus did not wash his hands$^n$ before the meal. ³⁹The Lord said to him, "You Pharisees clean the outside of the cup and the dish, but inside you are full of greed and evil. ⁴⁰You foolish people! The same one who made what is outside also made what is inside. ⁴¹So give what is in your dishes to the poor, and then you will be fully clean. ⁴²How terrible for you Pharisees! You give God one-tenth of even your mint, your rue, and every other plant in your garden. But you fail to be fair to others and to love God. These are the things you should do while continuing to do those other things. ⁴³How terrible for you Pharisees, because you love to have the most important seats in the synagogues, and you love to be greeted with respect in the marketplaces. ⁴⁴How terrible for you, because you are like hidden graves, which people walk on without knowing."

## Jesus Talks to Experts on the Law

⁴⁵One of the experts on the law said to Jesus, "Teacher, when you say these things, you are insulting us, too."

⁴⁶Jesus answered, "How terrible for you, you experts on the law! You make strict rules that are very hard for people to obey, but you yourselves don't even try to follow those rules. ⁴⁷How terrible for you, because you build tombs for the prophets whom your ancestors killed! ⁴⁸And now you show that you approve of what your ancestors did. They killed the prophets, and you build tombs for them! ⁴⁹This is why in his wisdom God said, 'I will send prophets and apostles to them. They will kill some, and they will treat others cruelly.' ⁵⁰So you who live now will be punished for the deaths of all the prophets who were killed since the beginning of the world— ⁵¹from the killing of Abel to the killing of Zechariah,$^n$ who died between the altar and the Temple. Yes, I tell you that you who are alive now will be punished for them all.

⁵²"How terrible for you, you experts on the law. You have taken away the key to learning about God. You yourselves would not learn, and you stopped others from learning, too."

**did you know?**

78% of girls agree it's more important to be smart than popular.

—*Business Wire, 10/10/03,* http://www.rab.com/newrst/article_view.cfm?id=308&type=article2

## cool

### Measuring Wealth

In 2004, the richest person in the world was "worth" $46.6 billion. Since there are about 6.4 billion people in the world, that means he has enough money to give every single person about seven dollars. Whoa! That's a lot of money!

But do you know what God thinks about judging people by how much money they have? Luke 12:15 says "Life is not measured by how much one owns." Make sure your focus in life isn't on being wealthy. Instead, try to be rich in love and faith . . . things that really matter and really last!

---

**11:29 sign of Jonah** *Jonah's three days in the fish are like Jesus' three days in the tomb. See Matthew 12:40.* **11:31 Queen of the South** *The Queen of Sheba. She traveled a thousand miles to learn God's wisdom from Solomon. Read 1 Kings 10:1–3.* **11:38 wash his hands** *This was a Jewish religious custom that the Pharisees thought was very important.* **11:51 Abel . . . Zechariah** *In the Hebrew Old Testament, the first and last men to be murdered.*

⁵³When Jesus left, the teachers of the law and the Pharisees began to give him trouble, asking him questions about many things, ⁵⁴trying to catch him saying something wrong.

## Don't Be Like the Pharisees

**12** So many thousands of people had gathered that they were stepping on each other. Jesus spoke first to his followers, saying, "Beware of the yeast of the Pharisees, because they are hypocrites. ²Everything that is hidden will be shown, and everything that is secret will be made known. ³What you have said in the dark will be heard in the light, and what you have whispered in an inner room will be shouted from the housetops.

⁴"I tell you, my friends, don't be afraid of people who can kill the body but after that can do nothing more to hurt you. ⁵I will show you the one to fear. Fear the one who has the power to kill you and also to throw you into hell. Yes, this is the one you should fear.

⁶"Five sparrows are sold for only two pennies, and God does not forget any of them. ⁷But God even knows how many hairs you have on your head. Don't be afraid. You are worth much more than many sparrows.

## Don't Be Ashamed of Jesus

⁸"I tell you, all those who stand before others and say they believe in me, I, the Son of Man, will say before the angels of God that they belong to me. ⁹But all who stand before others and say they do not believe in me, I will say before the angels of God that they do not belong to me.

¹⁰"Anyone who speaks against the Son of Man can be forgiven, but anyone who speaks against the Holy Spirit will not be forgiven.

¹¹"When you are brought into the synagogues before the leaders and other powerful people, don't worry about how to defend yourself or what to say. ¹²At that time the Holy Spirit will teach you what you must say."

## Jesus Warns Against Selfishness

¹³Someone in the crowd said to Jesus, "Teacher, tell my brother to divide with me the property our father left us."

¹⁴But Jesus said to him, "Who said I should judge or decide between you?" ¹⁵Then Jesus said to them, "Be careful and guard against all kinds of greed. Life is not measured by how much one owns."

¹⁶Then Jesus told this story: "There was a rich man who had some land, which grew a good crop. ¹⁷He thought to himself, 'What will I do? I have no place to keep all my crops.' ¹⁸Then he said, 'This is what I will do: I will tear down my barns and build bigger ones, and there I will store all my grain and other goods. ¹⁹Then I can say to myself, "I have enough good things stored to last for many years. Rest, eat, drink, and enjoy life!"'

²⁰"But God said to him, 'Foolish man! Tonight your life will be taken from you. So who will get those things you have prepared for yourself?'

²¹"This is how it will be for those who store up things for themselves and are not rich toward God."

### god's promises

Luke 15:7

Imagine your parents invited your whole class to your birthday party and they all came. Even that girl who used to make fun of you showed up . . . with a gift! Would you feel glad she came? Would you treat her extra nice? Would you give her the biggest piece of cake?

Sound strange? Well, it's the kind of thing Jesus would do. In Luke 15:7, he explains that God and his angels get more excited about one sinner who changes her life than about ninety-nine people who already live good lives. Jesus would feel happier about the classmate who had changed her attitude than about the rest of his friends who already treated him well.

Jesus wasn't saying that he doesn't love people who are good. No, he loves them, too! But some people are far from God, and he really wants them to come to him. Does that describe you? Maybe you have sins that you haven't confessed to him. You might even think that you're too "lost" for him to care. But God will never reject you. The Bible promises that God and his angels will have a huge celebration when you commit your life to him!

*God and his angels get excited about one sinner who changes her life.*

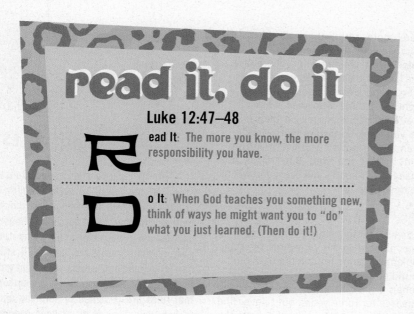

**read it, do it**

Luke 12:47—48

**R**ead It: The more you know, the more responsibility you have.

**D**o It: When God teaches you something new, think of ways he might want you to "do" what you just learned. (Then do it!)

## Don't Worry

²²Jesus said to his followers, "So I tell you, don't worry about the food you need to live, or about the clothes you need for your body. ²³Life is more than food, and the body is more than clothes. ²⁴Look at the birds. They don't plant or harvest, they don't have storerooms or barns, but God feeds them. And you are worth much more than birds. ²⁵You cannot add any time to your life by worrying about it. ²⁶If you cannot do even the little things, then why worry about the big things? ²⁷Consider how the lilies grow; they don't work or make clothes for themselves. But I tell you that even Solomon with his riches was not dressed as beautifully as one of these flowers. ²⁸God clothes the grass in the field, which is alive today but tomorrow is thrown into the fire. So how much more will God clothe you? Don't have so little faith! ²⁹Don't always think about what you will eat or what you will drink, and don't keep worrying. ³⁰All the people in the world are trying to get these things, and your Father knows you need them. ³¹But seek God's kingdom, and all your other needs will be met as well.

## Don't Trust in Money

³²"Don't fear, little flock, because your Father wants to give you the kingdom. ³³Sell your possessions and give to the poor. Get for yourselves purses that will not wear out, the treasure in heaven that never runs out, where thieves can't steal and moths can't destroy. ³⁴Your heart will be where your treasure is.

## Always Be Ready

³⁵"Be dressed, ready for service, and have your lamps shining. ³⁶Be like servants who are waiting for their master to come home from a wedding party. When he comes and knocks, the servants immediately open the door for him. ³⁷They will be blessed when their master comes home, because he sees that they were watching for him. I tell you the truth, the master will dress himself to serve and tell the servants to sit at the table, and he will serve them. ³⁸Those servants will be blessed when he comes in and finds them still waiting, even if it is midnight or later. ³⁹"Remember this: If the owner of the house knew what time a thief was coming, he would not allow the thief to enter his house. ⁴⁰So you also must be ready, because the Son of Man will come at a time when you don't expect him!"

## Who Is the Trusted Servant?

⁴¹Peter said, "Lord, did you tell this story to us or to all people?"

⁴²The Lord said, "Who is the wise and trusted servant that the master trusts to give the other servants their food at the right time? ⁴³When the master comes and finds the servant doing his work, the servant will be blessed. ⁴⁴I tell you the truth, the master will choose that servant to take care of everything he owns. ⁴⁵But suppose the servant thinks to himself, 'My master will not come back soon,' and he begins to beat the other servants, men and women, and to eat and drink and get drunk. ⁴⁶The master will come when that servant is not ready and is not expecting him. Then the master will cut him in pieces and send him away to be with the others who don't obey.

⁴⁷"The servant who knows what his master wants but is not ready, or who does not do what the master wants, will be beaten with many blows! ⁴⁸But the servant who does not know what his master wants and does things that should be punished will be beaten with few blows. From everyone who has been given much, much will be demanded. And from the one trusted with much, much more will be expected.

## Jesus Causes Division

⁴⁹"I came to set fire to the world, and I wish it were already burning! ⁵⁰I have a baptism[n] to suffer through, and I feel very troubled until it is over. ⁵¹Do you think I came to give peace to the earth? No, I tell you, I came to divide it. ⁵²From now on, a family with five people will be divided, three against two, and two against three. ⁵³They will be divided: father against son and son against father, mother against daughter and daughter

# Q&A

**Q** Was there really a "big bang?"

**A** The Bible says nothing about a "big bang" theory, but we *do* know that God created the whole world (check out Genesis 1—3). These chapters give us a beautiful description of our creative, all-powerful God in action!

**12:50 I . . . baptism** *Jesus was talking about the suffering he would soon go through.*

against mother, mother-in-law against daughter-in-law and daughter-in-law against mother-in-law."

## Understanding the Times

⁵⁴Then Jesus said to the people, "When you see clouds coming up in the west, you say, 'It's going to rain,' and it happens. ⁵⁵When you feel the wind begin to blow from the south, you say, 'It will be a hot day,' and it happens. ⁵⁶Hypocrites! You know how to understand the appearance of the earth and sky. Why don't you understand what is happening now?

## Settle Your Problems

⁵⁷"Why can't you decide for yourselves what is right? ⁵⁸If your enemy is taking you to court, try hard to settle it on the way. If you don't, your enemy might take you to the judge, and the judge might turn you over to the officer, and the officer might throw you into jail. ⁵⁹I tell you, you will not get out of there until you have paid everything you owe."

## Change Your Hearts

**13** At that time some people were there who told Jesus that Pilate⁷ had killed some people from Galilee while they were worshiping. He mixed their blood with the blood of the animals they were sacrificing to God. ²Jesus answered, "Do you think this happened to them because they

were more sinful than all others from Galilee? ³No, I tell you. But unless you change your hearts and lives, you will be destroyed as they were! ⁴What about those eighteen people who died when the tower of Siloam fell on them? Do you think they were more sinful than all the others who live in Jerusalem? ⁵No, I tell you. But unless you change your hearts and lives, you will all be destroyed too!"

## The Useless Tree

⁶Jesus told this story: "A man had a fig tree planted in his vineyard. He came looking for some fruit on the tree, but he found none. ⁷So the man said to his gardener, 'I have been looking for fruit on this tree for three years, but I never find any. Cut it down. Why should it waste the ground?' ⁸But the servant answered, 'Master, let the tree have one more year to produce fruit. Let me dig up the dirt around it and put on some fertilizer. ⁹If the tree produces fruit next year, good. But if not, you can cut it down.' "

## Jesus Heals on the Sabbath

¹⁰Jesus was teaching in one of the synagogues on the Sabbath day. ¹¹A woman was there who, for eighteen years, had an evil spirit in her that made her crippled. Her back was always bent; she could not stand up straight. ¹²When Jesus saw her, he called her over and said,

"Woman, you are free from your sickness." ¹³Jesus put his hands on her, and immediately she was able to stand up straight and began praising God.

¹⁴The synagogue leader was angry because Jesus healed on the Sabbath day. He said to the people, "There are six days when one has to work. So come to be healed on one of those days, and not on the Sabbath day."

¹⁵The Lord answered, "You hypocrites! Doesn't each of you untie your work animals and lead them to drink water every day—even on the Sabbath day? ¹⁶This woman that I healed, a daughter of Abraham, has been held by Satan for eighteen years. Surely it is not wrong for her to be freed from her sickness on a Sabbath day!" ¹⁷When Jesus said this, all of those who were criticizing him were ashamed, but the entire crowd rejoiced at all the wonderful things Jesus was doing.

## Stories of Mustard Seed and Yeast

¹⁸Then Jesus said, "What is God's kingdom like? What can I compare it with? ¹⁹It is like a mustard seed that a man plants

## read it, do it

### Luke 22:40

**R**ead It: Ask God to help you fight temptation.

**D**o It: Don't wait until you're tempted to pray for help! Every morning (and whenever you remember), ask God to help you say no to sin that day.

**13:1 Pilate** *Pontius Pilate was the Roman governor of Judea from A.D. 26 to A.D. 36.*

in his garden. The seed grows and becomes a tree, and the wild birds build nests in its branches."

²⁰Jesus said again, "What can I compare God's kingdom with? ²¹It is like yeast that a woman took and hid in a large tub of flour until it made all the dough rise."

## The Narrow Door

²²Jesus was teaching in every town and village as he traveled toward Jerusalem. ²³Someone said to Jesus, "Lord, will only a few people be saved?"

Jesus said, ²⁴"Try hard to enter through the narrow door, because many people will try to enter there, but they will not be able. ²⁵When the owner of the house gets up and closes the door, you can stand outside and knock on the door and say, 'Sir, open the door for us.' But he will answer, 'I don't know you or where you come from.' ²⁶Then you will say, 'We ate and drank with you, and you taught in the streets of our town.' ²⁷But he will say to you, 'I don't know you or where you come from. Go away from me, all you who do evil!' ²⁸You will cry and grind your teeth with pain when you see Abraham, Isaac, Jacob, and all the prophets in God's kingdom, but you yourselves thrown outside. ²⁹People will come from the east, west, north, and south and will sit down at the table in the kingdom of God. ³⁰There are those who are last now who will be first in the future. And there are those who are first now who will be last in the future."

## Jesus Will Die in Jerusalem

³¹At that time some Pharisees came to Jesus and said, "Go away from here! Herod wants to kill you!"

³²Jesus said to them, "Go tell that fox Herod, 'Today and tomorrow I am forcing demons out and healing people. Then, on the third day, I will reach my goal.' ³³Yet I must be on my way today and tomorrow and the next day. Surely it cannot be right for a prophet to be killed anywhere except in Jerusalem.

³⁴"Jerusalem, Jerusalem! You kill the prophets and stone to death those who are sent to you. Many times I wanted to gather your people as a hen gathers her chicks under her wings, but you would not let me. ³⁵Now your house is left completely empty. I tell you, you will not see

# Q & A

**Q** My parents died when I was little, and I've grown up in different foster homes. How can I stop feeling so lonely?

**A** Loneliness comes to everyone at different times so you might not be able to get rid of it completely, but God can help it hurt less. Psalm 34:18 says that "the Lord is close to the brokenhearted." Also, Jesus understands what loneliness feels like. Isaiah 53:3 says that Jesus was "hated and rejected by people. He had much pain and suffering. People would not even look at him." Talk to God when you're lonely. He's the best friend any of us could ever have!

me until that time when you will say, 'God bless the One who comes in the name of the Lord.' "ⁿ

## Healing on the Sabbath

**14** On a Sabbath day, when Jesus went to eat at the home of a leading Pharisee, the people were watching Jesus very closely. ²And in front of him was a man with dropsy.ⁿ ³Jesus said to the Pharisees and experts on the law, "Is it right or wrong to heal on the Sabbath day?" ⁴But they would not answer his question. So Jesus took the man, healed him, and sent him away. ⁵Jesus said to the Pharisees and teachers of the law, "If your childⁿ or ox falls into a well on the Sabbath day, will you not pull him out quickly?" ⁶And they could not answer him.

## Don't Make Yourself Important

⁷When Jesus noticed that some of the guests were choosing the best places to sit, he told this story: ⁸"When someone invites you to a wedding feast, don't take the most important seat, because someone more important than you may have been invited. ⁹The host, who invited both

of you, will come to you and say, 'Give this person your seat.' Then you will be embarrassed and will have to move to the last place. ¹⁰So when you are invited, go sit in a seat that is not important. When the host comes to you, he may say, 'Friend, move up here to a more important place.' Then all the other guests will respect you. ¹¹All who make themselves great will be made humble, but those who make themselves humble will be made great."

## You Will Be Rewarded

¹²Then Jesus said to the man who had invited him, "When you give a lunch or a dinner, don't invite only your friends, your family, your other relatives, and your rich neighbors. At another time they will invite you to eat with them, and you will be repaid. ¹³Instead, when you give a feast, invite the poor, the crippled, the lame, and the blind. ¹⁴Then you will be blessed, because they have nothing and cannot pay you back. But you will be repaid when the good people rise from the dead."

## A Story About a Big Banquet

¹⁵One of those at the table with Jesus heard these things and said to him, "Blessed are the people who will share in the meal in God's kingdom."

¹⁶Jesus said to him, "A man gave a big banquet and invited many people. ¹⁷When it was time to eat, the man sent his servant to tell the guests, 'Come. Everything is ready.'

¹⁸"But all the guests made excuses. The first one said, 'I have just bought a field, and I must go look at it. Please excuse me.' ¹⁹Another said, 'I have just bought five pairs of oxen; I must go and try them. Please excuse me.' ²⁰A third person said, 'I just got married; I can't come.' ²¹So the servant returned and told his master what had happened. Then the master became angry and said, 'Go at once into the streets and alleys of the town, and bring in the poor, the crippled, the blind, and the lame.' ²²Later the servant said to him, 'Master, I did what you commanded, but we still have room.' ²³The master said to the servant, 'Go out to the roads and country lanes, and urge the people there to come so my house will be full. ²⁴I tell you, none of those whom I invited first will eat with me.' "

**Luke**

---

**13:35** 'God . . . Lord.' *Quotation from Psalm 118:26.* **14:2** dropsy *A sickness that causes the body to swell larger and larger.* **14:5** child *Some Greek copies read "donkey."*

## The Cost of Being Jesus' Follower

<sup>25</sup>Large crowds were traveling with Jesus, and he turned and said to them, <sup>26</sup>"If anyone comes to me but loves his father, mother, wife, children, brothers, or sisters—or even life—more than me, he cannot be my follower. <sup>27</sup>Whoever is not willing to carry his cross and follow me cannot be my follower. <sup>28</sup>If you want to build a tower, you first sit down and decide how much it will cost, to see if you have enough money to finish the job. <sup>29</sup>If you don't, you might lay the foundation, but you would not be able to finish. Then all who would see it would make fun of you, <sup>30</sup>saying, 'This person began to build but was not able to finish.'

<sup>31</sup>"If a king is going to fight another king, first he will sit down and plan. He will decide if he and his ten thousand soldiers can defeat the other king who has twenty thousand soldiers. <sup>32</sup>If he can't, then while the other king is still far away, he will send some people to speak to him and ask for peace. <sup>33</sup>In the same way, you must give up everything you have to be my follower.

## Don't Lose Your Influence

<sup>34</sup>"Salt is good, but if it loses its salty taste, you cannot make it salty again. <sup>35</sup>It is no good for the soil or for manure; it is thrown away.

"Let those with ears use them and listen."

## A Lost Sheep, a Lost Coin

**15** The tax collectors and sinners all came to listen to Jesus. <sup>2</sup>But the Pharisees and the teachers of the law began to complain: "Look, this man welcomes sinners and even eats with them."

<sup>3</sup>Then Jesus told them this story: <sup>4</sup>"Suppose one of you has a hundred sheep but loses one of them. Then he will leave the other ninety-nine sheep in the open field and go out and look for the lost sheep until he finds it. <sup>5</sup>And when he finds it, he happily puts it on his shoulders <sup>6</sup>and goes home. He calls to his friends and neighbors and says, 'Be happy with me because I found my lost sheep.' <sup>7</sup>In the same way, I tell you there is more joy in heaven over one sinner who changes his heart and life, than over ninety-nine good people who don't need to change.

<sup>8</sup>"Suppose a woman has ten silver coins,<sup>n</sup> but loses one. She will light a lamp, sweep the house, and look carefully for the coin until she finds it. <sup>9</sup>And when she finds it, she will call her friends and neighbors and say, 'Be happy with me because I have found the coin that I lost.' <sup>10</sup>In the same way, there is joy in the presence of the angels of God when one sinner changes his heart and life."

## The Son Who Left Home

<sup>11</sup>Then Jesus said, "A man had two sons. <sup>12</sup>The younger son said to his father, 'Give me my share of the property.' So the father divided the property between his two sons. <sup>13</sup>Then the younger son gathered up all that was his and traveled far away to another country.

# Christian Girls Around the World
## Myrthe: *The Netherlands*

Ten-year-old Myrthe lives in Nieuw-Vennep, a town on the busy west side of the Netherlands (also known as Holland) and near the capital city of Amsterdam. It's also very close to the Schiphol Airport, so she can hear an airplane go by every five minutes or so! She says the prettiest thing about her area is the windmills.

When people think about the Netherlands, they often imagine those windmills, as well as tulips . . . and bicycles! Everybody has a bike in Holland. That's how most Dutch kids get to school (although some of them just walk) and even moms ride their bikes to do their daily shopping.

Holland is a very small country, but about 16 million people live there. To get a feeling of how crowded that is, imagine the entire population of Canada living in New Jersey!

The kids there enjoy playing outside, watching TV, playing sports, participating in clubs, and playing computer games. Myrthe enjoys doing crafts when she's on her own, but when she's with her friends, she likes talking, listening to CDs, going for a walk, shopping, or riding her bike. She also enjoys hanging out with her grandmother. Myrthe has a very good relationship with her whole family . . . even her older brother!

When Myrthe's friends find out that she's a Christian, they don't make fun of her because many people in Holland go to church. This makes it a little easier for her to talk with them about God. That's a good thing for Myrthe because she's very shy! At church, she enjoys participating in preteen Sunday School programs where the kids sing, learn from the Bible, watch movies, and do drama. Being surrounded by Christians, she gets a lot of encouragement to stay strong in her faith. Myrthe also enjoys using a special corner of her home that her mom prepared for anyone who wants to have a peaceful and quiet place to pray and read their Bible—and she's been going there more and more!

By the way, just in case you were wondering . . . people don't wear wooden shoes in Holland anymore!

**15:8 silver coins** *Roman denarii. One coin was the average pay for one day's work.*

your son.'[n] [22]But the father said to his servants, 'Hurry! Bring the best clothes and put them on him. Also, put a ring on his finger and sandals on his feet. [23]And get our fat calf and kill it so we can have a feast and celebrate. [24]My son was dead, but now he is alive again! He was lost, but now he is found!' So they began to celebrate.

[25]"The older son was in the field, and as he came closer to the house, he heard the sound of music and dancing. [26]So he called to one of the servants and asked what all this meant. [27]The servant said, 'Your brother has come back, and your father killed the fat calf, because your brother came home safely.' [28]The older son was angry and would not go in to the feast. So his father went out and begged him to come in. [29]But the older son said to his father, 'I have served you like a slave for many years and have always obeyed your commands. But you never gave me even a young goat to have at a feast with my friends. [30]But your other son, who wasted all your money on prostitutes, comes home, and you kill the fat calf for him!' [31]The father said to him, 'Son, you are always with me, and all that I have is yours. [32]We had to celebrate and be happy because your brother was dead, but now he is alive. He was lost, but now he is found.'"

## True Wealth

**16** Jesus also said to his followers, "Once there was a rich man who had a manager to take care of his business. This manager was accused of cheating him. [2]So he called the manager in and said to him, 'What is this I hear about you? Give me a report of what you have done with my money, because you can't be my manager any longer.' [3]The manager thought to himself, 'What will I do since my master is taking my job away from me? I am

## dig deeper

### Luke 17:22—27

You might be planning to go to school tomorrow. Or if it's the weekend or vacation, your plans could include relaxing in front of the TV. We make plans according to what we *think* will happen. But does anyone really *know* what tomorrow will be like? The Bible says that only God knows what the future holds—not weathermen, astrologers, or anyone else.

Luke 17:22—27 tells us that we can make plans and carry on with life, but we should never forget that Jesus Christ could come back at any moment. The climax of history could happen anytime.

Every day, people experience surprising things that change the rest of their lives. A person might suddenly die in an accident. Or a young teenager might find out she is very ill. We never know when something might happen that will change our lives and the lives of those around us.

If life is so uncertain, how are Christians supposed to act? The Bible says we should always give top priority to our relationship with the Lord, including Bible reading and prayer. That doesn't mean that we can't make plans for the future. It does mean, however, that those plans could be interrupted. Don't forget who the real Planner is!

There he wasted his money in foolish living. [14]After he had spent everything, a time came when there was no food anywhere in the country, and the son was poor and hungry. [15]So he got a job with one of the citizens there who sent the son into the fields to feed pigs. [16]The son was so hungry that he wanted to eat the pods the pigs were eating, but no one gave him anything. [17]When he realized what he was doing, he thought, 'All of my father's servants have plenty of food. But I am here, almost dying with hunger. [18]I will leave and return to my father and say to him, "Father, I have sinned against God and against you. [19]I am no longer worthy to be called your son, but let me be like one of your servants."' [20]So the son left and went to his father.

"While the son was still a long way off, his father saw him and felt sorry for his son. So the father ran to him and hugged and kissed him. [21]The son said, 'Father, I have sinned against God and against you. I am no longer worthy to be called

> FATHER, I HAVE SINNED AGAINST GOD AND AGAINST YOU. I AM NO LONGER WORTHY TO BE CALLED YOUR SON . . .

**15:21 son** *Some Greek copies continue, "but let me be like one of your servants" (see verse 19).*

not strong enough to dig ditches, and I am ashamed to beg. [4]I know what I'll do so that when I lose my job people will welcome me into their homes.'

[5]"So the manager called in everyone who owed the master any money. He asked the first one, 'How much do you owe?' [6]He answered, 'Eight hundred gallons of olive oil.' The manager said to him, 'Take your bill, sit down quickly, and write four hundred gallons.' [7]Then the manager asked another one, 'How much do you owe?' He answered, 'One thousand bushels of wheat.' Then the manager said to him, 'Take your bill and write eight hundred bushels.' [8]So, the master praised the dishonest manager for being clever. Yes, worldly people are more clever with their own kind than spiritual people are.

[9]"I tell you, make friends for yourselves using worldly riches so that when those riches are gone, you will be welcomed in those homes that continue forever. [10]Whoever can be trusted with a little can also be trusted with a lot, and whoever is dishonest with a little is dishonest with a lot. [11]If you cannot be trusted with worldly riches, then who will trust you with true riches? [12]And if you cannot be trusted with things that belong to someone else, who will give you things of your own?

[13]"No servant can serve two masters. The servant will hate one master and love the other, or will follow one master and refuse to follow the other. You cannot serve both God and worldly riches."

## God's Law Cannot Be Changed

[14]The Pharisees, who loved money, were listening to all these things and made fun of Jesus. [15]He said to them, "You make yourselves look good in front of people, but God knows what is really in your hearts. What is important to people is hateful in God's sight.

[16]"The law of Moses and the writings of the prophets were preached until John[n] came. Since then the Good News about the kingdom of God is being told, and everyone tries to enter it by force. [17]It would be easier for heaven and earth to pass away than for the smallest part of a letter in the law to be changed.

## Divorce and Remarriage

[18]"If a man divorces his wife and marries another woman, he is guilty of adultery, and the man who marries a divorced woman is also guilty of adultery."

## The Rich Man and Lazarus

[19]Jesus said, "There was a rich man who always dressed in the finest clothes and lived in luxury every day. [20]And a very poor man named Lazarus, whose body was covered with sores, was laid at the rich man's gate. [21]He wanted to eat only the small pieces of food that fell from the rich man's table. And the dogs would come and lick his sores. [22]Later, Lazarus died, and the angels carried him to the arms of Abraham. The rich man died, too, and was buried. [23]In the place of the dead, he was in much pain. The rich man saw Abraham far away with Lazarus at his side. [24]He called, 'Father Abraham, have mercy on me! Send Lazarus to dip his finger in water and cool my tongue, because I am suffering in this fire!' [25]But Abraham said, 'Child, remember when you were alive you had the good things in life, but bad things happened to Lazarus. Now he is comforted here, and you are suffering. [26]Besides, there is a big pit between you and us, so no one can cross over to you, and no one can leave there and come here.' [27]The rich man said, 'Father, then please send Lazarus to my father's house. [28]I have five brothers, and Lazarus could warn them so that they will not come to this place of pain.' [29]But Abraham said, 'They have the

## Shine Your Light

Joleen doesn't have to go downtown or across the country to show God's love to troubled children. When she steps out of her bedroom, two energetic little girls beg for her attention. Amy and Jessie live with Joleen's family while their mom works at getting her life clean from drugs and learns how to be a good parent.

Joleen isn't the foster parent—that's her mom and dad's job. But she does play an important role in Amy and Jessie's lives. The sisters watch Joleen and see what a Christian girl lives like—how she relates to her parents, treats her friends, works hard at school, and has fun just being a girl.

Kids who live with abusive or drug addicted parents don't necessarily know what a healthy family life looks like. They often have to take care of themselves instead of having a loving parent meet their needs. Every time Joleen reads them stories, paints their nails, or takes them outside to play, they experience her love—and God's.

Even if you don't have foster brothers or sisters, you probably know children in your school or your neighborhood who are hurting and could experience God's love through you!

16:16 **John** *John the Baptist, who preached to people about Christ's coming (Matthew 3, Luke 3).*

# WHAT'S YOUR LOVE STYLE?

Mark 12:30 says, "Love the Lord your God with all your heart, all your soul, all your mind and all your strength." Take this quiz to find out what your love style is.

**1. Your favorite types of books or movies are:**

   a. Romance
   b. Drama
   c. Mysteries or documentaries
   d. Adventure or sports

**2. Your idea of serving God is:**

   a. Being a kind friend to a lonely girl at school.
   b. Praying for people going through difficult times.
   c. Going to Sunday school or a Bible study.
   d. Helping your non-Christian elderly neighbors paint their fence.

**3. You think you should probably remember this verse:**

   a. "With all your heart you must do what God wants as people who are obeying Christ" (Ephesians 6:6).
   b. "It is worthless to have the whole world if they lose their souls" (Matthew 16:26).
   c. "Think only about the things in heaven, not the things on earth" (Colossians 3:2).
   d. "Finally, be strong in the Lord and in his great power" (Ephesians 6:10).

**4. The thing about God that you're most grateful for is:**

   a. That he loves you so much.
   b. That he has forgiven you for your sins.
   c. That he's always there to show you the way to live.
   d. That he gives you strength in tough situations.

## Are you all heart, soul, mind, or strength?

**If you answered mostly As,** you have a loving heart! You are sensitive about the feelings of others and can be very emotional at times. Sometimes your heart just bubbles over with love for God.

**If you answered mostly Bs,** you're very spiritual! Being a Christian is something you're thankful for deep down inside, in your soul. You love to spend time worshiping God and talking with him.

**If you answered mostly Cs,** you're a real thinker! You love to learn about God and enjoy studying his Word. You think a lot about things you learn and make a real effort to apply them in your life.

**If you answered mostly Ds,** you're a servant! You don't want to just be a Christian, you want to do the things God asks Christians to do. You love challenges and enjoy helping out people who need help.

All four of these qualities are wonderful! Keep doing what you're doing, but ask God to help you to love him with all four parts of you: your heart, your soul, your mind, and your strength!

law of Moses and the writings of the prophets; let them learn from them.' ³⁰The rich man said, 'No, father Abraham! If someone goes to them from the dead, they would believe and change their hearts and lives.' ³¹But Abraham said to him, 'If they will not listen to Moses and the prophets, they will not listen to someone who comes back from the dead.' "

## Sin and Forgiveness

**17** Jesus said to his followers, "Things that cause people to sin will happen, but how terrible for the person who causes them to happen! ²It would be better for you to be thrown into the sea with a large stone around your neck than to cause one of these little ones to sin. ³So be careful!

"If another follower sins, warn him, and if he is sorry and stops sinning, forgive him. ⁴If he sins against you seven times in one day and says that he is sorry each time, forgive him."

## How Big Is Your Faith?

⁵The apostles said to the Lord, "Give us more faith!"

⁶The Lord said, "If your faith were the size of a mustard seed, you could say to this mulberry tree, 'Dig yourself up and plant yourself in the sea,' and it would obey you.

## Be Good Servants

⁷"Suppose one of you has a servant who has been plowing the ground or

caring for the sheep. When the servant comes in from working in the field, would you say, 'Come in and sit down to eat'? ⁸No, you would say to him, 'Prepare something for me to eat. Then get yourself ready and serve me. After I finish eating and drinking, you can eat.' ⁹The servant does not get any special thanks for doing what his master commanded. ¹⁰It is the same with you. When you have done everything you are told to do, you should say, 'We are unworthy servants; we have only done the work we should do.' "

## Be Thankful

¹¹While Jesus was on his way to Jerusalem, he was going through the area between Samaria and Galilee. ¹²As he came into a small town, ten men who had a skin disease met him there. They did not come close to Jesus ¹³but called to him, "Jesus! Master! Have mercy on us!"

¹⁴When Jesus saw the men, he said, "Go and show yourselves to the priests."[n]

As the ten men were going, they were healed. ¹⁵When one of them saw that he was healed, he went back to Jesus, praising God in a loud voice. ¹⁶Then he bowed down at Jesus' feet and thanked him. (And this man was a Samaritan.) ¹⁷Jesus said, "Weren't ten men healed? Where are the other nine? ¹⁸Is this Samaritan the only one who came back to thank God?" ¹⁹Then Jesus said to him, "Stand up and go on your way. You were healed because you believed."

## God's Kingdom Is Within You

²⁰Some of the Pharisees asked Jesus, "When will the kingdom of God come?"

Jesus answered, "God's kingdom is coming, but not in a way that you will be able to see with your eyes. ²¹People will not say, 'Look, here it is!' or, 'There it is!' because God's kingdom is within[n] you."

²²Then Jesus said to his followers, "The time will come when you will want very much to see one of the days of the Son of Man. But you will not see it. ²³People will say to you, 'Look, there he is!' or, 'Look, here he is!' Stay where you are; don't go away and search.

## When Jesus Comes Again

²⁴"When the Son of Man comes again, he will shine like lightning, which flashes across the sky and lights it up from one side to the other. ²⁵But first he must suffer many things and be rejected by the people of this time. ²⁶When the Son of Man comes again, it will be as it was when Noah lived. ²⁷People were eating, drinking, marrying, and giving their children to be married until the day Noah entered the boat. Then the flood came and killed them all. ²⁸It will be the same as during the time of Lot. People were eating, drinking, buying, selling, planting, and building. ²⁹But the day Lot left Sodom,[n] fire and sulfur rained down from the sky and killed them all. ³⁰This is how it will be when the Son of Man comes again.

³¹"On that day, a person who is on the roof and whose belongings are in the house should not go inside to get them. A person who is in the field should not go back home. ³²Remember Lot's wife.[n] ³³Those who try to keep their lives will lose them. But those who give up their lives will save them. ³⁴I tell you, on that night two people will be sleeping in one bed; one will be taken and the other will be left. ³⁵There will be two women grinding grain together; one will be taken, and the other will be left. [³⁶Two people will be in the field. One will be taken, and the other will be left.]"[n]

³⁷The followers asked Jesus, "Where will this be, Lord?"

**17:14 show . . . priests** The Law of Moses said a priest must say when a person with a skin disease became well. **17:21 within** Or "among." **17:29 Sodom** City that God destroyed because the people were so evil. **17:32 Lot's wife** A story about what happened to Lot's wife is found in Genesis 19:15–17, 26. **17:36 Two . . . left.** Some Greek copies do not contain the bracketed text.

Jesus answered, "Where there is a dead body, there the vultures will gather."

## God Will Answer His People

**18** Then Jesus used this story to teach his followers that they should always pray and never lose hope. [2]"In a certain town there was a judge who did not respect God or care about people. [3]In that same town there was a widow who kept coming to this judge, saying, 'Give me my rights against my enemy.' [4]For a while the judge refused to help her. But afterwards, he thought to himself, 'Even though I don't respect God or care about

**On average, kids only spend 15 minutes a day with their parents.**

—Sonna, Linda, Ph.D. *The Everything Tween Book*. Avon, Massachusetts: Adams Media Corporation, 2003. p. 96

**did you know?**

people, [5]I will see that she gets her rights. Otherwise she will continue to bother me until I am worn out.' "

[6]The Lord said, "Listen to what the unfair judge said. [7]God will always give what is right to his people who cry to him night and day, and he will not be slow to answer them. [8]I tell you, God will help his people quickly. But when the Son of Man comes again, will he find those on earth who believe in him?"

## Being Right with God

[9]Jesus told this story to some people who thought they were very good and looked down on everyone else: [10]"A Pharisee and a tax collector both went to the Temple to pray. [11]The Pharisee stood alone and prayed, 'God, I thank you that I am not like other people who steal, cheat, or take part in adultery, or even like this tax collector. [12]I fast[n] twice a week, and I give one-tenth of everything I get!'

[13]"The tax collector, standing at a distance, would not even look up to heaven. But he beat on his chest because he was so sad. He said, 'God, have mercy on me, a sinner.' [14]I tell you, when this man went home, he was right with God, but the Pharisee was not. All who make themselves great will be made humble, but all who make themselves humble will be made great."

## Who Will Enter God's Kingdom?

[15]Some people brought even their babies to Jesus so he could touch them. When the followers saw this, they told them to stop. [16]But Jesus called for the children, saying, "Let the little children come to me. Don't stop them, because the kingdom of God belongs to people who are like these children. [17]I tell you the truth, you must accept the kingdom of God as if you were a child, or you will never enter it."

## A Rich Man's Question

[18]A certain leader asked Jesus, "Good Teacher, what must I do to have life forever?"

[19]Jesus said to him, "Why do you call me good? Only God is good. [20]You know the commands: 'You must not be guilty of adultery. You must not murder anyone. You must not steal. You must not tell lies about your neighbor. Honor your father and mother.' "[n]

[21]But the leader said, "I have obeyed all these commands since I was a boy."

[22]When Jesus heard this, he said to him, "There is still one more thing you need to do. Sell everything you have and give it to the poor, and you will have treasure in heaven. Then come and follow me." [23]But when the man heard this, he became very sad, because he was very rich.

[24]Jesus looked at him and said, "It is very hard for rich people to enter the kingdom of God. [25]It is easier for a camel to go through the eye of a needle than for a rich person to enter the kingdom of God."

# Relationships

**W**hat is a best friend? Someone who likes hanging out with you, laughs at your jokes, and tells you her secrets? Probably. For sure, the Bible says that a best friend will always love you (Proverbs 17:17). She won't criticize you to other people or pretend she doesn't know you when you mess up big time. She tells you she likes you, but she's also honest when you hurt her feelings. Then she forgives you and still wants to be your friend. Having a best friend doesn't happen every day, but Jesus will be your best friend for always!

**18:12 fast** *The people would give up eating for a special time of prayer and worship to God. It was also done to show sadness and disappointment.* **18:20 'You . . . mother.'** *Quotation from Exodus 20:12–16; Deuteronomy 5:16–20.*

## Who Can Be Saved?

²⁶When the people heard this, they asked, "Then who can be saved?"

²⁷Jesus answered, "The things impossible for people are possible for God."

²⁸Peter said, "Look, we have left everything and followed you."

²⁹Jesus said, "I tell you the truth, all those who have left houses, wives, brothers, parents, or children for the kingdom of God ³⁰will get much more in this life. And in the age that is coming, they will have life forever."

## Jesus Will Rise from the Dead

³¹Then Jesus took the twelve apostles aside and said to them, "We are going to Jerusalem. Everything the prophets wrote about the Son of Man will happen. ³²He will be turned over to those who are evil. They will laugh at him, insult him, spit on him, ³³beat him with whips, and kill him. But on the third day, he will rise to life again." ³⁴The apostles did not understand this; the meaning was hidden from them, and they did not realize what was said.

## Jesus Heals a Blind Man

³⁵As Jesus came near the city of Jericho, a blind man was sitting beside the road, begging. ³⁶When he heard the people coming down the road, he asked, "What is happening?"

³⁷They told him, "Jesus, from Nazareth, is going by."

³⁸The blind man cried out, "Jesus, Son of David, have mercy on me!"

³⁹The people leading the group warned the blind man to be quiet. But the blind man shouted even more, "Son of David, have mercy on me!"

⁴⁰Jesus stopped and ordered the blind man to be brought to him. When he came near, Jesus asked him, ⁴¹"What do you want me to do for you?"

He said, "Lord, I want to see."

⁴²Jesus said to him, "Then see. You are healed because you believed."

⁴³At once the man was able to see, and he followed Jesus, thanking God. All the people who saw this praised God.

## Zacchaeus Meets Jesus

**19** Jesus was going through the city of Jericho. ²A man was there named Zacchaeus, who was a very important tax collector, and he was wealthy. ³He wanted to see who Jesus was, but he was not able because he was too short to see above the crowd. ⁴He ran ahead to a place where Jesus would come, and he climbed a sycamore tree so he could see him. ⁵When Jesus came to that place, he looked up and said to him, "Zacchaeus, hurry and come down! I must stay at your house today."

⁶Zacchaeus came down quickly and welcomed him gladly. ⁷All the people saw this and began to complain, "Jesus is staying with a sinner!"

⁸But Zacchaeus stood and said to the Lord, "I will give half of my possessions to the poor. And if I have cheated anyone, I will pay back four times more."

⁹Jesus said to him, "Salvation has come to this house today, because this man also belongs to the family of Abraham. ¹⁰The Son of Man came to find lost people and save them."

## A Story About Three Servants

¹¹As the people were listening to this, Jesus told them a story because he was

### dig deeper

**Luke 18:23–34**

Has this ever happened to you? You think, *Oh! If I could just have that cool shirt, I'd be so happy!* Your mom buys the shirt for you and you're all excited for a few hours. And then? Are you happy for the rest of the year? No? Well, how about all month? The excitement doesn't really last long, does it?

Humans can be so greedy. We want money and we want things! Some people love money so much that they'll do anything to get money or nice things. They might steal. They might lie. They might even kill people or destroy other people's lives. Money is a big temptation for lots of people!

Does that make money bad? Is it a sin to be rich? No, the Bible doesn't say that at all. What it does say is that *loving* money causes all kinds of temptations and sins. The Bible warns us not to love money. You can still work hard and earn what you deserve. You can still enjoy buying nice things sometimes. And you can certainly use your money to serve God and help others.

But be careful. You cannot love God *and* money.

near Jerusalem and they thought God's kingdom would appear immediately. [12]He said: "A very important man went to a country far away to be made a king and then to return home. [13]So he called ten of his servants and gave a coin[n] to each servant. He said, 'Do business with this money until I get back.' [14]But the people in the kingdom hated the man. So they sent a group to follow him and say, 'We don't want this man to be our king.'

[15]"But the man became king. When he returned home, he said, 'Call those servants who have my money so I can know how much they earned with it.'

[16]"The first servant came and said, 'Sir, I earned ten coins with the one you gave me.' [17]The king said to the servant, 'Excellent! You are a good servant. Since I can trust you with small things, I will let you rule over ten of my cities.'

[18]"The second servant said, 'Sir, I earned five coins with your one.' [19]The king said to this servant, 'You can rule over five cities.'

[20]"Then another servant came in and said to the king, 'Sir, here is your coin which I wrapped in a piece of cloth and hid. [21]I was afraid of you, because you are a hard man. You even take money that you didn't earn and gather food that you didn't plant.' [22]Then the king said to the servant, 'I will condemn you by your own words, you evil servant. You knew that I am a hard man, taking money that I didn't earn and gathering food that I didn't plant. [23]Why then didn't you put my money in the bank? Then when I came back, my money would have earned some interest.'

[24]"The king said to the men who were standing by, 'Take the coin away from this servant and give it to the servant who earned ten coins.' [25]They said, 'But sir, that servant already has ten coins.' [26]The king said, 'Those who have will be given more, but those who do not have anything will have everything taken away from them. [27]Now where are my enemies who didn't want me to be king? Bring them here and kill them before me.' "

## Jesus Enters Jerusalem as a King

[28]After Jesus said this, he went on toward Jerusalem. [29]As Jesus came near Bethphage and Bethany, towns near the hill called the Mount of Olives, he sent out two of his followers. [30]He said, "Go to the town you can see there. When you enter it, you will find a colt tied there, which no one has ever ridden. Untie it and bring it here to me. [31]If anyone asks you why you are untying it, say that the Master needs it."

[32]The two followers went into town and found the colt just as Jesus had told them. [33]As they were untying it, its owners came out and asked the followers, "Why are you untying our colt?"

[34]The followers answered, "The Master needs it." [35]So they brought it to Jesus, threw their coats on the colt's back, and put Jesus on it. [36]As Jesus rode toward Jerusalem, others spread their coats on the road before him.

## god's promises

*Luke 21:17-18*

Being a Christian doesn't seem too dangerous, does it? As long as you don't bother anyone, no one seems to bother you. Okay, but what happens when your classmates decide to play a trick on your teacher and they tell you to lie? Uh oh . . . doing the right thing could make you *very* unpopular, very fast!

What about when your teacher says that we evolved from monkeys and you feel like you should speak up about your beliefs? The other students might laugh at you. Or worse, the teacher might grade you unfairly.

Jesus honestly told his followers that they—and we today—would not always get the best treatment from people who don't believe in him. In fact, some people *hate* Christians! But Jesus gave a promise: "None of these things can really harm you."

He didn't mean that we'll never get physically or emotionally hurt. We probably will! But no matter what people do to us, they can't destroy the things that really matter. They can't harm our relationship with God, our hope, our salvation, or our eternal home in heaven! When you find yourself losing courage in your Christian life, ask God for strength. And remember: nothing can harm you because you belong to him!

*No matter what people do to us,*
*they can't destroy the things that really matter!*

19:13 **coin** *A Greek "mina." One mina was enough money to pay a person for working three months.*

³⁷As he was coming close to Jerusalem, on the way down the Mount of Olives, the whole crowd of followers began joyfully shouting praise to God for all the miracles they had seen. ³⁸They said,

"God bless the king who comes in the name of the Lord!

*Psalm 118:26*

There is peace in heaven and glory to God!"

³⁹Some of the Pharisees in the crowd said to Jesus, "Teacher, tell your followers not to say these things."

⁴⁰But Jesus answered, "I tell you, if my followers didn't say these things, then the stones would cry out."

## Jesus Cries for Jerusalem

⁴¹As Jesus came near Jerusalem, he saw the city and cried for it, ⁴²saying, "I wish you knew today what would bring you peace. But now it is hidden from you. ⁴³The time is coming when your enemies will build a wall around you and will hold you in on all sides. ⁴⁴They will destroy you and all your people, and not one stone will be left on another. All this will happen because you did not recognize the time when God came to save you."

## Jesus Goes to the Temple

⁴⁵Jesus went into the Temple and began to throw out the people who were selling things there. ⁴⁶He said, "It is written in the Scriptures, 'My Temple will be a house for prayer.'ⁿ But you have changed it into a 'hideout for robbers'!"ⁿ

⁴⁷Jesus taught in the Temple every day. The leading priests, the experts on the law, and some of the leaders of the people wanted to kill Jesus. ⁴⁸But they did not know how they could do it, because all the people were listening closely to him.

## Jewish Leaders Question Jesus

**20** One day Jesus was in the Temple, teaching the people and telling them the Good News. The leading priests, teachers of the law, and elders came up to talk with him, ²saying, "Tell us what authority you have to do these things? Who gave you this authority?"

³Jesus answered, "I will also ask you a question. Tell me: ⁴When John baptized people, was that authority from God or just from other people?"

⁵They argued about this, saying, "If we answer, 'John's baptism was from God,' Jesus will say, 'Then why did you not believe him?' ⁶But if we say, 'It was from other people,' all the people will stone us to death, because they believe John was a prophet." ⁷So they answered that they didn't know where it came from.

⁸Jesus said to them, "Then I won't tell you what authority I have to do these things."

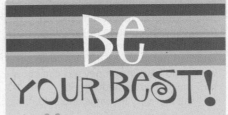

## Be YOUR BEST!

**E**ver tried getting ready in front of a dirty mirror? You can see yourself much better when you start with a clean mirror. As Christians, we reflect Christ to people around us. Make sure your life is always clean of sin, so people will see a good "reflection" of what Jesus is like.

## A Story About God's Son

⁹Then Jesus told the people this story: "A man planted a vineyard and leased it to some farmers. Then he went away for a long time. ¹⁰When it was time for the grapes to be picked, he sent a servant to the farmers to get some of the grapes. But they beat the servant and sent him away empty-handed. ¹¹Then he sent another servant. They beat this servant also, and showed no respect for him, and sent him away empty-handed. ¹²So the man sent a third servant. The farmers wounded him and threw him out. ¹³The owner of the vineyard said, 'What will I do now? I will send my son whom I love. Maybe they will respect him.' ¹⁴But when the farmers saw the son, they said to each other, 'This son will inherit the vineyard. If we kill him, it will be ours.' ¹⁵So the farmers threw the son out of the vineyard and killed him.

"What will the owner of this vineyard do to them? ¹⁶He will come and kill those farmers and will give the vineyard to other farmers."

When the people heard this story, they said, "Let this never happen!"

¹⁷But Jesus looked at them and said, "Then what does this verse mean:

'The stone that the builders rejected became the cornerstone'?

*Psalm 118:22*

¹⁸Everyone who falls on that stone will be broken, and the person on whom it falls, that person will be crushed!"

## ■ Bible Bios

### Young Jesus
### (Luke 2:39–52)

**E**ver wonder about Jesus' childhood? There's actually a story about him when he was twelve years old. With his parents, Jesus had gone to Jerusalem for a religious holiday. When it was time to leave, a huge group of people began traveling together. Mary and Joseph figured Jesus was somewhere in the group so they didn't keep an eye on him. But at the end of the first day, they couldn't find him! It took three days to discover he had stayed in Jerusalem and was in the Temple with the religious teachers, discussing God's Word.

When they seemed surprised, Jesus told his parents that he belonged in his Father's house . . . but they didn't understand. From a young age, Jesus loved studying God's Word and going to the Temple. Do you get excited about church and reading your Bible?

**19:46** 'My Temple . . . prayer.' *Quotation from Isaiah 56:7.* **19:46** 'hideout for robbers' *Quotation from Jeremiah 7:11.*

## cool

### Plastic Flamingos

You know those crazy-looking plastic pink birds some people put on their front lawns? Well, maybe not so much in colder states . . . but you can see lots of them in the south. In fact, it's been discovered that there are more plastic flamingos in the United States than there are *real* flamingos!

Sadly, there are a lot of fake Christians, too. These are people who call themselves Christians but don't truly love, worship, and obey Jesus Christ. God wants you to be a *real* Christian . . . not a "plastic" one.

---

¹⁹The teachers of the law and the leading priests wanted to arrest Jesus at once, because they knew the story was about them. But they were afraid of what the people would do.

### Is It Right to Pay Taxes or Not?

²⁰So they watched Jesus and sent some spies who acted as if they were sincere. They wanted to trap Jesus in saying something wrong so they could hand him over to the authority and power of the governor. ²¹So the spies asked Jesus, "Teacher, we know that what you say and teach is true. You pay no attention to who people are, and you always teach the truth about God's way. ²²Tell us, is it right for us to pay taxes to Caesar or not?"

²³But Jesus, knowing they were trying to trick him, said, ²⁴"Show me a coin. Whose image and name are on it?"

They said, "Caesar's."

²⁵Jesus said to them, "Then give to Caesar the things that are Caesar's, and give to God the things that are God's."

²⁶So they were not able to trap Jesus in anything he said in the presence of the people. And being amazed at his answer, they became silent.

### Some Sadducees Try to Trick Jesus

²⁷Some Sadducees, who believed people would not rise from the dead, came to Jesus. ²⁸They asked, "Teacher, Moses wrote that if a man's brother dies and leaves a wife but no children, then that man must marry the widow and have children for his brother. ²⁹Once there were seven brothers. The first brother married and died, but had no children. ³⁰Then the second brother married the widow, and he died. ³¹And the third brother married the widow, and he died. The same thing happened with all seven brothers; they died and had no children. ³²Finally, the woman died also. ³³Since all seven brothers had married her, whose wife will she be when people rise from the dead?"

³⁴Jesus said to them, "On earth, people marry and are given to someone to marry. ³⁵But those who will be worthy to be raised from the dead and live again will not marry, nor will they be given to someone to marry. ³⁶In that life they are like angels and cannot die. They are children of God, because they have been raised from the dead. ³⁷Even Moses clearly showed that the dead are raised to life. When he wrote about the burning bush,ⁿ he said that the Lord is 'the God of Abraham, the God of Isaac, and the God of Jacob.'ⁿ ³⁸God is the God of the living, not the dead, because all people are alive to him."

³⁹Some of the teachers of the law said, "Teacher, your answer was good." ⁴⁰No one was brave enough to ask him another question.

### Is the Christ the Son of David?

⁴¹Then Jesus said, "Why do people say that the Christ is the Son of David? ⁴²In the book of Psalms, David himself says:

'The Lord said to my Lord,
"Sit by me at my right side,
⁴³  until I put your enemies under your control." 'ⁿ          *Psalm 110:1*

⁴⁴David calls the Christ 'Lord,' so how can the Christ be his son?"

### Jesus Accuses Some Leaders

⁴⁵While all the people were listening, Jesus said to his followers, ⁴⁶"Beware of the teachers of the law. They like to walk around wearing fancy clothes, and they love for people to greet them with respect

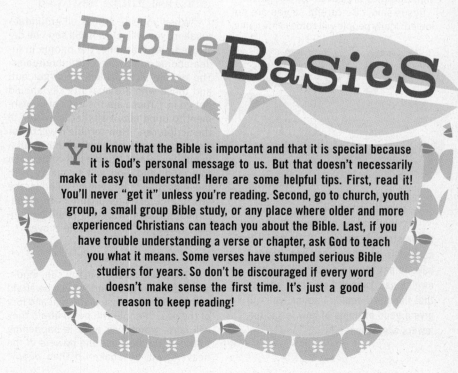

## BibLe BaSicS

You know that the Bible is important and that it is special because it is God's personal message to us. But that doesn't necessarily make it easy to understand! Here are some helpful tips. First, read it! You'll never "get it" unless you're reading. Second, go to church, youth group, a small group Bible study, or any place where older and more experienced Christians can teach you about the Bible. Last, if you have trouble understanding a verse or chapter, ask God to teach you what it means. Some verses have stumped serious Bible studiers for years. So don't be discouraged if every word doesn't make sense the first time. It's just a good reason to keep reading!

---

**20:37 burning bush** *Read Exodus 3:1–12 in the Old Testament.*     **20:37 'the God of . . . Jacob'** *These words are taken from Exodus 3:6.*     **20:43 until . . . control** *Literally, "until I make your enemies a footstool for your feet."*

**111**

in the marketplaces. They love to have the most important seats in the synagogues and at feasts. [47]But they cheat widows and steal their houses and then try to make themselves look good by saying long prayers. They will receive a greater punishment."

## True Giving

**21** As Jesus looked up, he saw some rich people putting their gifts into the Temple money box.[n] [2]Then he saw a poor widow putting two small copper coins into the box. [3]He said, "I tell you the truth, this poor widow gave more than all those rich people. [4]They gave only what they did not need. This woman is very poor, but she gave all she had to live on."

## The Temple Will Be Destroyed

[5]Some people were talking about the Temple and how it was decorated with beautiful stones and gifts offered to God.

But Jesus said, [6]"As for these things you are looking at, the time will come when not one stone will be left on another. Every stone will be thrown down."

[7]They asked Jesus, "Teacher, when will these things happen? What will be the sign that they are about to take place?"

[8]Jesus said, "Be careful so you are not fooled. Many people will come in my name,

# Q & A

**Q** If a cashier gives me too much change, do I have to give it back?

**A** Yes! First of all, that's not your money. It belongs to the store. At the end of the day, if the cashier is missing money, she might have to pay for the mistake with her own money. Even if it's a small amount that the store wouldn't notice, you will give a good example of how Jesus' followers are honest.

saying, 'I am the One' and, 'The time has come!' But don't follow them. [9]When you hear about wars and riots, don't be afraid, because these things must happen first, but the end will come later."

[10]Then he said to them, "Nations will fight against other nations, and kingdoms against other kingdoms. [11]In various places there will be great earthquakes, sicknesses, and a lack of food. Fearful events and great signs will come from heaven.

[12]"But before all these things happen, people will arrest you and treat you cruelly. They will judge you in their synagogues and put you in jail and force you to stand before kings and governors, because you follow me. [13]But this will give you an opportunity to tell about me. [14]Make up your minds not to worry ahead of time about what you will say. [15]I will give you the wisdom to say things that none of your enemies will be able to stand against or prove wrong. [16]Even your parents, brothers, relatives, and friends will turn against you, and they will kill some of you. [17]All people will hate you because you follow me. [18]But none of these things can really harm you. [19]By continuing to have faith you will save your lives.

## Jerusalem Will Be Destroyed

[20]"When you see armies all around Jerusalem, you will know it will soon be destroyed. [21]At that time, the people in Judea should run away to the mountains. The people in Jerusalem must get out, and those who are near the city should not go in. [22]These are the days of punishment to bring about all that is written in the Scriptures. [23]How terrible it will be for women who are pregnant or have nursing babies! Great trouble will come upon this land, and God will be angry with these people. [24]They will be killed by the sword and taken as prisoners to all nations. Jerusalem will be crushed by non-Jewish people until their time is over.

## Don't Fear

[25]"There will be signs in the sun, moon, and stars. On earth, nations will be afraid and confused because of the roar and fury of the sea. [26]People will be so afraid they will faint, wondering what is happening to the world, because the powers of the heavens will be shaken. [27]Then people

# top ten

## top ten ways to...
### Fight Temptation

**1** Study your Bible and memorize your favorite verses.

**2** Ask God for help!

**3** Plan ahead of time to say no to sin.

**4** Worship God throughout the day.

**5** Avoid people, places, or activities that tempt you.

**6** Start doing something different as a distraction.

**7** Confess sins right away to keep your heart pure.

**8** Fill your mind with good things.

**9** Get to know other Christians.

**10** Ask someone older and wiser to check up on you.

will see the Son of Man coming in a cloud with power and great glory. [28]When these things begin to happen, look up and hold your heads high, because the time when God will free you is near!"

## Jesus' Words Will Live Forever

[29]Then Jesus told this story: "Look at the fig tree and all the other trees. [30]When their leaves appear, you know that sum-

21:1 **money box** *A special box in the Jewish place of worship where people put their gifts to God.*

# dig deeper

## Luke 24:13–32

Two men talked with Jesus after he rose from the dead—but they didn't know it was him (Luke 24:13–32)! Maybe he looked different after dying and coming back to life. Maybe he kept them from recognizing him on purpose. If they had realized who he was, they might have been too excited to listen to what he had to say!

Jesus wanted these men to understand that his life on earth had been part of God's plan since the beginning. The Old Testament is a collection of messages God gave to his people, the Jews, over hundreds of years. These messages show how God was carefully preparing for Jesus' arrival. Through his life, death, and return to heaven, Jesus made a way for people to know God. *That* was God's plan. These men were Jews who probably knew the Old Testament well. They had not understood God's plan before, but when Jesus explained it, they could see that what he said was true.

God has plans. Plans for history; plans for your life. First, he wants you to follow Jesus. His other plans may not be clear, but he will always show you as much as you need to know. Have you decided to follow Jesus? Have you asked him about his plans for your life?

## Judas Becomes an Enemy of Jesus

**22** It was almost time for the Feast of Unleavened Bread, called the Passover Feast. ²The leading priests and teachers of the law were trying to find a way to kill Jesus, because they were afraid of the people.

³Satan entered Judas Iscariot, one of Jesus' twelve apostles. ⁴Judas went to the leading priests and some of the soldiers who guarded the Temple and talked to them about a way to hand Jesus over to them. ⁵They were pleased and agreed to give Judas money. ⁶He agreed and watched for the best time to hand Jesus over to them when he was away from the crowd.

## Jesus Eats the Passover Meal

⁷The Day of Unleavened Bread came when the Passover lambs had to be sacrificed. ⁸Jesus said to Peter and John, "Go and prepare the Passover meal for us to eat."

⁹They asked, "Where do you want us to prepare it?" ¹⁰Jesus said to them, "After you go into the city, a man carrying a jar of water will meet you. Follow him into the house that he enters, ¹¹and tell the owner of the house, 'The Teacher says: "Where is the guest room in which I may eat the Passover meal with my followers?" ' ¹²Then he will show you a large, furnished room upstairs. Prepare the Passover meal there."

¹³So Peter and John left and found everything as Jesus had said. And they prepared the Passover meal.

## The Lord's Supper

¹⁴When the time came, Jesus and the apostles were sitting at the table. ¹⁵He said to them, "I wanted very much to eat this Passover meal with you before I suffer. ¹⁶I will not eat another Passover meal until it is given its true meaning in the kingdom of God."

¹⁷Then Jesus took a cup, gave thanks, and said, "Take this cup and share it among yourselves. ¹⁸I will not drink again from the fruit of the vine[n] until God's kingdom comes."

¹⁹Then Jesus took some bread, gave thanks, broke it, and gave it to the apostles, saying, "This is my body,[n] which I am giving for you. Do this to remember me."

mer is near. ³¹In the same way, when you see these things happening, you will know that God's kingdom is near.

³²"I tell you the truth, all these things will happen while the people of this time are still living. ³³Earth and sky will be destroyed, but the words I have spoken will never be destroyed.

## Be Ready All the Time

³⁴"Be careful not to spend your time feasting, drinking, or worrying about worldly things. If you do, that day might come on you suddenly, ³⁵like a trap on all people on earth. ³⁶So be ready all the time. Pray that you will be strong enough to escape all these things that will happen and that you will be able to stand before the Son of Man."

³⁷During the day, Jesus taught the people in the Temple, and at night he went out of the city and stayed on the Mount of Olives. ³⁸Every morning all the people got up early to go to the Temple to listen to him.

22:18 **fruit of the vine** *Product of the grapevine; this may also be translated "wine."* 22:19b–20 **body** *Some Greek copies do not have the rest of verse 19 or verse 20.*

²⁰In the same way, after supper, Jesus took the cup and said, "This cup is the new agreement that God makes with his people. This new agreement begins with my blood which is poured out for you.

## Who Will Turn Against Jesus?

²¹"But one of you will turn against me, and his hand is with mine on the table. ²²What God has planned for the Son of Man will happen, but how terrible it will be for that one who turns against the Son of Man."

²³Then the apostles asked each other which one of them would do that.

## Be Like a Servant

²⁴The apostles also began to argue about which one of them was the most important. ²⁵But Jesus said to them, "The kings of the non-Jewish people rule over them, and those who have authority over others like to be called 'friends of the people.' ²⁶But you must not be like that.

Instead, the greatest among you should be like the youngest, and the leader should be like the servant. ²⁷Who is more important: the one sitting at the table or the one serving? You think the one at the table is more important, but I am like a servant among you.

²⁸"You have stayed with me through my struggles. ²⁹Just as my Father has given me a kingdom, I also give you a kingdom ³⁰so you may eat and drink at my table in my kingdom. And you will sit on thrones, judging the twelve tribes of Israel.

## Don't Lose Your Faith!

³¹"Simon, Simon, Satan has asked to test all of you as a farmer sifts his wheat. ³²I have prayed that you will not lose your faith! Help your brothers be stronger when you come back to me."

³³But Peter said to Jesus, "Lord, I am ready to go with you to prison and even to die with you!"

³⁴But Jesus said, "Peter, before the rooster crows this day, you will say three times that you don't know me."

## Be Ready for Trouble

³⁵Then Jesus said to the apostles, "When I sent you out without a purse, a bag, or sandals, did you need anything?"

They said, "No."

³⁶He said to them, "But now if you have a purse or a bag, carry that with you. If you don't have a sword, sell your coat and buy one. ³⁷The Scripture says, 'He was treated like a criminal,'ⁿ and I tell you this scripture must have its full meaning. It was written about me, and it is happening now."

³⁸His followers said, "Look, Lord, here are two swords."

He said to them, "That is enough."

## Jesus Prays Alone

³⁹Jesus left the city and went to the Mount of Olives, as he often did, and his followers went with him. ⁴⁰When he reached the place, he said to them, "Pray for strength against temptation."

⁴¹Then Jesus went about a stone's throw away from them. He kneeled down and prayed, ⁴²"Father, if you are willing, take away this cupⁿ of suffering. But do what you want, not what I want." ⁴³Then an angel from heaven appeared to him to strengthen him. ⁴⁴Being full of pain, Jesus prayed even harder. His sweat was like drops of blood falling to the ground. ⁴⁵When he finished praying, he went to his followers and found them asleep because of their sadness. ⁴⁶Jesus said to them, "Why are you sleeping? Get up and pray for strength against temptation."

## Jesus Is Arrested

⁴⁷While Jesus was speaking, a crowd came up, and Judas, one of the twelve apostles, was leading them. He came close to Jesus so he could kiss him. ⁴⁸But Jesus said to him, "Judas, are you using the kiss to give the Son of Man to his enemies?"

⁴⁹When those who were standing around him saw what was happening, they said, "Lord, should we strike them with our swords?" ⁵⁰And one of them struck the servant of the high priest and cut off his right ear.

⁵¹Jesus said, "Stop! No more of this." Then he touched the servant's ear and healed him.

⁵²Those who came to arrest Jesus were the leading priests, the soldiers who guarded the Temple, and the elders. Jesus said to them, "You came out here with swords and clubs as though I were a criminal. ⁵³I was with you every day in the Temple, and you didn't arrest me there. But this is your time—the time when darkness rules."

## Peter Says He Doesn't Know Jesus

⁵⁴They arrested Jesus, and led him away, and brought him into the house of the high priest. Peter followed far behind them. ⁵⁵After the soldiers started a fire in the middle of the courtyard and sat together, Peter sat with them. ⁵⁶A servant girl saw Peter sitting

> BEING FULL OF PAIN, JESUS PRAYED EVEN HARDER. HIS SWEAT WAS LIKE DROPS OF BLOOD FALLING TO THE GROUND.

## did you know?

Girls spend 4.5 hours per week on homework.
—*Business Wire*, 10/10/03, http://www.rab.com/newrst/article_view.cfm?id=308&type=article2

## speakout!

**Q** What do you do to stay close to God?

**A** For me, praying is what brings me closer. Reading the Bible, going to church, and all that helps, but I really feel close to God when I am able to take an hour and pray. —Rachel, 12

22:37 'He . . . criminal.' *Quotation from Isaiah 53:12.*  22:42 cup *Jesus is talking about the painful things that will happen to him. Accepting these things will be hard, like drinking a cup of something bitter.*

Luke

## BE YOUR BEST!

**W**hen you need to do something you find difficult or boring, like exercising or walking the dog, ask a friend to be your "buddy." Having someone along helps get the job done. Try to find some Christian "buddies," too, who can help you grow in your faith.

there in the firelight, and looking closely at him, she said, "This man was also with him."

57But Peter said this was not true; he said, "Woman, I don't know him."

58A short time later, another person saw Peter and said, "You are also one of them."

But Peter said, "Man, I am not!"

59About an hour later, another man insisted, "Certainly this man was with him, because he is from Galilee, too."

60But Peter said, "Man, I don't know what you are talking about!"

At once, while Peter was still speaking, a rooster crowed. 61Then the Lord turned and looked straight at Peter. And Peter remembered what the Lord had said: "Before the rooster crows this day, you will say three times that you don't know me." 62Then Peter went outside and cried painfully.

### The People Make Fun of Jesus

63The men who were guarding Jesus began making fun of him and beating him.

64They blindfolded him and said, "Prove that you are a prophet, and tell us who hit you." 65They said many cruel things to Jesus.

### Jesus Before the Leaders

66When day came, the council of the elders of the people, both the leading priests and the teachers of the law, came together and led Jesus to their highest court. 67They said, "If you are the Christ, tell us."

Jesus said to them, "If I tell you, you will not believe me. 68And if I ask you, you will not answer. 69But from now on, the Son of Man will sit at the right hand of the powerful God."

70They all said, "Then are you the Son of God?"

Jesus said to them, "You say that I am."

71They said, "Why do we need witnesses now? We ourselves heard him say this."

### Pilate Questions Jesus

**23** Then the whole group stood up and led Jesus to Pilate.[n] 2They began to accuse Jesus, saying, "We caught this man telling things that mislead our people. He says that we should not pay taxes to Caesar, and he calls himself the Christ, a king."

3Pilate asked Jesus, "Are you the king of the Jews?"

Jesus answered, "Those are your words."

4Pilate said to the leading priests and the people, "I find nothing against this man."

5They were insisting, saying, "But Jesus makes trouble with the people, teaching all around Judea. He began in Galilee, and now he is here."

### Pilate Sends Jesus to Herod

6Pilate heard this and asked if Jesus was from Galilee. 7Since Jesus was under Herod's authority, Pilate sent Jesus to Herod, who was in Jerusalem at that time. 8When Herod saw Jesus, he was very glad, because he had heard about Jesus and had wanted to meet him for a long time. He was hoping to see Jesus work a miracle. 9Herod asked Jesus many questions, but Jesus said nothing. 10The leading priests and teachers of the law were standing there, strongly accusing Jesus. 11After Herod and his soldiers had made fun of Jesus, they dressed him in a kingly robe and sent him back to Pilate. 12In the past, Pilate and Herod had always been enemies, but on that day they became friends.

### Jesus Must Die

13Pilate called the people together with the leading priests and the rulers. 14He said to them, "You brought this man to me, saying he makes trouble among the people. But I have questioned him before you all, and I have not found him guilty of what you say. 15Also, Herod found nothing wrong with him; he sent him back to us. Look, he has done nothing for which he should die. 16So, after I punish him, I will let him go free." [17Every year at the Passover Feast, Pilate had to release one prisoner to the people.][n]

18But the people shouted together, "Take this man away! Let Barabbas go free!" 19(Barabbas was a man who was in prison for his part in a riot in the city and for murder.)

20Pilate wanted to let Jesus go free and told this to the crowd. 21But they shouted again, "Crucify him! Crucify him!"

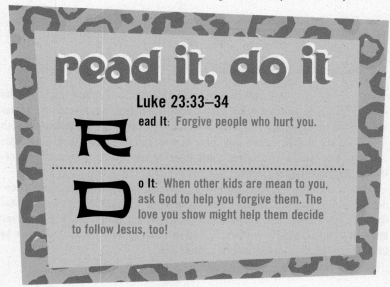

## read it, do it

### Luke 23:33–34

**R**ead It: Forgive people who hurt you.

**D**o It: When other kids are mean to you, ask God to help you forgive them. The love you show might help them decide to follow Jesus, too!

23:1 **Pilate** Pontius Pilate was the Roman governor of Judea from A.D. 26 to A.D. 36.   23:17 **Every . . . people.** Some Greek copies do not contain the bracketed text.

A third time Pilate said to them, "Why? What wrong has he done? I can find no reason to kill him. So I will have him punished and set him free."

[23]But they continued to shout, demanding that Jesus be crucified. Their yelling became so loud that [24]Pilate decided to give them what they wanted. [25]He set free the man who was in jail for rioting and murder, and he handed Jesus over to them to do with him as they wished.

## Jesus Is Crucified

[26]As they led Jesus away, Simon, a man from Cyrene, was coming in from the fields. They forced him to carry Jesus' cross and to walk behind him.

[27]A large crowd of people was following Jesus, including some women who were sad and crying for him. [28]But Jesus turned and said to them, "Women of Jerusalem, don't cry for me. Cry for yourselves and for your children. [29]The time is coming when people will say, 'Blessed are the women who cannot have children and who have no babies to nurse.' [30]Then people will say to the mountains, 'Fall on us!' And they will say to the hills, 'Cover us!' [31]If they act like this now when life is good, what will happen when bad times come?"[n]

[32]There were also two criminals led out with Jesus to be put to death. [33]When they came to a place called the Skull, the soldiers crucified Jesus and the criminals—one on his right and the other on his left. [34]Jesus said, "Father, forgive them, because they don't know what they are doing."[n]

The soldiers threw lots to decide who would get his clothes. [35]The people stood there watching. And the leaders made fun of Jesus, saying, "He saved others. Let him save himself if he is God's Chosen One, the Christ."

[36]The soldiers also made fun of him, coming to Jesus and offering him some vinegar. [37]They said, "If you are the king of the Jews, save yourself!" [38]At the top of the cross these words were written: THIS IS THE KING OF THE JEWS.

[39]One of the criminals on a cross began to shout insults at Jesus: "Aren't you the Christ? Then save yourself and us."

[40]But the other criminal stopped him and said, "You should fear God! You are getting the same punishment he is. [41]We are punished justly, getting what we deserve for what we did. But this man has done nothing wrong." [42]Then he said, "Jesus, remember me when you come into your kingdom."

[43]Jesus said to him, "I tell you the truth, today you will be with me in paradise."[n]

## Jesus Dies

[44]It was about noon, and the whole land became dark until three o'clock in the afternoon, [45]because the sun did not shine. The curtain in the Temple[n] was torn in two. [46]Jesus cried out in a loud voice, "Father, I give you my life." After Jesus said this, he died.

[47]When the army officer there saw what happened, he praised God, saying, "Surely this was a good man!"

[48]When all the people who had gathered there to watch saw what happened, they returned home, beating their chests because they were so sad. [49]But those who were close friends of Jesus, including the women who had followed him from Galilee, stood at a distance and watched.

## Joseph Takes Jesus' Body

[50]There was a good and religious man named Joseph who was a member of the council. [51]But he had not agreed to the other leaders' plans and actions against Jesus. He was from the town of Arimathea and was waiting for the kingdom of God to come. [52]Joseph went to Pilate to ask for the body of Jesus. [53]He took the body down from the cross, wrapped it in cloth, and put it in a tomb that was cut out of a wall of rock. This tomb had never been used before. [54]This was late on Preparation Day, and when the sun went down, the Sabbath day would begin.

[55]The women who had come from Galilee with Jesus followed Joseph and saw the tomb and how Jesus' body was laid. [56]Then the women left to prepare spices and perfumes.

On the Sabbath day they rested, as the law of Moses commanded.

## Jesus Rises from the Dead

**24** Very early on the first day of the week, at dawn, the women came to the tomb, bringing the spices they had prepared. [2]They found the stone rolled away from the entrance of the tomb, [3]but when they went in, they did not find the body of the Lord Jesus. [4]While they were wondering about this, two men in shining clothes suddenly stood beside them. [5]The women were very afraid and bowed their heads to the ground. The men said to them, "Why are you looking for a living person in this place for the dead? [6]He is not here; he has risen from the dead. Do you remember what he told you in Galilee? [7]He said the Son of Man must be handed over to sinful people, be crucified, and rise from the dead on the third day." [8]Then the women remembered what Jesus had said.

## ■ Bible Bios

### Mary of Bethany
### (Luke 10:38–42)

Mary lived with her sister Martha and brother Lazarus in the town of Bethany (about two miles from Jerusalem). As far as we know, none of them were married. Jesus and his followers often stayed at their house when they were in Jerusalem and they all became friends. Mary was a bit of a free spirit. Cooking and serving were not as important to her as being with Jesus.

Mary was always eager to learn from Jesus and would sit near his feet listening when he spoke, just like she was one of Jesus' followers! Jesus appreciated Martha's hard work, but Mary's interest in spiritual things pleased him even more. It's important to serve God . . . but don't forget to show him your love by taking time to talk with him and learn from him.

**23:31 If . . . come?** Literally, "If they do these things in the green tree, what will happen in the dry?" **23:34 Jesus . . . doing.** Some Greek copies do not have this first part of verse 34. **23:43 paradise** Another word for heaven. **23:45 curtain in the Temple** A curtain divided the Most Holy Place from the other part of the Temple, the special building in Jerusalem where God commanded the Jewish people to worship him.

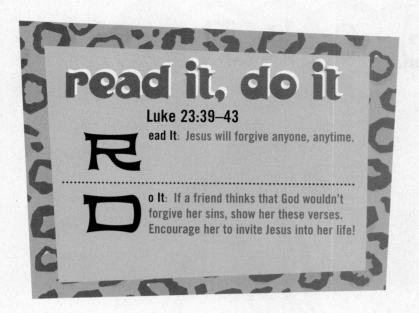

[9]The women left the tomb and told all these things to the eleven apostles and the other followers. [10]It was Mary Magdalene, Joanna, Mary the mother of James, and some other women who told the apostles everything that had happened at the tomb. [11]But they did not believe the women, because it sounded like nonsense. [12]But Peter got up and ran to the tomb. Bending down and looking in, he saw only the cloth that Jesus' body had been wrapped in. Peter went away to his home, wondering about what had happened.

## Jesus on the Road to Emmaus

[13]That same day two of Jesus' followers were going to a town named Emmaus, about seven miles from Jerusalem. [14]They were talking about everything that had happened. [15]While they were talking and discussing, Jesus himself came near and began walking with them, [16]but they were kept from recognizing him. [17]Then he said, "What are these things you are talking about while you walk?"

The two followers stopped, looking very sad. [18]The one named Cleopas answered, "Are you the only visitor in Jerusalem who does not know what just happened there?"

[19]Jesus said to them, "What are you talking about?"

They said, "About Jesus of Nazareth. He was a prophet who said and did many powerful things before God and all the people. [20]Our leaders and the leading priests handed him over to be sentenced to death, and they crucified him. [21]But we were hoping that he would free Israel. Besides this, it is now the third day since this happened. [22]And today some women among us amazed us. Early this morning they went to the tomb, [23]but they did not find his body there. They came and told us that they had seen a vision of angels who said that Jesus was alive! [24]So some of our group went to the tomb, too. They found it just as the women said, but they did not see Jesus."

[25]Then Jesus said to them, "You are foolish and slow to believe everything the prophets said. [26]They said that the Christ must suffer these things before he enters his glory." [27]Then starting with what Moses and all the prophets had said about him, Jesus began to explain everything that had been written about himself in the Scriptures.

[28]They came near the town of Emmaus, and Jesus acted as if he were going farther. [29]But they begged him, "Stay with us, because it is late; it is almost night." So he went in to stay with them.

[30]When Jesus was at the table with them, he took some bread, gave thanks, divided it, and gave it to them. [31]And then, they were allowed to recognize Jesus. But when they saw who he was, he disappeared. [32]They said to each other, "It felt like a fire burning in us when Jesus talked to us on the road and explained the Scriptures to us."

[33]So the two followers got up at once and went back to Jerusalem. There they found the eleven apostles and others gathered. [34]They were saying, "The Lord really has risen from the dead! He showed himself to Simon."

[35]Then the two followers told what had happened on the road and how they recognized Jesus when he divided the bread.

## Jesus Appears to His Followers

[36]While the two followers were telling this, Jesus himself stood right in the middle of them and said, "Peace be with you."

[37]They were fearful and terrified and thought they were seeing a ghost. [38]But Jesus said, "Why are you troubled? Why do you doubt what you see? [39]Look at my hands and my feet. It is I myself! Touch me and see, because a ghost does not have a living body as you see I have."

[40]After Jesus said this, he showed them his hands and feet. [41]While they still could not believe it because they were amazed and happy, Jesus said to them, "Do you have any food here?" [42]They gave him a piece of broiled fish. [43]While the followers watched, Jesus took the fish and ate it.

[44]He said to them, "Remember when I was with you before? I said that everything written about me must happen—everything in the law of Moses, the books of the prophets, and the Psalms."

[45]Then Jesus opened their minds so they could understand the Scriptures. [46]He said to them, "It is written that the Christ would suffer and rise from the dead on the third day [47]and that a change of hearts and lives and forgiveness of sins would be preached in his name to all nations, starting at Jerusalem. [48]You are witnesses of these things. [49]I will send you what my Father has promised, but you must stay in Jerusalem until you have received that power from heaven."

## Jesus Goes Back to Heaven

[50]Jesus led his followers as far as Bethany, and he raised his hands and blessed them. [51]While he was blessing them, he was separated from them and carried into heaven. [52]They worshiped him and returned to Jerusalem very happy. [53]They stayed in the Temple all the time, praising God.

# JOHN

**H**ave you ever heard someone describe an event you witnessed firsthand . . . but they get the story wrong? You want to set them straight, don't you? In fact, it's almost impossible not to! The apostle John might have felt that way. He was one of Jesus' closest friends. He was with him even at times when most of the other followers were not. Now, twenty, thirty, maybe fifty years later, many people had their own version of the truth. (You probably know how rumors can spread!)

Maybe John reacted to these rumors. Maybe he just wanted to give people another chance to hear about Jesus. Either way, he wrote this book full of pictures of Jesus' power and love. For example:

➡ John 1:1–18 contains a poetic description of who Jesus is and what he did. John calls him "The true Light that gives light to all" (verse 9).

➡ Jesus turned water into wine at a wedding (John 2:1–11)!

➡ Jesus shows kindness to a woman who was probably a social outcast (John 4:4–42).

➡ Chapter 11 contains the incredible story of how Jesus brought his good friend Lazarus back to life—*after* Lazarus had been dead three days!

➡ Jesus washes his followers' feet. Now *that's* love (John 13:1–17)!

➡ Jesus gave a second chance to his good friend Peter, who had denied knowing Jesus three times (John 18:15–18, 25–27; John 21:15–19).

# JOHN TELLS ABOUT JESUS, THE SON WHO REVEALS THE FATHER

**THINGS TO TALK WITH GOD ABOUT . . .**

## Christ Comes to the World

1 In the beginning there was the Word.[n] The Word was with God, and the Word was God. [2]He was with God in the beginning. [3]All things were made by him, and nothing was made without him. [4]In him there was life, and that life was the light of all people. [5]The Light shines in the darkness, and the darkness has not overpowered[n] it.

[6]There was a man named John[n] who was sent by God. [7]He came to tell people the truth about the Light so that through him all people could hear about the Light and believe. [8]John was not the Light, but he came to tell people the truth about the

**73% of girls believe they can make a difference in their community.**
—*Business Wire, 10/10/03,* http://www.rab.com/newrst/article_view.cfm?id=308&type=article2

**did you know?**

Light. [9]The true Light that gives light to all was coming into the world!

[10]The Word was in the world, and the world was made by him, but the world did not know him. [11]He came to the world that was his own, but his own people did not accept him. [12]But to all who did accept him and believe in him he gave the right to become children of God. [13]They did not become his children in any human way—by any human parents or human desire. They were born of God.

[14]The Word became a human and lived among us. We saw his glory—the glory that belongs to the only Son of the Father—and he was full of grace and truth. [15]John tells the truth about him and cries out, saying, "This is the One I told you about: 'The One who comes after me is greater than I am, because he was living before me.'"

[16]Because he was full of grace and truth, from him we all received one gift after another. [17]The law was given through Moses, but grace and truth came through Jesus Christ. [18]No one has ever seen God. But God the only Son is very close to the Father,[n] and he has shown us what God is like.

## John Tells People About Jesus

[19]Here is the truth John[n] told when the leaders in Jerusalem sent priests and Levites to ask him, "Who are you?"

[20]John spoke freely and did not refuse to answer. He said, "I am not the Christ."

[21]So they asked him, "Then who are you? Are you Elijah?"[n]

He answered, "No, I am not."

"Are you the Prophet?"[n] they asked.

He answered, "No."

[22]Then they said, "Who are you? Give us an answer to tell those who sent us. What do you say about yourself?"

[23]John told them in the words of the prophet Isaiah:

"I am the voice of one
  calling out in the desert:
'Make the road straight for the Lord.'"
        *Isaiah 40:3*

[24]Some Pharisees who had been sent asked John: [25]"If you are not the Christ or Elijah or the Prophet, why do you baptize people?"

[26]John answered, "I baptize with water, but there is one here with you that you don't know about. [27]He is the One who

**"I AM THE VOICE OF ONE CALLING OUT IN THE DESERT: MAKE THE ROAD STRAIGHT FOR THE LORD."**

## speakout!

**Q** What's the best thing about being a Christian?

**A** I'd have to say the best thing is knowing Jesus is in my heart and that I'll be going to heaven someday.
—Emily, 10

**1:1 Word** *The Greek word is "logos," meaning any kind of communication; it could be translated "message." Here, it means Christ, because Christ was the way God told people about himself.* **1:5 overpowered** *This can also be translated, "understood."* **1:6 John** *John the Baptist, who preached to people about Christ's coming (Matthew 3, Luke 3).* **1:18 But . . . Father** *This could be translated, "But the only God is very close to the Father." Also, some Greek copies read "But the only Son is very close to the Father."* **1:19 John** *John the Baptist, who preached to people about Christ's coming (Matthew 3, Luke 3).* **1:21 Elijah** *A prophet who spoke for God. He lived hundreds of years before Christ and was expected to return before Christ (Malachi 4:5–6).* **1:21 Prophet** *They probably meant the prophet that God told Moses he would send (Deuteronomy 18:15–19).*

comes after me. I am not good enough to untie the strings of his sandals."

[28]This all happened at Bethany on the other side of the Jordan River, where John was baptizing people.

[29]The next day John saw Jesus coming toward him. John said, "Look, the Lamb of God,[n] who takes away the sin of the world! [30]This is the One I was talking about when I said, 'A man will come after me, but he is greater than I am, because he was living before me.' [31]Even I did not know who he was, although I came baptizing with water so that the people of Israel would know who he is."

[32-33]Then John said, "I saw the Spirit come down from heaven in the form of a dove and rest on him. Until then I did not know who the Christ was. But the God who sent me to baptize with water told me, 'You will see the Spirit come down and rest on a man; he is the One who will baptize with the Holy Spirit.' [34]I have seen this happen, and I tell you the truth: This man is the Son of God."[n]

## The First Followers of Jesus

[35]The next day John[n] was there again with two of his followers. [36]When he saw Jesus walking by, he said, "Look, the Lamb of God!"[n]

[37]The two followers heard John say this, so they followed Jesus. [38]When Jesus turned and saw them following him, he asked, "What are you looking for?"

They said, "Rabbi, where are you staying?" ("Rabbi" means "Teacher.")

[39]He answered, "Come and see." So the two men went with Jesus and saw where he was staying and stayed there with him that day. It was about four o'clock in the afternoon.

[40]One of the two men who followed Jesus after they heard John speak about him was Andrew, Simon Peter's brother.

# dig deeper

## John 1:14–18

You've probably seen the initials "WWJD" on a bracelet, key chain, or poster. The letters are meant to encourage people to ask themselves, "What Would Jesus Do?" That's a good idea, but we can't always know what Jesus would do. We can't see into the mind of God or use the same wisdom he does. But we *can* study the Bible to learn how Jesus lived his life and then try to be more like him. We can read about how he treated people, how he handled difficult situations, and how he obeyed God. Jesus set a perfect example for us.

Even though he was God, he didn't use his powers in a selfish way, such as to become rich or popular . . . or even to save himself when people crucified him on the cross! He gave up everything he had in heaven to come down to earth and live with humans. He obeyed God in every situation—even to the point of death. In every situation, all through his life, Jesus was "full of grace and truth" (John 1:14). May that be true of us today.

[41]The first thing Andrew did was to find his brother Simon and say to him, "We have found the Messiah." ("Messiah" means "Christ.")

[42]Then Andrew took Simon to Jesus. Jesus looked at him and said, "You are Simon son of John. You will be called Cephas." ("Cephas" means "Peter."[n])

[43]The next day Jesus decided to go to Galilee. He found Philip and said to him, "Follow me."

[44]Philip was from the town of Bethsaida, where Andrew and Peter lived. [45]Philip found Nathanael and told him, "We have found the man that Moses wrote about in the law, and the prophets also wrote about him. He is Jesus, the son of Joseph, from Nazareth."

[46]But Nathanael said to Philip, "Can anything good come from Nazareth?"

Philip answered, "Come and see."

[47]As Jesus saw Nathanael coming toward him, he said, "Here is truly an Israelite. There is nothing false in him."

[48]Nathanael asked, "How do you know me?"

Jesus answered, "I saw you when you were under the fig tree, before Philip told you about me."

[49]Then Nathanael said to Jesus, "Teacher, you are the Son of God; you are the King of Israel."

:29, 36 **Lamb of God** *Name for Jesus. Jesus is like the lambs that were offered for a sacrifice to God.* 1:34 **the Son of God** *Some Greek copies read "God's Chosen One."* 1:35 **John** *John the Baptist, who preached to people about Christ's coming (Matthew 3, Luke 3).* 1:42 **Peter** *The Greek name "Peter," like the Aramaic name "Cephas," means "rock."*

> ## SO IN CANA OF GALILEE JESUS DID HIS FIRST MIRACLE. THERE HE SHOWED HIS GLORY, AND HIS FOLLOWERS BELIEVED IN HIM.

[50]Jesus said to Nathanael, "Do you believe simply because I told you I saw you under the fig tree? You will see greater things than that." [51]And Jesus said to them, "I tell you the truth, you will all see heaven open and 'angels of God going up and coming down'[n] on the Son of Man."

### The Wedding at Cana

**2** Two days later there was a wedding in the town of Cana in Galilee. Jesus' mother was there, [2]and Jesus and his followers were also invited to the wedding. [3]When all the wine was gone, Jesus' mother said to him, "They have no more wine."

[4]Jesus answered, "Dear woman, why come to me? My time has not yet come."

[5]His mother said to the servants, "Do whatever he tells you to do."

[6]In that place there were six stone water jars that the Jews used in their washing ceremony.[n] Each jar held about twenty or thirty gallons.

[7]Jesus said to the servants, "Fill the jars with water." So they filled the jars to the top.

[8]Then he said to them, "Now take some out and give it to the master of the feast."

So they took the water to the master. [9]When he tasted it, the water had become wine. He did not know where the wine came from, but the servants who had brought the water knew. The master of the wedding called the bridegroom [10]and said to him, "People always serve the best wine first. Later, after the guests have been drinking awhile, they serve the cheaper wine. But you have saved the best wine till now."

[11]So in Cana of Galilee Jesus did his first miracle. There he showed his glory, and his followers believed in him.

### Jesus in the Temple

[12]After this, Jesus went to the town of Capernaum with his mother, brothers, and followers. They stayed there for just a few days. [13]When it was almost time for the Jewish Passover Feast, Jesus went to Jerusalem. [14]In the Temple he found people selling cattle, sheep, and doves. He saw others sitting at tables, exchanging different kinds of money. [15]Jesus made a whip out of cords and forced all of them, both the sheep and cattle, to leave the Temple. He turned over the tables and scattered the money of those who were exchanging it. [16]Then he said to those who were selling pigeons, "Take these things out of here! Don't make my Father's house a place for buying and selling!"

[17]When this happened, the followers remembered what was written in the Scriptures: "My strong love for your Temple completely controls me."[n]

[18]Some of his people said to Jesus, "Show us a miracle to prove you have the right to do these things."

## god's promises

John 1:47–51

Do you know who God is? Have you ever experienced something great that he did? Have you ever thought about the things he can do and the things we will someday see when we get to heaven?

When Jesus was on earth, he did many amazing things and many people believed he was truly God. When Nathanael met Jesus, he experienced God's awesomeness in an unusual way. Jesus knew Nathanael and where he had been *before they even met!* When he heard this, Nathanael believed Jesus was God and said so out loud. Then Jesus told Nathanael and the other followers that they would see even more wonderful things.

Every day we can see God's greatness just by looking at the world around us and at the unique people he has made. We see Jesus changing the lives of people we know. But someday we will see more amazing things. We will see Jesus himself in heaven!

Jesus promised his followers they would see great things. In the same way, he will show us great things when we believe he is awesome and mighty.

***Someday we will see Jesus in heaven!***

---

1:51 **'angels . . . down'** *These words are from Genesis 28:12.* 2:6 **washing ceremony** *The Jewish people washed themselves in special ways before eating, before worshiping in the Temple, and at other special times.* 2:17 **"My . . . me."** *Quotation from Psalm 69:9.*

# Christian Girls Around the World
## Rachel: *Philippines*

Did you know that the Philippines, a country in Southeast Asia, has more than seven thousand islands? Thirteen-year-old Rachel feels proud of the beautiful scenery and nice beaches. She especially likes the people in her country and says they are kind, friendly, and respectful.

Rachel has many friends. Kids her age enjoy playing computer games, going out with their friends, and watching TV. They especially enjoy anime (a type of cartoons). Girls in the Philippines don't act as boldly as those in North America, Rachel says. For example, Filipinas (Filipino girls) don't approach boys to make friends. This is because Filipino people believe that the boy has to make the first move. Also, girls in the Philippines don't dress in the "daring" way that many North American girls do, but many are beginning to copy the North American styles.

To keep her faith strong, Rachel goes to church every Sunday and joins her younger brother at Sunday school. She feels thankful that God always reminds her of what is wrong and right to help keep her relationship with him growing. At her church, many of the kids participate in the dance min-istry—they do special dances and play the tambourine during the praise and worship time. Rachel hopes to join this group soon. Some of them also attend a special discipleship training class.

Most of the people in the Philippines belong to the Roman Catholic Church. A lot of them are also *superstitious,* which means they believe that certain things can bring bad or good luck. Rachel knows that many Catholic people haven't been taught that a Christian is someone who has accepted Jesus Christ as their Lord and Savior. So when she tells her Catholic friends that she's a Christian, they don't seem surprised. They call themselves Christians, too. Some of Rachel's "Christian" friends use bad language, which makes her uncomfortable. They tell Rachel they get bored at church services, which are too long for them.

When Rachel explains she's a "born again" Christian, they don't know what that means. They ask her how she could be born twice. That's when Rachel tells them about Jesus and how he died on the cross to save us from our sins!

---

[19] Jesus answered them, "Destroy this temple, and I will build it again in three days."

[20] They answered, "It took forty-six years to build this Temple! Do you really believe you can build it again in three days?"

[21] (But the temple Jesus meant was his own body. [22] After Jesus was raised from the dead, his followers remembered that Jesus had said this. Then they believed the Scripture and the words Jesus had said.)

[23] When Jesus was in Jerusalem for the Passover Feast, many people believed in him because they saw the miracles he did. [24] But Jesus did not believe in them because he knew them all. [25] He did not need anyone to tell him about people, because he knew what was in people's minds.

## Nicodemus Comes to Jesus

3 There was a man named Nicodemus who was one of the Pharisees and an important Jewish leader. [2] One night Nicodemus came to Jesus and said, "Teacher, we know you are a teacher sent from God, because no one can do the miracles you do unless God is with him."

[3] Jesus answered, "I tell you the truth, unless you are born again, you cannot be in God's kingdom."

[4] Nicodemus said, "But if a person is already old, how can he be born again? He cannot enter his mother's womb again. So how can a person be born a second time?"

[5] But Jesus answered, "I tell you the truth, unless you are born from water and the Spirit, you cannot enter God's kingdom. [6] Human life comes from human parents, but spiritual life comes from the Spirit. [7] Don't be surprised when I tell you, 'You must all be born again.' [8] The wind blows where it wants to and you hear the sound of it, but you don't know where the wind comes from or where it is going. It is the same with every person who is born from the Spirit."

[9] Nicodemus asked, "How can this happen?"

[10] Jesus said, "You are an important teacher in Israel, and you don't understand these things? [11] I tell you the truth, we talk about what we know, and we tell about what we have seen, but you don't accept what we tell you. [12] I have told you about things here on earth, and you do not believe me. So you will not believe me if I tell you about things of heaven. [13] The only one who has ever gone up to heaven is the One who came down from heaven—the Son of Man.[n]

[14] "Just as Moses lifted up the snake in the desert,[n] the Son of Man must also be lifted up. [15] So that everyone who believes can have eternal life in him.

[16] "God loved the world so much that he gave his one and only Son so that whoever believes in him may not be lost, but have eternal life. [17] God did not send his Son into the world to judge the world guilty, but to save the world through him. [18] People who believe in God's Son are not judged guilty. Those who do not believe have already been judged guilty, because they have not believed in God's one and only Son. [19] They are judged by this fact: The Light has come into the world, but they did not want light. They

---

**3:13 the Son of Man** Some Greek copies continue, "who is in heaven." **3:14 Moses . . . desert** When the Israelites were dying from snakebites, God told Moses to put a bronze snake on a pole. The people who looked at the snake were healed (Numbers 21:4–9).

wanted darkness, because they were doing evil things. [20]All who do evil hate the light and will not come to the light, because it will show all the evil things they do. [21]But those who follow the true way come to the light, and it shows that the things they do were done through God."

### Jesus and John the Baptist

[22]After this, Jesus and his followers went into the area of Judea, where he stayed with his followers and baptized people. [23]John was also baptizing in Aenon, near Salim, because there was plenty of water there. People were going there to be baptized. [24](This was before John was put into prison.)

[25]Some of John's followers had an argument with a Jew about religious washing.[n] [26]So they came to John and said, "Teacher, remember the man who was with you on the other side of the Jordan River, the one you spoke about so much? He is baptizing, and everyone is going to him."

[27]John answered, "A man can get only what God gives him. [28]You yourselves heard me say, 'I am not the Christ, but I am the one sent to prepare the way for him.' [29]The bride belongs only to the bridegroom. But the friend who helps the bridegroom stands by and listens to him. He is thrilled

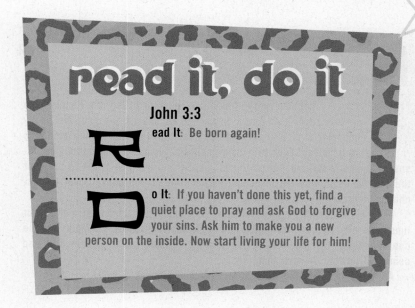

## read it, do it

### John 3:3

**R**ead It: Be born again!

**D**o It: If you haven't done this yet, find a quiet place to pray and ask God to forgive your sins. Ask him to make you a new person on the inside. Now start living your life for him!

# Q & A

**Q** My friend is having a sleepover birthday party and the only chaperone will be her big sister, who is seventeen. My parents won't let me go! What's the big deal?

**A** Your parents are probably concerned because they can't know what will happen at this party. You really need to trust their judgment in these types of issues. Without her parents there, there will much more likely be extra temptations to sin—and God wants you to stay far away from wrong things (1 Thessalonians 5:22).

that he gets to hear the bridegroom's voice. In the same way, I am really happy. [30]He must become greater, and I must become less important.

### The One Who Comes from Heaven

[31]"The One who comes from above is greater than all. The one who is from the earth belongs to the earth and talks about things on the earth. But the One who comes from heaven is greater than all. [32]He tells what he has seen and heard, but no one accepts what he says. [33]Whoever accepts what he says has proven that God is true. [34]The One whom God sent speaks the words of God, because God gives him the Spirit fully. [35]The Father loves the Son and has given him power over everything. [36]Those who believe in the Son have eternal life, but those who do not obey the Son will never have life. God's anger stays on them."

### Jesus and a Samaritan Woman

**4** The Pharisees heard that Jesus was making and baptizing more followers than John, [2]although Jesus himself did not baptize people, but his followers did. [3]Jesus knew that the Pharisees had heard about him, so he left Judea and went back to Galilee. [4]But on the way he had to go through the country of Samaria.

[5]In Samaria Jesus came to the town called Sychar, which is near the field Jacob gave to his son Joseph. [6]Jacob's well was there. Jesus was tired from his long trip, so he sat down beside the well. It was about twelve o'clock noon. [7]When a Samaritan woman came to the well to get some water, Jesus said to her, "Please give me a drink." [8](This happened while Jesus' followers were in town buying some food.)

[9]The woman said, "I am surprised that you ask me for a drink, since you are a Jewish man and I am a Samaritan woman." (Jewish people are not friends with Samaritans.[n])

[10]Jesus said, "If you only knew the free gift of God and who it is that is asking you for water, you would have asked him, and he would have given you living water."

[11]The woman said, "Sir, where will you get this living water? The well is very deep, and you have nothing to get water with. [12]Are you greater than Jacob, our father, who gave us this well and drank from it himself along with his sons and flocks?"

[13]Jesus answered, "Everyone who drinks this water will be thirsty again, [14]but whoever drinks the water I give will never be thirsty. The water I give will become a spring of water gushing up inside that person, giving eternal life."

[15]The woman said to him, "Sir, give me this water so I will never be thirsty again and will not have to come back here to get more water."

[16]Jesus told her, "Go get your husband and come back here."

[17]The woman answered, "I have no husband."

---

3:25 **religious washing** *The Jewish people washed themselves in special ways before eating, before worshiping in the Temple, and at other special times.* 4:9 **Jewish people . . . Samaritans.** *This can also be translated "Jewish people don't use things that Samaritans have used."*

## Bible Bios

### Zacchaeus
### (Luke 19:1–10)

**Z**acchaeus worked as a tax collector in Jericho. People have never liked paying taxes—so Zacchaeus' job made him pretty unpopular. It didn't help that he cheated people out of their money to get rich himself! Even with his greediness, when Zacchaeus found out Jesus had come to Jericho, he ran to see him. He had to climb a tree to see over the crowds, but it worked! Jesus spotted him and invited himself over to Zacchaeus' house.

Zacchaeus not only gladly welcomed Jesus, but he promised to give back four times whatever he had ever stolen *and* to give half of whatever remained to the poor. People complained about Jesus visiting a sinner, but he explained he had come just for that: to save sinners!

Are *you* willing to do anything it takes to know Jesus?

Jesus said to her, "You are right to say you have no husband. 18Really you have had five husbands, and the man you live with now is not your husband. You told the truth."

19The woman said, "Sir, I can see that you are a prophet. 20Our ancestors worshiped on this mountain, but you say that Jerusalem is the place where people must worship."

21Jesus said, "Believe me, woman. The time is coming when neither in Jerusalem nor on this mountain will you actually worship the Father. 22You Samaritans worship something you don't understand. We understand what we worship, because salvation comes from the Jews. 23The time is coming when the true worshipers will worship the Father in spirit and truth, and that time is here already. You see, the Father too is actively seeking such people to worship him. 24God is spirit, and those who worship him must worship in spirit and truth."

25The woman said, "I know that the Messiah is coming." (Messiah is the One called Christ.) "When the Messiah comes, he will explain everything to us."

26Then Jesus said, "I am he—I, the one talking to you."

27Just then his followers came back from town and were surprised to see him talking with a woman. But none of them asked, "What do you want?" or "Why are you talking with her?"

28Then the woman left her water jar and went back to town. She said to the people, 29"Come and see a man who told me everything I ever did. Do you think he might be the Christ?" 30So the people left the town and went to see Jesus.

31Meanwhile, his followers were begging him, "Teacher, eat something."

32But Jesus answered, "I have food to eat that you know nothing about."

33So the followers asked themselves, "Did somebody already bring him food?"

34Jesus said, "My food is to do what the One who sent me wants me to do and to finish his work. 35You have a saying, 'Four more months till harvest.' But I tell you, open your eyes and look at the fields ready for harvest now. 36Already, the one who harvests is being paid and is gathering crops for eternal life. So the one who plants and the one who harvests celebrate at the same time. 37Here the saying is true, 'One person plants, and another harvests.' 38I sent you to harvest a crop that you did not work on. Others did the work, and you get to finish up their work."[n]

39Many of the Samaritans in that town believed in Jesus because of what the woman said: "He told me everything I ever did." 40When the Samaritans came to Jesus, they begged him to stay with them, so he stayed there two more days. 41And many more believed because of the things he said.

42They said to the woman, "First we believed in Jesus because of what you said, but now we believe because we heard him ourselves. We know that this man really is the Savior of the world."

## Jesus Heals an Officer's Son

43Two days later, Jesus left and went to Galilee. 44(Jesus had said before that a prophet is not respected in his own country.) 45When Jesus arrived in Galilee, the people there welcomed him. They had seen all the things he did at the Passover Feast in Jerusalem, because they had been there, too.

46Jesus went again to visit Cana in Galilee where he had changed the water into wine. One of the king's important officers lived in the city of Capernaum, and his son was sick. 47When he heard that Jesus had come from Judea to Galilee, he went to Jesus and begged him to come to Capernaum and heal his son, because his son was almost dead. 48Jesus said to him, "You people must see signs and miracles before you will believe in me."

49The officer said, "Sir, come before my child dies."

50Jesus answered, "Go. Your son will live."

The man believed what Jesus told him and went home. 51On the way the man's servants came and met him and told him, "Your son is alive."

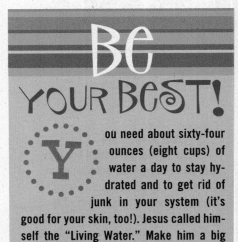

## Be YOUR BEST!

**Y**ou need about sixty-four ounces (eight cups) of water a day to stay hydrated and to get rid of junk in your system (it's good for your skin, too!). Jesus called himself the "Living Water." Make him a big part of your life to keep your soul refreshed and clean!

4:38 I . . . their work. *As a farmer sends workers to harvest grain, Jesus sends his followers out to bring people to God.*

# cool

## Thirsty?

Considering that water covers 75 percent of the earth, you'd think there would be enough for everyone to drink, right? But only about 3 percent of our water is good for drinking, and many people in the world have very little or no clean water. How important is water? A human being can live about a month without food . . . but only about a week without water!

Did you know your soul needs Jesus the way your body needs water? John 4:13–14 and John 7:37–39 says if you trust in Jesus, he will satisfy your thirsty soul!

⁵²The man asked, "What time did my son begin to get well?"

They answered, "Yesterday at one o'clock the fever left him."

⁵³The father knew that one o'clock was the exact time that Jesus had said, "Your son will live." So the man and all the people who lived in his house believed in Jesus.

⁵⁴That was the second miracle Jesus did after coming from Judea to Galilee.

## Jesus Heals a Man at a Pool

5 Later Jesus went to Jerusalem for a special feast. ²In Jerusalem there is a pool with five covered porches, which is called Bethesda*ⁿ* in the Hebrew language.*ⁿ* This pool is near the Sheep Gate. ³Many sick people were lying on the porches beside the pool. Some were blind, some were crippled, and some were paralyzed [, and they waited for the water to move. ⁴Sometimes an angel of the Lord came down to the pool and stirred up the water. After the angel did this, the first person to go into the pool was healed from any sickness he had].*ⁿ* ⁵A man was lying there who had been sick for thirty-eight years. ⁶When Jesus saw the man and knew that he had

been sick for such a long time, Jesus asked him, "Do you want to be well?"

⁷The sick man answered, "Sir, there is no one to help me get into the pool when the water starts moving. While I am coming to the water, someone else always gets in before me."

⁸Then Jesus said, "Stand up. Pick up your mat and walk." ⁹And immediately the man was well; he picked up his mat and began to walk.

The day this happened was a Sabbath day. ¹⁰So the Jews said to the man who had been healed, "Today is the Sabbath. It is against our law for you to carry your mat on the Sabbath day."

¹¹But he answered, "The man who made me well told me, 'Pick up your mat and walk.' "

¹²Then they asked him, "Who is the man who told you to pick up your mat and walk?"

¹³But the man who had been healed did not know who it was, because there were many people in that place, and Jesus had left.

¹⁴Later, Jesus found the man at the Temple and said to him, "See, you are well now. Stop sinning so that something worse does not happen to you."

¹⁵Then the man left and told his people that Jesus was the one who had made him well.

¹⁶Because Jesus was doing this on the Sabbath day, some evil people began to persecute him. ¹⁷But Jesus said to them,

"My Father never stops working, and so I keep working, too."

¹⁸This made them try still harder to kill him. They said, "First Jesus was breaking the law about the Sabbath day. Now he says that God is his own Father, making himself equal with God!"

## Jesus Has God's Authority

¹⁹But Jesus said, "I tell you the truth, the Son can do nothing alone. The Son does only what he sees the Father doing, because the Son does whatever the Father does. ²⁰The Father loves the Son and shows the Son all the things he himself does. But the Father will show the Son even greater things than this so that you can all be amazed. ²¹Just as the Father raises the dead and gives them life, so also the Son gives life to those he wants to. ²²In fact, the Father judges no one, but he has given the Son power to do all the judging ²³so that all people will honor the Son as much as they honor the Father. Anyone who does not honor the Son does not honor the Father who sent him.

²⁴"I tell you the truth, whoever hears what I say and believes in the One who sent me has eternal life. That person will not be judged guilty but has already left death and entered life. ²⁵I tell you the truth, the time is coming and is already here when the dead will hear the voice of the Son of God, and those who hear will have life. ²⁶Life comes from the Father himself, and he has allowed the Son to

## read it, do it

### John 3:6

**R**ead It: God is your spiritual Father.

**D**o It: This June, make a special Father's Day card for God! Thank him for giving you a new life through Jesus.

5:2 **Bethesda** *Some Greek copies read "Bethzatha" or "Bethsaida," different names for the pool of Bethesda.* 5:2 **Hebrew language** *Or Aramaic, the languages of many people in this region in the first century.* 5:3–4 **and . . . had** *Some Greek copies do not contain all or most of the bracketed text.*

have life in himself as well. ²⁷And the Father has given the Son the approval to judge, because he is the Son of Man. ²⁸Don't be surprised at this: A time is coming when all who are dead and in their graves will hear his voice. ²⁹Then they will come out of their graves. Those who did good will rise and have life forever, but those who did evil will rise to be judged guilty.

## Jesus Is God's Son

³⁰"I can do nothing alone. I judge only the way I am told, so my judgment is fair. I don't try to please myself, but I try to please the One who sent me.

³¹"If only I tell people about myself, what I say is not true. ³²But there is another who tells about me, and I know that the things he says about me are true.

³³"You have sent people to John, and he has told you the truth. ³⁴It is not that I need what humans say; I tell you this so you can be saved. ³⁵John was like a burning and shining lamp, and you were happy to enjoy his light for a while.

³⁶"But I have a proof about myself that is greater than that of John. The things I do, which are the things my Father gave me to do, prove that the Father sent me. ³⁷And the Father himself who sent me has

# Q & A

**Q** I'm not sure if I'm a Christian. How can I know?

**A** "Christian" describes someone who follows Christ. Do you believe that Jesus died on the cross to pay the punishment for your sins? Have you admitted your sins and asked God to forgive you? Are you willing to live for him and obey him from now on? If so, then you can be confident that you are a Christian. If not, ask God to save you today! Salvation is a free gift because God loves us! (Check out John 3:16.)

# Bible Basics

**L**isten to what the Bible has to say about itself: "God's Word is alive and working . . . it judges the thoughts and feelings in our hearts" (Hebrews 4:12). How can a book be living, working, and judging? God's Word is so much more than any other book. It contains words straight from God, and it is used by God to change people's lives. No matter how many times you read the Bible, there's always something fresh from God for you. He may use it to teach you about who he is, how people are created to be, or how he wants you to change. That's how the Bible lives and works!

given proof about me. You have never heard his voice or seen what he looks like. ³⁸His teaching does not live in you, because you don't believe in the One the Father sent. ³⁹You carefully study the Scriptures because you think they give you eternal life. They do in fact tell about me, ⁴⁰but you refuse to come to me to have that life.

⁴¹"I don't need praise from people. ⁴²But I know you—I know that you don't have God's love in you. ⁴³I have come from my Father and speak for him, but you don't accept me. But when another person comes, speaking only for himself, you will accept him. ⁴⁴You try to get praise from each other, but you do not try to get the praise that comes from the only God. So how can you believe? ⁴⁵Don't think that I will stand before the Father and say you are wrong. The one who says you are wrong is Moses, the one you hoped would save you. ⁴⁶If you really believed Moses, you would believe me, because Moses wrote about me. ⁴⁷But if you don't believe what Moses wrote, how can you believe what I say?"

## More than Five Thousand Fed

**6** After this, Jesus went across Lake Galilee (or, Lake Tiberias). ²Many people followed him because they saw the miracles he did to heal the sick.

³Jesus went up on a hill and sat down there with his followers. ⁴It was almost the time for the Jewish Passover Feast.

⁵When Jesus looked up and saw a large crowd coming toward him, he said to Philip, "Where can we buy enough bread for all these people to eat?" ⁶(Jesus asked Philip this question to test him, because Jesus already knew what he planned to do.)

⁷Philip answered, "Someone would have to work almost a year to buy enough bread for each person to have only a little piece."

⁸Another one of his followers, Andrew, Simon Peter's brother, said, ⁹"Here is a boy with five loaves of barley bread and two little fish, but that is not enough for so many people."

¹⁰Jesus said, "Tell the people to sit down." There was plenty of grass there, and about five thousand men sat down there. ¹¹Then Jesus took the loaves of bread, thanked God for them, and gave them to the people who were sitting there. He did the same with the fish, giving as much as the people wanted.

¹²When they had all had enough to eat, Jesus said to his followers, "Gather the leftover pieces of fish and bread so that nothing is wasted." ¹³So they gathered up the pieces and filled twelve baskets with the pieces left from the five barley loaves.

## The People Seek Jesus

[22]The next day the people who had stayed on the other side of the lake knew that Jesus had not gone in the boat with his followers but that they had left without him. And they knew that only one boat had been there. [23]But then some boats came from Tiberias and landed near the place where the people had eaten the bread after the Lord had given thanks. [24]When the people saw that Jesus and his followers were not there now, they got into boats and went to Capernaum to find Jesus.

## Jesus, the Bread of Life

[25]When the people found Jesus on the other side of the lake, they asked him, "Teacher, when did you come here?"

[26]Jesus answered, "I tell you the truth, you aren't looking for me because you saw me do miracles. You are looking for me because you ate the bread and were satisfied. [27]Don't work for the food that spoils. Work for the food that stays good always and gives eternal life. The Son of Man will give you this food, because on him God the Father has put his power."

[28]The people asked Jesus, "What are the things God wants us to do?"

[29]Jesus answered, "The work God wants you to do is this: Believe the One he sent."

[30]So the people asked, "What miracle will you do? If we see a miracle, we will believe you. What will you do? [31]Our ancestors ate the manna in the desert. This is written in the Scriptures: 'He gave them bread from heaven to eat.'"[n]

[32]Jesus said, "I tell you the truth, it was not Moses who gave you bread from heaven; it is my Father who is giving you the true bread from heaven. [33]God's bread is the One who comes down from heaven and gives life to the world."

[34]The people said, "Sir, give us this bread always."

[35]Then Jesus said, "I am the bread that gives life. Whoever comes to me will never be hungry, and whoever believes in me will never be thirsty. [36]But as I told you before, you have seen me and still don't believe. [37]The Father gives me the people who are mine. Every one of them will come to me, and I will always accept them. [38]I came down from heaven to do what God wants me to do, not what I want to do. [39]Here is what the One who

## god's promises

**John 5:24** There's a saying that unsaved people are born once and die twice, but Christians are born twice and die only once! What does that mean? The Bible tells us that the punishment for sin is death. Not just physical death (when your body stops living), but spiritual death! That's the second death.

Spiritual death means being separated from God and heaven forever. Even worse, it also means suffering in hell forever. And because we all have sin in our lives since the day of our birth, we all deserve to die spiritually!

Could this get any more depressing? Actually . . . it gets better! We can escape the punishment of eternal death! In John 5:24, Jesus says that whoever listens to his Word and believes in him has eternal life. "That person will not be judged guilty but has already left death and entered life."

When someone becomes a Christian we call that being "born again." (Check out John 3:3.) So it's true! Christians are born twice: once physically and once spiritually. And we only have to go through one type of death: physical. We don't even need to fear physical death—it actually takes us to eternal life with Jesus in heaven!

***Christians are born twice and die only once!***

[14]When the people saw this miracle that Jesus did, they said, "He must truly be the Prophet[n] who is coming into the world." [15]Jesus knew that the people planned to come and take him by force and make him their king, so he left and went into the hills alone.

## Jesus Walks on the Water

[16]That evening Jesus' followers went down to Lake Galilee. [17]It was dark now, and Jesus had not yet come to them. The followers got into a boat and started across the lake to Capernaum. [18]By now a strong wind was blowing, and the waves on the lake were getting bigger. [19]When they had rowed the boat about three or four miles, they saw Jesus walking on the water, coming toward the boat. The followers were afraid, [20]but Jesus said to them, "It is I. Do not be afraid." [21]Then they were glad to take him into the boat. At once the boat came to land at the place where they wanted to go.

6:14 **Prophet** *They probably meant the prophet that God told Moses he would send (Deuteronomy 18:15–19).* 6:31 **'He gave . . . eat.'** *Quotation from Psalm 78:24.*

sent me wants me to do: I must not lose even one whom God gave me, but I must raise them all on the last day. ⁴⁰Those who see the Son and believe in him have eternal life, and I will raise them on the last day. This is what my Father wants."

⁴¹Some people began to complain about Jesus because he said, "I am the bread that comes down from heaven." ⁴²They said, "This is Jesus, the son of Joseph. We know his father and mother. How can he say, 'I came down from heaven'?"

⁴³But Jesus answered, "Stop complaining to each other. ⁴⁴The Father is the One who sent me. No one can come to me unless the Father draws him to me, and I will raise that person up on the last day. ⁴⁵It is written in the prophets, 'They will all be taught by God.' Everyone who listens to the Father and learns from him comes to me. ⁴⁶No one has seen the Father except the One who is from God; only he has seen the Father. ⁴⁷I tell you the truth, whoever believes has eternal life. ⁴⁸I am the bread that gives life. ⁴⁹Your ancestors ate the manna in the desert, but still they died. ⁵⁰Here is the bread that comes down from heaven. Anyone who eats this bread will never die. ⁵¹I am the living bread that came down from heaven. Anyone who eats this bread will live forever. This bread is my flesh, which I will give up so that the world may have life."

⁵²Then the evil people began to argue among themselves, saying, "How can this man give us his flesh to eat?"

⁵³Jesus said, "I tell you the truth, you must eat the flesh of the Son of Man and drink his blood. Otherwise, you won't have real life in you. ⁵⁴Those who eat my flesh and drink my blood have eternal life, and I will raise them up on the last day. ⁵⁵My flesh is true food, and my blood is true drink. ⁵⁶Those who eat my flesh and drink my blood live in me, and I live in them. ⁵⁷The living Father sent me, and I live be-

cause of the Father. So whoever eats me will live because of me. ⁵⁸I am not like the bread your ancestors ate. They ate that bread and still died. I am the bread that came down from heaven, and whoever eats this bread will live forever." ⁵⁹Jesus said all these things while he was teaching in the synagogue in Capernaum.

### The Words of Eternal Life

⁶⁰When the followers of Jesus heard this, many of them said, "This teaching is hard. Who can accept it?"

⁶¹Knowing that his followers were complaining about this, Jesus said, "Does this teaching bother you? ⁶²Then will it also bother you to see the Son of Man

> ## NO ONE CAN COME TO ME UNLESS THE FATHER DRAWS HIM TO ME, AND I WILL RAISE THAT PERSON UP ON THE LAST DAY.

6:45 'They . . . God.' *Quotation from Isaiah 54:13.*

## dig deeper

### John 6:66–69

Many people followed Jesus besides his twelve closest followers. But when Jesus said they must eat his flesh and drink his blood in order to have eternal life (John 6:53–58), many of these people decided to go home. Maybe they hadn't thought much about what they were doing. Maybe they had been looking for adventure. Maybe this teaching just sounded too crazy for them. The twelve followers might have thought about leaving, too. Maybe Peter had a conversation with himself that went something like this:

"Maybe I should just go home. It's been a nice adventure, but I should get back to work! But then what? Who has ever taught like Jesus? Who else shows such love? I'm different since I started hanging out with Jesus. If he's not from God, who is he? A crazy man? A liar? No. I *know* him. He's not crazy. And he never lies."

When Jesus asked his twelve followers, "Do you want to leave, too?" Peter was ready with his answer. He asked, "Who would we go to?" (John 6:68).

Are you a follower of Jesus? Who else might you follow? There has never been anyone like Jesus. But you don't have to study world religions to learn that. Just "listen" to him and you'll see what Peter meant.

# Shine Your Light

Lily was just two years old when her family moved to Burkina Faso, Western Africa, to serve God as missionaries. She couldn't help very much at that age, but now that she's older, she serves God, too! One way she does this is by cheering up sick children.

Lily and some of her friends went with an older friend to visit hospitals and orphanages. That friend gave Lily a list of children who had terminal diseases (which means they won't get better) with information about their age, birthday, interests, and type of sickness. Lily started writing letters to some of the kids. She still writes to them about different subjects. She tries to make her letters funny to make the children smile. In her letters, Lily talks about things that interest each kid.

You could send letters and cards to sick children, too! Maybe you could even put small care packages together for them. Ask your parents to help you find out if a nearby hospital would give you a list of sick children. There are also special charities that organize projects like this. Pull out your markers and stickers and share God's love with a sick kid!

6Jesus said to his brothers, "The right time for me has not yet come, but any time is right for you. 7The world cannot hate you, but it hates me, because I tell it the evil things it does. 8So you go to the feast. I will not go yet[n] to this feast, because the right time for me has not yet come." 9After saying this, Jesus stayed in Galilee.

10But after Jesus' brothers had gone to the feast, Jesus went also. But he did not let people see him. 11At the feast some people were looking for him and saying, "Where is that man?"

12Within the large crowd there, many people were whispering to each other about Jesus. Some said, "He is a good man."

Others said, "No, he fools the people." 13But no one was brave enough to talk about Jesus openly, because they were afraid of the elders.

## Jesus Teaches at the Feast

14When the feast was about half over, Jesus went to the Temple and began to teach. 15The people were amazed and said, "This man has never studied in school. How did he learn so much?"

# Q & A

**Q** The Bible talks a lot about idols. Do idols still exist today?

going back to the place where he came from? 63It is the Spirit that gives life. The flesh doesn't give life. The words I told you are spirit, and they give life. 64But some of you don't believe." (Jesus knew from the beginning who did not believe and who would turn against him.) 65Jesus said, "That is the reason I said, 'If the Father does not bring a person to me, that one cannot come.'"

66After Jesus said this, many of his followers left him and stopped following him.

67Jesus asked the twelve followers, "Do you want to leave, too?"

68Simon Peter answered him, "Lord, who would we go to? You have the words that give eternal life. 69We believe and know that you are the Holy One from God."

70Then Jesus answered, "I chose all twelve of you, but one of you is a devil."

71Jesus was talking about Judas, the son of Simon Iscariot. Judas was one of the twelve, but later he was going to turn against Jesus.

## Jesus' Brothers Don't Believe

**7** After this, Jesus traveled around Galilee. He did not want to travel in Judea, because some evil people there wanted to kill him. 2It was time for the Feast of Shelters. 3So Jesus' brothers said to him, "You should leave here and go to Judea so your followers there can see the miracles you do. 4Anyone who wants to be well known does not hide what he does. If you are doing these things, show yourself to the world." 5(Even Jesus' brothers did not believe in him.)

**A** An idol is anything (or anyone) that we worship or give our best attention to. Not everyone bows down to statues, but that doesn't mean they don't have idols. Idols today can include money, popular singers, actors or athletes, clothes, and television. If anything takes more of your time and interest than God, ask yourself if you have an idol. Confess it to God and ask him to help you not put anything before him. Only God deserves our worship!

7:8 **yet** *Some Greek copies do not have this word.*

# Q&A

**Q** My friends sometimes steal jewelry or clothes from the mall. How can I get them to stop and still be their friend?

**A** Check out Exodus 20:15. Explain to your friends that stealing is wrong and that you won't do it with them. If they listen to you, that's great! If they think you're weird or get upset, don't back down. Stick to your beliefs. If they stop being your friend just because you want to do the right thing, you need to start looking for better friends!

[16]Jesus answered, "The things I teach are not my own, but they come from him who sent me. [17]If people choose to do what God wants, they will know that my teaching comes from God and not from me. [18]Those who teach their own ideas are trying to get honor for themselves. But those who try to bring honor to the one who sent them speak the truth, and there is nothing false in them. [19]Moses gave you the law,[n] but none of you obeys that law. Why are you trying to kill me?"

[20]The people answered, "A demon has come into you. We are not trying to kill you."

[21]Jesus said to them, "I did one miracle, and you are all amazed. [22]Moses gave you the law about circumcision. (But really Moses did not give you circumcision; it came from our ancestors.) And yet you circumcise a baby boy on a Sabbath day. [23]If a baby boy can be circumcised on a Sabbath day to obey the law of Moses, why are you angry at me for healing a person's whole body on the Sabbath day? [24]Stop judging by the way things look, but judge by what is really right."

## Is Jesus the Christ?

[25]Then some of the people who lived in Jerusalem said, "This is the man they are trying to kill. [26]But he is teaching where everyone can see and hear him, and no one is trying to stop him. Maybe the leaders have decided he really is the Christ. [27]But we know where this man is from. Yet when the real Christ comes, no one will know where he comes from."

[28]Jesus, teaching in the Temple, cried out, "Yes, you know me, and you know where I am from. But I have not come by my own authority. I was sent by the One who is true, whom you don't know. [29]But I know him, because I am from him, and he sent me."

[30]When Jesus said this, they tried to seize him. But no one was able to touch him, because it was not yet the right time. [31]But many of the people believed in Jesus. They said, "When the Christ comes, will he do more miracles than this man has done?"

## The Leaders Try to Arrest Jesus

[32]The Pharisees heard the crowd whispering these things about Jesus. So the leading priests and the Pharisees sent some Temple guards to arrest him. [33]Jesus said, "I will be with you a little while longer. Then I will go back to the One who sent me. [34]You will look for me, but you will not find me. And you cannot come where I am."

[35]Some people said to each other, "Where will this man go so we cannot find him? Will he go to the Greek cities where our people live and teach the Greek people there? [36]What did he mean when he said, 'You will look for me, but you will not find me,' and 'You cannot come where I am'?"

## Jesus Talks About the Spirit

[37]On the last and most important day of the feast Jesus stood up and said in a loud voice, "Let anyone who is thirsty come to me and drink. [38]If anyone believes in me, rivers of living water will flow out from that person's heart, as the Scripture says." [39]Jesus was talking about the Holy Spirit. The Spirit had not yet been given, because Jesus had not yet been raised to glory. But later, those who believed in Jesus would receive the Spirit.

## The People Argue About Jesus

[40]When the people heard Jesus' words, some of them said, "This man really is the Prophet."[n]

[41]Others said, "He is the Christ."

Still others said, "The Christ will not come from Galilee. [42]The Scripture says that the Christ will come from David's family and from Bethlehem, the town where David lived." [43]So the people did not agree with each other about Jesus. [44]Some of them wanted to arrest him, but no one was able to touch him.

## Some Leaders Won't Believe

[45]The Temple guards went back to the leading priests and the Pharisees, who asked, "Why didn't you bring Jesus?"

[46]The guards answered, "The words he says are greater than the words of any other person who has ever spoken!"

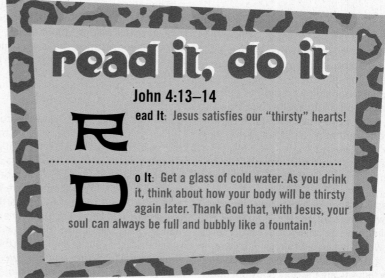

## read it, do it

### John 4:13–14

**R**ead It: Jesus satisfies our "thirsty" hearts!

**D**o It: Get a glass of cold water. As you drink it, think about how your body will be thirsty again later. Thank God that, with Jesus, your soul can always be full and bubbly like a fountain!

7:19 **law** Moses gave God's people the Law that God gave him on Mount Sinai (Exodus 34:29–32).   7:40 **Prophet** They probably meant the prophet God told Moses he would send (Deuteronomy 18:15–19).

⁴⁷The Pharisees answered, "So Jesus has fooled you also! ⁴⁸Have any of the leaders or the Pharisees believed in him? No! ⁴⁹But these people, who know nothing about the law, are under God's curse."

⁵⁰Nicodemus, who had gone to see Jesus before, was in that group.ⁿ He said, ⁵¹"Our law does not judge a person without hearing him and knowing what he has done."

⁵²They answered, "Are you from Galilee, too? Study the Scriptures, and you will learn that no prophet comes from Galilee."

---

Some of the earliest surviving Greek copies do not contain 7:53—8:11.

[⁵³And everyone left and went home.

¹¹She answered, "No one, sir."

Then Jesus said, "I also don't judge you guilty. You may go now, but don't sin anymore."]

---

## Jesus Is the Light of the World

¹²Later, Jesus talked to the people again, saying, "I am the light of the world. The person who follows me will never live in darkness but will have the light that gives life."

¹³The Pharisees said to Jesus, "When you talk about yourself, you are the only one to say these things are true. We cannot accept what you say."

¹⁴Jesus answered, "Yes, I am saying these things about myself, but they are true. I

**Preteens need about 10 hours of sleep each night.**
—Sonna, Linda, Ph.D. *The Everything Tween Book.* Avon, Massachusetts: Adams Media Corporation, 2003. p. 194

**did you know?**

know where I came from and where I am going. But you don't know where I came from or where I am going. ¹⁵You judge by human standards. I am not judging anyone. ¹⁶But when I do judge, I judge truthfully, because I am not alone. The Father who sent me is with me. ¹⁷Your own law says that when two witnesses say the same thing, you must accept what they say. ¹⁸I am one of the witnesses who speaks about myself, and the Father who sent me is the other witness."

¹⁹They asked, "Where is your father?"

Jesus answered, "You don't know me or my Father. If you knew me, you would know my Father, too." ²⁰Jesus said these things while he was teaching in the Temple, near where the money is kept. But no one arrested him, because the right time for him had not yet come.

## The People Misunderstand Jesus

²¹Again, Jesus said to the people, "I will leave you, and you will look for me, but you will die in your sins. You cannot come where I am going."

²²So the Jews asked, "Will he kill himself? Is that why he said, 'You cannot come where I am going'?"

²³Jesus said, "You people are from here below, but I am from above. You belong to this world, but I don't belong to this world. ²⁴So I told you that you would die in your sins. Yes, you will die in your sins if you don't believe that I am he."

²⁵They asked, "Then who are you?"

Jesus answered, "I am what I have told you from the beginning. ²⁶I have many things to say and decide about you. But I tell people only the things I have heard from the One who sent me, and he speaks the truth."

²⁷The people did not understand that he was talking to them about the Father. ²⁸So Jesus said to them, "When you lift up the Son of Man, you will know that I am he. You will know that these things I do are not by my own authority but that I say only what the Father has taught me. ²⁹The One who sent me is with me. I always do what is pleasing to him, so he has not left me alone." ³⁰While Jesus was saying these things, many people believed in him.

## Freedom from Sin

³¹So Jesus said to the Jews who believed in him, "If you continue to obey my teaching, you are truly my followers. ³²Then you will know the truth, and the truth will make you free."

³³They answered, "We are Abraham's children, and we have never been anyone's slaves. So why do you say we will be free?"

³⁴Jesus answered, "I tell you the truth, everyone who lives in sin is a slave to sin. ³⁵A

## The Woman Caught in Adultery

**8** Jesus went to the Mount of Olives. ²But early in the morning he went back to the Temple, and all the people came to him, and he sat and taught them. ³The teachers of the law and the Pharisees brought a woman who had been caught in adultery. They forced her to stand before the people. ⁴They said to Jesus, "Teacher, this woman was caught having sexual relations with a man who is not her husband. ⁵The law of Moses commands that we stone to death every woman who does this. What do you say we should do?" ⁶They were asking this to trick Jesus so that they could have some charge against him.

But Jesus bent over and started writing on the ground with his finger. ⁷When they continued to ask Jesus their question, he raised up and said, "Anyone here who has never sinned can throw the first stone at her." ⁸Then Jesus bent over again and wrote on the ground.

⁹Those who heard Jesus began to leave one by one, first the older men and then the others. Jesus was left there alone with the woman standing before him. ¹⁰Jesus raised up again and asked her, "Woman, where are they? Has no one judged you guilty?"

**speakout!**

**Q** Have you ever been tempted to cheat at school? What did you do?

**A** Yes. I put my hands around my eyes and remembered that God wouldn't want me to do that. —Hannah, 10

**7:50 Nicodemus . . . group.** *The story about Nicodemus going and talking to Jesus is in John 3:1—21.*

# Q & A

**Q** Is it wrong to play with Ouija boards?

**A** Yes! Ouija boards are a form of *divination* (trying to get hidden information from angels, demons, or dead people). Divination goes against God because it's like saying we don't think his Word and prayer are enough to give us the knowledge that we need. Also, the Old Testament has many warnings about talking to spirits and the devil. John 8:44 tells us that Satan is a liar! Don't let anyone convince you to participate in divination, even if they say "it's just a game."

slave does not stay with a family forever, but a son belongs to the family forever. [36]So if the Son makes you free, you will be truly free. [37]I know you are Abraham's children, but you want to kill me because you don't accept my teaching. [38]I am telling you what my Father has shown me, but you do what your father has told you."

[39]They answered, "Our father is Abraham."

Jesus said, "If you were really Abraham's children, you would do[n] the things Abraham did. [40]I am a man who has told you the truth which I heard from God, but you are trying to kill me. Abraham did nothing like that. [41]So you are doing the things your own father did."

But they said, "We are not like children who never knew who their father was. God is our Father; he is the only Father we have."

[42]Jesus said to them, "If God were really your Father, you would love me, because I came from God and now I am here. I did not come by my own authority; God sent me. [43]You don't understand what I say, because you cannot accept my teaching. [44]You belong to your father the devil, and you want to do what he wants. He was a

murderer from the beginning and was against the truth, because there is no truth in him. When he tells a lie, he shows what he is really like, because he is a liar and the father of lies. [45]But because I speak the truth, you don't believe me. [46]Can any of you prove that I am guilty of sin? If I am telling the truth, why don't you believe me? [47]The person who belongs to God accepts what God says. But you don't accept what God says, because you don't belong to God."

## Jesus Is Greater than Abraham

[48]They answered, "We say you are a Samaritan and have a demon in you. Are we not right?"

[49]Jesus answered, "I have no demon in me. I give honor to my Father, but you dishonor me. [50]I am not trying to get honor for myself. There is One who wants this honor for me, and he is the judge. [51]I tell you the truth, whoever obeys my teaching will never die."

[52]They said to Jesus, "Now we know that you have a demon in you! Even Abraham and the prophets died. But you say, 'Whoever obeys my teaching will never die.' [53]Do you think you are greater than our father Abraham, who died? And the prophets died, too. Who do you think you are?"

[54]Jesus answered, "If I give honor to myself, that honor is worth nothing. The One who gives me honor is my Father, and you say he is your God. [55]You don't really know him, but I know him. If I said I did not know him, I would be a liar like you. But I do know him, and I obey what he says. [56]Your father Abraham was very happy that he would see my day. He saw that day and was glad."

[57]They said to him, "You have never seen Abraham! You are not even fifty years old."

[58]Jesus answered, "I tell you the truth, before Abraham was even born, I am!" [59]When Jesus said this, the people picked up stones to throw at him. But Jesus hid himself, and then he left the Temple.

## Jesus Heals a Man Born Blind

**9** As Jesus was walking along, he saw a man who had been born blind. [2]His followers asked him, "Teacher, whose sin caused this man to be born blind—his own sin or his parents' sin?"

[3]Jesus answered, "It is not this man's sin or his parents' sin that made him blind. This man was born blind so that God's power could be shown in him. [4]While it is daytime, we must continue doing the work of the One who sent me. Night is coming, when no one can work. [5]While I am in the world, I am the light of the world."

[6]After Jesus said this, he spit on the ground and made some mud with it and put the mud on the man's eyes. [7]Then he told the man, "Go and wash in the Pool of Siloam." (Siloam means Sent.) So the man went, washed, and came back seeing.

[8]The neighbors and some people who had earlier seen this man begging said, "Isn't this the same man who used to sit and beg?"

[9]Some said, "He is the one," but others said, "No, he only looks like him."

The man himself said, "I am the man."

[10]They asked, "How did you get your sight?"

[11]He answered, "The man named Jesus made some mud and put it on my eyes.

## Get It

### Heaven

Heaven is the beautiful, perfect place where God lives. He created all of heaven, including the heavenly beings, such as angels. When this world ends, he will create a new heaven where his children will live with him forever. Heaven is pure and nothing bad can enter—that means no evil thoughts or actions, no pain or death, and no sin. When Christians die, they go to heaven. The apostle John had a vision of heaven from God (check out Revelation 4:1–11 for details). The best part about going to heaven is that we'll be with God!

8:39 **If . . . do** *Some Greek copies read "If you are really Abraham's children, you will do."*

# HOW ADVENTUROUS ARE YOU?

Jesus' followers, and many of the other early Christians, had courage and did bold things for God. You can read many of these adventures in the Gospels and Acts (the first five books of the New Testament).

How adventurous are you? Take this quiz to find out!

1. **You discover that a girl at school lives very close to your church. You:**
   a. Hope that she'll visit your church one day.
   b. Tell your pastor and suggest that he visit her family.
   c. Invite her to church and offer to stop at her house on the way so you can go together.

2. **Your Sunday school teacher asks for ideas of how you can serve God as a group. You suggest:**
   a. Praying for the sick people in your church.
   b. Sending Christmas cards to prisoners.
   c. Going downtown and giving out Bibles and sandwiches to street kids.

3. **You go out for a hamburger with some friends. When you get back to the table with your food you:**
   a. Start eating right away.
   b. Say a quick prayer in your head before you eat.
   c. Say, "Hey, guys! Let's thank God for the food first!"

4. **Everyone at church has been challenged to give at least one person an invitation to a special event. You give yours to:**
   a. Your best friend.
   b. A nice girl you met just last week.
   c. The school bully.

## How adventurous are you?

**If you answered mostly As,** you're playing it safe. You probably don't really enjoy adventure or taking risks. That's fine—everyone has different abilities. But God wants you to be courageous in your Christian life (1 Corinthians 16:13). Ask him to take away any fears you have and to make you bold about your faith. He'll help you!

**If you answered mostly Bs,** you enjoy serving God. You don't try to hide your relationship with Jesus and you look for things you can do for God. Try to take it to the next level, though. Ask God to help your courage grow so you can share his love with more people!

**If you answered mostly Cs,** your Christian life is an adventure! You don't let what other people think bother you. That's great! Keep on trusting God to take care of you as you get out there and show people how awesome it is to know Jesus. He'll use your life in wonderful ways!

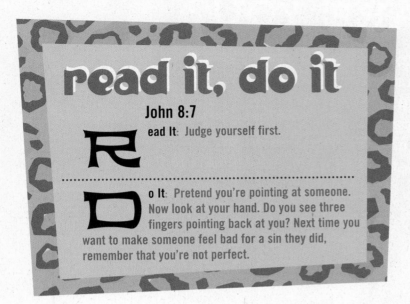

Then he told me to go to Siloam and wash. So I went and washed, and then I could see."

[12] They asked him, "Where is this man?"

"I don't know," he answered.

## Pharisees Question the Healing

[13] Then the people took to the Pharisees the man who had been blind. [14] The day Jesus had made mud and healed his eyes was a Sabbath day. [15] So now the Pharisees asked the man, "How did you get your sight?"

He answered, "He put mud on my eyes, I washed, and now I see."

[16] So some of the Pharisees were saying, "This man does not keep the Sabbath day, so he is not from God."

But others said, "A man who is a sinner can't do miracles like these." So they could not agree with each other.

[17] They asked the man again, "What do you say about him since it was your eyes he opened?"

The man answered, "He is a prophet."

[18] These leaders did not believe that he had been blind and could now see again. So they sent for the man's parents [19] and asked them, "Is this your son who you say was born blind? Then how does he now see?"

[20] His parents answered, "We know that this is our son and that he was born blind. [21] But we don't know how he can now see. We don't know who opened his eyes. Ask him. He is old enough to speak for himself." [22] His parents said this because they were afraid of the elders, who had already decided that anyone who said Jesus was the Christ would be avoided. [23] That is why his parents said, "He is old enough. Ask him."

[24] So for the second time, they called the man who had been blind. They said, "You should give God the glory by telling the truth. We know that this man is a sinner."

[25] He answered, "I don't know if he is a sinner. One thing I do know: I was blind, and now I see."

[26] They asked, "What did he do to you? How did he make you see again?"

[27] He answered, "I already told you, and you didn't listen. Why do you want to hear it again? Do you want to become his followers, too?"

[28] Then they insulted him and said, "You are his follower, but we are followers of Moses. [29] We know that God spoke to Moses, but we don't even know where this man comes from."

[30] The man answered, "This is a very strange thing. You don't know where he comes from, and yet he opened my eyes. [31] We all know that God does not listen to sinners, but he listens to anyone who worships and obeys him. [32] Nobody has ever heard of anyone giving sight to a man born blind. [33] If this man were not from God, he could do nothing."

[34] They answered, "You were born full of sin! Are you trying to teach us?" And they threw him out.

## Spiritual Blindness

[35] When Jesus heard that they had thrown him out, Jesus found him and said, "Do you believe in the Son of Man?"

[36] He asked, "Who is the Son of Man, sir, so that I can believe in him?"

[37] Jesus said to him, "You have seen him. The Son of Man is the one talking with you."

[38] He said, "Lord, I believe!" Then the man worshiped Jesus.

[39] Jesus said, "I came into this world so that the world could be judged. I came so that the blind[n] would see and so that those who see will become blind."

[40] Some of the Pharisees who were nearby heard Jesus say this and asked, "Are you saying we are blind, too?"

[41] Jesus said, "If you were blind, you would not be guilty of sin. But since you keep saying you see, your guilt remains."

## The Shepherd and His Sheep

**10** Jesus said, "I tell you the truth, the person who does not enter the sheepfold by the door, but climbs in some other way, is a thief and a robber. [2] The one who enters by the door is the shepherd of the sheep. [3] The one who guards the door opens it for him. And the sheep listen to the voice of the shepherd. He calls his own sheep by name and leads them out. [4] When he brings all his sheep out, he goes ahead of them, and they follow him because they know his voice. [5] But they will never follow a stranger. They will run away from him because they don't know his voice." [6] Jesus told the people this story, but they did not understand what it meant.

**9:39 blind** *Jesus is talking about people who are spiritually blind, not physically blind.*

John

# dig deeper

## John 12:1–8

When your parents take you somewhere cool on vacation, do you think to yourself, "They could have saved that money for when I go to college"? When someone buys you a special gift, do you wonder why they didn't send the money to a charity instead? No . . . you probably appreciate these gifts!

In John 12:1–8, we read about a woman who came to Jesus a few days before he was crucified. She pulled out a jar of very expensive perfume and poured it on Jesus' head. That might seem odd to us today but in those days it was a way to honor someone very special. The problem? The other people around them got upset! They complained to Jesus that she had wasted the perfume! They said it could have been sold and then the money given to poor people.

Jesus told everyone to leave the woman alone. He appreciated what she had done because it was the best way she knew to worship him. He wouldn't be around much longer and, after he returned to heaven, his followers would have many opportunities to help poor people. Jesus also understood that they cared more about the money than the poor people. But this woman loved him . . . and proved it!

When you worship God, do it enthusiastically! He deserves your best.

---

the Father knows me, and I know the Father. I give my life for the sheep. [16]I have other sheep that are not in this flock, and I must bring them also. They will listen to my voice, and there will be one flock and one shepherd. [17]The Father loves me because I give my life so that I can take it back again. [18]No one takes it away from me; I give my own life freely. I have the right to give my life, and I have the right to take it back. This is what my Father commanded me to do."

[19]Again the leaders did not agree with each other because of these words of Jesus. [20]Many of them said, "A demon has come into him and made him crazy. Why listen to him?"

[21]But others said, "A man who is crazy with a demon does not say things like this. Can a demon open the eyes of the blind?"

### Jesus Is Rejected

[22]The time came for the Feast of Dedication at Jerusalem. It was winter, [23]and Jesus was walking in the Temple in Solomon's Porch. [24]Some people gathered around him and said, "How long will you make us wonder about you? If you are the Christ, tell us plainly."

[25]Jesus answered, "I told you already, but you did not believe. The miracles I do in my Father's name show who I am. [26]But you don't believe, because you are not my sheep. [27]My sheep listen to my voice; I know them, and they follow me. [28]I give them eternal life, and they will never die, and no one can steal them out of my hand. [29]My Father gave my sheep to me. He is greater than all, and no person can steal my sheep out of my Father's hand. [30]The Father and I are one."

[31]Again some of the people picked up stones to kill Jesus. [32]But he said to them, "I have done many good works from the Father. Which of these good works are you killing me for?"

[33]They answered, "We are not killing you because of any good work you did, but because you speak against God. You are only a human, but you say you are the same as God!"

[34]Jesus answered, "It is written in your law that God said, 'I said, you are gods.'[n] [35]This Scripture called those people gods who received God's message, and Scripture is always true. [36]So why do you say that I speak against God because I said,

---

### Jesus Is the Good Shepherd

[7]So Jesus said again, "I tell you the truth, I am the door for the sheep. [8]All the people who came before me were thieves and robbers. The sheep did not listen to them. [9]I am the door, and the person who enters through me will be saved and will be able to come in and go out and find pasture. [10]A thief comes to steal and kill and destroy, but I came to give life—life in all its fullness.

[11]"I am the good shepherd. The good shepherd gives his life for the sheep. [12]The worker who is paid to keep the sheep is different from the shepherd who owns them. When the worker sees a wolf coming, he runs away and leaves the sheep alone. Then the wolf attacks the sheep and scatters them. [13]The man runs away because he is only a paid worker and does not really care about the sheep.

[14]"I am the good shepherd. I know my sheep, and my sheep know me, [15]just as

---

10:34 'I . . . gods.' *Quotation from Psalm 82:6.*

# Relationships

You might not be allowed to have a boyfriend yet, but you probably have friends that are boys. Boys are probably the hottest topic of conversation . . . and can sometimes be the most frustrating people on the planet! How does God want you to interact with guys? Paul instructed Timothy to treat young women as sisters, in a pure way (1 Timothy 5:2). He would probably say the same thing to you today: treat boys as brothers—that is, with respect. After all, Jesus said that "people will know that you are my followers if you love each other" (John 13:35).

'I am God's Son'? I am the one God chose and sent into the world. ³⁷If I don't do what my Father does, then don't believe me. ³⁸But if I do what my Father does, even though you don't believe in me, believe what I do. Then you will know and understand that the Father is in me and I am in the Father."

³⁹They tried to take Jesus again, but he escaped from them.

⁴⁰Then he went back across the Jordan River to the place where John had first baptized. Jesus stayed there, ⁴¹and many people came to him and said, "John never did a miracle, but everything John said about this man is true." ⁴²And in that place many believed in Jesus.

## The Death of Lazarus

**11** A man named Lazarus was sick. He lived in the town of Bethany, where Mary and her sister Martha lived. ²Mary was the woman who later put perfume on the Lord and wiped his feet with her hair. Mary's brother was Lazarus, the man who was now sick. ³So Mary and Martha sent someone to tell Jesus, "Lord, the one you love is sick."

⁴When Jesus heard this, he said, "This sickness will not end in death. It is for the glory of God, to bring glory to the Son of God." ⁵Jesus loved Martha and her sister and Lazarus. ⁶But when he heard that Lazarus was sick, he stayed where he was for two more days. ⁷Then Jesus said to his followers, "Let's go back to Judea."

⁸The followers said, "But Teacher, some people there tried to stone you to death only a short time ago. Now you want to go back there?"

⁹Jesus answered, "Are there not twelve hours in the day? If anyone walks in the daylight, he will not stumble, because he can see by this world's light. ¹⁰But if anyone walks at night, he stumbles because there is no light to help him see."

¹¹After Jesus said this, he added, "Our friend Lazarus has fallen asleep, but I am going there to wake him."

¹²The followers said, "But Lord, if he is only asleep, he will be all right."

¹³Jesus meant that Lazarus was dead, but his followers thought he meant Lazarus was really sleeping. ¹⁴So then Jesus said plainly, "Lazarus is dead. ¹⁵And I am glad for your sakes I was not there so that you may believe. But let's go to him now."

¹⁶Then Thomas (the one called Didymus) said to the other followers, "Let us also go so that we can die with him."

## Jesus in Bethany

¹⁷When Jesus arrived, he learned that Lazarus had already been dead and in the tomb for four days. ¹⁸Bethany was about two miles from Jerusalem. ¹⁹Many of the Jews had come there to comfort Martha and Mary about their brother.

²⁰When Martha heard that Jesus was coming, she went out to meet him, but Mary stayed home. ²¹Martha said to Jesus, "Lord, if you had been here, my brother would not have died. ²²But I know that even now God will give you anything you ask."

²³Jesus said, "Your brother will rise and live again."

²⁴Martha answered, "I know that he will rise and live again in the resurrection[n] on the last day."

²⁵Jesus said to her, "I am the resurrection and the life. Those who believe in me will have life even if they die. ²⁶And everyone who lives and believes in me will never die. Martha, do you believe this?"

²⁷Martha answered, "Yes, Lord. I believe that you are the Christ, the Son of God, the One coming to the world."

## Jesus Cries

²⁸After Martha said this, she went back and talked to her sister Mary alone. Martha said, "The Teacher is here and he is asking for you." ²⁹When Mary heard this, she got up quickly and went to Jesus. ³⁰Jesus had not yet come into the town but was still at the place where Martha had met him. ³¹The Jews were with Mary in the house, comforting her. When they saw her stand and leave quickly,

> JESUS SAID TO HER, "I AM THE RESURRECTION AND THE LIFE. THOSE WHO BELIEVE IN ME WILL HAVE LIFE EVEN IF THEY DIE."

**11:24 resurrection** *Being raised from the dead to live again.*

## Looking Ahead

### NEW FRIENDS

As you meet people and choose friends to spend time with, remember that who your friends are says a lot about who *you* are. Hopefully you'll keep some of your close friendships your whole life, but you'll also continue to make new friends as you grow older. Proverbs 13:20 says that if you surround yourself with friends who make good choices, you'll keep yourself out of trouble. It also says that "the friends of fools will suffer." You can be friends to people with different backgrounds, but be careful of those with dangerous lifestyles. Friends have a lot of influence on us, so make good choices!

they followed her, thinking she was going to the tomb to cry there.

32But Mary went to the place where Jesus was. When she saw him, she fell at his feet and said, "Lord, if you had been here, my brother would not have died."

33When Jesus saw Mary crying and the Jews who came with her also crying, he was upset and was deeply troubled. 34He asked, "Where did you bury him?"

"Come and see, Lord," they said.

35Jesus cried.

36So the Jews said, "See how much he loved him."

37But some of them said, "If Jesus opened the eyes of the blind man, why couldn't he keep Lazarus from dying?"

### Jesus Raises Lazarus

38Again feeling very upset, Jesus came to the tomb. It was a cave with a large stone covering the entrance. 39Jesus said, "Move the stone away."

Martha, the sister of the dead man, said, "But, Lord, it has been four days since he died. There will be a bad smell."

40Then Jesus said to her, "Didn't I tell you that if you believed you would see the glory of God?"

41So they moved the stone away from the entrance. Then Jesus looked up and said, "Father, I thank you that you heard me. 42I know that you always hear me, but I said these things because of the people here around me. I want them to believe that you sent me." 43After Jesus said this, he cried out in a loud voice, "Lazarus, come out!" 44The dead man came out, his hands and feet wrapped with pieces of cloth, and a cloth around his face.

Jesus said to them, "Take the cloth off of him and let him go."

### The Plan to Kill Jesus

45Many of the people, who had come to visit Mary and saw what Jesus did, believed in him. 46But some of them went to the Pharisees and told them what Jesus had done. 47Then the leading priests and Pharisees called a meeting of the council. They asked, "What should we do? This man is doing many miracles. 48If we let him continue doing these things, everyone will believe in him. Then the Romans will come and take away our Temple and our nation."

49One of the men there was Caiaphas, the high priest that year. He said, "You people know nothing! 50You don't realize that it is better for one man to die for the people than for the whole nation to be destroyed."

51Caiaphas did not think of this himself. As high priest that year, he was really prophesying that Jesus would die for their nation 52and for God's scattered children to bring them all together and make them one.

53That day they started planning to kill Jesus. 54So Jesus no longer traveled openly among the people. He left there and went to a place near the desert, to a town called Ephraim and stayed there with his followers.

55It was almost time for the Passover Feast. Many from the country went up to Jerusalem before the Passover to do the special things to make themselves pure. 56The people looked for Jesus and stood in the Temple asking each other, "Is he coming to the Feast? What do you think?" 57But the leading priests and the Pharisees had given orders that if anyone knew where Jesus was, he must tell them. Then they could arrest him.

### Jesus with Friends in Bethany

**12** Six days before the Passover Feast, Jesus went to Bethany, where Lazarus lived. (Lazarus is the man Jesus raised from the dead.) 2There they had a dinner for Jesus. Martha served the food, and Lazarus was one of the people eating with Jesus. 3Mary brought in a pint of very expensive perfume made from pure nard. She poured the perfume on Jesus' feet, and then she wiped his feet with

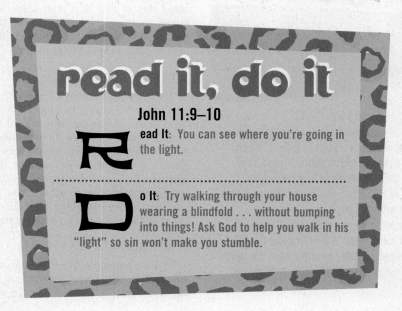

## read it, do it

### John 11:9–10

**R**ead It: You can see where you're going in the light.

**D**o It: Try walking through your house wearing a blindfold . . . without bumping into things! Ask God to help you walk in his "light" so sin won't make you stumble.

her hair. And the sweet smell from the perfume filled the whole house.

[4]Judas Iscariot, one of Jesus' followers who would later turn against him, was there. Judas said, [5]"This perfume was worth an entire year's wages. Why wasn't it sold and the money given to the poor?" [6]But Judas did not really care about the poor; he said this because he was a thief. He was the one who kept the money box, and he often stole from it.

[7]Jesus answered, "Leave her alone. It was right for her to save this perfume for today, the day for me to be prepared for burial. [8]You will always have the poor with you, but you will not always have me."

### The Plot Against Lazarus

[9]A large crowd of people heard that Jesus was in Bethany. So they went there to see not only Jesus but Lazarus, whom Jesus raised from the dead. [10]So the leading priests made plans to kill Lazarus, too. [11]Because of Lazarus many of the Jews were leaving them and believing in Jesus.

### Jesus Enters Jerusalem

[12]The next day a great crowd who had come to Jerusalem for the Passover Feast heard that Jesus was coming there. [13]So they took branches of palm trees and went out to meet Jesus, shouting,

# Q & A

**Q** Are the lyrics of a song important if I usually just listen to the music?

**A** Our brains remember messages that we hear, even if we don't realize it. When you listen to lyrics that dishonor God, talk dirty, or contain bad language, you're filling up your brain with garbage. That affects your heart, your words, your actions, and attitudes. God wants your mind filled only with good things (Philippians 4:8), so make sure the lyrics to your music are pleasing to him.

# Bible Basics

**P**eople study many old books whose authors lived around the time the Bible was written. Compared with other older books, the Bible is the one that has been proven to be the most reliable! There are no original copies of the books of the Bible that are written by the hands of the authors. But the earliest copies we do have were made shortly after the originals. There are *many* old copies of the Bible, and they are almost exactly the same. The differences between them are very small (for example, some copies spell a few names differently). It's easy to see that the Bible was carefully copied and that the message we have is what God wanted us to read!

"Praise[n] God!
God bless the One who comes in the name of the Lord!
God bless the King of Israel!"
*Psalm 118:25–26*

[14]Jesus found a colt and sat on it. This was as the Scripture says,

[15]"Don't be afraid, people of Jerusalem!
Your king is coming,
sitting on the colt of a donkey."
*Zechariah 9:9*

[16]The followers of Jesus did not understand this at first. But after Jesus was raised to glory, they remembered that this had been written about him and that they had done these things to him.

### People Tell About Jesus

[17]There had been many people with Jesus when he raised Lazarus from the dead and told him to come out of the tomb. Now they were telling others about what Jesus did. [18]Many people went out to meet Jesus, because they had heard about this miracle. [19]So the Pharisees said to each other, "You can see that nothing is going right for us. Look! The whole world is following him."

### Jesus Talks About His Death

[20]There were some Greek people, too, who came to Jerusalem to worship at the Passover Feast. [21]They went to Philip, who was from Bethsaida in Galilee, and said, "Sir, we would like to see Jesus." [22]Philip told Andrew, and then Andrew and Philip told Jesus.

[23]Jesus said to them, "The time has come for the Son of Man to receive his glory. [24]I tell you the truth, a grain of wheat must fall to the ground and die to make many seeds. But if it never dies, it remains only a single seed. [25]Those who love their lives will lose them, but those who hate their lives in this world will keep true life forever. [26]Whoever serves me must follow me. Then my servant will be with me everywhere I am. My Father will honor anyone who serves me.

[27]"Now I am very troubled. Should I say, 'Father, save me from this time'? No, I came to this time so I could suffer. [28]Father, bring glory to your name!"

Then a voice came from heaven, "I have brought glory to it, and I will do it again."

[29]The crowd standing there, who heard the voice, said it was thunder.

But others said, "An angel has spoken to him."

[30]Jesus said, "That voice was for your sake, not mine. [31]Now is the time for the world to be judged; now the ruler of this world will be thrown down. [32]If I am lifted up from the earth, I will draw all people toward me." [33]Jesus said this to show how he would die.

12:13 **Praise** *Literally, "Hosanna," a Hebrew word used at first in praying to God for help, but at this time it was probably a shout of joy used in praising God or his Messiah.*

John

³⁴The crowd said, "We have heard from the law that the Christ will live forever. So why do you say, 'The Son of Man must be lifted up'? Who is this 'Son of Man'?"

³⁵Then Jesus said, "The light will be with you for a little longer, so walk while you have the light. Then the darkness will not catch you. If you walk in the darkness, you will not know where you are going. ³⁶Believe in the light while you still have it so that you will become children of light." When Jesus had said this, he left and hid himself from them.

## Some People Won't Believe in Jesus

³⁷Though Jesus had done many miracles in front of the people, they still did not believe in him. ³⁸This was to bring about what Isaiah the prophet had said:

"Lord, who believed what we told them?
Who saw the Lord's power in this?"
*Isaiah 53:1*

³⁹This is why the people could not believe: Isaiah also had said,

⁴⁰"He has blinded their eyes,
and he has closed their minds.
Otherwise they would see with their eyes
and understand in their minds
and come back to me and be healed."
*Isaiah 6:10*

⁴¹Isaiah said this because he saw Jesus' glory and spoke about him.

⁴²But many believed in Jesus, even many of the leaders. But because of the Pharisees, they did not say they believed in him for fear they would be put out of the synagogue. ⁴³They loved praise from people more than praise from God.

⁴⁴Then Jesus cried out, "Whoever believes in me is really believing in the One who sent me. ⁴⁵Whoever sees me sees the One who sent me. ⁴⁶I have come as light into the world so that whoever believes in me would not stay in darkness.

⁴⁷"Anyone who hears my words and does not obey them, I do not judge, because I did not come to judge the world, but to save the world. ⁴⁸There is a judge for those who refuse to believe in me and do not accept my words. The word I have taught will be their judge on the last day. ⁴⁹The things I taught were not from myself.

The Father who sent me told me what to say and what to teach. ⁵⁰And I know that eternal life comes from what the Father commands. So whatever I say is what the Father told me to say."

## Jesus Washes His Followers' Feet

**13** It was almost time for the Passover Feast. Jesus knew that it was time for him to leave this world and go back to the Father. He had always loved those who were his own in the world, and he loved them all the way to the end.

²Jesus and his followers were at the evening meal. The devil had already persuaded Judas Iscariot, the son of Simon, to turn against Jesus. ³Jesus knew that the Father had given him power over everything and that he had come from God and was going back to God. ⁴So during the meal Jesus stood up and took off his outer clothing. Taking a towel, he wrapped it around his waist. ⁵Then he poured water into a bowl and began to wash the followers' feet, drying them with the towel that was wrapped around him.

⁶Jesus came to Simon Peter, who said to him, "Lord, are you going to wash my feet?"

⁷Jesus answered, "You don't understand now what I am doing, but you will understand later."

⁸Peter said, "No, you will never wash my feet."

Jesus answered, "If I don't wash your feet, you are not one of my people."

⁹Simon Peter answered, "Lord, then wash not only my feet, but wash my hands and my head, too!"

¹⁰Jesus said, "After a person has had a bath, his whole body is clean. He needs only to wash his feet. And you men are clean, but not all of you." ¹¹Jesus knew who would turn against him, and that is why he said, "Not all of you are clean."

¹²When he had finished washing their feet, he put on his clothes and sat down again. He asked, "Do you understand what I have just done for you? ¹³You call me 'Teacher' and 'Lord,' and you are right, because that is what I am. ¹⁴If I, your Lord and Teacher, have washed your feet, you also should wash each other's feet. ¹⁵I did this as an example so that you should do as I have done for you. ¹⁶I tell you the truth, a servant is not greater than his master. A messenger is

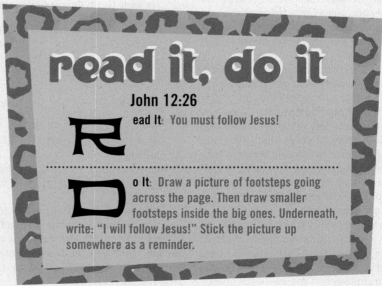

## read it, do it

**John 12:26**

**R**ead It: You must follow Jesus!

**D**o It: Draw a picture of footsteps going across the page. Then draw smaller footsteps inside the big ones. Underneath, write: "I will follow Jesus!" Stick the picture up somewhere as a reminder.

not greater than the one who sent him. [17]If you know these things, you will be blessed if you do them.

[18]"I am not talking about all of you. I know those I have chosen. But this is to bring about what the Scripture said: 'The man who ate at my table has turned against me.'[n] [19]I am telling you this now before it happens so that when it happens, you will believe that I am he. [20]I tell you the truth, whoever accepts anyone I send also accepts me. And whoever accepts me also accepts the One who sent me."

## Jesus Talks About His Death

[21]After Jesus said this, he was very troubled. He said openly, "I tell you the truth, one of you will turn against me."

[22]The followers all looked at each other, because they did not know whom Jesus was talking about. [23]One of the followers sitting[n] next to Jesus was the follower Jesus loved. [24]Simon Peter motioned to him to ask Jesus whom he was talking about.

[25]That follower leaned closer to Jesus and asked, "Lord, who is it?"

[26]Jesus answered, "I will dip this bread into the dish. The man I give it to is the man who will turn against me." So Jesus took a piece of bread, dipped it, and gave it to Judas Iscariot, the son of Simon. [27]As soon as Judas took the bread, Satan entered him. Jesus said to him, "The thing that you will do—do it quickly." [28]No one at the table understood why Jesus said this to Judas. [29]Since he was the one who kept the money box, some of the followers thought Jesus was telling him to buy what was needed for the feast or to give something to the poor.

[30]Judas took the bread Jesus gave him and immediately went out. It was night.

[31]When Judas was gone, Jesus said, "Now the Son of Man receives his glory, and God receives glory through him. [32]If God receives glory through him,[n] then God will give glory to the Son through himself. And God will give him glory quickly."

[33]Jesus said, "My children, I will be with you only a little longer. You will look for me, and what I told the Jews, I tell you now: Where I am going you cannot come. [34]"I give you a new command: Love each other. You must love each other as I have loved you. [35]All people will know that you are my followers if you love each other."

## god's promises

John 14:23–26

Have you ever gone to see a guidance counselor at school or another counselor who has helped you through a problem or given you advice? When Jesus was on earth, he promised that he would send Christians a special counselor. The name of this counselor, whom Jesus calls "the Helper," is the Holy Spirit.

In a way, the Holy Spirit is our spiritual counselor. He helps us understand the Bible. He also guides us in our daily life as Christians so we can know what Jesus wants us to do. Jesus promised us that the Holy Spirit will help us remember all of the things Jesus said. Jesus knew we couldn't do it on our own. He knew we would need help, and that is why he sent us a personal helper and counselor—the Holy Spirit!

As a Christian, have you ever felt in your heart that you should or should not do something? That could be the Holy Spirit doing his job, reminding you of what Jesus wants you to do! You can learn more about the jobs of the Holy Spirit in John 16:13, Romans 8:26, and Ephesians 4:30.

*Jesus promised us that the Holy Spirit will help us remember all of the things Jesus said.*

## Peter Will Say He Doesn't Know Jesus

[36]Simon Peter asked Jesus, "Lord, where are you going?"

Jesus answered, "Where I am going you cannot follow now, but you will follow later."

[37]Peter asked, "Lord, why can't I follow you now? I am ready to die for you!"

[38]Jesus answered, "Are you ready to die for me? I tell you the truth, before the rooster crows, you will say three times that you don't know me."

"I GIVE YOU A NEW COMMAND: LOVE EACH OTHER. YOU MUST LOVE EACH OTHER AS I HAVE LOVED YOU. ALL PEOPLE WILL KNOW THAT YOU ARE MY FOLLOWERS IF YOU LOVE EACH OTHER."

**13:18** 'The man . . . me.' *Quotation from Psalm 41:9.* **13:23** sitting *Literally, "lying." The people of that time ate lying down and leaning on one arm.* **13:32** If . . . him *Some Greek copies do not have this phrase.*

## Jesus Comforts His Followers

**14** Jesus said, "Don't let your hearts be troubled. Trust in God, and trust in me. [2]There are many rooms in my Father's house; I would not tell you this if it were not true. I am going there to prepare a place for you. [3]After I go and prepare a place for you, I will come back and take you to be with me so that you may be where I am. [4]You know the way to the place where I am going."[n]

[5]Thomas said to Jesus, "Lord, we don't know where you are going. So how can we know the way?"

[6]Jesus answered, "I am the way, and the truth, and the life. The only way to the Father is through me. [7]If you really knew me, you would know my Father, too. But now you do know him, and you have seen him."

[8]Philip said to him, "Lord, show us the Father. That is all we need."

[9]Jesus answered, "I have been with you a long time now. Do you still not know me, Philip? Whoever has seen me has seen the Father. So why do you say, 'Show us the Father'? [10]Don't you believe that I am in the Father and the Father is in me? The words I say to you don't come from me, but the Father lives in me and does his own work. [11]Believe me when I say that I am in the Father and the Father is in me. Or believe because of the miracles I have done. [12]I tell you the truth, whoever believes in me will do the same things that I do. Those who believe will do even greater things than these, because I am going to the Father. [13]And if you ask for anything in my name, I will do it for you so that the Father's glory will be shown through the Son. [14]If you ask me for anything in my name, I will do it.

## The Promise of the Holy Spirit

[15]"If you love me, you will obey my commands. [16]I will ask the Father, and he will give you another Helper[n] to be with you forever— [17]the Spirit of truth. The world cannot accept him, because it does not see him or know him. But you know him, because he lives with you and he will be in you.

[18]"I will not leave you all alone like orphans; I will come back to you. [19]In a little while the world will not see me anymore, but you will see me. Because I live, you will live, too. [20]On that day you will know that I am in my Father, and that you are in me and I am in you. [21]Those who know my commands and obey them are the ones who love me, and my Father will love those who love me. I will love them and will show myself to them."

[22]Then Judas (not Judas Iscariot) said, "But, Lord, why do you plan to show yourself to us and not to the rest of the world?"

[23]Jesus answered, "If people love me, they will obey my teaching. My Father will love them, and we will come to them and make our home with them. [24]Those who do not love me do not obey my teaching. This teaching that you hear is not really mine; it is from my Father, who sent me.

[25]"I have told you all these things while I am with you. [26]But the Helper will teach you everything and will cause you to remember all that I told you. This Helper is the Holy Spirit whom the Father will send in my name.

## dig deeper

### John 14:26–27

Have you ever wished you had someone to help you do the right thing? Someone who would encourage you to follow Jesus Christ by reminding you of the things he said and did? Guess what? You do have a helper!

Before Jesus returned to heaven, he told his worried followers, "The Helper will teach you everything and will cause you to remember all that I told you. This Helper is the Holy Spirit whom the Father will send in my name" (John 14:26). Jesus went on to say, "I leave you peace; my peace I give you. I do not give it to you as the world does. So don't let your hearts be troubled or afraid" (14:27).

And after Jesus left earth, the Holy Spirit did come (Acts 2:1–4)! The Holy Spirit is a gift that God gives to every Christian. He is always with us, and his full time job is to point us to God.

Some people refer to the Holy Spirit as their "conscience." But he's more than that; he also will bring to mind Jesus' words at just the right time. The more you listen to his voice, the clearer it will become!

---

14:4 *You . . . going. Some Greek copies read "You know where I am going and the way to the place I am going."*   14:16 *Helper "Counselor" or "Comforter." Jesus is talking about the Holy Spirit.*

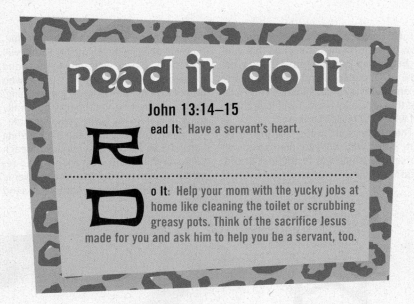

## read it, do it

### John 13:14–15

**R**ead It: Have a servant's heart.

- - - - - - - - - - - - - - - - - - - - - - - - - - -

**D**o It: Help your mom with the yucky jobs at home like cleaning the toilet or scrubbing greasy pots. Think of the sacrifice Jesus made for you and ask him to help you be a servant, too.

27"I leave you peace; my peace I give you. I do not give it to you as the world does. So don't let your hearts be troubled or afraid. 28You heard me say to you, 'I am going, but I am coming back to you.' If you loved me, you should be happy that I am going back to the Father, because he is greater than I am. 29I have told you this now, before it happens, so that when it happens, you will believe. 30I will not talk with you much longer, because the ruler of this world is coming. He has no power over me, 31but the world must know that I love the Father, so I do exactly what the Father told me to do.

"Come now, let us go.

### Jesus Is Like a Vine

**15** "I am the true vine; my Father is the gardener. 2He cuts off every branch of mine that does not produce fruit. And he trims and cleans every branch that produces fruit so that it will produce even more fruit. 3You are already clean because of the words I have spoken to you. 4Remain in me, and I will remain in you. A branch cannot produce fruit alone but must remain in the vine. In the same way, you cannot produce fruit alone but must remain in me.

5"I am the vine, and you are the branches. If any remain in me and I remain in them, they produce much fruit. But without me they can do nothing. 6If any do not remain in me, they are like a branch that is thrown away and then dies. People pick up dead branches, throw them into the fire, and burn them. 7If you remain in me and follow my teachings, you can ask anything you want, and it will be given to you. 8You should produce much fruit and show that you are my followers, which brings glory to my Father. 9I loved you as the Father loved me. Now remain in my love. 10I have obeyed my Father's commands, and I remain in his love. In the same way, if you obey my commands, you will remain in my love. 11I have told you these things so that you can have the same joy I have and so that your joy will be the fullest possible joy.

12"This is my command: Love each other as I have loved you. 13The greatest love a person can show is to die for his friends. 14You are my friends if you do what I command you. 15I no longer call you servants, because a servant does not know what his master is doing. But I call you friends, because I have made known to you everything I heard from my Father. 16You did not choose me; I chose you. And I gave you this work: to go and produce fruit, fruit that will last. Then the Father will give you anything you ask for in my name. 17This is my command: Love each other.

### Jesus Warns His Followers

18"If the world hates you, remember that it hated me first. 19If you belonged to the world, it would love you as it loves its own. But I have chosen you out of the world, so you don't belong to it. That is why the world hates you. 20Remember what I told you: A servant is not greater than his master. If people did wrong to me, they will do wrong to you, too. And if they obeyed my teaching, they will obey yours, too. 21They will do all this to you on account of me, because they do not know the One who sent me. 22If I had not come and spoken to them, they would not be guilty of sin, but now they have no excuse for their sin. 23Whoever hates me also hates my Father. 24I did works among them that no one else has ever done. If I had not done these works, they would not be guilty of sin. But now they have seen what I have done, and yet they have hated both me and my Father. 25But this happened so that what is written in their law would be true: 'They hated me for no reason.'[n]

26"I will send you the Helper[n] from the Father; he is the Spirit of truth who comes from the Father. When he comes, he will tell about me, 27and you also must tell people about me, because you have been with me from the beginning.

## cool

### That's Impossible!

**T**ry to lick your elbow (most people can't do it). You can't sneeze with your eyes open (please don't try this one!). You can't lift yourself by pulling on your shoelaces, you can't draw a square circle, and you can't use your hairbrush to clip your toenails!

Know what else is impossible? Getting into heaven without giving your life to Jesus. In John 14:6, Jesus said, "I am the way, and the truth, and the life. The only way to the Father is through me." Don't try to do the impossible. Put your faith in Jesus today!

---

**15:25** '*They . . . reason.*' *These words could be from Psalm 35:19 or Psalm 69:4.*  **15:26** **Helper** *"Counselor" or "Comforter." Jesus is talking about the Holy Spirit.*

**16** "I have told you these things to keep you from giving up. ²People will put you out of their synagogues. Yes, the time is coming when those who kill you will think they are offering service to God. ³They will do this because they have not known the Father and they have not known me. ⁴I have told you these things now so that when the time comes you will remember that I warned you.

## The Work of the Holy Spirit

"I did not tell you these things at the beginning, because I was with you then. ⁵Now I am going back to the One who sent me. But none of you asks me, 'Where are you going?' ⁶Your hearts are filled with sadness because I have told you these things. ⁷But I tell you the truth, it is better for you that I go away. When I go away, I will send the Helper*ⁿ* to you. If I do not go away, the Helper will not come. ⁸When the Helper comes, he will prove to the people of the world the truth about sin, about being right with God, and about judgment. ⁹He will prove to them that sin is not believing in me. ¹⁰He will prove to them that being right with God comes from my going to the Father and not being seen anymore. ¹¹And the Helper will prove to them that judgment happened when the ruler of this world was judged.

**Q** What does it mean to be a good friend?

**A** Jesus gave us the best example of a good friend: he gave up his life so that we would not get the punishment that our sins deserve (see John 15:13). You'll probably never have to sacrifice your life for your friend, but you can still love her in an unselfish and generous way. Keep in mind that being a good friend doesn't mean doing everything your friend wants. Sometimes it means honestly telling her that what she wants will harm her or will not please God.

¹²"I have many more things to say to you, but they are too much for you now. ¹³But when the Spirit of truth comes, he will lead you into all truth. He will not speak his own words, but he will speak only what he hears, and he will tell you what is to come. ¹⁴The Spirit of truth will bring glory to me, because he will take what I have to say and tell it to you. ¹⁵All that the Father has is mine. That is why I said that the Spirit will take what I have to say and tell it to you.

## Sadness Will Become Happiness

¹⁶"After a little while you will not see me, and then after a little while you will see me again."

¹⁷Some of the followers said to each other, "What does Jesus mean when he says, 'After a little while you will not see me, and then after a little while you will see me again'? And what does he mean when he says, 'Because I am going to the Father'?" ¹⁸They also asked, "What does he mean by 'a little while'? We don't understand what he is saying."

¹⁹Jesus saw that the followers wanted to ask him about this, so he said to them, "Are you asking each other what I meant when I said, 'After a little while you will not see me, and then after a little while you will see me again'? ²⁰I tell you the truth, you will cry and be sad, but the world will be happy. You will be sad, but your sadness will become joy. ²¹When a woman gives birth to a baby, she has pain, because her time has come. But when her baby is born, she forgets the pain, because she is so happy that a child has been born into the world. ²²It is the same with you. Now you are sad, but I will see you again and you will be happy, and no one will take away your joy. ²³In that day you will not ask me for anything. I tell you the truth, my Father will give you anything you ask for in my name. ²⁴Until now you have not asked for anything in my name. Ask and you will receive, so that your joy will be the fullest possible joy.

# Relationships

**H**ow many people are in your family? Maybe you only have a mom, or just a dad—or maybe you have ten siblings! Your family might include half brothers and sisters or stepbrothers and sisters. You could be living with people who aren't blood related to you. But that doesn't change one fact: they're still family. God asks us to "love each other as I have loved you" (John 15:12). That's a lot of love! First Peter 4:8 says that "love will cause people to forgive each other for many sins." Try it out!

**16:7 Helper** *"Counselor" or "Comforter." Jesus is talking about the Holy Spirit.*

## Victory over the World

25"I have told you these things indirectly in stories. But the time will come when I will not use stories like that to tell you things; I will speak to you in plain words about the Father. 26In that day you will ask the Father for things in my name. I mean, I will not need to ask the Father for you. 27The Father himself loves you. He loves you because you loved me and believed that I came from God. 28I came from the Father into the world. Now I am leaving the world and going back to the Father."

29Then the followers of Jesus said, "You are speaking clearly to us now and are not using stories that are hard to understand. 30We can see now that you know all things. You can answer a person's question even before it is asked. This makes us believe you came from God."

31Jesus answered, "So now you believe? 32Listen to me; a time is coming when you will be scattered, each to your own home. That time is now here. You will leave me alone, but I am never really alone, because the Father is with me.

33"I told you these things so that you can have peace in me. In this world you will have trouble, but be brave! I have defeated the world."

## Jesus Prays for His Followers

**17** After Jesus said these things, he looked toward heaven and prayed, "Father, the time has come. Give glory to your Son so that the Son can give glory to you. 2You gave the Son power over all people so that the Son could give eternal life to all those you gave him. 3And this is eternal life: that people know you, the only true God, and that they know Jesus Christ, the One you sent. 4Having finished the work you gave me to do, I brought you glory on earth. 5And now, Father, give me glory with you; give me the glory I had with you before the world was made.

6"I showed what you are like to those you gave me from the world. They belonged to you, and you gave them to me, and they have obeyed your teaching. 7Now they know that everything you gave me comes from you. 8I gave them the teachings you gave me, and they accepted them. They knew that I truly came from you, and they believed that you

sent me. 9I am praying for them. I am not praying for people in the world but for those you gave me, because they are yours. 10All I have is yours, and all you have is mine. And my glory is shown through them. 11I am coming to you; I will not stay in the world any longer. But they are still in the world. Holy Father, keep them safe by the power of your name,

the name you gave me, so that they will be one, just as you and I are one. 12While I was with them, I kept them safe by the power of your name, the name you gave me. I protected them, and only one of them, the one worthy of destruction, was lost so that the Scripture would come true.

13"I am coming to you now. But I pray these things while I am still in the world

# dig deeper

## John 16:33

Somehow the suspenseful parts aren't quite so scary the second time you read a book or see a movie. You still might jump when Godzilla roars or scream when the lights go out, but you aren't really worried. You know the good guy will get there in time and that everything will work out great.

Jesus knew he was going to be arrested and put to death, but he also knew he would come back to life. Jesus told his followers ahead of time because he wanted them to be comforted and he wanted them to be brave. Most of all, Jesus wanted them to find peace in him—

that no matter how terrible things looked, he really would defeat death. The good guy really would get there in time and save the day!

Jesus knows we will have trouble in our lives, too. He's honest with us about that. In John 16:33, he says, "In this world you will have trouble, but be brave! I have defeated the world."

Instead of pretending everything will be okay and telling you to just be happy, Jesus gives you comfort you can really use. He reminds you that he has defeated the world—anything and everything that is against God and hurtful to people. That's peace you can really count on!

so that these followers can have all of my joy in them. [14]I have given them your teaching. And the world has hated them, because they don't belong to the world, just as I don't belong to the world. [15]I am not asking you to take them out of the world but to keep them safe from the Evil One. [16]They don't belong to the world, just as I don't belong to the world. [17]Make them ready for your service through your truth; your teaching is truth. [18]I have sent them into the world, just as you sent me into the world. [19]For their sake, I am making myself ready to serve so that they can be ready for their service of the truth.

[20]"I pray for these followers, but I am also praying for all those who will believe in me because of their teaching. [21]Father, I pray that they can be one. As you are in me and I am in you, I pray that they can also be one in us. Then the world will believe that you sent me. [22]I have given these people the glory that you gave me so that they can be one, just as you and I are one. [23]I will be in them and you will be in me so that they will be completely one. Then the world will know that you sent me and that you loved them just as much as you loved me.

[24]"Father, I want these people that you gave me to be with me where I am. I want them to see my glory, which you gave me because you loved me before the world was made. [25]Father, you are the One who is good. The world does not know you, but I know you, and these people know you sent me. [26]I showed them

## Be YOUR BEST!

**S**tart learning how to manage money while you're young. If you waste it, you won't enjoy it for long. Either save it in the bank for later or use it for good things. Same thing goes for the talents and gifts God gave you. It pleases him if you use them responsibly!

what you are like, and I will show them again. Then they will have the same love that you have for me, and I will live in them."

### Jesus Is Arrested

**18** When Jesus finished praying, he went with his followers across the Kidron Valley. On the other side there was a garden, and Jesus and his followers went into it.

[2]Judas knew where this place was, because Jesus met there often with his followers. Judas was the one who turned against Jesus. [3]So Judas came there with a group of soldiers and some guards from the leading priests and the Pharisees. They were carrying torches, lanterns, and weapons.

[4]Knowing everything that would happen to him, Jesus went out and asked, "Who is it you are looking for?"

[5]They answered, "Jesus from Nazareth."

"I am he," Jesus said. (Judas, the one who turned against Jesus, was standing there with them.) [6]When Jesus said, "I am he," they moved back and fell to the ground.

[7]Jesus asked them again, "Who is it you are looking for?"

They said, "Jesus of Nazareth."

[8]"I told you that I am he," Jesus said. "So if you are looking for me, let the

others go." [9]This happened so that the words Jesus said before would come true: "I have not lost any of the ones you gave me."

[10]Simon Peter, who had a sword, pulled it out and struck the servant of the high priest, cutting off his right ear. (The servant's name was Malchus.) [11]Jesus said to Peter, "Put your sword back. Shouldn't I drink the cup[n] the Father gave me?"

### Jesus Is Brought Before Annas

[12]Then the soldiers with their commander and the guards arrested Jesus. They tied him [13]and led him first to Annas, the father-in-law of Caiaphas, the high priest that year. [14]Caiaphas was the one who told the Jews that it would be better if one man died for all the people.

### Peter Says He Doesn't Know Jesus

[15]Simon Peter and another one of Jesus' followers went along after Jesus. This follower knew the high priest, so he went with Jesus into the high priest's courtyard. [16]But Peter waited outside near the door. The follower who knew the high priest came back outside, spoke to the girl at the door, and brought Peter inside. [17]The girl at the door said to Peter, "Aren't you also one of that man's followers?"

Peter answered, "No, I am not!"

[18]It was cold, so the servants and guards had built a fire and were standing around it, warming themselves. Peter also was standing with them, warming himself.

### The High Priest Questions Jesus

[19]The high priest asked Jesus questions about his followers and his teaching. [20]Jesus answered, "I have spoken openly to everyone. I have always taught in synagogues and in the Temple, where all the Jews come together. I never said anything in secret. [21]So why do you question me? Ask the people who heard my teaching. They know what I said."

[22]When Jesus said this, one of the guards standing there hit him. The guard said, "Is that the way you answer the high priest?"

[23]Jesus answered him, "If I said something wrong, then show what it was. But if what I said is true, why do you hit me?"

[24]Then Annas sent Jesus, who was still tied, to Caiaphas the high priest.

## speakout!

**Q** How do you tell your friends about your faith in Jesus?

**A** At first I will talk about "regular" stuff with them, to build up a friendship, and then share more about Jesus.
—Robin, 12

**18:11 cup** *Jesus is talking about the painful things that will happen to him. Accepting these things will be very hard, like drinking a cup of something bitter.*

## Peter Says Again He Doesn't Know Jesus

25As Simon Peter was standing and warming himself, they said to him, "Aren't you one of that man's followers?"

Peter said it was not true; he said, "No, I am not."

26One of the servants of the high priest was there. This servant was a relative of the man whose ear Peter had cut off. The servant said, "Didn't I see you with him in the garden?"

27Again Peter said it wasn't true. At once a rooster crowed.

## Jesus Is Brought Before Pilate

28Early in the morning they led Jesus from Caiaphas's house to the Roman governor's palace. They would not go inside the palace, because they did not want to make themselves unclean;n they wanted to eat the Passover meal. 29So Pilate went outside to them and asked, "What charges do you bring against this man?"

30They answered, "If he were not a criminal, we wouldn't have brought him to you."

31Pilate said to them, "Take him yourselves and judge him by your own law."

"But we are not allowed to put anyone to death," the Jews answered. 32(This happened so that what Jesus said about how he would die would come true.)

33Then Pilate went back inside the palace and called Jesus to him and asked, "Are you the king of the Jews?"

34Jesus said, "Is that your own question, or did others tell you about me?"

35Pilate answered, "I am not one of you. It was your own people and their leading priests who handed you over to me. What have you done wrong?"

36Jesus answered, "My kingdom does not belong to this world. If it belonged to this world, my servants would have fought to keep me from being given over to the Jewish leaders. But my kingdom is from another place."

37Pilate said, "So you are a king!"

Jesus answered, "You are the one saying I am a king. This is why I was born and came into the world: to tell people the truth. And everyone who belongs to the truth listens to me."

38Pilate said, "What is truth?" After he said this, he went out to the crowd again and said to them, "I find nothing against this man. 39But it is your custom that I free one prisoner to you at Passover time. Do you want me to free the 'king of the Jews'?"

40They shouted back, "No, not him! Let Barabbas go free!" (Barabbas was a robber.)

19 Then Pilate ordered that Jesus be taken away and whipped. 2The soldiers made a crown from some thorny branches and put it on Jesus' head and put a purple robe around him. 3Then they came to him many times and said, "Hail, King of the Jews!" and hit him in the face.

4Again Pilate came out and said to them, "Look, I am bringing Jesus out to you. I want you to know that I find nothing against him." 5So Jesus came out, wearing the crown of thorns and the purple robe. Pilate said to them, "Here is the man!"

6When the leading priests and the guards saw Jesus, they shouted, "Crucify him! Crucify him!"

But Pilate answered, "Crucify him yourselves, because I find nothing against him."

7The leaders answered, "We have a law that says he should die, because he said he is the Son of God."

8When Pilate heard this, he was even more afraid. 9He went back inside the palace and asked Jesus, "Where do you come from?" But Jesus did not answer him. 10Pilate said, "You refuse to speak to me? Don't you know I have power to set you free and power to have you crucified?"

## top ten

### top ten ways to...
### Be a Good Neighbor

1 Pick up trash from your neighbors' lawns.

2 Keep the noise level down when playing outside.

3 When running errands, ask if your neighbors need anything.

4 Smile at them.

5 Help them carry in groceries.

6 Offer to wash their car.

7 Invite them to special events at your church.

8 Leave a bouquet of flowers at their front door.

9 Carry back their empty recycling bins and trash can.

10 Plant flowers in your neighborhood park.

## Q&A

Q I don't agree with some of the rules at my house. Do I always have to obey my parents?

A The Bible answers that question quite clearly: "Children, obey your parents as the Lord wants, because this is the right thing to do" (Ephesians 6:1). If you're ever concerned that one of their rules goes against what God wants, talk it over with them. Otherwise, yes, you need to obey them.

18:28 unclean Going into the Roman palace would make them unfit to eat the Passover Feast, according to their Law.

# *April

start here

**1** April Fool's Day. Instead of playing a joke on someone, do something nice!

**2**

**3**

**4** Pray for a person of influence: Today is Jamie Lynn Spears's birthday.

**5**

**6**

**7** Read James 1:5. Ask God to give you wisdom.

**8**

**9**

**10** Pray for a person of influence: Today is singer/actress Mandy Moore's birthday.

**11** Give your sister or best friend a really big hug!

**12**

**13** Skip watching TV today.

**14** Ask your grandma to tell you a story about her childhood.

**15**

**16**

**17** Pray for a person of influence: Today is actress Jennifer Garner's birthday.

**18** Wash the dishes after supper—without being asked to!

**19**

**20**

**21** Pray for a person of influence: Today is Queen Elizabeth II's birthday.

**22**

**23** Give your teacher a thank-you card.

**24**

**25**

**26** Pull out a photo album and enjoy some memories.

**27**

**28**

**29** Have a piece of fruit instead of cookies as a snack.

**30** Pray for a person of influence: Today is actress Kirsten Dunst's birthday.

Boots says, "Make a list!"

[11]Jesus answered, "The only power you have over me is the power given to you by God. The man who turned me in to you is guilty of a greater sin."

[12]After this, Pilate tried to let Jesus go. But some in the crowd cried out, "Anyone who makes himself king is against Caesar. If you let this man go, you are no friend of Caesar."

[13]When Pilate heard what they were saying, he brought Jesus out and sat down on the judge's seat at the place called The Stone Pavement. (In the Hebrew language[n] the name is Gabbatha.) [14]It was about noon on Preparation Day of Passover week. Pilate said to the crowd, "Here is your king!"

[15]They shouted, "Take him away! Take him away! Crucify him!"

Pilate asked them, "Do you want me to crucify your king?"

The leading priests answered, "The only king we have is Caesar."

[16]So Pilate handed Jesus over to them to be crucified.

## Jesus Is Crucified

The soldiers took charge of Jesus. [17]Carrying his own cross, Jesus went out to a place called The Place of the Skull, which in the Hebrew language[n] is called Golgotha. [18]There they crucified Jesus. They also crucified two other men, one on each side, with Jesus in the middle. [19]Pilate wrote a sign and put it on the cross. It read: JESUS OF

## Shine Your Light

Ruth's grandparents took her to Mexico—but not for a vacation. Instead, Ruth traveled with a group from her grandparents' church to help build houses in a community just outside Tijuana, Mexico. Las Floritas isn't really a town—it's just miles of shacks, some made of cardboard or covered with plastic bags.

Missionaries who live there invite teams of all ages to come and help build houses. Each house is about the size of Ruth's room, with one door, one window, and a dirt floor, but strong wooden walls and a roof. Each family prepares the spot for their new home, and the team builds the frames and lifts the walls. Meanwhile, the mothers prepare their best meals for the workers. Ruth enjoyed the tamales but avoided the chicken foot in the soup!

When Ruth wasn't on the roof hammering, she enjoyed playing games with the children who crowded around. After just two days, Ruth knew she would never forget how it felt to share God's love with people who had so little.

Maybe you can't go to Mexico, but you can ask your parents to pray about making your next family trip into a chance to share God's love!

## speakout!

**Q** What *kind* of television shows are best for tweens to watch?

**A** Action shows—shows about going places and seeing things all over the world.
—Erika, 10

NAZARETH, THE KING OF THE JEWS. [20]The sign was written in Hebrew, in Latin, and in Greek. Many of the people read the sign, because the place where Jesus was crucified was near the city. [21]The leading priests said to Pilate, "Don't write, 'The King of the Jews.' But write, 'This man said, "I am the King of the Jews."'"

[22]Pilate answered, "What I have written, I have written."

[23]After the soldiers crucified Jesus, they took his clothes and divided them into four parts, with each soldier getting one part. They also took his long shirt, which was all one piece of cloth, woven from top to bottom. [24]So the soldiers said to each other, "We should not tear this into parts. Let's throw lots to see who will get it." This happened so that this Scripture would come true:

"They divided my clothes among them,
 and they threw lots for my clothing."
*Psalm 22:18*

So the soldiers did this.

[25]Standing near his cross were Jesus' mother, his mother's sister, Mary the wife of Clopas, and Mary Magdalene. [26]When Jesus saw his mother and the follower he loved standing nearby, he said to his mother, "Dear woman, here is your son." [27]Then he said to the follower, "Here is your mother." From that time on, the follower took her to live in his home.

## Jesus Dies

[28]After this, Jesus knew that everything had been done. So that the Scripture would come true, he said, "I am thirsty."[n] [29]There was a jar full of vinegar there, so

**19:13, 17** Hebrew language *Or Aramaic, the languages of many people in this region in the first century.* **19:28** "I am thirsty." *Read Psalms 22:15; 69:21.*

148

# Q&A

**Q** How can God hear my prayers at the same time as everyone else's?

**A** It's important to remember that God can do anything he wants because he's not limited by space and time. If millions of people can watch one TV show at the exact same time, God could certainly reverse that and listen to millions of people at the same time. Even if you can't understand how he does it, you can trust that God always hear your prayers.

the soldiers soaked a sponge in it, put the sponge on a branch of a hyssop plant, and lifted it to Jesus' mouth. [30]When Jesus tasted the vinegar, he said, "It is finished." Then he bowed his head and died.

[31]This day was Preparation Day, and the next day was a special Sabbath day. Since the religious leaders did not want the bodies to stay on the cross on the Sabbath day, they asked Pilate to order that the legs of the men be broken[n] and the bodies be taken away. [32]So the soldiers came and broke the legs of the first man on the cross beside Jesus. Then they broke the legs of the man on the other cross beside Jesus. [33]But when the soldiers came to Jesus and saw that he was already dead, they did not break his legs. [34]But one of the soldiers stuck his spear into Jesus' side, and at once blood and water came out. [35](The one who saw this happen is the one who told us this, and whatever he says is true. And he knows that he tells the truth, and he tells it so that you might believe.) [36]These things happened to make the Scripture come true: "Not one of his bones will be broken."[n] [37]And another Scripture says, "They will look at the one they stabbed."[n]

## Jesus Is Buried

[38]Later, Joseph from Arimathea asked Pilate if he could take the body of Jesus. (Joseph was a secret follower of Jesus, because he was afraid of some of the leaders.) Pilate gave his permission, so Joseph came and took Jesus' body away. [39]Nicodemus, who earlier had come to Jesus at night, went with Joseph. He brought about seventy-five pounds of myrrh and aloes. [40]These two men took Jesus' body and wrapped it with the spices in pieces of linen cloth, which is how they bury the dead. [41]In the place where Jesus was crucified, there was a garden. In the garden was a new tomb that had never been used before. [42]The men laid Jesus in that tomb because it was nearby, and they were preparing to start their Sabbath day.

## Jesus' Tomb Is Empty

**20** Early on the first day of the week, Mary Magdalene went to the tomb while it was still dark. When she saw that the large stone had been moved away from the tomb, [2]she ran to Simon Peter and the follower whom Jesus loved. Mary said, "They have taken the Lord out of the tomb, and we don't know where they have put him."

[3]So Peter and the other follower started for the tomb. [4]They were both running, but the other follower ran faster than Peter and reached the tomb first. [5]He bent down and looked in and saw the strips of linen cloth lying there, but he did not go in. [6]Then following him, Simon Peter arrived and went into the tomb and saw the strips of linen lying there. [7]He also saw the cloth that had been around Jesus' head, which was folded up and laid in a different place from the strips of linen. [8]Then the other follower, who had reached the tomb first, also went in. He saw and believed. [9](They did not yet understand from the Scriptures that Jesus must rise from the dead.)

## Jesus Appears to Mary Magdalene

[10]Then the followers went back home. [11]But Mary stood outside the tomb, crying. As she was crying, she bent down and looked inside the tomb. [12]She saw two angels dressed in white, sitting where Jesus' body had been, one at the head and one at the feet.

[13]They asked her, "Woman, why are you crying?"

She answered, "They have taken away my Lord, and I don't know where they have put him." [14]When Mary said this, she turned around and saw Jesus standing there, but she did not know it was Jesus.

[15]Jesus asked her, "Woman, why are you crying? Whom are you looking for?"

Thinking he was the gardener, she said to him, "Did you take him away, sir? Tell me where you put him, and I will get him."

[16]Jesus said to her, "Mary."

Mary turned toward Jesus and said in the Hebrew language,[n] "Rabboni." (This means "Teacher.")

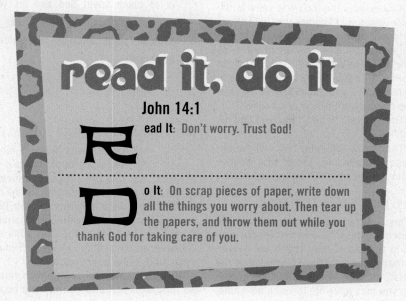

## read it, do it

**John 14:1**

**R** **ead It:** Don't worry. Trust God!

**D** **o It:** On scrap pieces of paper, write down all the things you worry about. Then tear up the papers, and throw them out while you thank God for taking care of you.

19:31 **broken** The breaking of their bones would make them die sooner. 19:36 **"Not one . . . broken."** Quotation from Psalm 34:20. The idea is from Exodus 12:46; Numbers 9:12. 19:37 **"They . . . stabbed."** Quotation from Zechariah 12:10. 20:16 **Hebrew language** Or Aramaic, the languages of many people in this region in the first century.

¹⁷Jesus said to her, "Don't hold on to me, because I have not yet gone up to the Father. But go to my brothers and tell them, 'I am going back to my Father and your Father, to my God and your God.'"

¹⁸Mary Magdalene went and said to the followers, "I saw the Lord!" And she told them what Jesus had said to her.

## Jesus Appears to His Followers

¹⁹When it was evening on the first day of the week, Jesus' followers were together. The doors were locked, because they were afraid of the elders. Then Jesus came and stood right in the middle of them and said, "Peace be with you." ²⁰After he said this, he showed them his hands and his side. His followers were thrilled when they saw the Lord.

²¹Then Jesus said again, "Peace be with you. As the Father sent me, I now send you." ²²After he said this, he breathed on them and said, "Receive the Holy Spirit. ²³If you forgive anyone his sins, they are forgiven. If you don't forgive them, they are not forgiven."

## Jesus Appears to Thomas

²⁴Thomas (called Didymus), who was one of the twelve, was not with them when Jesus came. ²⁵The other followers kept telling Thomas, "We saw the Lord."

But Thomas said, "I will not believe it until I see the nail marks in his hands and put my finger where the nails were and put my hand into his side."

²⁶A week later the followers were in the house again, and Thomas was with them. The doors were locked, but Jesus came in and stood right in the middle of them. He said, "Peace be with you." ²⁷Then he said to Thomas, "Put your finger here, and look at my hands. Put your hand here in my side. Stop being an unbeliever and believe."

²⁸Thomas said to him, "My Lord and my God!"

²⁹Then Jesus told him, "You believe because you see me. Those who believe without seeing me will be truly blessed."

## Why John Wrote This Book

³⁰Jesus did many other miracles in the presence of his followers that are not written in this book. ³¹But these are written so that you may believe that Jesus is the Christ, the Son of God. Then, by believing, you may have life through his name.

## dig deeper

### John 20:24—29

*It would be so much easier to believe if I could just see God!* Have you ever felt like that? Ever wished you could hear God's voice? Our society teaches us to believe only what we can prove to be true. In many cases, that's wise. The Bible tells us God does give us evidence of himself through creation and through what he does in our lives. But the Bible also says we need *faith* because there is so much about God and his Word that we *can't* experience with our five senses—sight, hearing, taste, touch, and smell.

Sometimes when we read the Bible it seems that miracles happened all the time when Jesus was alive. It must have been easy for people to believe! But Thomas's reaction to the news that Jesus was alive tells us that wasn't the case. He had trouble believing just like we do.

Isn't it amazing that when Jesus spoke to Thomas, he was thinking about *us?* He knew that people who believed after he was gone would only be able to learn by hearing about him from other people. We haven't seen Jesus, but he said that when we believe in him we "will be truly blessed" (John 20:29).

## Jesus Appears to Seven Followers

**21** Later, Jesus showed himself to his followers again—this time at Lake Galilee.ⁿ This is how he showed himself: ²Some of the followers were together: Simon Peter, Thomas (called Didymus), Nathanael from Cana in Galilee, the two sons of Zebedee, and two other followers. ³Simon Peter said, "I am going out to fish."

The others said, "We will go with you." So they went out and got into the boat. They fished that night but caught nothing. ⁴Early the next morning Jesus stood on the shore, but the followers did not know it was Jesus. ⁵Then he said to them, "Friends, did you catch any fish?"

They answered, "No."

⁶He said, "Throw your net on the right side of the boat, and you will find some." So they did, and they caught so many fish they could not pull the net back into the boat.

⁷The follower whom Jesus loved said to Peter, "It is the Lord!" When Peter heard

**21:1 Lake Galilee** *Literally, "Sea of Tiberias."*

him say this, he wrapped his coat around himself. (Peter had taken his clothes off.) Then he jumped into the water. [8]The other followers went to shore in the boat, dragging the net full of fish. They were not very far from shore, only about a hundred yards. [9]When the followers stepped out of the boat and onto the shore, they saw a fire of hot coals. There were fish on the fire, and there was bread.

[10]Then Jesus said, "Bring some of the fish you just caught."

[11]Simon Peter went into the boat and pulled the net to the shore. It was full of big fish, one hundred fifty-three in all, but even though there were so many, the net did not tear. [12]Jesus said to them, "Come and eat." None of the followers dared ask him, "Who are you?" because they knew it was the Lord. [13]Jesus came and took the bread and gave it to them, along with the fish.

[14]This was now the third time Jesus showed himself to his followers after he was raised from the dead.

## Jesus Talks to Peter

[15]When they finished eating, Jesus said to Simon Peter, "Simon son of John, do you love me more than these?"

He answered, "Yes, Lord, you know that I love you."

Jesus said, "Feed my lambs."

[16]Again Jesus said, "Simon son of John, do you love me?"

He answered, "Yes, Lord, you know that I love you."

Jesus said, "Take care of my sheep."

[17]A third time he said, "Simon son of John, do you love me?"

Peter was hurt because Jesus asked him the third time, "Do you love me?" Peter said, "Lord, you know everything; you know that I love you!"

He said to him, "Feed my sheep. [18]I tell you the truth, when you were younger, you tied your own belt and went where you wanted. But when you are old, you will put out your hands and someone else will tie you and take you where you don't want to go." [19](Jesus said this to show how Peter would die to give glory to God.) Then Jesus said to Peter, "Follow me!"

[20]Peter turned and saw that the follower Jesus loved was walking behind them. (This was the follower who had leaned against Jesus at the supper and had said, "Lord, who will turn against you?") [21]When Peter saw him behind them, he asked Jesus, "Lord, what about him?"

[22]Jesus answered, "If I want him to live until I come back, that is not your business. You follow me."

[23]So a story spread among the followers that this one would not die. But Jesus did not say he would not die. He only said, "If I want him to live until I come back, that is not your business."

[24]That follower is the one who is telling these things and who has now written them down. We know that what he says is true.

[25]There are many other things Jesus did. If every one of them were written down, I suppose the whole world would not be big enough for all the books that would be written.

## god's promises

John 20:30–31

Have you ever tried to earn someone's trust after you did something wrong to them? Maybe you told your best friend's secret and now she doesn't want to talk to you anymore. Or maybe you disobeyed a rule at home and now you're not allowed to have your old privileges.

No matter how many times you apologize, sometimes it's hard to prove that you're really sorry for what you did. You might promise never to do it again . . . yet the other person wants proof. Sometimes "I'm sorry" isn't enough.

God needs more than just words from you, too. Thankfully, he can see into your heart! That might not always seem like such a great thing—especially if you're feeling ashamed about something. But when you love and trust in God in your heart, he knows it! You don't have to try to convince him. He can see that you want to change . . . and he's ready to forgive you and give you eternal life!

John 20:31 promises that "by believing, you may have life through his name." It's a done deal—he'll save you when you believe in him. What a great promise!

*When you love and trust in God in your heart, he knows it!*

# ACTS

Isn't it disappointing to reach the end of a really good book? You say, "Is that *all*? I want to know what happens *next!*" Maybe that's what Theophilus said when he got to the end of Luke's description of Jesus' life. (See the introduction to the Book of Luke.) Maybe he said, "But I want to know the rest of the story!" Or maybe Luke just had so much fun writing the first part, he wanted to keep going.

In part two of the story, Doctor Luke describes what happened after Jesus returned to heaven. Before he left, Jesus told his followers to take the message about him to the rest of the world! Acts describes how they started to do that.

In Acts 8:1 we meet a character named Saul. He turns up again in chapter 9 and plays an im-

portant role in the rest of the book (where we know him as the apostle Paul—see Acts 13:9). When we first read about Saul, he is killing Christians. No one guessed he would become God's special messenger to the non-Jewish world!

The men and women God used to carry his message were normal people just like you. The Book of Acts tells their part . . . and encourages us to finish the story!

# THE GOOD NEWS OF JESUS SPREADS

## THINGS TO TALK WITH GOD ABOUT . . .

dates and times. These things are not for you to know. [8]But when the Holy Spirit comes to you, you will receive power. You will be my witnesses—in Jerusalem, in all of Judea, in Samaria, and in every part of the world."

[9]After he said this, as they were watching, he was lifted up, and a cloud hid him from their sight. [10]As he was going, they were looking into the sky. Suddenly, two men wearing white clothes stood beside them. [11]They said, "Men of Galilee, why are you standing here looking into the sky? Jesus, whom you

saw taken up from you into heaven, will come back in the same way you saw him go."

### A New Apostle Is Chosen

[12]Then they went back to Jerusalem from the Mount of Olives. (This mountain is about half a mile from Jerusalem.) [13]When they entered the city, they went

### Luke Writes Another Book

**1** To Theophilus.
The first book I wrote was about everything Jesus began to do and teach [2]until the day he was taken up into heaven. Before this, with the help of the Holy Spirit, Jesus told the apostles he had chosen what they should do. [3]After his death, he showed himself to them and proved in many ways that he was alive. The apostles saw Jesus during the forty days after he was raised from the dead, and he spoke to them about the kingdom of God. [4]Once when he was eating with them, he told them not to leave Jerusalem. He said, "Wait here to receive the promise from the Father which I told you about. [5]John baptized people with water, but in a few days you will be baptized with the Holy Spirit."

### Jesus Is Taken Up into Heaven

[6]When the apostles were all together, they asked Jesus, "Lord, are you now going to give the kingdom back to Israel?"

[7]Jesus said to them, "The Father is the only One who has the authority to decide

Could you imagine eating rice for every meal, every day? Actually, millions of kids do just that! In fact, one group of tweens from a church in Jefferson, Oregon, found out that some kids at a refugee center in Sierra Leone, Africa, only got *one* meal of rice each day. They also had only one hundred bowls to feed five hundred kids.

These tweens started a project to raise money to buy bowls for the children. They called it the "Rice Bowl" because it happened to be the same time as the college football bowl games in early January.

The group divided up and looked for ways to gather the donation money needed. Their goal was $750. They made phone calls, set up a booth at the church, and told their friends about the Rice Bowl. Guess what? They raised over nineteen hundred dollars for the kids in Africa! They were able to buy not just bowls, but also spoons and plenty of rice.

Do you know of a group of people who could use your help? Ask God to show you how *you* can make a difference in your community and your world.

# Q & A

**Q** Why are some girls my age already developing breasts when I'm not?

**A** Every body develops differently and at different times, so give yours a chance to grow the way God meant it to. He created you just right, so be patient while you continue to grow (physically and spiritually!). If you are concerned that something might be wrong, you should talk to your mom or another older woman you trust.

to the upstairs room where they were staying. Peter, John, James, Andrew, Philip, Thomas, Bartholomew, Matthew, James son of Alphaeus, Simon (known as the Zealot), and Judas son of James were there. [14]They all continued praying together with some women, including Mary the mother of Jesus, and Jesus' brothers.

[15]During this time there was a meeting of the believers (about one hundred twenty of them). Peter stood up and said, [16-17]"Brothers and sisters, in the Scriptures the Holy Spirit said through David something that must happen involving Judas. He was one of our own group and served together with us. He led those who arrested Jesus." [18](Judas bought a field with the money he got for his evil act. But he fell to his death, his body burst open, and all his intestines poured out. [19]Everyone in Jerusalem learned about this so they named this place Akeldama. In their language Akeldama means "Field of Blood.") [20]"In the Book of Psalms," Peter said, "this is written:

'May his place be empty;
    leave no one to live in it.'
                    *Psalm 69:25*

And it is also written:

'Let another man replace him as
        leader.'            *Psalm 109:8*

[21-22]"So now a man must become a witness with us of Jesus' being raised from

the dead. He must be one of the men who were part of our group during all the time the Lord Jesus was among us—from the time John was baptizing people until the day Jesus was taken up from us to heaven."

[23]They put the names of two men before the group. One was Joseph Barsabbas, who was also called Justus. The other was Matthias. [24-25]The apostles prayed, "Lord, you know the thoughts of everyone. Show us which one of these two you have chosen to do this work. Show us who should be an apostle in place of Judas, who turned away and went where he belongs." [26]Then they used lots to choose between them, and the lots showed that Matthias was the one. So he became an apostle with the other eleven.

## The Coming of the Holy Spirit

**2** When the day of Pentecost came, they were all together in one place. [2]Suddenly a noise like a strong, blowing wind came from heaven and filled the whole house where they were sitting. [3]They saw something like flames of fire that were separated and stood over each person there. [4]They were all filled with the Holy Spirit, and they began to speak different languages[n] by the power the Holy Spirit was giving them.

[5]There were some religious Jews staying in Jerusalem who were from every country in the world. [6]When they heard this noise, a crowd came together. They were all surprised, because each one heard them speaking in his own language. [7]They were completely amazed at this. They said, "Look! Aren't all these people that we hear speaking from Galilee? [8]Then how is it possible that we each hear them in our own languages? We are from different places: [9]Parthia, Media, Elam, Mesopotamia, Judea, Cappadocia, Pontus, Asia, [10]Phrygia, Pamphylia, Egypt, the areas of Libya near Cyrene, Rome [11](both Jews and those who had become Jews), Crete, and Arabia. But we hear them telling in our own languages about the great things God has done!" [12]They were all amazed and confused, asking each other, "What does this mean?"

[13]But others were making fun of them, saying, "They have had too much wine."

## Peter Speaks to the People

[14]But Peter stood up with the eleven apostles, and in a loud voice he spoke to the crowd: "My fellow Jews, and all of you who are in Jerusalem, listen to me. Pay attention to what I have to say. [15]These people are not drunk, as you think; it is only nine o'clock in the morning! [16]But Joel the prophet wrote about what is happening here today:

[17]'God says: In the last days
    I will pour out my Spirit on all
        kinds of people.
    Your sons and daughters will
        prophesy.
    Your young men will see visions,
        and your old men will dream
        dreams.
[18]At that time I will pour out my Spirit
        also on my male slaves and female
        slaves,
    and they will prophesy.
[19]I will show miracles
    in the sky and on the earth:
        blood, fire, and thick smoke.
[20]The sun will become dark,
    the moon red as blood,
    before the overwhelming and
        glorious day of the Lord will
        come.
[21]Then anyone who calls on the Lord
        will be saved.'    *Joel 2:28–32*

[22]"People of Israel, listen to these words: Jesus from Nazareth was a very

# BE YOUR BEST!

**J** unk food might be more fun to eat than vegetables, bread, and meat, but it'll eventually make you sick. It will keep you from getting the nutrition you need. To make sure you're growing spiritually, be careful that your music, TV shows, books and Web sites don't feed your soul "junk."

---

**2:4 languages** *This can also be translated "tongues."*

## dig deeper

### Acts 4:32–35

At your house, when you want to eat supper, do you have to make reservations or tip the waitress? When you watch a video from your family's collection, do you dig into your piggy bank to rent it? Do you have to ask for permission before using a tissue, a plate, a pillow, or soap? Probably not!

You're part of a family, and families share things, right? Okay, so maybe sometimes you fight over the remote control or a toy or something; that's normal. But God wants us to *enjoy* sharing and being generous!

As Christians we're also part of a family: God's family! And as "brothers" and "sisters," we have to treat each other a lot like we treat our actual family members (the good parts).

The first Christians gave us a great example of how this works. In Acts 4:32 we read that they were "united in their hearts and spirits." These people shared everything! Whatever they owned belonged to everyone else. If someone had very little, a wealthier person would sell something, such as land, and bring the money to the church so that the poor person could be taken care of. The believers loved and trusted each other!

Ask God to show you how you and your family can share your blessings with others in your Christian family!

---

of death, because death could not hold him. [25]For David said this about him:
 'I keep the Lord before me always.
   Because he is close by my side,
   I will not be hurt.
 [26]So I am glad, and I rejoice.
   Even my body has hope,
 [27]because you will not leave me in the grave.
   You will not let your Holy One rot.
 [28]You will teach me how to live a holy life.
   Being with you will fill me with joy.'
                                    *Psalm 16:8–11*
[29]"Brothers and sisters, I can tell you truly that David, our ancestor, died and was buried. His grave is still here with us today. [30]He was a prophet and knew God had promised him that he would make a person from David's family a king just as he was.[n] [31]Knowing this before it happened, David talked about the Christ rising from the dead. He said:
 'He was not left in the grave.
   His body did not rot.'
[32]So Jesus is the One whom God raised from the dead. And we are all witnesses to this. [33]Jesus was lifted up to heaven and is now at God's right side. The Father has given the Holy Spirit to Jesus as he promised. So Jesus has poured out that Spirit, and this is what you now see and hear. [34]David was not the one who was lifted up to heaven, but he said:
 'The Lord said to my Lord,
   "Sit by me at my right side,
 [35]  until I put your enemies under your control." '[n]        *Psalm 110:1*
[36]"So, all the people of Israel should know this truly: God has made Jesus—the man you nailed to the cross—both Lord and Christ."

[37]When the people heard this, they felt guilty and asked Peter and the other apostles, "What shall we do?"

[38]Peter said to them, "Change your hearts and lives and be baptized, each one of you, in the name of Jesus Christ for the forgiveness of your sins. And you will receive the gift of the Holy Spirit. [39]This promise is for you, for your children, and for all who are far away. It is for everyone the Lord our God calls to himself."

[40]Peter warned them with many other words. He begged them, "Save yourselves from the evil of today's people!"

---

**GOD SAYS: IN THE LAST DAYS I WILL POUR OUT MY SPIRIT ON ALL KINDS OF PEOPLE. YOUR SONS AND DAUGHTERS WILL PROPHESY.**

special man. God clearly showed this to you by the miracles, wonders, and signs he did through Jesus. You all know this, because it happened right here among you. [23]Jesus was given to you, and with the help of those who don't know the law, you put him to death by nailing him to a cross. But this was God's plan which he had made long ago; he knew all this would happen. [24]God raised Jesus from the dead and set him free from the pain

---

2:30 **God . . . was** *See 2 Samuel 7:13; Psalm 132:11.*   2:35 **until . . . control** *Literally, "until I make your enemies a footstool for your feet."*

[41]Then those people who accepted what Peter said were baptized. About three thousand people were added to the number of believers that day. [42]They spent their time learning the apostles' teaching, sharing, breaking bread,[n] and praying together.

## The Believers Share

[43]The apostles were doing many miracles and signs, and everyone felt great respect for God. [44]All the believers were together and shared everything. [45]They would sell their land and the things they owned and then divide the money and give it to anyone who needed it. [46]The believers met together in the Temple every day. They ate together in their homes, happy to share their food with joyful hearts. [47]They praised God and were liked by all the people. Every day the Lord added those who were being saved to the group of believers.

## Peter Heals a Crippled Man

**3** One day Peter and John went to the Temple at three o'clock, the time set each day for the afternoon prayer service. [2]There, at the Temple gate called Beautiful Gate, was a man who had been crippled all his life. Every day he was carried to this gate to beg for money from the people going into the Temple. [3]The man saw Peter and John going into the Temple and asked them for money. [4]Peter and John looked straight at him and said, "Look at us!"

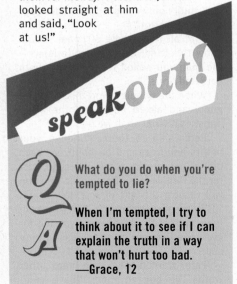

[5]The man looked at them, thinking they were going to give him some money. [6]But Peter said, "I don't have any silver or gold, but I do have something else I can give you. By the power of Jesus Christ from Nazareth, stand up and walk!" [7]Then Peter took the man's right hand and lifted him up. Immediately the man's feet and ankles became strong. [8]He jumped up, stood on his feet, and began to walk. He went into the Temple with them, walking and jumping and praising God. [9-10]All the people recognized him as the crippled man who always sat by the Beautiful Gate begging for money. Now they saw this same man walking and praising God, and they were amazed. They wondered how this could happen.

## Peter Speaks to the People

[11]While the man was holding on to Peter and John, all the people were amazed and ran to them at Solomon's Porch. [12]When Peter saw this, he said to them, "People of Israel, why are you surprised? You are looking at us as if it were our own power or goodness that made this man walk. [13]The God of Abraham, Isaac, and Jacob, the God of our ancestors, gave glory to Jesus, his servant. But you handed him over to be killed. Pilate decided to let him go free, but you told Pilate you did not want Jesus. [14]You did not want the One who is holy and good but asked Pilate to give you a murderer[n] instead. [15]And so you killed the One who gives life, but God raised him from the dead. We are witnesses to this. [16]It was faith in Jesus that made this crippled man well. You can see this man, and you know him. He was made completely well because of trust in Jesus, and you all saw it happen!

[17]"Brothers and sisters, I know you did those things to Jesus because neither you nor your leaders understood what you were doing. [18]God said through the prophets that his Christ would suffer and die. And now God has made these things come true in this way. [19]So you must change your hearts and lives! Come back to God, and he will forgive your sins. Then the Lord will send the time of rest. [20]And he will send Jesus, the One he chose to be the Christ. [21]But Jesus must stay in heaven until the time comes when all things will be made right again.

## Heart of Gold

Even the most expensive gold jewelry you see is not pure gold. You can't wear absolutely pure gold because it doesn't hold its shape—it's so soft you can mold it in your hands! But when gold is mixed with other things, it becomes hard and solid.

When your heart is pure and not cluttered with sinful thoughts like hatred, selfishness, and a disobedient attitude, God can take it and shape it into something beautiful. Don't let your heart get hard. Keep it pure so God can work with it.

God told about this time long ago when he spoke through his holy prophets. [22]Moses said, 'The Lord your God will give you a prophet like me, who is one of your own people. You must listen to everything he tells you. [23]Anyone who does not listen to that prophet will die, cut off from God's people.'[n] [24]Samuel, and all the other prophets who spoke for God after Samuel, told about this time now. [25]You are descendants of the prophets. You have received the agreement God made with your ancestors. He said to your father Abraham, 'Through your descendants all the nations on the earth will be blessed.'[n] [26]God has raised up his servant Jesus and sent him to you first to bless you by turning each of you away from doing evil."

## Peter and John at the Council

**4** While Peter and John were speaking to the people, priests, the captain of the soldiers that guarded the Temple, and Sadducees came up to them. [2]They were upset because the two apostles were teaching the people and were preaching that

---

**2:42 breaking bread** This may mean a meal as in verse 46, or the Lord's Supper, the special meal Jesus told his followers to eat to remember him (Luke 22:14–20).   **3:14 murderer** Barabbas, the man the crowd asked Pilate to set free instead of Jesus (Luke 23:18).   **3:22–23 'The Lord . . . people.'** Quotation from Deuteronomy 18:15, 19.   **3:25 'Through . . . blessed.'** Quotation from Genesis 22:18; 26:4.

## Get It

### Trinity

The word "trinity" can't be found anywhere in your Bible—but the idea is all over the place! Trinity means that God is *one* God who is known as *three* persons—Father, Son (Jesus), and the Holy Spirit. This concept has puzzled Christians for thousands of years. It's simply too big for our brains! A good way to think about the trinity is to imagine water. It appears in three forms: liquid (such as rivers), gas (such as steam), and frozen (such as ice cubes). The Father, Son, and Holy Spirit have different "forms"—but are all God!

people will rise from the dead through the power of Jesus. [3]The older leaders grabbed Peter and John and put them in jail. Since it was already night, they kept them in jail until the next day. [4]But many of those who had heard Peter and John preach believed the things they said. There were now about five thousand in the group of believers.

[5]The next day the rulers, the elders, and the teachers of the law met in Jerusalem. [6]Annas the high priest, Caiaphas, John, and Alexander were there, as well as everyone from the high priest's family. [7]They made Peter and John stand before them and then asked them, "By what power or authority did you do this?"

JESUS IS THE STONE THAT YOU BUILDERS REJECTED, WHICH HAS BECOME THE CORNERSTONE.

4:11 **stone** *A symbol meaning Jesus.*

[8]Then Peter, filled with the Holy Spirit, said to them, "Rulers of the people and you elders, [9]are you questioning us about a good thing that was done to a crippled man? Are you asking us who made him well? [10]We want all of you and all the people to know that this man was made well by the power of Jesus Christ from Nazareth. You crucified him, but God raised him from the dead. This man was crippled, but he is now well and able to stand here before you because of the power of Jesus. [11]Jesus is

'the stone[n] that you builders rejected, which has become the cornerstone.'

*Psalm 118:22*

[12]Jesus is the only One who can save people. No one else in the world is able to save us."

[13]The leaders saw that Peter and John were not afraid to speak, and they understood that these men had no special training or education. So they were amazed. Then they realized that Peter and John had been with Jesus. [14]Because they saw the healed man standing there beside the two apostles, they could say nothing against them. [15]After the leaders ordered them to leave the meeting, they began to talk to each other. [16]They said, "What shall we do with these men? Everyone in Jerusalem knows they have done a great miracle, and we cannot say it is not true. [17]But to keep it from spreading among the people, we must warn them not to talk to people anymore using that name."

[18]So they called Peter and John in again and told them not to speak or to teach at all in the name of Jesus. [19]But Peter and John answered them, "You decide what God would want. Should we obey you or God? [20]We cannot keep quiet. We must speak about what we have seen and heard." [21]The leaders warned the apostles again and let them go free. They could not find a way to punish them, because all the people were praising God for what had been done. [22]The man who received the miracle of healing was more than forty years old.

### The Believers Pray

[23]After Peter and John left the meeting of leaders, they went to their own group and told them everything the leading priests and the elders had said to them.

[24]When the believers heard this, they prayed to God together, "Lord, you are the One who made the sky, the earth, the sea, and everything in them. [25]By the Holy Spirit, through our father David your servant, you said:

'Why are the nations so angry? Why are the people making useless plans?
[26]The kings of the earth prepare to fight,
and their leaders make plans together
against the Lord
and his Christ.' *Psalm 2:1–2*

[27]These things really happened when Herod, Pontius Pilate, and some Jews and non-Jews all came together against Jesus here in Jerusalem. Jesus is your holy servant, the One you made to be the Christ. [28]These people made your plan happen because of your power and your will. [29]And now, Lord, listen to their threats. Lord, help us, your servants, to speak your word without fear. [30]Show us your power to heal. Give proofs and make miracles happen by the power of Jesus, your holy servant."

[31]After they had prayed, the place where they were meeting was shaken. They were all filled with the Holy Spirit, and they spoke God's word without fear.

## Q&A

**Q** My science teacher talks a lot about evolution. What should I say since I believe that God created the earth?

**A** Show respect to your teacher, but don't feel shy to say what you believe. Your teacher or other kids might try to make you feel like your beliefs are silly, but trust that God is watching you and that you're pleasing him! Pray these words from Acts 4:29—"Lord, help [me, your servant], to speak your word without fear."

## The Believers Share

32The group of believers were united in their hearts and spirit. All those in the group acted as though their private property belonged to everyone in the group. In fact, they shared everything. 33With great power the apostles were telling people that the Lord Jesus was truly raised from the dead. And God

blessed all the believers very much. 34There were no needy people among them. From time to time those who owned fields or houses sold them, brought the money, 35and gave it to the apostles. Then the money was given to anyone who needed it.

36One of the believers was named Joseph, a Levite born in Cyprus. The apostles called him Barnabas (which means "one who encourages"). 37Joseph owned a field, sold it, brought the money, and gave it to the apostles.

## Ananias and Sapphira Die

5 But a man named Ananias and his wife Sapphira sold some land. 2He kept back part of the money for himself; his wife knew about this and agreed to it. But he brought the rest of the money and gave it to the apostles. 3Peter said, "Ananias, why did you let Satan rule your thoughts to lie to the Holy Spirit and to keep for yourself part of the money you received for the land? 4Before you sold the land, it belonged to you. And even after you sold it, you could have used the money any way you wanted. Why did you think of doing this? You lied to God, not to us!" 5–6When Ananias heard this, he fell down and died. Some young men came in, wrapped up his body, carried it out, and buried it. And everyone who heard about this was filled with fear.

7About three hours later his wife came in, but she did not know what had happened. 8Peter said to her, "Tell me, was the money you got for your field this much?"

Sapphira answered, "Yes, that was the price."

9Peter said to her, "Why did you and your husband agree to test the Spirit of the Lord? Look! The men who buried your husband are at the door, and they will carry you out." 10At that moment Sapphira fell down by his feet and died. When the young men came in and saw that she was dead, they carried her out and buried her beside her husband. 11The

whole church and all the others who heard about these things were filled with fear.

## The Apostles Heal Many

12The apostles did many signs and miracles among the people. And they would all meet together on Solomon's Porch. 13None of the others dared to join them, but all the people respected them. 14More and more men and women believed in the Lord and were added to the group of believers. 15The people placed their sick on beds and mats in the streets, hoping that when Peter passed by at least his shadow might fall on them. 16Crowds came from all the towns around Jerusalem, bringing their sick and those who were bothered by evil spirits, and all of them were healed.

## Leaders Try to Stop the Apostles

17The high priest and all his friends (a group called the Sadducees) became very jealous. 18They took the apostles and put them in jail. 19But during the night, an angel of the Lord opened the doors of the jail and led the apostles outside. The angel said, 20"Go stand in the Temple and tell the people everything about this new life." 21When the apostles heard this, they obeyed and went into the Temple early in the morning and continued teaching.

When the high priest and his friends arrived, they called a meeting of the leaders and all the important elders. They sent some men to the jail to bring the apostles to them. 22But, upon arriving, the officers could not find the apostles. So they went back and reported to the leaders. 23They said, "The jail was closed and locked, and the guards were standing at the doors. But when we opened the doors, the jail was empty!" 24Hearing this, the captain of the Temple guards and the leading priests were confused and wondered what was happening.

25Then someone came and told them, "Listen! The men you put in jail are standing in the Temple teaching the people." 26Then the captain and his men went out and brought the apostles back. But the soldiers did not use force, because they were afraid the people would stone them to death.

27The soldiers brought the apostles to the meeting and made them stand before the leaders. The high priest ques-

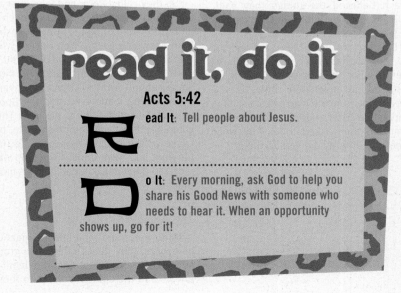

## read it, do it

**Acts 5:42**

**Read It:** Tell people about Jesus.

**Do It:** Every morning, ask God to help you share his Good News with someone who needs to hear it. When an opportunity shows up, go for it!

# dig deeper

## Acts 5:29

Have you ever played a game with a friend that kept cheating or trying to change the rules? It's so annoying! Even when you're having fun, you still need rules. When people don't follow the rules, it spoils everything.

The same goes for sports competitions. There always seems to be someone who wants to cheat. The problem is, when you break a rule in a real contest, you get a penalty or you're kicked out of the game!

Rules are important during games and sports, but they're even more important in life! Ultimately, God's rules matter most. It's not that he wants to make our lives boring. It's because he knows that rules help us do things the right way. And when we do things the right way, the results are always so much better!

No matter what anyone else says, we can't make up our own rules. There's only one way to get to heaven: trust Jesus Christ. Going to church, wearing a cross around your neck, or calling yourself a "believer" won't work. There's only one way to live on earth: keep following Jesus Christ. Ask God to help you follow his rules. Then you'll be a true winner!

---

him. He ordered the apostles to leave the meeting for a little while. [35]Then he said, "People of Israel, be careful what you are planning to do to these men. [36]Remember when Theudas appeared? He said he was a great man, and about four hundred men joined him. But he was killed, and all his followers were scattered; they were able to do nothing. [37]Later, a man named Judas came from Galilee at the time of the registration.[n] He also led a group of followers and was killed, and all his followers were scattered. [38]And so now I tell you: Stay away from these men, and leave them alone. If their plan comes from human authority, it will fail. [39]But if it is from God, you will not be able to stop them. You might even be fighting against God himself!"

The leaders agreed with what Gamaliel said. [40]They called the apostles in, beat them, and told them not to speak in the name of Jesus again. Then they let them go free. [41]The apostles left the meeting full of joy because they were given the honor of suffering disgrace for Jesus. [42]Every day in the Temple and in people's homes they continued teaching the people and telling the Good News—that Jesus is the Christ.

## Seven Leaders Are Chosen

6 The number of followers was growing. But during this same time, the Greek-speaking followers had an argument with the other followers. The Greek-speaking widows were not getting their share of the food that was given out every day. [2]The twelve apostles called the whole group of followers together and said, "It is not right for us to stop our work of teaching God's word in order to serve tables. [3]So, brothers and sisters, choose seven of your own

---

tioned them, [28]saying, "We gave you strict orders not to continue teaching in that name. But look, you have filled Jerusalem with your teaching and are trying to make us responsible for this man's death."

[29]Peter and the other apostles answered, "We must obey God, not human authority! [30]You killed Jesus by hanging him on a cross. But God, the God of our ancestors, raised Jesus up from the dead! [31]Jesus is the One whom God raised to be on his right side, as Leader and Savior. Through him, all people could change their hearts and lives and have their sins forgiven. [32]We saw all these things happen. The Holy Spirit, whom God has given to all who obey him, also proves these things are true."

[33]When the leaders heard this, they became angry and wanted to kill them. [34]But a Pharisee named Gamaliel stood up in the meeting. He was a teacher of the law, and all the people respected

**5:37 registration** *Census. A counting of all the people and the things they own.*

## ■ Bible Bios — Andrew (John 1:40–42)

Andrew, one of Jesus' followers, isn't mentioned too often in the Bible. But he did one very important thing that made a big difference! After Andrew heard about Jesus, he ran to tell his brother Simon he had found the Messiah (the Hebrew word for Christ). Simon, also known as Peter, went to meet Jesus, too. Later, they both became Jesus' followers. We read much more about Peter in the New Testament; many people became Christians because of his teachings about Jesus.

Maybe Andrew didn't have an outgoing personality like Peter. He might have preferred working "behind the scenes." But he pleased God by telling someone else about Jesus. Ask God for courage to tell someone about Jesus. You never know how God will use the other person's life for good . . . all because *you* obeyed!

men who are good, full of the Spirit and full of wisdom. We will put them in charge of this work. [4]Then we can continue to pray and to teach the word of God."

[5]The whole group liked the idea, so they chose these seven men: Stephen (a man with great faith and full of the Holy Spirit), Philip,[n] Procorus, Nicanor, Timon, Parmenas, and Nicolas (a man from Antioch who had become a follower of the Jewish religion). [6]Then they put these men before the apostles, who prayed and laid their hands[n] on them.

[7]The word of God was continuing to spread. The group of followers in Jerusalem increased, and a great number of the Jewish priests believed and obeyed.

### Stephen Is Accused

[8]Stephen was richly blessed by God who gave him the power to do great miracles and signs among the people. [9]But some people were against him. They belonged to the synagogue of Free Men[n] (as it was called), which included people from Cyrene, Alexandria, Cilicia, and Asia. They all came and argued with Stephen. [10]But the Spirit was helping him to speak with wisdom, and his words were so strong that they could not argue with him. [11]So they secretly urged some men to say, "We heard Stephen speak against Moses and against God."

[12]This upset the people, the elders, and the teachers of the law. They came and grabbed Stephen and brought him to a meeting of the leaders. [13]They brought in some people to tell lies about Stephen, saying, "This man is always speaking against this holy place and the law of Moses. [14]We heard him say that Jesus from Nazareth will destroy this place and that Jesus will change the customs Moses gave us." [15]All the people in the meeting were watching Stephen closely and saw that his face looked like the face of an angel.

### Stephen's Speech

7 The high priest said to Stephen, "Are these things true?"

[2]Stephen answered, "Brothers and fathers, listen to me. Our glorious God appeared to Abraham, our ancestor, in Mesopotamia before he lived in Haran. [3]God said to Abraham, 'Leave your country and your relatives, and go to the land I will show you.'[n] [4]So Abraham left the country of Chaldea and went to live in Haran. After Abraham's father died, God sent him to this place where you now live. [5]God did not give Abraham any of this land, not even a foot of it. But God promised that he would give this land to him and his descendants, even before Abraham had a child. [6]This is what God said to him: 'Your descendants will be strangers in a land they don't own. The people there will make them slaves and will mistreat them for four hundred years. [7]But I will punish the nation where they are slaves. Then your descendants will leave that land and will worship me in this place.'[n] [8]God made an agreement with Abraham, the sign of which was circumcision. And so when Abraham had his son Isaac, Abraham circumcised him when he was eight days old. Isaac also circumcised his son Jacob, and Jacob did the same for his sons, the twelve ancestors[n] of our people.

[9]"Jacob's sons became jealous of Joseph and sold him to be a slave in Egypt. But God was with him [10]and saved him from all his troubles. The king of Egypt liked Joseph and respected him because of the wisdom God gave him. The king made him governor of Egypt and put him in charge of all the people in his palace.

[11]"Then all the land of Egypt and Canaan became so dry that nothing would grow, and the people suffered very much. Jacob's sons, our ancestors, could not find anything to eat. [12]But when Jacob heard there was grain in Egypt, he sent his sons there. This was their first trip to Egypt. [13]When they went there a second time, Joseph told his brothers who he was, and the king learned about Joseph's family. [14]Then Joseph sent messengers to

## Q & A

**Q** When my friends ask me why I go to church, I'm not sure how to answer. What should I tell them?

**A** Be honest about why you go. Don't hide the fact that you enjoy going (if you do), but also don't try to sound overly religious. Explain that going to church is important because Christians can worship God there together, they can learn from the Bible, they can pray together, and they can encourage each other through friendships and different activities. Hebrews 10:25 is a good verse to remember.

6:5 **Philip** *Not the apostle named Philip.*  6:6 **laid their hands** *The laying on of hands had many purposes, including the giving of a blessing, power, or authority.*  6:9 **Free Men** *Jewish people who had been slaves or whose fathers had been slaves, but were now free.*  7:3 **'Leave . . . you.'** *Quotation from Genesis 12:1.*  7:6–7 **'Your descendants . . . place.'** *Quotation from Genesis 15:13–14 and Exodus 3:12.*  7:8 **twelve ancestors** *Important ancestors of the people of Israel; the leaders of the twelve tribes of Israel.*

his own people, the people of Israel. [24]Moses saw an Egyptian mistreating one of his people, so he defended the Israelite and punished the Egyptian by killing him. [25]Moses thought his own people would understand that God was using him to save them, but they did not. [26]The next day when Moses saw two men of Israel fighting, he tried to make peace between them. He said, 'Men, you are brothers. Why are you hurting each other?' [27]The man who was hurting the other pushed Moses away and said, 'Who made you our ruler and judge? [28]Are you going to kill me as you killed the Egyptian yesterday?'[n] [29]When Moses heard him say this, he left Egypt and went to live in the land of Midian where he was a stranger. While Moses lived in Midian, he had two sons.

[30]"Forty years later an angel appeared to Moses in the flames of a burning bush as he was in the desert near Mount Sinai. [31]When Moses saw this, he was amazed and went near to look closer. Moses heard the Lord's voice say, [32]'I am the God of your ancestors, the God of Abraham, Isaac, and Jacob.'[n] Moses began to shake with fear and was afraid to look. [33]The Lord said to him, 'Take off your sandals, because you are standing on holy ground. [34]I have seen the troubles my people have suffered in Egypt. I have heard their cries and have come down to save them. And now, Moses, I am sending you back to Egypt.'[n]

[35]"This Moses was the same man the two men of Israel rejected, saying, 'Who made you a ruler and judge?'[n] Moses is the same man God sent to be a ruler and savior, with the help of the angel that Moses saw in the burning bush. [36]So Moses led the people out of Egypt. He worked miracles and signs in Egypt, at the Red Sea, and then in the desert for forty years. [37]This is the same Moses that said to the people of Israel, 'God will give you a prophet like me, who is one of your own people.'[n] [38]This is the Moses who was with the gathering of the Israelites in the desert. He was with the angel that spoke to him at Mount Sinai, and he was with our ancestors. He received commands from God that give life, and he gave those commands to us.

[39]"But our ancestors did not want to obey Moses. They rejected him and

## god's promises

**Acts 9:36** — When someone at school constantly wants attention or is always bragging, don't you feel like avoiding that person? Sometimes it seems like nothing or no one else is ever good enough for her.

Now think about people you really respect. They're probably humble. In other words, they don't talk much about themselves; they just work hard and help others. They don't act like something they're not and they're satisfied with whatever they have. These people might never get public attention, but God sees what they do and he will bless them!

Tabitha was a woman just like that! She didn't have an important job or a fancy title; she just sewed clothes for poor women and children. People didn't love her because she was rich; they loved her for her kindness to poor and ordinary people. All through the Bible, God says that he gives special attention to the humble. For Tabitha, that meant that God raised her from the dead!

Do you consider yourself as more important than other people? Or do you have a humble attitude that puts other people first? God always notices and he will reward you!

***God gives special attention to the humble!***

invite Jacob, his father, to come to Egypt along with all his relatives (seventy-five persons altogether). [15]So Jacob went down to Egypt, where he and his sons died. [16]Later their bodies were moved to Shechem and put in a grave there. (It was the same grave Abraham had bought for a sum of money from the sons of Hamor in Shechem.)

[17]"The promise God made to Abraham was soon to come true, and the number of people in Egypt grew large. [18]Then a new king, who did not know who Joseph was, began to rule Egypt. [19]This king tricked our people and was cruel to our ancestors, forcing them to leave their babies outside to die. [20]At this time Moses was born, and he was very beautiful. For three months Moses was cared for in his father's house. [21]When they put Moses outside, the king's daughter adopted him and raised him as if he were her own son. [22]The Egyptians taught Moses everything they knew, and he was a powerful man in what he said and did.

[23]"When Moses was about forty years old, he thought it would be good to visit

# Relationships

**W**hen God commanded the Israelites in the Old Testament to "honor your father and your mother" (Deuteronomy 5:16), he gave a promise. If children honored their parents, they would live long lives, and things would go well for them.

Paul tells us in Ephesians 6:1–3 that the same is true for us today! Honoring your mom and dad includes respecting their authority, obeying their instructions, and letting them know you value them. God says that you will be blessed for obeying this command! How can you show your parents honor today?

wanted to go back to Egypt. 40They said to Aaron, 'Make us gods who will lead us. Moses led us out of Egypt, but we don't know what has happened to him.'n 41So the people made an idol that looked like a calf. Then they brought sacrifices to it and were proud of what they had made with their own hands. 42But God turned against them and did not try to stop them from worshiping the sun, moon, and stars. This is what is written in the book of the prophets: God says,

'People of Israel, you did not bring
    me sacrifices and offerings
while you traveled in the desert for
    forty years.
43You have carried with you
    the tent to worship Molech
and the idols of the star god
    Rephan that you made to
    worship.
So I will send you away beyond
    Babylon.'        Amos 5:25–27

44"The Holy Tent where God spoke to our ancestors was with them in the desert. God told Moses how to make this Tent, and he made it like the plan God showed him. 45Later, Joshua led our ancestors to capture the lands of the other nations. Our people went in, and God forced the other people out. When our people went into this new land, they took with them this same Tent they had received from their ancestors. They kept it until the time of David, 46who pleased God and asked God to let him build a house for him, the God of Jacob.n 47But Solomon was the one who built the Temple.

48"But the Most High does not live in houses that people build with their hands. As the prophet says:

49'Heaven is my throne,
    and the earth is my footstool.
So do you think you can build a
    house for me? says the Lord.
Do I need a place to rest?
50Remember, my hand made all these
    things!' "        Isaiah 66:1–2

51Stephen continued speaking: "You stubborn people! You have not given your hearts to God, nor will you listen to him! You are always against what the Holy Spirit is trying to tell you, just as your ancestors were. 52Your ancestors tried to hurt every prophet who ever lived. Those prophets said long ago that the One who is good would come, but your ancestors killed them. And now you have turned against and killed the One who is good. 53You received the law of Moses, which God gave you through his angels, but you haven't obeyed it."

## Stephen Is Killed

54When the leaders heard this, they became furious. They were so mad they were grinding their teeth at Stephen. 55But Stephen was full of the Holy Spirit. He looked up to heaven and saw the glory of God and Jesus standing at God's right side. 56He said, "Look! I see heaven open and the Son of Man standing at God's right side."

57Then they shouted loudly and covered their ears and all ran at Stephen. 58They took him out of the city and began to throw stones at him to kill him. And those who told lies against Stephen left their coats with a young man named Saul. 59While they were throwing stones, Stephen prayed, "Lord Jesus, receive my spirit." 60He fell on his knees and cried in a loud voice, "Lord, do not hold this sin against them." After Stephen said this, he died.

**8** Saul agreed that the killing of Stephen was good.

## Troubles for the Believers

On that day the church of Jerusalem began to be persecuted, and all the believers, except the apostles, were scattered throughout Judea and Samaria.

2And some religious people buried Stephen and cried loudly for him. 3Saul was also trying to destroy the church, going from house to house, dragging out men and women and putting them in jail. 4And wherever they were scattered, they told people the Good News.

## Philip Preaches in Samaria

5Philip went to the city of Samaria and preached about the Christ. 6When the people there heard Philip and saw the miracles he was doing, they all listened carefully to what he said. 7Many of these

---

7:40 'Make . . . him.' *Quotation from Exodus 32:1.*  7:46 Jacob *Some Greek copies read "the house of Jacob." This means the people of Israel.*

# May

start here

**1** Research how Mother's Day was started and explain it to your friends.

**2**

**3**

**4** Make up a tongue twister to challenge your friends.

**5**

**6** Pray for your best friend's parents.

**7**

**8**

**9** Memorize Ephesians 2:8. Thank God for his gift of salvation.

**10**

**11** Pray for your school principal.

**12**

**13** Ask your mom or dad if there's anything you can help them with.

**14**

**15**

**16** Ask someone to help you flip your mattress over. You should do it twice a year!

**17**

**18**

**19** Pray for a person of influence: Today is NBA player Kevin Garnett's birthday.

**20** Instead of watching TV, look out your window and make up a story about whatever you see.

**21**

**22**

**23** Pray for a person of influence: Today is singer Jewel's birthday.

**24**

**25** Pray for a person of influence: Today is singer Lauryn Hill's birthday.

**26** Call a relative you haven't seen for a while...just to say hi!

**27**

**28** Write down 5 things you would love to do this summer. Discuss the list with your parents.

**29** Pray for a person of influence: Today is Christian singer Bebo Norman's birthday.

**30**

**31** Pray for a person of influence: Today is actor Colin Farrell's birthday.

Fritz says, "Make a list!"

people had evil spirits in them, but Philip made the evil spirits leave. The spirits made a loud noise when they came out. Philip also healed many weak and crippled people there. ⁸So the people in that city were very happy.

⁹But there was a man named Simon in that city. Before Philip came there, Simon had practiced magic and amazed all the people of Samaria. He bragged and called himself a great man. ¹⁰All the people—the least important and the most important—paid attention to Simon, saying, "This man has the power of God, called 'the Great Power'!" ¹¹Simon had amazed them with his magic so long that the people became his followers. ¹²But when Philip told them the Good News about the kingdom of God and the power of Jesus Christ, men and women believed Philip and were baptized. ¹³Simon himself believed, and after he was baptized, he stayed very close to Philip. When he saw the miracles and the powerful things Philip did, Simon was amazed.

¹⁴When the apostles who were still in Jerusalem heard that the people of Samaria had accepted the word of God, they sent Peter and John to them. ¹⁵When Peter and John arrived, they prayed that the Samaritan believers might receive the Holy Spirit. ¹⁶These people had been baptized in the name of the Lord Jesus, but the Holy Spirit had not yet come upon any of them. ¹⁷Then, when the two apostles began laying their hands on the people, they received the Holy Spirit.

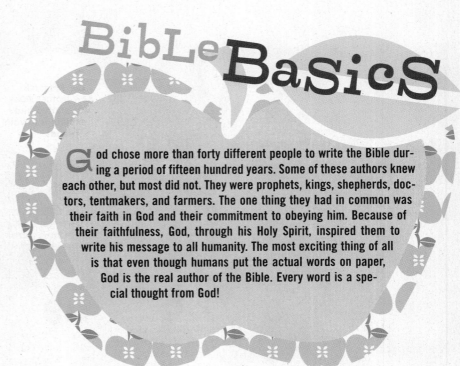

# Bible Basics

**G**od chose more than forty different people to write the Bible during a period of fifteen hundred years. Some of these authors knew each other, but most did not. They were prophets, kings, shepherds, doctors, tentmakers, and farmers. The one thing they had in common was their faith in God and their commitment to obeying him. Because of their faithfulness, God, through his Holy Spirit, inspired them to write his message to all humanity. The most exciting thing of all is that even though humans put the actual words on paper, God is the real author of the Bible. Every word is a special thought from God!

## speak out!

**Q** What do you use the Internet for the most?

**A** Research for school reports.
—Erika, 10

¹⁸Simon saw that the Spirit was given to people when the apostles laid their hands on them. So he offered the apostles money, ¹⁹saying, "Give me also this power so that anyone on whom I lay my hands will receive the Holy Spirit."

²⁰Peter said to him, "You and your money should both be destroyed, because you thought you could buy God's gift with money. ²¹You cannot share with us in this work since your heart is not right before God. ²²Change your heart! Turn away from this evil thing you have done, and pray to the Lord. Maybe he will forgive you for thinking this. ²³I see that you are full of bitter jealousy and ruled by sin."

²⁴Simon answered, "Both of you pray for me to the Lord so the things you have said will not happen to me."

²⁵After Peter and John told the people what they had seen Jesus do and after they had spoken the message of the Lord, they went back to Jerusalem. On the way, they went through many Samaritan towns and preached the Good News to the people.

## Philip Teaches an Ethiopian

²⁶An angel of the Lord said to Philip, "Get ready and go south to the road that leads down to Gaza from Jerusalem—the desert road." ²⁷So Philip got ready and went. On the road he saw a man from Ethiopia, a eunuch. He was an important officer in the service of Candace, the queen of the Ethiopians; he was responsible for taking care of all her money. He had gone to Jerusalem to worship. ²⁸Now, as he was on his way home, he was sitting in his chariot reading from the Book of Isaiah, the prophet. ²⁹The Spirit said to Philip, "Go to that chariot and stay near it."

³⁰So when Philip ran toward the chariot, he heard the man reading from Isaiah the prophet. Philip asked, "Do you understand what you are reading?"

³¹He answered, "How can I understand unless someone explains it to me?" Then he invited Philip to climb in and sit with him. ³²The portion of Scripture he was reading was this:

"He was like a sheep being led to be killed.
He was quiet, as a lamb is quiet while its wool is being cut;
he never opened his mouth.
³³ He was shamed and was treated unfairly.
He died without children to continue his family.
His life on earth has ended."
*Isaiah 53:7–8*

Acts

[34]The officer said to Philip, "Please tell me, who is the prophet talking about—himself or someone else?" [35]Philip began to speak, and starting with this same Scripture, he told the man the Good News about Jesus.

[36]While they were traveling down the road, they came to some water. The officer said, "Look, here is water. What is stopping me from being baptized?" [[37]Philip answered, "If you believe with all your heart, you can." The officer said, "I believe that Jesus Christ is the Son of God."][n] [38]Then the officer commanded the chariot to stop. Both Philip and the officer went down into the water, and Philip baptized him. [39]When they came up out of the water, the Spirit of the Lord took Philip away; the officer never saw him again. And the officer continued on his way home, full of joy. [40]But Philip appeared in a city called Azotus and preached the Good News in all the towns on the way from Azotus to Caesarea.

## Saul Is Converted

9 In Jerusalem Saul was still threatening the followers of the Lord by saying he would kill them. So he went to the high priest [2]and asked him to write letters to the synagogues in the city of Damascus. Then if Saul found any followers of Christ's Way, men or women, he would arrest them and bring them back to Jerusalem.

[3]So Saul headed toward Damascus. As he came near the city, a bright light from heaven suddenly flashed around him. [4]Saul fell to the ground and heard a voice saying to him, "Saul, Saul! Why are you persecuting me?"

[5]Saul said, "Who are you, Lord?"

The voice answered, "I am Jesus, whom you are persecuting. [6]Get up now and go into the city. Someone there will tell you what you must do."

[7]The people traveling with Saul stood there but said nothing. They heard the voice, but they saw no one. [8]Saul got up from the ground and opened his eyes, but he could not see. So those with Saul took his hand and led him into Damascus. [9]For three days Saul could not see and did not eat or drink.

[10]There was a follower of Jesus in Damascus named Ananias. The Lord spoke to Ananias in a vision, "Ananias!"

Ananias answered, "Here I am, Lord."

[11]The Lord said to him, "Get up and go to Straight Street. Find the house of Judas,[n] and ask for a man named Saul from the city of Tarsus. He is there now, praying. [12]Saul has seen a vision in which a man named Ananias comes to him and lays his hands on him. Then he is able to see again."

[13]But Ananias answered, "Lord, many people have told me about this man and the terrible things he did to your holy people in Jerusalem. [14]Now he has come here to Damascus, and the leading priests have given him the power to arrest everyone who worships you."

[15]But the Lord said to Ananias, "Go! I have chosen Saul for an important work. He must tell about me to those who are not Jews, to kings, and to the people of Israel. [16]I will show him how much he must suffer for my name."

[17]So Ananias went to the house of Judas. He laid his hands on Saul and said, "Brother Saul, the Lord Jesus sent me. He is the one you saw on the road on your way here. He sent me so that you can see again and be filled with the Holy Spirit." [18]Immediately, something that looked like fish scales fell from Saul's eyes, and he was able to see again! Then Saul got up and was baptized. [19]After he ate some food, his strength returned.

## Saul Preaches in Damascus

Saul stayed with the followers of Jesus in Damascus for a few days. [20]Soon he began to preach about Jesus in the synagogues, saying, "Jesus is the Son of God."

[21]All the people who heard him were amazed. They said, "This is the man who was in Jerusalem trying to destroy those who trust in this name! He came here to arrest the followers of Jesus and take them back to the leading priests."

[22]But Saul grew more powerful. His proofs that Jesus is the Christ were so strong that his own people in Damascus could not argue with him.

[23]After many days, they made plans to kill Saul. [24]They were watching the city gates day and night, but Saul learned about their plan. [25]One night some followers of Saul helped him leave the city by lowering him in a basket through an opening in the city wall.

## Saul Preaches in Jerusalem

[26]When Saul went to Jerusalem, he tried to join the group of followers, but they were all afraid of him. They did not believe he was really a follower. [27]But Barnabas accepted Saul and took him to the apostles. Barnabas explained to them that Saul had seen the Lord on the road and the Lord had spoken to Saul. Then he told them how boldly Saul had preached in the name of Jesus in Damascus.

[28]And so Saul stayed with the followers, going everywhere in Jerusalem, preaching boldly in the name of the Lord. [29]He

### did you know?

**46% of girls participate in sports teams.**
—Ten Emerging Truths Executive Summary, Girl Scouts research report

# Q & A

Q I'm not as pretty or athletic as other girls in my class. How can I be more popular?

A **Popularity can't really make you happy in the long run. Start by moving it down your list of priorities and goals. You're better off caring about your *reputation*—the impression people have of your character—not about your beauty or talents. Do people think of you as honest, kind, generous, fun, and confident? A good reputation will always bring you more friends and more respect than a pretty face or a tennis trophy. (And it'll last longer, too!)**

**8:37 Philip . . . God."** *Some Greek copies do not contain the bracketed text.* **9:11 Judas** *This is not either of the apostles named Judas.*

would often talk and argue with the Jewish people who spoke Greek, but they were trying to kill him. ³⁰When the followers learned about this, they took Saul to Caesarea and from there sent him to Tarsus.

³¹The church everywhere in Judea, Galilee, and Samaria had a time of peace and became stronger. Respecting the Lord by the way they lived, and being encouraged by the Holy Spirit, the group of believers continued to grow.

### Peter Heals Aeneas

³²As Peter was traveling through all the area, he visited God's people who lived in Lydda. ³³There he met a man named Aeneas, who was paralyzed and had not

## BE YOUR BEST!

Some things can't wait. Things like cavities, broken bones, infections, and splinters need immediate attention or they get more painful and harder to treat later. It's the same way with sin. Ask God for forgiveness right away, and don't give sin a chance to grow in your life!

been able to leave his bed for the past eight years. ³⁴Peter said to him, "Aeneas, Jesus Christ heals you. Stand up and make your bed." Aeneas stood up immediately. ³⁵All the people living in Lydda and on the Plain of Sharon saw him and turned to the Lord.

### Peter Heals Tabitha

³⁶In the city of Joppa there was a follower named Tabitha (whose Greek name was Dorcas). She was always doing good deeds and kind acts. ³⁷While Peter was in Lydda, Tabitha became sick and died. Her body was washed and put in a room upstairs. ³⁸Since Lydda is near Joppa and the followers in Joppa heard that Peter was in Lydda, they sent two messengers to Peter. They begged him, "Hurry, please come to us!" ³⁹So Peter got ready and went with them. When he arrived, they took him to the upstairs room where all the widows stood around Peter, crying. They showed him the shirts and coats Tabitha had made when she was still alive. ⁴⁰Peter sent everyone out of the room and kneeled and prayed. Then he turned to the body and said, "Tabitha, stand up." She opened her eyes, and when she saw Peter, she sat up. ⁴¹He gave her his hand and helped her up. Then he called the saints and the widows into the room and showed them that Tabitha was alive. ⁴²People everywhere in Joppa learned about this, and many believed in the Lord. ⁴³Peter stayed in Joppa for many days with a man named Simon who was a tanner.

## dig deeper

### Acts 11:27–30

One afternoon, you notice the older lady next door trying to mow her lawn. Later, a friend calls because she's having a hard time with a school assignment. Your mom has been too busy lately to dust and vacuum. Before bed, you find your little sister crying. In each situation, you have a choice. You can ignore the needs of others or you can take the opportunity to help. Can you guess what God wants you to do?

Acts 11:27–30 is one of many stories illustrating how eager the early followers of Jesus Christ were to assist others in need—especially fellow believers. Helping others whenever we can is one of the best ways to share God's love. That's exactly what Jesus did, too! He told people about God's love, and then he showed them God's love by meeting their needs.

God wants us to follow Jesus' example of serving others! This means we need to:

- Take time to find out what others need.
- Be willing to miss a favorite TV show or cut phone time a little short in order to help someone.
- Think about others and not just ourselves.

When you have an attitude that says, "How can I help?" you'll find opportunities around every corner!

## Peter Teaches Cornelius

**10** At Caesarea there was a man named Cornelius, an officer in the Italian group of the Roman army. ²Cornelius was a religious man. He and all the other people who lived in his house worshiped the true God. He gave much of his money to the poor and prayed to God often. ³One afternoon about three o'clock, Cornelius clearly saw a vision. An angel of God came to him and said, "Cornelius!"

⁴Cornelius stared at the angel. He became afraid and said, "What do you want, Lord?"

The angel said, "God has heard your prayers. He has seen that you give to the poor, and he remembers you. ⁵Send some men now to Joppa to bring back a man named Simon who is also called Peter. ⁶He is staying with a man, also named Simon, who is a tanner and has a house beside the sea." ⁷When the angel who spoke to Cornelius left, Cornelius called two of his servants and a soldier, a religious man who worked for him. ⁸Cornelius explained everything to them and sent them to Joppa.

⁹About noon the next day as they came near Joppa, Peter was going up to the roof⁷ to pray. ¹⁰He was hungry and wanted to eat, but while the food was being prepared, he had a vision. ¹¹He saw heaven opened and something coming down that looked like a big sheet being lowered to earth by its four corners. ¹²In it were all kinds of animals, reptiles, and birds. ¹³Then a voice said to Peter, "Get up, Peter; kill and eat."

¹⁴But Peter said, "No, Lord! I have never eaten food that is unholy or unclean."

¹⁵But the voice said to him again, "God has made these things clean, so don't call them 'unholy'!" ¹⁶This happened three times, and at once the sheet was taken back to heaven.

¹⁷While Peter was wondering what this vision meant, the men Cornelius sent had found Simon's house and were standing at the gate. ¹⁸They asked, "Is Simon Peter staying here?"

¹⁹While Peter was still thinking about the vision, the Spirit said to him, "Listen, three men are looking for you. ²⁰Get up and go downstairs. Go with them without doubting, because I have sent them to you."

²¹So Peter went down to the men and said, "I am the one you are looking for. Why did you come here?"

²²They said, "A holy angel spoke to Cornelius, an army officer and a good man; he worships God. All the people respect him. The angel told Cornelius to ask you to come to his house so that he can hear what you have to say." ²³So Peter asked the men to come in and spend the night.

The next day Peter got ready and went with them, and some of the followers from Joppa joined him. ²⁴On the following day they came to Caesarea. Cornelius was waiting for them and had called together his relatives and close friends. ²⁵When Peter entered, Cornelius met him, fell at his feet, and worshiped him. ²⁶But Peter helped him up, saying, "Stand up. I too am only a human." ²⁷As he talked with Cornelius, Peter went inside where he saw many people gathered. ²⁸He said, "You people understand that it is against our law for Jewish people to associate with or visit anyone who is not Jewish. But God has shown me that I should not call any person 'unholy' or 'unclean.' ²⁹That is why I did not argue when I was asked to come here. Now, please tell me why you sent for me."

³⁰Cornelius said, "Four days ago, I was praying in my house at this same time—three o'clock in the afternoon. Suddenly, there was a man standing before me wearing shining clothes. ³¹He said, 'Cornelius, God has heard your prayer and has seen that you give to the poor and remembers you. ³²So send some men to Joppa and ask Simon Peter to come. Peter is staying in the house of a man, also named Simon, who is a tanner and has a house beside the sea.' ³³So I sent for you immediately, and it was very good of you to come. Now we are all here before God to hear everything the Lord has commanded you to tell us."

³⁴Peter began to speak: "I really understand now that to God every person is the same. ³⁵In every country God accepts anyone who worships him and does what is right. ³⁶You know the message that God has sent to the people of Israel is the Good News that peace has come through Jesus Christ. Jesus is the Lord of all people! ³⁷You know what has

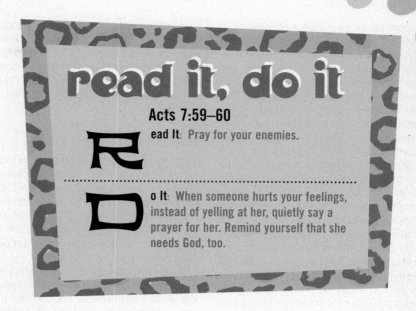

# read it, do it

## Acts 7:59–60

**R**ead It: Pray for your enemies.

**D**o It: When someone hurts your feelings, instead of yelling at her, quietly say a prayer for her. Remind yourself that she needs God, too.

**Tweens spend 11 hours a week listening to music.**
*—Laboratory* Research on Tweens by Creative Consumer Concepts

**did you know?**

**10:9 roof** *In Bible times houses were built with flat roofs. The roof was used for drying things such as flax and fruit. And it was used as an extra room, as a place for worship, and as a cool place to sleep in the summer.*

happened all over Judea, beginning in Galilee after John[n] preached to the people about baptism. [38]You know about Jesus from Nazareth, that God gave him the Holy Spirit and power. You know how Jesus went everywhere doing good and healing those who were ruled by the devil, because God was with him. [39]We saw what Jesus did in Judea and in Jerusalem, but the Jews in Jerusalem killed him by hanging him on a cross. [40]Yet, on the third day, God raised Jesus to life and caused him to be seen, [41]not by all the people, but only by the witnesses God had already chosen. And we are those witnesses who ate and drank with him after he was raised from the dead. [42]He told us to preach to the people and to tell them that he is the one whom God chose to be the judge of the living and the dead. [43]All the prophets say it is true that all who believe in Jesus will be forgiven of their sins through Jesus' name."

[44]While Peter was still saying this, the Holy Spirit came down on all those who were listening. [45]The Jewish believers who came with Peter were amazed that the gift of the Holy Spirit had been given even to the nations. [46]These believers heard them speaking in different languages[n] and praising God. Then Peter

# Q&A

**Q** Why do a lot of girls act like my friend one day and then act mean the next?

**A** Ephesians 4:22 says that "people are fooled by the evil things they want to do." The behavior of these girls has very little to do with you. You're not the problem! It's common for tweens to have trouble making up their minds about what—and who—they like. Try not to let it get you down too much. Make sure you don't do what they're doing . . . and pray for more loyal friends!

said, [47]"Can anyone keep these people from being baptized with water? They have received the Holy Spirit just as we did!" [48]So Peter ordered that they be baptized in the name of Jesus Christ. Then they asked Peter to stay with them for a few days.

## Peter Returns to Jerusalem

**11** The apostles and the believers in Judea heard that some who were not Jewish had accepted God's teaching too. [2]But when Peter came to Jerusalem, some people argued with him. [3]They said, "You went into the homes of people who are not circumcised and ate with them!"

[4]So Peter explained the whole story to them. [5]He said, "I was in the city of Joppa, and while I was praying, I had a vision. I saw something that looked like a big sheet being lowered from heaven by its four corners. It came very close to me. [6]I looked inside it and saw animals, wild beasts, reptiles, and birds. [7]I heard a voice say to me, 'Get up, Peter. Kill and eat.' [8]But I said, 'No, Lord! I have never eaten anything that is unholy or unclean.' [9]But the voice from heaven spoke again, 'God has made these things clean, so don't call them unholy.' [10]This happened three times. Then the whole thing was taken back to heaven. [11]Right then three men who were sent to me from Caesarea came to the house where I was staying. [12]The Spirit told me to go with them without doubting. These six believers here also went with me, and we entered the house of Cornelius. [13]He told us about the angel he saw standing in his house. The angel said to him, 'Send some men to Joppa and invite Simon Peter to come. [14]By the words he will say to you, you and all your family will be saved.' [15]When I began my speech, the Holy Spirit came on them just as he came on us at the beginning. [16]Then I remembered the words of the Lord. He said, 'John baptized with water, but you will be baptized with the Holy Spirit.' [17]Since God gave them the same gift he gave us who believed in the Lord Jesus Christ, how could I stop the work of God?"

[18]When the believers heard this, they stopped arguing. They praised God and said, "So God is allowing even other nations to turn to him and live."

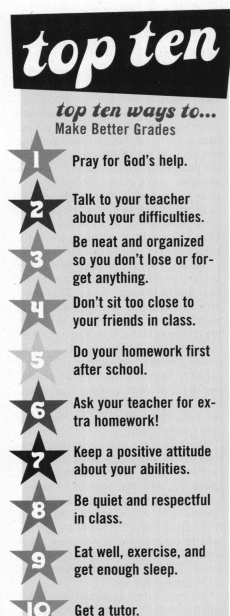

## top ten

### top ten ways to...
**Make Better Grades**

1. **Pray for God's help.**

2. **Talk to your teacher about your difficulties.**

3. **Be neat and organized so you don't lose or forget anything.**

4. **Don't sit too close to your friends in class.**

5. **Do your homework first after school.**

6. **Ask your teacher for extra homework!**

7. **Keep a positive attitude about your abilities.**

8. **Be quiet and respectful in class.**

9. **Eat well, exercise, and get enough sleep.**

10. **Get a tutor.**

## The Good News Comes to Antioch

[19]Many of the believers were scattered when they were persecuted after Stephen was killed. Some of them went as far as Phoenicia, Cyprus, and Antioch telling the message to others, but only to Jews. [20]Some of these believers were people from Cyprus and Cyrene. When they came to Antioch, they spoke also to Greeks,[n] telling them the Good News about the Lord Jesus. [21]The Lord was help-

**10:37 John** *John the Baptist, who preached to people about Christ's coming (Luke 3).* **10:46 languages** *This can also be translated "tongues."* **11:20 Greeks** *Some Greek copies read "Hellenists," non-Greeks who spoke Greek.*

## cool

### Wormy Diet

Guess how many earthworms a baby robin eats in a day (besides other food)? Fourteen feet (about 170 inches) of them! Imagine a basketball player standing on the shoulders of another. That's how long the line of worms would be. That's a lot of worms! But the baby robin needs them to grow. He doesn't complain that he's bored of worms. He just eats them because he knows they're good for him . . . and he's hungry!

As Christians, we should be just as hungry for God's Word. Don't ever get bored of reading your Bible . . . it's your spiritual food!

ing the believers, and a large group of people believed and turned to the Lord.

²²The church in Jerusalem heard about all of this, so they sent Barnabas to Antioch. ²³⁻²⁴Barnabas was a good man, full of the Holy Spirit and full of faith. When he reached Antioch and saw how God had blessed the people, he was glad. He encouraged all the believers in Antioch always to obey the Lord with all their hearts, and many people became followers of the Lord.

²⁵Then Barnabas went to the city of Tarsus to look for Saul, ²⁶and when he found Saul, he brought him to Antioch. For a whole year Saul and Barnabas met with the church and taught many people there. In Antioch the followers were called Christians for the first time.

²⁷About that time some prophets came from Jerusalem to Antioch. ²⁸One of them, named Agabus, stood up and spoke with the help of the Holy Spirit. He said, "A very hard time is coming to the whole world. There will be no food to eat." (This happened when Claudius ruled.) ²⁹The

followers all decided to help the believers who lived in Judea, as much as each one could. ³⁰They gathered the money and gave it to Barnabas and Saul, who brought it to the elders in Judea.

### Herod Agrippa Hurts the Church

**12** During that same time King Herod began to mistreat some who belonged to the church. ²He ordered James, the brother of John, to be killed by the sword. ³Herod saw that some of the people liked this, so he decided to arrest Peter, too. (This happened during the time of the Feast of Unleavened Bread.)

⁴After Herod arrested Peter, he put him in jail and handed him over to be guarded by sixteen soldiers. Herod planned to bring Peter before the people for trial after the Passover Feast. ⁵So Peter was kept in jail, but the church prayed earnestly to God for him.

### Peter Leaves the Jail

⁶The night before Herod was to bring him to trial, Peter was sleeping between two soldiers, bound with two chains. Other soldiers were guarding the door of the jail. ⁷Suddenly, an angel of the Lord stood there, and a light shined in the cell. The angel struck Peter on the side and woke him up. "Hurry! Get up!" the angel said. And the chains fell off Peter's hands. ⁸Then the angel told him, "Get dressed

and put on your sandals." And Peter did. Then the angel said, "Put on your coat and follow me." ⁹So Peter followed him out, but he did not know if what the angel was doing was real; he thought he might be seeing a vision. ¹⁰They went past the first and second guards and came to the iron gate that separated them from the city. The gate opened by itself for them, and they went through it. When they had walked down one street, the angel suddenly left him.

¹¹Then Peter realized what had happened. He thought, "Now I know that the Lord really sent his angel to me. He rescued me from Herod and from all the things the people thought would happen."

¹²When he considered this, he went to the home of Mary, the mother of John Mark. Many people were gathered there, praying. ¹³Peter knocked on the outside door, and a servant girl named Rhoda came to answer it. ¹⁴When she recognized Peter's voice, she was so happy she forgot to open the door. Instead, she ran inside and told the group, "Peter is at the door!"

¹⁵They said to her, "You are crazy!" But she kept on saying it was true, so they said, "It must be Peter's angel."

¹⁶Peter continued to knock, and when they opened the door, they saw him and were amazed. ¹⁷Peter made a sign with his hand to tell them to be quiet. He explained how the Lord led him out of the jail, and he said, "Tell James and the other

## Bible Bios — The Samaritan Woman (John 4)

Jesus met a woman by a well in Samaria and amazed her by asking for water. People from Samaria (Samaritans) didn't usually talk with Jews (like Jesus). Jesus amazed the woman even more by continuing to talk with her. He spoke about things in her private life most people didn't know about—things she was ashamed of. But he spoke kindly and began to explain who he was.

When she realized he was someone very special, she ran back to her village to tell people about him! Many of them went back with her, listened to Jesus, and believed in him. This woman who was living a sinful life changed in a dramatic way after meeting Jesus. When you invite Jesus to change your life, you'll have an exciting story to tell others, too!

believers what happened." Then he left to go to another place.

[18]The next day the soldiers were very upset and wondered what had happened to Peter. [19]Herod looked everywhere for him but could not find him. So he questioned the guards and ordered that they be killed.

## The Death of Herod Agrippa

Later Herod moved from Judea and went to the city of Caesarea, where he stayed. [20]Herod was very angry with the people of Tyre and Sidon, but the people of those cities all came in a group to him. After convincing Blastus, the king's personal servant, to be on their side, they asked Herod for peace, because their country got its food from his country.

[21]On a chosen day Herod put on his royal robes, sat on his throne, and made a speech to the people. [22]They shouted, "This is the voice of a god, not a human!" [23]Because Herod did not give the glory to God, an angel of the Lord immediately caused him to become sick, and he was eaten by worms and died.

[24]God's message continued to spread and reach people.

[25]After Barnabas and Saul finished their task in Jerusalem, they returned to Antioch, taking John Mark with them.

## Barnabas and Saul Are Chosen

**13** In the church at Antioch there were these prophets and teachers: Barnabas, Simeon (also called Niger), Lucius (from the city of Cyrene), Manaen (who had grown up with Herod, the ruler), and Saul. [2]They were all worshiping the Lord and fasting[n] for a certain time. During this time the Holy Spirit said to them, "Set apart for me Barnabas and Saul to do a special work for which I have chosen them."

[3]So after they fasted and prayed, they laid their hands on[n] Barnabas and Saul and sent them out.

## Barnabas and Saul in Cyprus

[4]Barnabas and Saul, sent out by the Holy Spirit, went to the city of Seleucia. From there they sailed to the island of Cyprus. [5]When they came to Salamis, they preached the Good News of God in the synagogues. John Mark was with them to help.

### dig deeper

### Acts 14:22

Have you ever been the "teacher's pet?" Classes always seem to have one kid who gets a little extra attention from the teacher. Usually it's a student who works really hard and treats the teacher with more respect than the other kids do. The problem is that the teacher's pet often gets picked on by other kids. Nobody says anything to the kids who misbehave, but they make fun of the student who is doing her best and not bothering anyone. It doesn't seem fair!

Our Christian lives can be like that, too. Maybe you go to church twice a week, obey your parents, dress properly, and treat everyone kindly. When someone starts bugging you because you believe in Jesus, it can feel awful inside. You might wonder why bad things are happening to you when you're trying to be so good.

Don't be surprised! The apostle Paul warned that Christians aren't exempt from suffering. People who don't believe in Jesus sometimes treat Christians very badly.

What should you do? Keep trusting in God! He knows what's going on, and he's watching over you. He'll help you through the hard times.

[6]They went across the whole island to Paphos where they met a magician named Bar-Jesus. He was a false prophet [7]who always stayed close to Sergius Paulus, the governor and a smart man. He asked Barnabas and Saul to come to him, because he wanted to hear the message of God. [8]But Elymas, the magician, was against them. (Elymas is the name for Bar-Jesus in the Greek language.) He tried to stop the governor from believing in Jesus. [9]But Saul, who was also called Paul, was filled with the Holy Spirit. He looked straight at Elymas [10]and said, "You son of the devil! You are an enemy of everything that is right! You are full of evil tricks and lies, always trying to change the Lord's truths into lies. [11]Now the Lord will touch you, and you will be blind. For a time you will not be able to see anything—not even the light from the sun."

Then everything became dark for Elymas, and he walked around, trying to find someone to lead him by the hand. [12]When the governor saw this, he be-

**13:2 fasting** The people would give up eating for a special time of prayer and worship to God. It was also done sometimes to show sadness and disappointment. **13:3 laid their hands on** The laying on of hands had many purposes, including the giving of a blessing, power, or authority.

Acts

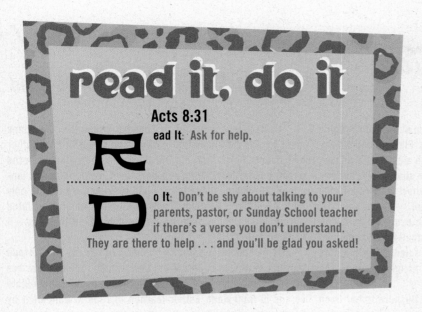

lieved because he was amazed at the teaching about the Lord.

## Paul and Barnabas Leave Cyprus

[13]Paul and those with him sailed from Paphos and came to Perga, in Pamphylia. There John Mark left them to return to Jerusalem. [14]They continued their trip from Perga and went to Antioch, a city in Pisidia. On the Sabbath day they went into the synagogue and sat down. [15]After the law of Moses and the writings of the prophets were read, the leaders of the synagogue sent a message to Paul and Barnabas: "Brothers, if you have any message that will encourage the people, please speak."

[16]Paul stood up, raised his hand, and said, "You Israelites and you who worship God, please listen! [17]The God of the Israelites chose our ancestors. He made the people great during the time they lived in Egypt, and he brought them out of that country with great power. [18]And he was patient with them[n] for forty years in the desert. [19]God destroyed seven nations in the land of Canaan and gave the

**GOD RAISED JESUS FROM THE DEAD, AND HE WILL NEVER GO BACK TO THE GRAVE AND BECOME DUST.**

land to his people. [20]All this happened in about four hundred fifty years.

"After this, God gave them judges until the time of Samuel the prophet. [21]Then the people asked for a king, so God gave them Saul son of Kish. Saul was from the tribe of Benjamin and was king for forty years. [22]After God took him away, God made David their king. God said about him: 'I have found in David son of Jesse the kind of man I want. He will do all I want him to do.' [23]So God has brought Jesus, one of David's descendants, to Israel to be its Savior, as he promised. [24]Before Jesus came, John[n] preached to all the people of Israel about a baptism of changed hearts and lives. [25]When he was finishing his work, he said, 'Who do you think I am? I am not the Christ. He is coming later, and I am not worthy to untie his sandals.'

[26]"Brothers, sons of the family of Abraham, and others who worship God, listen! The news about this salvation has been sent to us. [27]Those who live in Jerusalem and their leaders did not realize that Jesus was the Savior. They did not understand the words that the prophets wrote, which are read every Sabbath day. But they made them come true when they said Jesus was guilty. [28]They could not find any real reason for Jesus to be put to death, but they asked Pilate to have him killed. [29]When they had done to him all that the Scriptures had said, they took him down from the cross and laid

him in a tomb. [30]But God raised him up from the dead! [31]After this, for many days, those who had gone with Jesus from Galilee to Jerusalem saw him. They are now his witnesses to the people. [32]We tell you the Good News about the promise God made to our ancestors. [33]God has made this promise come true for us, his children, by raising Jesus from the dead. We read about this also in Psalm 2:

'You are my Son.
Today I have become your Father.'
*Psalm 2:7*

[34]God raised Jesus from the dead, and he will never go back to the grave and become dust. So God said:

'I will give you the holy and sure blessings
that I promised to David.'
*Isaiah 55:3*

[35]But in another place God says:

'You will not let your Holy One rot.'
*Psalm 16:10*

[36]David did God's will during his lifetime. Then he died and was buried beside his ancestors, and his body did rot in the grave. [37]But the One God raised from the dead did not rot in the grave. [38-39]Brothers, understand what we are telling you: You can have forgiveness of your sins

# Q&A

**Q** Is it okay to have non-Christian friends?

**A** The Bible tells us to separate ourselves from non-Christians (2 Corinthians 6:14–17), but that doesn't mean you can only talk to or be friends with other Christians. If you did that, how would non-Christians ever learn about Jesus? But God does want you to separate yourself from any of your friends' activities, conversations, or behaviors that don't honor him. So your very closest friends should be other Christians who live how God wants us to live.

**13:18 And . . . them** *Some Greek copies read "And he cared for them."* **13:24 John** *John the Baptist, who preached to people about Christ's coming (Luke 3).*

## Christian Girls Around the World

### Esther: Chad

The sun is just coming over the horizon in the Guera region of Chad, right in the heart of Africa. Eleven-year-old Esther wakes up to the sound of the neighbor's donkey braying and rolls off the bamboo bed she shares with her two sisters. Wrapping a scarf around her short black hair, she rushes off to get water from the local well.

School's out for the rainy season so everyone can work in the fields. Esther looks after her own small field of peanuts, and, after they've grown, she'll roast some to sell at the market. She'd really like to buy those dangly earrings she saw there!

Later, Esther straps her baby sister Bushera to her back and meets her friends. They'll be gathering leaves to make sauce for the boule (boiled and baked millet grain)—and giggling and sharing secrets at the same time. Esther's mother is working in her field today so Esther will make the sauce herself. She's much better at it than she was last year! Before supper, Esther holds the water pot and pours out water for her family members to wash their hands. That's important when the family eats with their hands from one dish!

Esther especially loves Sundays when the Christians meet to sing and hear God's Word. She sits with her mother and sisters; her father sits with the men. She's glad when the pastor reads the Scripture in Dangaleat, Esther's native language. The main language for Chad is French, so people only have the Bible in French. Slowly the Bible is being translated into Dangaleat. It's much easier to understand that way—if you can read it.

Most people in Esther's village can't read. She's proud that her mother was one of the first women to learn. Now her mother helps other women learn to read and understand Bible verses in Dangaleat. Esther learned to read in Dangaleat by listening in on her father teaching other grown ups, so now she is at the top of her class in school, even though it's taught in French. Only one boy is ahead of her!

Esther hopes to be a wife and mother and have her own business at the market someday. Maybe she will even teach other women to read. Most of all, she hopes one day she will be able to read the whole Bible for herself.

---

through Jesus. The law of Moses could not free you from your sins. But through Jesus everyone who believes is free from all sins. [40]Be careful! Don't let what the prophets said happen to you:

[41]"Listen, you people who doubt!
You can wonder, and then die.
I will do something in your lifetime
that you won't believe even when
you are told about it!' "

*Habakkuk 1:5*

[42]While Paul and Barnabas were leaving the synagogue, the people asked them to tell them more about these things on the next Sabbath. [43]When the meeting was over, many people with those who had changed to worship God followed Paul and Barnabas from that place. Paul and Barnabas were persuading them to continue trusting in God's grace.

[44]On the next Sabbath day, almost everyone in the city came to hear the word of the Lord. [45]Seeing the crowd, the Jewish people became very jealous and said insulting things and argued against what Paul said. [46]But Paul and Barnabas spoke very boldly, saying, "We must speak the message of God to you first. But you refuse to listen. You are judging yourselves not worthy of having eternal life! So we will now go to the people of other nations. [47]This is what the Lord told us to do, saying:

'I have made you a light for the
nations;
you will show people all over the
world the way to be saved.' "

*Isaiah 49:6*

[48]When those who were not Jewish heard Paul say this, they were happy and gave honor to the message of the Lord. And the people who were chosen to have life forever believed the message.

[49]So the message of the Lord was spreading through the whole country. [50]But the Jewish people stirred up some of the important religious women and the leaders of the city. They started trouble against Paul and Barnabas and forced them out of their area. [51]So Paul and Barnabas shook the dust off their feet[n] and went to Iconium. [52]But the followers were filled with joy and the Holy Spirit.

### Paul and Barnabas in Iconium

**14** In Iconium, Paul and Barnabas went as usual to the synagogue. They spoke so well that a great many Jews and Greeks believed. [2]But some people who did not believe excited the others and turned them against the believers. [3]Paul and Barnabas stayed in Iconium a long time and spoke bravely for the Lord. He showed that their message about his grace was true by giving them the power to work miracles and signs. [4]But the city was divided. Some of the people agreed with the Jews, and others believed the apostles.

[5]Some who were not Jews, some Jews, and some of their rulers wanted to mistreat Paul and Barnabas and to stone them to death. [6]When Paul and Barnabas

---

**13:51 shook . . . feet** *A warning. It showed that they had rejected these people.*

## dig deeper

### Acts 16:22-31

Acts 16:22-31 tells the story of Paul and Silas's imprisonment and rescue. The two men had cast a demon out of a young girl—and made the whole city mad in the process. They were thrown in prison and the guard was ordered to make sure that they were securely locked up.

Paul and Silas were not threatened. In fact, they were singing songs and praying in the middle of the night—in the middle of the jail cell! When God sent a strong earthquake that opened the prison doors and broke their chains off, Paul and Silas could have run for it. Instead, they stayed put and got the chance to share the Good News with the prison guard and his family. Because of their faithfulness to God, the jailer and his household came to know Jesus Christ.

These men could have taken the easy road out, but they saw the value in staying where God had them. They must have known the truth that "in everything God works for the good of those who love him" (Romans 8:28). When you find yourself in an uncomfortable situation, remember God can work miracles through difficulties! Don't be afraid to praise God, even during dark times. You can be sure that he hasn't forgotten about you!

14But when the apostles, Barnabas and Paul, heard about it, they tore their clothes. They ran in among the people, shouting, 15"Friends, why are you doing these things? We are only human beings like you. We are bringing you the Good News and are telling you to turn away from these worthless things and turn to the living God. He is the One who made the sky, the earth, the sea, and everything in them. 16In the past, God let all the nations do what they wanted. 17Yet he proved he is real by showing kindness, by giving you rain from heaven and crops at the right times, by giving you food and filling your hearts with joy." 18Even with these words, they were barely able to keep the crowd from offering sacrifices to them.

19Then some evil people came from Antioch and Iconium and persuaded the people to turn against Paul. So they threw stones at him and dragged him out of town, thinking they had killed him. 20But the followers gathered around him, and he got up and went back into the town. The next day he and Barnabas left and went to the city of Derbe.

### The Return to Antioch in Syria

21Paul and Barnabas told the Good News in Derbe, and many became followers. Paul and Barnabas returned to Lystra, Iconium, and Antioch, 22making the followers of Jesus stronger and helping them stay in the faith. They said, "We must suffer many things to enter God's kingdom." 23They chose elders for each church, by praying and fasting[n] for a certain time. These elders had trusted the Lord, so Paul and Barnabas put them in the Lord's care.

24Then they went through Pisidia and came to Pamphylia. 25When they had preached the message in Perga, they went down to Attalia. 26And from there they sailed away to Antioch where the believers had put them into God's care and had sent them out to do this work. Now they had finished.

27When they arrived in Antioch, Paul and Barnabas gathered the church together. They told the church all about what God had done with them and how God had made it possible for those who were not Jewish to believe. 28And they stayed there a long time with the followers.

learned about this, they ran away to Lystra and Derbe, cities in Lycaonia, and to the areas around those cities. 7They announced the Good News there, too.

### Paul in Lystra and Derbe

8In Lystra there sat a man who had been born crippled; he had never walked. 9As this man was listening to Paul speak, Paul looked straight at him and saw that he believed God could heal him. 10So he cried out, "Stand up on your feet!" The man jumped up and began walking around. 11When the crowds saw what Paul did, they shouted in the Lycaonian language, "The gods have become like humans and have come down to us!" 12Then the people began to call Barnabas "Zeus"[n] and Paul "Hermes,"[n] because he was the main speaker. 13The priest in the temple of Zeus, which was near the city, brought some bulls and flowers to the city gates. He and the people wanted to offer a sacrifice to Paul and Barnabas.

14:12 "Zeus" The Greeks believed in many false gods, of whom Zeus was most important. 14:12 "Hermes" The Greeks believed he was a messenger for the other gods. 14:23 fasting The people would give up eating for a special time of prayer and worship to God. It was also done sometimes to show sadness and disappointment.

## The Meeting at Jerusalem

**15** Then some people came to Antioch from Judea and began teaching the non-Jewish believers: "You cannot be saved if you are not circumcised as Moses taught us." [2]Paul and Barnabas were against this teaching and argued with them about it. So the church decided to send Paul, Barnabas, and some others to Jerusalem where they could talk more about this with the apostles and elders.

[3]The church helped them leave on the trip, and they went through the countries of Phoenicia and Samaria, telling all about how the other nations had turned to God. This made all the believers very happy. [4]When they arrived in Jerusalem, they were welcomed by the apostles, the elders, and the church. Paul, Barnabas, and the others told about everything God had done with them. [5]But some of the believers who belonged to the Pharisee group came forward and said, "The non-Jewish believers must be circumcised. They must be told to obey the law of Moses."

[6]The apostles and the elders gathered to consider this problem. [7]After a long debate, Peter stood up and said to them, "Brothers, you know that in the early days God chose me from among you to preach the Good News to the nations.

They heard the Good News from me, and they believed. [8]God, who knows the thoughts of everyone, accepted them. He showed this to us by giving them the Holy Spirit, just as he did to us. [9]To God, those people are not different from us. When they believed, he made their hearts pure. [10]So now why are you testing God by putting a heavy load around the necks of the non-Jewish believers? It is a load that neither we nor our ancestors were able to carry. [11]But we believe that we and they too will be saved by the grace of the Lord Jesus."

[12]Then the whole group became quiet. They listened to Paul and Barnabas tell about all the miracles and signs that God did through them among the people.

## Q & A

**Q** What's the difference between Christianity and other religions?

**A** The *main* difference is that we believe the only way to heaven is through accepting God's forgiveness for our sins (Ephesians 2:8), which Jesus made possible by dying on the cross. Most other religions believe you have to work your way to heaven (and some don't even believe in a heaven or hell). Other religions also worship idols or a leader who has died. But we believe our leader, the Lord Jesus, is alive (Acts 1:3)!

[13]After they finished speaking, James said, "Brothers, listen to me. [14]Simon has told us how God showed his love for those people. For the first time he is accepting from among them a people to be

his own. [15]The words of the prophets agree with this too:
[16]'After these things I will return.
    The kingdom of David is like a fallen tent.
But I will rebuild its ruins,
    and I will set it up.
[17]Then those people who are left alive may ask the Lord for help,
    and the other nations that belong to me,
says the Lord,
    who will make it happen.
[18]And these things have been known for a long time.' *Amos 9:11–12*
[19]"So I think we should not bother the other people who are turning to God. [20]Instead, we should write a letter to them

telling them these things: Stay away from food that has been offered to idols (which makes it unclean), any kind of sexual sin, eating animals that have been strangled, and blood. [21]They should do these things, because for a long time in every city the law of Moses has been taught. And it is still read in the synagogue every Sabbath day."

## Letter to Non-Jewish Believers

[22]The apostles, the elders, and the whole church decided to send some of their men with Paul and Barnabas to Antioch. They chose Judas Barsabbas and Silas, who were respected by the believers. [23]They sent the following letter with them:

From the apostles and elders, your brothers.
To all the non-Jewish believers in Antioch, Syria, and Cilicia:
Greetings!
[24]We have heard that some of our group have come to you and said things that trouble and upset you. But we did not tell them to do this. [25]We have all agreed to choose some messengers and send them to you with our dear friends Barnabas and Paul— [26]people who have given their lives to serve our Lord Jesus Christ. [27]So we are sending Judas and Silas, who will tell you the same things. [28]It has pleased the Holy Spirit that you should not have a heavy load to carry, and we agree. You need to do only these things: [29]Stay away from any food that has been offered to idols, eating any animals that have been strangled, and blood, and any kind of sexual sin. If you stay away from these things, you will do well.
Good-bye.

[30]So they left Jerusalem and went to Antioch where they gathered the church and gave them the letter. [31]When they read it, they were very happy because of the encouraging message. [32]Judas and Silas, who were also prophets, said many things to encourage the believers and make them stronger. [33]After some time Judas and Silas were sent off in peace by the believers, and they went back to those who had sent them [, [34]but Silas decided to remain there]."

15:34 **but . . . there** *Some Greek copies do not contain the bracketed text.*

# WHAT'S YOUR SPIRITUAL GIFT?

Romans 12:6–8 talks about different gifts (or abilities) God has given us. Rate each answer below by how true it is (1 = "I don't think so!" and 6 = "That is so me!")

### 1. At church you:

____ **a.** Listen to the pastor and think, "I need to tell Emma what I just learned!"
____ **b.** Hear about a volunteer opportunity and sign up right after the service.
____ **c.** Sometimes help in the nursery and read Bible stories to the little kids.
____ **d.** Are known for your big smiles and warm hugs.
____ **e.** Feel great whenever you bring a bag of clothes and toys for poor children.
____ **f.** Come up with great ideas for kids' activities (and they're used).

### 2. When you're with your friends:

____ **a.** They enjoy listening to you talk about your relationship with Jesus.
____ **b.** You always help one of them out with something.
____ **c.** You enjoy explaining homework assignments they have difficulty with.
____ **d.** You give them little notes telling them how much you appreciate them.
____ **e.** You're always ready to share your lunch or lend your sweater.
____ **f.** Everyone asks you what you're going to do that day.

### 3. When you grow up, you want to be:

____ **a.** A writer or missionary
____ **b.** A nurse or a chef
____ **c.** A teacher
____ **d.** A counselor
____ **e.** A social worker
____ **f.** A politician or company president

## What special abilities has God given you?

Count the points you gave each letter. The ones that scored 12 to 18 are probably your spiritual gifts. (You can have more than one.) If you scored highest on…

**A answers, your gift might be prophecy.** You have a good understanding of God's Word and love to share what you know with others. Ask God to give you wisdom as you tell people about him.

**B answers, your gift might be serving.** You prefer helping others rather than getting attention for yourself. Pray that God will help you stay humble and kind. And keep looking for ways to serve him (and others)!

**C answers, your gift might be teaching.** You enjoy helping others improve and grow. Pray for patience and gentleness as you teach. And, when you're a bit older, find out if there's training for Sunday School teachers at your church!

**D answers, your gift might be encouraging others.** You're happy when others are happy! Ask God to help you see when someone is hurting and to give you wisdom to know how to encourage her.

**E answers, your gift might be giving.** You notice when people need something…and you're generous! As you get into your teen years, pray that God will keep you from becoming materialistic. And ask for wisdom to know when to give and how much.

**F answers, your gift might be being a leader.** You're confident and creative! Ask God to help you use your gift to be a courageous but wise leader. Remember: follow God in order to be a good leader!

[35]But Paul and Barnabas stayed in Antioch and, along with many others, preached the Good News and taught the people the message of the Lord.

## Paul and Barnabas Separate

[36]After some time, Paul said to Barnabas, "We should go back to all those towns where we preached the message of the Lord. Let's visit the believers and see how they are doing." [37]Barnabas wanted to take John Mark with them, [38]but he had left them at Pamphylia; he did not continue with them in the work. So Paul did not think it was a good idea to take him. [39]Paul and Barnabas had such a serious argument about this that they separated and went different ways. Barnabas took Mark and sailed to Cyprus, [40]but Paul chose Silas and left. The believers in Antioch put Paul into the Lord's care, [41]and he went through Syria and Cilicia, giving strength to the churches.

## Timothy Goes with Paul

**16** Paul came to Derbe and Lystra, where a follower named Timothy lived. Timothy's mother was Jewish and a believer, but his father was a Greek.

[2]The believers in Lystra and Iconium respected Timothy and said good things about him. [3]Paul wanted Timothy to travel with him, but all the people living in that area knew that Timothy's father was Greek. So Paul circumcised Timothy to please his mother's people. [4]Paul and those with him traveled from town to town and gave the decisions made by the apostles and elders in Jerusalem for the people to obey. [5]So the churches became stronger in the faith and grew larger every day.

## Paul Is Called Out of Asia

[6]Paul and those with him went through the areas of Phrygia and Galatia since the Holy Spirit did not let them preach the Good News in Asia. [7]When they came near the country of Mysia, they tried to go into Bithynia, but the Spirit of Jesus did not let them. [8]So they passed by Mysia and went to Troas. [9]That night Paul saw in a vision a man from Macedonia. The man stood and begged, "Come over to Macedonia and help us." [10]After Paul had seen the vision, we immediately prepared to leave for Macedonia, understanding that God had called us to tell the Good News to those people.

## Lydia Becomes a Christian

[11]We left Troas and sailed straight to the island of Samothrace. The next day we sailed to Neapolis.[n] [12]Then we went by land to Philippi, a Roman colony[n] and the leading city in that part of Macedonia. We stayed there for several days. [13]On the Sabbath day we went outside the city gate to the river where we thought we would find a special place for prayer. Some women had gathered there, so we sat down and talked with them. [14]One of the listeners was a woman named Lydia from the city of Thyatira whose job was selling purple cloth. She worshiped God, and he opened her mind to pay attention to what Paul was saying. [15]She and all the people in her house were baptized. Then she invited us to her home, saying, "If you think I am truly a believer in the Lord, then come stay in my house." And she persuaded us to stay with her.

## Paul and Silas in Jail

[16]Once, while we were going to the place for prayer, a servant girl met us. She had a special spirit[n] in her, and she earned a lot of money for her owners by telling fortunes. [17]This girl followed Paul and us, shouting, "These men are servants of the Most High God. They are telling you how you can be saved."

[18]She kept this up for many days. This bothered Paul, so he turned and said to the spirit, "By the power of Jesus Christ, I command you to come out of her!" Immediately, the spirit came out. [19]When the owners of the servant girl saw this, they knew that now they could not use her to make money. So they grabbed Paul and Silas and dragged them before the city rulers in the marketplace. [20]They brought Paul and Silas to the Roman rulers and said, "These men are Jews and are making trouble in our city. [21]They are teaching things that are not right for us as Romans to do." [22]The crowd joined the attack against them. The Roman officers tore the clothes

**SUDDENLY, THERE WAS A STRONG EARTHQUAKE THAT SHOOK THE FOUNDATION OF THE JAIL. THEN ALL THE DOORS OF THE JAIL BROKE OPEN, . . .**

## speakout!

**Q** How do you feel about the way kids your age dress?

**A** Stylish and nice. They look good. —Kathleen, 11

16:11 **Neapolis** *City in Macedonia. It was the first city Paul visited on the continent of Europe.* 16:12 **Roman colony** *A town begun by Romans with Roman laws, customs, and privileges.* 16:16 **spirit** *This was a spirit from the devil, which caused her to say she had special knowledge.*

of Paul and Silas and had them beaten with rods. ²³Then Paul and Silas were thrown into jail, and the jailer was ordered to guard them carefully. ²⁴When he heard this order, he put them far inside the jail and pinned their feet down between large blocks of wood.

²⁵About midnight Paul and Silas were praying and singing songs to God as the other prisoners listened. ²⁶Suddenly, there was a strong earthquake that shook the foundation of the jail. Then all the doors of the jail broke open, and all the prisoners were freed from their chains. ²⁷The jailer woke up and saw that the jail doors were open. Thinking that the prisoners had already escaped, he got his sword and was about to kill himself.ⁿ ²⁸But Paul shouted, "Don't hurt yourself! We are all here."

²⁹The jailer told someone to bring a light. Then he ran inside and, shaking with fear, fell down before Paul and Silas. ³⁰He brought them outside and said, "Men, what must I do to be saved?"

³¹They said to him, "Believe in the Lord Jesus and you will be saved—you and all the people in your house." ³²So Paul and Silas told the message of the Lord to the jailer and all the people in his house. ³³At that hour of the night the jailer took Paul and Silas and washed their wounds. Then he and all his people were baptized immediately. ³⁴After this the jailer took Paul and Silas home and gave them food. He and his family were very happy because they now believed in God.

³⁵The next morning, the Roman officers sent the police to tell the jailer, "Let these men go free."

³⁶The jailer said to Paul, "The officers have sent an order to let you go free. You can leave now. Go in peace."

³⁷But Paul said to the police, "They beat us in public without a trial, even though we are Roman citizens.ⁿ And they threw us in jail. Now they want to make us go away quietly. No! Let them come themselves and bring us out."

³⁸The police told the Roman officers what Paul said. When the officers heard that Paul and Silas were Roman citizens, they were afraid. ³⁹So they came and told Paul and Silas they were sorry and took them out of jail and asked them to leave the city. ⁴⁰So when they came out of the jail, they went to Lydia's house where they saw some of the believers and encouraged them. Then they left.

## Paul and Silas in Thessalonica

**17** Paul and Silas traveled through Amphipolis and Apollonia and came to Thessalonica where there was a synagogue. ²Paul went into the synagogue as he always did, and on each Sabbath day for three weeks, he talked with his fellow Jews about the Scriptures. ³He explained and proved that the Christ must die and then rise from the dead. He said, "This Jesus I am telling you about is the Christ." ⁴Some of them were convinced and joined Paul and Silas, along with many of the Greeks who worshiped God and many of the important women.

⁵But some others became jealous. So they got some evil men from the marketplace, formed a mob, and started a riot.

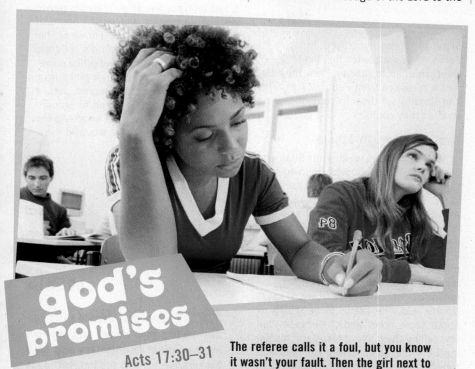

## god's promises

### Acts 17:30–31

The referee calls it a foul, but you know it wasn't your fault. Then the girl next to you in class copies your test and doesn't get caught. You watch TV and it makes you mad when you see people getting away with hurting others. You could wonder if God cares—or you could remember that God promises that, one day, he'll make everything right. The Bible says that there will be a day when God will judge the whole world—and he'll be completely fair. Jesus Christ, who was perfect in every way, will be the perfect judge. How do we know?

So don't get anxious when people don't get what they deserve. They won't get away with it forever. It's not God's judgment day yet. Besides, God is waiting so that people who don't trust him will turn to him and be saved first. You see, God is better than fair. He's gracious and patient and kind!

*God promises that one day, he'll make everything right!*

BELIEVE IN THE LORD JESUS AND YOU WILL BE SAVED . . .

16:27 **kill himself** *He thought the leaders would kill him for letting the prisoners escape.*     16:37 **Roman citizens** *Roman law said that Roman citizens must not be beaten before they had a trial.*

They ran to Jason's house, looking for Paul and Silas, wanting to bring them out to the people. ⁶But when they did not find them, they dragged Jason and some other believers to the leaders of the city. The people were yelling, "These people have made trouble everywhere in the world, and now they have come here too! ⁷Jason is keeping them in his house. All of them do things against the laws of Caesar, saying there is another king, called Jesus."

⁸When the people and the leaders of the city heard these things, they became very upset. ⁹They made Jason and the others put up a sum of money. Then they let the believers go free.

## Paul and Silas Go to Berea

¹⁰That same night the believers sent Paul and Silas to Berea where they went to the synagogue. ¹¹These people were more willing to listen than the people in Thessalonica. The Bereans were eager to hear what Paul and Silas said and studied the Scriptures every day to find out if these things were true. ¹²So, many of them believed, as well as many important Greek women and men. ¹³But the people in Thessalonica learned that Paul was preaching the word of God in Berea, too. So they came there, upsetting the people and making trouble.

¹⁴The believers quickly sent Paul away to the coast, but Silas and Timothy stayed in Berea. ¹⁵The people leading Paul went with him to Athens. Then they carried a message from Paul back to Silas and Timothy for them to come to him as soon as they could.

## Paul Preaches in Athens

¹⁶While Paul was waiting for Silas and Timothy in Athens, he was troubled because he saw that the city was full of idols. ¹⁷In the synagogue, he talked with the Jews and the Greeks who worshiped God. He also talked every day with people in the marketplace.

¹⁸Some of the Epicurean and Stoic philosophers[n] argued with him, saying, "This man doesn't know what he is talking about. What is he trying to say?" Others said, "He seems to be telling us about some other gods," because Paul was telling them about Jesus and his rising from the dead. ¹⁹They got Paul and took him to a meeting of the Areopagus,[n] where they said, "Please explain to us this new idea you have been teaching. ²⁰The things you are saying are new to us, and we want to know what this teaching means." ²¹(All the people of Athens and those from other countries who lived there always used their time to talk about the newest ideas.)

²²Then Paul stood before the meeting of the Areopagus and said, "People of Athens, I can see you are very religious in all things. ²³As I was going through your city, I saw the objects you worship. I found an altar that had these words written on it: TO A GOD WHO IS NOT KNOWN. You worship a god that you don't know, and this is the God I am telling you about! ²⁴The God who made the whole world and everything in it is the Lord of the land and the sky. He does not live in temples built by human hands. ²⁵This God is the One who gives life, breath, and everything else to people. He does not need any help from them; he has everything he needs. ²⁶God began by making one person, and from him came all the different people who live everywhere in the world. God decided exactly when and where they must live. ²⁷God wanted them to look for him and perhaps search all around for him and find him, though he is not far from any of us: ²⁸'By his power we live and move and exist.' Some of your own poets have said: 'For we are his children.' ²⁹Since we are God's children, you must not think that God is like something that people imagine or make from gold, silver, or rock. ³⁰In the past, people did not understand God, and he ignored this. But now, God tells all people in the world to change their hearts and lives.

**did you know?**

59% of preteens regularly play cards or board games with their families.

—CPYU.org, "Be-tween" by Doug West  https://www.cpyu.org/Page.aspx?id=76783

# Q & A

**Q** My parents got me a puppy, but it's so much work to look after him! What do I do now?

**A** Tell your parents that you love having a puppy but need some help. Maybe you can get a friend to give you a hand, or your parents might agree to give you a break sometimes. Just don't expect them to do *everything*. If you still can't manage, talk about the possibility of giving the puppy to someone who can care for him.

## Looking Ahead

### PARENTS

If you've ever worried about getting good enough grades or being the perfect daughter, you're in for a big surprise: parents don't expect you to be perfect! Sometimes it might seem like your parents expect too much from you, which can feel unfair. On the other hand, if your parents seem like they are always embarrassing you when you're with your friends, don't get mad at them. Parents aren't perfect either! You won't live with them forever, so relax; don't put extra pressure on yourself or your parents. Just remember Colossians 3:20: "Children, obey your parents in all things, because this pleases the Lord."

**17:18 Epicurean and Stoic philosophers** *Philosophers were those who searched for truth. Epicureans believed that pleasure, especially pleasures of the mind, were the goal of life. Stoics believed that life should be without feelings of joy or grief.* **17:19 Areopagus** *A council or group of important leaders in Athens. They were like judges.*

# Q & A

**Q** My pastor says that Christians will have eternal life. What does that mean?

**A** Something that is "eternal" has no end. As Christians, we will live forever with God in heaven. It's hard to imagine what "forever" is like because we're so used to measuring time with minutes, days, or years. You might think eternal life sounds boring . . . but the Bible tells us heaven will be awesome! Eternity won't seem long at all.

[31]"God has set a day that he will judge all the world with fairness, by the man he chose long ago. And God has proved this to everyone by raising that man from the dead!"

[32]When the people heard about Jesus being raised from the dead, some of them laughed. But others said, "We will hear more about this from you later." [33]So Paul went away from them. [34]But some of the people believed Paul and joined him. Among those who believed was Dionysius, a member of the Areopagus, a woman named Damaris, and some others.

## Paul in Corinth

**18** Later Paul left Athens and went to Corinth. [2]Here he met a Jew named Aquila who had been born in the country of Pontus. But Aquila and his wife, Priscilla, had recently moved to Corinth from Italy, because Claudius[n] commanded that all Jews must leave Rome. Paul went to visit Aquila and Priscilla. [3]Because they were tentmakers, just as he was, he stayed with them and worked with them. [4]Every Sabbath day he talked with the Jews and Greeks in the synagogue, trying to persuade them to believe in Jesus.

[5]Silas and Timothy came from Macedonia and joined Paul in Corinth. After this,

Paul spent all his time telling people the Good News, showing them that Jesus is the Christ. [6]But they would not accept Paul's teaching and said some evil things. So he shook off the dust from his clothes[n] and said to them, "If you are not saved, it will be your own fault! I have done all I can do! After this, I will go to other nations." [7]Paul left the synagogue and moved into the home of Titius Justus, next to the synagogue. This man worshiped God. [8]Crispus was the leader of that synagogue, and he and all the people living in his house believed in the Lord. Many others in Corinth also listened to Paul and believed and were baptized.

[9]During the night, the Lord told Paul in a vision: "Don't be afraid. Continue talking to people and don't be quiet. [10]I am with you, and no one will hurt you because many of my people are in this city." [11]Paul stayed there for a year and a half, teaching God's word to the people.

## Paul Is Brought Before Gallio

[12]When Gallio was the governor of the country of Southern Greece, some people came together against Paul and took him to the court. [13]They said, "This man is teaching people to worship God in a way that is against our law."

[14]Paul was about to say something, but Gallio spoke, saying, "I would listen to you if you were complaining about a crime or some wrong. [15]But the things you are saying are only questions about words and names—arguments about your own law. So you must solve this problem yourselves. I don't want to be a judge of these things." [16]And Gallio made them leave the court.

[17]Then they all grabbed Sosthenes, the leader of the synagogue, and beat him there before the court. But this did not bother Gallio.

## Paul Returns to Antioch

[18]Paul stayed with the believers for many more days. Then he left and sailed for Syria, with Priscilla and Aquila. At Cenchrea Paul cut off his hair,[n] because he had made a promise to God. [19]Then they went to Ephesus, where Paul left Priscilla and Aquila. While Paul was there, he went into the synagogue and talked with the people. [20]When they asked him to stay with them longer, he refused.

[21]But as he left, he said, "I will come back to you again if God wants me to." And so he sailed away from Ephesus.

[22]When Paul landed at Caesarea, he went and gave greetings to the church in Jerusalem. After that, Paul went to Antioch. [23]He stayed there for a while and then left and went through the regions of Galatia and Phrygia. He traveled from town to town in these regions, giving strength to all the followers.

## Apollos in Ephesus and Corinth

[24]A Jew named Apollos came to Ephesus. He was born in the city of Alexandria and was a good speaker who knew the Scriptures well. [25]He had been taught about the way of the Lord and was always very excited when he spoke and taught the truth about Jesus. But the only baptism Apollos knew about was the baptism that John[n] taught. [26]Apollos began to speak very boldly in the synagogue, and when Priscilla and Aquila heard him, they took him to their home and helped him better understand the way of God. [27]Now Apollos wanted to go to the country of Southern Greece. So the believers helped him and wrote a letter to the followers there, asking them to accept him. These followers had believed in Jesus because of God's grace, and when Apollos arrived, he helped them very much. [28]He argued very strongly

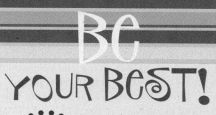

# Be YOUR BEST!

**M**ake a habit of sending thank-you cards or e-mails when people do things you appreciate. That way, the other person will know that you care about what they did. God also deserves our thanks! Try to thank him for something (or lots of things!) each day.

---

**18:2 Claudius** The emperor (ruler) of Rome, A.D. 41–54.   **18:6 shook . . . clothes** This was a warning to show that Paul was finished talking to the people in that city.   **18:18 cut . . . hair** Jews did this to show that the time of a special promise to God was finished.   **18:25 John** John the Baptist, who preached to people about Christ's coming (Luke 3).

# Relationships

**H**ave you ever started liking a school subject (such as math), that you used to hate . . . all because the teacher was so good? Teachers play a huge role in your life, and they deserve to be treated correctly.

The best teacher ever was Jesus Christ. He said, "You call me 'Teacher' . . . and you are right, because that is what I am" (John 13:13). His "students" (followers) showed respect for his teachings by listening closely, asking questions, and trying to live like him. How can you treat your teachers with honor?

with the Jews before all the people, clearly proving with the Scriptures that Jesus is the Christ.

## Paul in Ephesus

**19** While Apollos was in Corinth, Paul was visiting some places on the way to Ephesus. There he found some followers [2]and asked them, "Did you receive the Holy Spirit when you believed?"

They said, "We have never even heard of a Holy Spirit."

[3]So he asked, "What kind of baptism did you have?"

They said, "It was the baptism that John taught."

[4]Paul said, "John's baptism was a baptism of changed hearts and lives. He told people to believe in the one who would come after him, and that one is Jesus."

[5]When they heard this, they were baptized in the name of the Lord Jesus. [6]Then Paul laid his hands on them,[n] and the Holy Spirit came upon them. They began speaking different languages[n] and prophesying. [7]There were about twelve people in this group.

[8]Paul went into the synagogue and spoke out boldly for three months. He talked with the people and persuaded them to accept the things he said about the kingdom of God. [9]But some of them became stubborn. They refused to believe and said evil things about the Way of Jesus before all the people. So Paul

left them, and taking the followers with him, he went to the school of a man named Tyrannus. There Paul talked with people every day [10]for two years. Because of his work, every Jew and Greek in Asia heard the word of the Lord.

## The Sons of Sceva

[11]God used Paul to do some very special miracles. [12]Some people took handkerchiefs and clothes that Paul had used and put them on the sick. When they did this, the sick were healed and evil spirits left them.

[13]But some people also were traveling around and making evil spirits go out of people. They tried to use the name of the Lord Jesus to force the evil spirits out. They would say, "By the same Jesus that Paul talks about, I order you to come out!" [14]Seven sons of Sceva, a leading priest, were doing this.

[15]But one time an evil spirit said to them, "I know Jesus, and I know about Paul, but who are you?"

[16]Then the man who had the evil spirit jumped on them. Because he was so

> BUT ONE TIME AN EVIL SPIRIT SAID TO THEM, "I KNOW JESUS, AND I KNOW ABOUT PAUL, BUT WHO ARE YOU?"

much stronger than all of them, they ran away from the house naked and hurt. [17]All the people in Ephesus—Jews and Greeks—learned about this and were filled with fear and gave great honor to the Lord Jesus. [18]Many of the believers began to confess openly and tell all the evil things they had done. [19]Some of them who had used magic brought their magic books and burned them before everyone. Those books were worth about fifty thousand silver coins.[n]

[20]So in a powerful way the word of the Lord kept spreading and growing.

[21]After these things, Paul decided to go to Jerusalem, planning to go through the countries of Macedonia and Southern Greece and then on to Jerusalem. He said, "After I have been to Jerusalem, I must also visit Rome." [22]Paul sent Timothy and Erastus, two of his helpers, ahead to Macedonia, but he himself stayed in Asia for a while.

## Trouble in Ephesus

[23]And during that time, there was some serious trouble in Ephesus about the Way of Jesus. [24]A man named Demetrius, who worked with silver, made little silver models that looked like the temple of the goddess Artemis.[n] Those who did this work made much money. [25]Demetrius had a meeting with them and some others who did the same kind of work. He told them, "Men, you know that we make a lot of money from our business. [26]But look at what this man Paul is doing. He

---

**19:6 laid his hands on them** *The laying on of hands had many purposes, including the giving of a blessing, power, or authority.* **19:6 languages** *This can also be translated "tongues."* **19:19 fifty thousand silver coins** *Probably drachmas. One coin was enough to pay a worker for one day's labor.* **19:24 Artemis** *A Greek goddess that the people of Asia Minor worshiped.*

has convinced and turned away many people in Ephesus and in almost all of Asia! He says the gods made by human hands are not real. 27There is a danger that our business will lose its good name, but there is also another danger: People will begin to think that the temple of the great goddess Artemis is not important. Her greatness will be destroyed, and Artemis is the goddess that everyone in Asia and the whole world worships."

28When the others heard this, they became very angry and shouted, "Artemis, the goddess of Ephesus, is great!" 29The whole city became confused. The people grabbed Gaius and Aristarchus, who were from Macedonia and were traveling with Paul, and ran to the theater. 30Paul wanted to go in and talk to the crowd, but the followers did not let him. 31Also, some leaders of Asia who were friends of Paul sent him a message, begging him not to go into the theater. 32Some people were shouting one thing, and some were shouting another. The meeting was completely confused; most of them did not know why they had come together. 33They put a man named Alexander in front of the people, and some of them told him what to do. Alexander waved his hand so he could explain things to the people. 34But when they saw that Alexander was a Jew, they all shouted the same thing for two hours: "Great is Artemis of Ephesus!"

35Then the city clerk made the crowd be quiet. He said, "People of Ephesus, everyone knows that Ephesus is the city that keeps the temple of the great goddess Artemis and her holy stone[n] that fell from heaven. 36Since no one can say this is not true, you should be quiet. Stop and think before you do anything. 37You brought these men here, but they have not said anything evil against our goddess or stolen anything from her temple. 38If Demetrius and those who work with him have a charge against anyone they should go to the courts and judges where they can argue with each other. 39If there is something else you want to talk about, it can be decided at the regular town meeting of the people. 40I say this because some people might see this trouble today and say that we are rioting. We could not explain this, because there is no real reason for this meeting." 41After the city clerk said these things, he told the people to go home.

## Paul in Macedonia and Greece

20 When the trouble stopped, Paul sent for the followers to come to him. After he encouraged them and then told them good-bye, he left and went to the country of Macedonia. 2He said many things to strengthen the followers in the different places on his way through Macedonia. Then he went to Greece, 3where he stayed for three months. He was ready to sail for Syria, but some evil people were planning something against him. So Paul decided to go back through Macedonia to Syria. 4The men who went with him were Sopater son of Pyrrhus, from the city of Berea; Aristarchus and Secundus, from the city of Thessalonica; Gaius, from Derbe; Timothy; and Tychicus and Trophimus, two men from Asia. 5These men went on ahead and waited for us at Troas. 6We sailed from Philippi after the Feast of Unleavened Bread. Five days later we met them in Troas, where we stayed for seven days.

## Paul's Last Visit to Troas

7On the first day of the week,[n] we all met together to break bread,[n] and Paul spoke to the group. Because he was planning to leave the next day, he kept on talking until midnight. 8We were all together in a room upstairs, and there were many lamps in the room. 9A young man named Eutychus was sitting in the window. As Paul continued talking, Eutychus was falling into a deep sleep. Finally, he went sound asleep and fell to the ground from the third floor. When they picked him up, he was dead. 10Paul went down to Eutychus, knelt down, and put his arms around him. He said, "Don't worry. He is alive now." 11Then Paul went upstairs again, broke bread, and ate. He spoke to them a long time, until it was early morning, and then he left. 12They took the young man home alive and were greatly comforted.

## The Trip from Troas to Miletus

13We went on ahead of Paul and sailed for the city of Assos, where he wanted to join us on the ship. Paul planned it this way because he wanted to go to Assos by land. 14When he met us there,

"I TAUGHT YOU TO REMEMBER THE WORDS JESUS SAID: 'IT IS MORE BLESSED TO GIVE THAN TO RECEIVE.'"

## Bible Bios
### Mary Magdalene
(Luke 8:2–3; John 20:10–18)

Mary Magdalene's story shows us how God can make beautiful changes in people's lives. Jesus freed Mary from seven demons, and she became one of his most faithful followers!

After Jesus' death, Mary was the first person to go to his tomb. She's the one who discovered the stone was rolled away . . . and that Jesus' body was gone! Even after Jesus' followers came to see for themselves and then went back home, Mary stayed near the tomb, crying because she didn't know where Jesus was.

Suddenly a man appeared. Mary thought it was a gardener, but it was Jesus! He talked with her, and then she ran back to the followers, excited to tell them, "I saw the Lord!" Do you, like Mary, appreciate everything Jesus has saved you from? Do you love and trust him, too?

19:35 holy stone Probably a meteorite or stone that the people thought looked like Artemis. 20:7 first day of the week Sunday, which for Jews began at sunset on our Saturday. But if in this part of Asia a different system of time was used, then the meeting was on our Sunday night. 20:7 break bread Probably the Lord's Supper, the special meal that Jesus told his followers to eat to remember him (Luke 22:14–20).

THE MOST IMPORTANT THING IS THAT I COMPLETE MY MISSION, THE WORK THAT THE LORD JESUS GAVE ME—TO TELL PEOPLE THE GOOD NEWS ABOUT GOD'S GRACE.

## dig deeper

### Acts 20:33–35

Do you know people who act a certain way just to get you to like them or do favors for them? If you like chocolate ice cream, she says *she* likes chocolate ice cream. If you get a new bike, she says she's got a nicer one at home and, if you let her ride yours for a day, she'll let you try hers. If you have difficulty in math, she says she'll give you the answers during the next test . . . *if* you write her book report for her.

Why do people act like this? It really gets bad when dishonest people tell you that they are Christians to make you

trust them. Then they say things about God that confuse you, or they tempt you to do things you know are wrong.

In Acts 20:33–35, the apostle Paul told the believers that they could trust him as a Christian leader and teacher. He had proven himself by treating the other Christians the way Jesus would have. He never asked for help or money when he could take care of himself. In fact, he worked as hard as everyone else and set a good example of someone serving God. Ask God to give you wisdom when someone says she's a Christian but you feel funny about her words and actions.

did not hold back anything that would help you. You know that I taught you in public and in your homes. [21]I warned both Jews and Greeks to change their lives and turn to God and believe in our Lord Jesus. [22]But now I must obey the Holy Spirit and go to Jerusalem. I don't know what will happen to me there. [23]I know only that in every city the Holy Spirit tells me that troubles and even jail wait for me. [24]I don't care about my own life. The most important thing is that I complete my mission, the work that the Lord Jesus gave me—to tell people the Good News about God's grace.

[25]"And now, I know that none of you among whom I was preaching the kingdom of God will ever see me again. [26]So today I tell you that if any of you should be lost, I am not responsible, [27]because I have told you everything God wants you to know. [28]Be careful for yourselves and for all the people the Holy Spirit has given to you to oversee. You must be like shepherds to the church of God,[n] which he bought with the death of his own son. [29]I know that after I leave, some people will come like wild wolves and try to destroy the flock. [30]Also, some from your own group will rise up and twist the truth and will lead away followers after them. [31]So be careful! Always remember that for three years, day and night, I never stopped warning each of you, and I often cried over you.

[32]"Now I am putting you in the care of God and the message about his grace. It is able to give you strength, and it will give you the blessings God has for all his holy people. [33]When I was with you, I never wanted anyone's money or fine clothes. [34]You know I always worked to take care of my own needs and the needs of those who were with me. [35]I showed

we took him aboard and went to Mitylene. [15]We sailed from Mitylene and the next day came to a place near Kios. The following day we sailed to Samos, and the next day we reached Miletus. [16]Paul had already decided not to stop at Ephesus, because he did not want to stay too long in Asia. He was hurrying to be in Jerusalem on the day of Pentecost, if that were possible.

### The Elders from Ephesus

[17]Now from Miletus Paul sent to Ephesus and called for the elders of the church. [18]When they came to him, he said, "You know about my life from the first day I came to Asia. You know the way I lived all the time I was with you. [19]The evil people made plans against me, which troubled me very much. But you know I always served the Lord unselfishly, and I often cried. [20]You know I preached to you and

**20:28 of God** *Some Greek copies read "of the Lord."*

you in all things that you should work as I did and help the weak. I taught you to remember the words Jesus said: 'It is more blessed to give than to receive.' "

36When Paul had said this, he knelt down with all of them and prayed. 37-38And they all cried because Paul had said they would never see him again. They put their arms around him and kissed him. Then they went with him to the ship.

## Paul Goes to Jerusalem

**21** After we all said good-bye to them, we sailed straight to the island of Cos. The next day we reached Rhodes, and from there we went to Patara. 2There we found a ship going to Phoenicia, so we went aboard and sailed away. 3We sailed near the island of Cyprus, seeing it to the north, but we sailed on to Syria. We stopped at Tyre because the ship needed to unload its cargo there. 4We found some followers in Tyre and stayed with them for seven days. Through the Holy Spirit they warned Paul not to go to Jerusalem. 5When we finished our visit, we left and continued our trip. All the followers, even the women and children, came outside the city with us. After we all knelt on the beach and prayed, 6we said good-bye and got on the ship, and the followers went back home.

7We continued our trip from Tyre and arrived at Ptolemais, where we greeted the believers and stayed with them for a day. 8The next day we left Ptolemais and went to the city of Caesarea. There we went into the home of Philip the preacher, one of the seven helpers,[n] and stayed with him. 9He had four unmarried daughters who had the gift of prophesying. 10After we had been there for some time, a prophet named Agabus arrived from Judea. 11He came to us and borrowed Paul's belt and used it to tie his own hands and feet. He said, "The Holy Spirit says, 'This is how evil people in Jerusalem will tie up the man who wears this belt. Then they will give him to the older leaders.' "

12When we all heard this, we and the people there begged Paul not to go to Jerusalem. 13But he said, "Why are you crying and making me so sad? I am not only ready to be tied up in Jerusalem; I am ready to die for the Lord Jesus!"

14We could not persuade him to stay away from Jerusalem. So we stopped begging him and said, "We pray that what the Lord wants will be done."

15After this, we got ready and started on our way to Jerusalem. 16Some of the followers from Caesarea went with us and took us to the home of Mnason, where we would stay. He was from Cyprus and was one of the first followers.

## Paul Visits James

17In Jerusalem the believers were glad to see us. 18The next day Paul went with us to visit James, and all the elders were there. 19Paul greeted them and told them everything God had done among the other nations through him. 20When they heard this, they praised God. Then they said to Paul,

"Brother, you can see that many thousands of our people have become believers. And they think it is very important to obey the law of Moses. 21They have heard about your teaching, that you tell our people who live among the nations to leave the law of Moses. They have heard that you tell them not to circumcise their children and not to obey customs. 22What should we do? They will learn that you have come. 23So we will tell you what to do: Four of our men have made a promise to God. 24Take these men with you and share in their cleansing ceremony.[n] Pay their expenses so they can shave their heads.[n] Then it will prove to everyone that what they have heard about you is

# Shine Your Light

Uhen Rebekah was living on a ranch in Montana, she and her sister had very special people to give Valentine's cards to. Their mom encouraged the two girls to reach out to *widows* (women whose husbands had died) in their church. So for Valentine's Day, the sisters would make cards and bake cookies to give to the widows. They also surprised the older ladies with these treats on their birthdays, on other holidays, or on just any regular day!

Rebekah says that the cards and cookies weren't fancy, but the widows loved them! And she got to see what special people they were . . . just because of a little effort she made.

Widows often feel lonely because their children are all grown and their husbands are gone, so it means a lot to them when someone shows they care . . . especially kids! Do *you* know any widows, *widowers* (men whose wives have died), or older people who never got married and have no family? You can do simple things, too, to brighten their day. Think of something you can do this week!

21:8 **helpers** The seven men chosen for a special work described in Acts 6:1–6. Sometimes they are called "deacons." 21:24 **cleansing ceremony** The special things Jews did to end the Nazirite promise. 21:24 **shave their heads** Jews did this to show that their promise was finished.

# dig deeper

## Acts 22:14–15

What do you do when your grandma gives you a very special gold necklace? You probably put it in a safe place, like a jewelry box. If your parents give you a large amount of money for your birthday, you might decide to put it in the bank so that you don't lose it (or spend it!). Maybe you have a favorite doll, a private diary, or some nice gel pens that you don't want anyone to touch. You really try to protect the things that mean a lot to you, don't you?

In Acts 22:14–15, the apostle Paul explained how he had received a message from God years before. Amazingly, Paul could still quote exactly what he had been told. He could state with confidence what God wanted him to do and say. He had treasured every word.

You, too, can treasure the truth that God teaches you. Take time every day to read your Bible and to talk with God. Ask him to make your faith strong and to give you courage as a Christian. Never hide the fact that you're a follower of Jesus Christ. Know what you believe—and why!

³⁰All the people in Jerusalem became upset. Together they ran, took Paul, and dragged him out of the Temple. The Temple doors were closed immediately. ³¹While they were trying to kill Paul, the commander of the Roman army in Jerusalem learned that there was trouble in the whole city. ³²Immediately he took some officers and soldiers and ran to the place where the crowd was gathered. When the people saw them, they stopped beating Paul. ³³The commander went to Paul and arrested him. He told his soldiers to tie Paul with two chains. Then he asked who he was and what he had done wrong. ³⁴Some in the crowd were yelling one thing, and some were yelling another. Because of all this confusion and shouting, the commander could not learn what had happened. So he ordered the soldiers to take Paul to the army building. ³⁵When Paul came to the steps, the soldiers had to carry him because the people were ready to hurt him. ³⁶The whole mob was following them, shouting, "Kill him!"

³⁷As the soldiers were about to take Paul into the army building, he spoke to the commander, "May I say something to you?"

# Q&A

**Q** None of the other girls on my soccer team are Christians. I'm embarrassed to say that I am—what if they laugh?

**A** They might laugh . . . or they might not. A couple of them might want to know what it means to be a Christian. You could be a light that shows them Jesus' love (Matthew 5:16). If they do laugh, don't let it get you down. People laughed at Jesus—in fact, they did much worse to him! God will bless you for your courage. Keep your chin up, enjoy the game, and show them what a great soccer player a Christian girl can be!

not true and that you follow the law of Moses in your own life. ²⁵We have already sent a letter to the non-Jewish believers. The letter said: 'Do not eat food that has been offered to idols, or blood, or animals that have been strangled. Do not take part in sexual sin.' "

²⁶The next day Paul took the four men and shared in the cleansing ceremony with them. Then he went to the Temple and announced the time when the days of the cleansing ceremony would be finished. On the last day an offering would be given for each of the men.

²⁷When the seven days were almost over, some of his people from Asia saw Paul at the Temple. They caused all the people to be upset and grabbed Paul. ²⁸They shouted, "People of Israel, help us! This is the man who goes everywhere teaching against the law of Moses, against our people, and against this Temple. Now he has brought some Greeks into the Temple and has made this holy place unclean!" ²⁹(They said this because they had seen Trophimus, a man from Ephesus, with Paul in Jerusalem. They thought that Paul had brought him into the Temple.)

The commander said, "Do you speak Greek? [38]I thought you were the Egyptian who started some trouble against the government not long ago and led four thousand killers out to the desert."

[39]Paul said, "No, I am a Jew from Tarsus in the country of Cilicia. I am a citizen of that important city. Please, let me speak to the people."

[40]The commander gave permission, so Paul stood on the steps and waved his hand to quiet the people. When there was silence, he spoke to them in the Hebrew language.

## Paul Speaks to the People

**22** Paul said, "Brothers and fathers, listen to my defense to you." [2]When they heard him speaking the Hebrew language,[n] they became very quiet. Paul said, [3]"I am a Jew, born in Tarsus in the country of Cilicia, but I grew up in this city. I was a student of Gamaliel,[n] who carefully taught me everything about the law of our ancestors. I was very serious about serving God, just as are all of you here today. [4]I persecuted the people who followed the Way of Jesus, and some of them were even killed. I arrested men and women and put them in jail. [5]The high priest and the whole council of elders can tell you this is true. They gave me letters to the brothers in Damascus. So I was going there to arrest these people and bring them back to Jerusalem to be punished.

[6]"About noon when I came near Damascus, a bright light from heaven suddenly flashed all around me. [7]I fell to the ground and heard a voice saying, 'Saul, Saul, why are you persecuting me?' [8]I asked, 'Who are you, Lord?' The voice said, 'I am Jesus from Nazareth whom you are persecuting.' [9]Those who were with me did not understand the voice, but they saw the light. [10]I said, 'What shall I do, Lord?' The Lord answered, 'Get up and go to Damascus. There you will be told about all the things I have

planned for you to do.' [11]I could not see, because the bright light had made me blind. So my companions led me into Damascus.

[12]"There a man named Ananias came to me. He was a religious man; he obeyed the law of Moses, and all the Jews who lived there respected him. [13]He stood by me and said, 'Brother Saul, see again!' Immediately I was able to see him. [14]He said, 'The God of our ancestors chose you long ago to know his plan, to see the Righteous One, and to hear words from him. [15]You will be his witness to all people, telling them about what you have seen and heard. [16]Now, why wait any longer? Get up, be baptized, and wash your sins away, trusting in him to save you.'

[17]"Later, when I returned to Jerusalem, I was praying in the Temple, and I saw a vision. [18]I saw the Lord saying to me, 'Hurry! Leave Jerusalem now! The people here will not accept the truth about me.' [19]But I said, 'Lord, they know that in every synagogue I put the believers in jail and beat them. [20]They also know I was there when Stephen, your witness, was killed. I stood there agreeing and holding the coats of those who were killing him!' [21]But the Lord said to me, 'Leave now. I will send you far away to the other nations.' "

[22]The crowd listened to Paul until he said this. Then they began shouting, "Get rid of him! He doesn't deserve to live!" [23]They shouted, threw off their coats,[n] and threw dust into the air.[n]

[24]Then the commander ordered the soldiers to take Paul into the army building and beat him. He wanted to make Paul tell why the people were shouting against him like this. [25]But as the soldiers were tying him up, preparing to beat him, Paul said to an officer nearby, "Do you have the right to beat a Roman citizen[n] who has not been proven guilty?"

[26]When the officer heard this, he went to the commander and reported it. The officer said, "Do you know what you are doing? This man is a Roman citizen."

[27]The commander came to Paul and said, "Tell me, are you really a Roman citizen?"

He answered, "Yes."

[28]The commander said, "I paid a lot of money to become a Roman citizen."

But Paul said, "I was born a citizen."

[29]The men who were preparing to question Paul moved away from him immediately. The commander was frightened because he had already tied Paul, and Paul was a Roman citizen.

## Paul Speaks to Leaders

[30]The next day the commander decided to learn why the Jews were accusing Paul. So he ordered the leading priests and the council to meet. The commander took Paul's chains off. Then he brought Paul out and stood him before their meeting.

**23** Paul looked at the council and said, "Brothers, I have lived my life without guilt feelings before God up to this day." [2]Ananias,[n] the high priest, heard this and told the men who were standing near Paul to hit him on the

---

### cool

### Dangerous Pets!

You're probably more afraid of Great White Sharks than your pets, right? Well, think about this: more people are injured each year by cats, dogs, and pigs than they are by sharks! You can probably guess why. People are around pets more often than they are near sharks.

You might feel confident because you don't commit "big" sins. But Satan doesn't usually tempt us with things that are obviously wrong and horrible. Watch out for the little temptations that you think aren't so dangerous or serious. Those are the ones that usually get you!

---

**57% of kids consider family the most important thing in their lives.**
— Tween Audience Analysis Profile, The Health Communication Unit, 2004

**did you know?**

---

22:2 **Hebrew language** *Or Aramaic, the languages of many people in this region in the first century.* 22:3 **Gamaliel** *A very important teacher of the Pharisees, a Jewish religious group (Acts 5:34).* 22:23 **threw off their coats** *This showed that the people were very angry with Paul.* 22:23 **threw dust into the air** *This showed even greater anger.* 22:25 **Roman citizen** *Roman law said that Roman citizens must not be beaten before they had a trial.* 23:2 **Ananias** *This is not the same man named Ananias in Acts 22:12.*

mouth. [3]Paul said to Ananias, "God will hit you, too! You are like a wall that has been painted white. You sit there and judge me, using the law of Moses, but you are telling them to hit me, and that is against the law."

[4]The men standing near Paul said to him, "You cannot insult God's high priest like that!"

[5]Paul said, "Brothers, I did not know this man was the high priest. It is written in the Scriptures, 'You must not curse a leader of your people.' "[n]

[6]Some of the men in the meeting were Sadducees, and others were Pharisees. Knowing this, Paul shouted to them, "My brothers, I am a Pharisee, and my father was a Pharisee. I am on trial here because I believe that people will rise from the dead."

[7]When Paul said this, there was an argument between the Pharisees and the Sadducees, and the group was divided. [8](The Sadducees do not believe in angels or spirits or that people will rise from the dead. But the Pharisees believe in them all.) [9]So there was a great uproar. Some of the teachers of the law, who were Pharisees, stood up and argued, "We find nothing wrong with this man. Maybe

# Q&A

an angel or a spirit did speak to him."

[10]The argument was beginning to turn into such a fight that the commander was afraid some evil people would tear Paul to pieces. So he told the soldiers to go down and take Paul away and put him in the army building.

[11]The next night the Lord came and stood by Paul. He said, "Be brave! You have told people in Jerusalem about me. You must do the same in Rome."

[12]In the morning some evil people made a plan to kill Paul, and they took an oath not to eat or drink anything until they had killed him. [13]There were more than forty men who made this plan. [14]They went to the leading priests and the elders and said, "We have taken an oath not to eat or drink until we have killed Paul. [15]So this is what we want you to do: Send a message to the commander to bring Paul out to you as though you want to ask him more questions. We will be waiting to kill him while he is on the way here."

[16]But Paul's nephew heard about this plan and went to the army building and told Paul. [17]Then Paul called one of the officers and said, "Take this young man to the commander. He has a message for him."

[18]So the officer brought Paul's nephew to the commander and said, "The prisoner, Paul, asked me to bring this young man to you. He wants to tell you something."

[19]The commander took the young man's hand and led him to a place where they could be alone. He asked, "What do you want to tell me?"

[20]The young man said, "The Jews have decided to ask you to bring Paul down to their council meeting tomorrow. They want you to think they are going to ask him more questions. [21]But don't believe them! More than forty men are hiding and waiting to kill Paul. They have all taken an oath not to eat or drink until they have killed him. Now they are waiting for you to agree."

[22]The commander sent the young man away, ordering him, "Don't tell anyone that you have told me about their plan."

## Paul Is Sent to Caesarea

[23]Then the commander called two officers and said, "I need some men to go to Caesarea. Get two hundred soldiers, sev-

## Looking Ahead

### EXAMS

enty horsemen, and two hundred men with spears ready to leave at nine o'clock tonight. [24]Get some horses for Paul to ride so he can be taken to Governor Felix safely." [25]And he wrote a letter that said:

[26]From Claudius Lysias.

To the Most Excellent Governor Felix:

Greetings.

[27]Some of the Jews had taken this man and planned to kill him. But I learned that he is a Roman citizen, so I went with my soldiers and saved him. [28]I wanted to know why they were accusing him, so I brought him before their council meeting. [29]I learned that these people said Paul did some things that were wrong by their own laws, but no charge was worthy of jail or death. [30]When I was told that some of them were planning to kill Paul, I sent him to you at once. I also told them to tell you what they have against him.

[31]So the soldiers did what they were told and took Paul and brought him to the city of Antipatris that night. [32]The next day the horsemen went with Paul to

Acts

## god's promises

### Acts 23:16—22

Your best friend dumps you over a boy. You fail the math test *again,* even though you studied—*hard.* Or maybe you learn that one of your good friends is doing drugs or that your dad is moving out. Do these kinds of things make you ask yourself, "Why is this happening to me? Is God out to get me?"

The apostle Paul could have felt that way when he was stuck in jail with people trying to assassinate him. But the Bible tells us God's not out to get us. In fact, it says that quite the opposite is true. God loves us so much—and he is so powerful—that he brings good out of *everything* that happens to us. Everything. Even the bad stuff.

We don't always know right away what God's doing through the hard things that happen to us. Sometimes it takes a long, long time, and sometimes we never find out exactly what God had in mind.

Paul saw how God guided him and kept him safe. Most of all, Paul experienced God's love and care every step of the way. The next time you feel like everything is going wrong, remember to look for the good thing God is doing through your situation.

***God brings good out of everything that happens to us.***

Caesarea, but the other soldiers went back to the army building in Jerusalem. [33]When the horsemen came to Caesarea and gave the letter to the governor, they turned Paul over to him. [34]The governor read the letter and asked Paul, "What area are you from?" When he learned that Paul was from Cilicia, [35]he said, "I will hear your case when those who are against you come here, too." Then the governor gave orders for Paul to be kept under guard in Herod's palace.

### Paul Is Accused

**24** Five days later Ananias, the high priest, went to the city of Caesarea with some of the elders and a lawyer named Tertullus. They had come to make charges against Paul before the governor. [2]Paul was called into the meeting, and Tertullus began to accuse him, saying, "Most Excellent Felix! Our people enjoy much peace because of you, and many wrong things in our country are be-ing made right through your wise help. [3]We accept these things always and in every place, and we are thankful for them. [4]But not wanting to take any more of your time, I beg you to be kind and listen to our few words. [5]We have found this man to be a troublemaker, stirring up his people everywhere in the world. He is a leader of the Nazarene group. [6]Also, he was trying to make the Temple unclean, but we stopped him. [And we wanted to judge him by our own law. [7]But the officer Lysias came and used much force to take him from us. [8]And Lysias commanded those who wanted to accuse Paul to come to you.][n] By asking him questions yourself, you can decide if all these things are true." [9]The others agreed and said that all of this was true.

[10]When the governor made a sign for Paul to speak, Paul said, "Governor Felix, I know you have been a judge over this nation for a long time. So I am happy to defend myself before you. [11]You can learn for yourself that I went to worship in Jerusalem only twelve days ago. [12]Those who are accusing me did not find me arguing with anyone in the Temple or stirring up the people in the synagogues or in the city. [13]They cannot prove the things they are saying against me now. [14]But I will tell you this: I worship the God of our ancestors as a follower of the Way of Jesus. The others say that the Way of Jesus is not the right way. But I believe everything that is taught in the law of Moses and that is written in the books of the Prophets. [15]I have the same hope in God that they have—the hope that all people, good and bad, will surely be raised from the dead. [16]This is why I always try to do what I believe is right before God and people.

[17]"After being away from Jerusalem for several years, I went back to bring money to my people and to offer sacrifices. [18]I was doing this when they found me in the Temple. I had finished the cleansing ceremony and had not made any trouble; no people were gathering around me. [19]But there were some people from Asia who should be here, standing before you. If I have really done anything wrong, they are the ones who should accuse me. [20]Or ask these people here if they found any wrong in me when I stood before the council in Jerusalem. [21]But I did shout

24:6–8 **And . . . you.** *Some Greek copies do not contain the bracketed text.*

one thing when I stood before them: 'You are judging me today because I believe that people will rise from the dead!'"

²²Felix already understood much about the Way of Jesus. He stopped the trial

and said, "When commander Lysias comes here, I will decide your case." ²³Felix told the officer to keep Paul guarded but to give him some freedom and to let his friends bring what he needed.

## Paul Speaks to Felix and His Wife

²⁴After some days Felix came with his wife, Drusilla, who was Jewish, and asked for Paul to be brought to him. He listened to Paul talk about believing in Christ Jesus. ²⁵But Felix became afraid when Paul spoke about living right, self-control, and the time when God will judge the world. He said, "Go away now. When I have more time, I will call for you." ²⁶At the same time Felix hoped that

Paul would give him some money, so he often sent for Paul and talked with him. ²⁷But after two years, Felix was replaced by Porcius Festus as governor. But Felix had left Paul in prison to please the Jews.

## Paul Asks to See Caesar

**25** Three days after Festus became governor, he went from Caesarea to Jerusalem. ²There the leading priests and the important leaders made charges against Paul before Festus. ³They asked Festus to do them a favor. They wanted him to send Paul back to Jerusalem, because they had a plan to kill him on the way. ⁴But Festus answered that Paul would be kept in Caesarea and that he himself was returning there soon. ⁵He said, "Some of your leaders should go with me. They can accuse the man there in Caesarea, if he has really done something wrong."

⁶Festus stayed in Jerusalem another eight or ten days and then went back to Caesarea. The next day he told the soldiers to bring Paul before him. Festus was seated on the judge's seat ⁷when Paul came into the room. The people who had come from Jerusalem stood around him, making serious charges against him, which they could not prove. ⁸This is what Paul said to defend himself: "I have done nothing wrong against the law, against the Temple, or against Caesar."

⁹But Festus wanted to please the people. So he asked Paul, "Do you want to go to Jerusalem for me to judge you there on these charges?"

¹⁰Paul said, "I am standing at Caesar's judgment seat now, where I should be judged. I have done nothing wrong to them; you know this is true. ¹¹If I have done something wrong and the law says I must die, I do not ask to be saved from death. But if these charges are not true, then no one can give me to them. I want Caesar to hear my case!"

¹²Festus talked about this with his advisers. Then he said, "You have asked to see Caesar, so you will go to Caesar!"

## Paul Before King Agrippa

¹³A few days later King Agrippa and Bernice came to Caesarea to visit Festus. ¹⁴They stayed there for some time, and Festus told the king about Paul's case. Festus said, "There is a man that Felix left in prison. ¹⁵When I went to Jerusalem, the leading priests and the elders there made charges against him, asking me to sentence him to death. ¹⁶But I answered, 'When a man is accused of a crime, Romans do not hand him over until he has been allowed to face his accusers and defend himself against their charges.' ¹⁷So when these people came here to Caesarea for the trial, I did not waste time. The next day I sat on the judge's seat and commanded that the man be brought in. ¹⁸They stood up and accused him, but not of any serious crime as I thought they would. ¹⁹The things they said were about their own religion and about a man named Jesus who died. But Paul said that he is still alive. ²⁰Not knowing how to find out about these questions, I asked Paul, 'Do you want to go to Jerusalem and be judged there?' ²¹But he asked to be kept in Caesarea. He wants a decision from the emperor.ⁿ So I ordered that he be held until I could send him to Caesar."

²²Agrippa said to Festus, "I would also like to hear this man myself."

Festus said, "Tomorrow you will hear him."

# Q & A

**speakout!**

---

**25:21 emperor** *The ruler of the Roman Empire, which was almost all the known world.*

Acts

## ■ Bible Bios  Stephen (Acts 6—7)

Stephen left us a great example of following in Jesus' footsteps. He served God faithfully and told many people about Jesus . . . and ended up getting killed for it!

Some men had tried arguing with Stephen, but God gave him so much wisdom and strength that they could never prove him wrong. They finally decided to just kill him. Standing in front of a group of leaders while men lied about him, Stephen didn't feel afraid. In fact, his face looked like an angel's!

After he gave a long speech about how Jesus had come to save sinners, the people threw stones at Stephen until he died. And while they stoned him, Stephen prayed that God would forgive them. The next time you hear someone call Christians wimps, remember Stephen's story. Nothing could stop him from serving God!

[23]The next day Agrippa and Bernice appeared with great show, acting like very important people. They went into the judgment room with the army leaders and the important men of Caesarea. Then Festus ordered the soldiers to bring Paul in. [24]Festus said, "King Agrippa and all who are gathered here with us, you see this man. All the people, here and in Jerusalem, have complained to me about him, shouting that he should not live any longer. [25]When I judged him, I found no reason to order his death. But since he asked to be judged by Caesar, I decided to send him. [26]But I have nothing definite to write the emperor about him. So I have brought him before all of you—especially you, King Agrippa. I hope you can question him and give me something to write. [27]I think it is foolish to send a prisoner to Caesar without telling what charges are against him."

### Paul Defends Himself

**26** Agrippa said to Paul, "You may now speak to defend yourself."

Then Paul raised his hand and began to speak. [2]He said, "King Agrippa, I am very blessed to stand before you and will answer all the charges the evil people make against me. [3]You know so much about all the customs and the things they argue about, so please listen to me patiently.

[4]"All my people know about my whole life, how I lived from the beginning in my own country and later in Jerusalem. [5]They have known me for a long time. If they want to, they can tell you that I was a good Pharisee. And the Pharisees obey the laws of my tradition more carefully than any other group. [6]Now I am on trial because I hope for the promise that God made to our ancestors. [7]This is the promise that the twelve tribes of our people hope to receive as they serve God day and night. My king, they have accused me because I hope for this same promise! [8]Why do any of you people think it is impossible for God to raise people from the dead?

[9]"I, too, thought I ought to do many things against Jesus from Nazareth. [10]And that is what I did in Jerusalem. The leading priests gave me the power to put many of God's people in jail, and when they were being killed, I agreed it was a good thing. [11]In every synagogue, I often punished them and tried to make them speak against Jesus. I was so angry against them I even went to other cities to find them and punish them.

[12]"One time the leading priests gave me permission and the power to go to Damascus. [13]On the way there, at noon, I saw a light from heaven. It was brighter than the sun and flashed all around me and those who were traveling with me. [14]We all fell to the ground. Then I heard a voice speaking to me in the Hebrew language,[n] saying, 'Saul, Saul, why are you persecuting me? You are only hurting yourself by fighting me.' [15]I said, 'Who are you, Lord?' The Lord said, 'I am Jesus, the one you are persecuting. [16]Stand up! I have chosen you to be my servant and my witness—you will tell people the things that you have seen and the things that I will show you. This is why I have come to you today. [17]I will keep you safe from your own people and also from the others. I am sending you to them [18]to open their eyes so that they may turn away from darkness to the light, away from the power of Satan and to God. Then their sins can be forgiven, and they can have a place with those people who have been made holy by believing in me.'

[19]"King Agrippa, after I had this vision from heaven, I obeyed it. [20]I began telling people that they should change their hearts and lives and turn to God and do things to show they really had changed. I told this first to those in Damascus, then in Jerusalem, and in every part of Judea,

## Looking Ahead

### MISSIONS TRIPS

When you are older, you may have the chance to go on a mission or ministry trip with your church or youth group. Usually these trips are to another city or even another country! It can be frightening to be in an unfamiliar place. But mission trips can be life-changing experiences and lots of fun! You'll have the opportunity to help others and see God working in a different place. Galatians 5:13 tells us to "serve each other with love." You'll learn a lot by spending time with people and by helping them. Talk to your youth leaders to find out how you can be involved.

26:14 **Hebrew language** *Or Aramaic, the languages of many people in this region in the first century.*

and also to the other people. <sup>21</sup>This is why the Jews took me and were trying to kill me in the Temple. <sup>22</sup>But God has helped me, and so I stand here today, telling all people, small and great, what I have seen. But I am saying only what Moses and the prophets said would happen— <sup>23</sup>that the Christ would die, and as the first to rise from the dead, he would bring light to all people."

## Paul Tries to Persuade Agrippa

<sup>24</sup>While Paul was saying these things to defend himself, Festus said loudly, "Paul, you are out of your mind! Too much study has driven you crazy!"

<sup>25</sup>Paul said, "Most excellent Festus, I am not crazy. My words are true and sensible. <sup>26</sup>King Agrippa knows about these things, and I can speak freely to him. I know he has heard about all of these things, because they did not happen off in a corner. <sup>27</sup>King Agrippa, do you believe what the prophets wrote? I know you believe."

<sup>28</sup>King Agrippa said to Paul, "Do you think you can persuade me to become a Christian in such a short time?"

<sup>29</sup>Paul said, "Whether it is a short or a long time, I pray to God that not only you but every person listening to me today would be saved and be like me—except for these chains I have."

<sup>30</sup>Then King Agrippa, Governor Festus, Bernice, and all the people sitting with them stood up <sup>31</sup>and left the room. Talking to each other, they said, "There is no reason why this man should die or be put in jail." <sup>32</sup>And Agrippa said to Festus, "We could let this man go free, but he has asked Caesar to hear his case."

## Paul Sails for Rome

**27** It was decided that we would sail for Italy. An officer named Julius, who served in the emperor's[n] army, guarded Paul and some other prisoners. <sup>2</sup>We got on a ship that was from the city of Adramyttium and was about to sail to different ports in Asia. Aristarchus, a man from the city of Thessalonica in Macedonia, went with us. <sup>3</sup>The next day we came to Sidon. Julius was very good to Paul and gave him freedom to go visit his friends, who took care of his needs. <sup>4</sup>We left Sidon and sailed close to the island of Cyprus, because the wind was blowing against us. <sup>5</sup>We went across the sea by Cilicia and Pamphylia and landed at the city of Myra, in Lycia. <sup>6</sup>There the officer found a ship from Alexandria that was going to Italy, so he put us on it.

<sup>7</sup>We sailed slowly for many days. We had a hard time reaching Cnidus because the wind was blowing against us, and we could not go any farther. So we sailed by the south side of the island of Crete near Salmone. <sup>8</sup>Sailing past it was hard. Then we came to a place called Fair Havens, near the city of Lasea.

<sup>9</sup>We had lost much time, and it was now dangerous to sail, because it was already after the Day of Cleansing.[n] So Paul warned them, <sup>10</sup>"Men, I can see there will be a lot of trouble on this trip. The ship, the cargo, and even our lives may be lost." <sup>11</sup>But the captain and the owner of the ship did not agree with Paul, and the officer believed what the captain and owner of the ship said. <sup>12</sup>Since that harbor was not a good place for the ship to stay

for the winter, most of the men decided that the ship should leave. They hoped we could go to Phoenix and stay there for the winter. Phoenix, a city on the island of Crete, had a harbor which faced southwest and northwest.

### The Storm

<sup>13</sup>When a good wind began to blow from the south, the men on the ship thought, "This is the wind we wanted, and now we have it." So they pulled up the anchor, and we sailed very close to the island of Crete. <sup>14</sup>But then a very strong wind named the "northeaster" came from the island. <sup>15</sup>The ship was caught in it and could not sail against it. So we stopped trying and let the wind carry us. <sup>16</sup>When we went below a small island named Cauda, we were barely able to bring in the lifeboat. <sup>17</sup>After the men took the lifeboat in, they tied ropes around the ship to hold it together. The men were afraid that the ship would hit the sandbanks of Syrtis,[n] so they lowered the sail and let the wind carry the ship. <sup>18</sup>The next day the storm was blowing us so hard that the men threw out some of the cargo. <sup>19</sup>A day later with their own hands they threw out the ship's equipment. <sup>20</sup>When we could not see the sun or the stars for many days, and the storm was very bad, we lost all hope of being saved.

## cool

### Stick to It!

They used to just come in yellow squares, but now you can get sticky notes in all kinds of shapes and sizes. But did you know that Post-It Notes®, invented by 3M Company, were the result of a failure? A scientist developed a glue that didn't stick very well . . . and then came the idea for sticky notes!

Have you ever tried to do something good and it turned out badly? Did you feel discouraged, like you didn't want to try anymore? Next time, ask God to take over. He can use even your failures for good!

**27:1 emperor** The ruler of the Roman Empire, which was almost all the known world. **27:9 Day of Cleansing** An important Jewish holy day in the fall of the year. This was the time of year that bad storms arose on the sea. **27:17 Syrtis** Shallow area in the sea near the Libyan coast.

Acts

²¹After the men had gone without food for a long time, Paul stood up before them and said, "Men, you should have listened to me. You should not have sailed from Crete. Then you would not have all this trouble and loss. ²²But now I tell you to cheer up because none of you will die. Only the ship will be lost. ²³Last night an angel came to me from the God I belong to and worship. ²⁴The angel said, 'Paul, do not be afraid. You must stand before Caesar. And God has promised you that he will save the lives of everyone sailing with you.' ²⁵So men, have courage. I trust in God that everything will happen as his angel told me. ²⁶But we will crash on an island."

²⁷On the fourteenth night we were still being carried around in the Adriatic Sea.ⁿ About midnight the sailors thought we were close to land, ²⁸so they lowered a rope with a weight on the end of it into the water. They found that the water was one hundred twenty feet deep. They went a little farther and lowered the rope again. It was ninety feet deep. ²⁹The sailors were afraid that we would hit the rocks, so they threw four anchors into the water and prayed for daylight to come. ³⁰Some of the sailors wanted to leave the ship, and they lowered the lifeboat, pretending they were throwing more anchors from the front of the ship. ³¹But Paul told the officer and the other soldiers, "If these men do not stay in the ship, your lives cannot be saved." ³²So the soldiers cut the ropes and let the lifeboat fall into the water.

³³Just before dawn Paul began persuading all the people to eat something. He said, "For the past fourteen days you have been waiting and watching and not eating. ³⁴Now I beg you to eat something. You need it to stay alive. None of you will lose even one hair off your heads." ³⁵After he said this, Paul took some bread and thanked God for it before all of them. He broke off a piece and began eating. ³⁶They all felt better and started eating, too. ³⁷There were two hundred seventy-six people on the ship. ³⁸When they had eaten all they wanted, they began making the ship lighter by throwing the grain into the sea.

## The Ship Is Destroyed

³⁹When daylight came, the sailors saw land. They did not know what land it was, but they saw a bay with a beach and wanted to sail the ship to the beach if they could. ⁴⁰So they cut the ropes to the anchors and left the anchors in the sea. At the same time, they untied the ropes that were holding the rudders. Then they raised the front sail into the wind and sailed toward the beach. ⁴¹But the ship hit a sandbank. The front of the ship stuck there and could not move, but the back of the ship began to break up from the big waves.

⁴²The soldiers decided to kill the prisoners so none of them could swim away and escape. ⁴³But Julius, the officer, wanted to let Paul live and did not allow the soldiers to kill the prisoners. Instead

# god's promises

### Acts 26:18

When your room looks like a disaster zone, don't you hate turning on the light? It just makes the mess look worse! It's easier to hide dirt in the dark. But when your room looks good, you can enjoy the light!

That's a lot like our spiritual lives. Most people try to hide their sins. When you do something wrong, do you try to cover it up by lying or getting rid of the "evidence?" You probably don't want someone discovering your sin. You might get embarrassed or have to apologize . . . or even get punished!

But who wants to hide in darkness all the time? Darkness can be scary, lonely, and even dangerous if we can't see what's around us. That's why Jesus sent Paul with some Good News for the non-Jewish people—people who didn't know anything about God. Jesus said that believing in him meant turning to the light and being in God's power, not Satan's. He promised that, by believing in him, they would be forgiven and made clean and good.

When we turn to Jesus, we don't have to be afraid of the dark anymore. God fills our heart with his light when we believe—and it shows that Jesus has made us clean inside!

*God fills our heart with his light!*

27:27 **Adriatic Sea** *The sea between Greece and Italy, including the central Mediterranean.*

he ordered everyone who could swim to jump into the water first and swim to land. ⁴⁴The rest were to follow using wooden boards or pieces of the ship. And this is how all the people made it safely to land.

## Paul on the Island of Malta

**28** When we were safe on land, we learned that the island was called Malta. ²The people who lived there were very good to us. Because it was raining and very cold, they made a fire and welcomed all of us. ³Paul gathered a pile of sticks and was putting them on the fire when a poisonous snake came out because of the heat and bit him on the hand. ⁴The people living on the island saw the snake hanging from Paul's hand and said to each other, "This man must be a murderer! He did not die in the sea, but Justice*ⁿ* does not want him to live." ⁵But Paul shook the snake off into the fire and was not hurt. ⁶The people thought that Paul would swell up or fall down dead. They waited and watched him for a long time, but nothing bad happened to him. So they changed their minds and said, "He is a god!"

⁷There were some fields around there owned by Publius, an important man on the island. He welcomed us into his home and was very good to us for three days. ⁸Publius' father was sick with a fever and dysentery.*ⁿ* Paul went to him, prayed, and put his hands on the man and healed him. ⁹After this, all the other sick people on the island came to Paul, and he healed them, too. ¹⁰⁻¹¹The people on the island gave us many honors. When we were ready to leave, three months later, they gave us the things we needed.

## Paul Goes to Rome

We got on a ship from Alexandria that had stayed on the island during the winter. On the front of the ship was the sign of the twin gods.*ⁿ* ¹²We stopped at Syracuse for three days. ¹³From there we sailed to Rhegium. The next day a wind began to blow from the south, and a day later we came to Puteoli. ¹⁴We found some believers there who asked us to stay with them for a week. Finally, we came to Rome. ¹⁵The believers in Rome heard that we were there and came out as far as the Market of Appius*ⁿ* and the Three Inns*ⁿ* to meet us. When Paul saw them, he was encouraged and thanked God.

## Paul in Rome

¹⁶When we arrived at Rome, Paul was allowed to live alone, with the soldier who guarded him.

¹⁷Three days later Paul sent for the leaders there. When they came together, he said, "Brothers, I have done nothing against our people or the customs of our ancestors. But I was arrested in Jerusalem and given to the Romans. ¹⁸After they asked me many questions, they could find no reason why I should be killed. They wanted to let me go free, ¹⁹but the evil people there argued against that. So

**dig deeper**

### Acts 27:35

Your friend's mom just found out she has cancer. Your older brother's in trouble with the law, and your English teacher is completely unfair with grading. How do you feel? How do you think God wants you to feel?

During a fierce storm, everyone on board a ship thought they were going to die. The only one who disagreed was the apostle Paul, who publicly gave thanks to God.

God expects you to feel *thankful* when bad stuff is going on? Yes! We can do this when we trust that God controls everything. Even awful, sinful situations are under his watchful eye. Because of this, we can feel peaceful and trust God to handle things. He knows what's best, and he'll take care of us no matter what!

Most of us have trouble starting our prayers with, "Thank you for . . . "—but that's exactly what God asks of us. Thank God for giving you loving parents and an ability to figure out math (or whatever else you're good at!). Thank him for your funny looking toes or the snotty girl on the school bus. Whatever it is, give him thanks—and watch to see how God changes your heart through thankfulness. With God's help, you will be able to be thankful in all situations!

---

**28:4 Justice** The people thought there was a god named Justice who would punish bad people.   **28:8 dysentery** A sickness like diarrhea.   **28:10–11 twin gods** Statues of Castor and Pollux, gods in old Greek tales.
**28:15 Market of Appius** A town about twenty-seven miles from Rome.   **28:15 Three Inns** A town about thirty miles from Rome.

# Q & A

**Q** What is a good way to memorize Bible verses?

**A** Different things work for different people. Here are some ideas: Say the verse in your own words to make sure you understand it, then repeat the original verse until you learn it. Or write the verse over and over until you can do it without looking. You could also cover one word each time you recite it until you know it. Or make up a tune for it and sing it to yourself all day!

I had to ask to come to Rome to have my trial before Caesar. But I have no charge to bring against my own people. [20]That is why I wanted to see you and talk with you. I am bound with this chain because I believe in the hope of Israel."

[21]They answered Paul, "We have received no letters from Judea about you. None of our Jewish brothers who have come from there brought news or told us anything bad about you. [22]But we want to hear your ideas, because we know that people everywhere are speaking against this religious group."

[23]Paul and the people chose a day for a meeting and on that day many more of the Jews met with Paul at the place he was staying. He spoke to them all day long. Using the law of Moses and the prophets' writings, he explained the kingdom of God, and he tried to persuade them to believe these things about Jesus. [24]Some believed what Paul said, but others did not. [25]So they argued and began leaving after Paul said one more thing to them: "The Holy Spirit spoke the truth to your ancestors through Isaiah the prophet, saying,

[26]'Go to this people and say:
You will listen and listen, but you will not understand.
You will look and look, but you will not learn,
[27]because these people have become stubborn.
They don't hear with their ears, and they have closed their eyes.
Otherwise, they might really understand
what they see with their eyes and hear with their ears.
They might really understand in their minds
and come back to me and be healed.'          *Isaiah 6:9–10*

[28]"I want you to know that God has also sent his salvation to all nations, and they will listen!" [[29]After Paul said this, the Jews left. They were arguing very much with each other.][n]

[30]Paul stayed two full years in his own rented house and welcomed all people who came to visit him. [31]He boldly preached about the kingdom of God and taught about the Lord Jesus Christ, and no one stopped him.

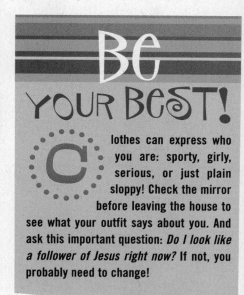

# Be YOUR BEST!

**C** lothes can express who you are: sporty, girly, serious, or just plain sloppy! Check the mirror before leaving the house to see what your outfit says about you. And ask this important question: *Do I look like a follower of Jesus right now?* If not, you probably need to change!

**28:29 After . . . other.** *Some Greek copies do not contain the bracketed text.*

# ROMANS

The Book of Romans is like a handbook for the Christian life—everything you need to know all in one place. Christian churches had only been around for about twenty years when the apostle Paul wrote this letter to the Christians in Rome. They needed clear explanations of what Jesus taught and what it meant for them. Paul wanted to answer their questions and help them understand the most important points of their faith. This letter has value for us, too. It answers important questions that people still ask, like:

➡ Who needs God?
➡ Why do we need God?
➡ How can we know God?
➡ What is faith?
➡ What about the Old Testament rules?
➡ Why do we struggle with sin?
➡ Why do we have hard times?

➡ What about Christians who have different beliefs than other Christians?
➡ What about people who have never heard about Jesus?

Most of all, Paul wants to let us know how to please God. How do you try to please God? By being a good person? Through loving others? Maybe by listening to your parents? All these are good. But Paul says no one can do all these things all the time. What God wants most of all is faith. He wants us to believe what he says about himself and about Jesus. When we do, he changes us on the inside. To find out more about how this works, read on!

# GOD'S PLAN TO SAVE US

## THINGS TO TALK WITH GOD ABOUT . . .

**1** From Paul, a servant of Christ Jesus. God called me to be an apostle and chose me to tell the Good News. [2]God promised this Good News long ago through his prophets, as it is written in the Holy Scriptures. [3-4]The Good News is about God's Son, Jesus Christ our Lord. As a man, he was born from the family of David. But through the Spirit of holiness he was declared to be God's Son with great power by rising from the dead. [5]Through Christ, God gave me the special work of an apostle, which was to lead people of all nations to believe and obey. I do this work for him. [6]And you who are in Rome are also called to belong to Jesus Christ.

[7]To all of you in Rome whom God loves and has called to be his holy people:

Grace and peace to you from God our Father and the Lord Jesus Christ.

### A Prayer of Thanks

[8]First I want to say that I thank my God through Jesus Christ for all of you, because

people everywhere in the world are talking about your faith. [9]God, whom I serve with my whole heart by telling the Good News about his Son, knows that I always mention you [10]every time I pray. I pray that I will be allowed to come to you, and this will happen if God wants it. [11]I want very much to see you, to give you some spiritual gift to make you strong. [12]I mean that I want us to help each other with the faith we have. Your faith will help me, and my faith will help you. [13]Brothers and sisters, I want you to know that I planned many times to come to you, but this has not been possible. I wanted to come so that I could help you grow spiritually as I have helped the other non-Jewish people.

[14]I have a duty to all people—Greeks and those who are not Greeks, the wise and the foolish. [15]That is why I want so much to preach the Good News to you in Rome.

[16]I am not ashamed of the Good News, because it is the power God uses to save everyone who believes—to save the Jews first, and then to save non-Jews. [17]The Good News shows how God makes people right with himself—that it begins and ends with faith. As the Scripture says, "But those who are right with God will live by faith."[n]

### All People Have Done Wrong

[18]God's anger is shown from heaven against all the evil and wrong things people do. By their own evil lives they hide the truth. [19]God shows his anger because some knowledge of him has been made clear to them. Yes, God has shown himself to them. [20]There are things about him that people cannot see—his eternal power and all the things that make him God. But since the beginning of the world those things have been easy to understand by what God has made. So people have no excuse for the bad things they do. [21]They knew God, but they did not give glory to God or thank him. Their thinking became useless. Their foolish minds were filled with darkness. [22]They said they were wise, but they became fools. [23]They traded the glory of God who lives forever for the worship of idols made to look like earthly people, birds, animals, and snakes.

[24]Because they did these things, God left them and let them go their sinful way, wanting only to do evil. As a result, they became full of sexual sin, using their bodies wrongly with each other.

**THEY KNEW GOD, BUT THEY DID NOT GIVE GLORY TO GOD OR THANK HIM.**

1:17 **"But those . . . faith."** *Quotation from Habakkuk 2:4.*

# Q & A

Why would a kind and loving God send people to hell?

**A** Actually, God doesn't "send" people to hell. He *saves* people *from* hell! Romans 3:23 tell us that we have all sinned—no one deserves to go to heaven! But because of his love, God sent Jesus to die on the cross and take the punishment for our sins. Now we have a choice (because God won't force anyone to go to heaven). When we believe in him and ask for forgiveness for our sins, he saves us from an eternity in hell. That's how kind and loving God is!

²⁵They traded the truth of God for a lie. They worshiped and served what had been created instead of the God who created those things, who should be praised forever. Amen.

²⁶Because people did those things, God left them and let them do the shameful things they wanted to do. Women stopped having natural sex and started having sex with other women. ²⁷In the same way, men stopped having natural sex and began wanting each other. Men did shameful things with other men, and in their bodies they received the punishment for those wrongs.

²⁸People did not think it was important to have a true knowledge of God. So God left them and allowed them to have their own worthless thinking and to do things they should not do. ²⁹They are filled with every kind of sin, evil, selfishness, and hatred. They are full of jealousy, murder, fighting, lying, and thinking the worst about each other. They gossip ³⁰and say evil things about each other. They hate God. They are rude and conceited and brag about themselves. They invent ways of doing evil. They do not obey their parents. ³¹They are foolish, they do not keep their promises, and they show no kindness or mercy to others. ³²They know God's law says that those who live like this should die. But they themselves not only continue to do these evil things, they applaud others who do them.

## You People Also Are Sinful

**2** If you think you can judge others, you are wrong. When you judge them, you are really judging yourself guilty, because you do the same things they do. ²God judges those who do wrong things, and we know that his judging is right. ³You judge those who do wrong, but you do wrong yourselves. Do you think you will be able to escape the judgment of God? ⁴He has been very kind and patient, waiting for you to change, but you think nothing of his kindness. Perhaps you do not understand that God is kind to you so you will change your hearts and lives. ⁵But you are stubborn and refuse to change, so you are making your own punishment even greater on the day he shows his anger. On that day everyone will see God's right judgments. ⁶God will reward or punish every person for what that person has done. ⁷Some people, by always continuing to do good, live for God's glory, for honor, and for life that has no end. God will give them life forever. ⁸But other people are selfish. They refuse to follow truth and, instead, follow evil. God will give them his punishment and anger. ⁹He will give trouble and suffering to everyone who does evil—to the Jews first and also to those who are not Jews. ¹⁰But he will give glory, honor, and peace to everyone who does good—to the Jews first and also to those who are not Jews. ¹¹For God judges all people in the same way.

¹²People who do not have the law and who are sinners will be lost, although they do not have the law. And, in the same way, those who have the law and are sinners will be judged by the law. ¹³Hearing the law does not make people right with God. It is those who obey the law who will be right with him. ¹⁴(Those who are not Jews do not have the law, but when they freely do what the law commands, they are the law for themselves. This is true even though they do not have the law. ¹⁵They show that in their hearts they know what is right and wrong, just as the law commands. And they show this by their consciences. Sometimes their thoughts tell them they did wrong, and sometimes their thoughts tell them they did right.) ¹⁶All these things will happen on the day when God, through Christ Jesus, will judge people's secret thoughts. The Good News that I preach says this.

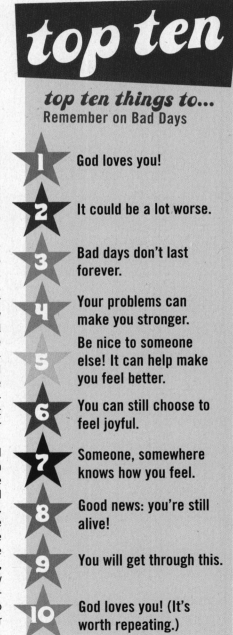

# top ten

## top ten things to...
Remember on Bad Days

**1** God loves you!

**2** It could be a lot worse.

**3** Bad days don't last forever.

**4** Your problems can make you stronger.

**5** Be nice to someone else! It can help make you feel better.

**6** You can still choose to feel joyful.

**7** Someone, somewhere knows how you feel.

**8** Good news: you're still alive!

**9** You will get through this.

**10** God loves you! (It's worth repeating.)

Romans

## The Jews and the Law

17What about you? You call yourself a Jew. You trust in the law of Moses and brag that you are close to God. 18You know what he wants you to do and what is important, because you have learned the law. 19You think you are a guide for the blind and a light for those who are in darkness. 20You think you can show foolish people what is right and teach those who know nothing. You have the law; so you think you know everything and have all truth. 21You teach others, so why don't you teach yourself? You tell others not to steal, but you steal. 22You say that others must not take part in adultery, but you are guilty of that sin. You hate idols, but you steal from temples. 23You brag about having God's law, but you bring shame to God by breaking his law, 24just as the Scriptures say: "Those who are not Jews speak against God's name because of you."[n]

25If you follow the law, your circumcision has meaning. But if you break the law, it is as if you were never circumcised. 26People who are not Jews are not circumcised, but if they do what the law says, it is as if they were circumcised. 27You Jews have the written law and circumcision, but you break the law. So those who are not circumcised in their bodies, but still obey the law, will show that you are guilty. 28They can do this because a person is not a true Jew if he is only a Jew in his physical body; true circumcision is not only on the outside of the body. 29A person is a Jew only if he is a Jew inside; true circumcision is done in the heart by the Spirit, not by the written law. Such a person gets praise from God rather than from people.

3 So, do Jews have anything that other people do not have? Is there anything special about being circumcised? 2Yes, of course, there is in every way. The most important thing is this: God trusted the Jews with his teachings. 3If some Jews were not faithful to him, will that stop God from doing what he promised? 4No! God will continue to be true even when every person is false. As the Scriptures say:

"So you will be shown to be right
    when you speak,
and you will win your case."

*Psalm 51:4*

5When we do wrong, that shows more clearly that God is right. So can we say that God is wrong to punish us? (I am talking as people might talk.) 6No! If God could not punish us, he could not judge the world.

7A person might say, "When I lie, it really gives him glory, because my lie shows God's truth. So why am I judged a sinner?" 8It would be the same to say, "We should do evil so that good will come." Some people find fault with us and say we teach this, but they are wrong and deserve the punishment they will receive.

# Christian Girls Around the World

## Vennila: *India*

Twelve-year-old Vennila loves babies. Where she lives, in an orphanage in India, there are lots of babies to cuddle! Vennila enjoys helping Shanthi, the housemother, after she is done with school and chores. She sings them the same song that Shanthi sang to her when she was a little girl.

In India, many people are educated and wealthy. Many more people are very, very poor. Vennila's mother brought her to the Christian orphanage when she was a baby because Vennila was very sick and her mother was too poor to care for her.

"You do so well with the little ones, Vennila," Shanthi praises her. "Perhaps when you grow up you will be a lady doctor and take care of children in the hospital. The directors have been praying that God will provide someone!"

"I would love to be a doctor—or at least a nurse. I was listening to the older girls studying for their exams—I think I could do it!"

"I'm sure you could, Vennila. And in a few years, you can become a warden and be in charge of the younger children." Shanthi's dark black eyes grow serious. "If you want to be a warden, you must follow Jesus completely. If you died tonight, would you go to be with the Lord?"

Vennila nods slowly. Most of the people in India are Hindus who worship many gods and idols. Vennila knows that there is only one true God. She remembers praying during daily Chapel when she was five and asking Jesus to come into her heart. But maybe Shanthi knows that she has not been careful to obey the Lord lately. Some of the girls have been using bad words. They have been making plans to break school rules. Vennila has sometimes gone along with them.

"You must decide if you will live for him, Vennila."

Vennila is quiet as she walks back to her room she shares with the other girls. She goes to her small cubby and takes out the little New Testament. This cubby is her only spot that belongs to her alone. Shanthi once told her that Jesus has gone to prepare a place for her—not just a cubby, but her own mansion! Vennila thinks about how much Jesus must love her to be doing that for her.

"Yes, Lord," she whispers, "I'll live for you my whole life."

2:24 "Those . . . you." *Quotation from Isaiah 52:5; Ezekiel 36:20.*

## All People Are Guilty

⁹So are we Jews better than others? No! We have already said that Jews and those who are not Jews are all guilty of sin. ¹⁰As the Scriptures say:

"There is no one who always does
what is right,
not even one.
¹¹There is no one who understands.
There is no one who looks to God
for help.
¹²All have turned away.
Together, everyone has become
useless.
There is no one who does anything
good;
there is not even one."
*Psalm 14:1–3*
¹³"Their throats are like open graves;
they use their tongues for telling
lies."
*Psalm 5:9*
"Their words are like snake poison."
*Psalm 140:3*
¹⁴ "Their mouths are full of cursing
and hate."
*Psalm 10:7*
¹⁵"They are always ready to kill
people.
¹⁶ Everywhere they go they cause
ruin and misery.
¹⁷They don't know how to live in
peace."
*Isaiah 59:7–8*
¹⁸ "They have no fear of God."
*Psalm 36:1*

¹⁹We know that the law's commands are for those who have the law. This stops all excuses and brings the whole world under God's judgment, ²⁰because no one can be made right with God by following the law. The law only shows us our sin.

## How God Makes People Right

²¹But God has a way to make people right with him without the law, and he has now shown us that way which the law and the prophets told us about. ²²God makes people right with himself through their faith in Jesus Christ. This is true for all who believe in Christ, because all people are the same: ²³Everyone has sinned and fallen short of God's glorious standard, ²⁴and all need to be made right with God by his grace, which is a free gift. They need to be made free from sin through Jesus Christ. ²⁵God sent him to die in our place to take away our sins. We receive forgiveness through

# dig deeper

## Romans 5:12

Beautiful eyes—baby blue, deep brown, or dark as night. Freckles sprinkled across your nose like your dad's, your mom's high cheekbones, or your grandma's wide smile. Many of your features have come from other people—even things about you like your sense of humor or your competitive spirit can be "gifts" from parents and grandparents!

Sadly, certain diseases and disabilities can get passed down in families, too. There's a disease that every single baby in the whole world is born with. It's called sin. Are you surprised? Did you think sin was just something you did? Like when Adam and Eve ate the forbidden fruit? You see, when Adam and Eve disobeyed God, they didn't just make a mistake—they died spiritually. That means they lost the purity that made it possible to be in God's presence. Sin and separation are the broken parts that got passed down to us instead. Romans 5:12 tells us that Adam started it—"sin came into the world because of what one man did." But we all did it, too—"This is why everyone must die—because everyone sinned."

This spiritual "death" separates us from God. That's why it's such Good News that Jesus died to forgive us and to make us God's children—alive and pure when we put our trust in him!

faith in the blood of Jesus' death. This showed that God always does what is right and fair, as in the past when he was patient and did not punish people for their sins. ²⁶And God gave Jesus to show today that he does what is right. God did this so he could judge rightly and so he could make right any person who has faith in Jesus.

²⁷So do we have a reason to brag about ourselves? No! And why not? It is the way of faith that stops all bragging, not the way of trying to obey the law. ²⁸A person is made right with God through faith, not through obeying the law. ²⁹Is God only the God of the Jews? Is he not also the God of those who are not Jews? ³⁰Of course he is, because there is only one

## Righteousness

Righteousness can mean goodness or holiness. It means doing good things, *right* things, not only because we want to be nice people but because we are obeying God. The Bible says that no one can be righteous on their own, no matter how hard they try (Romans 3:23–24). But when we accept salvation in Jesus, he makes us righteous in his sight. When he looks at us, he doesn't see all the sins and bad things we've done. Instead, he sees us as holy, without sin and *righteous* at that moment. He also helps Christians *continue* to follow him and do what's right each day.

God. He will make Jews right with him by their faith, and he will also make those who are not Jews right with him through their faith. [31]So do we destroy the law by following the way of faith? No! Faith causes us to be what the law truly wants.

### The Example of Abraham

4 So what can we say that Abraham,[n] the father of our people, learned about faith? [2]If Abraham was made right by the things he did, he had a reason to brag. But this is not God's view, [3]because the Scripture says, "Abraham believed God, and God accepted Abraham's faith, and that faith made him right with God."[n]

[4]When people work, their pay is not given as a gift, but as something earned. [5]But people cannot do any work that will make them right with God. So they must trust in him, who makes even evil people right in his sight. Then God accepts their faith, and that makes them right with him. [6]David said the same thing. He said that people are truly blessed when God, without paying attention to their deeds, makes people right with himself.

[7]"Blessed are they
     whose sins are forgiven,
     whose wrongs are pardoned.
[8]Blessed is the person
     whom the Lord does not consider
        guilty."          *Psalm 32:1–2*

[9]Is this blessing only for those who are circumcised or also for those who are not circumcised? We have already said that God accepted Abraham's faith and that faith made him right with God. [10]So how did this happen? Did God accept Abraham before or after he was circumcised? It was before his circumcision. [11]Abraham was circumcised to show that he was right with God through faith before he was circumcised. So Abraham is the father of all those who believe but are not circumcised; he is the father of all believers who are accepted as being right with God. [12]And Abraham is also the father of those who have been circumcised and who live following the faith that our father Abraham had before he was circumcised.

### God Keeps His Promise

[13]Abraham[n] and his descendants received the promise that they would get the whole world. He did not receive that promise through the law, but through being right with God by his faith. [14]If people could receive what God promised by following the law, then faith is worthless. And God's promise to Abraham is worthless, [15]because the law can only bring God's anger. But if there is no law, there is nothing to disobey.

[16]So people receive God's promise by having faith. This happens so the promise can be a free gift. Then all of Abraham's children can have that promise. It is not only for those who live under the law of Moses but for anyone who lives with faith like that of Abraham, who is the father of us all. [17]As it is written in the Scriptures: "I am making you a father of many nations."[n] This is true before God, the God Abraham believed, the God who gives life to the dead and who creates something out of nothing.

[18]There was no hope that Abraham would have children. But Abraham believed God and continued hoping, and so he became the father of many nations. As God told him, "Your descendants also will be too many to count."[n] [19]Abraham was almost a hundred years old, much past the age for having children, and Sarah could not have children. Abraham thought about all this, but his faith in

**Romans**

## Bible Basics

Do you call yourself a follower of Jesus Christ? Then you'll need to know his "map"—the Bible! The Bible is all about God's plan to save us and make us like his Son, Jesus. God doesn't usually speak directly to Christians in our time. But he has given us some pretty detailed explanations about himself and about what he expects from us. These can all be found in the pages between Genesis 1 and Revelation 22. Crack open your Bible and start reading; it's the best way to get to know God and his Son. Reading through the whole Bible, start to finish, could be the most exciting thing you've ever done. Give it a try!

4:1, 13 **Abraham** *Most respected ancestor of the Jews. Every Jew hoped to see Abraham.*    4:3 **"Abraham . . . God."** *Quotation from Genesis 15:6.*    4:17 **"I . . . nations."** *Quotation from Genesis 17:5.*    4:18 **"Your . . . count."** *Quotation from Genesis 15:5.*

God did not become weak. [20]He never doubted that God would keep his promise, and he never stopped believing. He grew stronger in his faith and gave praise to God. [21]Abraham felt sure that God was able to do what he had promised. [22]So, "God accepted Abraham's faith, and that faith made him right with God."[n] [23]Those words ("God accepted Abraham's faith") were written not only for Abraham [24]but also for us. God will accept us also because we believe in the One who raised Jesus our Lord from the dead. [25]Jesus was given to die for our sins, and he was raised from the dead to make us right with God.

of someone else. Although perhaps for a good person someone might possibly die. [8]But God shows his great love for us in this way: Christ died for us while we were still sinners.

[9]So through Christ we will surely be saved from God's anger, because we have been made right with God by the blood of Christ's death. [10]While we were God's enemies, he made us his friends through the death of his Son. Surely, now that we are his friends, he will save us through his Son's life. [11]And not only that, but now we are also very happy in God through our Lord Jesus

good act that Christ did makes all people right with God. And that brings true life for all. [19]One man disobeyed God, and many became sinners. In the same way, one man obeyed God, and many will be made right. [20]The law came to make sin worse. But when sin grew worse, God's grace increased. [21]Sin once used death to rule us, but God gave people more of his grace so that grace could rule by making people right with him. And this brings life forever through Jesus Christ our Lord.

## Dead to Sin but Alive in Christ

6 So do you think we should continue sinning so that God will give us even more grace? [2]No! We died to our old sinful lives, so how can we continue living with sin? [3]Did you forget that all of us became part of Christ when we were baptized? We shared his death in our baptism. [4]When we were baptized, we were buried with Christ and shared his death. So, just as Christ was raised from the dead by the wonderful

## Right with God

5 Since we have been made right with God by our faith, we have[n] peace with God. This happened through our Lord Jesus Christ, [2]who through our faith[n] has brought us into that blessing of God's grace that we now enjoy. And we are happy because of the hope we have of sharing God's glory. [3]We also have joy with our troubles, because we know that these troubles produce patience. [4]And patience produces character, and character produces hope. [5]And this hope will never disappoint us, because God has poured out his love to fill our hearts. He gave us his love through the Holy Spirit, whom God has given to us. [6]When we were unable to help ourselves, at the right time, Christ died for us, although we were living against God. [7]Very few people will die to save the life

**SO THROUGH CHRIST WE WILL SURELY BE SAVED FROM GOD'S ANGER, BECAUSE WE HAVE BEEN MADE RIGHT WITH GOD BY THE BLOOD OF CHRIST'S DEATH.**

Christ. Through him we are now God's friends again.

## Adam and Christ Compared

[12]Sin came into the world because of what one man did, and with sin came death. This is why everyone must die—because everyone sinned. [13]Sin was in the world before the law of Moses, but sin is not counted against us as breaking a command when there is no law. [14]But from the time of Adam to the time of Moses, everyone had to die, even those who had not sinned by breaking a command, as Adam had.

Adam was like the One who was coming in the future. [15]But God's free gift is not like Adam's sin. Many people died because of the sin of that one man. But the grace from God was much greater; many people received God's gift of life by the grace of the one man, Jesus Christ. [16]After Adam sinned once, he was judged guilty. But the gift of God is different. God's free gift came after many sins, and it makes people right with God. [17]One man sinned, and so death ruled all people because of that one man. But now those people who accept God's full grace and the great gift of being made right with him will surely have true life and rule through the one man, Jesus Christ.

[18]So as one sin of Adam brought the punishment of death to all people, one

4:22 **"God . . . God."** Quotation from Genesis 15:6.   5:1 **we have** Some Greek copies read "let us have."   5:2 **through our faith** Some Greek copies do not have this phrase.

Romans

# Relationships

What does every government leader in the world have in common? They all received their power to rule from God! Romans 13:1–7 gives clear instructions for how Christians should treat government leaders. You might not ever meet your country's leaders, but you can still show them respect by speaking only kind and true words about them, by obeying the law, and by praying for them. Romans 13:6, says "Rulers are working for God." In what ways can *you* treat them like God's specially picked leaders?

power of the Father, we also can live a new life.

⁵Christ died, and we have been joined with him by dying too. So we will also be joined with him by rising from the dead as he did. ⁶We know that our old life died with Christ on the cross so that our sinful selves would have no power over us and we would not be slaves to sin. ⁷Anyone who has died is made free from sin's control.

⁸If we died with Christ, we know we will also live with him. ⁹Christ was raised from the dead, and we know that he cannot die again. Death has no power over him now. ¹⁰Yes, when Christ died, he died to defeat the power of sin one time—enough for all time. He now has a new life, and his new life is with God. ¹¹In the same way, you should see yourselves as being dead to the power of sin and alive with God through Christ Jesus.

¹²So, do not let sin control your life here on earth so that you do what your sinful self wants to do. ¹³Do not offer the parts of your body to serve sin, as things to be used in doing evil. Instead, offer yourselves to God as people who have died and now live. Offer the parts of your body to God to be used in doing good. ¹⁴Sin will not be your master, because you are not under law but under God's grace.

## Be Slaves of Righteousness

¹⁵So what should we do? Should we sin because we are under grace and not un-

der law? No! ¹⁶Surely you know that when you give yourselves like slaves to obey someone, then you are really slaves of that person. The person you obey is your master. You can follow sin, which brings spiritual death, or you can obey God, which makes you right with him. ¹⁷In the past you were slaves to sin—sin controlled you. But thank God, you fully obeyed the things that you were taught. ¹⁸You were made free from sin, and now you are slaves to goodness. ¹⁹I use this example because this is hard for you to understand. In the past you offered the parts of your body to be slaves to sin and evil; you lived only for evil. In the same way now you must give yourselves to be slaves of goodness. Then you will live only for God.

²⁰In the past you were slaves to sin, and goodness did not control you. ²¹You did evil things, and now you are ashamed of them. Those things only bring death. ²²But now you are free from sin and have become slaves of God. This brings you a life that is only for God, and this gives you life forever. ²³The payment for sin is death. But God gives us the free gift of life forever in Christ Jesus our Lord.

## An Example from Marriage

7 Brothers and sisters, all of you understand the law of Moses. So surely you know that the law rules over people only while they are alive. ²For example, a woman must stay married to her husband as long as he is

alive. But if her husband dies, she is free from the law of marriage. ³But if she marries another man while her husband is still alive, the law says she is guilty of adultery. But if her husband dies, she is free from the law of marriage. Then if she marries another man, she is not guilty of adultery.

# Q&A

**Q** Why did God make zits?

**A** When God first created the world, it was perfect. But because humans decided to sin, all kinds of bad things have come into the world (like zits). Don't worry, you're not alone—millions of people have struggled with zits. Get good advice from your parents or a doctor on how to take care of your skin. But remember, outward beauty is not what makes people happy or popular. When you're enjoying life, people will notice that more than your pimples.

## god's promises

Romans 8:1–4

Do you ever feel like a *huge failure*? Like you've messed up so many times that God could never forgive you? We all feel that way at times. Even the apostle Paul felt that way sometimes. Read what he says about himself in Romans 7:17–25. He's describing what he calls "the law that brings sin and death" (Romans 8:2). As humans, we are powerless *not* to sin if we only rely on our own strength!

But you can see how happy Paul is when he gets to Romans 8:1. It's great news! If we believe in Jesus, God doesn't hold our wrong actions against us. If we confess them to him, he forgives us—*every* time!

Forgiveness is free for us because Jesus paid for it. He took the punishment for our sin, even though he never did anything wrong. This is "the law of the Spirit that brings life" (Romans 8:2). But this law doesn't apply to us automatically. We have to tell God that we accept what Jesus did for us and that we want to live for him, not for ourselves. That's what it means to be "in Christ Jesus" (8:1).

Don't give up when you feel like everything you do is wrong. Confess your mistakes to God and celebrate his forgiveness.

*Confess your mistakes to God and celebrate his forgiveness.*

⁴In the same way, my brothers and sisters, your old selves died, and you became free from the law through the body of Christ. This happened so that you might belong to someone else—the One who was raised from the dead—and so that we might be used in service to God. ⁵In the past, we were ruled by our sinful selves. The law made us want to do sinful things that controlled our bodies, so the things we did were bringing us death.

⁶In the past, the law held us like prisoners, but our old selves died, and we were made free from the law. So now we serve God in a new way with the Spirit, and not in the old way with written rules.

## Our Fight Against Sin

⁷You might think I am saying that sin and the law are the same thing. That is not true. But the law was the only way I could learn what sin meant. I would never have known what it means to want to take something belonging to someone else if the law had not said, "You must not want to take your neighbor's things."ⁿ ⁸And sin found a way to use that command and cause me to want all kinds of things I should not want. But without the law, sin has no power. ⁹I was alive before I knew the law. But when the law's command came to me, then sin began to live, ¹⁰and I died. The command was meant to bring life, but for me it brought death. ¹¹Sin found a way to fool me by using the command to make me die.

¹²So the law is holy, and the command is holy and right and good. ¹³Does this mean that something that is good brought death to me? No! Sin used something that is good to bring death to me. This happened so that I could see what sin is really like; the command was used to show that sin is very evil.

## The War Within Us

¹⁴We know that the law is spiritual, but I am not spiritual since sin rules me as if I were its slave. ¹⁵I do not understand the things I do. I do not do what I want to do, and I do the things I hate. ¹⁶And if I do not want to do the hated things I do, that means I agree that the law is good. ¹⁷But I am not really the one who is doing these hated things; it is sin living in me that does them. ¹⁸Yes, I know that nothing good lives in me—I mean nothing good lives in the part of me that is earthly and sinful. I want to do the things that are good, but I do not do them. ¹⁹I do not do the good things I want to do, but I do the bad things I do not want to do. ²⁰So if I do things I do not want to do, then I am not the one doing them. It is sin living in me that does those things.

²¹So I have learned this rule: When I want to do good, evil is there with me. ²²In my mind, I am happy with God's law. ²³But I see another law working in my body, which makes war against the law that my mind accepts. That other law working in my body is the law of sin, and it makes me its prisoner. ²⁴What a miser-

I THANK GOD FOR SAVING ME THROUGH JESUS CHRIST OUR LORD!

7:7 **"You . . . things."** *Quotation from Exodus 20:17.*

## Bible Bios — Philip (Acts 8)

**P**hilip, one of the earliest evangelists (Christians who tell others about Jesus), taught the people in Samaria how they could be saved from their sins if they believed in Jesus Christ. Many of them did believe and become Christians!

One day, God's angel told Philip that an important Ethiopian officer was reading the Book of Isaiah (in the Old Testament) on his way home. Philip obeyed God's orders to find him and stay near his chariot.

The man told Philip that he couldn't understand what he had read. Philip explained the verses and told him all about Jesus. Right away, the man believed! After Philip baptized him in some nearby water, the officer went home full of joy in his heart. Like Philip, be ready to tell others the Good News about Jesus! God can use you, too!

able man I am! Who will save me from this body that brings me death? [25]I thank God for saving me through Jesus Christ our Lord!

So in my mind I am a slave to God's law, but in my sinful self I am a slave to the law of sin.

### Be Ruled by the Spirit

**8** So now, those who are in Christ Jesus are not judged guilty.[n] [2]Through Christ Jesus the law of the Spirit that brings life made you[n] free from the law that brings sin and death. [3]The law was without power, because the law was made weak by our sinful selves. But God did what the law could not do. He sent his own Son to earth with the same human life that others use for sin. By sending his Son to be an offering for sin, God used a human life to destroy sin. [4]He did this so that we could be the kind of people the law correctly wants us to be. Now we do not live following our sinful selves, but we live following the Spirit.

[5]Those who live following their sinful selves think only about things that their sinful selves want. But those who live following the Spirit are thinking about the things the Spirit wants them to do. [6]If people's thinking is controlled by the sinful self, there is death. But if their thinking is controlled by the Spirit, there is life and peace. [7]When people's thinking is controlled by the sinful self, they are against God, because they refuse to

obey God's law and really are not even able to obey God's law. [8]Those people who are ruled by their sinful selves cannot please God.

[9]But you are not ruled by your sinful selves. You are ruled by the Spirit, if that Spirit of God really lives in you. But the person who does not have the Spirit of Christ does not belong to Christ. [10]Your body will always be dead because of sin. But if Christ is in you, then the Spirit gives you life, because Christ made you right with God. [11]God raised Jesus from the dead, and if God's Spirit is living in you, he will also give life to your bodies that die. God is the One who raised Christ from the dead, and he will give life through[n] his Spirit that lives in you.

[12]So, my brothers and sisters, we must not be ruled by our sinful selves or live the way our sinful selves want. [13]If you use your lives to do the wrong things your sinful selves want, you will die spiritually. But if you use the Spirit's help to stop doing the wrong things you do with your body, you will have true life.

[14]The true children of God are those who let God's Spirit lead them. [15]The Spirit we received does not make us slaves again to fear; it makes us children of God. With that Spirit we cry out, "Father."[n] [16]And the Spirit himself joins with our spirits to say we are God's children. [17]If we are God's children, we will receive blessings from God together with Christ. But we must suffer as Christ suffered so that we will have glory as Christ has glory.

### Our Future Glory

[18]The sufferings we have now are nothing compared to the great glory that will be shown to us. [19]Everything God made is waiting with excitement for God to show his children's glory completely. [20]Everything God made was changed to become useless, not by its own wish but because God wanted it and because all along there was this hope: [21]that everything God made would be set free from ruin to have the freedom and glory that belong to God's children.

[22]We know that everything God made has been waiting until now in pain, like a woman ready to give birth. [23]Not only the world, but we also have been waiting with pain inside us. We have the Spirit as the first part of God's promise. So we are waiting for God to finish making us his own children, which means our bodies will be made free. [24]We were saved, and we have this hope. If we see what we are waiting for, that is not really hope.

### Get It

### Resurrection (Easter)

**R**esurrection means coming back from the dead. Jesus' resurrection was the greatest miracle of all time. After he was brutally killed, his body was wrapped in "grave clothes" and put in a big tomb like a cave. Three days later, his body was missing. He had been brought back to life! He had risen! The Bible tells us that his resurrection was a display of God's amazing power (Ephesians 1:20). It is the resurrection of Jesus which proves we have a powerful God who can do anything! We celebrate this wonderful event each year on Easter Sunday.

**8:1 guilty** *Some Greek copies continue, "those who do not live in the power of their sinful selves, but in the power of the Spirit."* **8:2 you** *Some Greek copies read "me."* **8:11 through** *Some Greek copies read "because of."* **8:15 "Father"** *Literally, "Abba, Father." Jewish children called their fathers "Abba."*

called, he also made right with him; and those he made right, he also glorified.

## God's Love in Christ Jesus

[31]So what should we say about this? If God is for us, no one can defeat us. [32]He did not spare his own Son but gave him for us all. So with Jesus, God will surely give us all things. [33]Who can accuse the people God has chosen? No one, because God is the One who makes them right. [34]Who can say God's people are guilty? No one, because Christ Jesus died, but he was also raised from the dead, and now he is on God's right side, appealing to God for us. [35]Can anything separate us from the love Christ has for us? Can troubles or problems or sufferings or hunger or nakedness or danger or violent death? [36]As it is written in the Scriptures:

"For you we are in danger of death all the time.
People think we are worth no more than sheep to be killed."

*Psalm 44:22*

[37]But in all these things we are completely victorious through God who showed his love for us. [38]Yes, I am sure that neither death, nor life, nor angels, nor ruling spirits, nothing now, nothing in the future, no powers, [39]nothing above us,

## dig deeper

### Romans 8:38-39

Picture a big glass wall. You are on one side, and your parents are on the other. There's no way over the wall or around it. No sound can get through it. You can see your parents, but you're separated from their love. You can't feel it in a hug or hear them say, "I love you." You can't enjoy the special things they do to let you know they love you.

How would you feel?

Although most of us aren't stuck behind a big glass wall, sometimes things do happen to separate us from the love of someone special. But did you know there's one person whose love will *never* be taken from us?

Romans 8:38-39 promises, "I am sure that neither death, nor life, nor angels, nor ruling spirits, nothing now, nothing in the future, no powers, nothing above us, nothing below us, nor anything else in the whole world will be able to separate us from the love of God that is in Christ Jesus our Lord."

No matter where we go or what we do or what happens in our lives, God's love is always with us. He loves us so much and nothing will ever change that. We can never be separated from his love!

# Q & A

**Q** All my friends have boyfriends, but I don't. How can I make guys like me?

**A** Not having a boyfriend doesn't mean that boys don't like you. You can have great friendships with guys without worrying about dating. At your age, boyfriends don't last very long, so you might actually be better off than your friends who have boyfriends. Instead of suffering over a broken heart, you can have fun with your friends—girls and boys!

People do not hope for something they already have. [25]But we are hoping for something we do not have yet, and we are waiting for it patiently.

[26]Also, the Spirit helps us with our weakness. We do not know how to pray as we should. But the Spirit himself speaks to God for us, even begs God for us with deep feelings that words cannot explain. [27]God can see what is in people's hearts. And he knows what is in the mind of the Spirit, because the Spirit speaks to God for his people in the way God wants.

[28]We know that in everything God works for the good of those who love him.[n] They are the people he called, because that was his plan. [29]God knew them before he made the world, and he chose them to be like his Son so that Jesus would be the firstborn[n] of many brothers and sisters. [30]God planned for them to be like his Son; and those he planned to be like his Son, he also called; and those he

**8:28 We . . . him.** *Some Greek copies read "We know that everything works together for good for those who love God."* **8:29 firstborn** *Here this probably means that Christ was the first in God's family to share God's glory.*

# HOW DO YOU TREAT YOUR TEMPLE?

According to 1 Corinthians 6:19–20, when you became a Christian the Holy Spirit "moved in." Your body is now his temple.

Take this quiz to see if you are honoring God with your body.

**1. Your idea of exercise is:**
- **a.** Playing a video game.
- **b.** Walking around at the mall.
- **c.** Riding your bike or skateboarding.
- **d.** Being on a competitive basketball or soccer team.

**2. Your favorite things to eat are:**
- **a.** Ice cream, chips, cookies, and chocolate cake.
- **b.** Hot dogs, cheeseburgers, and pizza.
- **c.** Pasta, chicken, and ham sandwiches.
- **d.** Vegetables, fruit, fish, and eggs.

**3. When you choose books, CDs, and movies:**
- **a.** Anything is fine.
- **b.** A little bit of swearing, violence, or sex is okay.
- **c.** You ask your parents for their opinion first.
- **d.** You prefer the ones that are Christian and talk about God.

**4. If you have a day off you:**
- **a.** Sleep through most of it.
- **b.** Surf on the Internet or talk on the phone.
- **c.** Spend time playing with friends.
- **d.** Go to the library, volunteer somewhere, or work on a craft project.

## What condition is your temple in?

**If you answered mostly As,** you are not taking care of your temple! When you're lazy about exercise or eating properly, and when you aren't careful about what you feed your mind, you're telling God you don't care. And that doesn't honor him. Ask him to help you treat your body the way he meant you to. Remember: it belongs to him!

**If you answered mostly Bs,** you need a bit of a makeover! It takes some effort to think about how God wants you to live…and then to do it! You need some encouragement to try harder. Find a Christian friend who honors God with her life and try to pick up some of her habits. You can do it!

**If you answered mostly Cs,** you're making a real effort! You're not careless about your health and your activities, and that pleases God! Now look for ways to improve. Can you replace good habits with great ones? Ask God to help you aim for excellence—and honor him—in everything you do!

**If you answered mostly Ds,** you're right on target! You take good care of your body, and you spend time doing things that will develop your mind and character. To make sure you don't give up when you go through hard times, get to know Christians who can pray for you and encourage you. And pray your example will help other tweens want to honor God, too!

# Q & A

**Q** I'm homeschooled and I like it, but some of my friends think it's weird. How can I make them understand?

**A** Well, you can't *make* people understand things. You can't control the behavior and thoughts of others. But you *can* control yours. Continue to speak positively about your homeschooling, and don't let their reactions get you down. Or just change the subject. If you enjoy being homeschooled, that's what matters! What you *shouldn't* do is act like you're better than them because you're homeschooled.

nothing below us, nor anything else in the whole world will ever be able to separate us from the love of God that is in Christ Jesus our Lord.

44% of girls are involved in church youth groups.
—Ten Emerging Truths Executive Summary, Girl Scouts research report

**did you know?**

## God and the Jewish People

**9** I am in Christ, and I am telling you the truth; I do not lie. My conscience is ruled by the Holy Spirit, and it tells me I am not lying. [2]I have great sorrow and always feel much sadness. [3]I wish I could help my Jewish brothers and sisters, my people. I would even wish that I were cursed and cut off from Christ if that would help them. [4]They are the people of Israel, God's chosen children. They have seen the glory of God, and they have the agreements that God made between himself and his people. God gave them the law of Moses and the right way of worship and his promises. [5]They are the descendants of our great ancestors, and they are the earthly family into which Christ was born, who is God over all. Praise him forever![n] Amen.

[6]It is not that God failed to keep his promise to them. But only some of the people of Israel are truly God's people,[n] [7]and only some of Abraham's[n] descendants are true children of Abraham. But God said to Abraham: "The descendants I promised you will be from Isaac."[n] [8]This means that not all of Abraham's descendants are God's true children. Abraham's true children are those who become God's children because of the promise God made to Abraham. [9]God's promise to Abraham was this: "At the right time I will return, and Sarah will have a son."[n] [10]And that is not all. Rebekah's sons had the same father, our father Isaac. [11-12]But before the two boys were born, God told Rebekah, "The older will serve the younger."[n] This was before the boys had done anything good or bad. God said this so that the one chosen would be chosen because of God's own plan. He was chosen because he was the one God wanted to call, not because of anything he did. [13]As the Scripture says, "I loved Jacob, but I hated Esau."[n]

[14]So what should we say about this? Is God unfair? In no way. [15]God said to Moses, "I will show kindness to anyone to whom I want to show kindness, and I will show mercy to anyone to whom I want to show mercy."[n] [16]So God will choose the one to whom he decides to show mercy; his choice does not depend on what people want or try to do. [17]The Scripture says to the king of Egypt: "I made you king for this reason: to show my power in you so that my name will be talked about in all the earth."[n] [18]So God shows mercy where he wants to show mercy, and he makes stubborn the people he wants to make stubborn.

[19]So one of you will ask me: "Then why does God blame us for our sins? Who can fight his will?" [20]You are only human, and human beings have no right to question God. An object should not ask the person who made it, "Why did you make me like this?" [21]The potter can make anything he wants to make. He can use the same clay to make one thing for special use and another thing for daily use.

[22]It is the same way with God. He wanted to show his anger and to let people see his power. But he patiently stayed with those people he was angry with—people who were made ready to be destroyed. [23]He waited with patience so that he could make known his rich glory to the people who receive his mercy. He has prepared these people to have his glory, [24]and we are those people whom God called. He called us not from the Jews only but also from those who are not Jews. [25]As the Scripture says in Hosea:

"I will say, 'You are my people'
    to those I had called 'not my
    people.'
And I will show my love
    to those people I did not love."
                    *Hosea 2:1, 23*

[26]"They were called,
    'You are not my people,'
but later they will be called
    'children of the living God.'"
                    *Hosea 1:10*

[27]And Isaiah cries out about Israel:
"The people of Israel are many,
    like the grains of sand by the sea.
But only a few of them will be saved,
[28] because the Lord will quickly and
        completely punish the
        people on the earth."
                    *Isaiah 10:22-23*

[29]It is as Isaiah said:
"The Lord All-Powerful
    allowed a few of our descendants
        to live.
Otherwise we would have been
        completely destroyed
    like the cities of Sodom and
        Gomorrah."[n]      *Isaiah 1:9*
[30]So what does all this mean? Those who are not Jews were not trying to make

> IT IS WRITTEN, "HOW BEAUTIFUL IS THE PERSON WHO COMES TO BRING GOOD NEWS."

9:5 **born . . . forever!** This can also mean "born. May God, who rules over all things, be praised forever!" 9:6 **God's people** Literally, "Israel," the people God chose to bring his blessings to the world. 9:7 **Abraham** Most respected ancestor of the Jews. Every Jew hoped to see Abraham. 9:7 **"The descendants . . . Isaac."** Quotation from Genesis 21:12. 9:9 **"At . . . son."** Quotation from Genesis 18:10, 14. 9:11–12 **"The older . . . younger."** Quotation from Genesis 25:23. 9:13 **"I . . . Esau."** Quotation from Malachi 1:2–3. 9:15 **"I . . . mercy."** Quotation from Exodus 33:19. 9:17 **"I . . . earth."** Quotation from Exodus 9:16. 9:29 **Sodom and Gomorrah** Two cities that God destroyed because the people were so evil.

they do not know the right way. ³Because they did not know the way that God makes people right with him, they tried to make themselves right in their own way. So they did not accept God's way of making people right. ⁴Christ ended the law so that everyone who believes in him may be right with God.

⁵Moses writes about being made right by following the law. He says, "A person who obeys these things will live because of them."[n] ⁶But this is what the Scripture says about being made right through faith: "Don't say to yourself, 'Who will go up into heaven?'" (That means, "Who will go up to heaven and bring Christ down to earth?") ⁷"And do not say, 'Who will go down into the world below?'" (That means, "Who will go down and bring Christ up from the dead?") ⁸This is what the Scripture says: "The word is near you; it is in your mouth and in your heart."[n] That is the teaching of faith that we are telling. ⁹If you declare with your mouth, "Jesus is Lord," and if you believe in your heart that God raised Jesus from the dead, you will be saved. ¹⁰We believe with our hearts, and so we are made right with God. And we declare with our mouths that we believe, and so we are saved. ¹¹As the Scripture says, "Anyone who trusts in him will never be disappointed."[n] ¹²That Scripture says "anyone" because there is no difference between those who are Jews and those who are not. The same Lord is the Lord of all and gives many blessings to all

# god's promises

### Romans 11:29

You probably know some indecisive people—kids, or even adults, who just can't make up their minds! Sometimes it's not a big deal, like if they can't choose between Hawaiian pizza and a double cheeseburger. But there are people who change their minds very often and about bigger things. They buy clothes and then return them to the store. They start painting a room and then decide to switch colors. They tell you they're coming to your birthday party and then don't show up!

As people get older, these decisions can become more serious, like leaving a job because they're bored or dumping a boyfriend or husband because someone "nicer" came along. Do you ever wish people would just do what they said they were going to do? That they would keep their promises? Do you sometimes struggle with making up your mind and then sticking to your decisions?

If so, you'll like this promise from God: he never changes his mind about his people and the things he does for them. In other words, he promises to keep his promises. You can have confidence that he won't change his mind about *any* of his promises!

*God promises to keep his promises.*

themselves right with God, but they were made right with God because of their faith. ³¹The people of Israel tried to follow a law to make themselves right with God. But they did not succeed, ³²because they tried to make themselves right by the things they did instead of trusting in God to make them right. They stumbled over the stone that causes people to stumble. ³³As it is written in the Scripture:

"I will put in Jerusalem a stone that
causes people to stumble,
a rock that makes them fall.
Anyone who trusts in him will never
be disappointed."

*Isaiah 8:14; 28:16*

**10** Brothers and sisters, the thing I want most is for all the Jews to be saved. That is my prayer to God. ²I can say this about them: They really try to follow God, but

10:5 **"A person . . . them."** *Quotation from Leviticus 18:5.*   10:6–8 **But . . . heart.** *Quotations from Deuteronomy 9:4; 30:12–14; Psalm 107:26.*   10:11 **"Anyone . . . disappointed."** *Quotation from Isaiah 28:16.*

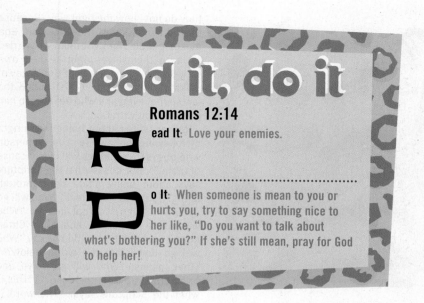

## read it, do it

### Romans 12:14

**R**ead It: Love your enemies.

**D**o It: When someone is mean to you or hurts you, try to say something nice to her like, "Do you want to talk about what's bothering you?" If she's still mean, pray for God to help her!

who trust in him, [13]as the Scripture says, "Anyone who calls on the Lord will be saved."[n]

[14]But before people can ask the Lord for help, they must believe in him; and before they can believe in him, they must hear about him; and for them to hear about the Lord, someone must tell them;

# Q&A

**Q** Everyone in my family is good at sports but I'm not. How can I stop feeling like a failure?

**A** It's always tough when you feel different or not as good as others. Keep in mind that God created each of us with different skills and talents. Sports might not be yours . . . and that's okay! Keep doing your best and ask your family to help you improve, but don't get stuck feeling bad. Focus on the things *you* are good at. God made you special . . . be thankful for that!

[15]and before someone can go and tell them, that person must be sent. It is written, "How beautiful is the person who comes to bring good news."[n] [16]But not all the Jews accepted the good news. Isaiah said, "Lord, who believed what we told them?"[n] [17]So faith comes from hearing the Good News, and people hear the Good News when someone tells them about Christ.

[18]But I ask: Didn't people hear the Good News? Yes, they heard—as the Scripture says:

"Their message went out through all
  the world;
their words go everywhere on
  earth."        *Psalm 19:4*

[19]Again I ask: Didn't the people of Israel understand? Yes, they did understand. First, Moses says:

"I will use those who are not a nation
  to make you jealous.
I will use a nation that does not
  understand to make you
  angry."        *Deuteronomy 32:21*

[20]Then Isaiah is bold enough to say:

"I was found by those who were not
  asking me for help.
I made myself known to people who
  were not looking for me."
                *Isaiah 65:1*

[21]But about Israel God says,

"All day long I stood ready to accept
  people who disobey and are
  stubborn."        *Isaiah 65:2*

## God Shows Mercy to All People

**11** So I ask: Did God throw out his people? No! I myself am an Israelite from the family of Abraham, from the tribe of Benjamin. [2]God chose the Israelites to be his people before they were born, and he has not thrown his people out. Surely you know what the Scripture says about Elijah, how he prayed to God against the people of Israel. [3]"Lord," he said, "they have killed your prophets, and they have destroyed your altars. I am the only prophet left, and now they are trying to kill me, too."[n] [4]But what answer did God give Elijah? He said, "But I have left seven thousand people in Israel who have never bowed down before Baal."[n] [5]It is the same now. There are a few people that God has chosen by his grace. [6]And if he chose them by grace, it is not for the things they have done. If they could be made God's people by what they did, God's gift of grace would not really be a gift.

[7]So this is what has happened: Although the Israelites tried to be right with God, they did not succeed, but the ones God chose did become right with him. The others were made stubborn and refused to listen to God. [8]As it is written in the Scriptures:

## Be YOUR BEST!

**E**veryone loves good news! Try to keep your conversations positive and encouraging. People will look forward to talking with you! Don't forget the Good News about Jesus, too! Romans 10:15 says that the people who bring God's message are beautiful! You can be, too, by telling others about Jesus.

10:13 **"Anyone . . . saved."** *Quotation from Joel 2:32.* 10:15 **"How . . . news."** *Quotation from Isaiah 52:7.* 10:16 **"Lord, . . . them?"** *Quotation from Isaiah 53:1.* 11:3 **"they . . . too"** *Quotation from 1 Kings 19:10, 14.* 11:4 **"But . . . Baal."** *Quotation from 1 Kings 19:18.*

Romans

# BibLe BaSicS

The Bible is a collection of God's messages to his people over centuries and centuries. God's Word is so important that *scribes* (people who wrote down important things for a living) made careful copies by hand of each book. That way people would always have God's Word to remind them how to live. The Israelite priests took care of these books, written on scrolls or papyrus (old-fashioned paper), and passed them down from generation to generation. After Jesus died, Christians needed a way to remember Jesus' teachings, too. Eventually all the different books of Scripture were put together as "the Bible." By the year 400 A.D.— over fifteen centuries ago—the Bible existed as we know it today!

"God gave the people a dull mind so
    they could not understand."
                            *Isaiah 29:10*
"He closed their eyes so they could
    not see
    and their ears so they could not
    hear.
This continues until today."
                            *Deuteronomy 29:4*
[9]And David says:
"Let their own feasts trap them and
    cause their ruin;
    let their feasts cause them to
    stumble and be paid back.
[10]Let their eyes be closed so they
    cannot see
    and their backs be forever weak
    from troubles."
                            *Psalm 69:22–23*
[11]So I ask: When the Jews fell, did that fall destroy them? No! But their failure brought salvation to those who are not Jews, in order to make the Jews jealous. [12]The Jews' failure brought rich blessings for the world, and the Jews' loss brought rich blessings for the non-Jewish people. So surely the world will receive much richer blessings when enough Jews become the kind of people God wants.

[13]Now I am speaking to you who are not Jews. I am an apostle to those who are not Jews, and since I have that work, I will make the most of it. [14]I hope I can make my own people jealous and, in that way, help some of them to be saved. [15]When God turned away from the Jews, he became friends with other people in the world. So when God accepts the Jews, surely that will bring them life after death.

[16]If the first piece of bread is offered to God, then the whole loaf is made holy. If the roots of a tree are holy, then the tree's branches are holy too.

[17]It is as if some of the branches from an olive tree have been broken off. You non-Jewish people are like the branch of a wild olive tree that has been joined to that first tree. You now share the strength and life of the first tree, the Jews. [18]So do not brag about those branches that were broken off. If you brag, remember that you do not support the root, but the root supports you. [19]You will say, "Branches were broken off so that I could be joined to their tree." [20]That is true. But those branches were broken off because they did not believe, and you continue to be part of the tree only because you believe. Do not be proud, but be afraid. [21]If God did not let the natural branches of that tree stay, then he will not let you stay if you don't believe.

[22]So you see that God is kind and also very strict. He punishes those who stop following him. But God is kind to you, if you continue following in his kindness. If you do not, you will be cut off from the tree. [23]And if the Jews will believe in God again, he will accept them back. God is able to put them back where they were. [24]It is not natural for a wild branch to be part of a good tree. And you who are not Jews are like a branch cut from a wild olive tree and joined to a good olive tree. But since those Jews are like a branch that grew from the good tree, surely they can be joined to their own tree again.

[25]I want you to understand this secret, brothers and sisters, so you will

## read it, do it

**Romans 12:15**

**R**ead It: Care about the feelings of others.

**D**o It: When your friend tells you about her day, really pay attention. Give a hug if she needs one or, if she's happy about something, show her that you're happy for her, too!

## cool

### I and You

**P**eople write the word "the" more than any other word in the English language. In fact, we use it almost twice as often as the next most frequently written word—"of." Count how often the word "the" appears on this page!

In *spoken* English, we use the word "I" most of all. The next most used words? "You," "the," and "a." We sure talk about ourselves a lot! You'd probably get tongue-tied if you tried talking without saying the word "I!" Romans 12:16 warns us against being proud. Pray that your words will make others feel important, too!

understand that you do not know everything: Part of Israel has been made stubborn, but that will change when many who are not Jews have come to God. [26]And that is how all Israel will be saved. It is written in the Scriptures:

"The Savior will come from
   Jerusalem;
he will take away all evil from the
   family of Jacob.[n]
[27]And I will make this agreement with
   those people
when I take away their sins."
       *Isaiah 59:20–21; 27:9*

[28]The Jews refuse to accept the Good News, so they are God's enemies. This has happened to help you who are not Jews. But the Jews are still God's chosen people, and he loves them very much because of the promises he made to their ancestors. [29]God never changes his mind about the people he calls and the things he gives them. [30]At one time you refused to obey God. But now you have received mercy, because those people refused to

obey. [31]And now the Jews refuse to obey, because God showed mercy to you. But this happened so that they also can[n] receive mercy from him. [32]God has given all people over to their stubborn ways so that he can show mercy to all.

### Praise to God

[33]Yes, God's riches are very great, and his wisdom and knowledge have no end! No one can explain the things God decides or understand his ways. [34]As the Scripture says,
"Who has known the mind of the
   Lord,
  or who has been able to give him
     advice?"     *Isaiah 40:13*
[35]"No one has ever given God anything
   that he must pay back."   *Job 41:11*
[36]Yes, God made all things, and everything continues through him and for him. To him be the glory forever! Amen.

### Give Your Lives to God

**12** So brothers and sisters, since God has shown us great mercy, I beg you to offer your lives as a living sacrifice to him. Your offering must be only for God and pleasing to him, which is the spiritual way for you to worship. [2]Do not be shaped by this world; instead be changed within by a new way of thinking. Then you will be able to decide what God wants for you; you will know what is good and pleasing to him and what is

LOVE EACH OTHER LIKE BROTHERS AND SISTERS. GIVE EACH OTHER MORE HONOR THAN YOU WANT FOR YOURSELVES.

perfect. [3]Because God has given me a special gift, I have something to say to everyone among you. Do not think you are better than you are. You must decide what you really are by the amount of faith God has given you. [4]Each one of us has a body with many parts, and these parts all have different uses. [5]In the same way, we are many, but in Christ we are all one body. Each one is a part of that body, and each part belongs to all the other parts. [6]We all have different gifts, each of which came because of the grace God gave us. The person who has the gift of prophecy should use that gift in agreement with the faith. [7]Anyone who has the gift of serving should serve. Anyone who has the gift of teaching should teach. [8]Whoever has the gift of encouraging others should encourage. Whoever has the gift of giving to others should give freely. Anyone who has the gift of being a leader should try hard when he leads. Whoever has the gift of showing mercy to others should do so with joy.

[9]Your love must be real. Hate what is evil, and hold on to what is good. [10]Love

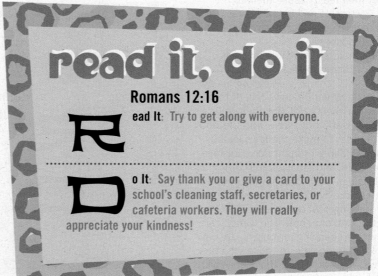

## read it, do it

### Romans 12:16

**R**ead It: Try to get along with everyone.

**D**o It: Say thank you or give a card to your school's cleaning staff, secretaries, or cafeteria workers. They will really appreciate your kindness!

**11:26 Jacob** *Father of the twelve family groups of Israel, the people God chose to be his people.*   **11:31 can** *Some Greek copies read "can now."*

## *Looking Ahead*

### DATING

**D**ating can be confusing! People casually use the word "love," and it seems like new couples are holding hands every week. You might wonder, *What's the deal with dating?* Some young people date because they feel special knowing someone likes them. But many people date just because others do. Dating relationships before and during high school usually don't last very long. So relax! There's nothing wrong with *not* dating. Many young people only group date. Try to save dating for when you're ready to get married. For now, enjoy making and keeping great friends—and remember to "love each other like brothers and sisters" (Romans 12:10).

each other like brothers and sisters. Give each other more honor than you want for yourselves. ¹¹Do not be lazy but work hard, serving the Lord with all your heart. ¹²Be joyful because you have hope. Be patient when trouble comes, and pray at all times. ¹³Share with God's people who need help. Bring strangers in need into your homes.

unimportant. Do not think how smart you are.

¹⁷If someone does wrong to you, do not pay him back by doing wrong to him. Try to do what everyone thinks is right. ¹⁸Do your best to live in peace with everyone. ¹⁹My friends, do not try to punish others when they wrong you, but wait for God to punish them with his anger. It is written: "I will punish those who do wrong; I will repay them,"[n] says the Lord. ²⁰But you should do this:

"If your enemy is hungry, feed him;
if he is thirsty, give him a drink.
Doing this will be like pouring burning
coals on his head."
*Proverbs 25:21–22*

²¹Do not let evil defeat you, but defeat evil by doing good.

### Christians Should Obey the Law

**13** All of you must yield to the government rulers. No one rules unless God has given him the power to rule, and no one rules now without that power from God. ²So those who are against the government are really against what God has commanded. And they will bring punishment on themselves. ³Those who do right do not have to fear the rulers; only those who do wrong fear them. Do you want to be unafraid of the rulers? Then do what is right, and they will praise you. ⁴The ruler is God's servant to help you. But if you do wrong, then be afraid. He has the power to punish; he is God's servant to punish those who do wrong. ⁵So you must yield to the government, not only because you might be punished, but because you know it is right.

### Loving Others

⁸Do not owe people anything, except always owe love to each other, because the person who loves others has obeyed all the law. ⁹The law says, "You must not be guilty of adultery. You must not murder anyone. You must not steal. You must not want to take your neighbor's things."[n] All these commands and all others are really only one rule: "Love your neighbor as you love yourself."[n] ¹⁰Love never hurts a neighbor, so loving is obeying all the law.

¹¹Do this because we live in an important time. It is now time for you to wake up from your sleep, because our salvation is nearer now than when we first believed. ¹²The "night"[n] is almost finished, and the "day"[n] is almost here. So we should stop doing things that belong to darkness and take up the weapons used for fighting in the light. ¹³Let us live in a right way, like people who belong to the day. We should not have wild parties or get drunk. There should be no sexual sins of any kind, no fighting or jealousy. ¹⁴But clothe yourselves with the Lord Jesus Christ and forget about satisfying your sinful self.

# Q&A

**Q** Why does God let things like earthquakes and tsunamis happen? So many people die!

**A** Many people struggle with this question. At some point, each person will die. It might be in an accident, from sickness, or just from getting old! That's the natural process of life. Some people will suffer while others die peacefully. What we must remember is that God suffers when we do because he made us and loves us. Read Romans 8:18–26 to learn how God cares about his people and the world he created.

**Kids multitask! 61% use the phone, TV, or computer while doing homework.**
—Trends & Tudes. Harris Interactive. May 2005.
http://www.harrisinteractive.com/news/newsletters/k12news/HI_Trends&TudesNews2005_v4_iss05.pdf

### did you know?

¹⁴Wish good for those who harm you; wish them well and do not curse them. ¹⁵Be happy with those who are happy, and be sad with those who are sad. ¹⁶Live in peace with each other. Do not be proud, but make friends with those who seem

⁶This is also why you pay taxes. Rulers are working for God and give their time to their work. ⁷Pay everyone, then, what you owe. If you owe any kind of tax, pay it. Show respect and honor to them all.

**Romans**

**12:19** "I . . . them." *Quotation from Deuteronomy 32:35.* **13:9** "You . . . things." *Quotation from Exodus 20:13–15, 17.* **13:9** "Love . . . yourself." *Quotation from Leviticus 19:18.* **13:12** "night" *This is used as a symbol of the sinful world we live in. This world will soon end.* **13:12** "day" *This is used as a symbol of the good time that is coming, when we will be with God.*

**211**

## dig deeper

### Romans 12:2

Have you ever watched a makeover show on TV? People completely change their looks, their houses, their families, or their wardrobes. They want a whole new look, and it can be exciting to see the results!

It's fun to get a makeover and feel and look like a whole new you. Maybe you and your friends have had makeover parties or spent time redecorating your bedroom.

But did you know God wants to give you a makeover, too? It's not the kind of makeover you see on TV. You may not look different on the outside, but you will be transformed in a more important way—from the inside out!

God cares most about how you think, what you say, and how you treat others. He wants to makeover your heart and mind! Romans 12:2 says, "Do not be shaped by this world; instead be changed within by a new way of thinking. Then you will be able to decide what God wants for you; you will know what is good and pleasing to him and what is perfect."

We shouldn't change ourselves to look or act or talk like celebrities or even our friends. Instead, we need to focus on being kind, gentle, caring, helpful, patient, and obedient to God. That's the ultimate makeover!

well because the Lord helps him do well.
⁵Some think that one day is more important than another, and others think that every day is the same. Let all be sure in their own mind. ⁶Those who think one day is more important than other days are doing that for the Lord. And those who eat all kinds of food are doing that for the Lord, and they give thanks to God. Others who refuse to eat some foods do that for the Lord, and they give thanks to God. ⁷We do not live or die for ourselves. ⁸If we live, we are living for the Lord, and if we die, we are dying for the Lord. So living or dying, we belong to the Lord.
⁹The reason Christ died and rose from the dead to live again was so he would be Lord over both the dead and the living. ¹⁰So why do you judge your brothers or sisters in Christ? And why do you think you are better than they are? We will all stand before God to be judged, ¹¹because it is written in the Scriptures:
"'As surely as I live,' says the Lord,
'Everyone will bow before me;
everyone will say that I am God.'"
*Isaiah 45:23*
¹²So each of us will have to answer to God.

### Do Not Cause Others to Sin

¹³For that reason we should stop judging each other. We must make up our minds not to do anything that will make another Christian sin. ¹⁴I am in the Lord Jesus, and I know that there is no food that is wrong to eat. But if a person believes

### Do Not Criticize Other People

**14** Accept into your group someone who is weak in faith, and do not argue about opinions. ²One person believes it is right to eat all kinds of food.ⁿ But another, who is weak, believes it is right to eat only vegetables. ³The one who knows that it is right to eat any kind of food must not reject the one who eats only vegetables. And the person who eats only vegetables must not think that the one who eats all foods is wrong, because God has accepted that person. ⁴You cannot judge another person's servant. The master decides if the servant is doing well or not. And the Lord's servant will do

14:2 **all . . . food** *The Jewish law said there were some foods Jews should not eat. When Jews became Christians, some of them did not understand they could now eat all foods.*

Romans

## Bible Bios — Paul (Acts 9:1–31)

Before he became a Christian and had his name changed to Paul, *Saul* wanted to destroy the early church. He was educated and knew the Jewish laws by heart. Yet he approved when some people killed Stephen, a Christian leader, for teaching about Jesus. Saul threatened Christians and arrested many of them!

But God loved Saul and wanted to save him from his evil heart. One day as Saul was traveling, God blinded him with a bright light and spoke to him loudly. When he understood he was wrong about Jesus, Saul's heart changed and he believed. It was a miracle! Instead of persecuting Christians, Paul began boldly preaching about Jesus. As you read the New Testament, you'll see how God used Paul to lead many people to Jesus.

Ask God to make a miracle out of *your* life!

---

something is wrong, that thing is wrong for him. [15]If you hurt your brother's or sister's faith because of something you eat, you are not really following the way of love. Do not destroy someone's faith by eating food he thinks is wrong, because Christ died for him. [16]Do not allow what you think is good to become what others say is evil. [17]In the kingdom of God, eating and drinking are not important. The important things are living right with God, peace, and joy in the Holy Spirit.

## BE YOUR BEST!

Braces can be a real pain! They hurt, you might have to avoid certain foods, and kids might tease you. But braces will eventually give you a beautiful smile! God's rules might not always seem fun to follow, but when you obey him, he shapes your life into something beautiful.

[18]Anyone who serves Christ by living this way is pleasing God and will be accepted by other people.

[19]So let us try to do what makes peace and helps one another. [20]Do not let the eating of food destroy the work of God. All foods are all right to eat, but it is wrong to eat food that causes someone else to sin. [21]It is better not to eat meat or drink wine or do anything that will cause your brother or sister to sin.

[22]Your beliefs about these things should be kept secret between you and God. People are happy if they can do what they think is right without feeling guilty. [23]But those who eat something without being sure it is right are wrong because they did not believe it was right. Anything that is done without believing it is right is a sin.

**15** We who are strong in faith should help the weak with their weaknesses, and not please only ourselves. [2]Let each of us please our neighbors for their good, to help them be stronger in faith. [3]Even Christ did not live to please himself. It was as the Scriptures said: "When people insult you, it hurts me."[n] [4]Everything that was written in the past was written to teach us. The Scriptures give us patience and encouragement so that we can have hope. [5]May the patience and encouragement that come from God allow you to live in harmony with each other the way Christ Jesus wants. [6]Then

you will all be joined together, and you will give glory to God the Father of our Lord Jesus Christ. [7]Christ accepted you, so you should accept each other, which will bring glory to God. [8]I tell you that Christ became a servant of the Jews to show that God's promises to the Jewish ancestors are true. [9]And he also did this so that those who are not Jews could give glory to God for the mercy he gives to them. It is written in the Scriptures:

"So I will praise you among the non-Jewish people.
I will sing praises to your name."
*Psalm 18:49*

[10]The Scripture also says,

"Be happy, you who are not Jews, together with his people."
*Deuteronomy 32:43*

[11]Again the Scripture says,

"All you who are not Jews, praise the Lord.
All you people, sing praises to him."
*Psalm 117:1*

[12]And Isaiah says,

"A new king will come from the family of Jesse.[n]
He will come to rule over the non-Jewish people,
and they will have hope because of him."
*Isaiah 11:10*

## Q&A

**Q** I fight a lot with my brother and sister. How can I get along with them?

**A** Choose a time when you're not fighting and tell them how much you wish you could get along better. Together, try to come up with some ideas of why you fight and how you can be more patient with each other. Even if they don't want to work on it, ask God to help you be kinder toward them. First John 4:20–21 tells us that if we love God, we must also love our brothers and sisters.

---

15:3 "When . . . me." *Quotation from Psalm 69:9.*   15:12 **Jesse** *Jesse was the father of David, king of Israel. Jesus was from their family.*

¹³I pray that the God who gives hope will fill you with much joy and peace while you trust in him. Then your hope will overflow by the power of the Holy Spirit.

## Paul Talks About His Work

¹⁴My brothers and sisters, I am sure that you are full of goodness. I know that you have all the knowledge you need and that you are able to teach each other. ¹⁵But I have written to you very openly about some things I wanted you to remember. I did this because God gave me this special gift: ¹⁶to be a minister of Christ Jesus to those who are not Jews. I served God by teaching his Good News, so that the non-Jewish people could be an offering that God would accept—an offering made holy by the Holy Spirit.

¹⁷So I am proud of what I have done for God in Christ Jesus. ¹⁸I will not talk about anything except what Christ has done through me in leading those who are not Jews to obey God. They have obeyed God because of what I have said and done, ¹⁹because of the power of miracles and the great things they saw, and because of the power of the Holy Spirit. I preached the Good News from Jerusalem all the way around to Illyricum, and so I have finished that part of my work. ²⁰I always want to preach the Good News in places where people have never heard of Christ, because I do not want to build on the work someone else has already started. ²¹But it is written in the Scriptures:

"Those who were not told about him
      will see,
and those who have not heard
      about him will understand."
                                        *Isaiah 52:15*

## Paul's Plan to Visit Rome

²²This is the reason I was stopped many times from coming to you. ²³Now I have finished my work here. Since for many

I PRAY THAT THE GOD WHO GIVES HOPE WILL FILL YOU WITH MUCH JOY AND PEACE WHILE YOU TRUST IN HIM.

# dig deeper

## Romans 15:1–3

Who are you trying to make happy? For most people, the answer is "Myself!" However, as Christians, we are called to live for others, rather than for ourselves. Why? Because that's what Jesus did, and he's our ultimate example.

Paul tells us in Romans 15:1–3, "We who are strong in faith should help the weak with their weaknesses, and not please only ourselves. Let each of us please our neighbors for their good, to help them be stronger in faith. Even Christ did not live to please himself." These verses are all about putting other people's needs above our own.

Paul wanted his readers to remember how Jesus lived. Sure, it wasn't always convenient or easy for Jesus to put other people first—but he did it anyway because of his love for God and for people.

You can help the "weak with their weaknesses" by living in a way that pleases God and by following all that he has commanded. This will help the Christians around you to become "stronger in faith." Is any of your sin making it harder for the people around you to follow Christ? Paul says you should get rid of it! Remember: "Even Christ did not live to please himself"!

years I have wanted to come to you, ²⁴I hope to visit you on my way to Spain. After I enjoy being with you for a while, I hope you can help me on my trip. ²⁵Now I am going to Jerusalem to help God's people. ²⁶The believers in Macedonia and Southern Greece were happy to give their money to help the poor among God's people at Jerusalem. ²⁷They were happy to do this, and really they owe it to them. These who are not Jews have shared in the Jews' spiritual blessings, so they should use their material possessions to help the Jews. ²⁸After I am sure the poor in Jerusalem get the money that has been given for them, I will leave for Spain and stop and visit you. ²⁹I know that when I come to you I will bring Christ's full blessing.

³⁰Brothers and sisters, I beg you to help me in my work by praying to God for me. Do this because of our Lord Jesus and the love that the Holy Spirit gives us. ³¹Pray

that I will be saved from the nonbelievers in Judea and that this help I bring to Jerusalem will please God's people there. [32]Then, if God wants me to, I will come to

lives to save my life. I am thankful to them, and all the non-Jewish churches are thankful as well. [5]Also, greet for me the church that meets at their house.

in prison with me. They are very important apostles. They were believers in Christ before I was. [8]Greetings to Ampliatus, my dear friend in the Lord. [9]Greetings to Urbanus, a worker together with me for Christ. And greetings to my dear friend Stachys. [10]Greetings to Apelles, who was tested and proved that he truly loves Christ. Greetings to all those who are in the family of Aristobulus. [11]Greetings to Herodion, my fellow citizen. Greetings to all those in the family of Narcissus who belong to the Lord. [12]Greetings to Tryphena and Tryphosa, women who work very hard for the Lord.

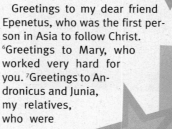

**64% of kids use e-mail to communicate with their friends.**
--Key Facts, Fall 2002 Report.
http://www.kff.org/entmedia/loader.cfm?url=/commonspot/security/getfile.cfm&PageID=14095

**did you know?**

you with joy, and together you and I will have a time of rest. [33]The God who gives peace be with you all. Amen.

## Greetings to the Christians

**16** I recommend to you our sister Phoebe, who is a helper* in the church in Cenchrea. [2]I ask you to accept her in the Lord in the way God's people should. Help her with anything she needs, because she has helped me and many other people also.

[3]Give my greetings to Priscilla and Aquila, who work together with me in Christ Jesus [4]and who risked their own

Greetings to my dear friend Epenetus, who was the first person in Asia to follow Christ. [6]Greetings to Mary, who worked very hard for you. [7]Greetings to Andronicus and Junia, my relatives, who were

# Q&A

**Q** Why do they always take an offering at church?

**A** Churches need money to function. Some support missionaries. Some have workers who get paid. Most of them have buildings that need to be taken care of and other expenses. Churches usually depend on donations to do God's work. But the most important reason for us to give is because it is a way to worship God and thank him for all he's given us. God loves cheerful givers (2 Corinthians 9:7)!

## Shine Your Light

Every year, a youth group in Portland, Oregon, has a "Prayer-a-Thon." The kids break into small groups, and from 7 P.M. to 7 A.M., they take turns praying in fifteen-minute shifts. Each group prays for requests from friends, family, teachers, and church members. They believe that intercessory prayer (praying for other people) is an important way to spread God's love.

Allisyn and Chris say the best part of Prayer-a-Thon is hearing how their prayers make a difference in people's lives. The youth group often gets letters from people, thanking them for their prayers and explaining how the prayer was answered.

At Prayer-a-Thon, Matt prays for people on the street, government leaders, and kids being hurt by war. He says that sometimes we never know how our prayers might affect someone. Matt knows that he might never see how his prayers change someone's life, but his words still matter to God.

You don't have to stay up all night for your prayers to make a difference. God loves to hear you talk anytime! Next time someone shares a problem with you, practice intercessory prayer by asking God to help that person.

**16:1 helper** Literally, "deaconess." This might mean the same as one of the special women helpers in 1 Timothy 3:11.

**read it, do it**

**Romans 16:19**

**R** ead It: Be wise and innocent.

**D** o It: Don't waste time learning about how people in the world live. Keep your mind pure and become an expert on living God's way by studying his Word and praying.

Greetings to my dear friend Persis, who also has worked very hard for the Lord. [13]Greetings to Rufus, who is a special person in the Lord, and to his mother, who has been like a mother to me also. [14]Greetings to Asyncritus, Phlegon, Hermes, Patrobas, Hermas, and all the brothers and sisters who are with them. [15]Greetings to Philologus and Julia, Nereus and his sister, and Olympas, and to all God's people with them. [16]Greet each other with a holy kiss. All of Christ's churches send greetings to you.

[17]Brothers and sisters, I ask you to look out for those who cause people to be against each other and who upset other people's faith. They are against the true teaching you learned, so stay away from them. [18]Such people are not serving our Lord Christ but are only doing what pleases themselves. They use fancy talk and fine words to fool the minds of those who do not know about evil. [19]All the believers have heard that you obey, so I am very happy because of you. But I want you to be wise in what is good and innocent in what is evil.

[20]The God who brings peace will soon defeat Satan and give you power over him.

The grace of our Lord Jesus be with you.

[21]Timothy, a worker together with me, sends greetings, as well as Lucius, Jason, and Sosipater, my relatives.

[22]I am Tertius, and I am writing this letter from Paul. I send greetings to you in the Lord.

[23]Gaius is letting me and the whole church here use his home. He also sends greetings to you, as do Erastus, the city treasurer, and our brother Quartus. [[24]The grace of our Lord Jesus Christ be with all of you. Amen.][n]

[25]Glory to God who can make you strong in faith by the Good News that I tell people and by the message about Jesus Christ. The message about Christ is the secret that was hidden for long ages past but is now made known. [26]It has been made clear through the writings of the prophets. And by the command of the eternal God it is made known to all nations that they might believe and obey.

[27]To the only wise God be glory forever through Jesus Christ! Amen.

**16:24 The . . . Amen.** Some Greek copies do not contain the bracketed text.

# 1CORINTHIANS

**T**he church in Corinth had serious problems. Some of the members were fighting with each other. Others were living in very sinful ways. But Paul didn't give up on them. Instead, he wrote this letter so they would know how to live like true followers of Christ.

No church is perfect. Your church might include people you don't like very much. Some of them might be hard to get along with. We're all still growing as Christians, and we all make mistakes. But in 1 Corinthians we read that a church is like a body with many parts. All the members belong together and need each other. Every person has a role—even kids! No one is "extra."

Paul told the Corinthians that "the best way of all" is love (2 Corinthians 12:31). Chapter 13 is the famous "love chapter." It tells us what real love is and what we'll do if we really love other people. Because God is love, this chapter describes him, too. Take a look—it's exciting to see how God loves you!

Paul patiently worked with the Corinthians to help them grow. In the same way, we need to love others, even when they make mistakes. This book will help you understand how to be a real part of a "body" of Christians.

# HELP FOR A CHURCH WITH PROBLEMS

## THiNGS TO TALK WiTH GOD ABOUT . . .

1 From Paul. God called me to be an apostle of Christ Jesus because that is what God wanted. Also from Sosthenes, our brother in Christ.

2 To the church of God in Corinth, to you who have been made holy in Christ Jesus. You were called to be God's holy people with all people everywhere who pray in the name of the Lord Jesus Christ—their Lord and ours:

3 Grace and peace to you from God our Father and the Lord Jesus Christ.

### Paul Gives Thanks to God

4 I always thank my God for you because of the grace God has given you in Christ Jesus.

**83% of students say it's cool to be smart.**
—OnMission.com "What's a Tween" by Dr. Mary Manz Simon
http://www.onmission.com/webzine/jul_aug01/tweens.htm

**did you know?**

5 I thank God because in Christ you have been made rich in every way, in all your speaking and in all your knowledge. 6 Just as our witness about Christ has been guaranteed to you, 7 so you have every gift from God while you wait for our Lord Jesus Christ to come again. 8 Jesus will keep you strong until the end so that there will be no wrong in you on the day our Lord Jesus Christ comes again. 9 God, who has called you into fellowship with his Son, Jesus Christ our Lord, is faithful.

### Problems in the Church

10 I beg you, brothers and sisters, by the name of our Lord Jesus Christ that all of you agree with each other and not be split into groups. I beg that you be completely joined together by having the same kind of thinking and the same purpose. 11 My brothers and sisters, some people from Chloe's family have told me quite plainly that there are quarrels among you. 12 This is what I mean: One of you says, "I follow Paul"; another says, "I follow Apollos"; another says, "I fol-

low Peter"; and another says, "I follow Christ." 13 Christ has been divided up into different groups! Did Paul die on the cross for you? No! Were you baptized in the name of Paul? No! 14 I thank God I did not baptize any of you except Crispus and Gaius 15 so that now no one can say you were baptized in my name. 16 (I also baptized the family of Stephanas, but I do not remember that I baptized anyone else.) 17 Christ did not send me to baptize people but to preach the Good News. And he sent me to preach the Good News without using words of human wisdom so that the cross[n] of Christ would not lose its power.

### Christ Is God's Power and Wisdom

18 The teaching about the cross is foolishness to those who are being lost, but to us who are being saved it is the power of God. 19 It is written in the Scriptures:

"I will cause the wise to lose their wisdom;
I will make the wise unable to understand."       *Isaiah 29:14*

20 Where is the wise person? Where is the educated person? Where is the skilled talker of this world? God has made the wisdom of the

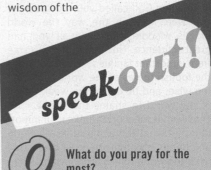

**speakout!**

Q What do you pray for the most?

A A good life and a dog.
—Nessa, 12

**DON'T YOU KNOW THAT YOU ARE GOD'S TEMPLE AND THAT GOD'S SPIRIT LIVES IN YOU?**

**1:17 cross** *Paul uses the cross as a picture of the Good News, the story of Christ's death and rising from the dead for people's sins. The cross, or Christ's death, was God's way to save people.*

219

# Relationships

**W**hen the apostle Paul wrote letters to his friends, he always started by saying he loved and appreciated them. His favorite phrase? "I always thank my God for you" (1 Corinthians 1:4). That's the kind of note everyone likes to receive! The Bible says, "Worry is a heavy load, but a kind word cheers you up" (Proverbs 12:25). Try saying, "What I like about you is . . . " or "You make me happy when . . . " and fill in the blank. You'll make your friends and family happy—and your own heart will feel happy, too!

world foolish. [21]In the wisdom of God the world did not know God through its own wisdom. So God chose to use the message that sounds foolish to save those who believe. [22]The Jews ask for miracles, and the Greeks want wisdom. [23]But we preach a crucified Christ. This causes the Jews to stumble and is foolishness to non-Jews. [24]But Christ is the power of God and the wisdom of God to those people God has called—Jews and Greeks. [25]Even the foolishness of God is wiser than human wisdom, and the weakness of God is stronger than human strength.

[26]Brothers and sisters, look at what you were when God called you. Not many of you were wise in the way the world judges wisdom. Not many of you had great influence. Not many of you came from important families. [27]But God chose the foolish things of the world to shame the wise, and he chose the weak things of the world to shame the strong. [28]He chose what the world thinks is unimportant and what the world looks down on and thinks is nothing in order to destroy what the world thinks is important. [29]God did this so that no one can brag in his presence. [30]Because of God you are in Christ Jesus, who has become for us wisdom from God. In Christ we are put right with God, and have been made holy, and have been set free from sin. [31]So, as the Scripture says, "If people want to brag, they should brag only about the Lord."[n]

## The Message of Christ's Death

**2** Dear brothers and sisters, when I came to you, I did not come preaching God's secret[n] with fancy words or a show of human wisdom. [2]I decided that while I was with you I would forget about everything except Jesus Christ and his death on the cross. [3]So when I came to you, I was weak and fearful and trembling. [4]My teaching and preaching were not with words of human wisdom that persuade people but with proof of the power that the Spirit gives. [5]This was so that your faith would be in God's power and not in human wisdom.

## God's Wisdom

[6]However, I speak a wisdom to those who are mature. But this wisdom is not from this world or from the rulers of this world, who are losing their power. [7]I speak God's secret wisdom, which he has kept hidden. Before the world began, God planned this wisdom for our glory. [8]None of the rulers of this world understood it. If they had, they would not have crucified the Lord of glory. [9]But as it is written in the Scriptures:

"No one has ever seen this,
    and no one has ever heard about it.
No one has ever imagined
    what God has prepared for those
        who love him."     *Isaiah 64:4*

[10]But God has shown us these things through the Spirit.

The Spirit searches out all things, even the deep secrets of God. [11]Who knows the thoughts that another person has? Only a person's spirit that lives within him knows his thoughts. It is the same with God. No one knows the thoughts of God except the Spirit of God. [12]Now we did not receive the spirit of the world, but we received the Spirit that is from God so that we can know all that God has given us. [13]And we speak about these things, not with words taught us by human wisdom but with words taught us by the Spirit.

# Q & A

**Q** What is a good way to show a boy that I like him?

**A** When you like someone, the best thing is to show respect and kindness. Some girls start acting silly or flirty around boys. Others become mean just to get their attention. These are not appropriate ways to behave (and they don't work with nice guys!). You don't need to be dating yet. If your goal is a pure friendship, just let your natural personality shine through. And, as usual, ask God to guide your thoughts, words, and actions.

**1:31** "If . . . Lord." *Quotation from Jeremiah 9:24.*   **2:1** **God's secret** *Some Greek copies read "God's message."*

220

1 Corinthians

## Get It

### Hell

Hell is the place where people who don't believe in Jesus go when they die. It is a place of separation from God where there is punishment for sins and for not believing in Jesus. The Bible tells us there will be suffering and "people will cry and grind their teeth with pain" (Matthew 8:12). God doesn't want *anyone* to go to hell (check out 2 Peter 3:9), but because he is holy, perfect, and sinless, he can't allow sinful people in heaven. We can thank God for providing a way for us to live with him in heaven forever!

And so we explain spiritual truths to spiritual people. ¹⁴A person who does not have the Spirit does not accept the truths that come from the Spirit of God. That person thinks they are foolish and cannot understand them, because they can only be judged to be true by the Spirit. ¹⁵The spiritual person is able to judge all things, but no one can judge him. The Scripture says:

¹⁶"Who has known the mind of the Lord?
Who has been able to teach him?"

*Isaiah 40:13*

But we have the mind of Christ.

### Following People Is Wrong

**3** Brothers and sisters, in the past I could not talk to you as I talk to spiritual people. I had to talk to you as I would to people without the Spirit—babies in Christ. ²The teaching I gave you was like milk, not solid food, because you were not able to take solid food. And even now you are not ready. ³You are still not spiritual, because there is jealousy and quarreling among you, and this shows that you are not spiritual. You are acting like people of the world.

⁴One of you says, "I belong to Paul," and another says, "I belong to Apollos." When you say things like this, you are acting like people of the world.

⁵Is Apollos important? No! Is Paul important? No! We are only servants of God who helped you believe. Each one of us did the work God gave us to do. ⁶I planted the seed, and Apollos watered it. But God is the One who made it grow. ⁷So the one who plants is not important, and the one who waters is not important. Only God, who makes things grow, is important. ⁸The one who plants and the one who waters have the same purpose, and each will be rewarded for his own work. ⁹We are God's workers, working together; you are like God's farm, God's house.

¹⁰Using the gift God gave me, I laid the foundation of that house like an expert

## dig deeper

### 1 Corinthians 1:26–29

If God had a softball team, you could be on it—even if you couldn't hit or pitch or run the bases. If God ran a student council, you could be treasurer—even if you didn't get good grades in math or weren't very popular. God does have a family—and you can be his child whether or not you come from a good family or live in a nice house or have many friends.

First Corinthians 1:26–29 says, "Look at what you were when God called you. Not many of you were wise in the way the world judges wisdom . . . but God chose . . . what the world thinks is unimportant and what the world looks down on and thinks is nothing in order to destroy what the world thinks is important. God did this so that no one can brag in his presence."

Most people want friends and teammates who are smart, rich, and important. But God doesn't leave anyone out—he cares for the people that others might think are unimportant or not good enough.

You don't ever need to be embarrassed that you don't match up to someone else. Be glad God chose you just the way you are. He wants to show the whole world the incredible things he does for people who love him!

builder. Others are building on that foundation, but all people should be careful how they build on it. [11]The foundation that has already been laid is Jesus Christ, and no one can lay down any other foundation. [12]But if people build on that foundation, using gold, silver, jewels, wood, grass, or straw, [13]their work will be clearly seen, because the Day of Judgment[n] will make it visible. That Day will appear with fire, and the fire will test everyone's work to show what sort of work it was. [14]If the building that has been put on the foundation still stands, the builder will get a reward. [15]But if the building is burned up, the builder will suffer loss. The builder will be saved, but it will be as one who escaped from a fire.

[16]Don't you know that you are God's temple and that God's Spirit lives in you? [17]If anyone destroys God's temple, God will destroy that person, because God's temple is holy and you are that temple.

[18]Do not fool yourselves. If you think you are wise in this world, you should become a fool so that you can become

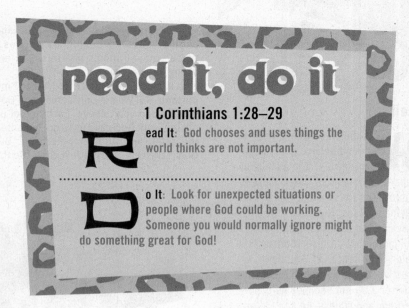

## read it, do it

### 1 Corinthians 1:28–29

**Read It**: God chooses and uses things the world thinks are not important.

**Do It**: Look for unexpected situations or people where God could be working. Someone you would normally ignore might do something great for God!

# Q & A

**Q** Is it okay for a Christian to do dangerous activities like skydiving or mountain climbing?

**A** The Bible doesn't specifically talk about that, so we should use wisdom when choosing our activities. Some people do dangerous sports because they're bored and empty inside and always need a new thrill. A good relationship with God should fill our lives with the excitement we need! But if you simply want to do some of these things for fun or exercise, you should make sure you follow *all* safety rules and not take foolish risks. Remember: our bodies belong to God! (1 Corinthians 3:16–17).

truly wise, [19]because the wisdom of this world is foolishness with God. It is written in the Scriptures, "He catches those who are wise in their own clever traps."[n] [20]It is also written in the Scriptures, "The Lord knows what wise people think. He knows their thoughts are just a puff of wind."[n] [21]So you should not brag about human leaders. All things belong to you: [22]Paul, Apollos, and Peter; the world, life, death, the present, and the future—all these belong to you. [23]And you belong to Christ, and Christ belongs to God.

## Apostles Are Servants of Christ

**4** People should think of us as servants of Christ, the ones God has trusted with his secrets. [2]Now in this way those who are trusted with something valuable must show they are worthy of that trust. [3]As for myself, I do not care if I am judged by you or by any human court. I do not even judge myself. [4]I know of no wrong I have done, but this does not make me right before the Lord. The Lord is the One who judges me. [5]So do not judge before the right time; wait until the Lord comes. He will bring to light things that are now hidden in darkness, and will make known the secret purposes of people's hearts. Then God will praise each one of them.

[6]Brothers and sisters, I have used Apollos and myself as examples so you could learn through us the meaning of the saying, "Follow only what is written in the Scriptures." Then you will not be more proud of one person than another. [7]Who says you are better than others? What do you have that was not given to you? And if it was given to you, why do you brag as if you did not receive it as a gift?

[8]You think you already have everything you need. You think you are rich. You think you have become kings without us. I wish you really were kings so we could be kings together with you. [9]But it seems to me that God has put us apostles in last place, like those sentenced to die. We are like a show for the whole world to see—angels and people. [10]We are fools for Christ's sake, but you are very wise in Christ. We are weak, but you are strong. You receive honor, but we are shamed. [11]Even to this very hour we do not have enough to eat or drink or to wear. We are often beaten, and we have no homes in which to live. [12]We work hard with our own hands for our food. When people curse us, we bless them. When they hurt us, we put up with it. [13]When they tell evil lies about us, we speak nice words about them. Even today, we are treated as though we were the garbage of the world—the filth of the earth.

[14]I am not trying to make you feel ashamed. I am writing this to give you a warning as my own dear children. [15]For though you may have ten thousand teachers in Christ, you do not have many fathers. Through the Good News I became your father in Christ Jesus, [16]so I beg you, please follow my example.

---

**3:13 Day of Judgment** *The day Christ will come to judge all people and take his people home to live with him.* **3:19 "He . . . traps."** *Quotation from Job 5:13.* **3:20 "The Lord . . . wind."** *Quotation from Psalm 94:11.*

## god's promises

### 1 Corinthians 2:2–5

Have you ever been scared of the dark or afraid to get onto a big roller coaster? Everyone has some kind of fear. Usually, we are afraid of something because we don't understand it or because it seems bigger than us. As Christians, we have a very real enemy—the devil, or Satan. Many Christians are afraid of him because he seems so powerful, dangerous, and evil.

Even though the devil does have great strength, you have something even stronger. Because you belong to God, you can have victory over the devil! God has defeated the devil, and his Spirit, who is in you, is greater than anyone, including Satan.

The devil will do everything he can to keep you from having a relationship with Jesus. He will tempt you to sin and send things into your life that could cause you to forget about God. We have a new battle to fight each day, kind of like a spiritual tug-of-war. God wants you to follow him, and the devil wants you to walk away from God. The choice is yours.

Remember, you have God's promise that his power in you is greater than the power of Satan. Pray that God will give you the desire to follow him always!

*Because you belong to God, you can have victory over the devil!*

---

your group. ³I am not there with you in person, but I am with you in spirit. And I have already judged the man who did that sin as if I were really there. ⁴When you meet together in the name of our Lord Jesus, and I meet with you in spirit with the power of our Lord Jesus, ⁵then hand this man over to Satan. So his sinful self[n] will be destroyed, and his spirit will be saved on the day of the Lord.

⁶Your bragging is not good. You know the saying, "Just a little yeast makes the whole batch of dough rise." ⁷Take out all the old yeast so that you will be a new batch of dough without yeast, which you really are. For Christ, our Passover lamb, has been sacrificed. ⁸So let us celebrate this feast, but not with the bread that has the old yeast—the yeast of sin and wickedness. Let us celebrate this feast with the bread that has no yeast—the bread of goodness and truth.

⁹I wrote you in my earlier letter not to associate with those who sin sexually. ¹⁰But I did not mean you should not associate with those of this world who sin sexually, or with the greedy, or robbers, or those who worship idols. To get away from them you would have to leave this world. ¹¹I am writing to tell you that you must not associate with those who call themselves believers in Christ but who sin sexually, or are greedy, or worship idols, or abuse others with words, or get

## Q&A

**Q** Is it wrong to return a sweater I bought after I've already worn it?

**A** If there's something wrong with the sweater, most stores don't mind giving your money back or letting you make an exchange. It's best to ask the store clerk if you can return a used item. If it's okay with them, there's no problem!

---

¹⁷That is why I am sending to you Timothy, my son in the Lord. I love Timothy, and he is faithful. He will help you remember my way of life in Christ Jesus, just as I teach it in all the churches everywhere.

¹⁸Some of you have become proud, thinking that I will not come to you again. ¹⁹But I will come to you very soon if the Lord wishes. Then I will know what the proud ones do, not what they say, ²⁰because the kingdom of God is present not in talk but in power. ²¹Which do you want: that I come to you with punishment or with love and gentleness?

### Wickedness in the Church

**5** It is actually being said that there is sexual sin among you. And it is a kind that does not happen even among people who do not know God. A man there has his father's wife. ²And you are proud! You should have been filled with sadness so that the man who did this should be put out of

5:5 **sinful self** Literally, "flesh." This could also mean his body.

drunk, or cheat people. Do not even eat with people like that.

[12-13] It is not my business to judge those who are not part of the church. God will judge them. But you must judge the people who are part of the church. The Scripture says, "You must get rid of the evil person among you."[n]

## Judging Problems Among Christians

6 When you have something against another Christian, how can you bring yourself to go before judges who are not right with God? Why do you not let God's people decide who is right? [2]Surely you know that

God's people will judge the world. So if you are to judge the world, are you not able to judge small cases as well? [3]You know that in the future we will judge angels, so surely we can judge the ordinary things of this life. [4]If you have ordinary cases that must be judged, are you going to appoint people as judges who mean nothing to the church? [5]I say this to shame you. Surely there is someone among you wise enough to judge a complaint between believers. [6]But now one believer goes to court against another believer— and you do this in front of unbelievers!

[7]The fact that you have lawsuits against each other shows that you are al-

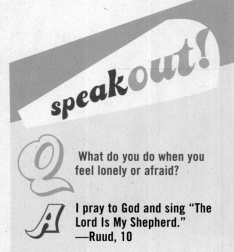

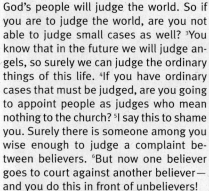

ready defeated. Why not let yourselves be wronged? Why not let yourselves be cheated? [8]But you yourselves do wrong and cheat, and you do this to other believers!

[9-10]Surely you know that the people who do wrong will not inherit God's kingdom. Do not be fooled. Those who sin sexually, worship idols, take part in adultery, those who are male prostitutes, or men who have sexual relations with other men, those who steal, are greedy, get drunk, lie about others, or rob— these people will not inherit God's kingdom. [11]In the past, some of you were like that, but you were washed clean. You were made holy, and you were made right with God in the name of the Lord Jesus Christ and in the Spirit of our God.

## Use Your Bodies for God's Glory

[12]"I am allowed to do all things," but not all things are good for me to do. "I am allowed to do all things," but I will not let anything make me its slave. [13]"Food is for the stomach, and the stomach for food," but God will destroy them both. The body is not for sexual sin but for the Lord, and the Lord is for the body. [14]By his power God has raised the Lord from the dead and will also raise us from the dead. [15]Surely you know that your bodies are parts of Christ himself. So I must never take the parts of Christ and join them to a prostitute! [16]It is written in the Scriptures, "The two will become one

## Shine Your Light

In our technological world, it seems like everyone should know how to use a computer, right? Actually, your grandparents probably never imagined what the invention of computers would do to our world.

When Beverly, a wonderful Christian woman in her eighties, received a new computer as a gift, she had no idea how to get started. So she was pleasantly surprised when her next door neighbor, thirteen-year-old Maria, offered to help!

Maria showed Beverly how to set up her e-mail so she could write to her children and grandchildren. She also explained to her how to open files and look at Web sites. In return, Beverly was always willing to answer Maria's questions about the Bible.

Do you know who your neighbors are? If you have never met them, ask God to show you a way to introduce yourself. Like Maria, you might find a new friend who shares your faith in Jesus! Or you might discover that your neighbors have never heard about Jesus. Maybe you could be the one to share the Good News with them. Ask God to give you the courage to tell others about him!

5:12–13 "You . . . you." *Quotation from Deuteronomy 17:7; 19:19; 22:21, 24; 24:7.*

# June

start here

**17**

**16** Organize all your jewelry and hair accessories. Give away anything you're not using. (Ask your mom first!)

**15**

**18**

**1** Pray for a person of influence: Today is singer Alanis Morissette's birthday.

**2** Think of ways kids who don't have dads can still celebrate Father's Day.

**3**

**19** Ask your youth pastor or Sunday School teacher what spiritual gifts they see in your life. Ask God to help you use them for him.

**27** Read Romans 12:14. Ask God to help you be kind toward someone who treats you badly.

**28**

**20**

**4** Surprise your parents: clean the bathroom, sink and toilet . . . without being asked to!

**14**

**26**

**29**

**13** Pray for a person of influence: Today is twin actresses Mary-Kate and Ashley Olsen's birthday.

**21** Pray for a person of influence: Today is Prince William of Great Britain's birthday.

**5**

**30** Send a postcard to one of your cousins—even if he or she lives in the same city!

**25** Try making a simple dessert tonight.

**12**

**22** Get a world map, randomly pick a country, and then see if you can learn something interesting about it (online or in an encyclopedia).

**6** Think of a hobby or skill you'd like to learn this summer, such as knitting, painting, playing chess, or throwing a football.

**24**

**23**

**11** Write down five things you want to accomplish when you grow up. Think of what it will take to succeed. Start now!

**7** Pray for a person of influence: Today is NBA player Allen Iverson's birthday.

**10** Pray for a person of influence: Today is actor Joey Zimmerman's birthday.

**9**

**8**

Patch, Cody, & Mittens say, "Make a list!"

body."[n] So you should know that anyone who joins with a prostitute becomes one body with the prostitute. [17]But the one who joins with the Lord is one spirit with the Lord.

[18]So run away from sexual sin. Every other sin people do is outside their bodies, but those who sin sexually sin against their own bodies. [19]You should know that your body is a temple for the Holy Spirit who is in you. You have received the Holy Spirit from God. So you do not belong to yourselves, [20]because you were bought by God for a price. So honor God with your bodies.

## About Marriage

**7** Now I will discuss the things you wrote me about. It is good for a man not to have sexual relations with a woman. [2]But because sexual sin is a danger, each man should have his own wife, and each woman should have her own husband. [3]The husband should give his wife all that he owes her as his wife. And the wife should give her husband

# dig deeper

## 1 Corinthians 4:5

Sometimes when you do something wrong, people know right away. For example, your parents told you to come home from your friend's house at seven o'clock, but you're in the middle of a game so you wait until it's finished before leaving. If you get home late, it's pretty obvious to your parents that you disobeyed, isn't it?

But what if you misbehaved in class and your teacher wrote a note for you to take home to your parents? You hide the note to avoid getting in trouble, but a few weeks later, during a parent-teacher interview, your mom finds out anyway. Now you're in bigger trouble!

The Bible says we can't hide our sins. Some are seen right away, some a little while later, and some only when we get to heaven. The same goes for good deeds. We often see kind things that people do, and we feel good about them. But many people do good things without anyone knowing. Maybe your family left a basket of food on the doorstep of a poor family. Or maybe you put your whole week's allowance in the offering at church one Sunday.

You might never get a "thank you" here on earth, but God saw . . . and he will reward you one day!

# Q & A

**Q** Should women be able to speak and teach in church?

**A** First Corinthians 14:34 says, "Women should keep quiet in the church meetings. They are not allowed to speak . . ." The next verse explains that women should wait until they get home to ask their husbands to explain things, instead of interrupting a meeting. But 1 Corinthians 11:5 mentions women praying and prophesying in public. So women can speak or teach at appropriate times, but they must do it with a humble attitude, remembering that God gave the role of spiritual leadership to men (1 Corinthians 11:3).

all that she owes him as her husband. [4]The wife does not have full rights over her own body; her husband shares them. And the husband does not have full rights over his own body; his wife shares them. [5]Do not refuse to give your bodies to each other, unless you both agree to stay away from sexual relations for a time so you can give your time to prayer. Then come together again so Satan cannot tempt you because of a lack of self-control. [6]I say this to give you permission to stay away from sexual relations for a time. It is not a command to do so. [7]I wish that everyone were like me, but each person has his own gift from God. One has one gift, another has another gift.

[8]Now for those who are not married and for the widows I say this: It is good for them to stay unmarried as I am. [9]But if they cannot control themselves, they should marry. It is better to marry than to burn with sexual desire.

6:16 **"The two . . . body."** *Quotation from Genesis 2:24.*

## top ten

### top ten ways to...
### Choose Good Friends

1. Ask God to give you friends.

2. Ask your parents what they think of your friends.

3. Be kind and good. You will attract other good people.

4. Get to know the other kids at your church.

5. Look for tweens who respect God.

6. Avoid people who want you to sin.

7. Look for someone who cares about others.

8. Pay more attention to who they are rather than their looks.

9. Choose people with interesting hobbies.

10. Consider older kids, too!

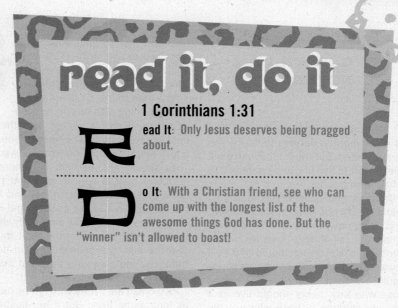

## read it, do it

### 1 Corinthians 1:31

**Read It**: Only Jesus deserves being bragged about.

**Do It**: With a Christian friend, see who can come up with the longest list of the awesome things God has done. But the "winner" isn't allowed to boast!

---

[10] Now I give this command for the married people. (The command is not from me; it is from the Lord.) A wife should not leave her husband. [11] But if she does leave, she must not marry again, or she should make up with her husband. Also the husband should not divorce his wife. [12] For all the others I say this (I am saying this, not the Lord): If a Christian man has a wife who is not a believer, and she is happy to live with him, he must not divorce her. [13] And if a Christian woman has a husband who is not a believer, and he is happy to live with her, she must not divorce him. [14] The husband who is not a believer is made holy through his believing wife. And the wife who is not a believer is made holy through her believing husband. If this were not true, your children would not be clean, but now your children are holy.

[15] But if those who are not believers decide to leave, let them leave. When this happens, the Christian man or woman is free. But God called us[n] to live in peace. [16] Wife, you don't know; maybe you will save your husband. And husband, you don't know; maybe you will save your wife.

### Live as God Called You

[17] But in any case each one of you should continue to live the way God has given you to live—the way you were when God called you. This is a rule I make in all the churches. [18] If a man was already circumcised when he was called, he should not undo his circumcision. If a man was without circumcision when he was called, he should not be circumcised. [19] It is not important if a man is circumcised or not. The important thing is obeying God's commands. [20] Each one of you should stay the way you were when God called you. [21] If you were a slave when God called you, do not let that bother you. But if you can be free, then make good use of your freedom. [22] Those who were slaves when the Lord called them are free persons who belong to the Lord. In the same way, those who were free when they were called are now Christ's slaves. [23] You all were bought at a great price, so do not become slaves of people. [24] Brothers and sisters, each of you should stay as you were when you were called, and stay there with God.

### Questions About Getting Married

[25] Now I write about people who are not married. I have no command from the Lord about this; I give my opinion. But I

> I MAY SPEAK IN DIFFERENT LANGUAGES OF PEOPLE OR EVEN ANGELS. BUT IF I DO NOT HAVE LOVE, I AM ONLY A NOISY BELL OR A CRASHING CYMBAL.

can be trusted, because the Lord has shown me mercy. [26] The present time is a time of trouble, so I think it is good for you to stay the way you are. [27] If you have a wife, do not try to become free from her. If you are not married, do not try to find a wife. [28] But if you decide to marry,

## IF I DO NOT HAVE LOVE, THEN I AM NOTHING.

you have not sinned. And if a girl who has never married decides to marry, she has not sinned. But those who marry will have trouble in this life, and I want you to be free from trouble.

29Brothers and sisters, this is what I mean: We do not have much time left. So starting now, those who have wives should live as if they had no wives. 30Those who are crying should live as if they were not crying. Those who are happy should live as if they were not happy. Those who buy things should live as if they own nothing. 31Those who use the things of the world should live as if they were not using them, because this world in its present form will soon be gone.

32I want you to be free from worry. A man who is not married is busy with the Lord's work, trying to please the Lord. 33But a man who is married is busy with things of the world, trying to please his wife. 34He must think about two things—pleasing his wife and pleasing the Lord. A woman who is not married or a girl who has never married is busy with the Lord's work. She wants to be holy in body and spirit. But a married woman is busy with things of the world, as to how she can please her husband. 35I am saying this to

help you, not to limit you. But I want you to live in the right way, to give yourselves fully to the Lord without concern for other things.

36If a man thinks he is not doing the right thing with the girl he is engaged to, if she is almost past the best age to marry and he feels he should marry her, he should do what he wants. They should get married. It is no sin. 37But if a man is sure in his mind that there is no need for marriage, and has his own desires under control, and has decided not to marry the one to whom he is engaged, he is doing the right thing. 38So the man who marries his girl does right, but the man who does not marry will do better.

39A woman must stay with her husband as long as he lives. But if her husband dies, she is free to marry any man she wants, but she must marry another believer. 40The woman is happier if she does not marry again. This is my opinion, but I believe I also have God's Spirit.

### About Food Offered to Idols

8 Now I will write about meat that is sacrificed to idols. We know that "we all have knowledge." Knowledge puffs you up with pride, but love builds up. 2If you think you know something, you do not yet know anything as you should. 3But if any person loves God, that person is known by God.

4So this is what I say about eating meat sacrificed to idols: We know that an idol

### Looking Ahead

### GETTING INVOLVED IN HIGH SCHOOL

Being on a sports team is just one way to be active in your future high school. There are also clubs for people with interests like chess, dance, reading, or speaking other languages. You can choose to be on the student council, be a cheerleader, or get involved with community service. Being involved with your school will help you feel like you belong and have a special place there. It is also a lot of fun! First Corinthians 7:7 tells us that "each person has his own gift from God." Look for ways to be involved in activities that you are gifted in and enjoy.

is really nothing in the world, and we know there is only one God. 5Even though there are things called gods, in heaven or on earth (and there are many "gods" and "lords"), 6for us there is only one God—our Father. All things came from him, and we live for him. And there is only one Lord—Jesus Christ. All things were made through him, and we also were made through him.

7But not all people know this. Some people are still so used to idols that when they eat meat, they still think of it as being sacrificed to an idol. Because their conscience is weak, when they eat it, they feel guilty. 8But food will not bring us closer to God. Refusing to eat does not make us less pleasing to God, and eating does not make us better in God's sight.

9But be careful that your freedom does not cause those who are weak in faith to fall into sin. 10Suppose one of you who has knowledge eats in an idol's temple.[n] Someone who is weak in faith might see you eating there and be encouraged to eat meat sacrificed to idols while think-

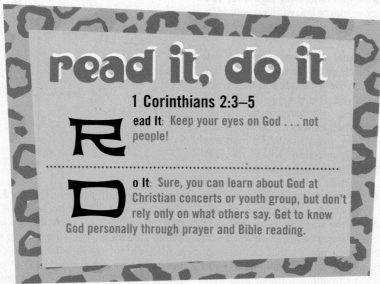

# read it, do it

### 1 Corinthians 2:3–5

**R**ead It: Keep your eyes on God . . . not people!

**D**o It: Sure, you can learn about God at Christian concerts or youth group, but don't rely only on what others say. Get to know God personally through prayer and Bible reading.

8:10 idol's temple Building where a god is worshiped.

## dig deeper

### 1 Corinthians 9:11–12

Can you guess what gives people more stress than almost anything else in life? Yup . . . money! Poor people might worry about how to buy the things they need or about the future. Rich people might worry about protecting their money, or they might want to become richer. People in between being poor and rich might have trouble saving their money because they have just enough to get some of the cool things they want. Very few people feel truly thankful for what they do have. It seems that money can't make people happy!

The apostle Paul had been rich once, but later, as he traveled and spent all his time telling people about Jesus, he became poor and had to depend on God and others for the things he needed. Some churches he started sent monetary gifts to him months, even years later when he was ministering in other cities. Most churches, however, never assisted him financially. That didn't bother him, though.

Paul was also happy to share his secret: feeling satisfied with whatever he had and keeping his heart thankful. Because he could trust God to meet all his needs, Paul didn't have to get stressed about money! And neither do you—when you trust God to meet all your needs.

---

the right to bring a believing wife with us when we travel as do the other apostles and the Lord's brothers and Peter? ⁶Are Barnabas and I the only ones who must work to earn our living? ⁷No soldier ever serves in the army and pays his own salary. No one ever plants a vineyard without eating some of the grapes. No person takes care of a flock without drinking some of the milk.

⁸I do not say this by human authority; God's law also says the same thing. ⁹It is

> LOVE IS PATIENT AND KIND. LOVE IS NOT JEALOUS, IT DOES NOT BRAG, AND IT IS NOT PROUD.

written in the law of Moses: "When an ox is working in the grain, do not cover its mouth to keep it from eating."ⁿ When God said this, was he thinking only about oxen? No. ¹⁰He was really talking about us. Yes, that Scripture was written for us, because it goes on to say: "The one who plows and the one who works in the grain should hope to get some of the

## Q & A

**Q** My parents are Christians, but I don't feel like one. How come?

**A** If your parents are Chinese, then you're Chinese. But having Christian parents doesn't automatically make you a Christian. Remember that you're not just following a religion. Christianity is all about putting *your* trust in Jesus, receiving forgiveness for *your* sins, and then having a *personal* relationship with God. Your parents can't make that decision for you. If you haven't asked Jesus to come into your life, do it today!

---

ing it is wrong to do so. ¹¹This weak believer for whom Christ died is ruined because of your "knowledge." ¹²When you sin against your brothers and sisters in Christ like this and cause them to do what they feel is wrong, you are also sinning against Christ. ¹³So if the food I eat causes them to fall into sin, I will never eat meat again so that I will not cause any of them to sin.

### Paul Is like the Other Apostles

**9** I am a free man. I am an apostle. I have seen Jesus our Lord. You people are all an example of my work in the Lord. ²If others do not accept me as an apostle, surely you do, because you are proof that I am an apostle in the Lord.

³This is the answer I give people who want to judge me: ⁴Do we not have the right to eat and drink? ⁵Do we not have

---

9:9 **"When an ox . . . eating."** *Quotation from Deuteronomy 25:4.*

grain for their work." [11]Since we planted spiritual seed among you, is it too much if we should harvest material things? [12]If others have the right to get something from you, surely we have this right, too. But we do not use it. No, we put up with everything ourselves so that we will not keep anyone from believing the Good News of Christ. [13]Surely you know that those who work at the Temple get their food from the Temple, and those who serve at the altar get part of what is offered at the altar. [14]In the same way, the Lord has commanded that those who tell

## LOVE IS NOT RUDE, IS NOT SELFISH, AND DOES NOT GET UPSET WITH OTHERS.

thing I must do. And how terrible it will be for me if I do not tell the Good News. [17]If I preach because it is my own choice, I have a reward. But if I preach and it is not my choice to do so, I am only doing the duty that was given to me. [18]So what re-

### cool

**61% of kids earn money from babysitting, mowing lawns, and caring for pets.**

—From Children's Business, article on reachadvisor.com "What a Tween Wants . . . Now: Market Research Experts Reveal What's New With This Important Demographic" by Erin E. Clack, April 1, 2004, http://www.reachadvisors.com/childrensbusinessarticle2.html

**did you know?**

the Good News should get their living from this work.

[15]But I have not used any of these rights. And I am not writing this now to get anything from you. I would rather die than to have my reason for bragging taken away. [16]Telling the Good News does not give me any reason for bragging. Telling the Good News is my duty—some-

ward do I get? This is my reward: that when I tell the Good News I can offer it freely. I do not use my full rights in my work of preaching the Good News.

[19]I am free and belong to no one. But I make myself a slave to all people to win as many as I can. [20]To the Jews I became like a Jew to win the Jews. I myself am not ruled by the law. But to those who are ruled by the law I became like a person who is ruled by the law. I did this to win those who are ruled by the law. [21]To those who are without the law I became like a person who is without the law. I did this to win those people who are without the law. (But really, I am not without God's law—I am ruled by Christ's law.) [22]To those who are weak, I became weak so I could win the weak. I have become all things to all people so I could save some of them in any way possible. [23]I do all this because of the Good News and so I can share in its blessings.

[24]You know that in a race all the runners run, but only one gets the prize. So run to win! [25]All those who compete in the games use self-control so they can win a crown. That crown is an earthly thing that lasts only a short time, but our crown will never be destroyed. [26]So I do not run without a goal. I fight like a boxer who is hitting something—not just the air. [27]I treat my body hard and make it my slave so that I myself will not be disqualified after I have preached to others.

### How Many Legs?

**D**on't you just love three-legged races? How would you like to try a thirty-one-legged race? In 2002, students at an elementary school in Japan ran fifty meters (about 164 feet) together in just 8.94 seconds! Every runner in this race became a winner . . . all because of great teamwork. No one tried to run faster than the other. They all had to help each other.

The Christian life is compared to a race, too. But it should never become a competition. We all need each other! Read 1 Corinthians 12:12–27 to learn more about Christian teamwork.

### Warnings from Israel's Past

**10** Brothers and sisters, I want you to know what happened to our ancestors who followed Moses. They were all under the cloud and all went through the sea. [2]They were all baptized as followers of Moses in the cloud and in the sea. [3]They all ate the same spiritual food, [4]and all drank the same spiritual drink. They drank from that spiritual rock that followed them, and that rock was Christ. [5]But God was not pleased with most of them, so they died in the desert.

[6]And these things happened as examples for us, to stop us from wanting evil things as those people did. [7]Do not worship idols, as some of them did. Just as it is written in the Scriptures: "They sat down to eat and drink, and then they got up and sinned sexually."[n] [8]We must not take part in sexual sins, as some of them did. In one day twenty-three thousand of them died because of their sins. [9]We must not test Christ as some of them did; they were killed by snakes. [10]Do not com-

## Q & A

**Q** What is the best way to talk to my friends about Jesus?

**A** Be yourself. Let Jesus become a natural subject in your conversations. If you try to plan it, it doesn't always work. Pray that God will create situations where you can talk about Jesus . . . and give you the courage to speak up! Most of all, remember that actions speak louder than words. Let your friends see the difference Jesus makes in your life. That will make your words more believable.

10:7 "They . . . sexually." Quotation from Exodus 32:6.

# HOW DO YOU RUN?

Read 1 Corinthians 9:24–27,
which compares the
Christian life to a race.
What kind of runner are you?

**1. How often do you read your Bible?**
   a. You forgot where it is, huh?
   b. Whenever someone gives you a verse to look up.
   c. You try to read it regularly but forget or get lazy sometimes.
   d. Every day…and you enjoy it!

**2. When it comes to telling others about Jesus:**
   a. You wouldn't know what to tell them.
   b. Isn't that the pastor's job?
   c. You invite friends to youth group sometimes.
   d. It comes naturally to you because you want your friends to be saved.

**3. When you're tempted to sin:**
   a. You can't help it…you just give in!
   b. Sometimes you feel guilty and don't sin.
   c. You ask God to help you fight the temptation.
   d. You say no right away and get away from the situation.

**4. How much do you love God?**
   a. You think he's kind of nice but don't know much about him.
   b. You go to church every week. Isn't that enough?
   c. You pray every day and try to obey him.
   d. You would do anything for him and tell him that every day!

## What kind of runner are you?

**If you answered mostly As,** you're a couch potato! You're just a spectator…you're not even in the race. If you haven't asked Jesus to be your Savior yet, you can do it today! Remember that only the runners get the prize, which is salvation from our sins and eternal life in heaven!

**If you answered mostly Bs,** you're not moving very much. When you don't make much of an effort, the race can seem really boring and long. Ask God to help you become more enthusiastic about your relationship with him. You've started the race, now pick up some speed!

**If you answered mostly Cs,** you're on the right track. Sometimes being a Christian seems difficult for you, but you're making a real effort. Ask God to help your faith get stronger. Hang in there; it's worth it!

**If you answered mostly Ds,** you're a sprinter! You love the race and nothing is going to stop you! It's wonderful you have a strong relationship with Christ. Just remember to pray for strength every day because you can't run the race alone. Ask God to run with you…and he will!

## god's promises

### 1 Corinthians 10:13

Have you ever been trapped somewhere? Maybe you fell into a ditch and couldn't get out or climbed a tree too high and couldn't find a way down. Or maybe you accidentally locked yourself in a closet! Whatever situations you've been in, you probably know the feeling of not being able to escape. As Christians, we often feel trapped. Every human has struggled with sins such as wanting evil things, complaining, lying, or being selfish.

God knows that you sometimes feel trapped by all the temptations around you. Jesus was tempted while he was on earth (see Matthew 4:1–11), so he knows what it is like to be tempted to do wrong things. But Jesus didn't give in!

The Bible says you can trust God to never let you be tempted more than you can stand. God promises that whenever you're tempted, he will give you a way to escape. No matter what sin you face, there is always a way out. When you are tempted to be mean to your brother or sister, or to disobey your parents, pray and ask God to show you the escape. He promises that it will always be there—you just have to be willing to take it!

*God promises that whenever you're tempted, he will give you a way to escape.*

## LOVE DOES NOT COUNT UP WRONGS THAT HAVE BEEN DONE.

[18]Think about the Israelites: Do not those who eat the sacrifices share in the altar? [19]I do not mean that the food sacrificed to an idol is important. I do not mean that an idol is anything at all. [20]But I say that what is sacrificed to idols is offered to demons, not to God. And I do not want you to share anything with demons. [21]You cannot drink the cup of the Lord and the cup of demons also. You cannot share in the Lord's table and the table of demons. [22]Are we trying to make the Lord jealous? We are not stronger than he is, are we?

### How to Use Christian Freedom

[23]"We are allowed to do all things," but not all things are good for us to do. "We are allowed to do all things," but not all things help others grow stronger. [24]Do not look out only for yourselves. Look out for the good of others also.

[25]Eat any meat that is sold in the meat market. Do not ask questions about it. [26]You may eat it, "because the earth belongs to the Lord, and everything in it."[n] [27]Those who are not believers may invite you to eat with them. If you want to

plain as some of them did; they were killed by the angel that destroys.

[11]The things that happened to those people are examples. They were written down to teach us, because we live in a time when all these things of the past have reached their goal. [12]If you think you are strong, you should be careful not to fall. [13]The only temptation that has come to you is that which everyone has. But you can trust God, who will not permit you to be tempted more than you can stand. But when you are tempted, he will also give you a way to escape so that you will be able to stand it.

[14]So, my dear friends, run away from the worship of idols. [15]I am speaking to you as to reasonable people; judge for yourselves what I say. [16]We give thanks for the cup of blessing,[n] which is a sharing in the blood of Christ. And the bread that we break is a sharing in the body of Christ. [17]Because there is one loaf of bread, we who are many are one body, because we all share that one loaf.

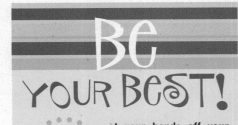

## Be YOUR BEST!

**G**et your hands off your face! Oil and dirt on your freshly washed faced can cause unfriendly pimples. When God forgives you, he washes away your sins. Stay far from tempting sins—and ask for forgiveness right away if you *do* sin—to keep your heart and life pure.

10:16 **cup of blessing** *The cup of the fruit of the vine that Christians thank God for and drink at the Lord's Supper.* 10:26 **"because . . . it"** *Quotation from Psalms 24:1; 50:12; 89:11.*

# cool

## That's the Limit!

Take a piece of paper and fold it as many times as you can. You won't be able to do it more than seven times. Go ahead . . . try it with a larger piece. How about a thinner sheet of paper? It doesn't make any difference; the paper just can't handle another fold!

Sometimes temptation might put that kind of pressure on you. But the Bible promises that no temptation can ever push you past your limit. God "will not permit you to be tempted more than you can stand" (1 Corinthians 10:13).

11 Follow my example, as I follow the example of Christ.

## Being Under Authority

²I praise you because you remember me in everything, and you follow closely the teachings just as I gave them to you. ³But I want you to understand this: The head of every man is Christ, the head of a woman is the man,ⁿ and the head of Christ is God. ⁴Every man who prays or prophesies with his head covered brings shame to his head. ⁵But every woman who prays or prophesies with her head uncovered brings shame to her head. She is the same as a woman who has her head shaved. ⁶If a woman does not cover her head, she should have her hair cut off. But since it is shameful for a woman to cut off her hair or to shave her head, she should cover her head. ⁷But a man should not cover his head, because he is the likeness and glory of God. But woman is man's glory. ⁸Man did not come from woman, but woman came from man.

**'LOVE TAKES NO PLEASURE IN EVIL BUT REJOICES OVER THE TRUTH.**

⁹And man was not made for woman, but woman was made for man. ¹⁰So that is why a woman should have a symbol of authority on her head, because of the angels.

¹¹But in the Lord women are not independent of men, and men are not independent of women. ¹²This is true because woman came from man, but also man is born from woman. But everything comes from God. ¹³Decide this for yourselves: Is it right for a woman to pray to God with her head uncovered? ¹⁴Even nature itself teaches you that wearing long hair is shameful for a man. ¹⁵But long hair is a woman's glory. Long hair is given to her as a covering. ¹⁶Some people may still want to argue about this, but I would add that neither we nor the churches of God have any other practice.

## The Lord's Supper

¹⁷In the things I tell you now I do not praise you, because when you come together you do more harm than good. ¹⁸First, I hear that when you meet together as a church you are divided, and I believe some of this. ¹⁹(It is necessary to have differences among you so that it may be

**did you know?**

13% of middle and high schoolers have a grandparent living in their home.

—Trends & Tudes. Harris Interactive. July 2005.
http://www.harrisinteractive.com/news/newsletters/k12news/HI_Trends&TudesNews2005_v4_iss07.pdf

go, eat anything that is put before you. Do not ask questions about it. ²⁸But if anyone says to you, "That food was offered to idols," do not eat it. Do not eat it because of that person who told you and because eating it might be thought to be wrong. ²⁹I don't mean you think it is wrong, but the other person might. But why, you ask, should my freedom be judged by someone else's conscience? ³⁰If I eat the meal with thankfulness, why am I criticized because of something for which I thank God?

³¹The answer is, if you eat or drink, or if you do anything, do it all for the glory of God. ³²Never do anything that might hurt others—Jews, Greeks, or God's church— ³³just as I, also, try to please everybody in every way. I am not trying to do what is good for me but what is good for most people so they can be saved.

**11:3 the man** This could also mean "her husband."

# read it, do it

## 1 Corinthians 11:27–29

**Read It**: Don't take communion if your heart's not right with God.

**Do It**: Before participating in communion at church, examine your heart. Confess any sins and thank Jesus for giving his life on the Cross.

clear which of you really have God's approval.) [20]When you come together, you are not really eating the Lord's Supper.[n] [21]This is because when you eat, each person eats without waiting for the others. Some people do not get enough to eat, while others have too much to drink. [22]You can eat and drink in your own homes! You seem to think God's church is not important, and you embarrass those who are poor. What should I tell you? Should I praise you? I do not praise you for doing this.

[23]The teaching I gave you is the same teaching I received from the Lord: On the night when the Lord Jesus was handed over to be killed, he took bread [24]and gave thanks for it. Then he broke the bread and said, "This is my body; it is[n] for you. Do this to remember me." [25]In the same way, after they ate, Jesus took the cup. He said, "This cup is the new agreement that is sealed with the blood of my death. When you drink this, do it to remember me." [26]Every time you eat this bread and drink this cup you are telling others about the Lord's death until he comes.

[27]So a person who eats the bread or drinks the cup of the Lord in a way that is not worthy of it will be guilty of sinning against the body and the blood of the Lord. [28]Look into your own hearts before you eat the bread and drink the cup, [29]because all who eat the bread and drink the cup without recognizing the body eat and drink judgment against themselves. [30]That is why many in your group are sick and weak, and some of you have died. [31]But if we judged ourselves in the right way, God would not judge us. [32]But when the Lord judges us, he disciplines us so that we will not be destroyed along with the world.

[33]So my brothers and sisters, when you come together to eat, wait for each other. [34]Anyone who is too hungry should eat at home so that in meeting together you will not bring God's judgment on

yourselves. I will tell you what to do about the other things when I come.

## Gifts from the Holy Spirit

**12** Now, brothers and sisters, I want you to understand about spiritual gifts. [2]You know the way you lived before you were believers. You let yourselves be influenced and led away to worship idols—things that could not speak. [3]So I want you to understand that no one who is speaking with the help of God's Spirit says, "Jesus be cursed." And no one can say, "Jesus is Lord," without the help of the Holy Spirit.

[4]There are different kinds of gifts, but they are all from the same Spirit. [5]There are different ways to serve but the same Lord to serve. [6]And there are different ways that God works through people but the same God. God works in all of us in everything we do. [7]Something from the Spirit can be seen in each person, for the common good. [8]The Spirit gives one person the ability to speak with wisdom, and the same Spirit gives another the ability to speak with knowledge. [9]The same Spirit gives faith to one person. And, to another, that one Spirit gives gifts of healing. [10]The Spirit gives to another person the power to do miracles, to another the ability to prophesy. And he gives to another the ability to know the difference between good and evil spirits. The Spirit gives one person the ability to speak in different kinds of languages[n] and to another the ability to interpret those languages. [11]One Spirit, the same Spirit, does all these things, and the Spirit decides what to give each person.

## The Body of Christ Works Together

[12]A person's body is one thing, but it has many parts. Though there are many parts to a body, all those parts make only one body. Christ is like that also. [13]Some

LOVE PATIENTLY
ACCEPTS ALL THINGS.
IT ALWAYS TRUSTS,
ALWAYS HOPES, AND
ALWAYS ENDURES.

## read it, do it

### 1 Corinthians 12:27

**R**ead It: Christians are connected together because we're connected to Christ.

**D**o It: Try to get along with other Christians you know. Be a team player by helping them whenever you can.

## The Church

**W**hen you think of "the church," you might picture the building where you go on Sundays to learn about God. But "the church" is also another name for *all* of the people who believe in Jesus! Think of it as one big family. Christians might be scattered all over the world, but we all belong to Jesus! Being part of God's family—the church—means we have other people to help us serve God and to teach us about him. Every person in the church has a special job to do, and by working together, we can honor God and share his love with others.

of us are Jews, and some are Greeks. Some of us are slaves, and some are free. But we were all baptized into one body through one Spirit. And we were all made to share in the one Spirit.

¹⁴The human body has many parts. ¹⁵The foot might say, "Because I am not a hand, I am not part of the body." But saying this would not stop the foot from being a part of the body. ¹⁶The ear might say, "Because I am not an eye, I am not part of the body." But saying this would not stop the ear from being a part of the body. ¹⁷If the whole body were an eye, it would not be able to hear. If the whole body were an ear, it would not be able to smell. ¹⁸⁻¹⁹If each part of the body were the same part, there would be no body. But truly God put all the parts, each one of them, in the body as he wanted them. ²⁰So then there are many parts, but only one body.

²¹The eye cannot say to the hand, "I don't need you!" And the head cannot say to the foot, "I don't need you!" ²²No! Those parts of the body that seem to be the weaker are really necessary. ²³And

### LOVE NEVER ENDS.

the parts of the body we think are less deserving are the parts to which we give the most honor. We give special respect to the parts we want to hide. ²⁴The more respectable parts of our body need no special care. But God put the body together and gave more honor to the parts that need it ²⁵so our body would not be divided. God wanted the different parts to care the same for each other. ²⁶If one part of the body suffers, all the other parts suffer with it. Or if one part of our body is honored, all the other parts share its honor.

²⁷Together you are the body of Christ,

and each one of you is a part of that body. ²⁸In the church God has given a place first to apostles, second to prophets, and third to teachers. Then God has given a place to those who do miracles, those who have gifts of healing, those who can help others, those who are able to govern, and those who can speak in different languages.ⁿ ²⁹Not all are apostles. Not all are prophets. Not all are teachers. Not all do miracles. ³⁰Not all have gifts of healing. Not all speak in different languages. Not all interpret those languages. ³¹But you should truly want to have the greater gifts.

**R**achael and Kristin love to sing, so they were very excited when their junior high youth group decided to give a Christmas concert at a local nursing home. Because the people who lived there were not able to attend the events in the city, the group was going to bring Christmas to them!

On the day of the concert, they piled into the church van and rode to the nursing home. They even brought along homemade Christmas cards. The residents smiled and clapped as the kids sang their Christmas carols. Afterward, the kids stopped to shake hands and talk with each person there.

God gave Rachael and Kristin beautiful voices, and they used their talent to praise God and give a special gift to others. Think about your talents. Do you sing or play an instrument? Do you like to bake cookies? Are you really good at encouraging people with your words?

God gave each one of us a special talent that we can use to benefit other Christians. He designed the church to work together just like all the parts of the body (see 1 Corinthians 12:12–27). You have a very special part in the family of God!

12:28 **languages** *This can also be translated "tongues."*

> WHEN I WAS A CHILD, I TALKED LIKE A CHILD, I THOUGHT LIKE A CHILD, I REASONED LIKE A CHILD. WHEN I BECAME A MAN, I STOPPED THOSE CHILDISH WAYS.

## Love Is the Greatest Gift

And now I will show you the best way of all.

**13** I may speak in different languages[n] of people or even angels. But if I do not have love, I am only a noisy bell or a crashing cymbal. [2]I may have the gift of prophecy. I may understand all the secret things of God and have all knowledge, and I may have faith so great I can move mountains. But even with all these things, if I do not have love, then I am nothing. [3]I may give away everything I have, and I may even give my body as an offering to be burned.[n] But I gain nothing if I do not have love.

[4]Love is patient and kind. Love is not jealous, it does not brag, and it is not proud. [5]Love is not rude, is not selfish, and does not get upset with others. Love does not count up wrongs that have been done. [6]Love takes no pleasure in evil but rejoices over the truth. [7]Love patiently accepts all things. It always trusts, always hopes, and always endures.

[8]Love never ends. There are gifts of prophecy, but they will be ended. There are gifts of speaking in different languages, but those gifts will stop. There is the gift of knowledge, but it will come to an end. [9]The reason is that our knowledge and our ability to prophesy are not perfect. [10]But when perfection comes, the things that are not perfect will end. [11]When I was a child, I talked like a child, I thought like a child, I reasoned like a child. When I became a man, I stopped those childish ways. [12]It is the same with us. Now we see a dim reflection, as if we were looking into a mirror, but then we shall see clearly. Now I know only a part, but then I will know fully, as God has

# dig deeper

## 1 Corinthians 13:4—8

Think about how people act when they love someone. If you love your grandma, you'll probably do whatever she asks you to, right? Or if you love your friend, you'll play the games she likes and hang out at her favorite places. When a wife loves her husband, she does things that will make him happy, like cook his favorite meal or say loving things to him. The more you love someone, the easier it is to please them and the harder it is to disobey or dishonor them.

The Bible tells us that if we love God, we must live the way God commanded us to live. What did he command? Live a life of love. Everything about God is love. He loves us. He wants us to love him. And he wants us to love others.

God doesn't ask us to do a lot of complicated things. He asks us to love him so much that we want to do the things that please him. When we love God and love people, we don't feel like sinning. We do the right things—not because we feel forced to, but because we want to. Ask God to help you start living a life of love today.

known me. [13]So these three things continue forever: faith, hope, and love. And the greatest of these is love.

## Desire Spiritual Gifts

**14** You should seek after love, and you should truly want to have the spiritual gifts, especially the gift of prophecy. [2]I will explain why. Those who have the gift of speaking in different languages[n] are not speaking to people; they are speaking to God. No one understands them; they are speaking secret things through the Spirit. [3]But those who prophesy are speaking to people to give them strength, encouragement, and comfort. [4]The ones who speak in different languages are helping only themselves, but those who prophesy are helping the whole church. [5]I wish all of you had the gift of speaking in different kinds of languages, but more, I wish you would prophesy. Those who prophesy are greater than those who can only speak in different languages—

---

13:1; 14:2 **languages** This can also be translated "tongues."    13:3 **give . . . burned** Other Greek copies read "hand over my body in order that I may brag."

# Relationships

When you become a Christian, you become God's child—and every other Christian in the world is your brother or sister in Christ! You won't know them all until you get to heaven, but you experience a smaller version of God's family in your church. When you go to church on Sunday, think about what others need and how you can share the good things that God has been teaching you (Colossians 3:16). Look for ways to help and pray for your church family (Ephesians 6:18). Don't forget to learn from them and let them love you, too!

unless someone is there who can explain what is said so that the whole church can be helped.

⁶Brothers and sisters, will it help you if I come to you speaking in different languages? No! It will help you only if I bring you a new truth or some new knowledge, or prophecy, or teaching. ⁷It is the same as with lifeless things that make sounds—like a flute or a harp. If they do not make clear musical notes, you will not know what is being played. ⁸And in a war, if the trumpet does not give a clear sound, who will prepare for battle? ⁹It is the same with you. Unless you speak clearly with your tongue, no one can understand what you are saying. You will be talking into the air! ¹⁰It may be true that there are all kinds of sounds in the world, and none is without meaning. ¹¹But unless I understand the meaning of what someone says to me, we will be like foreigners to each other. ¹²It is the same with you. Since you want spiritual gifts very much, seek most of all to have the gifts that help the church grow stronger.

¹³The one who has the gift of speaking in a different language should pray for the gift to interpret what is spoken. ¹⁴If I pray in a different language, my spirit is praying, but my mind does nothing. ¹⁵So what should I do? I will pray with my spirit, but I will also pray with my mind. I will sing with my spirit, but I will also sing with my mind. ¹⁶If you praise God with your spirit, those persons there without understanding cannot say amen[n] to your prayer of thanks, because they do not know what you are saying. ¹⁷You may be thanking God in a good way, but the other person is not helped.

¹⁸I thank God that I speak in different kinds of languages more than all of you. ¹⁹But in the church meetings I would rather speak five words I understand in order to teach others than thousands of words in a different language.

> NOW WE SEE A DIM REFLECTION, AS IF WE WERE LOOKING INTO A MIRROR, BUT THEN WE SHALL SEE CLEARLY.

# Bible Basics

The apostle John often calls Jesus Christ "the Word." *Wait a second,* you might think, *isn't that what the* Bible *is called?* You're right! Both Jesus and the Bible are called "the Word." The Bible says that, "the Word became a human and lived among us" (John 1:14). This means that Jesus was another way of God giving his message to the world. Jesus spoke God's words and taught people how to live in a way that pleases God. Just like the Bible, Jesus had an important and true message to bring to humans. Jesus was like the Bible in skin! Every word that he said was God's word—because Jesus is God!

14:16 **amen** *To say amen means to agree with the things that were said.*

## NOW I KNOW ONLY A PART, BUT THEN I WILL KNOW FULLY, AS GOD HAS KNOWN ME.

[20]Brothers and sisters, do not think like children. In evil things be like babies, but in your thinking you should be like adults. [21]It is written in the Scriptures:

"With people who use strange words
and foreign languages
I will speak to these people.
But even then they will not listen to
me,"                                    *Isaiah 28:11–12*
says the Lord.

[22]So the gift of speaking in different kinds of languages is a sign for those who do not believe, not for those who do believe. And prophecy is for people who believe, not for those who do not believe. [23]Suppose the whole church meets together and everyone speaks in different languages. If some people come in who do not understand or do not believe, they will say you are crazy. [24]But suppose everyone is prophesying and some people come in who do not believe or do not understand. If everyone is prophesying, their sin will be shown to them, and they will be judged by all that they hear. [25]The secret things in their hearts will be made known. So they will bow down and worship God saying, "Truly, God is with you."

### Meetings Should Help the Church

[26]So, brothers and sisters, what should you do? When you meet together, one person has a song, and another has a teaching. Another has a new truth from God. Another speaks in a different language,[n] and another person interprets that language. The purpose of all these things should be to help the church grow strong. [27]When you meet together, if anyone speaks in a different language, it should be only two, or not more than three, who speak. They should speak one after the other, and someone should interpret. [28]But if there is no interpreter, then those who speak in a different language should be quiet in the church meeting. They should speak only to themselves and to God.

[29]Only two or three prophets should speak, and the others should judge what they say. [30]If a message from God comes to another person who is sitting, the first speaker should stop. [31]You can all prophesy one after the other. In this way all the people can be taught and encouraged. [32]The spirits of prophets are under the control of the prophets themselves. [33]God is not a God of confusion but a God of peace.

As is true in all the churches of God's people, [34]women should keep quiet in the church meetings. They are not allowed to speak, but they must yield to this rule as the law says. [35]If they want to learn something, they should ask their own husbands at home. It is shameful for a woman to speak in the church meeting. [36]Did God's teaching come from you? Or are you the only ones to whom it has come?

[37]Those who think they are prophets or spiritual persons should understand that what I am writing to you is the Lord's command. [38]Those who ignore this will be ignored by God.[n]

[39]So my brothers and sisters, you should truly want to prophesy. But do not stop people from using the gift of speaking in different kinds of languages. [40]But let everything be done in a right and orderly way.

### The Good News About Christ

**15** Now, brothers and sisters, I want you to remember the Good News I brought to you. You received this Good News and continue strong in it. [2]And you are being saved by it if you continue believing what I told you. If you do not, then you believed for nothing.

[3]I passed on to you what I received, of which this was most important: that Christ died for our sins, as the Scriptures say; [4]that he was buried and was raised to life on the third day as the Scriptures say; [5]and that he was seen by Peter and then by the twelve apostles. [6]After that, Jesus was seen by more than five hundred of the believers at the same time. Most of them are still living today, but some have died. [7]Then he was seen by

## read it, do it

### 1 Corinthians 13:4–7

**R**ead It: True love always puts others first.

**D**o It: Replace each "love" in this passage with your name and read it again. If it's nowhere near a true description of you, ask God to fill your heart with true love!

---

14:26 **language** *This can also be translated "tongue."* 14:38 **Those . . . God.** *Some Greek copies read "Those who are ignorant of this will stay ignorant."*

# Q&A

**Q** How do I deal with people who make fun of me?

**A** Some kids have so many of their own insecurities that they end up making fun of others. Maybe they hope this will make them feel better. It usually doesn't! Depending on your relationship with them, talking it out might not work. Try ignoring the remarks and hang on to positive words others give you. If someone is really hurting you, ask an adult you trust for help. And don't forget to pray for those kids!

James and later by all the apostles. [8]Last of all he was seen by me—as by a person not born at the normal time. [9]All the other apostles are greater than I am. I am not even good enough to be called an apostle, because I persecuted the church of God. [10]But God's grace has made me what I am, and his grace to me was not wasted. I worked harder than all the other apostles. (But it was not I really; it was God's grace that was with me.) [11]So if I preached to you or the other apostles preached to you, we all preach the same thing, and this is what you believed.

## We Will Be Raised from the Dead

[12]Now since we preached that Christ was raised from the dead, why do some of you say that people will not be raised from the dead? [13]If no one is ever raised

SO THESE THREE
THINGS CONTINUE
FOREVER: FAITH,
HOPE, AND LOVE.
AND THE GREATEST
OF THESE
IS LOVE.

from the dead, then Christ has not been raised. [14]And if Christ has not been raised, then our preaching is worth nothing, and your faith is worth nothing. [15]And also, we are guilty of lying about God, because we testified of him that he raised Christ from the dead. But if people are not raised from the dead, then God never raised Christ. [16]If the dead are not raised, Christ has not been raised either. [17]And if Christ has not been raised, then your faith has nothing to it; you are still guilty of your sins. [18]And those in Christ who have already died are lost. [19]If our hope in Christ is for this life only, we should be pitied more than anyone else in the world.

[20]But Christ has truly been raised from the dead—the first one and proof that those who sleep in death will also be raised. [21]Death has come because of what one man did, but the rising from death also comes because of one man. [22]In Adam all of us die. In the same way, in Christ all of us will be made alive again. [23]But everyone will be raised to life in the right order. Christ was first to be raised. When Christ comes again, those who belong to him will be raised to life, [24]and then the end will come. At that time Christ will destroy all rulers, authorities, and powers, and he will hand over the kingdom to God the Father. [25]Christ must rule until he puts all enemies under his control. [26]The last enemy to be destroyed will be death. [27]The Scripture says that God put all things under his control.[n] When it says "all things" are under him, it is clear this does not include God himself. God is the One who put everything under his control. [28]After everything has been put under the Son, then he will put himself under God, who had put all things under him. Then God will be the complete ruler over everything.

[29]If the dead are never raised, what will people do who are being baptized for the dead? If the dead are not raised at all, why are people being baptized for them? [30]And what about us? Why do we put ourselves in danger every hour? [31]I die every day. That is true, brothers and sisters, just as it is true that I brag about you in Christ Jesus our Lord. [32]If I fought wild animals in Ephesus only with human hopes, I have gained nothing. If the dead are not raised, "Let us eat and drink, because tomorrow we will die."[n]

[33]Do not be fooled: "Bad friends will ruin good habits." [34]Come back to your right way of thinking and stop sinning. Some of you do not know God—I say this to shame you.

## What Kind of Body Will We Have?

[35]But someone may ask, "How are the dead raised? What kind of body will they have?" [36]Foolish person! When you sow a seed, it must die in the ground before it can live and grow. [37]And when you sow it, it does not have the same "body" it will have later. What you sow is only a bare seed, maybe wheat or something else. [38]But God gives it a body that he has planned for it, and God gives each kind of seed its own body. [39]All things made of flesh are not the same: People have one kind of flesh, animals have another, birds have another, and fish have another. [40]Also there are heavenly bodies and earthly bodies. But the beauty of the heavenly bodies is one kind, and the

## cool

### Skin-ny Dust

**W**here does it come from? Your mom cleans the room, and a week later you've got another thin layer of whitish dust everywhere! It might surprise you that most dust particles in your house come from dead skin. (Gross!) You lose *billions* of skin cells every day as your body gets rid of dirt and grows new cells.

Those of us who have asked Jesus to forgive and save us from our sins can look forward to an even greater skin change one day. Read 1 Corinthians 15 to learn about the new bodies we'll get in heaven!

**15:27 God put . . . control.** From Psalm 8:6. **15:32 "Let us . . . die."** Quotation from Isaiah 22:13; 56:12.

beauty of the earthly bodies is another. [41]The sun has one kind of beauty, the moon has another beauty, and the stars have another. And each star is different in its beauty.

[42]It is the same with the dead who are raised to life. The body that is "planted" will ruin and decay, but it is raised to a life that cannot be destroyed. [43]When the body is "planted," it is without honor, but it is raised in glory. When the body is "planted," it is weak, but when it is raised, it is powerful. [44]The body that is "planted" is a physical body. When it is raised, it is a spiritual body.

There is a physical body, and there is also a spiritual body. [45]It is written in the Scriptures: "The first man, Adam, became a living person."[n] But the last Adam became a spirit that gives life. [46]The spiritual did not come first, but the physical and then the spiritual. [47]The first man came from the dust of the earth. The second man came from heaven. [48]People who belong to the earth are like the first man of earth. But those people who belong to heaven are like the man of heaven. [49]Just as we were made like the man of earth, so we will[n] also be made like the man of heaven.

[50]I tell you this, brothers and sisters: Flesh and blood cannot have a part in the kingdom of God. Something that will ruin cannot have a part in something that never ruins. [51]But look! I tell you this secret: We will not all sleep in death, but we will all be changed. [52]It will take only a second—as quickly as an eye blinks—when the last trumpet sounds. The trumpet will sound, and those who have died will be raised to live forever, and we will all be changed. [53]This body that can be destroyed must clothe itself with something that can never be destroyed. And this body that dies must clothe itself with something that can never die. [54]So this body that can be destroyed will clothe itself with that which can never be destroyed, and this body that dies will clothe itself with that which can never die. When this happens, this Scripture will be made true:

"Death is destroyed forever in
        victory."                    *Isaiah 25:8*
[55]"Death, where is your victory?
    Death, where is your pain?"
                                    *Hosea 13:14*

## dig deeper

### 1 Corinthians 15:58

Don't you hate it when you work really hard on a project for school or a gift for your friend and it doesn't turn out the way you wanted? What a waste of time and effort! Sometimes serving God might feel like a waste, too. After all, people don't always appreciate when you try to help them, and kindness doesn't always make the mean girl your best friend.

Paul knew that Christians would feel like giving up living for God and doing his work, so he encouraged them to be strong. Paul said, "You know that your work in the Lord is never wasted"

(1 Corinthians 15:58). God always sees when you serve him because you love him. He knows how to use everything you do for him to help others, even if you never know about it in your lifetime. What you do for God *does* make a difference—to people now and in heaven later!

So when you help with the little kids at church or tell your friend about Jesus or buy the less expensive shoes so you can send some money to help kids in other countries—you're doing something good that will last forever. When you get to heaven, you'll see what happened because of it and you won't feel disappointed!

[56]Death's power to hurt is sin, and the power of sin is the law. [57]But we thank God! He gives us the victory through our Lord Jesus Christ.

[58]So my dear brothers and sisters, stand strong. Do not let anything move you. Always give yourselves fully to the work of the Lord, because you know that your work in the Lord is never wasted.

## The Gift for Other Believers

**16** Now I will write about the collection of money for God's people. Do the same thing I told the Galatian churches to do: [2]On the first day of every week, each one of you should put aside money as you have been blessed. Save it up so you will not have to collect money after I come.

**15:45** "The first . . . person." *Quotation from Genesis 2:7.*   **15:49** so we will *Some Greek copies read "so let us."*

240

³When I arrive, I will send whomever you approve to take your gift to Jerusalem. I will send them with letters of introduction, ⁴and if it seems good for me to go also, they will go along with me.

## Paul's Plans

⁵I plan to go through Macedonia, so I will come to you after I go through there. ⁶Perhaps I will stay with you for a time or even all winter. Then you can help me on my trip, wherever I go. ⁷I do not want to see you now just in passing. I hope to stay a longer time with you if the Lord allows it. ⁸But I will stay at Ephesus until Pentecost, ⁹because a good opportunity for a great and growing work has been given to me now. And there are many people working against me.

¹⁰If Timothy comes to you, see to it that he has nothing to fear with you, because he is working for the Lord just as I am.

¹¹So none of you should treat Timothy as unimportant, but help him on his trip in peace so that he can come back to me. I am expecting him to come with the brothers.

¹²Now about our brother Apollos: I strongly encouraged him to visit you with the other brothers. He did not at all want to come now; he will come when he has the opportunity.

## Paul Ends His Letter

¹³Be alert. Continue strong in the faith. Have courage, and be strong. ¹⁴Do everything in love.

¹⁵You know that the family of Stephanas were the first believers in Southern Greece and that they have given themselves to the service of God's people. I ask you, brothers and sisters, ¹⁶to follow the leading of people like these and anyone else who works and serves with them.

¹⁷I am happy that Stephanas, Fortunatus, and Achaicus have come. You are not here, but they have filled your place. ¹⁸They have refreshed my spirit and yours. You should recognize the value of people like these.

¹⁹The churches in Asia send greetings to you. Aquila and Priscilla greet you in the Lord, as does the church that meets in their house. ²⁰All the brothers and sisters here send greetings. Give each other a holy kiss when you meet.

²¹I, Paul, am writing this greeting with my own hand.

²²If anyone does not love the Lord, let him be separated from God—lost forever!

Come, O Lord!

²³The grace of the Lord Jesus be with you.

²⁴My love be with all of you in Christ Jesus.ⁿ

# Christian Girls Around the World

## Angie: *Hungary in the 1940s*

About sixty years ago, Angie lived in the suburbs of Budapest, Hungary. Life was a lot different for preteen girls living then than it is in North America today. Although they had a lot more grown-up responsibilities, in other ways, kids living in Hungary in the 1940s seemed like very young children. Most of the kids got jobs around the age of fifteen, and their money helped the family with expenses.

Angie started working at a younger age than other kids: thirteen. Her father had a very serious sickness, her mother couldn't work because of a handicap, and her younger sister had to go to school. Angie had to work in order for the family to have money. Every day, she left for work at 8:00 A.M. and didn't get home until 6:00 P.M. She didn't have time to play and have fun.

That same year, Angie asked Jesus into her heart. Afterward, she told her pastor she wanted to become a member of the church. This surprised him! Not too many kids her age became Christians and were involved in church.

The government in Hungary at that time was Commu-

nist . . . and against Christianity. This made life difficult for Christians. Angie remembers that, on the same day as a Communist holiday, she went with her family to a church picnic. On the way there, a girl she worked with saw her. When she asked if Angie was going to participate in the Communist activities that day, she said, "No, I'm going to a picnic with my church!"

The next day, the country's largest newspaper had a very mean article about Angie and her friends going to a picnic instead of the Communist activities. Angie had hoped to get a higher position (and more money) at her job soon, but because of the article, she didn't get it.

She knew her workplace had not treated her fairly, but Angie trusted God to take care of her. And he did! Several years later she got married, left Hungary, and moved to another country, where she has always had the freedom and right to be a Christian. Things have changed in Hungary since then. But stories about kids like Angie who trusted God help us have courage to stand up for him, too!

16:24 **My . . . Jesus.** *Some Greek copies add "Amen."*

# 2 CORINTHIANS

**H**as anyone ever spread rumors about you that weren't true? That's what happened to Paul. While he was in Ephesus, some false teachers got involved in the church in Corinth. They made accusations about Paul and taught wrong things about Jesus. Worse yet, the church members (the Corinthians) believed these lies! You can imagine how upset Paul was—the Corinthians had been his friends!

Paul wrote this letter to defend himself and set things straight. Second Corinthians is a very personal letter. Paul writes about himself, his plans, the hard times he's experienced, his goals for himself and for the believers. and about his love for the Corinthians.

This book was probably written later in the same year that Paul wrote his first letter to the Corinthians (see the introduction to 1 Corinthians).

It's like a sequel, but you don't have to read the first book to know what's going on in the second one! In this letter, Paul is responding to people in the church who were attacking his reputation and confusing the Christians. Other highlights from 2 Corinthians include:

→ Heaven: What's ahead for Christians?

→ Human weakness: How can God use imperfect people to serve him?

→ Relationships with non-Christians: What kind of relationship should we have with unbelievers? Read on to find out more!

# PAUL ANSWERS THOSE WHO ACCUSE HIM

## THINGS TO TALK WITH GOD ABOUT . . .

1 From Paul, an apostle of Christ Jesus. I am an apostle because that is what God wanted. Also from Timothy our brother in Christ.

To the church of God in Corinth, and to all of God's people everywhere in Southern Greece:

²Grace and peace to you from God our Father and the Lord Jesus Christ.

**Strong religious faith helps kids resist dangerous temptations like drugs and sex.**
—Sonna, Linda, Ph.D. *The Everything Tween Book.* Avon, Massachusetts: Adams Media Corporation, 2003. p. 240

### did you know?

### Paul Gives Thanks to God

³Praise be to the God and Father of our Lord Jesus Christ. God is the Father who is full of mercy and all comfort. ⁴He comforts us every time we have trouble, so when others have trouble, we can comfort them with the same comfort God gives us. ⁵We share in the many sufferings of Christ. In the same way, much comfort comes to us through Christ. ⁶If we have troubles, it is for your comfort and salvation, and if we have comfort, you also have comfort. This helps you to accept patiently the same sufferings we have. ⁷Our hope for you is strong, knowing that you share in our sufferings and also in the comfort we receive.

⁸Brothers and sisters, we want you to know about the trouble we suffered in Asia. We had great burdens there that were beyond our own strength. We even gave up hope of living. ⁹Truly, in our own hearts we believed we would die. But this happened so we would not trust in ourselves but in God, who raises people from the dead. ¹⁰God saved us from these great dangers of death, and he will continue to save us. We have put our hope in him, and he will save us again. ¹¹And you can help us with your prayers. Then many people will give thanks for us—

that God blessed us because of their many prayers.

### The Change in Paul's Plans

¹²This is what we are proud of, and I can say it with a clear conscience: In everything we have done in the world, and especially with you, we have had an honest[n] and sincere heart from God. We did this by God's grace, not by the kind of wisdom the world has. ¹³⁻¹⁴We write to you only what you can read and understand. And I hope that as you have understood some things about us, you may come to know everything about us. Then you can be proud of us, as we will be proud of you on the day our Lord Jesus Christ comes again.

### cool

### Eternal Glory

**D**id you know that you can see the Great Pyramid of Egypt from the moon? We're not sure *how* the ancient Egyptians built this huge pyramid (with a perfectly square base!) about forty-six hundred years ago. Each stone weighs over two tons. Lots of hard work resulted in something that has lasted for centuries.

When you serve God, remember that it will be worth the hard work in the long run, too! "We have small troubles for a while now, but they are helping us gain an eternal glory that is much greater than the troubles" (2 Corinthians 4:17).

**HE PUT HIS MARK ON US TO SHOW THAT WE ARE HIS, AND HE PUT HIS SPIRIT IN OUR HEARTS TO BE A GUARANTEE FOR ALL HE HAS PROMISED.**

1:12 **honest** *Some Greek copies read "holy."*

WE ARE THE SWEET SMELL OF CHRIST AMONG THOSE WHO ARE BEING SAVED AND AMONG THOSE WHO ARE BEING LOST.

## god's promises

**2 Corinthians 1:20**

When you go shopping, you can often hear young children calling out, "Mom! I need one of these!" or "Mom, I think we should buy this!" A lot of kids keep a wish list of gifts they want to receive for their birthdays or at Christmas. Some women write down shopping lists before they go to buy groceries or fold the corners of pages in catalogs if they see something they like. We all "need" so much stuff, right?

Actually, most of the things we say we need are really just things we *want*. You could pray and pray that God gives something to you, but he might not. He knows whether you really need that T-shirt, CD, game, or purse . . . or whether you're just being greedy.

But when it comes to the things you truly *need,* God is generous. He *loves* to bless his children with whatever they need. Sometimes he gives them things they didn't even realize they needed. Best of all, God keeps every one of his promises to his children. How can you be sure? Because Jesus is God's "Yes!" to everything you need and everything God promises. And he'll make sure it happens! You can't compare blessings from Jesus to anything else in the world!

*Jesus is God's "Yes!" to everything you need and everything God promises!*

---

mark on us to show that we are his, and he put his Spirit in our hearts to be a guarantee for all he has promised.

²³I tell you this, and I ask God to be my witness that this is true: The reason I did not come back to Corinth was to keep you from being punished or hurt. ²⁴We are not trying to control your faith. You are strong in faith. But we are workers with you for your own joy.

**2** So I decided that my next visit to you would not be another one to make you sad. ²If I make you sad, who will make me glad? Only you can make me glad—particularly the person whom I made sad. ³I wrote you a letter for this reason: that when I came to you I would not be made sad by the people who should make me happy. I felt sure of all of you, that you would share my joy. ⁴When I wrote to you before, I was very troubled and unhappy in my heart, and I wrote with many tears. I did not write to make you sad, but to let you know how much I love you.

### Forgive the Sinner

⁵Someone there among you has caused sadness, not to me, but to all of you. I mean he caused sadness to all in some way. (I do not want to make it sound worse than it really is.) ⁶The punishment that most of you gave him is enough for him. ⁷But now you should forgive him and comfort him to keep him from having too much sadness and giving up completely. ⁸So I beg you to show that you love him. ⁹I wrote you to test you and to see if you obey in everything. ¹⁰If you forgive someone, I also forgive him. And what I have forgiven—if I had anything to forgive—I forgave it for you, as if Christ were with me. ¹¹I did this so that Satan would not win anything from us, because we know very well what Satan's plans are.

---

¹⁵I was so sure of all this that I made plans to visit you first so you could be blessed twice. ¹⁶I planned to visit you on my way to Macedonia and again on my way back. I wanted to get help from you for my trip to Judea. ¹⁷Do you think that I made these plans without really meaning it? Or maybe you think I make plans as the world does, so that I say yes, yes and at the same time no, no.

¹⁸But since you can believe God, you can believe that what we tell you is never both yes and no. ¹⁹The Son of God, Jesus Christ, that Silas and Timothy and I preached to you, was not yes and no. In Christ it has always been yes. ²⁰The yes to all of God's promises is in Christ, and through Christ we say yes to the glory of God. ²¹Remember, God is the One who makes you and us strong in Christ. God made us his chosen people. ²²He put his

## ■ Bible Bios — Dorcas (Acts 9:36–43)

Dorcas (or Tabitha in Hebrew) lived in a city called Joppa. People knew her as a kind Christian woman who did many good things for others. One day she became very sick and died. This saddened the people who knew her because they loved Dorcas very much.

They called the apostle Peter, who was in a nearby city, to come and see her. When he arrived, there were widows in her room that were crying and showed him the clothes Dorcas had sewn for others while she was alive. They probably wanted him to know what a wonderful person she was.

Peter sent everyone out of the room, knelt by her bed, prayed, and then told her to get up. And Dorcas got up! The story of Dorcas reminds us that God notices the small kindnesses we do for others.

## Paul's Concern in Troas

¹²When I came to Troas to preach the Good News of Christ, the Lord gave me a good opportunity there. ¹³But I had no peace, because I did not find my brother Titus. So I said good-bye to them at Troas and went to Macedonia.

## Victory Through Christ

¹⁴But thanks be to God, who always leads us as captives in Christ's victory parade. God uses us to spread his knowledge everywhere like a sweet-smelling perfume. ¹⁵Our offering to God is this: We are the sweet smell of Christ among those who are being saved and among those who are being lost. ¹⁶To those who are lost, we are the smell of death that brings death, but to those who are being saved, we are the smell of life that brings life. So who is able to do this work? ¹⁷We do not sell the word of God for a profit as many other people do. But in Christ we speak the truth before God, as messengers of God.

> WE HAVE THIS
> TREASURE FROM
> GOD, BUT WE ARE
> LIKE CLAY JARS THAT
> HOLD THE TREASURE.

## Servants of the New Agreement

3 Are we starting to brag about ourselves again? Do we need letters of introduction to you or from you, like some other people? ²You yourselves are our letter, written on our hearts, known and read by everyone. ³You show that you are a letter from Christ sent through us. This letter is not written with ink but with the Spirit of the living God. It is not written on stone tablets[n] but on human hearts.

⁴We can say this, because through Christ we feel certain before God. ⁵We are not saying that we can do this work ourselves. It is God who makes us able to do all that we do. ⁶He made us able to be servants of a new agreement from himself to his people. This new agreement is not a written law, but it is of the Spirit. The written law brings death, but the Spirit gives life.

⁷The law that brought death was written in words on stone. It came with God's glory, which made Moses' face so bright that the Israelites could not continue to look at it. But that glory later disappeared. ⁸So surely the new way that brings the Spirit has even more glory. ⁹If the law that judged people guilty of sin had glory, surely the new way that makes people right with God has much greater glory. ¹⁰That old law had glory, but it really loses its glory when it is compared to the much greater glory of this new way.

¹¹If that law which disappeared came with glory, then this new way which continues forever has much greater glory.

¹²We have this hope, so we are very bold. ¹³We are not like Moses, who put a covering over his face so the Israelites would not see it. The glory was disappearing, and Moses did not want them to see it end. ¹⁴But their minds were closed, and even today that same covering hides the meaning when they read the old agreement. That covering is taken away only through Christ. ¹⁵Even today, when they read the law of Moses, there is a covering over their minds. ¹⁶But when a person changes and follows the Lord, that covering is taken away. ¹⁷The Lord is the Spirit, and where the Spirit of the Lord is, there is freedom. ¹⁸Our faces, then, are not covered. We all show the Lord's glory, and we are being changed to be like him. This change in us brings ever greater glory, which comes from the Lord, who is the Spirit.

## Preaching the Good News

4 God, with his mercy, gave us this work to do, so we don't give up. ²But we have turned away from secret and shameful ways. We use no trickery, and we do not change the teaching of God. We teach the truth plainly,

## Q&A

**Q** Sometimes I forget to pray. How can I get used to praying during the day?

**A** Start with a prayer! Tell God that you want to pray more but sometimes forget. He will help you. Also, try leaving notes for yourself in different places as reminders: on your mirror, in your notebook, or on your CD player, for example. As you get closer to God because of your prayers, it will become easier and more natural to pray often.

---

3:3 **stone tablets** Meaning the Law of Moses that was written on stone tablets (Exodus 24:12; 25:16).

## GOD RAISED THE LORD JESUS FROM THE DEAD, AND WE KNOW THAT GOD WILL ALSO RAISE US WITH JESUS.

showing everyone who we are. Then they can know in their hearts what kind of people we are in God's sight. [3]If the Good News that we preach is hidden, it is hidden only to those who are lost. [4]The devil who rules this world has blinded the minds of those who do not believe. They cannot see the light of the Good News— the Good News about the glory of Christ, who is exactly like God. [5]We do not preach about ourselves, but we preach that Jesus Christ is Lord and that we are your servants for Jesus. [6]God once said, "Let the light shine out of the darkness!" This is the same God who made his light shine in our hearts by letting us know the glory of God that is in the face of Christ.

### Spiritual Treasure in Clay Jars

[7]We have this treasure from God, but we are like clay jars that hold the treasure. This shows that the great power is from God, not from us. [8]We have troubles all around us, but we are not defeated.

### god's promises
### 2 Corinthians 4:7–9

What happens if you drop a mug? It breaks, right? It's not that durable—fine for drinking hot chocolate, but it doesn't stand up to rough use. That's what we're like. We may think we're strong, but we are really pretty weak. Our bodies, minds, and emotions don't stand up very well to sickness, stress, or attacks from other people.

But nothing is stronger than God. His amazing power made everything we see—and everything we can't see. He gave us life, and he even brought Jesus back from the dead! No human has found a way to escape death, but God defeated it.

Paul tells us in 2 Corinthians 4:7 that we are like fragile little jars that contain God's awesome strength! Isn't that incredible? In verses 8–9, Paul describes some of the difficulties a Christian might experience. But none of these problems can defeat us because we have God's Spirit inside us. He can give us victory in every situation.

If you feel like your problems are just too much for you, that's okay! If you have invited Jesus into your life, you have God's Spirit and his strength inside you. If you haven't, you can do it right now.

***God can give us victory in every situation.***

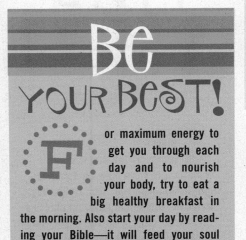

### Be YOUR BEST!

**F**or maximum energy to get you through each day and to nourish your body, try to eat a big healthy breakfast in the morning. Also start your day by reading your Bible—it will feed your soul and help you tap into God's strength and wisdom.

We do not know what to do, but we do not give up the hope of living. [9]We are persecuted, but God does not leave us. We are hurt sometimes, but we are not destroyed. [10]We carry the death of Jesus in our own bodies so that the life of Jesus can also be seen in our bodies. [11]We are alive, but for Jesus we are always in danger of death so that the life of Jesus can be seen in our bodies that die. [12]So death is working in us, but life is working in you.

[13]It is written in the Scriptures, "I believed, so I spoke."[n] Our faith is like this, too. We believe, and so we speak. [14]God raised the Lord Jesus from the dead, and we know that God will also raise us with Jesus. God will bring us together with you, and we will stand before him. [15]All these things are for you. And so the grace of God that is being given to more and more people will bring increasing thanks to God for his glory.

### Living by Faith

[16]So we do not give up. Our physical body is becoming older and weaker, but our spirit inside us is made new every day. [17]We have small troubles for a while

4:13 **"I . . . spoke."** *Quotation from Psalm 116:10.*

2 Corinthians

# Relationships

Alicia wants you to be on the soccer team with her, Danielle expects you to hang out with her every afternoon, and you're pretty sure Sara won't like you if she knows you can't afford to go shopping with her. Trying to please so many people can be exhausting! Of course, God wants you to show kindness and concern for other people. But don't do it just so they'll like you. As Christians, "our only goal is to please God" (2 Corinthians 5:9). He loves you no matter what!

now, but they are helping us gain an eternal glory that is much greater than the troubles. ¹⁸We set our eyes not on what we see but on what we cannot see. What we see will last only a short time, but what we cannot see will last forever. ⁵We know that our body—the tent we live in here on earth—will be destroyed. But when that happens, God will have a house for us. It will not be a house made by human hands; instead, it will be a home in heaven that will last forever. ²But now we groan in this tent. We want God to give us our heavenly home, ³because it will clothe us so we will not be naked. ⁴While we live in this body, we have burdens, and we groan. We do not want to be naked, but we want to be clothed with our heavenly home. Then this body that dies will be fully covered with life. ⁵This is what God made us for, and he has given us the Spirit to be a guarantee for this new life.

⁶So we always have courage. We know that while we live in this body, we are away from the Lord. ⁷We live by what we believe, not by what we can see. ⁸So I say that we have courage. We really want to be away from this body and be at home with the Lord. ⁹Our only goal is to please God whether we live here or there, ¹⁰because we must all stand before Christ to be judged. Each of us will receive what we should get—good or bad—for the things we did in the earthly body.

## Becoming Friends with God

¹¹Since we know what it means to fear the Lord, we try to help people accept the truth about us. God knows what we really are, and I hope that in your hearts you know, too. ¹²We are not trying to prove ourselves to you again, but we are telling you about ourselves so you will be proud of us. Then you will have an answer for those who are proud about things that can be seen rather than what is in the heart. ¹³If we are out of our minds, it is for God. If we have our right minds, it is for you. ¹⁴The love of Christ controls us, because we know that One died for all, so all have died. ¹⁵Christ died for all so that those who live would not continue to live for themselves. He died for them and was raised from the dead so that they would live for him.

¹⁶From this time on we do not think of anyone as the world does. In the past we thought of Christ as the world thinks, but we no longer think of him in that way. ¹⁷If anyone belongs to Christ, there is a new creation. The old things have gone; everything is made new! ¹⁸All this is from God. Through Christ, God made peace between us and himself, and God gave us the work of telling everyone about the peace we can have with him. ¹⁹God was in Christ, making peace between the world and himself. In Christ, God did not hold the world guilty of its sins. And he gave us this message of peace. ²⁰So we have been sent to speak for Christ. It is as if God is calling to you through us. We speak for Christ when we beg you to be at peace with God. ²¹Christ had no sin, but God made him become sin so that in Christ we could become right with God.

⁶We are workers together with God, so we beg you: Do not let the grace that you received from God be for nothing. ²God says,

"At the right time I heard your prayers.
On the day of salvation I helped
you."                    *Isaiah 49:8*

I tell you that the "right time" is now, and the "day of salvation" is now.

³We do not want anyone to find fault with our work, so nothing we do will be a problem for anyone. ⁴But in every way we show we are servants

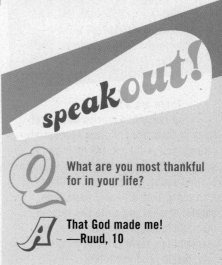

## speakout!

**Q** What are you most thankful for in your life?

**A** That God made me!
—Ruud, 10

of God: in accepting many hard things, in troubles, in difficulties, and in great problems. [5]We are beaten and thrown into prison. We meet those who become upset with us and start riots. We work hard, and sometimes we get no sleep or food. [6]We show we are servants of God by our pure lives, our understanding, patience, and kindness, by the Holy Spirit, by true love, [7]by speaking the truth, and by God's power. We use our right living to defend ourselves against everything. [8]Some people honor us, but others blame us. Some people say evil things about us, but others say good things. Some people say we are liars, but we speak the truth. [9]We are not known, but we are well known. We seem to be dying, but we continue to live. We are punished, but we are not killed. [10]We have much sadness, but we are always rejoicing. We are poor, but we are making many people rich in faith. We have nothing, but really we have everything.

[11]We have spoken freely to you in Corinth and have opened our hearts to you. [12]Our feelings of love for you have not stopped, but you have stopped your feelings of love for us. [13]I speak to you as if you were my children. Do to us as we have done—open your hearts to us.

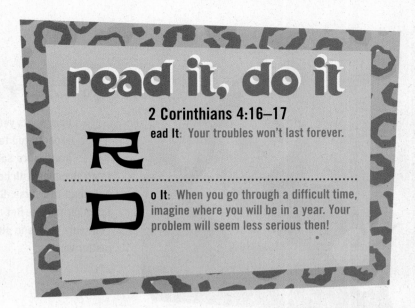

### read it, do it

**2 Corinthians 4:16–17**

**R**ead It: Your troubles won't last forever.

**D**o It: When you go through a difficult time, imagine where you will be in a year. Your problem will seem less serious then!

# Q & A

**Q** Why don't my parents let me go to movies with my friends?

**A** There are a lot of really bad movies out there! Many of them are not given appropriate ratings, so even if you tell them you're going to a PG movie, they can't be sure of what you're going to see. Until you're a bit older, they probably want to be careful of what you go to see without them. Be thankful that they care, and respect their wishes. If you trust them now, they'll trust you later.

## Warning About Non-Christians

[14]You are not the same as those who do not believe. So do not join yourselves to them. Good and bad do not belong together. Light and darkness cannot share together. [15]How can Christ and Belial, the devil, have any agreement? What can a believer have together with a nonbeliever? [16]The temple of God cannot have any agreement with idols, and we are the temple of the living God. As God said: "I will live with them and walk with them. And I will be their God, and they will be my people."[n]

[17]"Leave those people,
    and be separate, says the Lord.
Touch nothing that is unclean,
    and I will accept you."

*Isaiah 52:11; Ezekiel 20:34, 41*

[18]"I will be your father,
    and you will be my sons and
        daughters,
    says the Lord Almighty."

*2 Samuel 7:14*

**7** Dear friends, we have these promises from God, so we should make ourselves pure—free from anything that makes body or soul unclean. We should try to become holy in the way we live, because we respect God.

## Paul's Joy

[2]Open your hearts to us. We have not done wrong to anyone, we have not ruined the faith of anyone, and we have not cheated anyone. [3]I do not say this to blame you. I told you before that we love

you so much we would live or die with you. [4]I feel very sure of you and am very proud of you. You give me much comfort, and in all of our troubles I have great joy.

[5]When we came into Macedonia, we had no rest. We found trouble all around us. We had fighting on the outside and fear on the inside. [6]But God, who comforts those who are troubled, comforted us when Titus came. [7]We were comforted, not only by his coming but also by the comfort you gave him. Titus told us about your wish to see me and that you are very sorry for what you did. He also told me about your great care for me, and when I heard this, I was much happier.

[8]Even if my letter made you sad, I am not sorry I wrote it. At first I was sorry, because it made you sad, but you were sad only for a short time. [9]Now I am happy, not because you were made sad, but because your sorrow made you change your lives. You became sad in the way God wanted you to, so you were not hurt by us in any way. [10]The kind of sorrow God wants makes people change their hearts and lives. This leads to salvation, and you cannot be sorry for that.

> "I WILL BE YOUR FATHER, AND YOU WILL BE MY SONS AND DAUGHTERS, SAYS THE LORD ALMIGHTY."

6:16 **"I . . . people."** *Quotation from Leviticus 26:11–12; Jeremiah 32:38; Ezekiel 37:27.*

## dig deeper

### 2 Corinthians 5:17

No matter how hard we try to be good, we've all done wrong things—things God calls sin. Maybe you said something unkind to a friend, hit your brother when you were angry, stole from a store, or didn't obey your parents. Do you wish you could hit the delete button and start over?

Well, guess what? *We* can't get rid of our sins, but Jesus can! Second Corinthians 5:17 says, "If anyone belongs to Christ, there is a new creation. The old things have gone; everything is made new!"

When we accept Jesus' gift of salvation, he erases all the sin in our lives, all the bad things we've done. He doesn't just cover up our sins—he completely deletes them from our record, like they never happened!

We still have to face the consequences of our behavior, and we will still face temptation to sin. But because we are a "new creation," we can be free from our old, sinful behavior. God gives us the chance to start fresh and do *good* instead of evil! When we belong to Jesus, we are brand new. We become perfect in his eyes!

### Christian Giving

8 And now, brothers and sisters, we want you to know about the grace God gave the churches in Macedonia. [2]They have been tested by great troubles, and they are very poor. But they gave much because of their great joy. [3]I can tell you that they gave as much as they were able and even more than they could afford. No one told them to do it. [4]But they begged and pleaded with us to let them share in this service for God's people. [5]And they gave in a way we did not expect: They first gave themselves to the Lord and to us. This is what God wants. [6]So we asked Titus to help you finish this special work of grace since he is the one who started it. [7]You are rich in everything—in faith, in speaking, in knowledge, in truly wanting to help, and in the love you learned from us.[n] In the same way, be strong also in the grace of giving.

[8]I am not commanding you to give. But I want to see if your love is true by comparing you with others that really want to help. [9]You know the grace of our Lord Jesus Christ. You know that Christ was rich, but for you he became poor so that by his becoming poor you might become rich.

[10]This is what I think you should do: Last year you were the first to want to

# Q & A

**Q** My mom won't let me shave yet, but I have a lot of hair on my legs! What should I do?

But the kind of sorrow the world has brings death. [11]See what this sorrow—the sorrow God wanted you to have—has done to you: It has made you very serious. It made you want to restore yourselves. It made you angry and afraid. It made you want to see me. It made you care. It made you want to do the right thing. In every way you have regained your innocence. [12]I wrote that letter, not because of the one who did the wrong or because of the person who was hurt. I wrote the letter so you could see,

before God, the great care you have for us. [13]That is why we were comforted.

Not only were we very comforted, we were even happier to see that Titus was so happy. All of you made him feel much better. [14]I bragged to Titus about you, and you showed that I was right. Everything we said to you was true, and you have proved that what we bragged about to Titus is true. [15]And his love for you is stronger when he remembers that you were all ready to obey. You welcomed him with respect and fear. [16]I am very happy that I can trust you fully.

**A** Talk with your mom and find out why she doesn't want you to shave your legs. Maybe you can agree on something together. If she still says you have to wait, well . . . you have to wait, because God wants you to obey your mom. Try not to care about the hair, or stick to long skirts, tights, or pants for now. You can still look cool without showing your legs!

8:7 **in . . . us** *Some Greek copies read "in your love for us."*

## dig deeper

### 2 Corinthians 9:7–8

Don't you love it when you find just the right gift for your friend? You wrap it up in the brightest paper and top it with the best bow you can find. When she finally opens it up, she's smiling from ear to ear because she absolutely *loves* it! And you're smiling, too, because you're so happy that she's happy!

When the Bible talks about giving, it's not talking about birthdays or Christmas. You can give to God by sharing money with missionaries who tell people about Jesus. You can also give by helping a neighbor with her yard or babysitting someone's little kids for free.

But God doesn't want you to give because someone else is making you do it. He doesn't want you to give with a pout and a groan. Second Corinthians 9:7 says, "God loves the person who gives happily"—because that's how happy he is when he gives to us. You don't have to have a million dollars to give away to make God smile. When God gives you more than you need (and the Bible says he will!), you'll always have something to share with someone else! And when you have fun doing it, God's smiling, too!

---

give, and you were the first who gave. [11]So now finish the work you started. Then your "doing" will be equal to your "wanting to do." Give from what you have. [12]If you want to give, your gift will be accepted. It will be judged by what you have, not by what you do not have. [13]We do not want you to have troubles while other people are at ease, but we want everything to be equal. [14]At this time you have plenty. What you have can help others who are in need. Then later, when they have plenty, they can help you when you are in need, and all will be equal. [15]As it is written in the Scriptures, "The person who gathered more did not have too much, nor did the person who gathered less have too little."[n]

### Titus and His Companions Help

[16]I thank God because he gave Titus the same love for you that I have. [17]Titus accepted what we asked him to do. He wanted very much to go to you, and this was his own idea. [18]We are sending with him the brother who is praised by all the churches because of his service in preaching the Good News. [19]Also, this brother was chosen by the churches to go with us when we deliver this gift of money. We are doing this service to bring glory to the Lord and to show that we really want to help.

[20]We are being careful so that no one will criticize us for the way we are handling this large gift. [21]We are trying hard to do what the Lord accepts as right and also what people think is right.

[22]Also, we are sending with them our brother, who is always ready to help. He has proved this to us in many ways, and he wants to help even more now, because he has much faith in you. [23]Now about Titus—he is my partner who is working with me to help you. And about the other brothers—they are sent from the churches, and they bring glory to Christ. [24]So show these men the proof of your love and the reason we are proud of you. Then all the churches can see it.

### Help for Fellow Christians

**9** I really do not need to write you about this help for God's people. [2]I know you want to help. I have been bragging about this to the people in Macedonia, telling them that you in Southern Greece have been ready to give since last year. And your desire to give has made most of them ready to give also. [3]But I am sending the brothers to you so that our bragging about you in this will not be empty words. I want you to be ready, as I said you would be. [4]If any of the people from Macedonia come with me and find that you are not ready, we will be ashamed that we were so sure of you. (And you will be ashamed, too!) [5]So I thought I should ask these brothers to go to you before we do. They will finish getting in order the generous gift you promised so it will be ready when we come. And it will be a generous gift—not one that you did not want to give.

[6]Remember this: The person who plants a little will have a small harvest, but the person who plants a lot will have a big

> GOD LOVES THE PERSON WHO GIVES HAPPILY.

---

**8:15 "The person . . . little."** *Quotation from Exodus 16:18.*

2 Corinthians

# Q & A

**Q** After school, I just want to go to sleep forever. I'm sad all the time. Am I depressed?

**A** Maybe . . . or maybe you're not getting enough sleep, vitamins, or exercise. Talk to your mom or the school nurse. When our bodies don't get what they need, we can feel blue. But if changing your diet and schedule doesn't help, get your mom to take you to a doctor. Don't feel ashamed about it. Your body is just sending a signal that something's not right. A doctor can help you! And don't forget to pray for God's help, too.

harvest. ⁷Each of you should give as you have decided in your heart to give. You should not be sad when you give, and you should not give because you feel forced to give. God loves the person who gives happily. ⁸And God can give you more blessings than you need. Then you will always have plenty of everything—enough to give to every good work. ⁹It is written in the Scriptures:

"He gives freely to the poor.
The things he does are right and will
continue forever." *Psalm 112:9*

¹⁰God is the One who gives seed to the farmer and bread for food. He will give you all the seed you need and make it grow so there will be a great harvest from your goodness. ¹¹He will make you rich in every way so that you can always give freely. And your giving through us will cause many to give thanks to God. ¹²This service you do not only helps the needs of God's people, it also brings many more thanks to God. ¹³It is a proof of your faith. Many people will praise God because you obey the Good News of Christ—the gospel you say you believe—and because you freely share with them and with all others. ¹⁴And when they pray, they will wish they could be with you because of the great grace that God has

given you. ¹⁵Thanks be to God for his gift that is too wonderful for words.

## Paul Defends His Ministry

**10** I, Paul, am begging you with the gentleness and the kindness of Christ. Some people say that I am easy on you when I am with you and bold when I am away. ²They think we live in a worldly way, and I plan to be very bold with them when I come. I beg you that when I come I will not need to use that same boldness with you. ³We do live in the world, but we do not fight in the same way the world fights. ⁴We fight with weapons that are different from those the world uses. Our weapons have power from God that can destroy the enemy's strong places. We destroy people's arguments ⁵and every proud thing that raises itself against the knowledge of God. We capture every thought and make it give up and obey Christ. ⁶We are ready to punish anyone there who does not obey, but first we want you to obey fully.

⁷You must look at the facts before you. If you feel sure that you belong to Christ, you must remember that we belong to Christ just as you do. ⁸It is true that we brag freely about the authority the Lord gave us. But this authority is to build you

## Shine Your Light

Do you know when your next meal will be? If you do, then consider yourself more fortunate than much of the world's population! At least one billion people in the world do not get enough to eat every day. They live in remote African villages and in the middle of large American cities—and everywhere in between. Some of them are probably living in your town!

Two preteen girls, Elizabeth and Caitlin, found a way to help with this problem. Along with a group of their friends, they decided to plant a garden in an extra patch of land near their house. They planted rows of tomatoes, green beans, squash, potatoes, and pumpkins.

At the end of the summer, they had grown more than seven hundred pounds of food to donate to their local food bank! The food bank used the fresh vegetables as part of the food baskets they distribute to families who don't have enough to eat.

Do you see a need in your community? You can call your local rescue mission or food bank and ask what they need. Then ask God to show you how you can help. He loves a cheerful giver (2 Corinthians 9:7)!

## Bible Bios — Rhoda (Acts 12:13–16)

Rhoda, possibly around twelve years old, was a servant in the home of Mary, the mother of a missionary named John Mark. King Herod had put Peter in prison for preaching about Jesus, so some Christians met at Mary's house to pray for Peter. Meanwhile, an angel freed him from prison! He ran to Mary's house and knocked on the door.

Rhoda went to the door and, although she was young, she must have been part of the prayer group, because she recognized Peter's voice. She got so excited she ran back to tell everyone . . . but forgot to open the door! The adults thought she was crazy, but she kept insisting it was true. They finally opened the door . . . and there was Peter! Like Rhoda, don't let the doubts of other people stop you from believing what you know is true.

are very willing to accept a spirit or gospel that is different from the Spirit and Good News you received from us.

[5]I do not think that those "great apostles" are any better than I am. [6]I may not be a trained speaker, but I do have knowledge. We have shown this to you clearly in every way.

[7]I preached God's Good News to you without pay. I made myself unimportant to make you important. Do you think that was wrong? [8]I accepted pay from other churches, taking their money so I could serve you. [9]If I needed something when I

> **EVEN SATAN CHANGES HIMSELF TO LOOK LIKE AN ANGEL OF LIGHT.**

up, not to tear you down. So I will not be ashamed. [9]I do not want you to think I am trying to scare you with my letters. [10]Some people say, "Paul's letters are powerful and sound important, but when he is with us, he is weak. And his speaking is nothing." [11]They should know this: We are not there with you now, so we say these things in letters. But when we are there with you, we will show the same authority that we show in our letters.

[12]We do not dare to compare ourselves with those who think they are very important. They use themselves to measure themselves, and they judge themselves by what they themselves are. This shows that they know nothing. [13]But we will not brag about things outside the work that was given us to do. We will limit our bragging to the work that God gave us, and this includes our work with you. [14]We are not bragging too much, as we would be if we had not already come to you. But we have come to you with the Good News of Christ. [15]We limit our bragging to the work that is ours, not what others have done. We hope that as your faith continues to grow, you will help our work to grow much larger. [16]We want to tell the Good News in the areas beyond your city. We do not want to brag about work that has already been done in another person's area. [17]But, "If people want to brag, they should brag only about the Lord."[n] [18]It is not those who say they are good who are accepted but those the Lord thinks are good.

### Paul and the False Apostles

11 I wish you would be patient with me even when I am a little foolish, but you are already doing that. [2]I am jealous over you with a jealousy that comes from God. I promised to give you to Christ, as your only husband. I want to give you as his pure bride. [3]But I am afraid that your minds will be led away from your true and pure following of Christ just as Eve was tricked by the snake with his evil ways. [4]You are very patient with anyone who comes to you and preaches a different Jesus from the one we preached. You

was with you, I did not trouble any of you. The brothers who came from Macedonia gave me all that I needed. I did not allow myself to depend on you in any way, and I will never depend on you. [10]No one in Southern Greece will stop me from bragging about that. I say this with the truth of Christ in me. [11]And why do I not depend on you? Do you think it is because I do not love you? God knows that I love you.

[12]And I will continue doing what I am doing now, because I want to stop those people from having a reason to brag. They would like to say that the work they brag about is the same as ours. [13]Such

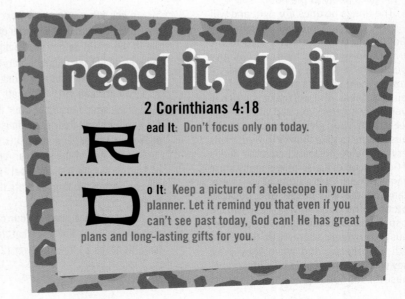

## read it, do it

**2 Corinthians 4:18**

**Read It:** Don't focus only on today.

**Do It:** Keep a picture of a telescope in your planner. Let it remind you that even if you can't see past today, God can! He has great plans and long-lasting gifts for you.

**10:17** **"If . . . Lord."** Quotation from Jeremiah 9:24.

men are not true apostles but are workers who lie. They change themselves to look like apostles of Christ. [14]This does not surprise us. Even Satan changes himself to look like an angel of light.[n] [15]So it does not surprise us if Satan's servants also make themselves look like servants who work for what is right. But in the end they will be punished for what they do.

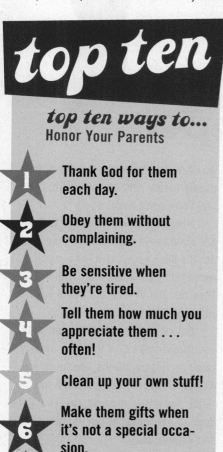

## top ten

### top ten ways to...
### Honor Your Parents

**1** Thank God for them each day.

**2** Obey them without complaining.

**3** Be sensitive when they're tired.

**4** Tell them how much you appreciate them . . . often!

**5** Clean up your own stuff!

**6** Make them gifts when it's not a special occasion.

**7** Speak respectfully to them in front of others.

**8** Speak respectfully about them with others.

**9** Show interest in their jobs or activities.

**10** Don't always ask for things. Instead, ask how you can help.

## Paul Tells About His Sufferings

[16]I tell you again: No one should think I am a fool. But if you think so, accept me as you would accept a fool. Then I can brag a little, too. [17]When I brag because I feel sure of myself, I am not talking as the Lord would talk but as a fool. [18]Many people are bragging about their lives in the world. So I will brag too. [19]You are wise, so you will gladly be patient with fools! [20]You are even patient with those who order you around, or use you, or trick you, or think they are better than you, or hit you in the face. [21]It is shameful to me to say this, but we were too "weak" to do those things to you!

But if anyone else is brave enough to brag, then I also will be brave and brag. (I am talking as a fool.) [22]Are they Hebrews?[n] So am I. Are they Israelites? So am I. Are they from Abraham's family? So am I. [23]Are they serving Christ? I am serving him more. (I am crazy to talk like this.) I have worked much harder than they. I have been in prison more often. I have been hurt more in beatings. I have been near death many times. [24]Five times the Jews have given me their punishment of thirty-nine lashes with a whip. [25]Three different times I was beaten with rods. One time I was almost stoned to death. Three times I was in ships that wrecked, and one of those times I spent a night and a day in the sea. [26]I have gone on many travels and have been in danger from rivers, thieves, my own people, the Jews, and those who are not Jews. I have been in danger in cities, in places where no one lives, and on the sea. And I have been in danger with false Christians. [27]I have done hard and tiring work, and many times I did not sleep. I have been hungry and thirsty, and many times I have been without food. I have been cold and without clothes. [28]Besides all this, there is on me every day the load of my concern for all the churches. [29]I feel weak every time someone is weak, and I feel upset every time someone is led into sin.

[30]If I must brag, I will brag about the things that show I am weak. [31]God knows I am not lying. He is the God and Father of the Lord Jesus Christ, and he is to be praised forever. [32]When I was in Damascus, the governor under King Aretas wanted to arrest me, so he put guards around the city. [33]But my friends lowered me in a basket through a hole in the city wall. So I escaped from the governor.

## A Special Blessing in Paul's Life

**12** I must continue to brag. It will do no good, but I will talk now about visions and revelations[n] from the Lord. [2]I know a man in Christ who was taken up to the third heaven fourteen years ago. I do not know whether the man was in his body or out of his body, but God knows. [3-4]And I know that this man was taken up to paradise.[n] I don't know if he was in his body or away from his body, but God knows. He heard things he is not able to explain, things that no human is allowed to tell. [5]I will brag about a man like that, but I will not brag about myself, except about my weaknesses. [6]But if I wanted to brag about myself, I would not be a fool, because I would be telling the truth. But I will not brag about myself. I do not want people to think more of me than what they see me do or hear me say.

[7]So that I would not become too proud of the wonderful things that were shown to me, a painful physical problem[n] was given to me. This problem was a messenger from Satan, sent to beat me and keep me from being too proud. [8]I begged the Lord three times to take this problem

## Q & A

**Q** What is a tithe?

**A** In the Old Testament, God told his followers to put aside 10 percent of whatever they had to bring to him as an offering and a way of saying "thank you" for blessing them. Many Christians still give a tithe today. Some give much less than 10 percent of their money, and others give much more. God cares most of all that, whatever we give, we give it happily (2 Corinthians 9:7).

---

**11:14 angel of light** *Messenger from God. The devil fools people so that they think he is from God.* **11:22 Hebrews** *A name for the Jews that some Jews were very proud of.* **12:1 revelations** *Revelation is making known a truth that was hidden.* **12:3–4 paradise** *Another word for heaven.* **12:7 painful physical problem** *Literally, "thorn in the flesh."*

## BUT HE SAID TO ME, "MY GRACE IS ENOUGH FOR YOU. WHEN YOU ARE WEAK, MY POWER IS MADE PERFECT IN YOU."

away from me. ⁹But he said to me, "My grace is enough for you. When you are weak, my power is made perfect in you." So I am very happy to brag about my weaknesses. Then Christ's power can live in me. ¹⁰For this reason I am happy when I have weaknesses, insults, hard times, sufferings, and all kinds of troubles for Christ. Because when I am weak, then I am truly strong.

### Paul's Love for the Christians

¹¹I have been talking like a fool, but you made me do it. You are the ones who should say good things about me. I am worth nothing, but those "great apostles" are not worth any more than I am! ¹²When I was with you, I patiently did the things that prove I am an apostle—

# Q&A

**Q** My teacher hugs me a lot and touches me even though I've told him I don't like it and asked him to stop. What should I do?

**A** Tell your parents! Don't feel embarrassed. *His* behavior is wrong. Let your parents talk to the school. Of course, he might say you're lying and then not get in trouble . . . or he might get fired. If he continues teaching, ask to be switched to another class. Whatever happens, make sure you're never around him alone, and don't let him scare you. Don't forget to talk to God about your concerns (1 Peter 5:7).

# dig deeper

### 2 Corinthians 13:11

Pink tops, striped jackets, layered skirts, flip-flops, scarves, running shoes, baggy overalls, snuggly turtlenecks . . . clothes, clothes, clothes! Don't you just love them? Most girls do, whether they're sporty, girly, "retro," or some other style. If you had enough money, your closets and drawers might be overflowing with the latest fashions, right?

There's nothing wrong with wanting to look nice, but sometimes we put too much emphasis on what we wear. In fact, we often end up being wasteful because we buy far more clothes than we need. And, if you think about it, most people hardly notice what you're wearing! Some won't notice at all.

What people *will* notice and remember about you is your character. No wonder the Bible says: "Live in harmony . . . Agree with each other, and live in peace. Then the God of love and peace will be with you" (2 Corinthians 13:11).

Before your outfit can be complete, you should make sure that your heart is ready to forgive anyone who hurts you. And to complete your look, add lots of faith! Tomorrow morning, as you get dressed, remember to put on your *spiritual* clothes, too!

signs, wonders, and miracles. ¹³So you received everything that the other churches have received. Only one thing was different: I was not a burden to you. Forgive me for this!

¹⁴I am now ready to visit you the third time, and I will not be a burden to you. I want nothing from you, except you. Children should not have to save up to give to their parents. Parents should save to give to their children. ¹⁵So I am happy to give everything I have for you, even myself. If I love you more, will you love me less?

¹⁶It is clear I was not a burden to you, but you think I was tricky and lied to catch you. ¹⁷Did I cheat you by using any of the messengers I sent to you? No, you know I did not. ¹⁸I asked Titus to go to you, and I sent our brother with him. Titus did not cheat you, did he? No, you know that Titus and I did the same thing and with the same spirit.

¹⁹Do you think we have been defending ourselves to you all this time? We have

# Relationships

**H**ow important is truth in a relationship? As important as air is for living! Paul told the Ephesians to stop lying and start telling the truth. Why? He said Christians must do this "because we all belong to each other in the same body" (Ephesians 4:25). If we don't tell the truth in our relationships, we are like a bunch of separated body parts. By telling the truth and not lying, our relationships form the complete body of Christ. Little lies may not seem dangerous, but they are enough to tear apart our body. Make sure you only speak truth!

been speaking in Christ and before God. You are our dear friends, and everything we do is to make you stronger. [20]I am afraid that when I come, you will not be what I want you to be, and I will not be what you want me to be. I am afraid that among you there may be arguing, jealousy, anger, selfish fighting, evil talk, gossip, pride, and confusion. [21]I am afraid that when I come to you again, my God will make me ashamed before you. I may be saddened by many of those who have sinned because they have not changed their hearts or turned from their sexual sins and the shameful things they have done.

## Final Warnings and Greetings

**13** I will come to you for the third time. "Every case must be proved by two or three witnesses."[n] [2]When I was with you the second time, I gave a warning to those who had sinned. Now I am away from you, and I give a warning to all the others. When I come to you again, I will not be easy with them. [3]You want proof that Christ is speaking through me. My proof is that he is not weak among you, but he is powerful. [4]It is true that he was weak when he was killed on the cross, but he lives now by God's power. It is true that we are weak in Christ, but for you we will be alive in Christ by God's power.

[5]Look closely at yourselves. Test yourselves to see if you are living in the faith. You know that Jesus Christ is in you—unless you fail the test. [6]But I hope you will see that we ourselves have not failed the test. [7]We pray to God that you will not do anything wrong. It is not important to see that we have passed the test, but it is important that you do what is right, even if it seems we have failed. [8]We cannot do anything against the truth, but only for the truth. [9]We are happy to be weak, if you are strong, and we pray that you will become complete. [10]I am writing this while I am away from you so that when I come I will not have to be harsh in my use of authority. The Lord gave me this authority to build you up, not to tear you down.

[11]Now, brothers and sisters, I say goodbye. Live in harmony. Do what I have asked you to do. Agree with each other, and live in peace. Then the God of love and peace will be with you.

[12]Greet each other with a holy kiss. [13]All of God's holy people send greetings to you.

[14]The grace of the Lord Jesus Christ, the love of God, and the fellowship of the Holy Spirit be with you all.

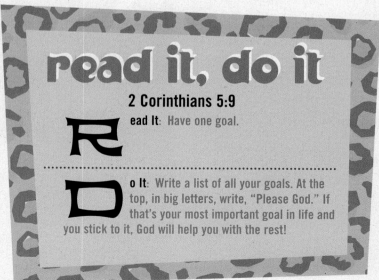

# read it, do it

## 2 Corinthians 5:9

**R**ead It: Have one goal.

**D**o It: Write a list of all your goals. At the top, in big letters, write, "Please God." If that's your most important goal in life and you stick to it, God will help you with the rest!

**13:1** "Every . . . witnesses." *Quotation from Deuteronomy 19:15.*

# GALATIANS

Think of the best gift you've ever received. Did you have to do anything to earn it? Did you have to pay for it? No! A gift is something we get for free. We don't deserve it or earn it. It's ours just because someone loves us and wants us to have it.

The Book of Galatians describes salvation exactly this way—as a free gift from God! But some of the Christians in Galatia (an area in the country of Turkey) tried to teach that people had to believe in Jesus *and* follow the old Jewish laws to be saved. They thought they had to *earn* the right to live in heaven with Jesus forever.

The apostle Paul wrote this letter to remind the Galatians that God gives us salvation as a special gift. Following certain rules or performing certain ceremonies won't make any difference in God's eyes. Nothing we do will make him love us more or less or get us closer to heaven. What's important is having faith in him.

Rules and laws help us understand we have sinned and can't measure up to God's standards. But we can't get to heaven just by following a set of rules. We can live out our faith by showing with our actions that God's love has changed us. The Book of Galatians reminds us that God has given us the best gift ever—the gift of salvation!

# CHRISTIANS ARE SAVED BY GRACE

this evil world we live in, as God the Father planned. [5]The glory belongs to God forever and ever. Amen.

## The Only Good News

[6]God, by his grace through Christ, called you to become his people. So I am amazed that you are turning away so quickly and believing something different than the Good News. [7]Really, there is no other Good News. But some people are confusing you; they want to change the Good News of Christ. [8]We preached to you the Good News. So if we ourselves, or even an angel from heaven, should preach to you something different, we should be judged guilty! [9]I said this before, and now I say it again: You have already accepted the Good News. If anyone is preaching something different to you, let that person be judged guilty!

[10]Do you think I am trying to make people accept me? No, God is the One I am trying to please. Am I trying to please people? If I still wanted to please people, I would not be a servant of Christ.

## Paul's Authority Is from God

[11]Brothers and sisters, I want you to know that the Good News I preached to you was not made up by human beings. [12]I did not get it from humans, nor did anyone teach it to me, but Jesus Christ showed it to me.

[13]You have heard about my past life in the Jewish religion. I attacked the church of God and tried to destroy it. [14]I was becoming a leader in the Jewish religion, doing better than most other Jews of my age. I tried harder than anyone else to follow the teachings handed down by our ancestors.

[15]But God had special plans for me and set me apart for his work even before I was born. He called me through his grace [16]and showed his son to me so that I might tell the Good News about him to those who are not Jewish. When God called me, I did not get advice or help from any person. [17]I did not go to Jerusalem to see those who were apostles before I was. But, without waiting, I went away to Arabia and later went back to Damascus.

[18]After three years I went to Jerusalem to meet Peter and stayed with him for fifteen days. [19]I met no other apostles, except James, the brother of the Lord. [20]God knows that these things I write are not lies. [21]Later, I went to the areas of Syria and Cilicia.

[22]In Judea the churches in Christ had never met me. [23]They had only heard it

54% of preteen girls have their own cell phone.
—Shopping In America Survey, April 2005. "What's in the Bag for Tween Shoppers." www.shoppinginamerica.biz/

**did you know?**

[1]From Paul, an apostle. I was not chosen to be an apostle by human beings, nor was I sent from human beings. I was made an apostle through Jesus Christ and God the Father who raised Jesus from the dead. [2]This letter is also from all those of God's family[n] who are with me.

To the churches in Galatia:[n]

[3]Grace and peace to you from God our Father and the Lord Jesus Christ. [4]Jesus gave himself for our sins to free us from

## cool

### Telephone Poles

The two most common types of trees used for telephone poles are chestnut and pine. Chestnut trees can grow up to one hundred feet! They also support a lot of weight and don't rot easily, making them a great choice for telephone poles. But first the wood needs a special chemical treatment to preserve it.

Just as telephone poles help messages to get sent, God can use *you* to communicate his message to people! Ask him to make you strong, "tall" in your faith, and easy to work with. Don't forget to ask for his protective "preservative," too!

**1:2 those . . . family** *The Greek text says "brothers."*  **1:2 Galatia** *Probably the same country where Paul preached and began churches on his first missionary trip. Read the Book of Acts, chapters 13 and 14.*

said, "This man who was attacking us is now preaching the same faith that he once tried to destroy." [24]And these believers praised God because of me.

## Other Apostles Accepted Paul

2 After fourteen years I went to Jerusalem again, this time with Barnabas. I also took Titus with me. [2]I went because God showed me I should go. I met with the believers there, and in private I told their leaders the Good News that I preach to the non-Jewish people. I did not want my past work and the work I am now doing to be wasted. [3]Titus was with me, but he was not forced to be circumcised, even though he was a Greek. [4]We talked about this problem because some false believers had come into our group secretly. They came in like spies to overturn the freedom we have in Christ Jesus. They wanted to make us slaves. [5]But we did not give in to those false believers for a minute. We wanted the truth of the Good News to continue for you.

[6]Those leaders who seemed to be important did not change the Good News that I preach. (It doesn't matter to me if they were "important" or not. To God everyone is the same.) [7]But these leaders saw that I had been given the work of telling the Good News to those who are not Jewish, just as Peter had the work of telling the Jews. [8]God gave Peter the power to work as an apostle for the Jewish people. But he also gave me the power to work as an apostle for those who are not Jews. [9]James, Peter, and John, who seemed to be the leaders, understood that God had given me this special grace, so they accepted Barnabas and me. They agreed that they would go to the Jewish people and that we should go to those who are not Jewish. [10]The only thing they asked us was to re-

> THIS GOOD NEWS WAS TOLD TO ABRAHAM BEFOREHAND, AS THE SCRIPTURE SAYS: "ALL NATIONS WILL BE BLESSED THROUGH YOU."

## god's promises

Galatians 4:28

In Genesis (the first book of the Bible), we read about a man named Abraham. Abraham loved and obeyed God long before Jesus' time. God promised that Abraham would be the father to many nations, but Abraham was one hundred years old and his wife Sarah was ninety—and they still had no children! They had almost given up hoping. Then an amazing thing happened. God appeared to Abraham and told him that Sarah would have a son!

Abraham and Sarah were so surprised that they each laughed to themselves! But God's promise came true; a year later Sarah had a son. They named him Isaac which means laughter—for good reason!

The Bible says that Isaac was born because of the promise God made to Abraham. The Bible also says that "you are God's children because of his promise"—just like Isaac was. God keeps his promise to make you his child when you believe in him.

Just as God kept his promise and did something impossible for Abraham and Sarah, he can also do unexpected things in our lives. We should be ready for him to do anything—nothing is too hard for the Lord!"

*God keeps his promise to make you his child!*

member to help the poor—something I really wanted to do.

## Paul Shows that Peter Was Wrong

[11]When Peter came to Antioch, I challenged him to his face, because he was wrong. [12]Peter ate with the non-Jewish people until some Jewish people sent from James came to Antioch. When they arrived, Peter stopped eating with those who weren't Jewish, and he separated himself from them. He was afraid of the Jews. [13]So Peter was a hypocrite, as were the other Jewish believers who joined with him. Even Barnabas was influenced by what these Jewish believers did. [14]When I saw they were not following the truth of the Good News, I spoke to Peter in front of them all. I said, "Peter, you are a Jew, but you are not living like a Jew. You are living like those who are not Jewish. So why do you now try to force those who are not Jewish to live like Jews?"

# Be YOUR BEST!

**I**f you want to have an interesting life, you need hobbies and interests other than watching TV or hanging out at the mall. It's the same for your Christianity. It's not enough to just go to church each week. Start *doing* things for God and you will attract people to him!

[15]We were not born as non-Jewish "sinners," but as Jews. [16]Yet we know that a person is made right with God not by following the law, but by trusting in Jesus Christ. So we, too, have put our faith in Christ Jesus, that we might be made right with God because we trusted in Christ. It is not because we followed the law, because no one can be made right with God by following the law.

[17]We Jews came to Christ, trying to be made right with God, and it became clear that we are sinners, too. Does this mean that Christ encourages sin? No! [18]But I would really be wrong to begin teaching again those things that I gave up. [19]It was the law that put me to death, and I died to the law so that I can now live for God. [20]I was put to death on the cross with Christ, and I do not live anymore—it is Christ who lives in me. I still live in my body, but I live by faith in the Son of God who loved me and gave himself to save me. [21]By saying these things I am not going against God's grace. Just the opposite, if the law could make us right with God, then Christ's death would be useless.

## Blessing Comes Through Faith

**3** You people in Galatia were told very clearly about the death of Jesus Christ on the cross. But you were foolish; you let someone trick you. [2]Tell me this one thing: How did you receive the Holy Spirit? Did you receive the Spirit by following the law? No, you received the Spirit because you heard the Good News and believed it. [3]You began your life in Christ by the Spirit. Now are you trying to make it complete by your own power? That is foolish. [4]Were all your experiences wasted? I hope not! [5]Does God give you the Spirit and work miracles among you because you follow the law? No, he does these things because you heard the Good News and believed it.

[6]The Scriptures say the same thing about Abraham: "Abraham believed God, and God accepted Abraham's faith, and that faith made him right with God."[n] [7]So you should know that the true children of Abraham are those who have faith. [8]The Scriptures, telling what would happen in the future, said that God would make the non-Jewish people right through their faith. This Good News was told to Abraham beforehand, as the Scripture says: "All nations will be blessed through you."[n] [9]So all who believe as Abraham believed are blessed just as Abraham was. [10]But those who depend on following the law to make them right are under a curse, because the Scriptures say, "Anyone will be cursed who does not always obey what is written in the Book of the Law."[n] [11]Now it is clear that no one can be made right with God by the law, because the Scriptures say, "Those who are right with God will live by faith."[n] [12]The law is not based on faith. It says, "A person who obeys these things will live because of them."[n] [13]Christ took away the curse the law put on us. He changed places with us and put himself under that curse. It is written in the Scriptures, "Anyone whose body is displayed on a tree[n] is cursed." [14]Christ did this so that God's blessing promised to Abraham might come through Jesus Christ to those who are not Jews. Jesus died so that by our believing we could receive the Spirit that God promised.

## The Law and the Promise

[15]Brothers and sisters, let us think in human terms: Even an agreement made

> ABRAHAM BELIEVED GOD, AND GOD ACCEPTED ABRAHAM'S FAITH, AND THAT FAITH MADE HIM RIGHT WITH GOD.

# BibLe BaSicS

**Y**ou may wonder why the Bible gets so much attention in church and at youth group. It seems like pastors are always saying, "the Bible says. . . ." Why all the fuss over this Book? Aren't there millions of great books out there? The Bible is different because it contains God's words to us. Wow! It's amazing to think that God took the time to communicate important messages and stories because of his deep love for his children. The Bible is unique because it offers what no other book can—a chance to get to know God better and to become more like him as we read his thoughts, written down for us!

---

**3:6** "Abraham . . . God." *Quotation from Genesis 15:6.* **3:8** "All . . . you." *Quotation from Genesis 12:3 and 18:18.* **3:10** "Anyone . . . Law." *Quotation from Deuteronomy 27:26.* **3:11** "Those . . . faith." *Quotation from Habakkuk 2:4.* **3:12** "A person . . . them." *Quotation from Leviticus 18:5.* **3:13** displayed on a tree *Deuteronomy 21:22–23 says that when a person was killed for doing wrong, the body was hung on a tree to show shame. Paul means that the cross of Jesus was like that.*

# dig deeper

### Galatians 5:22–23

What's your favorite fruit? Strawberries? Oranges? Bananas? There are hundreds of different types of fruit in the world; you probably haven't heard of many of them! If you know kids from different cultures, you might get to taste some interesting fruits, such as figs, pomegranates, guavas, or litchis.

Fruit is very important for your body; it contains vitamins and other good things that you need. Fruits also help you recognize trees. For example, you can't get papayas from a cherry tree or pears from a peach tree. If you see apples growing on a tree, you can be sure it's an apple tree!

Did you know that Christians are supposed to grow fruit also? The Bible says that if we have God's Spirit living in us, we will grow a special kind of fruit. This fruit has different flavors! It contains "love, joy, peace, patience, kindness, goodness, faithfulness, gentleness, self-control" (Galatians 5:22–23). When someone sees these things in your life, they should be able to recognize you as a Christian. Pray that as you grow in your relationship with Jesus, people will see the fruit of the Spirit in you.

## WE HAD NO FREEDOM UNTIL GOD SHOWED US THE WAY OF FAITH THAT WAS COMING.

been promised, came. The law was given through angels who used Moses for a mediator[n] to give the law to people. [20]But a mediator is not needed when there is only one side, and God is only one.

### The Purpose of the Law of Moses

[21]Does this mean that the law is against God's promises? Never! That would be true only if the law could make us right with God. But God did not give a law that can bring life. [22]Instead, the Scriptures showed that the whole world is bound by sin. This was so the promise would be given through faith to people who believe in Jesus Christ.

[23]Before this faith came, we were all held prisoners by the law. We had no freedom until God showed us the way of faith that was coming. [24]In other words, the law was our guardian leading us to Christ so that we could be made right

# Q&A

**A** *Don't* bug her about being anorexic. She might just have a small appetite. But *do* ask her, in a caring way, why she eats so little. If she gets upset or doesn't want to talk about it, tell her you love her and don't want her getting sick. Ask a school counselor or your mom for information on where people with anorexia can get help. Give your friend the information and encourage her to talk to someone. Pray for her and, if necessary, ask a trusted adult to help.

between two persons is firm. After that agreement is accepted by both people, no one can stop it or add anything to it. [16]God made promises both to Abraham and to his descendant. God did not say, "and to your descendants." That would mean many people. But God said, "and to your descendant." That means only one person; that person is Christ. [17]This is what I mean: God had an agreement with Abraham and promised to keep it. The law, which came four hundred thirty years later, cannot change that agreement and so destroy God's promise to Abraham. [18]If the law could give us Abraham's blessing, then the promise would not be necessary. But that is not possible, because God freely gave his blessings to Abraham through the promise he had made.

[19]So what was the law for? It was given to show that the wrong things people do are against God's will. And it continued until the special descendant, who had

3:19 **mediator** *A person who helps one person talk to or give something to another person.*

## Get It

### Communion

Communion is a special way for Christians to remember the meaning of Jesus' death on the cross—his promise to forgive all our sins if we believe in him. The bits of bread (or crackers) symbolize Jesus' body, and the wine (or grape juice) reminds us of his blood, which he sacrificed when he took the punishment for *our* sins. At the Last Supper (before he died), Jesus explained communion and said his followers should celebrate communion until he comes again (Matthew 26:26–29). When we take communion, we should remember how much Jesus loves us and thank him for dying for our sins.

came, God sent his Son who was born of a woman and lived under the law. ⁵God did this so he could buy freedom for those who were under the law and so we could become his children.

⁶Since you are God's children, God sent the Spirit of his Son into your hearts, and the Spirit cries out, "Father."ⁿ ⁷So now you are not a slave; you are God's child, and God will give you the blessing he promised, because you are his child.

### Paul's Love for the Christians

⁸In the past you did not know God. You were slaves to gods that were not real. ⁹But now you know the true God. Really, it is God who knows you. So why do you turn back to those weak and useless rules you followed before? Do you want to be slaves to those things again? ¹⁰You still follow

teachings about special days, months, seasons, and years. ¹¹I am afraid for you, that my work for you has been wasted.

¹²Brothers and sisters, I became like you, so I beg you to become like me. You were very good to me before. ¹³You remember that it was because of an illness that I came to you the first time, preaching the Good News. ¹⁴Though my sickness was a trouble for you, you did not hate me or make me leave. But you welcomed me as an angel from God, as if I were Jesus Christ himself! ¹⁵You were very happy then, but where is that joy now? I am ready to testify that you would have taken out your eyes and given them to me if that were possible. ¹⁶Now am I your enemy because I tell you the truth?

## Shine Your Light

with God through faith. ²⁵Now the way of faith has come, and we no longer live under a guardian.

²⁶⁻²⁷You were all baptized into Christ, and so you were all clothed with Christ. This means that you are all children of God through faith in Christ Jesus. ²⁸In Christ, there is no difference between Jew and Greek, slave and free person, male and female. You are all the same in Christ Jesus. ²⁹You belong to Christ, so you are Abraham's descendants. You will inherit all of God's blessings because of the promise God made to Abraham.

**4** I want to tell you this: While those who will inherit their fathers' property are still children, they are no different from slaves. It does not matter that the children own everything. ²While they are children, they must obey those who are chosen to care for them. But when the children reach the age set by their fathers, they are free. ³It is the same for us. We were once like children, slaves to the useless rules of this world. ⁴But when the right time

Have you ever had a great idea for something your youth group could do? Emily put her ideas into action by joining her youth group's planning team.

Each month, Emily and others kids from her group would get together and brainstorm interesting activities. The planning team helped the youth leaders organize unique opportunities. One example is an urban ministry experience. Thanks to Emily's ideas and planning, her group was able to "see" God in surprising places as they walked to well-known spots in their city. At each place, Emily talked about how the Lord was working in the lives of different people. The kids in Emily's youth group caught on to her excitement for seeing God at work.

Like Emily, you probably have ideas for cool activities that no one else has thought of. Your youth group will probably be glad to try your activity! Be bold in sharing these ideas with your youth leader. He or she will be excited to see your enthusiasm and will appreciate the help in planning!

**4:6 "Father"** *Literally, "Abba, Father." Jewish children called their fathers "Abba."*

[17]Those people[n] are working hard to persuade you, but this is not good for you. They want to persuade you to turn against us and follow only them. [18]It is good for people to show interest in you, but only if their purpose is good. This is always true, not just when I am with you. [19]My little children, again I feel the pain of childbirth for you until you truly become like Christ. [20]I wish I could be with you now and could change the way I am talking to you, because I do not know what to think about you.

## The Example of Hagar and Sarah

[21]Some of you still want to be under the law. Tell me, do you know what the law says? [22]The Scriptures say that Abraham had two sons. The mother of one son was a slave woman, and the mother of the other son was a free woman. [23]Abraham's son from the slave woman was born in the normal human way. But the son from the free woman was born because of the promise God made to Abraham.

[24]This story teaches something else: The two women are like the two agreements between God and his people. One

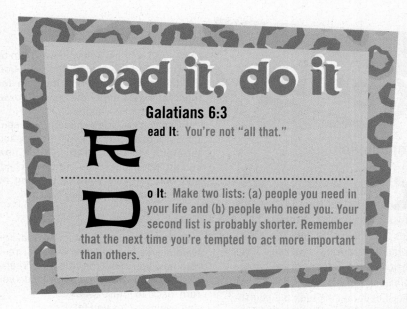

**read it, do it**

**Galatians 6:3**

**R**ead It: You're not "all that."

**D**o It: Make two lists: (a) people you need in your life and (b) people who need you. Your second list is probably shorter. Remember that the next time you're tempted to act more important than others.

agreement is the law that God made on Mount Sinai,[n] and the people who are under this agreement are like slaves. The mother named Hagar is like that agreement. [25]She is like Mount Sinai in Arabia and is a picture of the earthly city of Jerusalem. This city and its people are slaves to the law. [26]But the heavenly Jerusalem, which is above, is like the free woman. She is our mother. [27]It is written in the Scriptures:

> "Be happy, Jerusalem.
> You are like a woman who never gave birth to children.
> Start singing and shout for joy.
> You never felt the pain of giving birth,
> but you will have more children than the woman who has a husband."                *Isaiah 54:1*

[28]My brothers and sisters, you are God's children because of his promise, as Isaac was then. [29]The son who was born in the normal way treated the other son badly. It is the same today. [30]But what does the Scripture say? "Throw out the slave woman and her son. The son of the slave woman should not inherit anything. The son of the free woman should receive it all."[n] [31]So, my brothers and sisters, we are not children of the slave woman, but of the free woman.

## Keep Your Freedom

**5** We have freedom now, because Christ made us free. So stand strong. Do not change and go back into the slavery of the law. [2]Listen, I Paul tell you that if you go back to the law by being circumcised, Christ does you no good. [3]Again, I warn every man: If you allow yourselves to be circumcised, you must follow all the law. [4]If you try to be made right with God through the law, your life with Christ is over—you have left God's grace. [5]But we have the true hope that comes from being made right with God, and by the Spirit we wait eagerly for this hope. [6]When we are in

Christ Jesus, it is not important if we are circumcised or not. The important thing is faith—the kind of faith that works through love.

[7]You were running a good race. Who stopped you from following the true way? [8]This change did not come from the One who chose you. [9]Be careful! "Just a little yeast makes the whole batch of dough rise." [10]But I trust in the Lord that you will not believe those different ideas. Whoever is confusing you with such ideas will be punished.

[11]My brothers and sisters, I do not teach that a man must be circumcised. If I teach circumcision, why am I still being attacked? If I still taught circumcision, my preaching about the cross would not be a problem. [12]I wish the people who are bothering you would castrate[n] themselves!

[13]My brothers and sisters, God called you to be free, but do not use your freedom as an excuse to do what pleases your sinful self. Serve each other with love. [14]The whole law is made complete in this one command: "Love your neigh-

> **61% of girls who play sports play mainly to have fun.**
> —Taylor KidsPulse 2004 Report. Taylor Research & Consulting Group, http://www.thetaylorgroup.com/get_download.cfm

**did you know?**

**BUT WE HAVE THE TRUE HOPE THAT COMES FROM BEING MADE RIGHT WITH GOD, AND BY THE SPIRIT WE WAIT EAGERLY FOR THIS HOPE.**

---

**4:17 Those people** *They are the false teachers who were bothering the believers in Galatia (Galatians 1:7).* **4:24 Mount Sinai** *Mountain in Arabia where God gave his Law to Moses (Exodus 19 and 20).* **4:30 "Throw . . . all."** *Quotation from Genesis 21:10.* **5:12 castrate** *To cut off part of the male sex organ. Paul uses this word because it is similar to "circumcision." Paul wanted to show that he is very upset with the false teachers.*

# cool

## Fun Fruit Facts

**W**hy call it a *grape*fruit when it looks like an orange? Because grapefruits grow in clusters on a tree, just like bunches of grapes! *Pineapples,* which taste nothing like apples, got their name because they look like giant pinecones and they grow on trees (like apples). And "orange" comes from *naranj,* the ancient Indian name for them. Someone must have heard "an orange" instead of the original "a narange"!

Did you know Christians should have spiritual "fruit" in their lives? To learn about this fruit, look up Galatians 5:22–23.

bor as you love yourself."[n] [15]If you go on hurting each other and tearing each other apart, be careful, or you will completely destroy each other.

## The Spirit and Human Nature

[16]So I tell you: Live by following the Spirit. Then you will not do what your sinful selves want. [17]Our sinful selves want what is against the Spirit, and the Spirit wants what is against our sinful selves. The two are against each other, so you cannot do just what you please. [18]But if the Spirit is leading you, you are not under the law.

[19]The wrong things the sinful self does are clear: being sexually unfaithful, not being pure, taking part in sexual sins, [20]worshiping gods, doing witchcraft, hating, making trouble, being jealous, being angry, being selfish, making people angry with each other, causing divisions among people, [21]feeling envy, being drunk, having wild and wasteful parties, and doing other things like these. I warn you now as I warned you before: Those who do these things will not inherit God's kingdom. [22]But the Spirit produces the fruit of love, joy, peace, patience, kindness, goodness, faithfulness, [23]gentleness, self-control. There is no law that says these things are wrong. [24]Those who belong to Christ Jesus have crucified their own sinful selves. They have given up their old selfish feelings and the evil things they wanted to do. [25]We get our new life from the Spirit, so we should follow the Spirit. [26]We must not be proud or make trouble with each other or be jealous of each other.

## Help Each Other

**6** Brothers and sisters, if someone in your group does something wrong, you who are spiritual should go to that person and gently help make him right again. But be careful, because you might be tempted to sin, too. [2]By helping each other with your troubles, you truly obey the law of Christ. [3]If anyone thinks he is important when he really is not, he is only fooling himself. [4]Each person should judge his own actions and not compare himself with others. Then he can be proud for what he himself has done. [5]Each person must be responsible for himself.

[6]Anyone who is learning the teaching of God should share all the good things he has with his teacher.

## Life Is like Planting a Field

[7]Do not be fooled: You cannot cheat God. People harvest only what they plant. [8]If they plant to satisfy their sinful selves, their sinful selves will bring them ruin. But if they plant to please the Spirit, they will receive eternal life from the Spirit. [9]We must not become tired of doing good. We will receive our harvest of eternal life at the right time if we do not give up. [10]When we have the opportunity to help anyone, we should do it. But we should give special attention to those who are in the family of believers.

## Paul Ends His Letter

[11]See what large letters I use to write this myself. [12]Some people are trying to force you to be circumcised so the Jews will accept them. They are afraid they will be attacked if they follow only the cross of Christ.[n] [13]Those who are circumcised do not obey the law themselves, but they want you to be circumcised so they can brag about what they forced you to do. [14]I hope I will never brag about things like that. The cross of our Lord Jesus Christ is my only reason for bragging. Through the cross of Jesus my world was crucified, and I died to the world. [15]It is not important if a man is circumcised or uncircumcised. The important thing is being the new people God has made. [16]Peace and mercy to those who follow this rule—and to all of God's people.

[17]So do not give me any more trouble. I have scars on my body that show[n] I belong to Christ Jesus.

[18]My brothers and sisters, the grace of our Lord Jesus Christ be with your spirit. Amen.

> BUT THE SPIRIT PRODUCES THE FRUIT OF LOVE, JOY, PEACE, PATIENCE, KINDNESS, GOODNESS, FAITHFULNESS, GENTLENESS, SELF-CONTROL.

# Q & A

**Q** Why doesn't God answer our prayers right away?

**A** God does answer our prayers right away . . . but that doesn't mean he always says yes to what you ask for. Sometimes God says no, which is why it seems like nothing's happening. Other times he just wants us to wait for the right time for something to happen. Or he could be working in the background and you just don't see it yet. Keep praying! God loves you and always knows the best way to answer your prayers. You need to patiently trust him.

**5:14** "**Love . . . yourself.**" *Quotation from Leviticus 19:18.* **6:12 cross of Christ** *Paul uses the cross as a picture of the Good News, the story of Christ's death and rising from the dead to pay for our sins. The cross, or Christ's death, was God's way to save us.* **6:17 that show** *Many times Paul was beaten and whipped by people who were against him because he was teaching about Christ. The scars were from these beatings.*

# EPHESIANS

**W**hat can you see from the top of a mountain or the roof of a tall skyscraper? Everything, right? You see the big picture of how different parts of the world all fit together. The Book of Ephesians gives us a big picture, too. It shows us why it's special to be a Christian and tells us what we should do to make God special in our lives.

Paul wrote this letter to Christians in the city of Ephesus. He wanted to encourage them to keep serving God and loving each other. First, Paul reminded the Ephesians of all the ways God blesses those who believe in him. God made a way for *everyone* to receive salvation through his Son, Jesus Christ. Then, Paul told the Ephesians what

they could do to thank God for all his blessings.

Everyone who believes in God belongs to God's family, and we each have a special job to love and help each other, working together to serve God. When we get along with other Christians, it's like thanking God for everything he's done for us!

God gives us unique tools to help us obey him. Ephesians 6:10–18 talks about the armor of God. God gives his followers "spiritual armor" and "weapons" to fight temptation and sin.

If you're excited to learn about God's love for you and how you can show your love for him, then start reading! The Book of Ephesians has a lot to say to *you!*

# GOD UNITES HIS PEOPLE

THINGS TO TALK WITH
GOD ABOUT . . .

1 From Paul, an apostle of Christ Jesus. I am an apostle because that is what God wanted.

To God's holy people living in Ephesus,[n] believers in Christ Jesus:

²Grace and peace to you from God our Father and the Lord Jesus Christ.

## Spiritual Blessings in Christ

³Praise be to the God and Father of our Lord Jesus Christ. In Christ, God has given us every spiritual blessing in the heavenly world. ⁴That is, in Christ, he chose us before the world was made so that we would be his holy people—people without blame before him. ⁵Because of his love, God had already decided to

**64% of kids dream of being rich.**

—Lindstrom, Martin. *BRANDchild: Remarkable insights into the minds of today's global kids and their relationships with brands.* London: Kogan Page Limited, 2003. p. 27

**did you know?**

make us his own children through Jesus Christ. That was what he wanted and what pleased him, ⁶and it brings praise to God because of his wonderful grace. God gave that grace to us freely, in Christ, the One he loves. ⁷In Christ we are set free by the blood of his death, and so we have forgiveness of sins. How rich is God's grace, ⁸which he has given to us so fully and freely. God, with full wisdom and understanding, ⁹let us know his secret purpose. This was what God wanted, and he planned to do it through Christ. ¹⁰His goal was to carry out his plan, when the right time came, that all things in heaven and on earth would be joined together in Christ as the head.

¹¹In Christ we were chosen to be God's people, because from the very beginning God had decided this in keeping with his plan. And he is the One who makes everything agree with what he decides and wants. ¹²We are the first people who hoped in Christ, and we were chosen so that we would bring praise to God's

glory. ¹³So it is with you. When you heard the true teaching—the Good News about your salvation—you believed in Christ. And in Christ, God put his special mark of ownership on you by giving you the Holy Spirit that he had promised. ¹⁴That Holy Spirit is the guarantee that we will receive what God promised for his people until God gives full freedom to those who are his—to bring praise to God's glory.

## Paul's Prayer

¹⁵That is why since I heard about your faith in the Lord Jesus and your love for all God's people, ¹⁶I have not stopped giving thanks to God for you. I always remember you in my prayers, ¹⁷asking the God of our Lord Jesus Christ, the glorious Father, to give you a spirit of wisdom and revelation so that you will know him better. ¹⁸I pray also that you will have greater understanding in your heart so you will know the hope to which he has called us and that you will know how rich and glorious are the blessings God has promised his holy people. ¹⁹And you will know that God's power is very great for us who

# BE YOUR BEST!

**W**hen you're dirty and sweaty, perfume won't help for long. Until you take a shower, you're going to stink! It's the same with sin. You can try to cover it up, but it's going to reek. Instead of hiding your sin, ask God to wash it away with his forgiveness.

I ALWAYS
REMEMBER YOU IN
MY PRAYERS. . . .

**1:1 in Ephesus** *Some Greek copies do not have this phrase.*

believe. That power is the same as the great strength [20]God used to raise Christ from the dead and put him at his right side in the heavenly world. [21]God has put Christ over all rulers, authorities, powers, and kings, not only in this world but also in the next. [22]God put everything under his power and made him the head over everything for the church, [23]which is Christ's body. The church is filled with Christ, and Christ fills everything in every way.

## We Now Have Life

2 In the past you were spiritually dead because of your sins and the things you did against God. [2]Yes, in the past you lived the way the world lives, following the ruler of the evil powers that are above the earth. That same spirit is now working in those who refuse to obey God. [3]In the past all of us lived like them, trying to please our sinful selves and doing all the things our bodies and minds wanted. We should have suffered God's anger because we were sinful by nature. We were the same as all other people.

# Q & A

**Q** Kids make fun of me because I'm chubby. How can I make them stop?

**A** You probably can't change how people behave toward you, but you do have a choice about how you're going to react. *Do* remember God designed you just right. King David said, "I praise you because you made me in an amazing and wonderful way" (Psalm 139:14)—and that's true of you, too! *Don't* feel ashamed of your looks. *Do* get some exercise and eat carefully (God wants us to take care of our bodies). *Don't* do anything drastic, like starve yourself, to get other kids to like you more.

# dig deeper

## Ephesians 2:4–10

You can try your best to always obey your parents, be nice to your sister, not gossip, read your Bible, and pray every day . . . and still not feel good enough. That's because obeying all the rules is not what makes anybody a good Christian. A "good Christian" is someone who has Jesus Christ living inside.

There's nothing you can do to make yourself good enough for God—Jesus Christ already did everything when he died for you. Because of his death and resurrection, it's just like you died and became a new person. God "gave us new life with Christ" (Ephesians 2:5). What marvelous grace and mercy!

Remember, it's not *you* working hard for God so he will love you. From now on, trust *Jesus* to live in you. He will help you love God and give you the power to do good works that please him.

Ephesians 2:8–9 says it best: "You have been saved by grace through believing. You did not save yourselves; it was a gift from God. It was not the result of your own efforts, so you cannot brag about it."

We wouldn't need Jesus if we could be good enough on our own. But we do need him! It will always be Jesus who makes us right with God—more than good enough!

[4]But God's mercy is great, and he loved us very much. [5]Though we were spiritually dead because of the things we did against God, he gave us new life with Christ. You have been saved by God's grace. [6]And he raised us up with Christ and gave us a seat with him in the heavens. He did this for those in Christ Jesus [7]so that for all future time he could show the very great riches of his grace by being kind to us in Christ Jesus. [8]I mean that you have been saved by grace through believing. You did not save yourselves; it was a gift from God. [9]It was not the result of your own efforts, so you cannot brag about it. [10]God has made us what we are. In Christ Jesus, God made us to do good works, which God planned in advance for us to live our lives doing.

## One in Christ

[11]You were not born Jewish. You are the people the Jews call "uncircumcised."[n] Those who call you "uncircumcised" call themselves "circumcised." (Their circumcision is only something they themselves do on their bodies.) [12]Remember that in the past you were without Christ. You were not citizens of Israel, and you had no part in the agreements[n] with the promise that God made to his people. You had no hope, and you did not know God. [13]But now in Christ Jesus, you who were far away from God are brought near through the blood of Christ's death. [14]Christ himself is our peace. He made both Jewish people and those who are not Jews one people. They were separated as if there were a wall between them, but Christ broke down that wall of hate by giving his own body. [15]The Jewish law had many commands and rules, but Christ ended that law. His purpose was to make the two groups of people become one new people in him and in this way make peace. [16]It was also Christ's purpose to end the hatred between the two groups, to make them into one body, and to bring them back to God. Christ did all this with his death on the cross. [17]Christ came and preached peace to you who were far away from God, and to those who were near to God. [18]Yes, it is through Christ we all have the right to come to the Father in one Spirit.

[19]Now you who are not Jewish are not foreigners or strangers any longer, but are citizens together with God's holy people. You belong to God's family. [20]You are like a building that was built on the foundation of the apostles and prophets. Christ Jesus himself is the most important stone[n] in that building, [21]and that whole building is joined together in Christ. He makes it grow and become a holy temple in the Lord. [22]And in Christ you, too, are being built together with the Jews into a place where God lives through the Spirit.

## Paul's Work in Telling the Good News

**3** So I, Paul, am a prisoner of Christ Jesus for you who are not Jews. [2]Surely you have heard that God gave me this work to tell you about his grace. [3]He let me know his secret by showing it to me. I have already written a little about this. [4]If you read what I wrote then, you can see that I truly understand the secret about the Christ. [5]People who lived in other times were not told that secret. But now, through the Spirit, God has shown that secret to his holy apostles and prophets. [6]This is that secret: that through the Good News those who are not Jews will share with the Jews in God's blessing. They belong to the same body, and they share

IN CHRIST JESUS, GOD MADE US TO DO GOOD WORKS, WHICH GOD PLANNED IN ADVANCE FOR US TO LIVE OUR LIVES DOING.

## god's promises

Ephesians 3:12

Have you ever worried that something will keep you from being able to know God and talk to him? Do you worry about being good, smart, or spiritual enough to please him? What other fears do you have?

In Ephesians 3:12, Paul says that with faith in Christ, we are completely free to have a relationship with God—without any fear to hold us back. What does this promise from God mean for your life? It means that no matter what happens, you don't have to worry that God won't want you with him. Never!

Just think—if we have faith in Christ, we can go to God at any time, knowing that he will gladly welcome us. We don't have to be afraid that we aren't good enough or that he will be too busy to care for us. We don't have to be afraid of *anything!*

If you don't have any fears about praying and talking to God, then you understand what God's promise means for your life. If you do have fears, remember that when we have faith in Christ, God promises we can always come to him.

*With faith in Christ, we are completely free to have a relationship with God—without any fear.*

---

2:11 "uncircumcised" *People not having the mark of circumcision as the Jews had.* 2:12 agreements *The agreements that God gave to his people in the Old Testament.* 2:20 most important stone *Literally, "cornerstone." The first and most important stone in a building.*

# July

start here

**1** Canada Day (CAN)— Pray for the Prime Minister of Canada.

**2** Pray for a person of influence: Today is actress Lindsay Lohan's birthday.

**3**

**4** Independence Day (USA)— Wear only red, white, and blue today!

**5**

**6**

**7** Write a poem or draw a picture expressing how much you love God.

**8**

**9** Come up with a cool new way to make and decorate your bed.

**10** Pray for a person of influence: Today is singer/actress Jessica Simpson's birthday.

**11**

**12** Ask your mom if you can help with the laundry (or another task) today.

**13**

**14**

**15** Find out how to make lemonade from scratch and make some for your family!

**16**

**17** Go through your toys and books. Choose some things to give away (ask your parents first!)

**18**

**19**

**20**

**21** Pray for a person of influence: Today is actor Josh Hartnett's birthday.

**22** Pray for Christians around the world who are in prison (or danger) because of their faith in Jesus.

**23**

**24** Pray for a person of influence: Today is singer/actress Jennifer Lopez's birthday.

**25**

**26**

**27** If you have a garden, offer to water it today.

**28**

**29** Use your imagination to create a different salad tonight.

**30**

Jumper says, "Make a list!"

together in the promise that God made in Christ Jesus.

⁷By God's special gift of grace given to me through his power, I became a servant to tell that Good News. ⁸I am the least important of all God's people, but God gave me this gift—to tell those who are not Jews the Good News about the riches of Christ, which are too great to understand fully. ⁹And God gave me the work of telling all people about the plan for his secret, which has been hidden in him since the beginning of time. He is the One who created everything. ¹⁰His purpose was that through the church all the rulers and powers in the heavenly world will now know God's wisdom, which has so many forms. ¹¹This agrees with the purpose God had since the beginning of time, and he carried out his plan through Christ Jesus our Lord. ¹²In Christ we can come before God with freedom and without fear. We can do this through faith in Christ. ¹³So I ask you not to become discouraged because of the sufferings I am having for you. My sufferings are for your glory.

### The Love of Christ

¹⁴So I bow in prayer before the Father ¹⁵from whom every family in heaven and on earth gets its true name. ¹⁶I ask the Father in his great glory to give you the power to be strong inwardly through his Spirit. ¹⁷I pray that Christ will live in your hearts by faith and that your life will be strong in love and be built on love. ¹⁸And I pray that you and all God's holy people will have the power to understand the greatness of Christ's love—how wide and how long and how high and how deep that love is. ¹⁹Christ's love is greater than anyone can ever know, but I pray that you will be able to know that love. Then you can be filled with the fullness of God.

### YOU DID NOT SAVE YOURSELVES; IT WAS A GIFT FROM GOD.

²⁰With God's power working in us, God can do much, much more than anything we can ask or imagine. ²¹To him be glory in the church and in Christ Jesus for all time, forever and ever. Amen.

### The Unity of the Body

**4** I am in prison because I belong to the Lord. Therefore I urge you who have been chosen by God to live up to the life to which God called you. ²Always be humble, gentle, and patient, accepting each other in love. ³You are joined together with peace through the Spirit, so make every effort to continue together in this way. ⁴There is one body and one Spirit, and God called you to have one hope. ⁵There is one Lord, one faith, and one baptism. ⁶There is one God and Father of everything. He rules everything and is everywhere and is in everything.

⁷Christ gave each one of us the special gift of grace, showing how generous he is. ⁸That is why it says in the Scriptures,

"When he went up to the heights,
  he led a parade of captives,
  and he gave gifts to people."

*Psalm 68:18*

## top ten

### top ten ways to...
**Reuse/Recycle Stuff**

1. Use old comic books to wrap small gifts.
2. Make pretty magnets with old buttons.
3. Use old socks as dust rags.
4. Borrow books from the library instead of buying new ones.
5. Sew a pillow out of an old sweater.
6. Save envelopes for scratch paper.
7. Cut gift tags out of old cards.
8. Reuse wrapping paper.
9. Donate old newspapers to a pet shop.
10. Cover books with old maps.

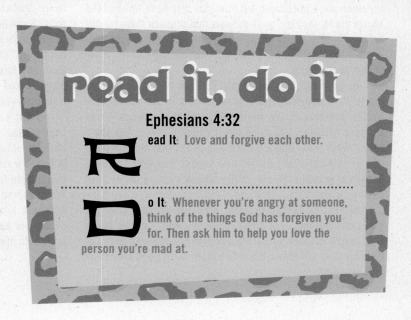

## read it, do it

**Ephesians 4:32**

**Read It**: Love and forgive each other.

**Do It**: Whenever you're angry at someone, think of the things God has forgiven you for. Then ask him to help you love the person you're mad at.

⁹When it says, "He went up," what does it mean? It means that he first came down to the earth. ¹⁰So Jesus came down, and he is the same One who went up above all the heaven. Christ did that to fill everything with his presence. ¹¹And Christ gave gifts to people—he made some to be apostles, some to be prophets, some to go and tell the Good News, and some to have the work of caring for and teaching God's people. ¹²Christ gave those gifts to prepare God's holy people for the work of serving, to make the body of Christ stronger. ¹³This work must continue until we are all joined together in the same faith and in the same knowledge of the Son of God. We must become like a mature person, growing until we become like Christ and have his perfection.

¹⁴Then we will no longer be babies. We will not be tossed about like a ship that the waves carry one way and then an-other. We will not be influenced by every new teaching we hear from people who are trying to fool us. They make plans and try any kind of trick to fool people into following the wrong path. ¹⁵No! Speaking the truth with love, we will grow up in every way into Christ, who is the head. ¹⁶The whole body depends on Christ, and all the parts of the body are joined and held together. Each part does its own work to make the whole body grow and be strong with love.

## The Way You Should Live

¹⁷In the Lord's name, I tell you this. Do not continue living like those who do not believe. Their thoughts are worth nothing. ¹⁸They do not understand, and they know nothing, because they refuse to listen. So they cannot have the life that God gives. ¹⁹They have lost all feeling of shame, and they use their lives for doing evil. They continually want to do all kinds

> WHEN YOU ARE ANGRY, DO NOT SIN, AND BE SURE TO STOP BEING ANGRY BEFORE THE END OF THE DAY.

of evil. ²⁰But what you learned in Christ was not like this. ²¹I know that you heard about him, and you are in him, so you were taught the truth that is in Jesus. ²²You were taught to leave your old self—to stop living the evil way you lived before. That old self becomes worse, because people are fooled by the evil things they want to do. ²³But you were taught to be made new in your hearts, ²⁴to become a new person. That new person is made to be like God—made to be truly good and holy.

# Christian Girls Around the World

## Birgit: *Austria*

Ten-year-old Birgit hugs her best friends, Dani and Dag-mar, and they kiss each other's cheeks as they say good-bye on the last day of school. They have gone to school together since preschool, but now that they have finished the fourth grade, they will go to schools that prepare them for different careers someday. At least they will still live in their same town together, but Birgit will ride the train to the trade school in Moedling.

Birgit loves going to the mall with her friends and listening to American music. She plays soccer in the fall and ice skates and skis in the winter. On special occasions, Birgit wears a traditional Austrian outfit called a *dirndl,* but she'd rather wear jeans and a T-shirt! She hopes that she will meet one or two Christians at her new school. Her only Christian friends at school before were two brothers whose family goes to Birgit's church.

In Austria, the government officially accepts only two kinds of churches, but these churches don't always teach people how to follow Jesus. Most people are baptized in one of the churches as babies, but they usually don't go to church as kids or adults.

Birgit started going to a small Bible-teaching church after her older brother joined the youth group. One day, he came home from youth group and told Birgit more about Jesus. She knew that Jesus had died on the cross, but she didn't know he was alive and cared about *her!*

Birgit's mom goes to church with her and her brother, but Birgit's step-dad makes fun of them. Birgit wishes that Dani and Dagmar would come, but Dani's mom says that Birgit is part of a *cult* (a strange religious group that controls the lives of their members).

Birgit would like to be baptized. When her brother was baptized last summer, their mom invited lots of relatives to the special service and the big church meal afterwards. Her grandma wasn't happy about it at all because being baptized told people that Birgit's brother was really going to follow Jesus instead of following the official church that his parents took him to when he was a baby. Baptism is a big decision, but Birgit already knows she wants to live for Jesus her whole life.

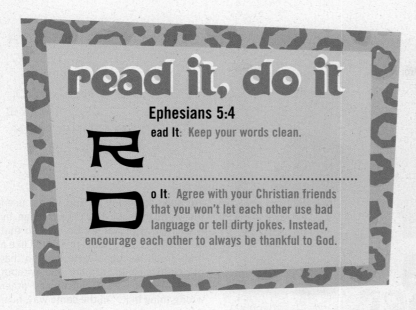

## read it, do it

**Ephesians 5:4**

**Read It**: Keep your words clean.

**Do It**: Agree with your Christian friends that you won't let each other use bad language or tell dirty jokes. Instead, encourage each other to always be thankful to God.

25So you must stop telling lies. Tell each other the truth, because we all belong to each other in the same body.[n] 26When you are angry, do not sin, and be sure to stop being angry before the end of the day. 27Do not give the devil a way to defeat you. 28Those who are stealing must stop stealing and start working. They should earn an honest living for them-selves. Then they will have something to share with those who are poor.

29When you talk, do not say harmful things, but say what people need—words that will help others become stronger. Then what you say will do good to those who listen to you. 30And do not make the Holy Spirit sad. The Spirit is God's proof that you belong to him. God gave you the Spirit to show that God will make you free when the final day comes. 31Do not be bitter or angry or mad. Never shout angrily or say things to hurt others. Never do anything evil. 32Be kind and loving to each other, and forgive each other just as God forgave you in Christ.

### Living in the Light

5 You are God's children whom he loves, so try to be like him. 2Live a life of love just as Christ loved us and gave himself for us as a sweet-smelling offering and sacrifice to God.

3But there must be no sexual sin among you, or any kind of evil or greed. Those things are not right for God's holy people. 4Also, there must be no evil talk among you, and you must not speak fool-ishly or tell evil jokes. These things are not right for you. Instead, you should be giving thanks to God. 5You can be sure of this: No one will have a place in the king-dom of Christ and of God who sins sexu-ally, or does evil things, or is greedy. Any-one who is greedy is serving a false god.

6Do not let anyone fool you by telling you things that are not true, because these things will bring God's anger on those who do not obey him. 7So have nothing to do with them. 8In the past you were full of darkness, but now you are full of light in the Lord. So live like chil-dren who belong to the light. 9Light brings every kind of goodness, right liv-ing, and truth. 10Try to learn what pleases the Lord. 11Have nothing to do with the things done in darkness, which are not worth anything. But show that they are wrong. 12It is shameful even to talk about what those people do in secret. 13But the light makes all things easy to see, 14and everything that is made easy to see can become light. This is why it is said:
"Wake up, sleeper!
Rise from death,
and Christ will shine on you."
15So be very careful how you live. Do not live like those who are not wise, but

## Q & A

**Q** Where did God come from?

**A** The Bible says that God has always existed. He has no beginning or end. That's hard for us to understand because we're used to schedules, expiration dates, and stop watches. Human babies are born, grow up, and die. But God exists outside the limits of time. He just is, which is why he calls himself "I am" in the Bible (John 8:58). Pray and ask God to help you trust in him even when you don't under-stand everything about him.

## Looking Ahead

### DRUGS AND ALCOHOL

As you get older, your peers may begin trying things that you know are wrong. Drugs and alcohol often seem attractive to young people, but they don't understand what can hap-pen from using them. In movies and on TV, drugs and alcohol look like the nor-mal thing to do. In reality, these sub-stances are against the law and are very harmful to your body. If you're around others who use drugs or alcohol, keep yourself safe by leaving as fast as you can! Remember Ephesians 5:18: "Do not be drunk with wine, which will ruin you." You can choose to stay away from drugs and alcohol!

4:25 **Tell . . . body.** *Quotation from Zechariah 8:16.*

# dig deeper

### Ephesians 5:1–2

What's your favorite smell? Chocolate chip cookies baking in the oven? Strawberry lip gloss? Fresh cut grass? Lemons? A campfire? Your sister's perfume? We usually enjoy the smells of good things. We like smells that remind us of yummy food, something clean, or a fun activity.

Did you know that people can "smell" your Christian life? Ephesians 5:1–2 says you should try to be like God and love people the way he does. Jesus set a good example for us by dying on the cross as a sacrifice for our sins. The Bible says what Jesus did was a "sweet-smelling offering" (verse 2).

When you truly love people and are not selfish, it's almost as if you leave a beautiful smell behind you wherever you go. The smell makes people feel good and attracts them to God's love in your life. But if you're mean and greedy and unkind, they will smell something fishy in your life and might feel doubtful about becoming a Christian. Pray that God will help you become more like him so that your life will smell sweet—and attract people to him.

---

DO YOUR WORK WITH ENTHUSIASM. WORK AS IF YOU WERE SERVING THE LORD, NOT AS IF YOU WERE SERVING ONLY MEN AND WOMEN.

[26]to make it belong to God. Christ used the word to make the church clean by washing it with water. [27]He died so that he could give the church to himself like a bride in all her beauty. He died so that the church could be pure and without fault, with no evil or sin or any other wrong thing in it. [28]In the same way, husbands should love their wives as they love their own bodies. The man who loves his wife loves himself. [29]No one ever hates his own body, but feeds and takes care of it. And that is what Christ does for the church, [30]because we are parts of his body. [31]The Scripture says, "So a man will leave his father and mother and be united with his wife, and the two will become one body."[n] [32]That secret is very important—I am talking about Christ and the

# Q & A

**Q** Most of my friends have cell phones, but my parents won't let me get one. Isn't that unfair?

**A** Your parents probably have a good reason for their decision. Cell phones are costly, time-consuming, distracting, and possibly even harmful to your health with too much use. Whatever their reasons, it's important to respect and obey your parents' rules. God promises to bless children who obey their parents (Ephesians 6:1–3). Try to find confidence in being different from your friends.

---

live wisely. [16]Use every chance you have for doing good, because these are evil times. [17]So do not be foolish but learn what the Lord wants you to do. [18]Do not be drunk with wine, which will ruin you, but be filled with the Spirit. [19]Speak to each other with psalms, hymns, and spiritual songs, singing and making music in your hearts to the Lord. [20]Always give thanks to God the Father for everything, in the name of our Lord Jesus Christ.

### Wives and Husbands

[21]Yield to obey each other as you would to Christ.

[22]Wives, yield to your husbands, as you do to the Lord, [23]because the husband is the head of the wife, as Christ is the head of the church. And he is the Savior of the body, which is the church. [24]As the church yields to Christ, so you wives should yield to your husbands in everything.

[25]Husbands, love your wives as Christ loved the church and gave himself for it

5:31 **"So . . . body."** *Quotation from Genesis 2:24.*

## cool

### Be a Toothpick!

**I**f you came face to face with a crocodile in Egypt, what would you do? Scream and run away? Or would you hang around and offer to clean its teeth? Probably not! But that's exactly what a little plover bird would do. In exchange for getting to ride on a crocodile's back, the plover will pick its teeth. Gross? Maybe . . . but the arrangement makes both animals happy.

Ephesians 4:32 encourages us to be kind to each other. You don't need to pick your friend's teeth, but you should look for ways to help each other!

church. <sup>33</sup>But each one of you must love his wife as he loves himself, and a wife must respect her husband.

### Children and Parents

**6** Children, obey your parents as the Lord wants, because this is the right thing to do. <sup>2</sup>The command says, "Honor your father and mother."[n] This is the first command that has a promise with it— <sup>3</sup>"Then everything will be well with you, and you will have a long life on the earth."[n]

<sup>4</sup>Fathers, do not make your children angry, but raise them with the training and teaching of the Lord.

### Slaves and Masters

<sup>5</sup>Slaves, obey your masters here on earth with fear and respect and from a sincere heart, just as you obey Christ. <sup>6</sup>You must do this not only while they are watching you, to please them. With all your heart you must do what God wants as people who are obeying Christ. <sup>7</sup>Do your work with enthusiasm. Work as if you were serving the Lord, not as if you were serving only men and women. <sup>8</sup>Remember that the Lord will give a reward to everyone, slave or free, for doing good.

<sup>9</sup>Masters, in the same way, be good to your slaves. Do not threaten them. Remember that the One who is your Master and their Master is in heaven, and he treats everyone alike.

### Wear the Full Armor of God

<sup>10</sup>Finally, be strong in the Lord and in his great power. <sup>11</sup>Put on the full armor of God so that you can fight against the devil's evil tricks. <sup>12</sup>Our fight is not against people on earth but against the rulers and authorities and the powers of this world's darkness, against the spiritual powers of evil in the heavenly world. <sup>13</sup>That is why you need to put on God's full armor. Then on the day of evil you will be able to stand strong. And when you have finished the whole fight, you will still be standing. <sup>14</sup>So stand strong, with the belt of truth tied around your waist and the protection of right living on your chest. <sup>15</sup>On your feet wear the Good News of peace to help you stand strong. <sup>16</sup>And also use the shield of faith with which you can stop all the burning arrows of the Evil One. <sup>17</sup>Accept God's salvation as your helmet, and take the sword of the Spirit, which is the word of God. <sup>18</sup>Pray in the Spirit at all times with all kinds of prayers, asking for everything

> PRAY IN THE SPIRIT AT ALL TIMES WITH ALL KINDS OF PRAYERS, ASKING FOR EVERYTHING YOU NEED.

you need. To do this you must always be ready and never give up. Always pray for all God's people.

<sup>19</sup>Also pray for me that when I speak, God will give me words so that I can tell the secret of the Good News without fear. <sup>20</sup>I have been sent to preach this Good News, and I am doing that now, here in prison. Pray that when I preach the Good News I will speak without fear, as I should.

### Final Greetings

<sup>21</sup>I am sending to you Tychicus, our brother whom we love and a faithful servant of the Lord's work. He will tell you everything that is happening with me. Then you will know how I am and what I am doing. <sup>22</sup>I am sending him to you for this reason—so that you will know how we are, and he can encourage you.

<sup>23</sup>Peace and love with faith to you brothers and sisters from God the Father and the Lord Jesus Christ. <sup>24</sup>Grace to all of you who love our Lord Jesus Christ with love that never ends.

## read it, do it

### Ephesians 5:8

**R**ead It: Live in the light.

**D**o It: Go into a dark room and think about how empty it looks. Turn on the light and thank God for saving you from spiritual darkness. Ask him to help you live in the light!

---

**6:2** "Honor . . . mother." *Quotation from Exodus 20:12; Deuteronomy 5:16.* **6:3** "Then . . . earth." *Quotation from Exodus 20:12; Deuteronomy 5:16.*

# PHILIPPIANS

**I**magine being made fun of at school, getting in a car accident, breaking your arm, having all your money stolen, and losing your best friend—all in one day. How would you feel? Angry? Sad? Probably anything but joyful, right?

In the Book of Philippians, Paul talks about being joyful in all things because of Jesus. Paul had more than a few bad days in his life. He was beaten, shipwrecked, and locked up in jail. He actually wrote this letter from prison! Yet he wanted to re-mind the Christians in the Greek city of Philippi of one important thing: the joy of serving God is much more important than any "unjoyful" times we face.

When we follow God, we can trust him to be with us, even in the hard things and the bad days. We might not be happy about what happens, but we can still have joy in serving God and sharing his love with others. We can be joyful because God forgives us for all our sins. We can be joyful because he promises to give us the strength to get through everything we face.

If you're having a bad day, try reading the Book of Philippians. You'll discover the exciting news that when we love and serve God, he helps us have joy in *any* situation!

# SERVE OTHERS WITH JOY

## THiNGS TO TALK WiTH GOD ABOUT . . .

## TO ME THE ONLY IMPORTANT THING ABOUT LIVING IS CHRIST, AND DYING WOULD BE PROFIT FOR ME.

good work in you, and I am sure he will continue it until it is finished when Jesus Christ comes again.

⁷And I know that I am right to think like this about all of you, because I have you in my heart. All of you share in God's grace with me while I am in prison and while I am defending and proving the truth of the Good News. ⁸God knows that I want to see you very much, because I love all of you with the love of Christ Jesus.

⁹This is my prayer for you: that your love will grow more and more; that you will have knowledge and understanding with your love; ¹⁰that you will see the difference between good and bad and will choose the good; that you will be pure and without wrong for the coming of Christ; ¹¹that you will be filled with the good things produced in your life by Christ to bring glory and praise to God.

### Paul's Troubles Help the Work

¹²I want you brothers and sisters to know that what has happened to me has helped to spread the Good News. ¹³All the palace guards and everyone else knows that I am in prison because I am a believer in Christ. ¹⁴Because I am in prison, most of the believers have become more bold in Christ and are not afraid to speak the word of God.

¹⁵It is true that some preach about Christ because they are jealous and ambitious, but others preach about Christ because they want to help. ¹⁶They preach because they have love, and they know that God gave me the work of defending the Good News. ¹⁷But the others preach about Christ for selfish and wrong reasons, wanting to make trouble for me in prison.

¹⁸But it doesn't matter. The important thing is that in every way, whether for right or wrong reasons, they are preaching about Christ. So I am happy, and I will continue to be happy. ¹⁹Because you are praying for me and the Spirit of Jesus Christ is helping me, I know this trouble will bring my freedom. ²⁰I expect and hope that I will not fail Christ in anything but that I will have the courage now, as always, to show the greatness of Christ in my life here on earth, whether I live or die. ²¹To me the only important thing about living is Christ, and dying would be profit for me. ²²If I continue living in my body, I will be able to work for the Lord. I do not know what to choose—living or dying. ²³It is hard to choose between the

## cool

### Bullet-Proof Faith

A strip of tough, see-through plastic (technically called polycarbonate laminate) placed between two layers of glass can stop bullets! How does it do this? The plastic's special design makes the force of the bullet move off to the sides, along the material instead of through it. The glass surrounding the plastic material shatters, but the bullet doesn't get through!

When you trust God with your life, he sends his Holy Spirit to live inside you and help you. He also gives you a "shield of faith" (Ephesians 6:16), which you can use to stop the devil's temptation "bullets!"

**1** From Paul and Timothy, servants of Christ Jesus.

To all of God's holy people in Christ Jesus who live in Philippi, including your overseers and deacons:

²Grace and peace to you from God our Father and the Lord Jesus Christ.

### Paul's Prayer

³I thank my God every time I remember you, ⁴always praying with joy for all of you. ⁵I thank God for the help you gave me while I preached the Good News—help you gave from the first day you believed until now. ⁶God began doing a

# Relationships

You can't just find a best friend online or out of a catalog. No one friend can meet all your needs, either. Whether or not you have a best friend, you should focus on being a good friend to lots of people. Most of all, get to know your very best friend, Jesus. In John 15:14, Jesus calls us his friends when we love and obey him. Get to know him better by talking to him every day. Trust him with your secrets. He's the one friend who will never get bored with you, stop loving you, or move away.

two. I want to leave this life and be with Christ, which is much better, 24but you need me here in my body. 25Since I am sure of this, I know I will stay with you to help you grow and have joy in your faith. 26You will be very happy in Christ Jesus when I am with you again.

27Only one thing concerns me: Be sure that you live in a way that brings honor to the Good News of Christ. Then whether I come and visit you or am away from you, I will hear that you are standing strong with one purpose, that you work together as one for the faith of the Good News, 28and that you are not afraid of those who are against you. All of this is proof that your enemies will be destroyed but that you will be saved by God. 29God gave you the honor not only of believing in Christ but also of suffering for him, both of which bring glory to Christ. 30When I was with you, you saw the struggles I had, and you hear about the struggles I am having now. You yourselves are having the same kind of struggles.

2 Does your life in Christ give you strength? Does his love comfort you? Do we share together in the spirit? Do you have mercy and kindness? 2If so, make me very happy by having the same thoughts, sharing the same love, and having one mind and purpose. 3When you do things, do not let selfishness or pride be your guide. Instead, be humble and give more honor to others than to yourselves. 4Do not be interested only in your own life, but be interested in the lives of others.

## Be Unselfish Like Christ

5In your lives you must think and act like Christ Jesus.
6Christ himself was like God in
    everything.
    But he did not think that being
        equal with God was something
        to be used for his own benefit.
7But he gave up his place with God
        and made himself nothing.
    He was born as a man
    and became like a servant.
8And when he was living as a man,
    he humbled himself and was fully
        obedient to God,
    even when that caused his death—
        death on a cross.
9So God raised him to the highest
        place.
    God made his name greater than
        every other name
10so that every knee will bow to the
        name of Jesus—
    everyone in heaven, on earth, and
        under the earth.
11And everyone will confess that Jesus
        Christ is Lord
    and bring glory to God the Father.

## read it, do it

**Philippians 2:14**

**R**ead It: Stop complaining!

**D**o It: When your mom asks you to fold the laundry, don't grumble. Do it cheerfully! And if she tells you that you're doing it wrong . . . listen and learn without arguing.

# HOW HUMBLE ARE YOU?

Philippians 2:3 says, "When you do things, do not let selfishness or pride be your guide. Instead, be humble and give more honor to others than to yourselves."

How humble are you? Take this quiz to see if you've got it right.

**1.** Someone says that you look beautiful today. You say:

    **a.** "No way! Look how flat my hair is today!"

    **b.** "Thanks! That's very nice of you."

    **c.** "What do you mean 'today?' Don't I always look beautiful?"

**2.** You teacher chooses another girl for the part you wanted in the school play. You:

    **a.** Tell yourself you're a loser and don't try out for any other parts.

    **b.** Congratulate the other girl and say, "I'm sure you'll be great!"

    **c.** Go around telling everyone that you could have played that part much better.

**3.** Your pastor asks if you would help set up chairs before a service at the church. You:

    **a.** Think, "He never asks me to do anything else. I guess I'm kind of useless."

    **b.** Smile and say, "I'd love to! Thanks for asking me."

    **c.** Say, "Oh, I can't do that. I'll get my clothes dirty!"

**4.** Some kids at school find out you're a Christian and ask, "So you think you're better than everyone else now?" You answer:

    **a.** "No…it really doesn't make a difference."

    **b.** "No, I'm not better. But I've asked God to forgive me for all the wrong things I've done."

    **c.** "Of course! I'm not going to hell like you sinners!"

**5.** Your best friend calls to say that something came up, and she can't come to your house today. You think:

    **a.** "She doesn't like me anymore. She thinks I'm boring. Maybe she's right."

    **b.** "Maybe her family has to do something important together. I hope she has fun anyway and that she can come over another time."

    **c.** "How could she do this to me? I'm not going to be her best friend anymore!"

## How's your humility?

**If you answered mostly As,** you've got poor self-esteem. Thinking badly of yourself is not the same as being humble…and it's not what God wants. If you always put yourself down or don't stand up for the things you believe in, you might not be trusting God enough. He's made you special and he wants you to try your best in everything!

**If you answered mostly Bs,** you've got it figured out! Don't feel proud about this, because that would just spoil it…but you've reached a good level of humility. You put others first but you're also secure about yourself. That's great! Ask God to help you stay humble.

**If you answered mostly Cs,** you are not very humble. You probably need to start thinking more about the feelings of others. Pray that God will give you a more humble heart. As you begin to love others more, you will change so much that even you will like yourself better. But in a healthier way!

offer my own blood with your sacrifice, I will be happy and full of joy with all of you. ¹⁸You also should be happy and full of joy with me.

## Timothy and Epaphroditus

¹⁹I hope in the Lord Jesus to send Timothy to you soon. I will be happy to learn how you are. ²⁰I have no one else like Timothy, who truly cares for you. ²¹Other people are interested only in their own lives, not in the work of Jesus Christ. ²²You know the kind of person Timothy is. You know he has served with me in telling the Good News, as a son serves his father. ²³I plan to send him to you quickly when I know what will happen to me. ²⁴I am sure that the Lord will help me to come to you soon.

²⁵Epaphroditus, my brother in Christ, works and serves with me in the army of Christ. When I needed help, you sent him to me. I think now that I must send him back to you, ²⁶because he wants very much to see all of you. He is worried because you heard that he was sick. ²⁷Yes,

## god's promises

**Philippians 1:6**

Have you ever started a project you didn't finish? It could have been a fort, a jigsaw puzzle, a book, a letter, or a drawing. God hasn't! He always finishes what he starts. In Philippians 1:6, Paul tells Christians that God is working on *us.* He is making us more beautiful on the inside. More kind, loving, patient—more like him! And he's not going to stop until he's done. That doesn't mean that we'll become perfect before we die, but the Bible tells us that those who believe in Jesus *will* be perfect when he returns—perfect like him!

That's a long time to wait, though. In the meantime, it's easy to get impatient and discouraged. Do you ever feel like there's no point in trying to do the right thing because you always do what's wrong? Are you tempted to give up? God doesn't give up working on you! He is making you more like Jesus every day, and he can see the progress much more clearly than you can.

Some projects aren't that important—some aren't even worth finishing. But you are! This verse assures us that God is going to finish what he started doing in us.

*Some projects aren't worth finishing. But you are!*

## Q & A

**Q** How can I stop lying all the time?

**A** *Wanting to* change is the first big step we always have to make. Try to figure out why you lie—are you afraid of telling the truth? Knowing *why* you lie can help you decide not to do it. Ask God to help you stop lying. He wants to help! And if you do lie again, make sure you admit the truth as soon as possible.

## Be the People God Wants You to Be

¹²My dear friends, you have always obeyed God when I was with you. It is even more important that you obey now while I am away from you. Keep on working to complete your salvation with fear and trembling, ¹³because God is working in you to help you want to do and be able to do what pleases him.

¹⁴Do everything without complaining or arguing. ¹⁵Then you will be innocent and without any wrong. You will be God's children without fault. But you are living with crooked and mean people all around you, among whom you shine like stars in the dark world. ¹⁶You offer the teaching that gives life. So when Christ comes again, I can be happy because my work was not wasted. I ran the race and won. ¹⁷Your faith makes you offer your lives as a sacrifice in serving God. If I have to

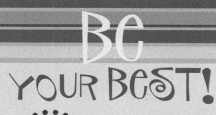

# BE YOUR BEST!

**G**et your eyes checked regularly . . . and wear glasses if you need them! When you can't focus or see properly, it gets difficult to do things without falling down or making mistakes! By focusing our spiritual "eyes" on Jesus, we can make sure we're always seeing straight and doing the right things.

he was sick, and nearly died, but God had mercy on him and me too so that I would not have more sadness. ²⁸I want very much to send him to you so that when you see him you can be happy, and I can stop worrying about you. ²⁹Welcome him in the Lord with much joy. Give honor to people like him, ³⁰because he almost died for the work of Christ. He risked his life to give me the help you could not give in your service to me.

## The Importance of Christ

**3** My brothers and sisters, be full of joy in the Lord. It is no trouble for me to write the same things to you again, and it will help you to be more ready. ²Watch out for those who do evil, who are like dogs, who demand to cut*ⁿ* the body. ³We are the ones who are truly circumcised. We worship God

> I WANT TO KNOW CHRIST AND THE POWER THAT RAISED HIM FROM THE DEAD. I WANT TO SHARE IN HIS SUFFERINGS AND BECOME LIKE HIM IN HIS DEATH.

through his Spirit, and our pride is in Christ Jesus. We do not put trust in ourselves or anything we can do, ⁴although I might be able to put trust in myself. If anyone thinks he has a reason to trust in himself, he should know that I have greater reason for trusting in myself. ⁵I was circumcised eight days after my birth. I am from the people of Israel and the tribe of Benjamin. I am a Hebrew, and my parents were Hebrews. I had a strict view of the law, which is why I became a Pharisee. ⁶I was so enthusiastic I tried to hurt the church. No one could find fault with the way I obeyed the law of Moses. ⁷Those things were important to me, but now I think they are worth nothing because of

Christ. ⁸Not only those things, but I think that all things are worth nothing compared with the greatness of knowing Christ Jesus my Lord. Because of him, I have lost all those things, and now I know they are worthless trash. This allows me to have Christ ⁹and to belong to him. Now I am right with God, not because I followed the law, but because I believed in Christ. God uses my faith to make me right with him. ¹⁰I want to know Christ and the power that raised him from the dead. I want to share in his sufferings and become like him in his death.

## Shine Your Light

**D**o you have a sweater that doesn't fit anymore? Or a bike that you never use? Did you know that you can use those things to help others? Julie, Evan, Yoshi, and Brian belong to a junior high club at their church that loves to help people in need. That's why, every year at Thanksgiving, they spread all over the town and collect donations for a rescue mission.

These kids collect everything from warm coats, hats, and mittens, to canned food, furniture, and bicycles that people no longer need. The rescue mission uses the donations to take care of the physical needs of thousands of people who are having hard times. And each person that comes in gets a chance to hear about Jesus!

The Bible says that we should think about others, not just ourselves (Philippians 2:3–4). Jesus wasn't thinking about himself when he died on the cross. He was thinking of us!

The next time you are about to buy something for yourself, take a moment to think of a way to put others first. Remember how Jesus set the example by looking out for the needs of others while he was on earth.

---

**3:2 cut** *The word in Greek is like the word "circumcise," but it means "to cut completely off."*

> FORGETTING THE PAST AND STRAINING TOWARD WHAT IS AHEAD, I KEEP TRYING TO REACH THE GOAL AND GET THE PRIZE FOR WHICH GOD CALLED ME THROUGH CHRIST TO THE LIFE ABOVE.

<sup>11</sup>Then I have hope that I myself will be raised from the dead.

### Continuing Toward Our Goal

<sup>12</sup>I do not mean that I am already as God wants me to be. I have not yet reached that goal, but I continue trying to reach it and to make it mine. Christ wants me to do that, which is the reason he made me his. <sup>13</sup>Brothers and sisters, I know that I have not yet reached that goal, but there is one thing I always do. Forgetting the past and straining toward what is ahead, <sup>14</sup>I keep trying to reach the goal and get

# Q&A

**Q** Is it okay to watch movies that have some violence or bad words in them?

**A** It's hard to know ahead of time that some movies have violence or swearing. If you *do* know, why not watch something else? Watching "bad" movies might not seem like a sin, but God wants us to keep our minds pure. "Think about the things that are good and worthy of praise . . . that are true and honorable and right and pure and beautiful and respected" (Philippians 4:8). Don't fill your mind with pictures and words that don't add goodness to your life.

## dig deeper

### Philippians 4:6

What makes you worry? A big test? Disagreements with friends? A sick pet? Parents who argue? A lot of things can cause us to worry, and we all handle worrying in different ways. Some people try to fix the problem, even when they can't. Others try to ignore it, hoping it will fix itself.

God says in Philippians 4:6, "Do not worry about anything, but pray and ask God for everything you need, always giving thanks."

Let's look at this verse carefully. What does it tell us to do?

1. *Don't* worry. God, who created the whole universe—including you!—has everything under control. We can trust him to take care of us in any situation.

2. *Do* pray. God loves it when we talk to him about our worries and ask him for the things we need. He loves us more than anyone else, and we can let go of our worries because we know he cares.

3. *Do* thank God. Thanking him for how he has cared for us in the past reminds us that we don't need to worry. We can trust him to keep providing everything we need.

It's easy to worry, but when we know that God cares, we can choose *not* to worry. Let's practice trusting God instead!

the prize for which God called me through Christ to the life above. <sup>15</sup>All of us who are spiritually mature should think this way, too. And if there are things you do not agree with, God will make them clear to you. <sup>16</sup>But we should continue following the truth we already have.

<sup>17</sup>Brothers and sisters, all of you should try to follow my example and to copy those who live the way we showed you. <sup>18</sup>Many people live like enemies of the cross of Christ. I have often told you about them, and it makes me cry to tell you about them now. <sup>19</sup>In the end, they will be destroyed. They do whatever their bodies want, they are proud of their

# Q & A

**Q** I stole a candy bar from the store the other day when my mom wasn't looking. Now I feel ashamed. Will God forgive me?

**A** God promises to forgive us whenever we admit we've done wrong and ask for forgiveness. First John 1:9 says, "But if we confess our sins, he will forgive our sins, because we can trust God to do what is right." You don't have to feel guilty after God forgives you. You should also talk to your parents about going back to the store and making things right. God will help give you courage!

shameful acts, and they think only about earthly things. ²⁰But our homeland is in heaven, and we are waiting for our Savior, the Lord Jesus Christ, to come from heaven. ²¹By his power to rule all things, he will change our humble bodies and make them like his own glorious body.

## What the Christians Are to Do

**4** My dear brothers and sisters, I love you and want to see you. You bring me joy and make me proud of you, so stand strong in the Lord as I have told you.

²I ask Euodia and Syntyche to agree in the Lord. ³And I ask you, my faithful friend, to help these women. They served with me in telling the Good News, together with Clement and others who worked with me, whose names are written in the book of life.ⁿ

⁴Be full of joy in the Lord always. I will say again, be full of joy.

⁵Let everyone see that you are gentle and kind. The Lord is coming soon. ⁶Do not worry about anything, but pray and ask God for everything you need, always giving thanks. ⁷And God's peace, which is so great we cannot understand it, will keep your hearts and minds in Christ Jesus.

⁸Brothers and sisters, think about the things that are good and worthy of praise. Think about the things that are true and honorable and right and pure and beautiful and respected. ⁹Do what you learned and received from me, what I told you, and what you saw me do. And the God who gives peace will be with you.

## Paul Thanks the Christians

¹⁰I am very happy in the Lord that you have shown your care for me again. You continued to care about me, but there was no way for you to show it. ¹¹I am not telling you this because I need anything. I have learned to be satisfied with the things I have and with everything that happens. ¹²I know how to live when I am poor, and I know how to live when I have plenty. I have learned the secret of being happy at any time in everything that happens, when I have enough to eat and when I go hungry, when I have more than I need and when I do not have enough. ¹³I can do all things through Christ, because he gives me strength.

¹⁴But it was good that you helped me when I needed it. ¹⁵You Philippians remember when I first preached the Good News there. When I left Macedonia, you were the only church that gave me help. ¹⁶Several times you sent me things I needed when I was in Thessalonica. ¹⁷Really, it is not that I want to receive gifts from you, but I want you to have the good that comes from giving. ¹⁸And now I have everything, and more. I have all I need, because Epaphroditus brought your gift to me. It is like a sweet-smelling sacrifice offered to God, who accepts that sacrifice and is pleased with it. ¹⁹My God will use his wonderful riches in Christ Jesus to give you everything you need. ²⁰Glory to our God and Father forever and ever! Amen.

²¹Greet each of God's people in Christ Jesus. Those who are with me send greetings to you. ²²All of God's people greet you, particularly those from the palace of Caesar.

²³The grace of the Lord Jesus Christ be with you all.

> ## LET EVERYONE SEE THAT YOU ARE GENTLE AND KIND. THE LORD IS COMING SOON.

# read it, do it

## Philippians 3:8

**R**ead It: Nothing compares with God!

**D**o It: Imagine life without all your stuff. Not fun? Well, now imagine life without God. Wow—pretty awful, huh? Make sure you show God your appreciation by spending time with him each day.

---

4:3 **book of life** *God's book that has the names of all God's chosen people (Revelation 3:5; 21:27).*

# COLOSSIANS

**D**o you know that God has a name for every star? Do you know that he makes the sun rise every morning and set each evening? Do you know that he is so great that he is the only thing we need to have eternal life?

The Colossians had a hard time understanding this. Some of them kept trying to mix other beliefs, rituals, and rules with faith in Jesus. They thought it was important to do something more than just believe in order to be saved.

Paul wrote this letter to remind the church in Colosse (a city in what is now Turkey) that Jesus is all we need. He is the one who created everything, and he has authority over everything. Nothing is

greater than Jesus, and we don't need to add even one thing to what the Bible teaches. Jesus has *all* the power to save us from our sins!

Because he's so great, living for Jesus is the greatest thing we can do! Paul explains in this letter that while we don't need to add anything to God's ways, we do need to follow certain guidelines. The guidelines help us honor God with our behavior and show him how thankful we are for his love.

Start reading Colossians . . . and be prepared to be amazed at how much the God who created *everything* loves you—just because you're you!

# ONLY CHRIST CAN SAVE PEOPLE

## THiNGS TO TALK WiTH GOD ABOUT . . .

**1** From Paul, an apostle of Christ Jesus. I am an apostle because that is what God wanted. Also from Timothy, our brother. [2]To the holy and faithful brothers and sisters in Christ that live in Colossae:

Grace and peace to you from God our Father.[n]

[3]In our prayers for you we always thank God, the Father of our Lord Jesus Christ, [4]because we have heard about the faith you have in Christ Jesus and the love you have for all of God's people. [5]You have this faith and love because of your hope, and what you hope for is kept safe for you in heaven. You learned about this hope

**29% of kids get an allowance.**
— Shopping In America Survey, April 2005. "What's in the Bag for Tween Shoppers." www.shoppinginamerica.biz/

**did you know?**

when you heard the message about the truth, the Good News [6]that was told to you. Everywhere in the world that Good News is bringing blessings and is growing. This has happened with you, too, since you heard the Good News and understood the truth about the grace of God. [7]You learned about God's grace from Epaphras, whom we love. He works together with us and is a faithful servant of Christ for us.[n] [8]He also told us about the love you have from the Holy Spirit.

[9]Because of this, since the day we heard about you, we have continued praying for you, asking God that you will know fully what he wants. We pray that you will also have great wisdom and understanding in spiritual things [10]so that you will live the kind of life that honors and pleases the Lord in every way. You will produce fruit in every good work and grow in the knowledge of God. [11]God will strengthen you with his own great power so that you will not give up when troubles come, but you will be patient. [12]And you will joyfully give thanks to the Father

## ALL THINGS WERE MADE THROUGH CHRIST AND FOR CHRIST.

who has made you[n] able to have a share in all that he has prepared for his people in the kingdom of light. [13]God has freed us from the power of darkness, and he brought us into the kingdom of his dear Son. [14]The Son paid for our sins,[n] and in him we have forgiveness.

### The Importance of Christ

[15]No one can see God, but Jesus Christ is exactly like him. He ranks higher than everything that has been made. [16]Through his power all things were made—things in heaven and on earth, things seen and unseen, all powers, authorities, lords, and rulers. All things were made through Christ and for Christ.

# Q&A

**Q** I have to get braces, and I'm afraid I'll look like a nerd. Help!

**A** **Braces** are cool now. Even some celebrities have them! Ask your orthodontist to let you pick out the colors for the elastics and have fun showing off your trendy new smile. If you still think they look awful, just remember: they'll be off in a while and then you'll have beautiful teeth! And don't stop smiling. Braces are always prettier than a frown!

1:2 **Father** *Some Greek copies continue, "and the Lord Jesus Christ."* 1:7 **for us** *Some Greek copies read "for you."* 1:12 **you** *Some Greek copies read "us."* 1:14 **sins** *Some Greek copies continue, "with his blood."*

# cool

## ACHOO!

In 1983, a twelve-year-old girl in the United Kingdom set the Guinness World Record for the longest sneezing fit: 978 days (over two-and-a-half years)! At first she sneezed every minute, but it slowed down to once every five minutes. "I'm determined not to let it stop me from doing the things I like," she said.

You might not sneeze for thirty-two straight months, but other situations could discourage you. Colossians 1:11 says, "God will strengthen you with his own great power so that you will not give up when troubles come, but you will be patient."

¹⁷He was there before anything was made, and all things continue because of him. ¹⁸He is the head of the body, which is the church. Everything comes from him. He is the first one who was raised from the dead. So in all things Jesus has first place. ¹⁹God was pleased for all of himself to live in Christ. ²⁰And through Christ, God has brought all things back to himself again—things on earth and things in heaven. God made peace through the blood of Christ's death on the cross. ²¹At one time you were separated from God. You were his enemies in your minds, and the evil things you did were against God. ²²But now God has made you his friends again. He did this through Christ's

> GOD MADE PEACE
> THROUGH THE BLOOD
> OF CHRIST'S DEATH
> ON THE CROSS.

death in the body so that he might bring you into God's presence as people who are holy, with no wrong, and with nothing of which God can judge you guilty. ²³This will happen if you continue strong and sure in your faith. You must not be moved away from the hope brought to you by the Good News that you heard. That same Good News has been told to everyone in the world, and I, Paul, help in preaching that Good News.

## Paul's Work for the Church

²⁴I am happy in my sufferings for you. There are things that Christ must still suffer through his body, the church. I am accepting, in my body, my part of these things that must be suffered. ²⁵I became a servant of the church because God gave me a special work to do that helps you, and that work is to tell fully the message of God. ²⁶This message is the secret that was hidden from everyone since the beginning of time, but now it is made known to God's holy people. ²⁷God decided to let his people know this rich and glorious secret which he has for all people. This secret is Christ himself, who is in you. He is our only hope for glory. ²⁸So we continue to preach Christ to each person, using all wisdom to warn and to teach everyone, in order to bring each one into God's presence as a mature person in Christ. ²⁹To do this, I work and struggle, using Christ's great strength that works so powerfully in me.

## Q & A

**Q** I hate changing in the locker room in front of other girls. What can I do?

**A** That's a common struggle for many girls . . . you're not alone! The best way not to attract attention is to act like you don't care. If you seem nervous, they'll watch you more. Be quick about it and ask God to help you not worry. If it really bothers you, learn to change with a towel wrapped around you, change in a bathroom stall, or talk to your mom or gym teacher about it.

**2** I want you to know how hard I work for you, those in Laodicea, and others who have never seen me. ²I want them to be strengthened and joined together with love so that they may be rich in their understanding. This leads to their knowing fully God's secret, that is, Christ himself. ³In him all the treasures of wisdom and knowledge are safely kept.

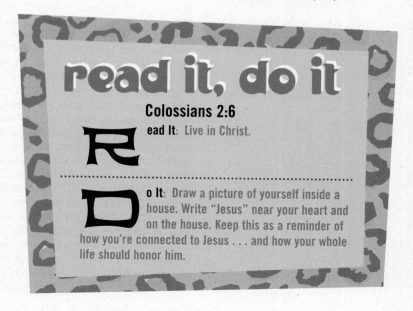

# read it, do it

### Colossians 2:6

**R**ead It: Live in Christ.

**D**o It: Draw a picture of yourself inside a house. Write "Jesus" near your heart and on the house. Keep this as a reminder of how you're connected to Jesus . . . and how your whole life should honor him.

# BibLe BasicS

The Bible contains many kinds of books. Some are historical—that is, collections of stories about things God has done. Others are letters to specific groups of people who lived long ago. The Book of Psalms contains songs that the Jews used in worship. For hundreds of years these "books" were all separate scrolls (rolled up "books"). Within one hundred years after Jesus died, Christians began to put some of the books together in one cover, like the books we read now. No book could contain *everything* about God—our human minds could never understand it all! But together, the books of the Bible tell us everything we *need* to know—how great he is, how much he loves us, and how we can know him.

⁴I say this so that no one can fool you by arguments that seem good, but are false. ⁵Though I am absent from you in my body, my heart is with you, and I am happy to see your good lives and your strong faith in Christ.

## Continue to Live in Christ

⁶As you received Christ Jesus the Lord, so continue to live in him. ⁷Keep your roots deep in him and have your lives built on him. Be strong in the faith, just as you were taught, and always be thankful.

⁸Be sure that no one leads you away with false and empty teaching that is only human, which comes from the rul-

ing spirits of this world, and not from Christ. ⁹All of God lives fully in Christ (even when Christ was on earth), ¹⁰and you have a full and true life in Christ, who is ruler over all rulers and powers.

¹¹Also in Christ you had a different kind of circumcision, a circumcision not done by hands. It was through Christ's circumcision, that is, his death, that you were made free from the power of your sinful self. ¹²When you were baptized, you were

buried with Christ, and you were raised up with him through your faith in God's power that was shown when he raised Christ from the dead. ¹³When you were spiritually dead because of your sins and because you were not free from the power of your sinful self, God made you alive with Christ, and he forgave all our sins. ¹⁴He canceled the debt, which listed all the rules we failed to follow. He took away that record with its rules and nailed it to the cross. ¹⁵God stripped the spiritual rulers and powers of their authority. With the cross, he won the victory and showed the world that they were powerless.

## Don't Follow People's Rules

¹⁶So do not let anyone make rules for you about eating and drinking or about a religious feast, a New Moon Festival, or a Sabbath day. ¹⁷These things were like a shadow of what was to come. But what is true and real has come and is found in Christ. ¹⁸Do not let anyone disqualify you by making you humiliate yourself and worship angels. Such people enter into visions, which fill them with foolish pride because of their human way of thinking. ¹⁹They do not hold tightly to Christ, the head. It is from him that all the parts of the body are cared for and held together. So it grows in the way God wants it to grow.

²⁰Since you died with Christ and were made free from the ruling spirits of the world, why do you act as if you still

WHEN YOU WERE BAPTIZED, YOU WERE BURIED WITH CHRIST, AND YOU WERE RAISED UP WITH HIM THROUGH YOUR FAITH IN GOD'S POWER THAT WAS SHOWN WHEN HE RAISED CHRIST FROM THE DEAD.

# read it, do it

## Colossians 2:8

**R**ead It: Beware of false teachers.

**D**o It: When someone tells you something about God that sounds strange, check it out with your pastor or parents. Don't follow people who make up their own beliefs!

belong to this world by following rules like these: [21]"Don't handle this," "Don't taste that," "Don't even touch that thing"? [22]These rules refer to earthly things that are gone as soon as they are used. They are only human commands and teachings. [23]They seem to be wise, but they are only part of a human religion. They make people pretend not to be proud and make them punish their bodies, but they do not really control the evil desires of the sinful self.

## Your New Life in Christ

**3** Since you were raised from the dead with Christ, aim at what is in heaven, where Christ is sitting at the right hand of God. [2]Think only about the things in heaven, not the things on earth. [3]Your old sinful self has died, and your new life is kept with Christ in God. [4]Christ is your[n] life, and when he comes again, you will share in his glory.

[5]So put all evil things out of your life: sexual sinning, doing evil, letting evil thoughts control you, wanting things that are evil, and greed. This is really serving a false god. [6]These things make God angry.[n] [7]In your past, evil life you also did these things.

[8]But now also put these things out of your life: anger, bad temper, doing or saying things to hurt others, and using evil words when you talk. [9]Do not lie to each other. You have left your old sinful life and the things you did before. [10]You have begun to live the new life, in which you are being made new and are becoming like the One who made you. This new life brings you the true knowledge of God. [11]In the new life there is no difference between Greeks and Jews, those who are circumcised and those who are not circumcised, or people who are foreigners, or Scythians.[n] There is no difference between slaves and free people.

# Q&A

**Q** Is it ever okay to lie?

**A** Colossians 3:9 says, "Do not lie to each other." Many verses in the Bible warn us that lying is a sin. The only time a lie might be "okay" is when the truth would help God's enemies do something evil (read Joshua 2:1–21 and 6:22–23 in the Old Testament). An example might be protecting your little sister by telling a robber she's not home (while she hides under the bed). But these situations are very rare, and God would show you the right thing to do. As a general rule, it's never okay to lie.

## dig deeper

### Colossians 3:23

Have you ever spent time near an ant hill watching the ants rush around? Ants always seem to be busy moving crumbs and bits of leaves bigger than themselves. Why do they work so hard? Because they are serving their queen! Everything they do in some way serves or honors her, and queens deserve only the best, right?

The Bible tells us we should have this same attitude in all the work we do. All our chores, all our schoolwork, and *everything* we do should be our best effort because we're doing it for God! Colossians 3:23 says, "In all the work you are doing, work the best you can. Work as if you were doing it for the Lord, not for people."

It's easy to grumble, complain, and be lazy when we do chores for our parents or schoolwork for our teachers. But imagine what would happen if you realized that everything you do isn't just for your parents or your teachers or any other person. You might see that everything you do is an opportunity to serve God!

When we love God, we want to work hard to do our best in everything. So learn a lesson from the ants. Always try to do your best because you are serving the greatest King!

---

**3:4 your** *Some Greek copies read "our."* **3:6 These . . . angry** *Some Greek copies continue, "against the people who do not obey God."* **3:11 Scythians** *The Scythians were known as very wild and cruel people.*

## Bible Bios — Lydia (Acts 16:13-15)

Only a few verses in the Bible talk about Lydia, but they tell us a lot about this special woman. We know she sold expensive purple fabric and had a successful business. She had money, a big house, and probably slaves, too. You might expect Lydia to act snobby, but she didn't!

She became one of the first people in Europe to accept Jesus as her Savior. After that, she really committed her life to God. People saw her as kind and generous . . . not proud or selfish. She invited Paul and his big group of traveling missionaries to stay at her home. She made her house a meeting place for the Christians in the city of Philippi. She also met with other women at a special place to pray. People looked up to Lydia because of her strong faith and love for God.

But Christ is in all believers, and Christ is all that is important.

¹²God has chosen you and made you his holy people. He loves you. So you should always clothe yourselves with mercy, kindness, humility, gentleness, and patience. ¹³Bear with each other, and forgive each other. If someone does wrong to you, forgive that person because the Lord forgave you. ¹⁴Even more than all this, clothe yourself in love. Love is what holds you all together in perfect unity. ¹⁵Let the peace that Christ gives control your thinking, because you were all called together in one body[n] to have peace. Always be thankful. ¹⁶Let the teaching of Christ live in you richly. Use all wisdom to teach and instruct each other by singing psalms, hymns, and spiritual songs with thankfulness in your hearts to God. ¹⁷Everything you do or say should be done to obey Jesus your Lord. And in all you do, give thanks to God the Father through Jesus.

### Your New Life with Other People

¹⁸Wives, yield to the authority of your husbands, because this is the right thing to do in the Lord.

¹⁹Husbands, love your wives and be gentle with them.

²⁰Children, obey your parents in all things, because this pleases the Lord. ²¹Fathers, do not nag your children. If you are too hard to please, they may want to stop trying.

²²Slaves, obey your masters in all things. Do not obey just when they are watching you, to gain their favor, but serve them honestly, because you respect the Lord. ²³In all the work you are doing, work the best you can. Work as if you were doing it for the Lord, not for people. ²⁴Remember that you will receive your reward from the Lord, which he promised to his people. You are serving the Lord Christ. ²⁵But remember that anyone who does wrong will be punished for that wrong, and the Lord treats everyone the same.

**4** Masters, give what is good and fair to your slaves. Remember that you have a Master in heaven.

### What the Christians Are to Do

²Continue praying, keeping alert, and always thanking God. ³Also pray for us that God will give us an opportunity to tell people his message. Pray that we can preach the secret that God has made known about Christ. This is why I am in prison. ⁴Pray that I can speak in a way that will make it clear, as I should.

⁵Be wise in the way you act with people who are not believers, making the most of every opportunity. ⁶When you talk, you should always be kind and pleasant so you will be able to answer everyone in the way you should.

SINCE YOU WERE RAISED FROM THE DEAD WITH CHRIST, AIM AT WHAT IS IN HEAVEN, WHERE CHRIST IS SITTING AT THE RIGHT HAND OF GOD.

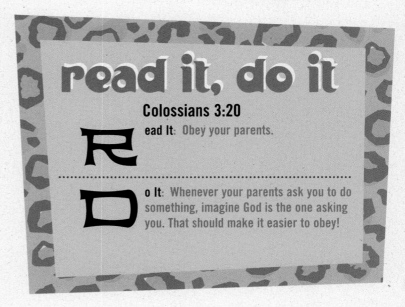

# read it, do it

### Colossians 3:20

**R**ead It: Obey your parents.

**D**o It: Whenever your parents ask you to do something, imagine God is the one asking you. That should make it easier to obey!

3:15 **body** The spiritual body of Christ, meaning the church or his people.

### News About the People with Paul

[7]Tychicus is my dear brother in Christ and a faithful minister and servant with me in the Lord. He will tell you all the things that are happening to me. [8]This is why I am sending him: so you may know how we are[n] and he may encourage you. [9]I send him with Onesimus, a faithful and dear brother in Christ, and one of your group. They will tell you all that has happened here.

> BEAR WITH EACH OTHER, AND FORGIVE EACH OTHER. IF SOMEONE DOES WRONG TO YOU, FORGIVE THAT PERSON BECAUSE THE LORD FORGAVE YOU.

[10]Aristarchus, a prisoner with me, and Mark, the cousin of Barnabas, greet you. (I have already told you what to do about Mark. If he comes, welcome him.) [11]Jesus, who is called Justus, also greets you. These are the only Jewish believers who work with me for the kingdom of God, and they have been a comfort to me.

[12]Epaphras, a servant of Jesus Christ, from your group, also greets you. He always prays for you that you will grow to be spiritually mature and have everything God wants for you. [13]I know he has worked hard for you and the people in Laodicea and in Hierapolis. [14]Demas and our dear friend Luke, the doctor, greet you.

[15]Greet the brothers and sisters in Laodicea. And greet Nympha and the church that meets in her house. [16]After this letter is read to you, be sure it is also read to the church in Laodicea. And you read the letter that I wrote to Laodicea. [17]Tell Archippus, "Be sure to finish the work the Lord gave you."

[18]I, Paul, greet you and write this with my own hand. Remember me in prison. Grace be with you.

## Looking Ahead

### FIRST JOB

Getting your first job is an opportunity to learn new skills and gain life experience. Dress nicely and be polite when you ask for an application. If you have an interview, be sure to speak slowly and clearly and make eye contact with the interviewer. You won't know how to do everything when you begin, so be patient and ask questions. Businesses appreciate employees who respect others and work hard to do their best. Colossians 3:23 says, "In all the work you are doing, work the best you can. Work as if you were doing it for the Lord, not for people."

---

**4:8 so . . . are** *Some Greek copies read "so he may know how you are."*

notes

# 1 THESSALONIANS

"**W**hy did they do that?" We ask that question a lot when we watch movies or read books. Only when we get to the end do we realize why characters did what they did. Sometimes we wonder why we do certain things, too. What's the point? In the Book of 1 Thessalonians, we can find out!

The apostle Paul wrote this letter to the Christians in Thessalonica (a city in Greece) to remind them that we live in obedience to Jesus because one day he's coming back to take us to heaven with him. When he comes, we want to be able to tell him that we lived for him every day!

Paul also wanted to remind the Thessalonians that Jesus *is* coming. He describes the excitement of the day when Jesus will come back through the clouds with angels and trumpets to gather everyone who believes in him. What a day that will be!

As you read 1 Thessalonians, remember there is a point to everything we do. We want to please Jesus and be ready to meet him when he comes!

# PAUL ENCOURAGES NEW CHRISTIANS

## THINGS TO TALK WITH GOD ABOUT . . .

**1** From Paul, Silas, and Timothy.
To the church in Thessalonica, the church in God the Father and the Lord Jesus Christ:
Grace and peace to you.

### The Faith of the Thessalonians

²We always thank God for all of you and mention you when we pray. ³We continually recall before God our Father the things you have done because of your faith

**50% of kids do chores every day.**
—Taylor KidsPulse 2004 Report. Taylor Research & Consulting Group.
http://www.thetaylorgroup.com/get_download.cfm

**did you know?**

and the work you have done because of your love. And we thank him that you continue to be strong because of your hope in our Lord Jesus Christ.

⁴Brothers and sisters, God loves you, and we know he has chosen you, ⁵because the Good News we brought to you came not only with words, but with power, with the Holy Spirit, and with sure knowledge that it is true. Also you know

how we lived when we were with you in order to help you. ⁶And you became like us and like the Lord. You suffered much, but still you accepted the teaching with the joy that comes from the Holy Spirit. ⁷So you became an example to all the believers in Macedonia and Southern Greece. ⁸And the Lord's teaching spread from you not only into Macedonia and Southern Greece, but now your faith in God has become known everywhere. So we do not need to say anything about it. ⁹People everywhere are telling about the way you accepted us when we were there with you. They tell how you stopped worshiping idols and began serving the living and true God. ¹⁰And you wait for God's Son, whom God raised from the dead, to come from heaven. He is Jesus, who saves us from God's angry judgment that is sure to come.

### Paul's Work in Thessalonica

**2** Brothers and sisters, you know our visit to you was not a failure. ²Before we came to you, we suffered in Philippi. People there insulted us, as you know, and many people were against us. But our God helped us to be brave and to tell you his Good

WE BELIEVE THAT
JESUS DIED AND
THAT HE ROSE AGAIN.
SO, BECAUSE OF HIM,
GOD WILL RAISE WITH
JESUS THOSE WHO
HAVE DIED.

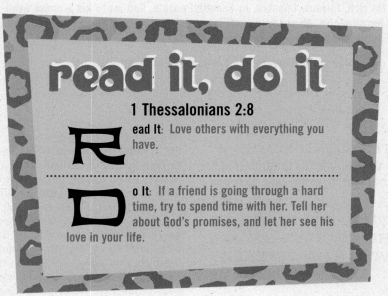

## read it, do it

### 1 Thessalonians 2:8

**R** ead It: Love others with everything you have.

**D** o It: If a friend is going through a hard time, try to spend time with her. Tell her about God's promises, and let her see his love in your life.

## god's promises

### 1 Thessalonians 1:2–6

Have you ever moaned that "life is not fair"? We don't all have the same life experiences or advantages. Some people have more than enough money, clothes, and food, while others are very poor. You might not have some of the things that other people have. That can feel unfair! But there is one special gift that is for everyone.

The apostle Paul was excited to tell people about the amazing gift that God promised to give to all people who accept it. When people receive forgiveness from Jesus and let God change their hearts, God promises that they will receive the gift of the Holy Spirit! The gift of the Holy Spirit is God's Spirit living inside of us.

Some people get to have special things while some do not. But this promise from God is not just for the people Paul spoke with thousands of years ago. It's not just for rich, famous, talented, or beautiful people. God made his promise available for *all* people. All you have to do is believe, and you will receive the gift of the Holy Spirit! What an exciting promise!

**The gift of the Holy Spirit is God's Spirit living inside of us!**

## BE YOUR BEST!

**W**hether you live on a farm or in the city, do everyone a favor and wipe (or remove!) your shoes before entering your house. In the same way, when you come home from school, don't drag in with you the dirty or foolish things you heard during the day.

---

THE LORD HIMSELF WILL COME DOWN FROM HEAVEN WITH A LOUD COMMAND, WITH THE VOICE OF THE ARCHANGEL, AND WITH THE TRUMPET CALL OF GOD.

---

News. [3]Our appeal does not come from lies or wrong reasons, nor were we trying to trick you. [4]But we speak the Good News because God tested us and trusted us to do it. When we speak, we are not trying to please people, but God, who tests our hearts. [5]You know that we never tried to influence you by saying nice things about you. We were not trying to get your money; we had no selfishness to hide from you. God knows that this is true. [6]We were not looking for human praise, from you or anyone else, [7]even though as apostles of Christ we could have used our authority over you.

But we were very gentle with you,[n] like a mother caring for her little children. [8]Because we loved you, we were happy to share not only God's Good News with you, but even our own lives. You had become so dear to us! [9]Brothers and sisters, I know you remember our hard work and difficulties. We worked night and day so we would not burden any of you while we preached God's Good News to you.

[10]When we were with you, we lived in a holy and honest way, without fault. You know this is true, and so does God. [11]You know that we treated each of you as a father treats his own children. [12]We encouraged you, we urged you, and we insisted that you live good lives for God, who calls you to his glorious kingdom.

[13]Also, we always thank God because when you heard his message from us, you accepted it as the word of God, not the words of humans. And it really is God's message which works in you who believe. [14]Brothers and sisters, your experiences have been like those of God's churches in Christ that are in Judea.[n] You suffered from the people of your own country, as they suffered from the Jews [15]who killed both the Lord Jesus and the prophets and forced us to leave that country. They do not please God and are against all people. [16]They try to stop us

---

**2:7 But . . . you** *Some Greek copies read "But we were like infants among you."*  **2:14 Judea** *The Jewish land where Jesus lived and taught and where the church first began.*

from teaching those who are not Jews so they may be saved. By doing this, they are increasing their sins to the limit. The anger of God has come to them at last.

## Paul Wants to Visit Them Again

[17]Brothers and sisters, though we were separated from you for a short time, our thoughts were still with you. We wanted very much to see you and tried hard to do so. [18]We wanted to come to you. I, Paul, tried to come more than once, but Satan stopped us. [19]You are our hope, our joy, and the crown we will take pride in when our Lord Jesus Christ comes. [20]Truly you are our glory and our joy.

**3** When we could not wait any longer, we decided it was best to stay in Athens alone [2]and send Timothy to you. Timothy, our brother, works with us for God and helps us tell people the Good News about Christ. We sent him to strengthen and encourage you in your faith [3]so none of you would be upset by these troubles. You yourselves know that we must face these troubles. [4]Even when we were with you, we told you we all would have to suffer, and you know it has happened. [5]Because of this, when I could wait no longer, I sent Timothy to you so I could learn about your faith. I was afraid the devil had tempted you, and perhaps our hard work would have been wasted.

[6]But Timothy now has come back to us from you and has brought us good news about your faith and love. He told us that you always remember us in a good way and that you want to see us just as much as we want to see you. [7]So, brothers and sisters, while we have much trouble and suffering, we are encouraged about you because of your faith. [8]Our life is really full if you stand

AND THOSE WHO HAVE DIED BELIEVING IN CHRIST WILL RISE FIRST. AFTER THAT, WE WHO ARE STILL ALIVE WILL BE GATHERED UP WITH THEM IN THE CLOUDS TO MEET THE LORD IN THE AIR. AND WE WILL BE WITH THE LORD FOREVER.

strong in the Lord. [9]We have so much joy before our God because of you. We cannot thank him enough for all the joy we feel. [10]Night and day we continue praying with all our heart that we can see you again and give you all the things you need to make your faith strong.

[11]Now may our God and Father himself and our Lord Jesus prepare the way for us to come to you. [12]May the Lord make your love grow more and multiply for each other and for all people so that you will love others as we love you. [13]May your hearts be made strong so that you will be holy and without fault before our God and Father when our Lord Jesus comes with all his holy ones.

## top ten

### top ten things to...
**Do on a Rainy Day**

1. Work on a jigsaw puzzle . . . or make one!

2. Thank God for watering the earth.

3. Write a letter to a friend or relative.

4. Take a bubble bath (clean the tub when you're done!)

5. Clean out your closet.

6. Draw or paint a sunny scene.

7. Share your umbrella with a friend.

8. Go to the library.

9. Make a list of things that make you happy.

10. Have a picnic indoors!

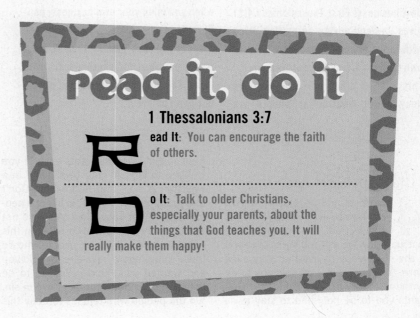

## read it, do it

**1 Thessalonians 3:7**

**R**ead It: You can encourage the faith of others.

**D**o It: Talk to older Christians, especially your parents, about the things that God teaches you. It will really make them happy!

## dig deeper

### 1 Thessalonians 4:11–12

"Mind your own business!" How often have you heard that expression . . . or said it to someone else? It sounds pretty rude, doesn't it? Well, it can be if we're trying to get someone to leave us alone or if we don't want others to see what we're doing.

It might be surprising to find out that the Bible tells us to mind our own business! First Thessalonians 4:11 gives us good advice on getting along with other people: "Take care of your own business, and do your own work." This means that you shouldn't be nosy about what other people are

doing and you shouldn't be quick to judge them.

You might not agree with the way they talk or dress or behave or sing . . . but it's not your job to tell them how to do things better. If you have a good relationship with a girl who *wants* your advice, then it is okay to share your thoughts. Otherwise, mind your own business!

These verses go on to explain that when you mind your own business, non-Christians will notice . . . and they will respect you! And gaining their respect is a great start for sharing Jesus with them. Remember: *do* care about people but *don't* be nosy!

## Q & A

**Q** Is it a sin to get a divorce? I think my parents might be getting one.

**A** In the Bible, God makes it clear that he designed marriage as a life-long commitment between a man and a woman. Divorce breaks God's heart because it hurts families. Divorce also breaks his rules (see 1 Corinthians 7:10–11). God wants married people to love each other and work through their problems, but they often still choose to divorce. Pray that your parents will ask God to help them with their marriage. Whatever happens, remember: it's not your fault.

> YOU KNOW VERY WELL THAT THE DAY THE LORD COMES AGAIN WILL BE A SURPRISE, LIKE A THIEF THAT COMES IN THE NIGHT.

### A Life that Pleases God

**4** Brothers and sisters, we taught you how to live in a way that will please God, and you are living that way. Now we ask and encourage you in the Lord Jesus to live that way even more. [2]You know what we told you to do by the authority of the Lord Jesus. [3]God wants you to be holy and to stay away from sexual sins. [4]He wants each of you to learn to control your own body[n] in a way that is holy and honorable. [5]Don't use your body for sexual sin like the people who do not know God. [6]Also, do not wrong or cheat another Christian in this way. The Lord will punish people who do those things as we have already told you and warned you. [7]God called us to be holy and does not want us to live in sin. [8]So the person who refuses to obey this teaching is disobeying God, not simply a human teaching. And God is the One who gives us his Holy Spirit.

[9]We do not need to write you about having love for your Christian family, because God has already taught you to love each other. [10]And truly you do love the Christians in all of Macedonia. Brothers and sisters, now we encourage you to love them even more.

[11]Do all you can to live a peaceful life. Take care of your own business, and do your own work as we have already told you. [12]If you do, then people who are not believers will respect you, and you will not have to depend on others for what you need.

---

4:4 **learn . . . body** This might also mean "learn to live with your own wife."

# August

start here

**1**

**2**

**17**

**16** Make a kite and see if it flies!

**18** Pick wildflowers with your sister or friend.

**19**

**3** Write a thank-you card to your pastor.

**15** Pray for a person of influence: Today is actor Ben Affleck's birthday.

**27**

**28** Pray for a person of influence: Today is singer LeAnn Rimes's birthday.

**29** Pray for a person of influence: Today is singer Michael Jackson's birthday.

**20**

**4**

**14**

**26** Set the table really fancy for dinner tonight.

**13** Write down 5 things you are sorry for. Cross them out as you ask God to forgive you for each one.

**31**

**30**

**21** Offer to give your mom or dad a back rub.

**5** If you go to a store today, be extra polite to the cashier.

**25**

**22**

**6**

**12**

**11** Memorize 1 Corinthians 13:4–7.

**24** Pray for a person of influence: Today is actor Chad Michael Murray's birthday.

**23** Pray for a person of influence: Today is NBA all-star Kobe Bryant's birthday.

**7**

**10**

**9** Start your shopping list for school supplies.

**8** Make up 10 crazy ice cream flavors and get people to vote on them, just for fun.

Rocky says, "Make a list!"

## The Lord's Coming

13Brothers and sisters, we want you to know about those Christians who have died so you will not be sad, as others who have no hope. 14We believe that Jesus died and that he rose again. So, because of him, God will raise with Jesus those who have died. 15What we tell you now is the Lord's own message. We who are living when the Lord comes again will not go before those who have already died. 16The Lord himself will come down from heaven with a loud command, with the voice of the archangel,[n] and with the trumpet call of God. And those who have died believing in Christ will rise first. 17After that, we who are still alive will be gathered up with them in the clouds to meet the Lord in the air. And we will be with the Lord forever. 18So encourage each other with these words.

## Be Ready for the Lord's Coming

5 Now, brothers and sisters, we do not need to write you about times and dates. 2You know very well that the day the Lord comes again will be a surprise, like a thief that comes in the night. 3While people are saying, "We have peace and we are safe," they will be destroyed quickly. It is like pains

> WHILE PEOPLE ARE SAYING, "WE HAVE PEACE AND WE ARE SAFE," THEY WILL BE DESTROYED QUICKLY. IT IS LIKE PAINS THAT COME QUICKLY TO A WOMAN HAVING A BABY. THOSE PEOPLE WILL NOT ESCAPE.

that come quickly to a woman having a baby. Those people will not escape. 4But you, brothers and sisters, are not living in darkness, and so that day will not surprise you like a thief. 5You are all people who belong to the light and to the day. We do not belong to the night or to darkness. 6So we should not be like other people who are sleeping, but we should be alert and have self-control. 7Those who sleep, sleep at night. Those who get drunk, get drunk at night. 8But we belong to the day, so we should control ourselves. We should wear faith and love to protect us, and the hope of salvation should be our helmet. 9God did not choose us to suffer his anger but to have salvation through our Lord Jesus Christ. 10Jesus died for us so that we can live together with him, whether we are alive or dead when he comes. 11So encourage each other and give each other strength, just as you are doing now.

## Final Instructions and Greetings

12Now, brothers and sisters, we ask you to appreciate those who work hard among you, who lead you in the Lord and teach you. 13Respect them with a very special love because of the work they do.

Live in peace with each other. 14We ask you, brothers and sisters, to warn those who do not work. Encourage the people who are afraid. Help those who are weak. Be patient with everyone. 15Be sure that no one pays back wrong for wrong, but always try to do what is good for each other and for all people.

16Always be joyful. 17Pray continually, 18and give thanks whatever happens. That is what God wants for you in Christ Jesus.

19Do not hold back the work of the Holy Spirit. 20Do not treat prophecy as if it were unimportant. 21But test everything. Keep what is good, 22and stay away from everything that is evil.

23Now may God himself, the God of peace, make you pure, belonging only to him. May your whole self—spirit, soul, and body—be kept safe and without fault when our Lord Jesus Christ comes. 24You can trust the One who calls you to do that for you.

25Brothers and sisters, pray for us.

26Give each other a holy kiss when you meet. 27I tell you by the authority of the Lord to read this letter to all the believers.

28The grace of our Lord Jesus Christ be with you.

## Rapture (Second Coming)

The rapture will take place one day when Jesus comes to earth again (also called the "second coming")! About two thousand years ago, Jesus died on the cross so that all who believe in him can be saved from punishment for their sins. When he comes again, he will come as the King of heaven. Check out 1 Thessalonians 4:16–17 for an exciting picture of that day. Trumpets will play and, faster than you can blink your eyes, Jesus will gather the Christians from every corner of the world and take them to heaven with him.

---

4:16 archangel *The leader among God's angels or messengers.*

# 2 THESSALONIANS

**H**ave you ever been so excited about something that you just *couldn't* wait for it? It might have felt like nothing else was important in comparison.

The Thessalonians felt that way, too. After they read the apostle Paul's first letter, they couldn't wait for Jesus to come back to earth and take them to live in heaven with him. In fact, they were so focused on waiting for Jesus that they quit working and ignored their responsibilities. They even depended on others to provide food for them!

It's great to be excited for Jesus' coming. As Christians, we *should* look forward to it eagerly.

But we can't stop doing everything else, no matter how soon we think Jesus might come. Paul wrote this second letter to the Thessalonians as a reminder that we don't know when Christ will come. Until then, God wants us to keep working, taking care of ourselves, and living for him.

Knowing Jesus will come someday—maybe soon!—isn't an excuse to be lazy. It's a reason to look forward with hope and excitement while we continue to live in obedience to God. Let's make the most of each day. You can start by reading the Book of 2 Thessalonians!

# THE PROBLEMS OF NEW CHRISTIANS

## THINGS TO TALK WITH GOD ABOUT . . .

**1** ¹From Paul, Silas, and Timothy.

To the church in Thessalonica in God our Father and the Lord Jesus Christ:

²Grace and peace to you from God the Father and the Lord Jesus Christ.

### Paul Talks About God's Judgment

³We must always thank God for you, brothers and sisters. This is only right, because your faith is growing more and more, and the love that every one of you has for each other is increasing. ⁴So we brag about you to the other churches of God. We tell them about the way you continue to be strong and have faith even though you are being treated badly and are suffering many troubles.

⁵This is proof that God is right in his judgment. He wants you to be counted worthy of his kingdom for which you are suffering. ⁶God will do what is right. He will give trouble to those who trouble you. ⁷And he will give rest to you who are troubled and to us also when the Lord Jesus appears with burning fire from heaven with his powerful angels. ⁸Then he will punish those who do not know God and who do not obey the Good News about our Lord Jesus Christ. ⁹Those people will be punished with a destruction that continues forever. They will be kept away from the Lord and from his great power. ¹⁰This will happen on the day when the Lord Jesus comes to receive glory because of his holy people. And all the people who have believed will be amazed at Jesus. You will be in that group, because you believed what we told you.

¹¹That is why we always pray for you, asking our God to help you live the kind of life he called you to live. We pray that with his power God will help you do the good things you want and perform the works that come from your faith. ¹²We pray all this so that the name of our Lord Jesus Christ will have glory in you, and you will have glory in him. That glory comes from the grace of our God and the Lord Jesus Christ.

### Evil Things Will Happen

**2** ¹Brothers and sisters, we have something to say about the coming of our Lord Jesus Christ and the time when we will meet together with him. ²Do not become easily upset in

WE PRAY THAT WITH HIS POWER GOD WILL HELP YOU DO THE GOOD THINGS YOU WANT AND PERFORM THE WORKS THAT COME FROM YOUR FAITH.

## read it, do it

### 2 Thessalonians 1:3

**R**ead It: Grow in faith and love.

**D**o It: In a notebook, keep track of what you learned in church, prayers God answered, and ways you showed love to others. Flip through the notebook sometimes to see how you're growing!

## Q & A

**Q** Does God see everything I do?

**A** God is "omni-scient" and "omnipresent," which means he knows everything and is everywhere. Psalm 33:13 says, "The Lord looks down from heaven and sees every person." We can't hide from him! So yes, he can see everything you do. That shouldn't worry you, though, if you obey him and live in a way that pleases him.

## god's promises

### 2 Thessalonians 3:3

Who do you think has the scariest job? Firemen, police officers, security guards, or pilots? Actually, even taxi drivers, builders, nurses, high school teachers, and many others can face scary situations. So don't feel bad when *you* find yourself in a situation where you wish someone would help and protect you. It could be a school bully, your neighbor's huge dog, or even taking the bus by yourself for the first time.

People usually outgrow the things that frightened them as a child, such as darkness or being alone. But when there's real danger around, it's perfectly okay for even an adult to feel scared!

You can try doing all kinds of things to protect yourself: hire a bodyguard, walk around with helmets and armor, or never leave the house. But those things aren't really realistic or necessary. None of those things will protect you from the scariest enemy we all have: the devil. But God will protect you from the devil!

In 2 Thessalonians 3:3 we learn that God "is faithful and will give you strength and will protect you from the Evil One." Who needs a bodyguard when you've got *God* watching out for you?!

***God will protect you from the devil.***

> DO NOT BECOME EASILY UPSET IN YOUR THINKING OR AFRAID IF YOU HEAR THAT THE DAY OF THE LORD HAS ALREADY COME.

your thinking or afraid if you hear that the day of the Lord has already come. Someone may have said this in a prophecy or in a message or in a letter as if it came from us. ³Do not let anyone fool you in any way. That day of the Lord will not come until the turning away[n] from God happens and the Man of Evil,[n] who is on his way to hell, appears. ⁴He will be against and put himself above any so-called god or anything that people worship. And that Man of Evil will even go into God's Temple and sit there and say that he is God.

⁵I told you when I was with you that all this would happen. Do you not remember? ⁶And now you know what is stopping that Man of Evil so he will appear at the right time. ⁷The secret power of evil is already working in the world, but there is one who is stopping that power. And he will continue to stop it until he is taken out of the way. ⁸Then that Man of Evil will appear, and the Lord Jesus will kill him with the breath that comes from his mouth and will destroy him with the glory of his coming. ⁹The Man of Evil will come by the power of Satan. He will have great power, and he will do many different false miracles, signs, and wonders. ¹⁰He will use every kind of evil to trick those who are lost. They will die, because they refused to love the truth. (If they loved the truth, they would be saved.) ¹¹For this reason God sends them something powerful that leads them away from the truth so they will believe a lie. ¹²So all those will be judged guilty who did not believe the truth, but enjoyed doing evil.

### You Are Chosen for Salvation

¹³Brothers and sisters, whom the Lord loves, God chose you from the begin-

---

**2:3 turning away** Or "the rebellion."  **2:3 Man of Evil** Some Greek copies read "Man of Sin."

MAY OUR LORD JESUS CHRIST HIMSELF AND GOD OUR FATHER ENCOURAGE YOU AND STRENGTHEN YOU IN EVERY GOOD THING YOU DO AND SAY.

# dig deeper

## 2 Thessalonians 3:6–13

What would you do if you were at the mall and saw a two-year-old boy wandering around, crying for his mommy? Would you ignore him? Or would you gently take his hand and go to the information booth so that they could make an announcement for his mom to hear? Hopefully you would help him find his mother!

It's good to help people find their way. It might be a visitor to your church looking for the pastor or a new girl at school trying to find her classroom. It's even better to help a Christian friend find her way back to God. Sometimes Christians get so busy in their lives that they start skipping their Bible reading, prayer time, or even church. Then, because they're not spending time with God, they start to think it is okay to do certain things that they used to know were sins. This is called *compromising*.

What does God want you to do when you have a friend like that? Ask God to show you how to help your friend get strong in her faith again. Then ask God to give you courage and love when you talk with her. Which friend of yours needs help finding her way back to God? Don't put it off: talk with her today.

## Q & A

**Q** I can't wait to go to camp this summer, but I'm afraid I'll get homesick. How can I make sure I like it?

**A** It's OK to feel a little homesick as long as you don't let it ruin your fun. Pack a few special reminders of home, such as your favorite teddy bear or a photo of your parents. Get to know other kids and remember they might feel homesick, too. When you feel sad, ask your counselor for a hug and to pray with you. Each night, instead of focusing on how much you miss home, write down all the fun things that happened during the day and thank God for them.

ning[n] to be saved. So we must always thank God for you. You are saved by the Spirit that makes you holy and by your faith in the truth. [14]God used the Good News that we preached to call you to be saved so you can share in the glory of our Lord Jesus Christ. [15]So, brothers and sisters, stand strong and continue to believe the teachings we gave you in our speaking and in our letter.

[16–17]May our Lord Jesus Christ himself and God our Father encourage you and strengthen you in every good thing you do and say. God loved us, and through his grace he gave us a good hope and encouragement that continues forever.

### Pray for Us

**3** And now, brothers and sisters, pray for us that the Lord's teaching will continue to spread quickly and that people will give honor to that teaching, just as happened with you. [2]And pray that we will be protected from stubborn and evil people, because not all people believe.

[3]But the Lord is faithful and will give you strength and will protect you from the Evil One. [4]The Lord makes us feel sure that you are doing and will continue to do the things we told you. [5]May the Lord lead your hearts into God's love and Christ's patience.

### The Duty to Work

[6]Brothers and sisters, by the authority of our Lord Jesus Christ we command you to stay away from any believer who refuses to work and does not follow the teaching we gave you. [7]You yourselves know that you should live as we live. We were not lazy when we were with you. [8]And when we ate another person's food,

2:13 **God . . . beginning** *Some Greek copies read "God chose you as the firstfruits of the harvest."*

# Christian Girls Around the World

## Rosita: *Peru*

The sunshine peeks in Rosita's window, waking her up. She looks out the window. It's a beautiful spring day in *November* (because Rosita lives *south* of the equator). Rosita jumps up and puts on a gray pleated skirt and a white blouse; then white socks and black shoes finish her school uniform. She wishes it were gym day so she could wear her gym clothes. Besides, she loves volleyball!

Now her mother is scolding her to hurry and eat her breakfast—liquid oatmeal and two rolls—it's almost 7:00 A.M.! Profesora Tonia greets Rosita as she slips into her seat next to Marta. Marta chatters to the girl behind them, but she gets quiet real quick when Profesora calls out her name. Rosita is happy just to listen as she arranges her papers and prepares to copy her lessons for today. She doesn't like to be the center of attention, but she does want to do her best. She loves math and hopes she can be a teacher someday.

After school, Rosita eats lunch with her family. Then she and her mother go downtown on the bus to get a gift for her cousin's birthday party. Peruvians love parties! They don't have much to spend on presents, but everyone will have a great time staying up late, listening to music, and playing games. Her *tia* (aunt) will serve sandwiches, popcorn, soda pop, and cake. Rosita's favorite part is singing "Happy Birthday"—in Spanish and English!

At the shop, they see *hermana* (sister) Malena, Rosita's Sunday school teacher. They greet her with a hug and a kiss on the cheek. Rosita blushes when *hermana* tells her mom what a great job she is doing memorizing the Scripture verses. Rosita wants to win the prize for memorizing the most verses. Even if she doesn't win, Rosita loves being able to say the verses over to herself and imagine God saying the words just to her.

Rosita accepted the Lord Jesus as her Savior when she was only seven years old. Now that she is eleven, she is trying to read her Bible every day. Her mom prays with her at night and talks to her about loving and obeying God. Tomorrow will be another day at school. Rosita asks God to help her shine Jesus' light to everyone around her.

---

we always paid for it. We worked very hard night and day so we would not be an expense to any of you. [9]We had the right to ask you to help us, but we worked to take care of ourselves so we would be an example for you to follow. [10]When we were with you, we gave you this rule: "Anyone who refuses to work should not eat."

[11]We hear that some people in your group refuse to work. They do nothing but busy themselves in other people's lives. [12]We command those people and beg them in the Lord Jesus Christ to work quietly and earn their own food. [13]But you, brothers and sisters, never become tired of doing good.

[14]If some people do not obey what we tell you in this letter, then take note of them. Have nothing to do with them so they will feel ashamed. [15]But do not treat them as enemies. Warn them as fellow believers.

### Final Words

[16]Now may the Lord of peace give you peace at all times and in every way. The Lord be with all of you.

[17]I, Paul, end this letter now in my own handwriting. All my letters have this to show they are from me. This is the way I write.

[18]The grace of our Lord Jesus Christ be with you all.

> GOD LOVED US, AND THROUGH HIS GRACE HE GAVE US A GOOD HOPE AND ENCOURAGEMENT THAT CONTINUES FOREVER.

# 1 TIMOTHY

**H**ow would you feel if you were suddenly asked to lead your youth group or Sunday school class? Would you know what to do? It might be kind of scary!

Timothy, a young pastor in New Testament times, might have felt the same way. He was excited to serve God as a church leader in Ephesus, but it was a big responsibility. Paul wrote this letter to encourage Timothy in his job and to teach him how to run the church.

Think of the Book of 1 Timothy as an instruction manual for a healthy church. It talks about prayer and worshiping God with other Christians. It talks about leaders in the church—what kind of people they should be and how they should act.

Plus, there is a special message for *you!* First Timothy 4:12 says, "Do not let anyone treat you as if you are unimportant because you are young." No matter what age you are, God wants each of us to set an example of right living and to help others in the body of Christ.

First Timothy helps us understand what it takes to serve as a leader in the church and to be an example for others. You're never too young to get started!

# ADVICE TO A YOUNG PREACHER

## THINGS TO TALK WITH GOD ABOUT . . .

1 From Paul, an apostle of Christ Jesus, by the command of God our Savior and Christ Jesus our hope. ²To Timothy, a true child to me because you believe:

Grace, mercy, and peace from God the Father and Christ Jesus our Lord.

### Warning Against False Teaching

³I asked you to stay longer in Ephesus when I went into Macedonia so you could command some people there to stop teaching false things. ⁴Tell them not to spend their time on stories that are not true and on long lists of names in family histories. These things only bring arguments; they do not help God's work, which is done in faith. ⁵The purpose of this command is for people to have love, a love that comes from a pure heart and a good conscience and a true faith. ⁶Some people have missed these things and turned to useless talk. ⁷They want to be teachers of the law, but they do not understand either what they are talking about or what they are sure about.

⁸But we know that the law is good if someone uses it lawfully. ⁹We also know that the law is not made for good people

> I THANK CHRIST JESUS OUR LORD, WHO GAVE ME STRENGTH, BECAUSE HE TRUSTED ME AND GAVE ME THIS WORK OF SERVING HIM.

but for those who are against the law and for those who refuse to follow it. It is for people who are against God and are sinful, who are unholy and ungodly, who kill their fathers and mothers, who murder, ¹⁰who take part in sexual sins, who have sexual relations with people of the same sex, who sell slaves, who tell lies, who speak falsely, and who do anything against the true teaching of God. ¹¹That teaching is part of the Good News of the blessed God that he gave me to tell.

### Thanks for God's Mercy

¹²I thank Christ Jesus our Lord, who gave me strength, because he trusted me and gave me this work of serving him. ¹³In the past I spoke against Christ

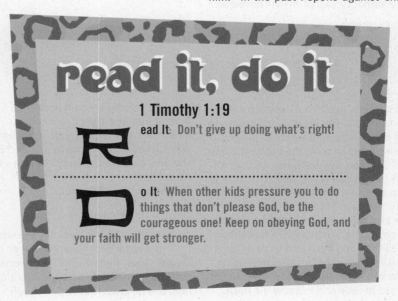

## read it, do it

**1 Timothy 1:19**

**R** ead It: Don't give up doing what's right!

**D** o It: When other kids pressure you to do things that don't please God, be the courageous one! Keep on obeying God, and your faith will get stronger.

and persecuted him and did all kinds of things to hurt him. But God showed me mercy, because I did not know what I was doing. I did not believe. [14]But the grace of our Lord was fully given to me, and with that grace came the faith and love that are in Christ Jesus.

[15]What I say is true, and you should fully accept it: Christ Jesus came into the world to save sinners, of whom I am the worst. [16]But I was given mercy so that in me, the worst of all sinners, Christ Jesus could show that he has patience without limit. His patience with me made me an example for those who would believe in him and have life forever. [17]To the King that rules forever, who will never die, who cannot be seen, the only God, be honor and glory forever and ever. Amen.

[18]Timothy, my child, I am giving you a command that agrees with the prophecies that were given about you in the past. I tell you this so you can follow them and fight the good fight. [19]Continue to have faith and do what you know is right. Some people have rejected this, and their faith has been shipwrecked. [20]Hymenaeus and Alexander have done that, and I have given them to Satan so they will learn not to speak against God.

## Some Rules for Men and Women

**2** First, I tell you to pray for all people, asking God for what they need and being thankful to him. [2]Pray for rulers and for all who have authority so that we can have quiet

and peaceful lives full of worship and respect for God. [3]This is good, and it pleases God our Savior, [4]who wants all people to be saved and to know the truth. [5]There is one God and one mediator so that human beings can reach God. That way is through Christ Jesus, who is himself human. [6]He gave himself as a payment to free all people. He is proof that came at the right time. [7]That is why I was chosen to tell the Good News and to be an apostle. (I am telling the truth; I am not lying.) I was chosen to teach those who are not Jews to believe and to know the truth.

[8]So, I want the men everywhere to pray, lifting up their hands in a holy manner, without anger and arguments.

[9]Also, women should wear proper clothes that show respect and self-control, not using braided hair or gold or pearls or expensive clothes. [10]Instead, they should do good deeds, which is right for women who say they worship God.

[11]Let a woman learn by listening quietly and being ready to cooperate in everything. [12]But I do not allow a woman to teach or to have authority over a man, but to listen quietly, [13]because Adam was formed first and then Eve. [14]And Adam was not tricked, but the woman was tricked and became a sinner. [15]But she will be saved through having children if she continues in faith, love, and holiness, with self-control.

## Elders in the Church

**3** What I say is true: Anyone wanting to become an overseer desires a good work. [2]An overseer must not give people a reason to criticize him, and he must have only one wife. He must be self-controlled, wise, respected by others, ready to welcome guests, and able to teach. [3]He must not drink too much wine or like to fight, but rather be gentle and peaceable, not loving money. [4]He must be a good family leader, having children who cooperate with full respect. [5](If someone does not know how to lead the family, how can that person take care

### ■ Bible Bios — Priscilla (Acts 18:18—28)

Priscilla and her husband were Jews living in Corinth (a city in Greece). They had a business making tents . . . just like the apostle Paul! Paul would stay with them and work with them when he was in Corinth.

Priscilla not only helped her husband with the business, but she was also a wise Christian woman who talked to people about Jesus and explained God's Word to them. This was pretty unusual for Jewish women in those days.

The way the Bible mentions her, we can tell that she had a strong relationship with God. Along with her husband, she explained God's Word to another teacher who had misunderstood things about Jesus. Priscilla is a great example for Christian girls today: you can help others by growing in your faith!

### did you know?

39% of kids say Chinese is their favorite kind of food.
—Center for Culinary Development. "Tween peeks." http://ccdsf.com/trendcornerjano4.html

### Q & A

**Q** What does it mean to love your neighbor as yourself?

**A** In Luke 10:25–37, Jesus told a story that gave a good picture of what it means to love your neighbor. Your neighbor is basically anyone around you, not just the person living next door. God wants you to treat others the way you would like to be treated—with patience, kindness, and generosity. You might not *like* your neighbors, but you should still show them God's love!

THERE IS ONE GOD AND ONE MEDIATOR SO THAT HUMAN BEINGS CAN REACH GOD. THAT WAY IS THROUGH CHRIST JESUS, WHO IS HIMSELF HUMAN.

# dig deeper

## 1 Timothy 4:12

Who is your role model? Is it someone smart or athletic? Someone funny or adventurous or talented? Why do you admire this person? Most importantly, does your role model set a good example of how God wants you to live?

Timothy, a young pastor in New Testament times, looked up to the apostle Paul as his role model. Paul was older and wiser, and Timothy wanted to follow his example of living for God.

But do you know what Paul told Timothy? He said Timothy could be a role model, too! In 1 Timothy 4:12, Paul wrote, "Do not let anyone treat you as if you are unimportant because you are young. Instead, be an example to the believers with your words, your actions, your love, your faith, and your pure life."

Just like Timothy, you are never too young to be an example to others! Do people know you belong to Jesus? Can they see a difference in your life because of it? By talking and behaving in a way that honors God, others will see that living for Jesus makes a difference in your life. What you say and do *is* important, no matter how old you are. Even when you're young, you can be an example every day!

# Q & A

**Q** My family goes on long road trips. What are some ideas for fun things to do in the car?

**A** Bring along lots of paper, pens, markers, books, and a few CDs. If you get bored with that stuff, make up funny songs with your family or have a contest for who can spot certain things first (some examples: something purple, a brown cow, or a certain type of car). See who can list the most things they are thankful about. Most of all, don't be selfish or rude. A nasty fight can ruin the trip for everyone!

---

of God's church?) [6]But an elder must not be a new believer, or he might be too proud of himself and be judged guilty just as the devil was. [7]An elder must also have the respect of people who are not in the church so he will not be criticized by others and caught in the devil's trap.

## Deacons in the Church

[8]In the same way, deacons must be respected by others, not saying things they do not mean. They must not drink too much wine or try to get rich by cheating others. [9]With a clear conscience they must follow the secret of the faith that God made known to us. [10]Test them first. Then let them serve as deacons if you find nothing wrong in them. [11]In the same way, women[n] must be respected by others. They must not speak evil of others. They must be self-controlled and trustworthy in everything. [12]Deacons must have only one wife and be good leaders of their children and their own families. [13]Those who serve well as deacons are making an honorable place for themselves, and they will be very bold in their faith in Christ Jesus.

## The Secret of Our Life

[14]Although I hope I can come to you soon, I am writing these things to you now. [15]Then, even if I am delayed, you will know how to live in the family of God. That family is the church of the living God, the support and foundation of the truth. [16]Without doubt, the secret of our life of worship is great:

He[n] was shown to us in a human body,
   proved right in spirit,
and seen by angels.
   He was proclaimed to the nations,
believed in by the world,
   and taken up in glory.

**3:11 women** *This might mean the wives of the deacons, or it might mean women who serve in the same way as deacons.* **3:16 He** *Some Greek copies read "God."*

## A Warning About False Teachers

**4** Now the Holy Spirit clearly says that in the later times some people will stop believing the faith. They will follow spirits that lie and teachings of demons. ²Such teachings come from the false words of liars whose consciences are destroyed as if by a hot iron. ³They forbid people to marry and tell them not to eat certain foods which God created to be eaten with thanks by people who believe and know the truth. ⁴Everything God made is good, and nothing should be refused if it is accepted with thanks, ⁵because it is made holy by what God has said and by prayer.

> BUT DO NOT FOLLOW FOOLISH STORIES THAT DISAGREE WITH GOD'S TRUTH, BUT TRAIN YOURSELF TO SERVE GOD.

## Be a Good Servant of Christ

⁶By telling these things to the brothers and sisters, you will be a good servant of Christ Jesus. You will be made strong by the words of the faith and the good teaching which you have been following. ⁷But do not follow foolish stories that disagree with God's truth, but train yourself to serve God. ⁸Training your body helps you in some ways, but serving God helps you in every way by bringing you blessings in this life and in the future life, too. ⁹What I say is true, and you should fully accept it. ¹⁰This is why we work and struggle:ⁿ We hope in the living God who is the Savior of all people, especially of those who believe.

¹¹Command and teach these things. ¹²Do not let anyone treat you as if you are unimportant because you are young. Instead, be an example to the believers with your words, your actions, your love, your faith, and your pure life. ¹³Until I come, continue to read the Scriptures to the people, strengthen them, and teach them. ¹⁴Use the gift you have, which was given to you through prophecy when the group of elders laid their hands onⁿ you. ¹⁵Continue to do those things; give your life to doing them so your progress may be seen by everyone. ¹⁶Be careful in your life and in your teaching. If you continue to live and teach rightly, you will save both yourself and those who listen to you.

## cool

### How Humerus . . .

Can't you just feel it now? You hit a certain spot on your elbow and . . . yow! Your whole arm and a few fingers tingle. Maybe you hop around, shaking your arm until the weird feeling goes away. People often call that spot on your elbow a "funny bone." Here's what really happens: your *ulnar nerve* bumps against your *humerus* (a long bone in your arm). This doesn't cause any damage; it just feels . . . funny!

Isn't it cool how God created our bodies? Take a moment to thank him for it today!

## Shine Your Light

Eleven-year-old Ashley loves to help her mom in the kitchen, whether it's making dinner or baking her favorite chocolate chip cookies. She also loves to give to others. Guess what? She found a way to do both things at once!

In Ashley's busy neighborhood, there is always something exciting going on. The neighbors two doors down just had a new baby, and across the street, an older gentleman is about to have surgery.

When situations like that happen, most people don't have time to think, "What will I make for dinner?" That's where Ashley comes in. She and her mom prepare one of their favorite meals and take it to their neighbors, warm and ready to eat. You can imagine how happy the neighbors are to have a delicious, home-cooked meal instead of another night of fast food or frozen dinners!

What do you like to do? Do you enjoy taking care of animals or reading books? You could volunteer at an animal shelter or hold a story time for the younger kids in your neighborhood. Ask God to show you how you can give to others by doing what you love to do!

---

4:10 **struggle** *Some Greek copies read "suffer."*  4:14 **laid their hands on** *The laying on of hands had many purposes, including the giving of a blessing, power, or authority.*

## read it, do it

**1 Timothy 5:3**

**R** ead It: Take care of widows.

**D** o It: If you know someone whose husband has died, or who is lonely and has no one to take care of her, talk with your parents about ways *you* can play a role in helping her out.

IF YOU CONTINUE TO LIVE AND TEACH RIGHTLY, YOU WILL SAVE BOTH YOURSELF AND THOSE WHO LISTEN TO YOU

### Rules for Living with Others

**5** Do not speak angrily to an older man, but plead with him as if he were your father. Treat younger men like brothers, ²older women like mothers, and younger women like sisters. Always treat them in a pure way.

³Take care of widows who are truly widows. ⁴But if a widow has children or grandchildren, let them first learn to do their duty to their own family and to repay their parents or grandparents. That pleases God. ⁵The true widow, who is all alone, puts her hope in God and continues to pray night and day for God's help. ⁶But the widow who uses her life to please herself is really dead while she is alive. ⁷Tell the believers to do these things so that no one can criticize them. ⁸Whoever does not care for his own relatives, especially his own family members, has turned against the faith and is worse than someone who does not believe in God.

⁹To be on the list of widows, a woman must be at least sixty years old. She must have been faithful to her husband. ¹⁰She must be known for her good works—works such as raising her children, welcoming strangers, washing the feet of God's people, helping those in trouble, and giving her life to do all kinds of good deeds.

¹¹But do not put younger widows on that list. After they give themselves to Christ, they are pulled away from him by their physical desires, and then they want to marry again. ¹²They will be judged for not doing what they first promised to do. ¹³Besides that, they learn to waste their time, going from house to house. And they not only waste their time but also begin to gossip and busy themselves with other people's lives, saying things they should not say. ¹⁴So I want the younger widows to marry, have children, and manage their homes. Then no enemy will have any reason to criticize them. ¹⁵But some have already turned away to follow Satan.

¹⁶If any woman who is a believer has widows in her family, she should care for them herself. The church should not have to care for them. Then it will be able to take care of those who are truly widows.

# Relationships

**H** ow do you treat older people? Do you treat some elders (people who are older than you) different from others? Paul told the young pastor, Timothy, to treat older men as fathers and older women as mothers (1 Timothy 5:1–2). In other words, he instructed Timothy to treat every elder as a special relative. Be sure to treat your elders with respect by honoring them in the same way you honor your parents.

## BE YOUR BEST!

Showing your belly or wearing short skirts will make boys attracted to you. But do you really want the attention of guys who only like your body? Find creative ways to look cool while staying covered, and trust God to bring you friends who care about *you*—not your looks.

## dig deeper

### 1 Timothy 5:1—2

A lot of adults say kids today don't respect older men and women. Unfortunately, that's true in many cases! Teenagers, tweens, and even younger children often speak rudely or just don't listen to adults. Are you respectful toward others, especially grown-ups? Or do you think that they're old-fashioned and just don't understand kids? Do you think that all they want is to keep you from having fun?

God wants you to respect your elders! First Timothy 5:1—2 says: "Do not speak angrily to an older man, but plead with him as if he were your father. Treat younger men like brothers, older women like mothers and younger women like sisters. Always treat them in a pure way."

Whether it's at church, school, or the mall, make an effort to treat everyone with respect, especially older people. Show them love the way you would to your family. Of course, if you're not respectful toward your parents or your brothers and sisters, it might be hard to figure out how to show respect to someone else. Ask God to help you speak kindly to everyone—adults *and* other kids.

If you're wondering what's in it for you . . . that's easy: you will have better relationships with the people in your life!

[17]The elders who lead the church well should receive double honor, especially those who work hard by speaking and teaching, [18]because the Scripture says: "When an ox is working in the grain, do not cover its mouth to keep it from eating,"[n] and "A worker should be given his pay."[n]

[19]Do not listen to someone who accuses an elder, without two or three witnesses. [20]Tell those who continue sinning that they are wrong. Do this in front of the whole church so that the others will have a warning.

[21]Before God and Christ Jesus and the chosen angels, I command you to do these things without showing favor of any kind to anyone.

[22]Think carefully before you lay your hands on[n] anyone, and don't share in the sins of others. Keep yourself pure.

[23]Stop drinking only water, but drink a little wine to help your stomach and your frequent sicknesses.

> ### WE BROUGHT NOTHING INTO THE WORLD, SO WE CAN TAKE NOTHING OUT.

[24]The sins of some people are easy to see even before they are judged, but the sins of others are seen only later. [25]So also good deeds are easy to see, but even those that are not easily seen cannot stay hidden.

**6** All who are slaves under a yoke should show full respect to their masters so no one will speak against God's name and our teaching. [2]The slaves whose masters are believers should not show their masters any less respect because they are believers. They should serve their masters even better, because they are helping believers they love.

You must teach and preach these things.

### False Teaching and True Riches

[3]Anyone who has a different teaching does not agree with the true teaching of our Lord Jesus Christ and the teaching

---

5:18 **"When . . . eating."** *Quotation from Deuteronomy 25:4.* 5:18 **"A worker . . . pay."** *Quotation from Luke 10:7.* 5:22 **lay your hands on** *The laying on of hands had many purposes, including the giving of a blessing, power, or authority.*

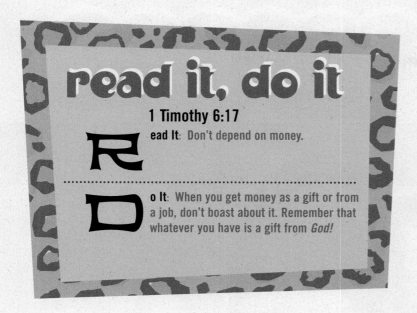

### read it, do it

**1 Timothy 6:17**

**R**ead It: Don't depend on money.

**D**o It: When you get money as a gift or from a job, don't boast about it. Remember that whatever you have is a gift from *God!*

THOSE WHO WANT TO BECOME RICH BRING TEMPTATION TO THEMSELVES AND ARE CAUGHT IN A TRAP.

that shows the true way to serve God. [4]This person is full of pride and understands nothing, but is sick with a love for arguing and fighting about words. This brings jealousy, fighting, speaking against others, evil mistrust, [5]and constant quarrels from those who have evil minds and have lost the truth. They think that serving God is a way to get rich.

[6]Serving God does make us very rich, if we are satisfied with what we have. [7]We brought nothing into the world, so we can take nothing out. [8]But, if we have food and clothes, we will be sat-

isfied with that. [9]Those who want to become rich bring temptation to themselves and are caught in a trap. They want many foolish and harmful things that ruin and destroy people. [10]The love of money causes all kinds of evil. Some people have left the faith, because they wanted to get more money, but they have caused themselves much sorrow.

### Some Things to Remember

[11]But you, man of God, run away from all those things. Instead, live in the right way, serve God, have faith, love, patience, and gentleness. [12]Fight the good fight of faith, grabbing hold of the life that continues forever. You were called to have that life when you confessed the good confession before many witnesses. [13]In the sight of God, who gives life to everything, and of Christ Jesus, I give you a command. Christ Jesus made the good confession when he stood before Pontius Pilate. [14]Do what you were commanded to do without wrong or blame until our Lord Jesus Christ comes again. [15]God will make that happen at the right time. He is the blessed and only Ruler, the King of all kings and the Lord of all lords. [16]He is the only One who never dies. He lives in light so bright no one can go near it. No one has ever seen God, or can see him. May honor and power belong to God forever. Amen.

[17]Command those who are rich with things of this world not to be proud. Tell

them to hope in God, not in their uncertain riches. God richly gives us everything to enjoy. [18]Tell the rich people to do good, to be rich in doing good deeds, to be generous and ready to share. [19]By doing that, they will be saving a treasure for themselves as a strong foundation for the future. Then they will be able to have the life that is true life.

[20]Timothy, guard what God has trusted to you. Stay away from foolish, useless talk and from the arguments of what is falsely called "knowledge." [21]By saying they have that "knowledge," some have missed the true faith.

Grace be with you.

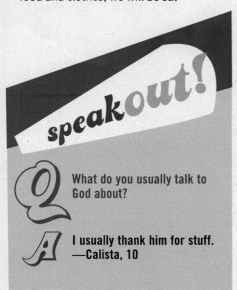

### speakout!

**Q** What do you usually talk to God about?

**A** I usually thank him for stuff.
—Calista, 10

## Q&A

**Q** What does it mean to be modest?

**A** Modesty means more than just making sure you cover your body properly when you get dressed, although that's important! Clothes that are too tight or show too much skin don't please God. First Timothy 2:9–10 says that we should be modest. That includes not trying to make people think we're rich or important by what we wear. It also means not drawing too much attention to ourselves with crazy hairstyles or heavy makeup. Go ahead . . . express your personality! But don't forget to ask, "Does this honor God?"

# 2 TIMOTHY

The Book of 2 Timothy teaches us to stand strong for Christ! Like soldiers focused on their mission, we need be dedicated to Christ. Our mission? Operation Faith. We can complete our assignment by obeying God's Word each day.

The apostle Paul wrote this second letter to Timothy near the end of his life. Already in prison in Rome, where the evil emperor Nero had ordered his death, Paul probably knew this was the last New Testament letter he would ever write.

Before he died, Paul wanted to give Timothy and other church leaders some final guidelines for ministry and Christian living. He wanted them to know how to continue leading the church after his death.

Second Timothy reminds us we must serve the Lord faithfully. We need to focus on our mission and not get distracted by things around us. It's not always easy to be a Christian. Sometimes, just like soldiers, we have to fight, but our battle is spiritual. We have to fight temptations to sin and stand up for what we know is right.

As you'll discover in 2 Timothy, God has given us his Word to guide us as we live for him each day. By claiming the promises and sharing the truths found in the Bible, we can serve him faithfully. So put on your combat boots and start reading. God has an important mission just for you!

# PAUL ENCOURAGES TIMOTHY

## THINGS TO TALK WITH GOD ABOUT . . .

1 From Paul, an apostle of Christ Jesus by the will of God. God sent me to tell about the promise of life that is in Christ Jesus.

²To Timothy, a dear child to me:

Grace, mercy, and peace to you from God the Father and Christ Jesus our Lord.

### Encouragement for Timothy

³I thank God as I always mention you in my prayers, day and night. I serve him, doing what I know is right as my ancestors did. ⁴Remembering that you cried for me,

**39% of kids have friends or relatives who live in other countries.**

—Lindstrom, Martin. *BRANDchild: Remarkable insights into the minds of today's global kids and their relationships with brands.* London: Kogan Page Limited, 2003. p. 5

**did you know?**

I want very much to see you so I can be filled with joy. ⁵I remember your true faith. That faith first lived in your grandmother Lois and in your mother Eunice, and I know you now have that same faith. ⁶This is why I remind you to keep using the gift God gave you when I laid my hands on[n] you. Now let it grow, as a small flame grows into a fire. ⁷God did not give us a spirit that makes us afraid but a spirit of power and love and self-control.

⁸So do not be ashamed to tell people about our Lord Jesus, and do not be ashamed of me, in prison for the Lord. But suffer with me for the Good News. God, who gives us the strength to do that, ⁹saved us and made us his holy people. That was not because of anything we did ourselves but because of God's purpose and grace. That grace was given to us through Christ Jesus before time began, ¹⁰but it is now shown to us by the coming of our Savior Christ Jesus. He destroyed death, and through the Good News he showed us the way to have life that cannot be destroyed. ¹¹I was chosen to tell that Good News and to be an apostle and a teacher. ¹²I am suffering now because I tell the Good News, but I am not

ashamed, because I know Jesus, the One in whom I have believed. And I am sure he is able to protect what he has trusted me with until that day.[n] ¹³Follow the pattern of true teachings that you heard from me in faith and love, which are in Christ Jesus. ¹⁴Protect the truth that you were given; protect it with the help of the Holy Spirit who lives in us.

¹⁵You know that everyone in Asia has left me, even Phygelus and Hermogenes. ¹⁶May the Lord show mercy to the family of Onesiphorus, who has often helped me and was not ashamed that I was in prison. ¹⁷When he came to Rome, he looked eagerly for me until he found me. ¹⁸May the Lord allow him to find mercy from the Lord on that day. You know how many ways he helped me in Ephesus.

## cool

### Hey, Honey!

How many different types of honey have you tried? Maybe your local grocery store has five or ten different flavors. Actually, there are about three hundred varieties of honey! It all depends on where the bees got the nectar they used to make the honey.

The Bible mentions honey quite a few times—people have enjoyed eating honey for thousands of years! King David said that God's commands "are sweeter than honey, even the finest honey" (Psalm 19:10). Yummy honey might make your mouth happy . . . but only God's Word can satisfy your soul!

## SO DO NOT BE ASHAMED TO TELL PEOPLE ABOUT OUR LORD JESUS, . . .

**1:6 laid my hands on** *The laying on of hands had many purposes, including the giving of a blessing, power, or authority.* **1:12 day** *The day Christ will come to judge all people and take his people to live with him.*

## god's promises

### 2 Timothy 3:14–17

Have you noticed how many kids don't live with both of their parents? Some kids have never known one of their parents . . . or even both. Others live with grandparents or in a foster home. Some kids live with both their parents but don't really have a good relationship with them. Most kids have wondered at some time in their lives what it would be like to have perfect parents.

God understands. He knows that, deep down inside, we all want a mom or dad who loves God and loves us no matter what. We all want a home where we belong and feel safe and can learn about God.

Because of God's amazing love for us, even the loneliest person on earth *can* belong to a wonderful family . . . God's family! When we put our trust in Jesus and ask him to take away our sins, we begin a relationship with God. He calls us sons and daughters! Think about how special that is. The Creator of the universe loves us and invites us to become part of his family. That's the message throughout God's Word, the Bible. And there's more good news about all God wants to do in and through us this side of heaven. Keep reading!

*The Creator of the universe invites us to become part of his family.*

## Q & A

**Q** Were there ever dinosaurs on the earth?

**A** For many years, some Christians thought that only people who believed in evolution could also believe that dinosaurs existed. As Christian researchers, scientists, and Bible experts have studied the question, though, many people now believe that dinosaurs *could* have existed. Some people believe that after the great flood (think Noah and the big boat), some of the very large animals did not have enough food to survive on for very long and became extinct. There isn't a definite yes or no answer, but it *is* possible. We'll know for sure when we get to heaven and can ask God questions like this!

## IF WE DIED WITH HIM, WE WILL ALSO LIVE WITH HIM.

preach, [9]and I am suffering because of it to the point of being bound with chains like a criminal. But God's teaching is not in chains. [10]So I patiently accept all these troubles so that those whom God has chosen can have the salvation that is in Christ Jesus. With that salvation comes glory that never ends.

[11]This teaching is true:
If we died with him, we will also live with him.
[12]If we accept suffering, we will also rule with him.
If we say we don't know him, he will say he doesn't know us.
[13]If we are not faithful, he will still be faithful,
because he must be true to who he is.

### A Loyal Soldier of Christ Jesus

**2** You then, Timothy, my child, be strong in the grace we have in Christ Jesus. [2]You should teach people whom you can trust the things you and many others have heard me say. Then they will be able to teach others. [3]Share in the troubles we have like a good soldier of Christ Jesus. [4]A soldier wants to please the enlisting officer, so no one serving in the army wastes time with everyday matters. [5]Also an athlete who takes part in a contest must obey all the rules in order to win. [6]The farmer who works hard should be the first person to get some of the food that was grown. [7]Think about what I am saying, because the Lord will give you the ability to understand everything.

[8]Remember Jesus Christ, who was raised from the dead, who is from the family of David. This is the Good News I

# WHAT KIND OF GIRL ARE YOU?

Are you a tomboy or a girly girl?
What kind of girl does God want you to be?
This fun quiz will give you some ideas!

**1.** Your parents tell you you're going to summer camp and you think:

a. "Alright! I can't wait to go hiking and look for crayfish in the lake!"

b. "I hope we have a campfire every night!"

c. "If Valerie is there this year, maybe we can take arts and crafts together again."

d. "I'll have to take my hair-straightener with me. My hair gets so frizzy after swimming!"

**2.** At your best friend's birthday party you wear:

a. Old jeans, a T-shirt, and sneakers.

b. Your black cords and a nice blue shirt.

c. Lime-green capris and a fun printed top.

d. A ruffled flowery skirt, a fancy beaded top, and fancy sandals.

**3.** Your parents agree to let you take lessons in one thing of your choice. You pick:

a. Soccer.

b. Piano.

c. Painting.

d. Hairdressing.

**4.** To get ready in the morning you:

a. Change out of your pajamas.

b. Brush your teeth, comb your hair, and wash your face.

c. Take time to fix your hair, put on a little perfume, and check yourself in the mirror.

d. Spend an hour in the bathroom styling your hair and putting on make-up.

## How feminine are you?

**If you answered mostly As,** you're a bit of a tomboy! You prefer being active and think it's crazy for girls to waste so much time getting dolled up. That's fine! But Deuteronomy 22:5 says that women should dress like women and men should dress like men. God made us different from boys. Ask him to show you if he wants you to sometimes behave or dress a little more like girls are expected to.

**If you answered mostly Bs,** you're a casual girl. You're satisfied with simple things and like to just blend into the background. Your modesty is a good quality, but make sure it's not because you're uncomfortable with your body and looks. Ask God to help you grow into the young woman he wants you to be.

**If you answered mostly Cs,** you're comfortable being a girl! You enjoy looking nice but you're quick about it. Your confidence and creativity make people enjoy being around you. Try to keep up this good balance of being fun and feminine at the same time!

**If you answered mostly Ds,** you're a real girly girl! You are becoming a woman and you know it! You love the attention you get when you're dressed up so you make sure people notice you. But remember, being feminine is one thing...being vain is another. Read 2 Timothy 2:9–10 for a reminder that true beauty comes from the inside!

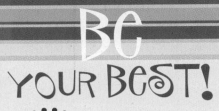

# Be YOUR BEST!

**G**ood posture when you sit, stand, and walk is very important for your back, and it makes you look more confident, too! As a Christian, don't be afraid to stand up tall for your beliefs. If you're tempted to "slouch," ask God to give you the courage you need!

## A Worker Pleasing to God

[14]Continue teaching these things, warning people in God's presence not to argue about words. It does not help anyone, and it ruins those who listen. [15]Make every effort to give yourself to God as the kind of person he will approve. Be a worker who is not ashamed and who uses the true teaching in the right way. [16]Stay away from foolish, useless talk, because that will lead people further away from God. [17]Their evil teaching will spread like a sickness inside the body. Hymenaeus and Philetus are like that. [18]They have left the true teaching, saying that the rising from the dead has already taken place, and so they are destroying the faith of some people. [19]But God's strong foundation continues to stand. These words are written on the seal: "The Lord knows those who belong to him,"[n] and "Everyone who wants to belong to the Lord must stop doing wrong."

[20]In a large house there are not only things made of gold and silver, but also things made of wood and clay. Some things are used for special purposes, and others are made for ordinary jobs. [21]All who make themselves clean from evil will be used for special purposes. They will be made holy, useful to the Master, ready to do any good work.

[22]But run away from the evil desires of youth. Try hard to live right and to have faith, love, and peace, together with those who trust in the Lord from pure hearts. [23]Stay away from foolish and stupid arguments, because you know they grow into quarrels. [24]And a servant of the Lord must not quarrel but must be kind to everyone, a good teacher, and patient. [25]The Lord's servant must gently teach those who disagree. Then maybe God will let them change their minds so they can accept the truth. [26]And they may wake up and escape from the trap of the devil, who catches them to do what he wants.

## The Last Days

**3** Remember this! In the last days there will be many troubles, [2]because people will love themselves, love money, brag, and be proud. They will say evil things against others and will not obey their parents or be thankful or be the kind of people God wants. [3]They will not love others, will refuse to forgive, will gossip, and will not control themselves. They will be cruel, will hate what is good, [4]will turn against their friends, and will do foolish things without thinking. They will be conceited, will love pleasure instead of God, [5]and will act as if they serve God but will not have his power. Stay away from those

> STAY AWAY FROM FOOLISH, USELESS TALK, BECAUSE THAT WILL LEAD PEOPLE FURTHER AWAY FROM GOD.

people. [6]Some of them go into homes and get control of silly women who are full of sin and are led by many evil desires. [7]These women are always learning new teachings, but they are never able to understand the truth fully. [8]Just as Jannes and Jambres were against Moses, these people are against the truth. Their thinking has been ruined, and they have failed in trying to follow the faith. [9]But they will not be successful in what they do, because as with Jannes and Jambres, everyone will see that they are foolish.

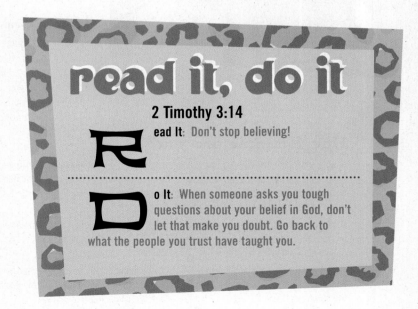

# read it, do it

## 2 Timothy 3:14

**R**ead It: Don't stop believing!

**D**o It: When someone asks you tough questions about your belief in God, don't let that make you doubt. Go back to what the people you trust have taught you.

2:19 **"The Lord . . . him."** Quotation from Numbers 16:5.

# Q & A

**Q** Why does God let us do bad things?

**A** When God created humans, he didn't make us robots. He gave us the ability to choose between wrong and right. God doesn't want us to sin, but if he always stopped us, we'd be just like puppets or robots . . . programmed to behave a certain way. That doesn't mean we're stuck with sin, though! When we choose to commit our lives to Christ, God's Spirit living in us helps us stop doing bad things. (Check out 1 John 3:6.)

## Obey the Teachings

¹⁰But you have followed what I teach, the way I live, my goal, faith, patience, and love. You know I never give up. ¹¹You know how I have been hurt and have suffered, as in Antioch, Iconium, and Lystra. I have suffered, but the Lord saved me from all those troubles. ¹²Everyone who wants to live as God desires, in Christ Jesus, will be persecuted. ¹³But people who are evil and cheat others will go from bad to worse. They will fool others, but they will also be fooling themselves.

¹⁴But you should continue following the teachings you learned. You know they are true, because you trust those who taught you. ¹⁵Since you were a child you have known the Holy Scriptures which are able to make you wise. And that wisdom leads to salvation through faith in Christ Jesus. ¹⁶All Scripture is inspired by God and is useful for teaching, for showing people what is wrong in their lives, for correcting faults, and for teaching how to live right. ¹⁷Using the Scriptures, the person who serves God will be capable, having all that is needed to do every good work.

# dig deeper

### 2 Timothy 4:7

How do you feel when you get a really high grade on a test or bring home a great report card? Or when you spend hours on a painting and it looks beautiful? Whenever we work really hard at something, it feels great to finally finish and see what we've done. While you're cleaning your room, even if it's not fun, imagining what it's going to look like later can help you keep going.

When the apostle Paul was old and knew that he wouldn't live much longer, he told Timothy that he had "fought the good fight," "finished the race," and "kept the faith" (2 Timothy 4:7). For many years, he had devoted his life to serving God. He was treated badly for believing in Jesus and was even put in prison. He traveled to different countries and used all his money to make it possible for people to hear about Jesus. As he got ready to die, he felt peaceful because he had pleased God with his life.

Can you say that you've been living for God? Do you do your best to share the Good News about Jesus with your friends? Ask God to help you "keep the faith." Then you'll be able to look back at your hard work and be proud of your "high grades!"

**4** I give you a command in the presence of God and Christ Jesus, the One who will judge the living and the dead, and by his coming and his kingdom: ²Preach the Good News. Be ready at all times, and tell people what they need to do. Tell them when they are wrong. Encourage them with great patience and careful teaching, ³because the time will come when people will not listen to the true teaching but will find many more teachers who please them by saying the things they want to hear. ⁴They will stop listening to the truth and will begin to follow false stories. ⁵But you should control yourself at all times, accept troubles, do the work of telling the Good News, and complete all the duties of a servant of God.

⁶My life is being given as an offering to God, and the time has come for me to

leave this life. [7]I have fought the good fight, I have finished the race, I have kept the faith. [8]Now, a crown is being held for me—a crown for being right with God. The Lord, the judge who judges rightly, will give the crown to me on that day[n]—not only to me but to all those who have waited with love for him to come again.

## Personal Words

[9]Do your best to come to me as soon as you can, [10]because Demas, who loved this world, left me and went to Thessalonica. Crescens went to Galatia, and Titus went to Dalmatia. [11]Luke is the only one still with me. Get Mark and bring him with you when you come, because he can help me in my work here. [12]I sent Tychicus to Ephesus. [13]When I was in Troas, I left my coat there with Carpus. So when you come, bring it to me, along with my books, particularly the ones written on parchment.[n]

[14]Alexander the metalworker did many harmful things against me. The Lord will punish him for what he did. [15]You also should be careful that he does not hurt you, because he fought strongly against our teaching.

### Bible Bios — Paul's Nephew (Acts 23:12–35)

Some people who didn't believe in Jesus got so upset by the apostle Paul's teachings they made a plan to kill him! Somehow Paul's nephew, a young man whose name we don't know, heard about this plan. He went to warn his uncle; then Paul sent him with an officer to give the information to the army's commander.

Paul's nephew bravely went to the commander, who met with him privately. The commander heard about the whole evil plan and believed everything the young man told him. Afterward, he sent Paul's nephew away, warning him not to tell anyone what he had done.

We read later in Acts 23 about how the commander's soldiers helped Paul escape. His nephew had saved his life! God can use *you* for great things, too, when you care about and look out for others.

[16]The first time I defended myself, no one helped me; everyone left me. May they be forgiven. [17]But the Lord stayed with me and gave me strength so I could fully tell the Good News to all those who are not Jews. So I was saved from the lion's mouth. [18]The Lord will save me when anyone tries to hurt me, and he will bring me safely to his heavenly kingdom. Glory forever and ever be the Lord's. Amen.

## Final Greetings

[19]Greet Priscilla and Aquila and the family of Onesiphorus. [20]Erastus stayed in Corinth, and I left Trophimus sick in Miletus. [21]Try as hard as you can to come to me before winter.

Eubulus sends greetings to you. Also Pudens, Linus, Claudia, and all the brothers and sisters in Christ greet you.

[22]The Lord be with your spirit. Grace be with you.

## Q & A

**Q** Is there life on other planets?

**A** No one has found life on other planets yet, though scientists keep trying to. The Bible doesn't specifically answer this question, but when you study the way God created the earth and his special relationship with humans, it's hard to imagine there's life somewhere else in the universe. But God can do whatever he wants, right? So . . . there's a mystery to ask him about when you get to heaven!

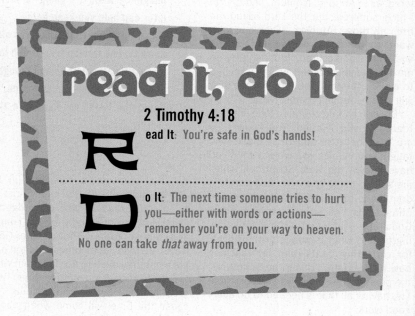

### read it, do it

**2 Timothy 4:18**

**Read It**: You're safe in God's hands!

**Do It**: The next time someone tries to hurt you—either with words or actions—remember you're on your way to heaven. No one can take *that* away from you.

---

**4:8 day** The day Christ will come to judge all people and take his people to live with him. **4:13 parchment** A writing paper made from the skins of sheep.

notes

# TITUS

**D**o you ever feel like you're the only one who cares about doing the right thing? With all the sin and evil in the world around us, sometimes it's hard to even know what's right.

If you want some help understanding how to live a godly (right) life in an evil world, start reading the Book of Titus!

Paul wrote this letter to a young Greek man named Titus. Titus had become a Christian because of Paul's preaching about the Good News. When Paul wrote this letter, Titus was working in the church on the island of Crete (in the Mediterranean Sea).

Titus needed to know how to run the church and what should make its members different from the rest of the world. Some important things you'll learn in this book:

➜ We shouldn't listen to people who try to teach us to do things that go against God's laws. Even if evil surrounds us, we can live pure lives.

➜ Church leaders need to be dedicated to following God. Their lives should show Christ's love to everyone!

➜ We should live as good citizens, obeying authority and treating our neighbors fairly.

Titus is a practical manual on how to live a life that pleases God, no matter what people around you do. Are you ready for the challenge?

# PAUL INSTRUCTS TITUS

## THINGS TO TALK WITH GOD ABOUT . . .

**1** From Paul, a servant of God and an apostle of Jesus Christ. I was sent to help the faith of God's chosen people and to help them know the truth that shows people how to serve God. [2]That faith and that knowledge come from the hope for life forever, which God promised to us before time began. And God cannot lie. [3]At the right time God let the world know about that life through preaching. He trusted me with that work,

**50% of preteens have divorced parents.**
—Lindstrom, Martin. *BRANDchild: Remarkable insights into the minds of today's global kids and their relationships with brands.* London: Kogan Page Limited, 2003. p. 11

**did you know?**

and I preached by the command of God our Savior.

[4]To Titus, my true child in the faith we share:

Grace and peace from God the Father and Christ Jesus our Savior.

### Titus' Work in Crete

[5]I left you in Crete so you could finish doing the things that still needed to be done and so you could appoint elders in every town, as I directed you. [6]An elder must not be guilty of doing wrong, must have only one wife, and must have believing children. They must not be known as children who are wild and do not cooperate. [7]As God's managers, overseers must not be guilty of doing wrong, being selfish, or becoming angry quickly. They must not drink too much wine, like to fight, or try to get rich by cheating others. [8]Overseers must be ready to welcome guests, love what is good, be wise, live right, and be holy and self-controlled. [9]By holding on to the trustworthy word just as we teach it, overseers can help people by using true teaching, and they can show those who are against the true teaching that they are wrong.

[10]There are many people who refuse to cooperate, who talk about worthless things and lead others into the wrong

## BibLe BaSicS

**A**ll the stories in the Bible are absolutely true! Through these stories, God shows how much he loves people and how he has guided and cared for his people in the past. These stories remind us that he'll be there for us, too, helping us through even the hardest situations. We know these stories are true because:

- The Bible says so! Psalm 33:4 says, "God's word is true."
- God wrote the Bible, and he doesn't lie! Titus 1:2 tells us "God cannot lie."
- Science and history have also proven that people and places in the Bible really existed and that the events in Bible stories really did happen!

## IN EVERY WAY BE AN EXAMPLE OF DOING GOOD DEEDS.

# September

start here

**1** Introduce yourself to a girl you don't know at school.

**2**

**3**

**4** Pray for a person of influence: Today is singer Beyoncé Knowles's birthday.

**5** Practice writing your name with your "opposite" hand.

**6** Before your favorite class, put a sticky note with a smiley face on your teacher's desk!

**7**

**8** Write down your 5 best memories from this past summer. Thank God for them!

**9**

**10** Treat your dad like a king today! (Or your mom like a queen.)

**11** Pray for a person of influence: Today is rap artist Ludacris's (Chris Bridges) birthday.

**12** Design a homemade puzzle for a younger kid at your church.

**13**

**14**

**15** Pray for a person of influence: Today is Prince Harry of Great Britain's birthday.

**16**

**17** Vacuum the family car today.

**18**

**19**

**20** Look out your window. Write down everything you see that God made and then thank him!

**21**

**22** Fluff all the pillows in the house today.

**23**

**24**

**25** Take turns with your best friend saying what you like about each other.

**26**

**27** Pray for a person of influence: Today is singer Avril Lavigne's birthday.

**28**

**29** Pray for a person of influence: Today is singer/actress Hilary Duff's birthday.

**30**

Murphy says, "Make a list!"

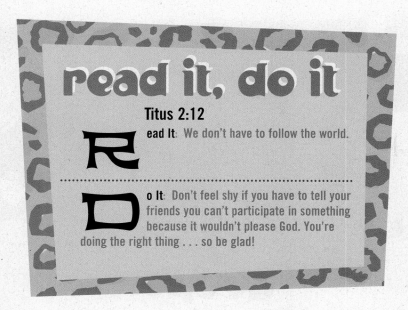

## read it, do it

**Titus 2:12**

**R**ead It: We don't have to follow the world.

**D**o It: Don't feel shy if you have to tell your friends you can't participate in something because it wouldn't please God. You're doing the right thing . . . so be glad!

way—mainly those who insist on circumcision to be saved. ¹¹These people must be stopped, because they are upsetting whole families by teaching things they should not teach, which they do to get rich by cheating people. ¹²Even one of their own prophets said, "Cretans are always liars, evil animals, and lazy people who do nothing but eat." ¹³The words that prophet said are true. So firmly tell those people they are wrong so they may become strong in the faith, ¹⁴not accepting Jewish false stories and the commands of people who reject the truth. ¹⁵To those who are pure, all things are pure, but to those who are full of sin and do not believe, nothing is pure. Both their minds and their consciences have been ruined. ¹⁶They say they know God, but their actions show they do not accept him. They are hateful people, they refuse to obey, and they are useless for doing anything good.

### Following the True Teaching

**2** But you must tell everyone what to do to follow the true teaching. ²Teach older men to be self-controlled, serious, wise, strong in faith, in love, and in patience.

³In the same way, teach older women to be holy in their behavior, not speaking against others or enslaved to too much wine, but teaching what is good. ⁴Then they can teach the young women to love their husbands, to love their children, ⁵to be wise and pure, to be good workers at home, to be kind, and to yield to their husbands. Then no one will be able to criticize the teaching God gave us.

⁶In the same way, encourage young men to be wise. ⁷In every way be an example of doing good deeds. When you teach, do it with honesty and seriousness. ⁸Speak the truth so that you cannot be criticized. Then those who are against you will be ashamed because there is nothing bad to say about us.

⁹Slaves should yield to their own masters at all times, trying to please them and not arguing with them. ¹⁰They should not steal from them but should show their masters they can be fully trusted so that in everything they do they will make the teaching of God our Savior attractive.

¹¹That is the way we should live, because God's grace that can save everyone has come. ¹²It teaches us not to live against God nor to do the evil things the world wants to do. Instead, that grace teaches us to live in the present age in a wise and right way and in a way that shows we serve God. ¹³We should live like that while we wait for our great hope and the coming of the glory of our great God and Savior Jesus Christ. ¹⁴He gave

## Relationships

**M**ost girls like to "trade in" their old clothes for something new and in style. But don't trade in your friends just because someone else more fun and popular comes along! Good friends are like puppies—they will always stick by you, and they think you're the best! The Bible says, "A friend loves you all the time" (Proverbs 17:17). And a loyal friend is even better than a puppy! Being loyal doesn't mean you have to do everything your friend wants to do or agree with everything she says, but it does mean caring about her no matter what.

BEING MADE RIGHT WITH GOD BY HIS GRACE, WE COULD HAVE THE HOPE OF RECEIVING THE LIFE THAT NEVER ENDS.

himself for us so he might pay the price to free us from all evil and to make us pure people who belong only to him—people who are always wanting to do good deeds.

¹⁵Say these things and encourage the people and tell them what is wrong in their lives, with all authority. Do not let anyone treat you as if you were unimportant.

## The Right Way to Live

**3** Remind the believers to yield to the authority of rulers and government leaders, to obey them, to be ready to do good, ²to speak no evil about anyone, to live in peace, and to be gentle and polite to all people.

³In the past we also were foolish. We did not obey, we were wrong, and we were slaves to many things our bodies wanted and enjoyed. We spent our lives doing evil and being jealous. People hated us, and we hated each other. ⁴But when the kindness and love of God our Savior was shown, ⁵he saved us because of his mercy. It was not because of good deeds we did to be right with him. He saved us through the washing that made us new people through the Holy Spirit. ⁶God poured out richly upon us that Holy Spirit through Jesus Christ our Savior. ⁷Being made right with God by his grace, we could have the hope of receiving the life that never ends.

⁸This teaching is true, and I want you to be sure the people understand these things. Then those who believe in God will be careful to use their lives for doing good. These things are good and will help everyone.

⁹But stay away from those who have foolish arguments and talk about useless family histories and argue and quarrel about the law. Those things are worth nothing and will not help anyone. ¹⁰After a first and second warning, avoid some-

### dig deeper

### Titus 3:9

Some people love to argue. They can go on and on, trying to prove that they're right about something that's not even very important. For example, let's say a few of your friends come over to your house. You pick a game and start to play, but one of the girls says you're playing the wrong way. She starts to explain the rules, pulling out the instructions and trying to show you the right way to play. You and your friends spend the next fifteen minutes arguing about the rules. What a waste of time! Instead of having fun, now you're all annoyed and probably don't even feel like playing anymore.

People can be like that about Christianity, too. When you talk with them about Jesus, they start asking questions about this and that, trying to get you to prove the Bible is true. They don't really want to understand the Bible. They want to confuse you and waste your time!

Ask God to help you know the difference between someone who really wants to know more about Jesus and someone who just likes to argue. Titus 3:9 tells us to "stay away from those who have foolish arguments and . . . quarrel about the law. Those things are worth nothing and will not help anyone."

one who causes arguments. ¹¹You can know that such people are evil and sinful; their own sins prove them wrong.

### Some Things to Remember

¹²When I send Artemas or Tychicus to you, make every effort to come to me at Nicopolis, because I have decided to stay there this winter. ¹³Do all you can to help Zenas the lawyer and Apollos on their journey so that they have everything they need. ¹⁴Our people must learn to use their lives for doing good deeds to provide what is necessary so that their lives will not be useless.

¹⁵All who are with me greet you. Greet those who love us in the faith.

Grace be with you all.

# PHILEMON

**P**aul doesn't beat around the bush in this tiny book! He wrote it to his friend Philemon as a letter. Philemon's slave, Onesimus, had run away from his master's home—and found his way to Paul's side.

In twenty-five verses, Paul makes a convincing argument. He was in jail and had benefited from Onesimus's help while he was in chains. But Paul knew that Onesimus needed to go home to his master, Philemon.

Paul reminds Philemon that he owes him his very life (since Paul had shared the Good News

with him). And then he asks for a big favor: take Onesimus back as a brother without giving him a hard time. Paul says, "I write this letter, knowing that you will do what I ask you and even more" (Philemon 21). He wasn't afraid to let Philemon know what the right thing to do was!

As you read this little letter, watch for Paul's boldness. When we know the right thing to do, we don't have to avoid or water down the truth. Paul wasn't afraid to be direct. He knew what the right thing to do was, and he wasn't going to let anything stop him from saying it!

# A SLAVE BECOMES A CHRISTIAN

**THiNGS TO TALK WiTH GOD ABOUT . . .**

[1]From Paul, a prisoner of Christ Jesus, and from Timothy, our brother.

To Philemon, our dear friend and worker with us; [2]to Apphia, our sister; to Archippus, a worker with us; and to the church that meets in your home:

[3]Grace and peace to you from God our Father and the Lord Jesus Christ.

## Philemon's Love and Faith

[4]I always thank my God when I mention you in my prayers, [5]because I hear about the love you have for all God's holy people and the faith you have in the Lord Jesus. [6]I pray that the faith you share may make you understand every blessing we have in Christ. [7]I have great joy and comfort, my brother, because the love you have shown to God's people has refreshed them.

## Accept Onesimus as a Brother

[8]So, in Christ, I could be bold and order you to do what is right. [9]But because I love you, I am pleading with you instead. I, Paul, an old man now and also a prisoner for Christ Jesus, [10]am pleading with you for my child Onesimus, who became my child while I was in prison. [11]In the past he was useless to you, but now he has become useful for both you and me.

[12]I am sending him back to you, and with him I am sending my own heart. [13]I wanted to keep him with me so that in your place he might help me while I am in prison for the Good News. [14]But I did not want to do anything without asking you first so that any good you do for me will be because you want to do it, not because I forced you. [15]Maybe Onesimus was separated from you for a short time so you could have him back forever— [16]no longer as a slave, but better than a slave, as a loved brother. I love him very much, but you will love him even more, both as a person and as a believer in the Lord.

[17]So if you consider me your partner, welcome Onesimus as you would welcome me. [18]If he has done anything wrong to you or if he owes you anything, charge that to me. [19]I, Paul, am writing this with my own hand. I will pay it back, and I will say nothing about what you owe me for your own life. [20]So, my brother, I ask that you do this for me in the Lord: Refresh my heart in Christ. [21]I write this letter, knowing that you will do what I ask you and even more.

[22]One more thing—prepare a room for me in which to stay, because I hope God will answer your prayers and I will be able to come to you.

## Final Greetings

[23]Epaphras, a prisoner with me for Christ Jesus, sends greetings to you. [24]And also Mark, Aristarchus, Demas, and Luke, workers together with me, send greetings.

[25]The grace of our Lord Jesus Christ be with your spirit.

**I ALWAYS THANK MY GOD WHEN I MENTION YOU IN MY PRAYERS**

# Be YOUR BEST!

**N**o matter how much they love you, your parents aren't your school friends. Speak—and listen—to them with extra respect. And when you talk to God, whether you're in church or praying, speak and act in a respectful way. If you really love God, it has to show!

# HEBREWS

**J**ewish Christians in the first century seemed to have many questions such as, "Why is Jesus so special?", "Are we still supposed to follow all the old rules from the Old Testament?", and "What does it mean to have faith?"

The Book of Hebrews answers all of these questions—and more! Jesus is greater than all of the Old Testament heroes (see chapters 1—4). Because Jesus offered the perfect sacrifice for sins, he fulfilled all of the rules and regulations of the old agreement (from the Old Testament) between God and people (see chapters 5—10).

Faith is explained through the examples of holy people from the Old Testament in chapter 11 (the "Hall of Faith"). Chapters 12—13 give instructions for how Christians should act based on Jesus' example of a pure life.

Don't give up having faith—Jesus is alive! He gave us a way to have a relationship with God and to have our sins removed.

# A BETTER LIFE THROUGH CHRIST

## God Spoke Through His Son

**1** In the past God spoke to our ancestors through the prophets many times and in many different ways. ²But now in these last days God has spoken to us through his Son. God has chosen his Son to own all things, and through him he made the world. ³The Son reflects the glory of God and shows exactly what God is like. He holds everything together with his powerful word. When the Son made people clean from their sins, he sat down at the right side of God, the Great One in heaven. ⁴The Son became much greater than the angels, and God gave him a name that is much greater than theirs.

⁵This is because God never said to any of the angels,

"You are my Son.
   Today I have become your Father."
*Psalm 2:7*

Nor did God say of any angel,
   "I will be his Father,
      and he will be my Son."
*2 Samuel 7:14*

⁶And when God brings his firstborn Son into the world, he says,

"Let all God's angels worship him."ⁿ
*Psalm 97:7*

⁷This is what God said about the angels:
   "God makes his angels become like winds.
      He makes his servants become like flames of fire." *Psalm 104:4*

⁸But God said this about his Son:
   "God, your throne will last forever and ever.
      You will rule your kingdom with fairness.

### THINGS TO TALK WITH GOD ABOUT . . .

**did you know?**

21% of kids believe it's easiest to make new friends online.

—Lindstrom, Martin. *BRANDchild: Remarkable insights into the minds of today's global kids and their relationships with brands.* London: Kogan Page Limited, 2003. p. 165

## BibLe BaSicS

**W**hat does it mean when we say the Bible was inspired? Creative writers often get "inspiration" for writing from a beautiful story or amazing work of art. With the Bible, however, inspiration means that the Bible's authors received the messages they wrote from God's own mouth! Like any creative writer, they wrote with their own personalities and individual styles. But the messages contained in the Bible are 100 percent approved and accepted by God himself. Second Timothy 3:16 says, "All Scripture is inspired by God and is useful . . . for teaching how to live right." You can be sure that every verse in your Bible actually contains God's own words and messages for your life.

### GOD HAS SPOKEN TO US THROUGH HIS SON.

1:6 **"Let . . . him."** These words are found in Deuteronomy 32:43 in the Septuagint, the Greek version of the Old Testament, and in a Hebrew copy among the Dead Sea Scrolls.

⁹You love right and hate evil,
　so God has chosen you from
　　among your friends;
　he has set you apart with much
　　joy." 　　　　*Psalm 45:6–7*

¹⁰God also says,
　"Lord, in the beginning you made the
　　earth,
　and your hands made the skies.

¹¹They will be destroyed, but you will
　　remain.
　They will all wear out like clothes.

¹²You will fold them like a coat.
　And, like clothes, you will change
　　them.
　But you never change,
　　and your life will never end."
　　　　　　　　*Psalm 102:25–27*

¹³And God never said this to an angel:
　"Sit by me at my right side
　　until I put your enemies under your
　　　control."ⁿ 　　*Psalm 110:1*

¹⁴All the angels are spirits who serve
God and are sent to help those who will
receive salvation.

# cool

## Brain Freeze

**Y**ou're having a bowl of delicious ice cream, but you're eating too fast and *bam!* You get a huge pain between your eyes. It only lasts about a minute but, boy, does it ever hurt! What's happening? The nerves in your palate (the smooth "ceiling" of your mouth) tell your body that your brain is too cold, and so your body rushes extra blood to your head. The extra blood in your veins causes a headache!

James 1:4 reminds us to have patience. Slow down. You'll enjoy your ice cream more . . . and most other things in life, too!

# dig deeper

## Hebrews 1:9–12

Did you like to play dress-up when you were little? Maybe you still do! It's fun to put on fancy clothes and try new hairstyles. You can pretend you're a beautiful princess or a famous actress or the next Miss Universe.

Like celebrities, we sometimes think we need to wear expensive clothes and fancy jewelry and have perfect hairstyles for people to think we're beautiful. But God has a different opinion. The Bible reminds us that God and his kingdom are eternal. Everything we can see—including the ground beneath us—is temporal. One day, God is going to recreate the entire universe. All those nice dresses in your closet will disappear!

So, what does God treasure? What does he find beautiful?

It's the inside—our hearts and what kind of people we are—that God values more than precious jewels. You probably know some girls who always look perfect but who act mean and selfish. They may look nice on the outside, but that doesn't matter to God. True beauty comes from living like God wants us to—being loving and kind and unselfish.

When we're beautiful on the inside, that will make us beautiful on the outside, too—no matter what kind of clothes we wear!

## Our Salvation Is Great

**2** So we must be more careful to follow what we were taught. Then we will not stray away from the truth. ²The teaching God spoke through angels was shown to be true, and anyone who did not follow it or obey it received the punishment that was earned. ³So surely we also will be punished if we ignore this great salvation. The Lord himself first told about this salvation, and those who heard him testified it was true. ⁴God also testified to the truth of the message by using wonders, great signs, many kinds of miracles, and by giving people gifts through the Holy Spirit, just as he wanted.

---

**1:13 until . . . control** *Literally, "until I make your enemies a footstool for your feet."*

# Q & A

**Q** I have a learning disability. Why couldn't God just make me normal?

**A** Don't think of yourself as not "normal." Every kid has something different about them, whether you can see it or not. And God has made every kid special in his or her own way. You might have difficulty with your studies, but maybe you're a better singer than the kid with the highest grade. Or maybe you're kind or funny or a fast runner. Thank God for making you *you* and for the special talents *you* have!

## Christ Became like Humans

⁵God did not choose angels to be the rulers of the new world that was coming, which is what we have been talking about. ⁶It is written in the Scriptures,

"Why are people even important to you?
  Why do you take care of human beings?
⁷You made them a little lower than the angels
  and crowned them with glory and honor.[n]
⁸You put all things under their control."          *Psalm 8:4–6*

When God put everything under their control, there was nothing left that they did not rule. Still, we do not yet see them ruling over everything. ⁹But we see Jesus, who for a short time was made lower than the angels. And now he is wearing a crown of glory and honor because he suffered and died. And by God's grace, he died for everyone.

**GOD IS THE ONE WHO MADE ALL THINGS, AND ALL THINGS ARE FOR HIS GLORY.**

¹⁰God is the One who made all things, and all things are for his glory. He wanted to have many children share his glory, so he made the One who leads people to salvation perfect through suffering.

¹¹Jesus, who makes people holy, and those who are made holy are from the same family. So he is not ashamed to call them his brothers and sisters. ¹²He says,

"Then, I will tell my brothers and sisters about you;
  I will praise you in the public meeting."          *Psalm 22:22*

¹³He also says,

"I will trust in God."          *Isaiah 8:17*

And he also says,

"I am here, and with me are the children God has given me."          *Isaiah 8:18*

¹⁴Since these children are people with physical bodies, Jesus himself became like them. He did this so that, by dying, he could destroy the one who has the power of death—the devil— ¹⁵and free those who were like slaves all their lives because of their fear of death. ¹⁶Clearly, it is not angels that Jesus helps, but the people who are from Abraham.[n] ¹⁷For this reason Jesus had to be made like his brothers and sisters in every way so he could be their merciful and faithful high priest in service to God. Then Jesus could die in their place to take away their sins. ¹⁸And now he can help those who are tempted, because he himself suffered and was tempted.

## Jesus Is Greater than Moses

**3** So all of you holy brothers and sisters, who were called by God, think about Jesus, who was sent to us and is the high priest of our faith. ²Jesus was faithful to God as Moses was in God's family. ³Jesus has more honor than Moses, just as the builder of a house has more honor than the house itself. ⁴Every house is built by someone, but the builder of everything is God himself. ⁵Moses was faithful in God's family as a servant, and he told what God would say in the future. ⁶But Christ is faithful as a Son over God's house. And we are God's house if we confidently maintain our hope.

## We Must Continue to Follow God

⁷So it is as the Holy Spirit says:
"Today listen to what he says.
⁸Do not be stubborn as in the past
  when you turned against God,
  when you tested God in the desert.
⁹There your ancestors tried me and tested me
  and saw the things I did for forty years.
¹⁰I was angry with them.
  I said, 'They are not loyal to me
  and have not understood my ways.'
¹¹I was angry and made a promise,
  'They will never enter my rest.' "[n]
          *Psalm 95:7–11*

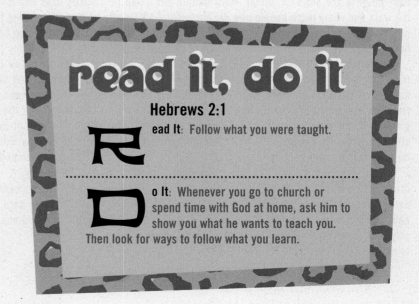

# read it, do it

**Hebrews 2:1**

**R** ead It: Follow what you were taught.

**D** o It: Whenever you go to church or spend time with God at home, ask him to show you what he wants to teach you. Then look for ways to follow what you learn.

---

**2:7 You . . . honor.** *Some Greek copies continue, "You put them in charge of everything you made." See Psalm 8:6.*   **2:16 Abraham** *Most respected ancestor of the Jews. Every Jew hoped to see Abraham.*   **3:11 rest** *A place of rest God promised to give his people.*

¹²So brothers and sisters, be careful that none of you has an evil, unbelieving heart that will turn you away from the living God. ¹³But encourage each other every day while it is "today."[n] Help each other so none of you will become hardened because sin has tricked you. ¹⁴We all share in Christ if we keep till the end the sure faith we had in the beginning. ¹⁵This is what the Scripture says:

"Today listen to what he says.
Do not be stubborn as in the past when you turned against God."

*Psalm 95:7–8*

¹⁶Who heard God's voice and was against him? It was all those people Moses led out of Egypt. ¹⁷And with whom was God angry for forty years? He was angry with those who sinned, who died in the desert. ¹⁸And to whom was God talking when he promised that they would never enter his rest? He was talking to those who did not obey him. ¹⁹So we see they were not allowed to enter and have God's rest, because they did not believe.

4 Now, since God has left us the promise that we may enter his rest, let us be very careful so none of you will fail to enter. ²The Good News was preached to us just as it was to them. But the teaching they heard did not help them, because they heard it but did not accept it with faith.[n] ³We who have believed are able to enter and have God's rest. As God has said,

"I was angry and made a promise,
'They will never enter my rest.'"

*Psalm 95:11*

But God's work was finished from the time he made the world. ⁴In the Scriptures he talked about the seventh day of the week: "And on the seventh day God

## Q & A

**Q** How and why should I pray?

**A** You can't be good friends with someone if you never talk to each other. Prayer is how we talk with God—and the more you do it, the better your relationship with him will be. Jesus gave a good lesson about prayer in Matthew 6:5–15. Read those verses and then ask God to help you learn how to pray.

## Christian Girls Around the World

### Merab: *Uganda*

People come to Uganda to see the famous gorillas that live in the lush jungles. Unfortunately, other kinds of *guerillas* (terrorist rebels) live in Uganda. In some areas, preteen boys are kidnapped to serve in the rebel army. Preteen girls are not safe, either. Many people have died in the wars and many more people now die because of AIDS and other diseases. It's not unusual for twelve-year-old girls or boys to care for their younger siblings after their parents die.

Nine-year-old Merab lives in Kabale, a town far away from the fighting—for now. She is grateful that her mother and father are alive and well. At home, Merab carries water from the communal tap (where she and her neighbors go to get water) and sweeps the floor with a broom made from the stiff fibers of the palm tree. She helps her mother peel plaintain bananas or sweet potatoes.

Each school morning, Merab puts on her uniform and drinks a cup of hot sweetened tea with her bread. School is hard—Merab learns her lessons by reciting after the teacher and copying everything down. But she is grateful to go to school. A family in America sends money to the missionaries to pay her school fees and to buy her uniform, notebooks, and

pens. Merab hopes they remember to pray that she will pass her exams every year!

School isn't all work. At recess, kids love to play soccer. The goal is marked by two rocks, and the ball is made up of plastic bags tied into a round shape with banana stalk pieces or any other string they can scrounge. Merab and her friends also love to jump rope and play jacks with rocks (no bouncing—just catching!)

At church on Sunday, Bugongi Bible Chapel kids rule! They take up half of the pews on the left side of the church and beat the drums during singing. Older kids like Merab usually sit through the whole sermon, but the littler ones often slip in and out of the service to go play outside. Merab also goes to Sunday school and AWANA Bible club on Saturdays. Memorizing verses is hard for her, but she loves the games and the singing.

Merab has been to church many times for funerals. People are crying hard, but they also sing loudly and praise God that their loved one is with Jesus—free and happy and without any pain.

**3:13 "today"** *This word is taken from verse 7. It means that it is important to do these things now.* **4:2 because . . . faith** *Some Greek copies read "because they did not share the faith of those who heard it."*

rested from all his works."[n] [5]And again in the Scripture God said, "They will never enter my rest."

[6]It is still true that some people will enter God's rest, but those who first heard the way to be saved did not enter, because they did not obey. [7]So God planned another day, called "today." He spoke about that day through David a long time later in the same Scripture used before:

## top ten

### top ten things to...
### Pray About

**1** Forgiveness of your sins.

**2** Wisdom! The Bible tells us to ask God for it.

**3** Strength to resist temptation.

**4** Courage to tell others about Jesus and his salvation.

**5** Your parents or guardians.

**6** Your country's leaders.

**7** God's help when you need to make a tough decision.

**8** Patience for dealing with difficult people.

**9** Prayer requests you hear about at church.

**10** Your future. God wants the best for you!

"Today listen to what he says.
Do not be stubborn."     *Psalm 95:7–8*

[8]We know that Joshua[n] did not lead the people into that rest, because God spoke later about another day. [9]This shows that the rest[n] for God's people is still coming. [10]Anyone who enters God's rest will rest from his work as God did. [11]Let us try as hard as we can to enter God's rest so that no one will fail by following the example of those who refused to obey.

[12]God's word is alive and working and is sharper than a double-edged sword. It cuts all the way into us, where the soul and the spirit are joined, to the center of our joints and bones. And it judges the thoughts and feelings in our hearts. [13]Nothing in all the world can be hidden from God. Everything is clear and lies open before him, and to him we must explain the way we have lived.

"YOU ARE A PRIEST FOREVER, A PRIEST LIKE MELCHIZEDEK."

### Jesus Is Our High Priest

[14]Since we have a great high priest, Jesus the Son of God, who has gone into heaven, let us hold on to the faith we have. [15]For our high priest is able to understand our weaknesses. He was tempted in every way that we are, but he

did not sin. [16]Let us, then, feel very sure that we can come before God's throne where there is grace. There we can receive mercy and grace to help us when we need it.

**5** Every high priest is chosen from among other people. He is given the work of going before God for them to offer gifts and sacrifices for sins. [2]Since he himself is weak, he is able to be gentle with those who do not understand and who are doing wrong things. [3]Because he is weak, the high priest must offer sacrifices for his own sins and also for the sins of the people.

[4]To be a high priest is an honor, but no one chooses himself for this work. He must be called by God as Aaron[n] was. [5]So also Christ did not choose himself to have the honor of being a high priest, but God chose him. God said to him,

"You are my Son.
Today I have become your Father."
*Psalm 2:7*

[6]And in another Scripture God says,

"You are a priest forever,
a priest like Melchizedek."[n]
*Psalm 110:4*

[7]While Jesus lived on earth, he prayed to God and asked God for help. He prayed with loud cries and tears to the One who could save him from death, and his prayer was heard because he trusted God. [8]Even though Jesus was the Son of God, he learned obedience by what he suffered. [9]And because his obedience was perfect, he was able to give eternal salvation to

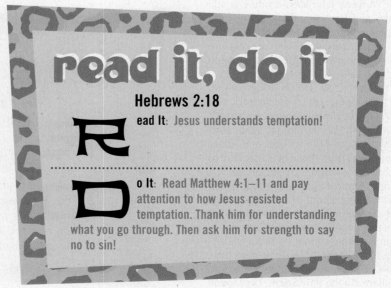

## read it, do it

### Hebrews 2:18

**R**ead It: Jesus understands temptation!

**D**o It: Read Matthew 4:1–11 and pay attention to how Jesus resisted temptation. Thank him for understanding what you go through. Then ask him for strength to say no to sin!

---

**4:4** **"And . . . works."** *Quotation from Genesis 2:2.*   **4:8** **Joshua** *After Moses died, Joshua became leader of the Jewish people and led them into the land that God promised to give them.*   **4:9** **rest** *Literally, "sabbath rest," meaning a sharing in the rest that God began after he created the world.*   **5:4** **Aaron** *Moses' brother and the first Jewish high priest.*   **5:6** **Melchizedek** *A priest and king who lived in the time of Abraham. (Read Genesis 14:17–24.)*

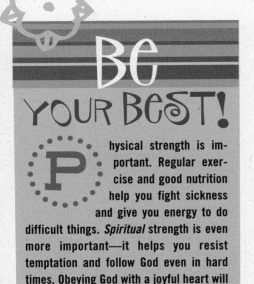

# Be YOUR BEST!

**P**hysical strength is important. Regular exercise and good nutrition help you fight sickness and give you energy to do difficult things. *Spiritual* strength is even more important—it helps you resist temptation and follow God even in hard times. Obeying God with a joyful heart will keep you spiritually strong.

all who obey him. ¹⁰In this way God made Jesus a high priest, a priest like Melchizedek.

## Warning Against Falling Away

¹¹We have much to say about this, but it is hard to explain because you are so slow to understand. ¹²By now you should be teachers, but you need someone to teach you again the first lessons of God's message. You still need the teaching that is like milk. You are not ready for solid food. ¹³Anyone who lives on milk is still a baby and knows nothing about right teaching. ¹⁴But solid food is for those who are grown up. They are mature enough to know the difference between good and evil.

**6** So let us go on to grown-up teaching. Let us not go back over the beginning lessons we learned about Christ. We should not again start teaching about faith in God and about turning away from those acts that lead to death. ²We should not return to the teaching about baptisms,ⁿ about laying on of hands,ⁿ about the raising of the dead and eternal judgment. ³And we will go on to grown-up teaching if God allows.

⁴Some people cannot be brought back again to a changed life. They were once in God's light, and enjoyed heaven's gift, and shared in the Holy Spirit. ⁵They found

out how good God's word is, and they received the powers of his new world. ⁶But they fell away from Christ. It is impossible to bring them back to a changed life again, because they are nailing the Son of God to a cross again and are shaming him in front of others.

⁷Some people are like land that gets plenty of rain. The land produces a good crop for those who work it, and it receives God's blessings. ⁸Other people are like land that grows thorns and weeds and is worthless. It is about to be cursed by God and will be destroyed by fire.

⁹Dear friends, we are saying this to you, but we really expect better things from you that will lead to your salvation. ¹⁰God is fair; he will not forget the work you did and the love you showed for him by helping his people. And he will remember that you are still helping them. ¹¹We want each of you to go on with the same hard work all your lives so you will surely get what you hope for. ¹²We do not want you to become lazy. Be like those who through faith and patience will receive what God has promised.

¹³God made a promise to Abraham. And as there is no one greater than God, he used himself when he swore to Abraham, ¹⁴saying, "I will surely bless you and give you many descendants."ⁿ ¹⁵Abraham waited patiently for this to happen, and he received what God promised.

¹⁶People always use the name of someone greater than themselves when they

swear. The oath proves that what they say is true, and this ends all arguing. ¹⁷God wanted to prove that his promise was true to those who would get what he promised. And he wanted them to understand clearly that his purposes never change, so he made an oath. ¹⁸These two things cannot change: God cannot lie when he makes a promise, and he cannot lie when he makes an oath. These things encourage us who came to God for safety. They give us strength to hold on to the hope we have been given. ¹⁹We have this hope as an anchor for the soul, sure and strong. It enters behind the curtain in the Most Holy Place in heaven,

## speakout!

**Q** What is one way that tweens can live for God?

**A** By choosing the right movies and games. —Rosalie, 9

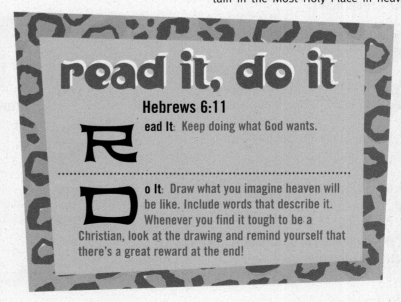

## read it, do it

### Hebrews 6:11

**R**ead It: Keep doing what God wants.

**D**o It: Draw what you imagine heaven will be like. Include words that describe it. Whenever you find it tough to be a Christian, look at the drawing and remind yourself that there's a great reward at the end!

---

6:2 **baptisms** The word here may refer to Christian baptism, or it may refer to the Jewish ceremonial washings.   6:2 **laying on of hands** The laying on of hands had many purposes, including the giving of a blessing, power, or authority.   6:14 **"I . . . descendants."** Quotation from Genesis 22:17.

Hebrews

### dig deeper

### Hebrews 6:10

Some pretty exciting things happen in your life, don't they? Like going to your favorite theme park on your family vacation this summer. You can't wait to tell your friends. This has got to be the most important news of the week!

But did you ever stop to think that a lot of people feel exactly the same way about their lives? They are just as excited about *their* summer vacation as you are. They get just as sad when their favorite pet dies as you would if it were your pet.

It's natural to think of ourselves first. After all, that's who we spend the most time with! But sometimes we get *so* wrapped up in our own lives that we forget about others. Hebrews 6:10 reminds us that God wants us to show love to him "by helping his people." He wants us to love others as much as we love ourselves.

What happens in your life *is* important, and it's great to have friends and family members to share things with. But God wants us to remember that other people are important, too. We need to take time to find out what's going on in their lives instead of only talking about ourselves. Being interested in others tells them they're special and important—to us and to God!

a tenth of everything that he won in battle. [5]Now the law says that those in the tribe of Levi who become priests must collect a tenth from the people—their own people—even though the priests and the people are from the family of Abraham. [6]Melchizedek was not from the tribe of Levi, but he collected a tenth from Abraham. And he blessed Abraham, the man who had God's promises. [7]Now everyone knows that the more important person blesses the less important person. [8]Priests receive a tenth, even though they are only men who live and then die. But Melchizedek, who received a tenth from Abraham, continues living, as the Scripture says. [9]We might even say that Levi, who receives a tenth, also paid it when Abraham paid Melchizedek a tenth. [10]Levi was not yet born, but he was in the body of his ancestor when Melchizedek met Abraham.

[11]The people were given the law[n] concerning the system of priests from the tribe of Levi, but they could not be made perfect through that system. So there was a need for another priest to come, a priest like Melchizedek, not Aaron. [12]And when a different kind of priest comes, the law must be changed, too. [13]We are saying these things about Christ, who belonged

## Q&A

**Q** Is there proof that Jesus existed, besides what the Bible says?

**A** Many people who lived around the time of Jesus—even non-Christians—wrote about him and his followers and their activities. In fact, there's so much good proof that even other religions believe he existed. They don't believe he was God's Son, but many say he was a good man, a prophet, or a *rabbi* (a Jewish teacher). No one has been able to prove that what the Bible says isn't true!

[20]where Jesus has gone ahead of us and for us. He has become the high priest forever, a priest like Melchizedek.[n]

### The Priest Melchizedek

**7** Melchizedek[n] was the king of Salem and a priest for God Most High. He met Abraham when Abraham was coming back after defeating the kings. When they met, Melchizedek blessed Abraham, [2]and Abraham gave him a tenth of everything he had brought back from the battle. First, Melchizedek's name means "king of goodness," and he is king of Salem, which means "king of peace." [3]No one knows who Melchizedek's father or mother was,[n] where he came from, when he was born, or when he died. Melchizedek is like the Son of God; he continues being a priest forever.

[4]You can see how great Melchizedek was. Abraham, the great father, gave him

6:20; 7:1 **Melchizedek** *A priest and king who lived in the time of Abraham. (Read Genesis 14:17–24.)* 7:3 **No . . . was** *Literally, "Melchizedek was without father, without mother, without genealogy."* 7:11 **The . . . law** *This refers to the people of Israel who were given the Law of Moses.*

335

## god's promises

### Hebrews 8:12

If you had to write a list of all the people who have hurt your feelings or done something mean to you, you might not remember every situation. But you could probably think of quite a few, right? In fact, you might have some bad memories that keep coming back to you and making you feel angry, sad, or jealous all over again.

It's quite normal for human beings to remember bad things that others have done. It's called resentment. We say we've forgiven someone, but no matter how hard we try, we just can't forget what they did. Sometimes we hold grudges for years.

But God is not like us. When you truly feel sorry for a sin and ask God to forgive you, he not only does it right away, but he also forgets all about your sin. He promises that he will not remember our sins anymore.

God chooses to not keep a record of the things we have done wrong. That might seem impossible, but God does it all the time. That's how much he loves us! God promises to forgive . . . and forget!

*God chooses to not keep a record of the things we have done wrong.*

out an oath, [21]but Christ became a priest with God's oath. God said:

> "The Lord has made a promise
> and will not change his mind.
> 'You are a priest forever.' "
>
> *Psalm 110:4*

[22]This means that Jesus is the guarantee of a better agreement[n] from God to his people.

[23]When one of the other priests died, he could not continue being a priest. So there were many priests. [24]But because Jesus lives forever, he will never stop serving as priest. [25]So he is able always to save those who come to God through him because he always lives, asking God to help them.

[26]Jesus is the kind of high priest we need. He is holy, sinless, pure, not influenced by sinners, and he is raised above the heavens. [27]He is not like the other priests who had to offer sacrifices every day, first for their own sins, and then for the sins of the people. Christ offered his sacrifice only once and for all time when he offered himself. [28]The law chooses high priests who are people with weaknesses, but the word of God's oath came later than the law. It made God's Son to be the high priest, and that Son has been made perfect forever.

## Q & A

**Q** My parents want me to baby-sit my little brother a lot. Why do I have to?

**A** Each member of a family has some responsibility for taking care of the others. Your parents have the big job of taking care of you and your brother, but sometimes they will need your help. It might not always seem fun, but if you remember that you are honoring your parents by helping out, it will be a little easier. You'll make your little brother happy . . . and God will bless you for it!

to a different tribe. No one from that tribe ever served as a priest at the altar. [14]It is clear that our Lord came from the tribe of Judah, and Moses said nothing about priests belonging to that tribe.

### Jesus Is like Melchizedek

[15]And this becomes even more clear when we see that another priest comes who is like Melchizedek.[n] [16]He was not made a priest by human rules and laws but through the power of his life, which continues forever. [17]It is said about him,

> "You are a priest forever,
> a priest like Melchizedek."
>
> *Psalm 110:4*

[18]The old rule is now set aside, because it was weak and useless. [19]The law of Moses could not make anything perfect. But now a better hope has been given to us, and with this hope we can come near to God. [20]It is important that God did this with an oath. Others became priests with-

---

**7:15 Melchizedek** *A priest and king who lived in the time of Abraham. (Read Genesis 14:17–24.)* **7:22 agreement** *God gives a contract or agreement to his people. For the Jews, this agreement was the Law of Moses. But now God has given a better agreement to his people through Christ.*

Hebrews

# Relationships

**W**ho can you trust to give you wise advice? Look for an older woman at your church to mentor you. Mentoring is when a more experienced Christian teaches a younger Christian to become more like Jesus. The apostle Paul mentored young Timothy (see 2 Timothy 2:1–2). Timothy was later a leader in the church! A mentoring relationship should be encouraging, challenging, and loving. Ask God to give you a mentor who will help you to love God even more!

## Jesus Is Our High Priest

**8** Here is the point of what we are saying: We have a high priest who sits on the right side of God's throne in heaven. [2]Our high priest serves in the Most Holy Place, the true place of worship that was made by God, not by humans.

[3]Every high priest has the work of offering gifts and sacrifices to God. So our high priest must also offer something to God. [4]If our high priest were now living on earth, he would not be a priest, because there are already priests here who follow the law by offering gifts to God. [5]The work they do as priests is only a copy and a shadow of what is in heaven. This is why God warned Moses when he was ready to build the Holy Tent: "Be very careful to make everything by the plan I showed you on the mountain."[n] [6]But the priestly work that has been given to Jesus is much greater than the work that was given to the other priests. In the same way, the new agreement that Jesus brought from God to his people is much greater than the old one. And the new agreement is based on promises of better things.

[7]If there had been nothing wrong with the first agreement,[n] there would have been no need for a second agreement. [8]But God found something wrong with his people. He says:[n]

"Look, the time is coming, says the Lord,
    when I will make a new agreement
  with the people of Israel
    and the people of Judah.
[9]It will not be like the agreement
    I made with their ancestors
  when I took them by the hand
    to bring them out of Egypt.
  But they broke that agreement,
    and I turned away from them, says the Lord.
[10]This is the agreement I will make
    with the people of Israel at that time, says the Lord.
  I will put my teachings in their minds
    and write them on their hearts.
  I will be their God,
    and they will be my people.
[11]People will no longer have to teach
    their neighbors and relatives
    to know the Lord,
  because all people will know me,
    from the least to the most important.
[12]I will forgive them for the wicked
    things they did,
  and I will not remember their sins
    anymore."    *Jeremiah 31:31–34*
[13]God called this a new agreement, so he has made the first agreement old. And anything that is old and worn out is ready to disappear.

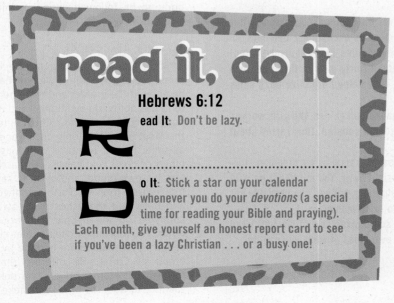

# read it, do it

## Hebrews 6:12

**R**ead It: Don't be lazy.

**D**o It: Stick a star on your calendar whenever you do your *devotions* (a special time for reading your Bible and praying). Each month, give yourself an honest report card to see if you've been a lazy Christian . . . or a busy one!

**8:5 "Be . . . mountain."** *Quotation from Exodus 25:40.*    **8:7 first agreement** *The contract God gave the Jewish people when he gave them the Law of Moses.*    **8:8 But . . . says** *Some Greek copies read "But God found something wrong and says to his people."*

## The Old Agreement

**9** The first agreement[n] had rules for worship and a place on earth for worship. [2]The Holy Tent was set up for this. The first area in the Tent was called the Holy Place. In it were the lamp and the table with the bread that was made holy for God. [3]Behind the second curtain was a room called the Most Holy Place. [4]In it was a golden altar for burning incense and the Ark covered with gold that held the old agreement. Inside this Ark was a golden jar of manna, Aaron's rod that once grew leaves, and the stone tablets of the old agreement. [5]Above the Ark were the creatures that showed God's glory, whose wings reached over the lid. But we cannot tell everything about these things now.

[6]When everything in the Tent was made ready in this way, the priests went into the first room every day to worship. [7]But only the high priest could go into the second room, and he did that only once a year. He could never enter the inner room without taking blood with him, which he offered to God for himself and for sins the people did without knowing they did them. [8]The Holy Spirit uses this to show that the way into the Most Holy Place was not open while the system of the old Holy Tent was still being used. [9]This is an example for the present time. It shows that the gifts and sacrifices offered cannot make the conscience of the worshiper perfect. [10]These gifts and sacrifices were only about food and drink and special washings. They were rules for the body, to be followed until the time of God's new way.

## The New Agreement

[11]But when Christ came as the high priest of the good things we now have,[n] he entered the greater and more perfect tent. It is not made by humans and does not belong to this world. [12]Christ entered the Most Holy Place only once—and for all time. He did not take with him the blood of goats and calves. His sacrifice was his own blood, and by it he set us free from sin forever. [13]The blood of goats and bulls and the ashes of a cow are sprinkled on the people who are unclean, and this makes their bodies clean again. [14]How much more is done by the blood of Christ. He offered himself through the eternal Spirit[n] as a perfect sacrifice to God. His blood will make our

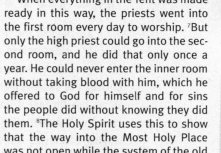

## Shine Your Light

When a *tsunami* (a large, powerful sea wave) hit Southeast Asia soon after Christmas 2004, many people lost their homes and even family members. All around the world, people started to send help to the victims. Kids got involved, too!

At a church in Matthews, North Carolina, about thirty girls in fifth and sixth grade participated in a special mission project. They helped organize bake sales to raise money for the tsunami victims.

During a couple of the church youth group basketball games, the girls worked at tables filled with goodies that people had baked and donated. They raised about three hundred dollars!

We often hear on the news about terrible disasters such as earthquakes, tornadoes, or floods. The victims usually need help right away. You might not be able to send three hundred or even thirty dollars to help them, but you can probably get some friends together and organize an activity to raise money.

Ask a teacher or parent to tell you about some disaster victims who need help, and then see if you can come up with your own ideas of what *you* can do!

## cool

### Beds, Lounges, and Leashes?

Animals usually stay in their own groups, which sometimes have funny names: a *bed* of oysters, a *lounge* of lizards, or a *leash* of foxes. Cows in a *herd* don't care if the others are brown, white, or black . . . as long as they're cows! The animals stick together to protect and help each other.

Christians also need to spend time with each other. *Fellowship* (the word to describe Christians meeting together) helps us feel loved, grow strong, and get help that we need. Best of all, we can worship God together! Who do *you* hang out with?

**9:1 first agreement** *The contract God gave the Jewish people when he gave them the Law of Moses.* **9:11 good . . . have** *Some Greek copies read "good things that are to come."* **9:14 Spirit** *This refers to the Holy Spirit, to Christ's own spirit, or to the spiritual and eternal nature of his sacrifice.*

338

consciences pure from useless acts so we may serve the living God.

[15]For this reason Christ brings a new agreement from God to his people. Those who are called by God can now receive the blessings he has promised, blessings that will last forever. They can have those things because Christ died so that the people who lived under the first agreement could be set free from sin.

[16]When there is a will,[n] it must be proven that the one who wrote that will is dead. [17]A will means nothing while the person is alive; it can be used only after the person dies. [18]This is why even the first agreement could not begin without blood to show death. [19]First, Moses told all the people every command in the law. Next he took the blood of calves and mixed it with water. Then he used red wool and a branch of the hyssop plant to sprinkle it on the book of the law and on all the people. [20]He said, "This is the blood that begins the Agreement that God commanded you to obey."[n] [21]In the same way, Moses sprinkled the blood on the Holy Tent and over all the things used in worship. [22]The law says that almost everything must be made clean by blood, and sins cannot be forgiven without blood to show death.

## Christ's Death Takes Away Sins

[23]So the copies of the real things in heaven had to be made clean by animal sacrifices. But the real things in heaven need much better sacrifices. [24]Christ did not go into the Most Holy Place made by humans, which is only a copy of the real one. He went into heaven itself and is there now before God to help us. [25]The high priest enters the Most Holy Place once every year with blood that is not his own. But Christ did not offer himself many times. [26]Then he would have had to suffer many times since the world was made. But Christ came only once and for all time at just the right time to take away all sin by sacrificing himself. [27]Just as everyone must die once and then be judged, [28]so

AND HE WILL COME A SECOND TIME, NOT TO OFFER HIMSELF FOR SIN, BUT TO BRING SALVATION TO THOSE WHO ARE WAITING FOR HIM.

Christ was offered as a sacrifice one time to take away the sins of many people. And he will come a second time, not to offer himself for sin, but to bring salvation to those who are waiting for him.

**10** The law is only an unclear picture of the good things coming in the future; it is not the real thing. The people under the law offer the same sacrifices every year, but these sacrifices can never make perfect those who come near to worship God. [2]If the law could make them perfect, the sacrifices would have already stopped. The worshipers would be made clean, and they would no longer have a sense of sin. [3]But these sacrifices remind them of their sins every year, [4]because it is impossible for the blood of bulls and goats to take away sins.

[5]So when Christ came into the world, he said:

"You do not want sacrifices and offerings,
but you have prepared a body for me.
[6]You do not ask for burnt offerings and offerings to take away sins.
[7]Then I said, 'Look, I have come.
It is written about me in the book.
God, I have come to do what you want.'"      *Psalm 40:6–8*

[8]In this Scripture he first said, "You do not want sacrifices and offerings. You do not ask for burnt offerings and offerings to take away sins." (These are all sacrifices that the law commands.) [9]Then he said, "Look, I have come to do what you want." God ends the first system of sacrifices so he can set up the new system. [10]And because of this, we are made holy through the sacrifice Christ made in his body once and for all time.

[11]Every day the priests stand and do their religious service, often offering the same sacrifices. Those sacrifices can never take away sins. [12]But after Christ offered one sacrifice for sins, forever, he sat down at the right side of God. [13]And now Christ waits there for his enemies to be put under his power. [14]With one sacrifice he made perfect forever those who are being made holy.

## Bible Bios

**Timothy (Acts 16:1–5; 1 and 2 Timothy)**

The Bible tells us that Timothy's mother and grandmother were believers in Jesus. There was no Sunday school in those days, but Timothy learned about God's Word at home when he was young. When Paul came to Lystra, where Timothy lived, he heard good things about Timothy from the other believers. In fact, young Timothy's faith impressed him so much he wanted to take him along on his missionary trips!

The Books of 1 and 2 Timothy are actually letters that Paul wrote to Timothy. They show us how much Paul loved his student and helper, and they also contain good advice for young Christians today! From Timothy's example, you can see that studying the Bible from a young age is important. Take time to read it each day so *you* can grow in your faith!

**9:16 will** *A legal document that shows how a person's money and property are to be distributed at the time of death. This is the same word in Greek as "agreement" in verse 15.* **9:20 "This . . . obey."** *Quotation from Exodus 24:8.*

## THEN HE SAYS: "THEIR SINS AND THE EVIL THINGS THEY DO— I WILL NOT REMEMBER ANYMORE."

15The Holy Spirit also tells us about this. First he says:

16"This is the agreement[n] I will make with them at that time, says the Lord.

I will put my teachings in their hearts and write them on their minds."

*Jeremiah 31:33*

17Then he says:

"Their sins and the evil things they do—

I will not remember anymore."

*Jeremiah 31:34*

18Now when these have been forgiven, there is no more need for a sacrifice for sins.

### Continue to Trust God

19So, brothers and sisters, we are completely free to enter the Most Holy Place without fear because of the blood of Jesus' death. 20We can enter through a new and living way that Jesus opened for us. It leads through the curtain—Christ's body. 21And since we have a great priest over God's house, 22let us come near to God with a sincere heart and a sure faith, because we have been made free from a guilty conscience, and our bodies have been washed with pure water. 23Let us hold firmly to the hope that we have confessed, because we can trust God to do what he promised.

24Let us think about each other and help each other to show love and do good deeds. 25You should not stay away from the church meetings, as some are doing, but you should meet together and encourage each other. Do this even more as you see the day[n] coming.

26If we decide to go on sinning after we have learned the truth, there is no longer any sacrifice for sins. 27There is nothing but fear in waiting for the judgment and the terrible fire that will destroy all those who live against God. 28Anyone who refused to obey the law of Moses was

## dig deeper

### Hebrews 11:8–10

Imagine that your parents came to you and said, "We're moving." And imagine how you'd feel if, when you asked them where you were headed, they said, "A different country—but we don't know which one. God will show us."

That's what Abraham did. "By faith Abraham obeyed God's call to go to another place" (Hebrews 11:8). After he had traveled for a while, God told him, "You're there! This is your country."

But Abraham still didn't get to settle down. He and his children were always on the move, with no permanent home. It was hundreds of years after Abraham's death when the Israelites, Abraham's descendants, returned to live in the land God had promised Abraham.

Did Abraham lose faith in God? Did he sulk? Did he go back to his comfortable home? No. The Bible says Abraham continued to camp out in that foreign country because he believed God would keep his promise. Abraham also knew that *no* home on earth can compare to the permanent home God has waiting for us in heaven. That was his real goal, so he didn't worry about looking for a comfortable place to build a house.

It's not bad to be comfortable. But when God puts us in uncomfortable situations, it's good to remember that our permanent home is in heaven and not to spend too much time looking for a good life here.

found guilty from the proof given by two or three witnesses. He was put to death without mercy. 29So what do you think should be done to those who do not respect the Son of God, who look at the blood of the agreement that made them holy as no different from others' blood, who insult the Spirit of God's grace? Surely they should have a much worse punishment. 30We know that God said, "I will punish those who do wrong; I will repay them."[n] And he also said, "The Lord will judge his people."[n] 31It is a terrible thing to fall into the hands of the living God.

32Remember those days in the past when you first learned the truth. You had a hard struggle with many sufferings, but you continued strong. 33Sometimes you were hurt and attacked before crowds of

---

10:16 **agreement** *God gives a contract or agreement to his people. For the Jews, this agreement was the Law of Moses. But now God has given a better agreement to his people through Christ.* 10:25 **day** *The day Christ will come to judge all people and take his people to live with him.* 10:30 **"I . . . them."** *Quotation from Deuteronomy 32:35.* 10:30 **"The Lord . . . people."** *Quotation from Deuteronomy 32:36; Psalm 135:14.*

# Q & A

people, and sometimes you shared with those who were being treated that way. [34]You helped the prisoners. You even had joy when all that you owned was taken from you, because you knew you had something better and more lasting.

[35]So do not lose the courage you had in the past, which has a great reward. [36]You must hold on, so you can do what God wants and receive what he has promised. [37]For in a very short time,

"The One who is coming will come
and will not be delayed.
[38]Those who are right with me
will live by faith.
But if they turn back with fear,
I will not be pleased with them."

*Habakkuk 2:3–4*

[39]But we are not those who turn back and are lost. We are people who have faith and are saved.

## What Is Faith?

**11** Faith means being sure of the things we hope for and knowing that something is real even if we do not see it. [2]Faith is the reason we remember great people who lived in the past.

[3]It is by faith we understand that the whole world was made by God's command so what we see was made by something that cannot be seen.

[4]It was by faith that Abel offered God a better sacrifice than Cain did. God said he was pleased with the gifts Abel offered and called Abel a good man because of his faith. Abel died, but through his faith he is still speaking.

> ANYONE WHO COMES TO GOD MUST BELIEVE THAT HE IS REAL AND THAT HE REWARDS THOSE WHO TRULY WANT TO FIND HIM.

**Q** My friend believes that when we die we come back as another person or animal *(reincarnation)*. Is that true?

**A** The Bible makes it very clear that we only die once (see Hebrews 9:27). There are only two places you can go after you die: either heaven or hell. Of course, that depends on whether you have asked Jesus to be your Savior . . . or not. Once your life is over, there is no more opportunity to decide to follow Jesus. The Bible tells us that we only get to live once—there aren't any "second chances" at life!

[5]It was by faith that Enoch was taken to heaven so he would not die. He could not be found, because God had taken him away. Before he was taken, the Scripture says that he was a man who truly pleased God. [6]Without faith no one can please God. Anyone who comes to God must believe that he is real and that he rewards those who truly want to find him.

[7]It was by faith that Noah heard God's warnings about things he could not yet see. He obeyed God and built a large boat to save his family. By his faith, Noah showed that the world was wrong, and he became one of those who are made right with God through faith.

[8]It was by faith Abraham obeyed God's call to go to another place God promised to give him. He left his own country, not knowing where he was to go. [9]It was by faith that he lived like a foreigner in the country God promised to give him. He lived in tents with Isaac and Jacob, who had received that same promise from God. [10]Abraham was waiting for the city[n] that has real foundations—the city planned and built by God.

[11]He was too old to have children, and Sarah could not have children. It was by faith that Abraham was made able to become a father, because he trusted God to do what he had promised.[n] [12]This man was so old he was almost dead, but from him came as many descendants as there are stars in the sky. Like the sand on the seashore, they could not be counted.

[13]All these great people died in faith. They did not get the things that God promised his people, but they saw them coming far in the future and were glad. They said they were like visitors and strangers on earth. [14]When people say such things, they show they are looking for a country that will be their own. [15]If they had been thinking about the country they had left, they could have gone back. [16]But they were waiting for a better country—a heavenly country. So God is

## Looking Ahead

### PEER PRESSURE

**P**eer pressure isn't just about drugs and alcohol. You'll probably experience it in many ways, including the pressure to be popular. To get others to like them more, people often change the way they dress and act. Sometimes they treat others hurtfully or act as if they are better than everyone else. If you feel pressured, remember that you're in charge of yourself and your actions. And remember Romans 12:2: "Do not be shaped by this world." Popularity is not worth being unkind or pretending to be someone you're not. You will earn respect by sticking to what you know is right.

**did you know?**

20% of preteens have their own checking account.
—Aquatics International. "Tween Spirit." by Judith L. Leblein
http://www.aquaticsintl.com/2005/apr/0504_bl.html

---

**11:10 city** The spiritual "city" where God's people live with him. Also called "the heavenly Jerusalem." (See Hebrews 12:22.)  **11:11 It . . . promised.** Some Greek copies refer to Sarah's faith, rather than Abraham's.

# Relationships

God gave you two ears and one mouth because being a good listener is twice as important as being a good talker! The Bible says, "Always be willing to listen and slow to speak" (James 1:19). Listening makes other people feel cared for and loved—and there are fewer misunderstandings when you listen carefully! You can be a better listener by not thinking about what you're going to say while the other person is talking. Instead, ask questions that help you better understand what she is trying to say. Everyone appreciates a good listener!

not ashamed to be called their God, because he has prepared a city for them.

¹⁷It was by faith that Abraham, when God tested him, offered his son Isaac as a sacrifice. God made the promises to Abraham, but Abraham was ready to offer his own son as a sacrifice. ¹⁸God had said, "The descendants I promised you will be from Isaac."ⁿ ¹⁹Abraham believed that God could raise the dead, and really,

# Q&A

**Q** How can I get my little sister to leave me and my friends alone when they come over to my house?

**A** Try talking to your parents about this. You probably can't expect your sister not to be around at all, but maybe your parents can make sure she has other activities to do while your friends are over. Still, try to be patient with her and treat her with respect. Your friends will copy whatever attitude you have.

it was as if Abraham got Isaac back from death.

²⁰It was by faith that Isaac blessed the future of Jacob and Esau. ²¹It was by faith that Jacob, as he was dying, blessed each one of Joseph's sons. Then he worshiped as he leaned on the top of his walking stick.

²²It was by faith that Joseph, while he was dying, spoke about the Israelites leaving Egypt and gave instructions about what to do with his body.

²³It was by faith that Moses' parents hid him for three months after he was born. They saw that Moses was a beautiful baby, and they were not afraid to disobey the king's order.

²⁴It was by faith that Moses, when he grew up, refused to be called the son of the king of Egypt's daughter. ²⁵He chose to suffer with God's people instead of enjoying sin for a short time. ²⁶He thought it was better to suffer for the Christ than to have all the treasures of Egypt, because he was looking for God's reward. ²⁷It was by faith that Moses left Egypt and was not afraid of the king's anger. Moses continued strong as if he could see the God that no one can see. ²⁸It was by faith that Moses prepared the Passover and spread the blood on the doors so the one who brings death would not kill the first-born sons of Israel.

²⁹It was by faith that the people crossed the Red Sea as if it were dry land. But when the Egyptians tried it, they were drowned.

³⁰It was by faith that the walls of Jericho fell after the people had marched around them for seven days.

³¹It was by faith that Rahab, the prostitute, welcomed the spies and was not killed with those who refused to obey God.

³²Do I need to give more examples? I do not have time to tell you about Gideon, Barak, Samson, Jephthah, David, Samuel, and the prophets. ³³Through their faith they defeated kingdoms. They did what was right, received God's promises, and shut the mouths of lions. ³⁴They stopped great fires and were saved from being killed with swords.
They were weak, and
yet were made

## speakout!

**Q** What is one important thing you've learned through reading the Bible?

**A** There is always a memory verse to help you.
—Nessa, 12

11:18 "The descendants . . . Isaac." *Quotation from Genesis 21:12.*

## Be YOUR BEST!

**P**art of having good manners is knowing when to be quiet, such as at a library, hospital, or funeral home. Don't forget to show the same respect to God when you go to church. It's a place of worship that we should take care of, not treat like a playground.

strong. They were powerful in battle and defeated other armies. [35]Women received their dead relatives raised back to life. Others were tortured and refused to accept their freedom so they could be raised from the dead to a better life. [36]Some were laughed at and beaten. Others were put in chains and thrown into prison. [37]They were stoned to death, they were cut in half,[n] and they were killed with swords. Some wore the skins of sheep and goats. They were poor, abused, and treated badly. [38]The world was not good enough for them! They wandered in deserts and mountains, living in caves and holes in the earth.

[39]All these people are known for their faith, but none of them received what God had promised. [40]God planned to give us something better so that they would be made perfect, but only together with us.

### Follow Jesus' Example

**12** We are surrounded by a great cloud of people whose lives tell us what faith means. So let us run the race that is before us and never give up. We should remove from our lives anything that would get in the way and the sin that so easily holds us back. [2]Let us look only to Jesus, the One who began our faith and who makes it perfect. He suffered death on the cross. But he accepted the shame as if it were nothing because of the joy that God put before him. And now he is sitting at the right side of God's throne. [3]Think about Jesus' example. He held on while wicked people were doing evil things to him. So do not get tired and stop trying.

### God Is like a Father

[4]You are struggling against sin, but your struggles have not yet caused you to be killed. [5]You have forgotten the encouraging words that call you his children:

"My child, don't think the Lord's
    discipline is worth nothing,
and don't stop trying when he
    corrects you.
[6]The Lord disciplines those he loves,
    and he punishes everyone he
    accepts as his child."

*Proverbs 3:11–12*

[7]So hold on through your sufferings, because they are like a father's discipline. God is treating you as children. All children are disciplined by their fathers. [8]If you are never disciplined (and every child must be disciplined), you are not true children. [9]We have all had fathers here on earth who disciplined us, and we respected them. So it is even more important that we accept discipline from the Father of our spirits so we will have life. [10]Our fathers on earth disciplined us for a short time in the way they thought was best. But God disciplines us to help us, so we can become holy as he is. [11]We do not enjoy being disciplined. It is painful at the time, but later, after we have learned from it, we have peace, because we start living in the right way.

### Be Careful How You Live

[12]You have become weak, so make yourselves strong again. [13]Keep on the right path, so the weak will not stumble but rather be strengthened.

[14]Try to live in peace with all people, and try to live free from sin. Anyone whose life is not holy will never see the Lord. [15]Be careful that no one fails to receive God's grace and begins to cause trouble among you. A person like that can ruin many of you. [16]Be careful that no one takes part in sexual sin or is like Esau and never thinks about God. As the oldest son, Esau would have received everything from his father, but he sold all that

> THE LORD DISCIPLINES THOSE HE LOVES, AND HE PUNISHES EVERYONE HE ACCEPTS AS HIS CHILD."

for a single meal. [17]You remember that after Esau did this, he wanted to get his father's blessing, but his father refused. Esau could find no way to change what he had done, even though he wanted the blessing so much that he cried.

[18]You have not come to a mountain that can be touched and that is burning with fire. You have not come to darkness, sadness, and storms. [19]You have not come to the noise of a trumpet or to the sound of a voice like the one the people of Israel heard and begged not to hear another word. [20]They did not want to hear the command: "If anything, even an animal,

### Messiah

**J**esus is the Messiah—the Savior whom God promised to send to his special people, the Jews. The Jews spent hundreds of years as slaves or prisoners of other countries. They couldn't wait for the Messiah to come save them and be their king. But Jesus is not an earthly king with a palace, an army, and a country. He is the Messiah, the King of heaven, and he came to rule our hearts. The exciting news is that he came to save *everyone*, not just the Jews. He came to give *eternal* life and freedom from sin to everyone who believes in him!

# Q & A

**Q** Why do countries fight against each other so much?

**A** Most wars start because people are greedy for something, such as money or power. It's like the fighting that goes on between two people. James 4:1 says, "Do you know where your fights and arguments come from? They come from the selfish desires that war within you." Many people pray for world peace, but that won't happen until each person makes things right with God in their lives.

HERE ON EARTH WE DO NOT HAVE A CITY THAT LASTS FOREVER, BUT WE ARE LOOKING FOR THE CITY THAT WE WILL HAVE IN THE FUTURE.

## dig deeper

### Hebrews 12:1–3

Imagine a crowd of people at the city park grab you and take you to court. There, they accuse you of evil things you've never done. They keep yelling, "She must die!" Besides being scared, you probably would feel angry and embarrassed. How could these people accuse *you?*

The same thing happened to Jesus, except that the people *did* kill him. But Hebrews 12:2 says that Jesus "accepted the shame as if it were nothing because of the joy that God put before him." The writer of Hebrews tells us we should be like Jesus by holding on and not getting tired—just like Jesus did when evil people accused and killed him.

What holds you back from following Jesus' example? Often little things such as not getting enough sleep or not getting our way make us give up. When you feel like you want to stop trying, look at Jesus! Even death couldn't keep him from following God!

touches the mountain, it must be put to death with stones."[n] [21]What they saw was so terrible that Moses said, "I am shaking with fear."[n]

[22]But you have come to Mount Zion,[n] to the city of the living God, the heavenly Jerusalem. You have come to thousands of angels gathered together with joy. [23]You have come to the meeting of God's firstborn[n] children whose names are written in heaven. You have come to God, the judge of all people, and to the spirits of good people who have been made perfect. [24]You have come to Jesus, the One who brought the new agreement from God to his people, and you have come to the sprinkled blood[n] that has a better message than the blood of Abel.[n]

[25]So be careful and do not refuse to listen when God speaks. Others refused to listen to him when he warned them on earth, and they did not escape. So it will be worse for us if we refuse to listen to God who warns us from heaven. [26]When he spoke before, his voice shook the earth, but now he has promised, "Once again I will shake not only the earth but also the heavens."[n] [27]The words "once again" clearly show us that everything that was made—things that can be shaken—will be destroyed. Only the things that cannot be shaken will remain. [28]So let us be thankful, because we have a kingdom that cannot be shaken.

We should worship God in a way that pleases him with respect and fear, [29]because our God is like a fire that burns things up.

**13** Keep on loving each other as brothers and sisters. [2]Remember to welcome strangers, because some who have done this have welcomed angels without knowing it. [3]Remember those who are in prison as if you were in prison with them. Remember those who are suffering as if you were suffering with them.

[4]Marriage should be honored by everyone, and husband and wife should keep their marriage pure. God will judge as guilty those who take part in sexual sins.

**12:20** "If . . . stones." *Quotation from Exodus 19:12–13.* **12:21** "I . . . fear." *Quotation from Deuteronomy 9:19.* **12:22** **Mount Zion** *Another name for Jerusalem, here meaning the spiritual city of God's people.* **12:23** **firstborn** *The first son born in a Jewish family was given the most important place in the family and received special blessings. All of God's children are like that.* **12:24** **sprinkled blood** *The blood of Jesus' death.* **12:24** **Abel** *The son of Adam and Eve, who was killed by his brother Cain (Genesis 4:8).* **12:26** "Once . . . heavens." *Quotation from Haggai 2:6, 21.*

> SO THROUGH JESUS LET US ALWAYS OFFER TO GOD OUR SACRIFICE OF PRAISE, COMING FROM LIPS THAT SPEAK HIS NAME.

[5] Keep your lives free from the love of money, and be satisfied with what you have. God has said,

"I will never leave you;
I will never abandon you."

*Deuteronomy 31:6*

[6] So we can be sure when we say,

"I will not be afraid, because the Lord
is my helper.
People can't do anything to me."

*Psalm 118:6*

[7] Remember your leaders who taught God's message to you. Remember how they lived and died, and copy their faith. [8] Jesus Christ is the same yesterday, today, and forever.

[9] Do not let all kinds of strange teachings lead you into the wrong way. Your hearts should be strengthened by God's grace, not by obeying rules about foods, which do not help those who obey them.

[10] We have a sacrifice, but the priests who serve in the Holy Tent cannot eat from it. [11] The high priest carries the blood of animals into the Most Holy Place where he offers this blood for sins. But the bodies of the animals are burned outside the camp. [12] So Jesus also suffered outside the city to make his people holy with his own blood. [13] So let us go to Jesus outside the camp, holding on as he did when we are abused.

[14] Here on earth we do not have a city that lasts forever, but we are looking for the city that we will have in the future. [15] So through Jesus let us always offer to God our sacrifice of praise, coming from lips that speak his name. [16] Do not forget to do good to others, and share with them, because such sacrifices please God.

[17] Obey your leaders and act under their authority. They are watching over you, because they are responsible for your souls. Obey them so that they will do this work with joy, not sadness. It will not help you to make their work hard.

[18] Pray for us. We are sure that we have a clear conscience, because we always want to do the right thing. [19] I especially beg you to pray so that God will send me back to you soon.

[20-21] I pray that the God of peace will give you every good thing you need so you can do what he wants. God raised from the dead our Lord Jesus, the Great Shepherd of the sheep, because of the blood of his death. His blood began the eternal agreement that God made with his people. I pray that God will do in us what pleases him, through Jesus Christ, and to him be glory forever and ever. Amen.

[22] My brothers and sisters, I beg you to listen patiently to this message I have written to encourage you, because it is not very long. [23] I want you to know that our brother Timothy has been let out of prison. If he arrives soon, we will both come to see you.

[24] Greet all your leaders and all of God's people. Those from Italy send greetings to you.

[25] Grace be with you all.

# cool

## Don't be Afraid!

**D**o you know what these words mean: *tonitrophobia, amaxophobia,* and *sesquipedalophobia?* Those strange words describe the fear of thunder, the fear of riding in a car, and the fear of long words. There are hundreds of types of phobias, and although some of them seem funny, others can cause real problems in someone's life. Some people with phobias even need a doctor's help.

God doesn't want you to be afraid. Hebrews 13:6 says that you can confidently say, "I will not be afraid, because the Lord is my helper." Talk to God about your fears. He'll help you!

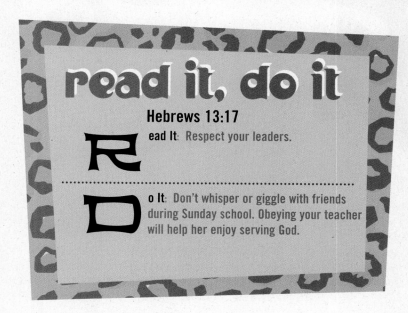

## read it, do it

### Hebrews 13:17

**R**ead It: Respect your leaders.

**D**o It: Don't whisper or giggle with friends during Sunday school. Obeying your teacher will help her enjoy serving God.

# JAMES

**H**ow can you know if your faith in Jesus Christ is real? James says, "Faith by itself—that does nothing—is dead" (James 2:17). This is the constant subject of the Book of James. His message to Christians is, "Do what God's teaching says; when you only listen and do nothing, you are fooling yourselves" (1:22).

Jesus' little brother James wrote this short, yet powerful book to Jewish Christians in the first century. He didn't sugar-coat the truth. In fact, his in-your-face instructions have been hard for many Christians to put into practice. For example, check out chapter 3 and what James has to say about our tongues: "But no one can tame the tongue. It is wild and evil and full of deadly poison . . . Praises and curses come from the same mouth! My brothers and sisters, this should not happen" (James 3:8, 10). Yikes! How does your tongue measure up?

As you read through this short book, take time to consider what James is saying. He's not just offering suggestions—he's serious! If we have faith in Christ, it should show in our lives. We might not become perfect overnight, but with God's help, we can become more and more like him. Our faith in Jesus should be reason for us to try to please God with our lives!

# HOW TO LIVE AS A CHRISTIAN

## THINGS TO TALK WITH GOD ABOUT . . .

**1** From James, a servant of God and of the Lord Jesus Christ.

To all of God's people who are scattered everywhere in the world:

Greetings.

### Faith and Wisdom

²My brothers and sisters, when you have many kinds of troubles, you should be full of joy, ³because you know that these troubles test your faith, and this will give

> **4 million kids in the United States and Canada wear braces.**
>
> —*The Telegraph. 7/11/05 "Fashionable looks have some kids smiling about braces." By Elizabeth Wellington http://www.macon.com/mld/telegraph/living/health/12087772.htm*

**did you know?**

you patience. ⁴Let your patience show itself perfectly in what you do. Then you will be perfect and complete and will have everything you need. ⁵But if any of you needs wisdom, you should ask God for it. He is generous to everyone and will give you wisdom without criticizing you. ⁶But when you ask God, you must believe and

not doubt. Anyone who doubts is like a wave in the sea, blown up and down by the wind. ⁷⁻⁸Such doubters are thinking two different things at the same time, and they cannot decide about anything they do. They should not think they will receive anything from the Lord.

### True Riches

⁹Believers who are poor should take pride that God has made them spiritually rich. ¹⁰Those who are rich should take pride that God has shown them that they are spiritually poor. The rich will die like a wild flower in the grass. ¹¹The sun rises with burning heat and dries up the plants. The flower falls off, and its beauty is gone. In the same way the rich will die while they are still taking care of business.

### Temptation Is Not from God

¹²When people are tempted and still continue strong, they should be happy. After they have proved their faith, God will reward them with life forever. God promised this to all those who love him. ¹³When people are tempted, they should not say, "God is tempting me." Evil cannot tempt God, and God himself does not tempt anyone. ¹⁴But people are tempted

WHEN YOU HAVE MANY KINDS OF TROUBLES, YOU SHOULD BE FULL OF JOY, BECAUSE YOU KNOW THAT THESE TROUBLES TEST YOUR FAITH, AND THIS WILL GIVE YOU PATIENCE.

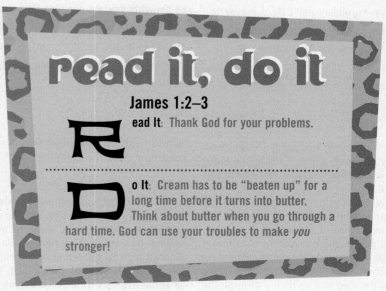

## read it, do it

**James 1:2–3**

**R**ead It: Thank God for your problems.

**D**o It: Cream has to be "beaten up" for a long time before it turns into butter. Think about butter when you go through a hard time. God can use your troubles to make *you* stronger!

## dig deeper

### James 2:1–4

Preteens sometimes complain that when they go into a nice store at the mall, the workers don't treat them politely and even seem annoyed to have young girls in there. But if an older lady with expensive clothes walks in, the workers go to her right away and try to help. Do you know why? Because they want to sell clothes, and they think that preteens—especially if they're dressed kind of sloppy—probably don't have money to spend and will just waste their time.

In many other situations in life, people get treated a certain way depending on their clothes and how rich or important they look. At a restaurant, famous people get the best tables. At a party, the prettiest girl gets the most attention. It doesn't seem fair, does it?

The apostle James would agree with you! He warned Christians not to play favorites. It upset him that, in some churches, rich people were asked to sit in the front while poor people were stuck in the back. He said, "What are you doing? You are making some people more important than others, and with evil thoughts you are deciding that one person is better" (James 2:4). Pray that God will help *you* not to judge people from the outside but be equally loving and kind to everyone.

## BE YOUR BEST!

**I**f you take music lessons or play sports, you know the importance of practicing. It's not always fun, but you have to do it to be your best. As a Christian, it's even more important to "practice" or live out what you learn at church and in the Bible.

---

when their own evil desire leads them away and traps them. [15]This desire leads to sin, and then the sin grows and brings death.

[16]My dear brothers and sisters, do not be fooled about this. [17]Every good action and every perfect gift is from God. These good gifts come down from the Creator of the sun, moon, and stars, who does not change like their shifting shadows. [18]God decided to give us life through the word of truth so we might be the most important of all the things he made.

### Listening and Obeying

[19]My dear brothers and sisters, always be willing to listen and slow to speak. Do not become angry easily, [20]because anger will not help you live the right kind of life God wants. [21]So put out of your life every evil thing and every kind of wrong. Then in gentleness accept God's teaching that is planted in your hearts, which can save you.

[22]Do what God's teaching says; when you only listen and do nothing, you are fooling yourselves. [23]Those who hear God's teaching and do nothing are like people who look at themselves in a mirror. [24]They see their faces and then go away and quickly forget what they looked like. [25]But the truly happy people are those who carefully study God's perfect law that makes people free, and they continue to study it. They do not forget what they heard, but they obey what God's teaching says. Those who do this will be made happy.

### The True Way to Worship God

[26]People who think they are religious but say things they should not say are just fooling themselves. Their "religion" is worth nothing. [27]Religion that God accepts as pure and without fault is this: caring for orphans or widows who need help, and keeping yourself free from the world's evil influence.

### Love All People

**2** My dear brothers and sisters, as believers in our glorious Lord Jesus Christ, never think some people are more important than others. [2]Suppose someone comes into your church meeting wearing nice clothes

## Bible Bios — Deborah (Judges 4–5)

In a time and place where men had more power than women, Deborah really stood out as an amazing woman. She served God as a judge and as a *prophetess* (someone who explained God's messages to the people).

Deborah's wisdom, strength, and confidence came from God, so she didn't worry about what other people thought. When God told her to do something, she just went ahead and obeyed . . . because she trusted him! And she never did more than God asked her to do.

With God's help, Deborah made wise decisions that freed her country (Israel) from its enemies. But she never boasted about the victory. Instead, she wrote a song thanking God for what *he* had done. (You can read more about her in the Old Testament Book of Judges, chapters 4—5).

and a gold ring. At the same time a poor person comes in wearing old, dirty clothes. [3]You show special attention to the one wearing nice clothes and say, "Please, sit here in this good seat." But you say to the poor person, "Stand over there," or, "Sit on the floor by my feet." [4]What are you doing? You are making some people more important than others, and with evil thoughts you are deciding that one person is better.

[5]Listen, my dear brothers and sisters! God chose the poor in the world to be rich with faith and to receive the kingdom God promised to those who love him. [6]But you show no respect to the poor. The rich are always trying to control your lives. They are the ones who take you to court. [7]And they are the ones who speak against Jesus, who owns you.

[8]This royal law is found in the Scriptures: "Love your neighbor as you love yourself."[n] If you obey this law, you are doing right. [9]But if you treat one person

as being more important than another, you are sinning. You are guilty of breaking God's law. [10]A person who follows all of God's law but fails to obey even one command is guilty of breaking all the commands in that law. [11]The same God who said, "You must not be guilty of adultery,"[n] also said, "You must not murder anyone."[n] So if you do not take part in adultery but you murder someone, you are guilty of breaking all of God's law. [12]In everything you say and do, remember that you will be judged by the

law that makes people free. [13]So you must show mercy to others, or God will not show mercy to you when he judges you. But the person who shows mercy can stand without fear at the judgment.

### Faith and Good Works

[14]My brothers and sisters, if people say they have faith, but do nothing, their faith is worth nothing. Can faith like that save them? [15]A brother or sister in Christ might need clothes or food. [16]If you say to that person, "God be with you! I hope you stay warm and get plenty to eat," but you do not give what that person needs, your words are worth nothing. [17]In the same way, faith by itself—that does nothing—is dead.

[18]Someone might say, "You have faith, but I have deeds." Show me your faith without doing anything, and I will show you my faith by what I do. [19]You believe there is one God. Good! But the demons believe that, too, and they tremble with fear.

[20]You foolish person! Must you be shown that faith that does nothing is worth nothing? [21]Abraham, our ancestor, was made right with God by what he did when he offered his son Isaac on the altar. [22]So you see that Abraham's faith and the things he did worked together. His faith was made perfect by what he did. [23]This shows the full meaning of the Scripture that says: "Abraham believed God, and God accepted Abraham's faith,

. . . IN GENTLENESS ACCEPT GOD'S TEACHING THAT IS PLANTED IN YOUR HEARTS, WHICH CAN SAVE YOU.

## read it, do it

**James 2:8**

**R**ead It: Love your neighbor as yourself.

**D**o It: Pick up trash from in front of your neighbor's lawn or offer to clear snow off her car. Treat people as you'd like to be treated!

**2:8** "Love . . . yourself." *Quotation from Leviticus 19:18.*   **2:11** "You . . . adultery." *Quotation from Exodus 20:14 and Deuteronomy 5:18.*   **2:11** "You . . . anyone." *Quotation from Exodus 20:13 and Deuteronomy 5:17.*

# Q&A

**Q** I get distracted easily in class and can't focus on the lesson. How can I pay more attention?

**A** Ask your teacher if you can sit in the first row so that you'll have less people and stuff to look at. Don't keep anything on your desk except what you need. Try writing down everything the teacher says to force yourself to listen. If none of this works, ask your teacher or a counselor for more ideas. They are there to help. And, of course, ask God to help you!

and that faith made him right with God."[n] And Abraham was called God's friend.[n] ²⁴So you see that people are made right with God by what they do, not by faith only.

²⁵Another example is Rahab, a prostitute, who was made right with God by something she did. She welcomed the spies into her home and helped them escape by a different road.

²⁶Just as a person's body that does not have a spirit is dead, so faith that does nothing is dead!

## Controlling the Things We Say

**3** My brothers and sisters, not many of you should become teachers, because you know that we who teach will be judged more strictly. ²We all make many mistakes. If people never said anything wrong, they would be perfect and able to control their entire selves, too. ³When we put bits into the mouths of horses to make them obey us, we can control their whole bodies. ⁴Also a ship is very big, and it is pushed by strong winds. But a very small rudder controls that big ship, making it go wherever the pilot wants. ⁵It is the same with the tongue. It is a small part of the body, but it brags about great things.

## god's promises

*James 4:6*

What do you do when you win a game or get an award? Do you give a victory shout or do a little victory dance? Do you brag to your friends that you are the best? James 4:6 reminds us that God doesn't want us to be proud. In fact, God gives grace to those who are humble. Giving grace to humble people means that God no longer see us as people who do wrong things. Instead, he sees us as perfect! We need God's grace because we would never be able to earn perfection by ourselves.

What does it mean to be humble? Humility is the opposite of pride and arrogance. It means that instead of acting *superior* (as though we're better than others), we treat others as better than ourselves. Being humble doesn't mean we can't feel happy about the good things in our lives. But it does mean that instead of taking the credit, we should give all the recognition to God.

The next time you feel like bragging, remember that God doesn't want you to take personal pride in your success. Instead, make sure you give him all the credit for the good things in your life. When you are humble, you can be sure God will give you grace—just as he promised.

***God gives grace to those who are humble!***

A big forest fire can be started with only a little flame. ⁶And the tongue is like a fire. It is a whole world of evil among the parts of our bodies. The tongue spreads its evil through the whole body. The tongue is set on fire by hell, and it starts a fire that influences all of life. ⁷People can tame every kind of wild animal, bird, reptile, and fish, and they have tamed them, ⁸but no one can tame the tongue. It is wild and evil and full of

A PERSON WHO FOLLOWS ALL OF GOD'S LAW BUT FAILS TO OBEY EVEN ONE COMMAND IS GUILTY OF BREAKING ALL THE COMMANDS IN THAT LAW.

2:23 **"Abraham . . . God."** *Quotation from Genesis 15:6.* 2:23 **God's friend** *These words about Abraham are found in 2 Chronicles 20:7 and Isaiah 41:8.*

# October

start here

**1** Make up a secret code with your best friends. Write funny messages to each other.

**2**

**3** Pray for a person of influence: Today is singer Ashlee Simpson's birthday.

**4**

**5** Write John 3:16 for your friends using your secret code.

**6** Organize all your CDs in alphabetical order of the artists names.

**7** Pray for a person of influence: Today is Christian singer Michael W. Smith's birthday.

**8**

**9** Work on a crossword puzzle with your dad today.

**10** Canadian Thanksgiving is on the 2nd Monday of October. Thank God for all he's done for you!

**11**

**12** Wear something orange today!

**13**

**14** Pray for a person of influence: Today is rap artist Usher's birthday.

**15** Pray for a person of influence: Today is Christian singer Jaci Velasquez's birthday.

**16**

**17** Pray for a person of influence: Today is rap artist Eminem's birthday.

**18**

**19** Call one of your grandparents just to say "I love you!"

**20**

**21**

**22** Read Romans 13:8. If you've borrowed anything from anyone, try to give it back this week.

**23**

**24**

**25** Start writing your Christmas list. Not things you want, but things you want to give others!

**26**

**27** Pray for the musicians at your church.

**28**

**29** Have a contest with your family to see who can go the longest without saying the word "I." It's pretty tough!

**30**

**31**

Ginger says, "Make a list!"

## read it, do it

### James 4:4

**R**ead It: Choose between God and the world.

**D**o It: Go through your magazines, CDs, and books. If anything would not please God, get rid of it! If you're not sure, ask your mom to help you.

deadly poison. ⁹We use our tongues to praise our Lord and Father, but then we curse people, whom God made like himself. ¹⁰Praises and curses come from the same mouth! My brothers and sisters, this should not happen. ¹¹Do good and bad water flow from the same spring? ¹²My brothers and sisters, can a fig tree make olives, or can a grapevine make figs? No! And a well full of salty water cannot give good water.

## True Wisdom

¹³Are there those among you who are truly wise and understanding? Then they should show it by living right and doing good things with a gentleness that comes from wisdom. ¹⁴But if you are selfish and have bitter jealousy in your hearts, do not brag. Your bragging is a lie that hides the truth. ¹⁵That kind of "wisdom" does not come from God but from the world. It is not spiritual; it is from the devil. ¹⁶Where jealousy and selfishness are, there will be confusion and every kind of evil. ¹⁷But the wisdom that comes from God is first of all pure, then peaceful, gentle, and easy to please. This wisdom is always ready to help those who are troubled and to do good for others. It is always fair and honest. ¹⁸People who work for peace in a peaceful way plant a good crop of right-living.

## Give Yourselves to God

**4** Do you know where your fights and arguments come from? They come from the selfish desires that war within you. ²You want things, but you do not have them. So you are ready to kill and are jealous of other people, but you still cannot get what you want. So you argue and fight. You do not get what you want, because you do not ask God. ³Or when you ask, you do not receive because the reason you ask is wrong. You want things so you can use them for your own pleasures.

⁴So, you are not loyal to God! You should know that loving the world is the same as hating God. Anyone who wants to be a friend of the world becomes God's enemy. ⁵Do you think the Scripture means nothing that says, "The Spirit that God made to live in us wants us for himself alone"?ⁿ ⁶But God gives us even more grace, as the Scripture says,

"God is against the proud,
but he gives grace to the humble."
*Proverbs 3:34*

⁷So give yourselves completely to God. Stand against the devil, and the devil will run from you. ⁸Come near to God, and God will come near to you. You sinners, clean sin out of your lives. You who are trying to follow God and the world at the same time, make your thinking pure. ⁹Be

# Q & A

**Q** My friend is thinking about committing suicide. What should I do?

**A** Ask your friend to talk about what's bothering her and really listen without judging her. Remind her of all the people who love her and would be upset if she killed herself. If she's still serious about wanting to commit suicide, encourage her to get help or else talk to a counselor, teacher, or parent yourself. You can also call a suicide crisis number for help. And pray! James 5:16 says that when a believer prays, "great things happen."

# cool

## Close Your Mouth!

**A**ccording to statistics, about four hundred thousand people around the world die from drowning every year. Many more people come very close to drowning but are safely rescued. Drowning happens when water fills up your lungs, so it's important to keep your mouth closed while under water. You don't want to accidentally breathe in water!

Even if you're not in the water, it can be a good idea to keep your mouth shut. It's easy to make our problems worse when we talk and talk, trying to explain ourselves or argue. James 1:19 gives good advice: talk less and listen more. You'll get in less trouble!

4:5 "The Spirit . . . alone." *These words may be from Exodus 20:5.*

# BibLe BaSicS

The Bible was first written in the languages of the ancient Middle East: Hebrew, Aramaic, and Greek. People translated the Bible so those of us who don't speak the original languages could understand it. You read an English translation of the Bible. But language is always changing. You have probably noticed that the way you speak is different from the way your parents or grandparents speak. New translations are always being made to keep up with language changes and to serve different purposes: some translations are good for close study of the Bible and others are good for easy reading. But they all have the same message: God loves us and wants to save us!

sad, cry, and weep! Change your laughter into crying and your joy into sadness. ¹⁰Humble yourself in the Lord's presence, and he will honor you.

## You Are Not the Judge

¹¹Brothers and sisters, do not tell evil lies about each other. If you speak against your fellow believers or judge them, you are judging and speaking against the law they follow. And when you are judging the law, you are no longer a follower of the law. You have become a judge. ¹²God is the only Lawmaker and Judge. He is the only One who can save and destroy. So it is not right for you to judge your neighbor.

## Let God Plan Your Life

¹³Some of you say, "Today or tomorrow we will go to some city. We will stay there a year, do business, and make money." ¹⁴But you do not know what will happen tomorrow! Your life is like a mist. You can see it for a short time, but then it goes away. ¹⁵So you should say, "If the Lord wants, we will live and do this or that." ¹⁶But now you are proud and you brag. All of this bragging is wrong. ¹⁷Anyone who knows the right thing to do, but does not do it, is sinning.

## A Warning to the Rich

5 You rich people, listen! Cry and be very sad because of the troubles that are coming to you. ²Your riches have rotted, and your clothes have been eaten by moths. ³Your gold and silver have rusted, and that rust will be a proof that you were wrong. It will eat your bodies like fire. You saved your treasure for the last days. ⁴The pay you did not give the workers who mowed your fields cries out against you, and the cries of the workers have been heard by the Lord All-Powerful. ⁵Your life on earth was full of rich living and pleasing yourselves with everything you wanted. You made yourselves fat, like an animal ready to be killed. ⁶You have judged guilty and then murdered innocent people, who were not against you.

## Be Patient

⁷Brothers and sisters, be patient until the Lord comes again. A farmer patiently waits for his valuable crop to grow from the earth and for it to receive the autumn and spring rains. ⁸You, too, must be patient. Do not give up hope, because the Lord is coming soon. ⁹Brothers and sisters, do not complain against each other or you will be judged guilty. And

the Judge is ready to come! ¹⁰Brothers and sisters, follow the example of the prophets who spoke for the Lord. They suffered many hard things, but they were patient. ¹¹We say they are happy because they did not give up. You have heard about Job's patience, and you know the Lord's purpose for him in the end. You know the Lord is full of mercy and is kind.

## Be Careful What You Say

¹²My brothers and sisters, above all, do not use an oath when you make a promise. Don't use the name of heaven, earth, or anything else to prove what you say. When you mean yes, say only yes, and when you mean no, say only no so you will not be judged guilty.

## The Power of Prayer

¹³Anyone who is having troubles should pray. Anyone who is happy should sing praises. ¹⁴Anyone who is sick should call the church's elders. They should pray for and pour oil on the person[n] in the name of the Lord. ¹⁵And the prayer that is said with faith will make the sick person well; the Lord will heal that person. And if the person has sinned, the sins will be forgiven. ¹⁶Confess your sins to each other and pray for each other so God can heal you. When a believing person prays, great things happen. ¹⁷Elijah was a human being just like us. He prayed that it would not rain, and it did not rain on the land for three and a half years! ¹⁸Then Elijah prayed again, and the rain came down from the sky, and the land produced crops again.

## Saving a Soul

¹⁹My brothers and sisters, if one of you wanders away from the truth, and someone helps that person come back, ²⁰remember this: Anyone who brings a sinner back from the wrong way will save that sinner's soul from death and will cause many sins to be forgiven.

ANYONE WHO BRINGS A SINNER BACK FROM THE WRONG WAY WILL SAVE THAT SINNER'S SOUL FROM DEATH . . .

5:14 **pour oil on the person** *Oil was used in the name of the Lord as a sign that the person was now set apart for God's special attention and care.*

# 1 PETER

**W**hat makes Christians different? And what are you supposed to do about it? Dive into 1 Peter for some honest answers.

The apostle Peter (the same man who hung out with Jesus during his time on earth and who is known for always having something to say) wrote this book to Christians throughout the world in the first century (and all Christians).

Peter wanted Christians to know that God had chosen them for a special purpose—even before he created the world! He reminded them to be true to who they were by living pure lives. "Now that you are obedient children of God do not live as you did in the past," he told them (1 Peter 1:14).

What about you? Don't miss Peter's beauty advice in 3:3–6.

And when you are worried, remember, "Give all your worries to him, because he cares about you" (1 Peter 5:7).

Check out what Peter has to say about who you are in Jesus: "But you are a chosen people, royal priests, a holy nation, a people for God's own possession. You were chosen to tell about the wonderful acts of God" (1 Peter 2:9). God has big plans for your life!

Here's a hint: 1 and 2 Peter are even better when read together!

# ENCOURAGEMENT FOR SUFFERING CHRISTIANS

## THINGS TO TALK WITH GOD ABOUT . . .

1 From Peter, an apostle of Jesus Christ.

To God's chosen people who are away from their homes and are scattered all around Pontus, Galatia, Cappadocia, Asia, and Bithynia. ²God planned long ago to choose you by making you his holy people, which is the Spirit's work. God wanted you to obey him and to be made clean by the blood of the death of Jesus Christ.

Grace and peace be yours more and more.

**20% of kids consider their grandparents role models.**
—Trends & Tudes. Harris Interactive. July 2005.
http://www.harrisinteractive.com/news/newsletters/k12news/HI_Trends&TudesNews2005_v4_iss07.pdf

**did you know?**

### We Have a Living Hope

³Praise be to the God and Father of our Lord Jesus Christ. In God's great mercy he has caused us to be born again into a living hope, because Jesus Christ rose from the dead. ⁴Now we hope for the blessings God has for his children. These blessings, which cannot be destroyed or be spoiled or lose their beauty, are kept in heaven for you. ⁵God's power protects you through your faith until salvation is shown to you at the end of time. ⁶This makes you very happy, even though now for a short time different kinds of troubles may make you sad. ⁷These troubles come to prove that your faith is pure. This purity of faith is worth more than gold, which can be proved to be pure by fire but will ruin. But the purity of your faith will bring you praise and glory and honor when Jesus Christ is shown to you. ⁸You have not seen Christ, but still you love him. You cannot see him now, but you believe in him. So you are filled with a joy that cannot be explained, a joy full of glory. ⁹And you are receiving the goal of your faith—the salvation of your souls.

¹⁰The prophets searched carefully and tried to learn about this salvation. They prophesied about the grace that was coming to you. ¹¹The Spirit of Christ was in the prophets, telling in advance about the sufferings of Christ and about the glory that would follow those sufferings. The prophets tried to learn about what the Spirit was showing them, when those things would happen, and what the world would be like at that time. ¹²It was shown them that their service was not for themselves but for you, when they told about the truths you have now heard. Those who preached the Good News to you told you those things with the help of the Holy Spirit who was sent from heaven—things into which angels desire to look.

**IN GOD'S GREAT MERCY HE HAS CAUSED US TO BE BORN AGAIN INTO A LIVING HOPE, BECAUSE JESUS CHRIST ROSE FROM THE DEAD.**

## cool

### Tongue Prints

You probably already knew every human has a unique fingerprint pattern, which is why the police are often able to track down criminals. Well, here's something interesting: everyone has a unique tongue print, too! (We don't recommend you test this one out.)

One thing our tongues all have in common, though, is that they're very difficult to control! We often say things that we wish we could take back. That's why we need God's help each day to keep our words truthful, kind, and pure.

## A Call to Holy Living

[13]So prepare your minds for service and have self-control. All your hope should be for the gift of grace that will be yours when Jesus Christ is shown to you. [14]Now that you are obedient children of God do not live as you did in the past. You did not understand, so you did the evil things you wanted. [15]But be holy in all you do, just as God, the One who called you, is holy. [16]It is written in the Scriptures: "You must be holy, because I am holy."[n]

[17]You pray to God and call him Father, and he judges each person's work equally. So while you are here on earth, you should live with respect for God. [18]You know that in the past you were living in a worthless way, a way passed down from the people who lived before you. But you were saved from that useless life. You were bought, not with something that ruins like gold or silver, [19]but with the precious blood of Christ, who was like a pure and perfect lamb. [20]Christ was chosen before the world was made, but he was shown to the world in these last times for your sake. [21]Through Christ you believe in God, who raised Christ from the dead and gave him glory. So your faith and your hope are in God.

[22]Now that your obedience to the truth has purified your souls, you can have true love for your Christian brothers and sisters. So love each other deeply with all your heart.[n] [23]You have been born again, and this new life did not come from something that dies, but from something that cannot die. You were born again through God's living message that continues forever. [24]The Scripture says,
"All people are like the grass,
    and all their glory is like the
        flowers of the field.
The grass dies and the flowers fall,
[25]    but the word of the Lord will live
        forever."          *Isaiah 40:6–8*
And this is the word that was preached to you.

> THE GRASS DIES AND
> THE FLOWERS FALL,
> BUT THE WORD OF
> THE LORD WILL LIVE
> FOREVER."

## Jesus Is the Living Stone

**2** So then, rid yourselves of all evil, all lying, hypocrisy, jealousy, and evil speech. [2]As newborn babies want milk, you should want the pure and simple teaching. By it you can mature in your salvation, [3]because you have already examined and seen how good the Lord is.

[4]Come to the Lord Jesus, the "stone"[n] that lives. The people of the world did not want this stone, but he was the stone God chose, and he was precious. [5]You also are like living stones, so let yourselves be used to build a spiritual temple—to be holy priests who offer spiritual sacrifices to God. He will accept those sacrifices through Jesus Christ. [6]The Scripture says:

## god's promises

### 1 Peter 2:9–10

Many people in the world feel like they don't belong anywhere . . . and some of them really don't. Maybe their parents died when they were little and they have no one to take care of them. Maybe they had to leave their country because of a terrible war and now have nowhere to live. Maybe they lost their job, their house burned down, or they had a terrible accident and now they feel helpless and alone. You might have an idea of what that's like if you've ever moved and had to try to fit into a new school where you didn't know anyone.

Before people become Christians, that's what their spiritual lives are like. They are lost, helpless, and hopeless. But when a person believes that Jesus died on the cross to take the punishment for their sins, and when they ask him to forgive and save them, they automatically belong somewhere! That's the way to belong to the special family of God. 1 Peter 2:10 says that "you are God's people" and that "you have received God's mercy."

No matter who you live with, how many friends you have, or what groups you belong to, you never have to feel alone or unimportant. If you've committed your life to Jesus, you belong to God!

*You never have to feel alone or unimportant.*

---

1:16 **"You must be . . . holy."** *Quotation from Leviticus 11:45; 19:2; 20:7.*  1:22 **with all your heart** *Some Greek copies read "with a pure heart."*  2:4 **"stone"** *The most important stone in God's spiritual temple or house (his people).*

**read it, do it**

**1 Peter 2:2**

**R**ead It: Drink your spiritual milk!

...........................................................

**D**o It: Keep a Bible in the kitchen. Whenever you have a glass of milk, read a few Bible verses, too!

"I will put a stone in the ground in
  Jerusalem.
Everything will be built on this
    important and precious rock.
Anyone who trusts in him
  will never be disappointed."
                        *Isaiah 28:16*
⁷This stone is worth much to you who believe. But to the people who do not believe,
  "the stone that the builders rejected
    has become the cornerstone."
                        *Psalm 118:22*
⁸Also, he is
  "a stone that causes people to
      stumble,
  a rock that makes them fall."
                        *Isaiah 8:14*
They stumble because they do not obey what God says, which is what God planned to happen to them.

⁹But you are a chosen people, royal priests, a holy nation, a people for God's own possession. You were chosen to tell about the wonderful acts of God, who called you out of darkness into his wonderful light. ¹⁰At one time you were not a people, but now you are God's people. In

## ALSO, HE IS "A STONE THAT CAUSES PEOPLE TO STUMBLE, A ROCK THAT MAKES THEM FALL."

the past you had never received mercy, but now you have received God's mercy.

### Live for God

¹¹Dear friends, you are like foreigners and strangers in this world. I beg you to avoid the evil things your bodies want to do that fight against your soul. ¹²People who do not believe are living all around you and might say that you are doing wrong. Live such good lives that they will see the good things you do and will give glory to God on the day when Christ comes again.

### Yield to Every Human Authority

¹³For the Lord's sake, yield to the people who have authority in this world: the king, who is the highest authority, ¹⁴and the leaders who are sent by him to punish those who do wrong and to praise those who do right. ¹⁵It is God's desire that by doing good you should stop foolish people from saying stupid things about you. ¹⁶Live as free people, but do not use your freedom as an excuse to do evil. Live as servants of God. ¹⁷Show respect for all people: Love the brothers and sisters of God's family, respect God, honor the king.

### Follow Christ's Example

¹⁸Slaves, yield to the authority of your masters with all respect, not only those who are good and kind, but also those

who are dishonest. ¹⁹A person might have to suffer even when it is unfair, but if he thinks of God and can stand the pain, God is pleased. ²⁰If you are beaten for doing wrong, there is no reason to praise you for being patient in your punishment. But if you suffer for doing good, and you are patient, then God is pleased. ²¹This is what you were called to do, because Christ suffered for you and gave you an example to follow. So you should do as he did.
²²"He had never sinned,
    and he had never lied." *Isaiah 53:9*
²³People insulted Christ, but he did not insult them in return. Christ suffered, but he did not threaten. He let God, the One who judges rightly, take care of him. ²⁴Christ carried our sins in his body on the cross so we would stop living for sin and start living for what is right. And you are healed because of his wounds. ²⁵You were like sheep that wandered away, but now you have come back to the Shepherd and Overseer of your souls.

## Looking Ahead

### DRIVING

**R**ight now you might not think much about the fact that someone drives you wherever you need to go. But one day you'll be on the road! The idea of driving (and taking the test) can be scary or exciting. Don't worry—you'll study and practice before you ever drive alone. The tests (written and behind-the-wheel) make sure you're ready to be in the driver's seat. Many people don't pass the first time, so don't feel bad if you have to try again. Remember 1 Peter 2:13 as you drive: "For the Lord's sake, yield to the people who have authority."

## dig deeper

### 1 Peter 4:12–13

"Why me? Why is life so *hard?*" Isn't that what we say when bad things happen? We expect life to be easy and assume problems mean something is wrong. But Peter says that just the opposite is true. He says, "Do not be surprised at the terrible trouble which now comes to test you . . . be happy that you are sharing in Christ's sufferings" (1 Peter 4:12–13). *That* is normal. Not very comforting, is it?

Maybe not. But on the other hand, Peter's words reassure us that hard times don't come just because we've done something wrong. God's not ignoring us. Jesus suffered, too—far more than we ever will. In Hebrews 12:7 we learn that God allows us to struggle because we are his children. He loves us and wants to teach us through hard times.

Any problems we have now are temporary. When we go to be with Jesus, we will never suffer again. Difficulties make us more excited that Jesus is coming back. When he does, we won't say, "Aw, man! Do I really have to go? But I was having so much *fun!*" Those who don't know God will have a lot to worry about when Jesus returns. But not his followers. When that happens, all our problems will be over—forever!

### Wives and Husbands

**3** In the same way, you wives should yield to your husbands. Then, if some husbands do not obey God's teaching, they will be persuaded to believe without anyone's saying a word to them. They will be persuaded by the way their wives live. ²Your husbands will see the pure lives you live with your respect for God. ³It is not fancy hair, gold jewelry, or fine clothes that should make you beautiful. ⁴No, your beauty should come from within you—the beauty of a gentle and quiet spirit that will never be destroyed and is very precious to God. ⁵In this same way the holy women who lived long ago and followed God made themselves beautiful, yielding to their own husbands. ⁶Sarah obeyed Abraham, her husband, and called him her master. And you women are true children of Sarah if you always do what is right and are not afraid.

⁷In the same way, you husbands should live with your wives in an understanding way, since they are weaker than you. But show them respect, because God gives them the same blessing he gives you—the grace that gives true life. Do this so that nothing will stop your prayers.

### Suffering for Doing Right

⁸Finally, all of you should be in agreement, understanding each other, loving each other as family, being kind and humble. ⁹Do not do wrong to repay a wrong, and do not insult to repay an insult. But repay with a blessing, because you yourselves were called to do this so that you might receive a blessing. ¹⁰The Scripture says,

"A person must do these things
　　to enjoy life and have many happy days.
He must not say evil things,
　　and he must not tell lies.
¹¹He must stop doing evil and do good.
　　He must look for peace and work for it.
¹²The Lord sees the good people
　　and listens to their prayers.
But the Lord is against
　　those who do evil." *Psalm 34:12–16*

## Q & A

**Q** I get really nervous when I'm up in front of a class. What can I do to calm my nerves?

**A** Figure out what makes you nervous. Then talk to your teacher or parents about it. Remember: some of the other students feel nervous, too. They're probably thinking about their own presentation . . . not waiting for you to mess up. Most importantly, pray before you go up! God can give you peace. He is right there with you!

# Relationships

Do you go to school with Muslim kids? Have you noticed a Buddhist temple around your neighborhood? With more religions than you can count, what's a Christian girl to do? Take a minute to think about what your life would be like without Jesus. That thought should make you eager to help other people know Jesus! The Bible says we should treat people of other religions with gentleness and respect (1 Peter 3:15–16). If someone asks you about Christ, tell them about him. Treat people of other religions with love, and let God take care of the rest!

¹³If you are trying hard to do good, no one can really hurt you. ¹⁴But even if you suffer for doing right, you are blessed.
"Don't be afraid of what they fear;
do not dread those things."
*Isaiah 8:12–13*
¹⁵But respect Christ as the holy Lord in your hearts. Always be ready to answer everyone who asks you to explain about the hope you have, ¹⁶but answer in a gentle way and with respect. Keep a clear conscience so that those who speak evil of your good life in Christ will be made ashamed. ¹⁷It is better to suffer for doing good than for doing wrong if that is what God wants. ¹⁸Christ himself suffered for sins once. He was not guilty, but he suffered for those who are guilty to bring you to God. His body was killed, but he was made alive in the spirit. ¹⁹And in the spirit he went and preached to the spirits in prison ²⁰who refused to obey God long ago in the time of Noah. God was waiting patiently for them while Noah was building the boat. Only a few people—eight in all—were saved by water. ²¹And that water is like baptism that now saves you—not the washing of dirt from the body,

but the promise made to God from a good conscience. And this is because Jesus Christ was raised from the dead. ²²Now Jesus has gone into heaven and is at God's right side ruling over angels, authorities, and powers.

## Change Your Lives

4 Since Christ suffered while he was in his body, strengthen yourselves with the same way of thinking Christ had. The person who has suffered in the body is finished with sin. ²Strengthen yourselves so that you will live here on earth doing what God wants, not the evil things people want. ³In the past you wasted too much time doing what nonbelievers enjoy. You were guilty of sexual sins, evil desires, drunkenness, wild and drunken parties, and hateful idol worship. ⁴Nonbelievers think it is strange that you do not do the many wild and wasteful things they do, so they insult you. ⁵But they will have to explain this to God, who is ready to judge the living and the dead. ⁶For this reason the Good News was preached to those who are now dead. Even though they were judged like all people, the Good News

**DO NOT DO WRONG TO REPAY A WRONG, AND DO NOT INSULT TO REPAY AN INSULT.**

## Bible Bios — Hannah (1 Samuel 1–2)

Hannah's husband, Elkanah, treated her very well, but something still made Hannah sad. She desperately wanted a son! Hannah believed in God, though, so she went to the *Holy Tent* (a place of worship) to pray about her problem. She became so emotional the priest Eli thought she was drunk!

Hannah explained the situation and Eli blessed her, saying: "May the God of Israel give you what you asked of him." This calmed Hannah's heart and she believed God would answer her prayer. In fact, she had so much faith, she promised to give her son back to God when he was born! God did give Hannah a baby boy. She named him Samuel and took him to the Holy Tent where he grew up learning to serve God. Like Hannah, we can go to God when our hearts are hurting and trust him to answer our prayers.

> MOST IMPORTANTLY, LOVE EACH OTHER DEEPLY, BECAUSE LOVE WILL CAUSE PEOPLE TO FORGIVE EACH OTHER FOR MANY SINS.

was preached to them so they could live in the spirit as God lives.

## Use God's Gifts Wisely

[7]The time is near when all things will end. So think clearly and control yourselves so you will be able to pray. [8]Most importantly, love each other deeply, because love will cause people to forgive each other for many sins. [9]Open your homes to each other, without complaining. [10]Each of you has received a gift to use to serve others. Be good servants of God's various gifts of grace. [11]Anyone who speaks should speak words from God. Anyone who serves should serve with the strength God gives so that in everything God will be praised through Jesus Christ. Power and glory belong to him forever and ever. Amen.

# Q&A

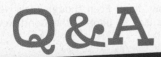

**Q** What will happen to people in other countries who never hear about Jesus?

**A** With so many missionaries around the world and Bible translations in most languages, many more people are learning about Jesus. For those who don't hear, the Holy Spirit can teach them about God in other ways and help them choose between wrong and right. You can trust that God will judge them fairly according to how they respond to what they *do* know.

## Shine Your Light

Some Christians have decided to spend their whole lives telling others about Jesus. We call them missionaries. Sometimes they share the Good News where they live, and sometimes they travel across the world. Someday, Brittany wants to be a missionary to another country. Of course, at twelve-and-a-half, she still has to grow up some more. But that doesn't mean that she sits around twiddling her thumbs!

Whenever she can, Brittany finds ways to help missionaries who are serving all over the world. Several missionaries have come to visit her church and, each time, Brittany gives some of her allowance to them. Brittany doesn't just give money, though! In her room, she has a list of all the missionaries she has met. She tries to pray for each of them at least once a week.

No matter how young you are, you can still be a part of spreading the Good News about Jesus all over the world. You can pray for missionaries, give money to support them, and even write letters to encourage them. You can make a difference for Jesus all over the world!

## Suffering as a Christian

[12]My friends, do not be surprised at the terrible trouble which now comes to test you. Do not think that something strange is happening to you. [13]But be happy that you are sharing in Christ's sufferings so that you will be happy and full of joy when Christ comes again in glory. [14]When people insult you because you follow Christ, you are blessed, because the glorious Spirit, the Spirit of God, is with you. [15]Do not suffer for murder, theft, or any other crime, nor because you trouble other people. [16]But if you suffer because you are a Christian, do not be ashamed. Praise God because you wear that name. [17]It is time for judgment to begin with God's family. And if that judging begins with us, what will happen to those people who do not obey the Good News of God?

[18]"If it is very hard for a good person to be saved,

the wicked person and the sinner will surely be lost!"[n]

[19]So those who suffer as God wants should trust their souls to the faithful Creator as they continue to do what is right.

## The Flock of God

**5** Now I have something to say to the elders in your group. I also am an elder. I have seen Christ's sufferings, and I will share in the glory

4:18 **"If . . . lost!"** *Quotation from Proverbs 11:31 in the Septuagint, the Greek version of the Old Testament.*

## "GOD IS AGAINST THE PROUD, BUT HE GIVES GRACE TO THE HUMBLE."

that will be shown to us. I beg you to ²shepherd God's flock, for whom you are responsible. Watch over them because you want to, not because you are forced. That is how God wants it. Do it because you are happy to serve, not because you want money. ³Do not be like a ruler over people you are responsible for, but be good examples to them. ⁴Then when Christ, the Chief Shepherd, comes, you will get a glorious crown that will never lose its beauty.

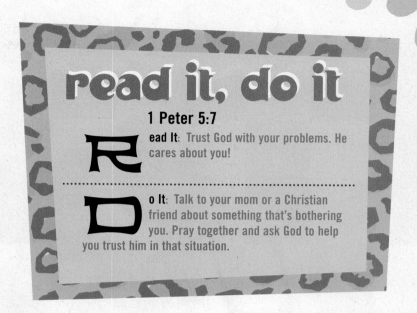

## read it, do it

### 1 Peter 5:7

**R** ead It: Trust God with your problems. He cares about you!

**D** o It: Talk to your mom or a Christian friend about something that's bothering you. Pray together and ask God to help you trust him in that situation.

## cool

### Emotional Intelligence?

To test the intelligence of some four-year-olds, researchers first gave each child a marshmallow. The children could either eat it or wait fifteen minutes to get a second one. Most of them quickly ate their marshmallow but a few patiently waited and got a second treat. Scientists call that "emotional intelligence". . . and the kids who had it grew up to do better in school!

You could also describe this "intelligence" as wisdom. It's not about how much stuff you know, but how well you make good decisions. God wants to give *you* wisdom, too (James 1:5)!

⁵In the same way, younger people should be willing to be under older people. And all of you should be very humble with each other.

"God is against the proud,
but he gives grace to the humble."

*Proverbs 3:34*

⁶Be humble under God's powerful hand so he will lift you up when the right time comes. ⁷Give all your worries to him, because he cares about you.

⁸Control yourselves and be careful! The devil, your enemy, goes around like a roaring lion looking for someone to eat. ⁹Refuse to give in to him, by standing strong in your faith. You know that your Christian family all over the world is having the same kinds of suffering.

¹⁰And after you suffer for a short time, God, who gives all grace, will make everything right. He will make you strong and support you and keep you from falling. He called you to share in his glory in Christ, a glory that will continue forever. ¹¹All power is his forever and ever. Amen.

### Final Greetings

¹²I wrote this short letter with the help of Silas, who I know is a faithful brother in Christ. I wrote to encourage you and to tell you that this is the true grace of God. Stand strong in that grace.

¹³The church in Babylon, who was chosen like you, sends you greetings. Mark, my son in Christ, also greets you. ¹⁴Give each other a kiss of Christian love when you meet.

Peace to all of you who are in Christ.

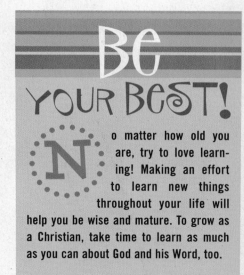

## BE YOUR BEST!

**N** o matter how old you are, try to love learning! Making an effort to learn new things throughout your life will help you be wise and mature. To grow as a Christian, take time to learn as much as you can about God and his Word, too.

# 2 PETER

**S**econd Peter is like 1 Peter in a few important ways. Both books are written by the apostle Peter to Christians everywhere. Both books are meant to encourage us to live pure lives.

Chapter 2 refers to several Old Testament Bible stories—Noah and the flood, Sodom and Gomorrah being destroyed by raining fire, and Balaam's talking donkey. Peter's point is this: if God punished sinful people in the past, he'll punish sinful people now, too. If people live as though there is no God, he will set them straight.

Have you ever wondered when Jesus will return to earth? Chapter 3 lets us know that it will be soon! We should remember that "the day of the Lord" will come like a thief in the night—when it is least expected. As Christians, we "are waiting for this to happen," and we should do our "best to be without sin and without fault" (2 Peter 3:14).

You don't have to worry about becoming "without fault" on your own, though. Second Peter 1:3 says, "Jesus has the power of God, by which he has given us everything we need to live and to serve God. We have these things because we know him." Jesus has made it possible for us to be clean before him!

# CORRECTING FALSE TEACHINGS

## THINGS TO TALK WITH GOD ABOUT . . .

## read it, do it

**2 Peter 1:5**

**R**ead It: Faith leads to goodness and knowledge.

**D**o It: Whenever you read your Bible, write down what the main lesson is. Then think of a way to practice it.

1 From Simon Peter, a servant and apostle of Jesus Christ.
To you who have received a faith as valuable as ours, because our God and Savior Jesus Christ does what is right.

²Grace and peace be given to you more and more, because you truly know God and Jesus our Lord.

### God Has Given Us Blessings

³Jesus has the power of God, by which he has given us everything we need to live and to serve God. We have these things because we know him. Jesus called us by his glory and goodness. ⁴Through these he gave us the very great and precious promises. With these gifts you can share in God's nature, and the world will not ruin you with its evil desires.

⁵Because you have these blessings, do your best to add these things to your lives: to your faith, add goodness; and to your goodness, add knowledge; ⁶and to your knowledge, add self-control; and to your self-control, add patience; and to your patience, add service for God; ⁷and to your service for God, add kindness for your brothers and sisters in Christ; and to this kindness, add love. ⁸If all these things are in you and are growing, they will help you to be useful and productive in your knowledge of our Lord Jesus Christ. ⁹But anyone who does not have these things cannot see clearly. He is blind and has forgotten that he was made clean from his past sins.

¹⁰My brothers and sisters, try hard to be certain that you really are called and chosen by God. If you do all these things, you will never fall. ¹¹And you will be given a very great welcome into the eternal kingdom of our Lord and Savior Jesus Christ.

¹²You know these things, and you are very strong in the truth, but I will always help you remember them. ¹³I think it is right for me to help you remember as long as I am in this body. ¹⁴I know I must soon leave this body, as our Lord Jesus Christ has shown me. ¹⁵I will try my best so that you may be able to remember these things even after I am gone.

## Be YOUR BEST!

**W**hen you eat, it's best to take small bites and chew well before swallowing. Not only is this more polite, but you'll digest better. Remember this principle when reading your Bible, too. Rather than rushing through it, take your time and try to "digest" what you read.

# BibLe Basics

F lip to the beginning of most Bibles and you'll find the Old Testament. It starts with Genesis and the incredible story of Creation. From there it covers everything from poetry and songs to history and prophecy. Hundreds of years before Jesus was born, God gave many men words from him to record and pass along as our present day Old Testament. It ends with the Book of Malachi, which was the last word anyone heard from God before Jesus appeared on the scene. Throughout the Old Testament, you can see hints of God's plan to save everyone through the life, death, and resurrection of his Son. The Old Testament certainly wasn't God's final word!

## We Saw Christ's Glory

[16]When we told you about the powerful coming of our Lord Jesus Christ, we were not telling just clever stories that someone invented. But we saw the greatness of Jesus with our own eyes. [17]Jesus heard the voice of God, the Greatest Glory, when he received honor and glory from God the Father. The voice said, "This is my Son, whom I love, and I am very pleased with him." [18]We heard that voice from heaven while we were with Jesus on the holy mountain.

[19]This makes us more sure about the message the prophets gave. It is good for you to follow closely what they said as you would follow a light shining in a dark place, until the day begins and the morning star rises in your hearts. [20]Most of all, you must understand this: No prophecy in the Scriptures ever comes from the prophet's own interpretation. [21]No prophecy ever came from what a person wanted to say, but people led by the Holy Spirit spoke words from God.

## False Teachers

2 There used to be false prophets among God's people, just as you will have some false teachers in your group. They will secretly teach things that are wrong—teachings that will cause people to be lost. They will even refuse to accept the Master, Jesus, who bought their freedom. So they will bring quick ruin on themselves. [2]Many will follow their evil ways and say evil things about the way of truth. [3]Those false teachers only want your money, so they will use you by telling you lies. Their judgment spoken against them long ago is still coming, and their ruin is certain.

[4]When angels sinned, God did not let them go free without punishment. He sent them to hell and put them in caves[n] of darkness where they are being held for judgment. [5]And God punished the world long ago when he brought a flood to the world that was full of people who were against him. But God saved Noah, who preached about being right with God, and seven other people with him. [6]And God also destroyed the evil cities of Sodom and Gomorrah[n] by burning them until they were ashes. He made those cities an example of what will happen to those who are against God. [7]But he saved Lot from those cities. Lot, a good man, was troubled because of the filthy lives of evil people. [8](Lot was a good man, but because he lived with evil people every day, his good heart was hurt by the evil things he saw and heard.) [9]So the Lord knows how to save those who serve him when troubles come. He will

THE VOICE SAID, "THIS IS MY SON, WHOM I LOVE, AND I AM VERY PLEASED WITH HIM."

## Bible Bios — Abigail (1 Samuel 25)

A bigail's husband was a rich rancher named Nabal, which means "fool." He lived up to his name by doing something so foolish it made King David very angry! But Abigail came to his rescue with her quick and clever thinking. She used generosity, honesty, and a humble attitude to calm down the king. She apologized for her husband's foolishness and convinced David not to kill him. She reminded the king how God would want him to act and how much people respected him. When David saw how wise her arguments were, he agreed with her!

Abigail's wisdom and character impressed King David so much that when Nabal died naturally a few days later, he married her! *You* can be wise like Abigail, too! James 1:5 promises that if you ask for wisdom, God will give it to you!

2:4 **caves** Some Greek copies read "chains." 2:6 **Sodom and Gomorrah** Two cities God destroyed because the people were so evil.

into the trap of sin, and they have taught their hearts to be greedy. God will punish them! [15]These false teachers left the right road and lost their way, following the way Balaam went. Balaam was the son of Beor, who loved being paid for doing wrong. [16]But a donkey, which cannot talk, told Balaam he was sinning. It spoke with a man's voice and stopped the prophet's crazy thinking.

[17]Those false teachers are like springs without water and clouds blown by a storm. A place in the blackest darkness has been kept for them. [18]They brag with words that mean nothing. By their evil desires they lead people into the trap of sin—people who are just beginning to escape from others who live in error. [19]They promise them freedom, but they themselves are not free. They are slaves

# dig deeper

## 2 Peter 3:8–10

It has been about two thousand years since Jesus Christ died, rose from the dead, and went back to heaven. Before he left, Jesus promised he would come again. At that time, everyone will see Jesus for who he really is—the Son of God.

Do you ever wonder what's taking him so long to come back? You are not the first one to ask! The apostle Peter answered the question for some excited Christians who wanted Jesus to return right after he left! You might be surprised at what he said: "To the Lord one day is as a thousand years, and a thou-sand years is as one day" (2 Peter 3:8). To God, our days and years are not the important thing. Instead of being slow, God's actually being patient!

God is waiting to send Jesus back to earth. What is he waiting for? More people to accept Jesus as their Savior! But don't think that he will wait forever. Second Peter 3:10 says, "But the day of the Lord will come like a thief." When we don't expect it, Jesus will be back! While you wait for Jesus to return and take you to heaven, you can get ready by telling other people about Jesus and loving him every day of your life!

## Disciple

A disciple is anyone who chooses to *follow* Jesus Christ and become his "student." The original twelve disciples, or followers, were Jesus' best students and closest friends—Peter, Andrew, James, John, Philip, Bartholomew, Matthew, Thomas, James, Simon, Judas, and Judas Iscariot. Jesus chose them to help him during his ministry and to keep sharing his teachings and message of salvation after he returned to heaven. After Jesus' death and resurrection, these men shared the Good News all over the world and helped others learn to follow Christ. By believing in Jesus and learning from him, Christians today are also followers of Jesus!

hold evil people and punish them, while waiting for the Judgment Day. [10]That punishment is especially for those who live by doing the evil things their sinful selves want and who hate authority.

These false teachers are bold and do anything they want. They are not afraid to speak against the angels. [11]But even the angels, who are much stronger and more powerful than false teachers, do not accuse them with insults before[n] the Lord. [12]But these people speak against things they do not understand. They are like animals that act without thinking, animals born to be caught and killed. And, like animals, these false teachers will be destroyed. [13]They have caused many people to suffer, so they themselves will suffer. That is their pay for what they have done. They take pleasure in openly doing evil, so they are like dirty spots and stains among you. They delight in deceiving you while eating meals with you. [14]Every time they look at a woman they want her, and their desire for sin is never satisfied. They lead weak people

2:11 **before** *Some Greek copies read "from."*

## read it, do it

**2 Peter 1:8**

**R**ead It: God wants growing Christians!

**D**o It: Ask your parents if you can have a small plant to take care of. Every time you water it, take a moment to ask God to help you grow as a Christian.

**YOU SHOULD LIVE HOLY LIVES AND SERVE GOD, AS YOU WAIT FOR AND LOOK FORWARD TO THE COMING OF THE DAY OF GOD.**

of things that will be destroyed. For people are slaves of anything that controls them. ²⁰They were made free from the evil in the world by knowing our Lord and Savior Jesus Christ. But if they return to evil things and those things control them, then it is worse for them than it was before. ²¹Yes, it would be better for them to have never known the right way than to know it and to turn away from the holy teaching that was given to them. ²²What they did is like this true saying: "A dog goes back to what it has thrown up,"[n] and, "After a pig is washed, it goes back and rolls in the mud."

### Jesus Will Come Again

**3** My friends, this is the second letter I have written you to help your honest minds remember. ²I want you to think about the words the holy prophets spoke in the past, and remember the command our Lord and Savior gave us through your apostles. ³It is most important for you to understand what will happen in the last days. People will laugh at you. They will live doing the evil things they want to do. ⁴They will say, "Jesus promised to come again. Where is he? Our fathers have died, but the world continues the way it has been since it was made." ⁵But they do not want to remember what happened long ago. By the word of God heaven was made, and the earth was made from water and with water. ⁶Then the world was flooded and destroyed with water. ⁷And that same word of God is keeping heaven and earth that we now have in order to be destroyed by fire. They are being kept for the Judgment Day and the destruction of all who are against God.

⁸But do not forget this one thing, dear friends: To the Lord one day is as a thousand years, and a thousand years is as one day. ⁹The Lord is not slow in doing what he promised—the way some people understand slowness. But God is being patient with you. He does not want anyone to be lost, but he wants all people to change their hearts and lives.

¹⁰But the day of the Lord will come like a thief. The skies will disappear with a loud noise. Everything in them will be destroyed by fire, and the earth and everything in it will be exposed.[n] ¹¹In that way everything will be destroyed. So what kind of people should you be? You should live holy lives and serve God, ¹²as you wait for

# Q & A

**Q** I forgot to study for a test that I really need to pass. I'm sure I would have passed if I'd studied. Is it okay to cheat a little?

**A** No, it's not.
Everyone's being tested on what they know at the time of the test. It would be dishonest and unfair to cheat even a "little." It's like saying, "I would have paid for this candy bar if I hadn't forgotten my wallet at home. I'll just take it." You need to take responsibility for your actions. Besides, failing to obey God is much worse than failing a test!

## cool

### Chameleon Eyes

**C**hameleons have really cool features! Their skin changes color in response to temperature, light, and mood (it's *not* for camouflage). Their tongues can be twice as long as their bodies. And their two eyes can look in different directions at the same time, giving them almost 360-degree vision!

Wouldn't you like to have the ability to see all around you? 1 Peter 5:8 warns us that the devil prowls around us like a lion. We have to watch out! Ask God to help you keep your spiritual eyes open so you can recognize and avoid temptations.

---

**2:22** *"A dog . . . up."* Quotation from Proverbs 26:11. **3:10 and . . . exposed** Some Greek copies read "and everything in it will be burned up."

> BE CAREFUL SO YOU WILL NOT FALL FROM YOUR STRONG FAITH. BUT GROW IN THE GRACE AND KNOWLEDGE OF OUR LORD AND SAVIOR JESUS CHRIST.

# god's promises

2 Peter 3:13

Do you ever worry about what's happening to the world? The news tells many stories of war, diseases, famine, and pollution. Sometimes it seems like all the fighting and disasters will ruin this planet and the people who live here. Peter reminds us in 2 Peter 3:13 that this world won't last forever. Before you get upset that your home is going to be destroyed, realize that Peter's message is actually exciting! Instead of an old, worn out earth, God has promised to remake the world into a *new* heaven and a *new* earth!

The new heaven and new earth will be where goodness lives. That means that everyone who is there will be right with God. No more crying, diseases, war, or even pollution. It will be a perfect world!

Still, that doesn't mean that we can do whatever we want to this earth. We still need to treat the earth and one another carefully. After all, God's creation is a very special gift that we have been given. We don't know when God will make the new heaven and the new earth, but we can look forward to a day when the place where we live will be perfect.

*God has promised to remake the world into a* new *heaven and a* new *earth!*

and look forward to the coming of the day of God. When that day comes, the skies will be destroyed with fire, and everything in them will melt with heat. [13]But God made a promise to us, and we are waiting for a new heaven and a new earth where goodness lives.

[14]Dear friends, since you are waiting for this to happen, do your best to be without sin and without fault. Try to be at peace with God. [15]Remember that we are saved because our Lord is patient. Our dear brother Paul told you the same thing when he wrote to you with the wisdom that God gave him. [16]He writes about this in all his letters. Some things in Paul's letters are hard to understand, and people who are ignorant and weak in faith explain these things falsely. They also falsely explain the other Scriptures, but they are destroying themselves by doing this.

[17]Dear friends, since you already know about this, be careful. Do not let those evil people lead you away by the wrong they do. Be careful so you will not fall from your strong faith. [18]But grow in the grace and knowledge of our Lord and Savior Jesus Christ. Glory be to him now and forever! Amen.

# 1 JOHN

**L**ove. It is inspiration for mushy songs, strong enough to hold families together, and the greatest thing about God's character. But what is real love? You're about to find out!

First John was written to encourage Christians to love each other in the way that God loves us. The apostle John tells Christians, "The Father has loved us so much that we are called children of God. And we really are his children" (1 John 3:1). And by loving other believers, we prove that God's love is in our lives (2:10). Our example of how to love others is Jesus Christ. He gave his life for us and loved us with real actions, not just with words (3:18).

John says over and over that we must love each other (1 John 3:11). He even says that loving other people makes us alive and "whoever does not love is still dead" (3:14). Since love makes us alive, then as a Christian, you can have an exciting "love life"—without a boyfriend!

Want to know what real love is? First John 4:10 says that real love is not us loving God, but God loving us. He loved us so much that he sent Jesus to die for us and make us alive through his love.

The Book of 1 John is all about love—read it to find out how to improve your "love life" and become more like Christ!

# LOVE ONE ANOTHER

## THiNGS TO TALK WiTH GOD ABOUT . . .

**1** We write you now about what has always existed, which we have heard, we have seen with our own eyes, we have looked at, and we have touched with our hands. We write to you about the Word[n] that gives life. [2]He who gives life was shown to us. We saw him and can give proof about it. And now we announce to you that he has life that continues forever. He was with God the Father and was shown to us. [3]We announce to you what we have seen and heard, because we want you also to have fellowship with us. Our fellowship is with God the Father and with his Son, Jesus Christ. [4]We write this to you so we may be full of joy.[n]

### God Forgives Our Sins

[5]Here is the message we have heard from Christ and now announce to you: God is light,[n] and in him there is no darkness at all. [6]So if we say we have fellowship with God, but we continue living in darkness, we are liars and do not follow the truth. [7]But if we live in the light, as God is in the light, we can share fellowship with each other. Then the blood of Jesus, God's Son, cleanses us from every sin.

[8]If we say we have no sin, we are fooling ourselves, and the truth is not in us. [9]But if we confess our sins, he will forgive our sins, because we can trust God to do what is right. He will cleanse us from all the wrongs we have done. [10]If we say we have not sinned, we make God a liar, and we do not accept God's teaching.

### Jesus Is Our Helper

**2** My dear children, I write this letter to you so you will not sin. But if anyone does sin, we have a helper in the presence of the Father—

Jesus Christ, the One who does what is right. [2]He died in our place to take away our sins, and not only our sins but the sins of all people.

[3]We can be sure that we know God if we obey his commands. [4]Anyone who says, "I know God," but does not obey God's commands is a liar, and the truth is not in that person. [5]But if someone obeys God's teaching, then in that person God's love has truly reached its goal. This is how we can be sure we are living in God: [6]Whoever says that he lives in God must live as Jesus lived.

### The Command to Love Others

[7]My dear friends, I am not writing a new command to you but an old command you have had from the beginning. It is

**cool**

## Strong Hearts

**S**queeze a tennis ball as hard as you can. It takes your heart that much strength every time it beats (to pump your blood). What makes that even more amazing is that your heart beats about one hundred thousand times each day! You probably couldn't squeeze a tennis ball that hard one hundred thousand times, but that's how strong your heart is!

Even the strongest human heart can't compare with God. 1 John 3:20 says, "God is greater than our hearts, and he knows everything." Tell God today how great he is!

GOD IS LIGHT, AND IN HIM THERE IS NO DARKNESS AT ALL.

---

1:1 **Word** The Greek word is "logos," meaning any kind of communication. Here, it means Christ, who was the way God told people about himself.   1:4 **so . . . joy** Some Greek copies read "so you may be full of joy."
1:5 **light** Here, it is used as a symbol of God's goodness or truth.

the teaching you have already heard. [8]But also I am writing a new command to you, and you can see its truth in Jesus and in you, because the darkness is passing away, and the true light is already shining.

[9]Anyone who says, "I am in the light,"[n] but hates a brother or sister, is still in the darkness. [10]Whoever loves a brother or sister lives in the light and will not cause anyone to stumble in his faith. [11]But whoever hates a brother or sister is in darkness, lives in darkness, and does not know where to go, because the darkness has made that person blind.

[12]I write to you, dear children,
because your sins are forgiven
through Christ.
[13]I write to you, fathers,
because you know the One who
existed from the beginning.
I write to you, young people,
because you have defeated the Evil
One.
[14]I write to you, children,
because you know the Father.
I write to you, fathers,
because you know the One who
existed from the beginning.
I write to you, young people,
because you are strong;
the teaching of God lives in you,
and you have defeated the Evil
One.

[15]Do not love the world or the things in the world. If you love the world, the love of the Father is not in you. [16]These are the ways of the world: wanting to please our sinful selves, wanting the sinful things we see, and being too proud of what we have. None of these come from the Father, but all of them come from the world. [17]The world and everything that people want in it are passing away, but the person who does what God wants lives forever.

## Reject the Enemies of Christ

[18]My dear children, these are the last days. You have heard that the enemy of Christ is coming, and now many enemies of Christ are already here. This is how we know that these are the last days. [19]These enemies of Christ were in our fellowship, but they left us. They never really belonged to us; if they had been a part of us, they would have stayed with us. But they left, and this shows that none of them really belonged to us.

[20]You have the gift[n] that the Holy One gave you, so you all know the truth.[n] [21]I do not write to you because you do not know the truth but because you do know the truth. And you know that no lie comes from the truth. [22]Who is the liar? It is the person who does not accept Jesus as the Christ. This is the enemy of Christ: the person who does not accept the Father and his Son. [23]Whoever does not accept the Son does not have the Father. But whoever confesses the Son has the Father, too.

# Q & A

**Q** How often should I read my Bible?

**A** Jesus didn't give specific instructions on how many times a day or week we should read our Bibles. Still, many verses in the Bible talk about how important it is to study God's Word until we begin learning it by heart (Psalm 119:11)! Just as calcium keeps your bones strong and harder to break, reading and studying the Bible makes your heart strong against temptation and your mind protected from wrong messages. Try reading at least one or two chapters each day.

[24]Be sure you continue to follow the teaching you heard from the beginning. If you continue to follow what you heard from the beginning, you will stay in the Son and in the Father. [25]And this is what the Son promised to us—life forever.

[26]I am writing this letter about those people who are trying to lead you the wrong way. [27]Christ gave you a special gift that is still in you, so you do not need any other teacher. His gift teaches you about everything, and it is true, not false. So continue to live in Christ, as his gift taught you.

[28]Yes, my dear children, live in him so that when Christ comes back, we can be without fear and not be ashamed in his presence. [29]Since you know that Christ is righteous, you know that all who do right are God's children.

**BUT WE KNOW THAT WHEN CHRIST COMES AGAIN, WE WILL BE LIKE HIM, BECAUSE WE WILL SEE HIM AS HE REALLY IS.**

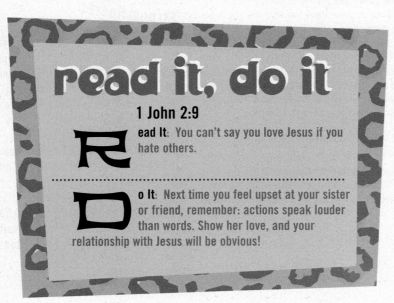

# read it, do it

## 1 John 2:9

**R**ead It: You can't say you love Jesus if you hate others.

**D**o It: Next time you feel upset at your sister or friend, remember: actions speak louder than words. Show her love, and your relationship with Jesus will be obvious!

---

**2:9 light** Here, it is used as a symbol of God's goodness or truth.    **2:20 gift** This might mean the Holy Spirit, or it might mean teaching or truth as in verse 24.    **2:20 you . . . truth** Some Greek copies read "so you know all things."

## dig deeper

### 1 John 2:14

There's professional hockey, international soccer competitions, the Olympics, and the craze for extreme sports. People all over the world enjoy competing in and watching sports! To succeed in their sports, athletes have to train. Many of them spend hours every day running, swimming, skating, climbing, lifting weights, or whatever exercise they need to make their bodies strong and ready for competition.

Exercise is great for your health. It's also good for your mind and emotions! Exercise is hard work at first, but athletes will tell you that it gets easier and more enjoyable after a while. And it's worth it!

But what about our spiritual fitness? The apostle John urged young people to have God's power and strength in their lives. How? By making sure "the teaching of God lives in you" (1 John 2:14). We might not think of reading, believing, and obeying God's word as *fun.* But every time we do it, we're getting a spiritual work out!

Obeying God's Word could mean helping out at church, being a kind neighbor, or praying for someone. It might mean telling someone about Jesus. You'll see some benefits to those things here on earth, such as feeling good inside or helping a friend believe in Jesus. But the greatest rewards will be waiting for you in heaven!

### We Are God's Children

**3** The Father has loved us so much that we are called children of God. And we really are his children. The reason the people in the world do not know us is that they have not known him. [2]Dear friends, now we are children of God, and we have not yet been shown what we will be in the future. But we know that when Christ comes again, we will be like him, because we will see him as he really is. [3]Christ is pure, and all who have this hope in Christ keep themselves pure like Christ.

[4]The person who sins breaks God's law. Yes, sin is living against God's law. [5]You know that Christ came to take away sins and that there is no sin in Christ. [6]So anyone who lives in Christ does not go on sinning. Anyone who goes on sinning has never really understood Christ and has never known him.

[7]Dear children, do not let anyone lead you the wrong way. Christ is righteous. So to be like Christ a person must do what is right. [8]The devil has been sinning since the beginning, so anyone who continues to sin belongs to the devil. The Son of God came for this purpose: to destroy the devil's work.

[9]Those who are God's children do not continue sinning, because the new life from God remains in them. They are not able to go on sinning, because they have become children of God. [10]So we can see who God's children are and who the devil's children are: Those who do not do what is right are not God's children, and those who do not love their brothers and sisters are not God's children.

### We Must Love Each Other

[11]This is the teaching you have heard from the beginning: We must love each other. [12]Do not be like Cain who belonged to the Evil One and killed his brother. And why did he kill him? Because the things Cain did were evil, and the things his brother did were good.

[13]Brothers and sisters, do not be surprised when the people of the world hate you. [14]We know we have left death and have come into life because we love each other. Whoever does not love is still dead.

## Be YOUR BEST!

**W**hen eating at your friend's house, show your appreciation by offering to help set the table or wash the dishes. You can do that at God's house, too. When there's something you can help with at church, go ahead and do it! God will be pleased . . . and you'll feel good, too.

# Relationships

Have you ever thought, "I would never be like *her*"? There are probably some kids in your class at school or in your neighborhood who are troublemakers—they're always picking on little kids or stealing stuff. But you can tell them about Jesus, too! When you talk to them, don't just complain about the wrong things they do, but share with them that God wants all people to know and love him. Remember that we have all sinned and we *all* need a Savior (Romans 3:10–11). Show love to everyone—and let God be the one to change people's behavior.

<sup>15</sup>Everyone who hates a brother or sister is a murderer,<sup>n</sup> and you know that no murderers have eternal life in them. <sup>16</sup>This is how we know what real love is: Jesus gave his life for us. So we should give our lives for our brothers and sisters. <sup>17</sup>Suppose someone has enough to live and sees a brother or sister in need, but does not help. Then God's love is not living in that person. <sup>18</sup>My children, we should love people not only with words and talk, but by our actions and true caring.

<sup>19–20</sup>This is the way we know that we belong to the way of truth. When our hearts make us feel guilty, we can still have peace before God. God is greater than our hearts, and he knows everything. <sup>21</sup>My dear friends, if our hearts do not make us feel guilty, we can come without fear into God's presence. <sup>22</sup>And God gives us what we ask for because we obey God's commands and do what pleases him. <sup>23</sup>This is what God commands: that we believe in his Son, Jesus Christ, and that we love each other, just as he commanded. <sup>24</sup>The people who obey God's commands live in God, and God lives in

WHERE GOD'S LOVE IS, THERE IS NO FEAR, BECAUSE GOD'S PERFECT LOVE DRIVES OUT FEAR.

them. We know that God lives in us because of the Spirit God gave us.

## Warning Against False Teachers

4 My dear friends, many false prophets have gone out into the world. So do not believe every spirit, but test the spirits to see if they are from God. <sup>2</sup>This is how you can know God's Spirit: Every spirit who confesses that Jesus Christ came to earth as a human is from God. <sup>3</sup>And every spirit who refuses to say this about Jesus is not from God. It is the spirit of the enemy of Christ, which you have heard is coming, and now he is already in the world.

<sup>4</sup>My dear children, you belong to God and have defeated them; because God's Spirit, who is in you, is greater than the devil, who is in the world. <sup>5</sup>And they belong to the world, so what they say is from the world, and the world listens to them. <sup>6</sup>But we belong to God, and those who know God listen to us. But those who are not from God do not listen to us. That is how we know the Spirit that is true and the spirit that is false.

## Love Comes from God

<sup>7</sup>Dear friends, we should love each other, because love comes from God. Everyone who loves has become God's child and knows God. <sup>8</sup>Whoever does not love does

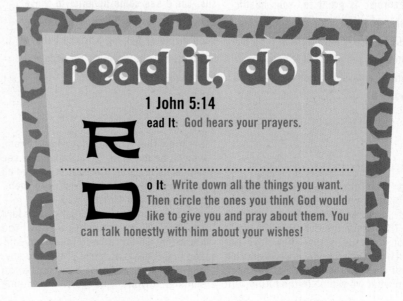

# read it, do it

### 1 John 5:14

**R**ead It: God hears your prayers.

**D**o It: Write down all the things you want. Then circle the ones you think God would like to give you and pray about them. You can talk honestly with him about your wishes!

**3:15 Everyone . . . murderer** *If one person hates a brother or sister, then in the heart that person has killed that brother or sister. Jesus taught about this sin to his followers (Matthew 5:21–26).*

## Salvation

Salvation means being saved from sin. It's what the Bible is all about! When we sin, we break God's laws and deserve to be punished. The punishment for sin is spiritual death—being separated from God forever. But because God loves us so much, he made a way for us to be saved! He sent his Son, Jesus Christ, to die on the cross so that anyone who believes in him can receive salvation and someday live in heaven forever (John 3:16). The best part about salvation? We don't have to earn it by doing good things. All we have to do is trust God!

not know God, because God is love. [9]This is how God showed his love to us: He sent his one and only Son into the world so that we could have life through him. [10]This is what real love is: It is not our love for God; it is God's love for us. He sent his Son to die in our place to take away our sins.

[11]Dear friends, if God loved us that much we also should love each other. [12]No one has ever seen God, but if we love each other, God lives in us, and his love is made perfect in us.

[13]We know that we live in God and he lives in us, because he gave us his Spirit. [14]We have seen and can testify that the Father sent his Son to be the Savior of the world. [15]Whoever confesses that Jesus is the Son of God has God living inside, and that person lives in God. [16]And so we know the love that God has for us, and we trust that love.

God is love. Those who live in love live in God, and God lives in them. [17]This is how love is made perfect in us: that we can be without fear on the day God judges us, because in this world we are like him. [18]Where God's love is, there is

no fear, because God's perfect love drives out fear. It is punishment that makes a person fear, so love is not made perfect in the person who fears.

[19]We love because God first loved us. [20]If people say, "I love God," but hate their brothers or sisters, they are liars. Those who do not love their brothers and sisters, whom they have seen, cannot love God, whom they have never seen. [21]And God gave us this command: Those who love God must also love their brothers and sisters.

### Faith in the Son of God

5 Everyone who believes that Jesus is the Christ is God's child, and whoever loves the Father also loves the Father's children. [2]This is how we know we love God's children: when we love God and obey his commands. [3]Loving God means obeying his commands. And God's commands are not too hard for us, [4]because everyone who is a child of God conquers the world. And this is the victory that conquers the world—our faith. [5]So the one who conquers the world is the person who believes that Jesus is the Son of God.

[6]Jesus Christ is the One who came by water[n] and blood.[n] He did not come by water only, but by water and blood. And the Spirit says that this is true, because the Spirit is the truth. [7]So there are three witnesses:[n] [8]the Spirit, the water, and the blood; and these three witnesses agree. [9]We believe people when they say something is true. But what God says is more important, and he has told us the truth about his own Son. [10]Anyone who believes in the Son of God has the truth that God told us. Anyone who does not believe makes God a liar, because that person does not believe what God told us about his Son. [11]This is what God told us: God has given us eternal life, and this life is in his Son. [12]Whoever has the Son has life, but whoever does not have the Son of God does not have life.

### We Have Eternal Life Now

[13]I write this letter to you who believe in the Son of God so you will know you have eternal life. [14]And this is the boldness we have in God's presence: that if we ask God for anything that agrees with what he wants, he hears us. [15]If we know

he hears us every time we ask him, we know we have what we ask from him.

[16]If anyone sees a brother or sister sinning (sin that does not lead to eternal death), that person should pray, and God will give the sinner life. I am talking about people whose sin does not lead to eternal death. There is sin that leads to death. I do not mean that a person should pray about that sin. [17]Doing wrong is always sin, but there is sin that does not lead to eternal death.

[18]We know that those who are God's children do not continue to sin. The Son of God keeps them safe, and the Evil One cannot touch them. [19]We know that we belong to God, but the Evil One controls the whole world. [20]We also know that the Son of God has come and has given us understanding so that we can know the True One. And our lives are in the True One and in his Son, Jesus Christ. He is the true God and the eternal life.

[21]So, dear children, keep yourselves away from false gods.

## cool

### A Father's Love

In the unbelievably cold Antarctic, when a female emperor penguin lays an egg, she passes it to the father to keep warm while she goes searching for food. For the next few months, "dad" hides the egg under a flap of skin on his belly. He stays huddled in the brutal cold with no food until the chick is born and the mother has returned. What a sacrifice!

What's so amazing is that God, your heavenly Father, loves you even more than a papa penguin loves his babies! "This is how we know what real love is: Jesus gave his life for us" (1 John 3:16).

**5:6 water** This probably means the water of Jesus' baptism. **5:6 blood** This probably means the blood of Jesus' death. **5:7–8 So . . . witnesses** A few very late Greek copies and the Latin Vulgate continue, "in heaven: the Father, the Word, and the Holy Spirit, and these three witnesses agree. [8]And there are three witnesses on earth:"

# 2 JOHN

**H**ave you ever had someone tell a lie about you? Have you ever believed a lie about someone else—only to find out it wasn't true at all? Then you probably know why the apostle John thought truth was so important.

This letter is more like a short note! In just thirteen verses, though, John says a lot! His main point is that truth is super important. Although the Book of 2 John doesn't have a writer's name in it, most people think that 2 John was written by the apostle John. It's hard to say who he's writing to when he says, "To the chosen lady and her children" (2 John 1). It could be a Christian woman and her kids. Or it could be a church ("lady") and the people who belong to the church ("children"). Either way, 2 John has special instructions about loving God by truthfully obeying him.

What does it mean to love God and other people? Saying kind, truthful words? Serving them? Telling them you love them? Second John tells us, "Love means living the way God commanded us to live" (2 John 6). So love is all of these things and more! The biggest and best way to prove our love for God is to follow the truth he's given us.

As you read 2 John, look for truth. You may be surprised by what you find!

# DO NOT HELP FALSE TEACHERS

## THINGS TO TALK WITH GOD ABOUT . . .

[1]From the Elder.[n]
To the chosen lady[n] and her children:
I love all of you in the truth,[n] and all those who know the truth love you. [2]We love you because of the truth that lives in us and will be with us forever.

[3]Grace, mercy, and peace from God the Father and his Son, Jesus Christ, will be with us in truth and love.

[4]I was very happy to learn that some of your children are following the way of truth, as the Father commanded us. [5]And now, dear lady, this is not a new command but is the same command we have had from the beginning. I ask you that we all love each other. [6]And love means living the way God commanded us to live. As you have heard from the beginning, his command is this: Live a life of love.

> GRACE, MERCY, AND PEACE FROM GOD THE FATHER AND HIS SON, JESUS CHRIST, WILL BE WITH US IN TRUTH AND LOVE.

> AS YOU HAVE HEARD FROM THE BEGINNING, HIS COMMAND IS THIS: LIVE A LIFE OF LOVE.

[7]Many false teachers are in the world now who do not confess that Jesus Christ came to earth as a human. Anyone who does not confess this is a false teacher and an enemy of Christ. [8]Be careful yourselves that you do not lose everything you[n] have worked for, but that you receive your full reward.

[9]Anyone who goes beyond Christ's teaching and does not continue to follow only his teaching does not have God. But whoever continues to follow the teaching of Christ has both the Father and the Son. [10]If someone comes to you and does not bring this teaching, do not welcome or accept that person into your house. [11]If you welcome such a person, you share in the evil work.

[12]I have many things to write to you, but I do not want to use paper and ink. Instead, I hope to come to you and talk face to face so we can be full of joy. [13]The children of your chosen sister[n] greet you.

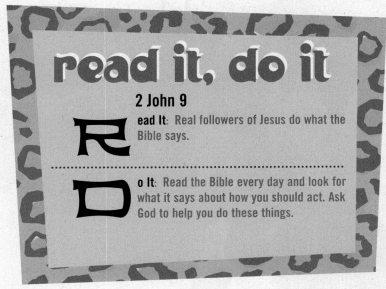

## read it, do it

### 2 John 9

**R**ead It: Real followers of Jesus do what the Bible says.

**D**o It: Read the Bible every day and look for what it says about how you should act. Ask God to help you do these things.

**1 Elder** *"Elder" means an older person. It can also mean a special leader in the church (as in Titus 1:5).* **1 lady** *This might mean a woman, or in this letter it might mean a church. If it is a church, then "her children" would be the people of the church.* **1 truth** *The truth or "Good News" about Jesus Christ that joins all believers together.* **8 you** *Some Greek copies read "we."* **13 sister** *Sister of the "lady" in verse 1. This might be another woman or another church.*

375

# November

start here →

**1** Pray for a person of influence: Today is rap artist Nelly's birthday.

**2**

**3** U.S. Thanksgiving is the 4th Thursday in November. Write a thank-you card to God and put it on your desk as a reminder to be thankful.

**4** Write a short story that begins with: "On my way to the library yesterday…"

**5**

**6**

**7** Make a few Christmas cards to get a head start on next month!

**8**

**9** Pray for a person of influence: Today is singer Nick Lachey's birthday.

**10**

**11** Pray for a person of influence: Today is actor Leonardo DiCaprio's birthday.

**12** When you see your mom doing a chore today, offer to help… or finish it for her!

**13**

**14** Memorize Ephesians 5:1-2. Write down five ways that you can be like God.

**15** Make up a song about how much you love your parents. Sing it for them!

**16** Pray for everyone you know whose name starts with the letter "B."

**17** Draw a picture using only green and purple pencils, crayons or markers.

**18**

**19**

**20** Pray for a person of influence: Today is singer Clay Aiken's birthday.

**21**

**22** Pray for a person of influence: Today is actress Scarlett Johansson's birthday.

**23**

**24**

**25** It's been 6 months! Time to flip your mattress again.

**26**

**27** At dinner, ask your parents about their day instead of just talking about yours.

**28**

**29** Before you start your homework, ask God to help you concentrate.

**30**

Shelby says, "Make a list!"

notes

# 3 John

**D**o you know what "proves" we know God and belong to him? Third John says that people who do good things and love truth have a relationship with God. In this little letter, we get to peek into one man's life to see what that means.

Third John was written to a Christian man named Gaius. "The Elder" (or author, most likely the apostle John) loved Gaius. It's easy to see why: Gaius loved truth (the Good News message) just like John did! Gaius believed the truth about Jesus, and it changed his life! He loved to help his brothers and sisters (other Christians); in this way, he helped spread the truth.

If Gaius is the "good guy," then Diotrephes is the "bad guy." In verses 9–10, Diotrephes is pointed out as a bad example for us. He didn't listen to truth. Instead, he believed—and told—lies. He also thought he was more important than anyone else.

But John couldn't have been happier about Gaius! John said, "Nothing gives me greater joy than to hear that my children are following the way of truth" (3 John 4). Following the way of truth means believing in the Good News and living like Jesus did. Just like it did for John, it gives God great joy to see his children following the way of truth.

# HELP CHRISTIANS WHO TEACH TRUTH

**THINGS TO TALK WITH GOD ABOUT . . .**

[1]From the Elder.[n]
To my dear friend Gaius, whom I love in the truth:[n]

[2]My dear friend, I know your soul is doing fine, and I pray that you are doing well in every way and that your health is good. [3]I was very happy when some brothers and sisters came and told me about the truth in your life and how you are following the way of truth. [4]Nothing gives me greater joy than to hear that my children are following the way of truth.

[5]My dear friend, it is good that you help the brothers and sisters, even those you

**THE ONE WHO DOES GOOD BELONGS TO GOD. BUT THE ONE WHO DOES EVIL HAS NEVER KNOWN GOD.**

[9]I wrote something to the church, but Diotrephes, who loves to be their leader, will not listen to us. [10]So if I come, I will talk about what Diotrephes is doing, about how he lies and says evil things about us. But more than that, he refuses to accept the other brothers and sisters; he even stops those who do want to accept them and puts them out of the church.

[11]My dear friend, do not follow what is bad; follow what is good. The one who does good belongs to God. But the one who does evil has never known God.

[12]Everyone says good things about Demetrius, and the truth agrees with what they say. We also speak well of him, and you know what we say is true.

[13]I have many things I want to write you, but I do not want to use pen and ink. [14]I hope to see you soon and talk face to face. [15]Peace to you. The friends here greet you. Please greet each friend there by name.

do not know. [6]They told the church about your love. Please help them to continue their trip in a way worthy of God. [7]They started out in service to Christ, and they have been accepting nothing from nonbelievers. [8]So we should help such people; when we do, we share in their work for the truth.

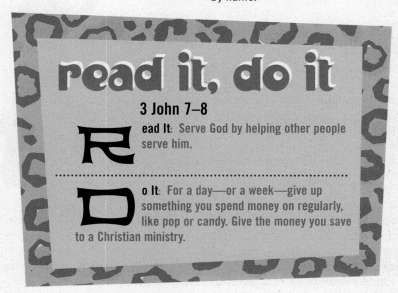

## read it, do it

**3 John 7–8**

**R**ead It: Serve God by helping other people serve him.

**D**o It: For a day—or a week—give up something you spend money on regularly, like pop or candy. Give the money you save to a Christian ministry.

---

**1 Elder** *"Elder" means an older person. It can also mean a special leader in the church (as in Titus 1:5).* **1 truth** *The truth or "Good News" about Jesus Christ that joins all believers together.*

# JUDE

**S**tand up for what you believe in! That's the message in the Book of Jude. Do you know anyone who makes fun of Christians or Jesus Christ? The people who first read Jude's letter sure did! Jude was a Christian who lived around Jesus' time; he wrote this short note to remind Christians to "fight hard for the faith" (Jude 3).

As Christians, we should stand up for *what* and *who* we believe in—and stand against people who teach lies. People who don't know God or trust Jesus Christ sometimes try to steer Christians away from Jesus. That's exactly what was happening in Jude's time.

Jude reminds us that even angels who didn't admit that Jesus is Lord were punished. If even angels couldn't get around it, then foolish people who deny God will definitely be judged by him. Jude says these people are like trees in the autumn: they have no fruit and have been pulled out by the roots. In other words, they are dead and completely useless.

This book was written to Christians to tell them about the future of ungodly people. It was supposed to inspire Christians, not scare them. *Because* there are evil people with evil intentions, we have to stand strong for Christ!

The prayer in Jude 24–25 shows the difference between those who hate Jesus and those who love him. Those who love him can happily say, "He is the only God, the One who saves us" (verse 25).

# WARNINGS ABOUT FALSE TEACHERS

## THINGS TO TALK WITH GOD ABOUT . . .

[1]From Jude, a servant of Jesus Christ and a brother of James.

To all who have been called by God. God the Father loves you, and you have been kept safe in Jesus Christ:

[2]Mercy, peace, and love be yours richly.

### God Will Punish Sinners

[3]Dear friends, I wanted very much to write you about the salvation we all share. But I felt the need to write you about something else: I want to encourage you to fight hard for the faith that was given the holy people of God once and for all time. [4]Some people have secretly entered your group. Long ago the prophets wrote about these people who will be judged guilty. They are against God and have changed the grace of our God into a reason for sexual sin. They also refuse to accept Jesus Christ, our only Master and Lord.

[5]I want to remind you of some things you already know: Remember that the

# Q&A

Q Sometimes I have a game on Sunday, so I don't go to church. Is that wrong?

A There will be lots of things that come up that you could do instead of going to church. It's okay to miss once in a while, but make sure that going to church is a priority for you. God thinks it's important for Christians to meet together (Hebrews 10:25). Don't let anything—whether it's sports, or hanging out with your friends, or watching television—get in the way!

> IN THE LAST TIMES THERE WILL BE PEOPLE WHO LAUGH ABOUT GOD, FOLLOWING THEIR OWN EVIL DESIRES WHICH ARE AGAINST GOD.

Lord[n] saved his people by bringing them out of the land of Egypt. But later he destroyed all those who did not believe. [6]And remember the angels who did not keep their place of power but left their proper home. The Lord has kept these angels in darkness, bound with everlasting chains, to be judged on the great day. [7]Also remember the cities of Sodom and Gomorrah[n] and the other towns around them. In the same way they were full of sexual sin and people who desired sexual relations that God does not allow. They suffer the punishment of eternal fire, as an example for all to see.

[8]It is the same with these people who have entered your group. They are guided by dreams and make themselves filthy with sin. They reject God's authority and speak against the angels. [9]Not even the archangel[n] Michael, when he argued with the devil about who would have the body of Moses, dared to judge the devil guilty. Instead, he said, "The Lord punish you." [10]But these people speak against things they do not understand. And what they do know, by feeling, as dumb animals know things, are the very things that destroy them. [11]It will be terrible for them. They have followed the way of Cain, and for money they have given themselves to doing the wrong that Balaam did. They have fought against God as Korah did, and like Korah, they surely will be destroyed. [12]They are like dirty spots in your special Christian meals you share. They eat with you and have no fear, caring only for themselves. They are clouds without rain, which the wind

---

5 **the Lord** *Some Greek copies read "Jesus."*    7 **Sodom and Gomorrah** *Two cities God destroyed because they were so evil.*    9 **archangel** *The leader among God's angels or messengers.*

blows around. They are autumn trees without fruit that are pulled out of the ground. So they are twice dead. ¹³They are like wild waves of the sea, tossing up their own shameful actions like foam. They are like stars that wander in the sky. A place in the blackest darkness has been kept for them forever.

¹⁴Enoch, the seventh descendant from Adam, said about these people: "Look, the Lord is coming with many thousands of his holy angels to ¹⁵judge every person. He is coming to punish all who are against God for all the evil they have done against him. And he will punish the sinners who are against God for all the evil they have said against him."

¹⁶These people complain and blame others, doing the evil things they want to do. They brag about themselves, and they flatter others to get what they want.

## A Warning and Things to Do

¹⁷Dear friends, remember what the apostles of our Lord Jesus Christ said before. ¹⁸They said to you, "In the last times there will be people who laugh about God, following their own evil desires which are against God." ¹⁹These are the people who divide you, people whose thoughts are only of this world, who do not have the Spirit.

²⁰But dear friends, use your most holy faith to build yourselves up, praying in the Holy Spirit. ²¹Keep yourselves in God's love as you wait for the Lord Jesus Christ with his mercy to give you life forever.

²²Show mercy to some people who have doubts. ²³Take others out of the fire, and save them. Show mercy mixed with fear to others, hating even their clothes which are dirty from sin.

## Praise God

²⁴God is strong and can help you not to fall. He can bring you before his glory without any wrong in you and can give you great joy. ²⁵He is the only God, the One who saves us. To him be glory, greatness, power, and authority through Jesus Christ our Lord for all time past, now, and forever. Amen.

# Q & A

**Q** My little sister is never punished for being bad. I always get blamed. It's not fair!

**A** Tell your parents how you feel (without yelling or talking badly about your sister). If nothing changes, pray for patience and do your best to be nice to your sister so your parents can see that you want to do the right thing. That might help!

# cool

## Can You Hear Me?

**D**ecibels measure the loudness of sounds humans can hear. A soft whisper is about 30 decibels, while a rocket blast has a sound level of 180 to 200 decibels. At 130 decibels your ears start to hurt because of the pressure on your eardrums. If you blare your music as loud as a chainsaw (110 decibels), turn it down!

You can protect your spiritual "hearing," too, by not cluttering your life with too many distractions. God sometimes speaks to us very softly and gently. Can you hear him?

KEEP YOURSELVES IN GOD'S LOVE AS YOU WAIT FOR THE LORD JESUS CHRIST WITH HIS MERCY TO GIVE YOU LIFE FOREVER.

# REVELATION

The Book of Revelation is like getting to the final chapter of a really good mystery novel! And it's perfectly fine to skip to the end to see what happens!

Revelation is often referred to as we talk about "end times"—what will happen when Jesus comes back to earth to rescue his church and the world as we know it ends. In the pages of Revelation, you will find more action than you could imagine. Revelation is the great clash between God and Satan. Those who oppose God—including Satan, evil, and death—will finally be judged. Those of us who believe in him have hope because we know how it will end . . . God wins! One of Revelation's messages is this: no matter what happens in this life, if we continue to obey God, we have no reason to worry about the end times.

Revelation was written by the apostle John at the end of his life. God sent an angel to give John the messages contained in this book. The original audience was seven churches (Revelation 1:4), yet Revelation was always meant to be for every Christian!

Sometimes the Book of Revelation can seem confusing. It wasn't written to make Christians worried or scared. Instead, John wrote the book to encourage us to live like Jesus and to give us hope because Jesus is more powerful than death, evil, and suffering. Don't forget that Jesus is coming to take us to be with him forever!

# CHRIST WILL WIN OVER EVIL

**THiNGS TO TALK WiTH GOD ABOUT . . .**

## John Tells About This Book

1 This is the revelation[n] of Jesus Christ, which God gave to him, to show his servants what must soon happen. And Jesus sent his angel to show it to his servant John, [2]who has told everything he has seen. It is the word of God; it is the message from Jesus Christ. [3]Blessed is the one who reads the words of God's message, and blessed are the people who hear this message and do what is written in it. The time is near when all of this will happen.

## Jesus' Message to the Churches

[4]From John.

To the seven churches in Asia:

Grace and peace to you from the One who is and was and is coming, and from the seven spirits before his throne, [5]and from Jesus Christ. Jesus is the faithful witness, the first among those raised from the dead. He is the ruler of the kings of the earth.

He is the One who loves us, who made us free from our sins with the blood of his death. [6]He made us to be a kingdom of priests who serve God his Father. To

## . . . AND BLESSED ARE THE PEOPLE WHO HEAR THIS MESSAGE AND DO WHAT IS WRITTEN IN IT.

Jesus Christ be glory and power forever and ever! Amen.

[7]Look, Jesus is coming with the clouds, and everyone will see him, even those who stabbed him. And all peoples of the earth will cry loudly because of him. Yes, this will happen! Amen.

[8]The Lord God says, "I am the Alpha and the Omega.[n] I am the One who is and was and is coming. I am the Almighty."

[9]I, John, am your brother. All of us share with Christ in suffering, in the kingdom, and in patience to continue. I was on the island of Patmos,[n] because I had preached the word of God and the message about Jesus. [10]On the Lord's day I was in the Spirit, and I heard a loud voice behind me that sounded like a trumpet. [11]The voice said, "Write what you see in a book and send it to the seven churches: to Ephesus, Smyrna, Pergamum, Thyatira, Sardis, Philadelphia, and Laodicea."

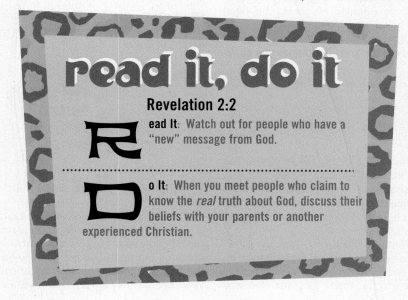

## read it, do it

### Revelation 2:2

**R**ead It: Watch out for people who have a "new" message from God.

**D**o It: When you meet people who claim to know the *real* truth about God, discuss their beliefs with your parents or another experienced Christian.

---

**1:1 revelation** *Making known truth that has been hidden.* **1:8 Alpha and the Omega** *The first and last letters of the Greek alphabet. This means "the beginning and the end."* **1:9 Patmos** *A small island in the Aegean Sea, near the coast of Asia Minor (modern Turkey).*

## Neat Knees!

**N**o other animal has the special type of knee joints humans have. In fact, our knees are completely different from the rest of the joints in our bodies! Two *ligaments* (tissue that holds bones together) cross each other between your thigh bone and calf bone, allowing you to stand, sit, or walk whenever you want to.

Because monkeys don't have knees like ours, it's awkward for them to stand straight or walk. (So don't believe that we evolved from monkeys!) Human knees are also great for praying! Why not kneel down and talk to God right now?

[12]I turned to see who was talking to me. When I turned, I saw seven golden lampstands [13]and someone among the lampstands who was "like a Son of Man."[n] He was dressed in a long robe and had a gold band around his chest. [14]His head and hair were white like wool, as white as snow, and his eyes were like flames of fire. [15]His feet were like bronze that glows

hot in a furnace, and his voice was like the noise of flooding water. [16]He held seven stars in his right hand, and a sharp double-edged sword came out of his mouth. He looked like the sun shining at its brightest time.

[17]When I saw him, I fell down at his feet like a dead man. He put his right hand on me and said, "Do not be afraid. I am the First and the Last. [18]I am the One who

lives; I was dead, but look, I am alive forever and ever! And I hold the keys to death and to the place of the dead. [19]So write the things you see, what is now and what will happen later. [20]Here is the secret of the seven stars that you saw in my right hand and the seven golden lampstands: The seven lampstands are the seven churches, and the seven stars are the angels of the seven churches.

## To the Church in Ephesus

**2** "Write this to the angel of the church in Ephesus:

"The One who holds the seven stars in his right hand and walks among the seven golden lampstands says this: [2]I know what you do, how you work hard and never give up. I know you do not put up with the false teachings of evil people. You have tested those who say they are apostles but really are not, and you found they are liars. [3]You have patience and have suffered troubles for my name and have not given up.

[4]"But I have this against you: You have left the love you had in the beginning. [5]So remember where you were before you fell. Change your hearts and do what you did at first. If you do not change, I will come to you and will take away your lampstand from its place. [6]But there is something you do that is right: You hate what the Nicolaitans[n] do, as much as I.

[7]"Every person who has ears should listen to what the Spirit says to the churches. To those who win the victory I will give the right to eat the fruit from the tree of life, which is in the garden of God.

## To the Church in Smyrna

[8]"Write this to the angel of the church in Smyrna:

"The One who is the First and the Last, who died and came to life again, says this: [9]I know your troubles and that you are poor, but really you are rich! I know the bad things some people say about you. They say they are Jews, but they are

not true Jews. They are a synagogue that belongs to Satan. [10]Do not be afraid of what you are about to suffer. I tell you, the devil will put some of you in prison to test you, and you will suffer for ten days. But be faithful, even if you have to die, and I will give you the crown of life.

[11]"Everyone who has ears should listen to what the Spirit says to the churches. Those who win the victory will not be hurt by the second death.

## To the Church in Pergamum

[12]"Write this to the angel of the church in Pergamum:

"The One who has the sharp, double-edged sword says this: [13]I know where you live. It is where Satan has his throne. But you are true to me. You did not refuse to tell about your faith in me even during the time of Antipas, my faithful witness who was killed in your city, where Satan lives.

[14]"But I have a few things against you: You have some there who follow the teaching of Balaam. He taught Balak how to cause the people of Israel to sin by eating food offered to idols and by taking part in sexual sins. [15]You also have some who follow the teaching of the Nicolaitans.[n] [16]So change your hearts and lives. If you do not, I will come to you quickly and fight against them with the sword that comes out of my mouth.

[17]"Everyone who has ears should listen to what the Spirit says to the churches.

"I will give some of the hidden manna to everyone who wins the victory. I will also give to each one who wins the victory a white stone with a new name written on it. No one knows this new name except the one who receives it.

## To the Church in Thyatira

[18]"Write this to the angel of the church in Thyatira:

"The Son of God, who has eyes that blaze like fire and feet like shining bronze, says this: [19]I know what you do. I know about your love, your faith, your service, and your patience. I know that you are doing more now than you did at first.

[20]"But I have this against you: You let that woman Jezebel spread false teachings. She says she is a prophetess, but by her teaching she leads my people to take part in sexual sins and to eat food

**1:13 "like . . . Man"** *"Son of Man" is a name Jesus called himself.* **2:6, 15 Nicolaitans** *This is the name of a religious group that followed false beliefs and ideas.*

# HOT OR COLD?

Are you hot or cold? We're not just talking about the temperature outside. In Revelation 3:16, God had something to say about being "hot" or "cold." Take this quiz to find out if you're hot, cold, or just lukewarm ... and which temperature God wants you to be.

1. **Your mom wakes you up on Sunday and says, "Time for church!" You say:**
   a. "I don't want to go!"
   b. Nothing. You just grumble and get up.
   c. "Okay, Mom! I'll be ready soon!"

2. **When your family gets to church you:**
   a. Wait outside or hang out in the bathroom.
   b. Go sit inside and pull out your notebook and pen to start drawing.
   c. Ask your teacher or the pastor if you can help out with anything.

3. **You pray:**
   a. Almost never.
   b. Before eating and going to bed.
   c. A few times during the day, whenever you remember.

4. **When it's time to sing at church you:**
   a. Yawn and stare at the funny hat a lady in the front is wearing.
   b. Sing along but don't pay attention to the words.
   c. Really get into the song. You know the words by heart!

5. **Someone at school asks you to explain what Christmas is about. You say:**
   a. "Don't you know? Santa Claus and getting presents!"
   b. "It's about baby Jesus being born in a manger."
   c. "That's when God sent his Son to the world so that we could be saved from our sins!"

6. **One of your friends tells a dirty joke. You:**
   a. Laugh and tell yourself you'll have to remember that one.
   b. Don't do anything and hope the subject changes soon.
   c. Say, "Hey! I don't think we should be talking like that!"

## What's your temperature?

**If you answered mostly As,** brrrr, you're cold! Maybe you've never made a serious decision to follow Jesus. You don't seem to have a relationship with him or any interest in serving him. First Thessalonians 5:2 warns: "You know very well that the day the Lord comes again will be a surprise, like a thief that comes in the night." Don't wait. Ask Jesus into your heart today!

**If you answered mostly Bs,** you're lukewarm. This is not good news. The church in Laodicea (in the book of Revelation) was lukewarm and God told them: "I am ready to spit you out of my mouth." (Imagine drinking lukewarm milk. Yuck!) God doesn't want you to be a sort-of Christian. He wants you to be honest if you haven't accepted him as your Savior (cold) or to really live your life for him (hot). Keep reading...

**If you answered mostly Cs,** you are hot! We don't mean "hot" the way the world does. God wants Christians to be "fired up" for him—excited, energetic, and bold! And it sounds like you're either very warm (which is still good) or nice and hot! Pray that God will help you to keep up the good work.

that is offered to idols. ²¹I have given her time to change her heart and turn away from her sin, but she does not want to change. ²²So I will throw her on a bed of suffering. And all those who take part in adultery with her will suffer greatly if they do not turn away from the wrongs she does. ²³I will also kill her followers. Then all the churches will know I am the One who searches hearts and minds, and I will repay each of you for what you have done.

²⁴"But others of you in Thyatira have not followed her teaching and have not learned what some call Satan's deep secrets. I say to you that I will not put any other load on you. ²⁵Only continue in your loyalty until I come.

²⁶"I will give power over the nations to everyone who wins the victory and continues to be obedient to me until the end.

²⁷"You will rule over them with an iron rod,
as when pottery is broken into pieces.'                    Psalm 2:9

²⁸This is the same power I received from my Father. I will also give him the morning star. ²⁹Everyone who has ears should listen to what the Spirit says to the churches.

## To the Church in Sardis

**3** "Write this to the angel of the church in Sardis:

"The One who has the seven spirits and the seven stars says this: I know what you do. People say that you are alive, but really you are dead. ²Wake up! Strengthen what you have left before it dies completely. I have found that what you are doing is less than what my God wants. ³So do not forget what you have received and heard. Obey it, and change your hearts and lives. So you must wake up, or I will come like a thief, and you will not know when I will come to you. ⁴But you have a few there in Sardis who have kept their clothes unstained, so they will walk with me and will wear white clothes, because they are worthy. ⁵Those who win the victory will be dressed in white clothes like them. And I will not erase their names from the book of life, but I will say they belong to me before my Father and before his angels. ⁶Everyone who has ears should listen to what the Spirit says to the churches.

## To the Church in Philadelphia

⁷"Write this to the angel of the church in Philadelphia:

"This is what the One who is holy and true, who holds the key of David, says. When he opens a door, no one can close it. And when he closes it, no one can open it. ⁸I know what you do. I have put an open door before you, which no one can close. I know you have little strength, but you have obeyed my teaching and were not afraid to speak my name. ⁹Those in the synagogue that belongs to Satan say they are Jews, but they are not true Jews; they are liars. I will make them come before you and bow at your feet, and they will know that I have loved you. ¹⁰You have obeyed my teaching about not giving up your faith. So I will keep you from the time of trouble that will come to the whole world to test those who live on earth.

¹¹"I am coming soon. Continue strong in your faith so no one will take away your crown. ¹²I will make those who win the victory pillars in the temple of my God, and they will never have to leave it. I will write on them the name of my God and the name of the city of my God, the new Jerusalem,ⁿ that comes down out of heaven from my God. I will also write on them my new name. ¹³Everyone who has ears should listen to what the Spirit says to the churches.

## To the Church in Laodicea

¹⁴"Write this to the angel of the church in Laodicea:

"The Amen,ⁿ the faithful and true witness, the ruler of all God has made, says this: ¹⁵I know what you do, that you are

---

# top ten

## top ten ways to...
### Be More Like Jesus

1. Get to know him by reading the Bible.
2. Make God #1 in your life.
3. Pray often! In fact, make extra time for it.
4. Love your enemies.
5. Be generous. Help the people you can help.
6. Forgive people quickly; don't hold grudges.
7. Trust and obey God even in the worst situations.
8. Choose to live a pure life, staying away from sin.
9. Be willing to give up anything for God.
10. Be satisfied with whatever you have.

---

# Q&A

**Q** One of my friends is really overweight. What can I do to help her?

**A** Don't talk about her weight unless she does. If she brings it up, encourage her that God loves her just the way she is. Also, try not to eat junk food around her; instead, suggest healthy foods when you're together. Organize fun games and activities that will get her moving but not feel like exercise. Set a good example by taking care of *your* body. Most of all . . . show her lots of love!

---

**3:12 Jerusalem** *This name is used to mean the spiritual city God built for his people. See Revelation 21–22.* **3:14 Amen** *Used here as a name for Jesus; it means to agree fully that something is true.*

HERE I AM! I STAND AT THE DOOR AND KNOCK. IF YOU HEAR MY VOICE AND OPEN THE DOOR, I WILL COME IN AND EAT WITH YOU, AND YOU WILL EAT WITH ME.

my Father on his throne. ²²Everyone who has ears should listen to what the Spirit says to the churches."

### John Sees Heaven

4 After the vision of these things I looked, and there before me was an open door in heaven. And the same voice that spoke to me before, that sounded like a trumpet, said, "Come up here, and I will show you what must happen after this." ²Immediately I was in the Spirit, and before me was a throne in heaven, and someone was sitting on it. ³The One who sat on the throne looked like precious stones, like jasper and carnelian. All around the throne was a rainbow the color of an emerald. ⁴Around the throne there were twenty-four other thrones with twenty-four elders sitting on them. They were dressed in white and had golden crowns on their heads. ⁵Lightning flashes and noises and thunder came from the throne. Before the throne seven lamps were burning, which are the seven spirits of God. ⁶Also before the throne there was something that looked like a sea of glass, clear like crystal.

In the center and around the throne were four living creatures with eyes all over them, in front and in back. ⁷The first living creature was like a lion. The second was like a calf. The third had a face like a man. The fourth was like a flying eagle. ⁸Each of these four living creatures had six wings and was covered all over with eyes, inside and out. Day and night they never stop saying:

"Holy, holy, holy is the Lord God
    Almighty.

He was, he is, and he is coming."

⁹These living creatures give glory, honor, and thanks to the One who sits on the throne, who lives forever and ever. ¹⁰Then the twenty-four elders bow down before

## god's promises

**Revelation 1:5**

Have you ever done something wrong and tried to hide it from your parents or your teachers? It's hard to admit when we do the wrong thing. We're afraid of getting in trouble or disappointing someone. But when we admit our mistakes to people, they respond differently. Often our parents or teachers thank us for telling the truth. Sometimes we *do* get in trouble, though it may not be as bad as we expected.

When we confess our wrong actions to God, he forgives us—always. He doesn't hold a grudge against us. He doesn't remind us later and tell us we're bad. This verse promises that Jesus made us *free* from our sins because he shed his blood for us. We still experience the consequences of our choices. This may include punishment by our parents or teachers. It might be an injury that results from our actions. But we don't have to go on feeling guilty if we have confessed our mistakes to God.

So if you've made bad choices, don't try to hide them from God. (He already knows anyway!) Tell him what you've done. Ask him to forgive you and help you to do the right thing in the future. He will—it's a promise!

*We don't have to go on feeling guilty if we have confessed our mistakes to God.*

not hot or cold. I wish that you were hot or cold! ¹⁶But because you are lukewarm—neither hot, nor cold—I am ready to spit you out of my mouth. ¹⁷You say, 'I am rich, and I have become wealthy and do not need anything.' But you do not know that you are really miserable, pitiful, poor, blind, and naked. ¹⁸I advise you to buy from me gold made pure in fire so you can be truly rich. Buy from me white clothes so you can be clothed and so you

can cover your shameful nakedness. Buy from me medicine to put on your eyes so you can truly see.

¹⁹"I correct and punish those whom I love. So be eager to do right, and change your hearts and lives. ²⁰Here I am! I stand at the door and knock. If you hear my voice and open the door, I will come in and eat with you, and you will eat with me.

²¹"Those who win the victory will sit with me on my throne in the same way that I won the victory and sat down with

# Relationships

What do you think when you see homeless people begging on the streets downtown or at the freeway exit? Jesus said, "If you are nice only to your friends, you are no better than other people" (Matthew 5:47). Being nice to homeless people could include donating some of your old clothing to a homeless shelter, volunteering with your family or youth group at a soup kitchen, or praying for people when you see them on the streets. Whatever you decide to do, don't forget God considers people without a home just as valuable as those who have one!

the One who sits on the throne, and they worship him who lives forever and ever. They put their crowns down before the throne and say:

¹¹"You are worthy, our Lord and God,
to receive glory and honor and power,
because you made all things.
Everything existed and was made,
because you wanted it."

**5** Then I saw a scroll in the right hand of the One sitting on the throne. The scroll had writing on both sides and was kept closed with seven seals. ²And I saw a powerful angel calling in a loud voice, "Who is worthy to break the seals and open the scroll?" ³But there was no one in heaven or on earth or under the earth who could open the scroll or look inside it. ⁴I cried bitterly because there was no one who was worthy to open the scroll or look inside. ⁵But one of the elders said to me, "Do not cry! The Lion[n] from the tribe of Judah, David's descendant, has won the victory so that he is able to open the scroll and its seven seals."

⁶Then I saw a Lamb standing in the center of the throne and in the middle of the four living creatures and the elders. The Lamb looked as if he had been killed. He had seven horns and seven eyes, which are the seven spirits of God that were sent into all the world. ⁷The Lamb came and took the scroll from the right hand of the One sitting on the throne. ⁸When he took the scroll, the four living creatures and the twenty-four elders bowed down before the Lamb. Each one of them had a harp and golden bowls full of incense, which are the prayers of God's holy people. ⁹And they all sang a new song to the Lamb:

"You are worthy to take the scroll
and to open its seals,
because you were killed,
and with the blood of your death
you bought people for God
from every tribe, language, people,
and nation.
¹⁰You made them to be a kingdom of
priests for our God,
and they will rule on the earth."

¹¹Then I looked, and I heard the voices of many angels around the throne, and the four living creatures, and the elders. There were thousands and thousands of angels, ¹²saying in a loud voice:

"The Lamb who was killed is worthy
to receive power, wealth, wisdom, and
strength,
honor, glory, and praise!"

¹³Then I heard all creatures in heaven and on earth and under the earth and in the sea saying:

"To the One who sits on the throne
and to the Lamb
be praise and honor and glory and
power
forever and ever."

¹⁴The four living creatures said, "Amen," and the elders bowed down and worshiped.

**6** Then I watched while the Lamb opened the first of the seven seals. I heard one of the four living creatures say with a voice like thunder, "Come!" ²I looked, and there before me was a white horse. The rider on the horse held a bow, and he was given a crown, and he rode out, determined to win the victory.

³When the Lamb opened the second seal, I heard the second living creature say, "Come!" ⁴Then another horse came out, a red one. Its rider was given power to take away peace from the earth and to make people kill each other, and he was given a big sword.

⁵When the Lamb opened the third seal, I heard the third living creature say, "Come!" I looked, and there before me was a black horse, and its rider held a pair of scales in his hand. ⁶Then I heard something that sounded like a voice coming from the middle of the four living creatures. The voice said, "A quart of wheat for a day's pay, and three quarts of barley for a day's pay, and do not damage the olive oil and wine!"

⁷When the Lamb opened the fourth seal, I heard the voice of the fourth living creature say, "Come!" ⁸I looked, and there before me was a pale horse. Its rider was named death, and Hades[n] was following close behind him. They were given power over a fourth of the earth to kill people by war, by starvation, by disease, and by the wild animals of the earth.

**5:5 Lion** *Here refers to Christ.*   **6:8 Hades** *The unseen world of the dead.*

## "YOU ARE WORTHY, OUR LORD AND GOD, TO RECEIVE GLORY AND HONOR AND POWER, . . ."

9When the Lamb opened the fifth seal, I saw under the altar the souls of those who had been killed because they were faithful to the word of God and to the message they had received. 10These souls shouted in a loud voice, "Holy and true Lord, how long until you judge the people of the earth and punish them for killing us?" 11Then each one of them was given a white robe and was told to wait a short time longer. There were still some of their fellow servants and brothers and sisters in the service of Christ who must be killed as they were. They had to wait until all of this was finished.

12Then I watched while the Lamb opened the sixth seal, and there was a great earthquake. The sun became black like rough black cloth, and the whole moon became red like blood. 13And the stars in the sky fell to the earth like figs falling from a fig tree when the wind blows. 14The sky disappeared as a scroll when it is rolled up, and every mountain and island was moved from its place.

15Then the kings of the earth, the rulers, the generals, the rich people, the powerful people, the slaves, and the free people hid themselves in caves and in the rocks on the mountains. 16They called to the mountains and the rocks, "Fall on us. Hide us from the face of the One who sits on the throne and from the anger of the Lamb! 17The great day for their anger has come, and who can stand against it?"

### The 144,000 People of Israel

7 After the vision of these things I saw four angels standing at the four corners of the earth. The angels were holding the four winds of the earth to keep them from blowing on the land or on the sea or on any tree. 2Then I saw another angel coming up from the east who had the seal of the living God. And he called out in a loud voice to the four angels to whom God had given

power to harm the earth and the sea. 3He said to them, "Do not harm the land or the sea or the trees until we mark with a sign the foreheads of the people who serve our God." 4Then I heard how many people were marked with the sign. There were one hundred forty-four thousand from every tribe of the people of Israel.

5From the tribe of Judah twelve thousand were marked with the sign,

from the tribe of Reuben twelve thousand,

from the tribe of Gad twelve thousand,

6from the tribe of Asher twelve thousand,

from the tribe of Naphtali twelve thousand,

from the tribe of Manasseh twelve thousand,

7from the tribe of Simeon twelve thousand,

from the tribe of Levi twelve thousand,

from the tribe of Issachar twelve thousand,

8from the tribe of Zebulun twelve thousand,

from the tribe of Joseph twelve thousand,

and from the tribe of Benjamin twelve thousand were marked with the sign.

### The Great Crowd Worships God

9After the vision of these things I looked, and there was a great number of people, so many that no one could count them. They were from every nation, tribe, people, and language of the earth. They were all standing before the throne and before the Lamb, wearing white robes and holding palm branches in their hands. 10They were shouting in a loud voice, "Salvation belongs to our God, who sits on the throne, and to the Lamb." 11All the angels were standing around the throne and the elders and the four living creatures. They all bowed down on their faces before the throne and worshiped God, 12saying, "Amen! Praise, glory, wisdom, thanks, honor, power, and strength belong to our God forever and ever. Amen!"

13Then one of the elders asked me, "Who are these people dressed in white robes? Where did they come from?"

14I answered, "You know, sir."

And the elder said to me, "These are the people who have come out of the great distress. They have washed their robes[n] and made them white in the blood of the Lamb. 15Because of this, they are before the throne of God. They worship him day and night in his temple. And the One who sits on the throne will be present with them. 16Those people will never

---

### ■ Bible Bios
### The Little Slave Girl
### (2 Kings 5)

One of the coolest Bible stories about great faith involves a young girl. We don't know her name or exact age, but her courage made it into Bible history! During a war in the country of Israel, this girl was captured and taken away from her home and family. How scary! But she trusted God . . . even when she became the servant of Naaman, an important military captain.

Naaman had a terrible sickness called leprosy. The young girl cared and wanted to help. She told Naaman's wife about a prophet in Israel who could heal him through God's power. Her masters trusted her so much that Naaman went to Israel to find the prophet . . . and God healed him! Naaman's thankfulness made him start worshiping God, too. This young girl bravely told someone about God, and a great miracle happened!

7:14 **washed their robes** This means they believed in Jesus so that their sins could be forgiven by Christ's blood.

be hungry again, and they will never be thirsty again. The sun will not hurt them, and no heat will burn them, [17]because the Lamb at the center of the throne will be their shepherd. He will lead them to springs of water that give life. And God will wipe away every tear from their eyes."

## The Seventh Seal

8 When the Lamb opened the seventh seal, there was silence in heaven for about half an hour. [2]And I saw the seven angels who stand before God and to whom were given seven trumpets.

[3]Another angel came and stood at the altar, holding a golden pan for incense. He was given much incense to offer with the prayers of all God's holy people. The angel put this offering on the golden altar before the throne. [4]The smoke from the incense went up from the angel's hand to God with the prayers of God's people. [5]Then the angel filled the incense pan with fire from the altar and threw it on the earth, and there were flashes of lightning, thunder and loud noises, and an earthquake.

## The Seven Angels and Trumpets

[6]Then the seven angels who had the seven trumpets prepared to blow them.

[7]The first angel blew his trumpet, and hail and fire mixed with blood were poured down on the earth. And a third of the earth, and all the green grass, and a third of the trees were burned up.

[8]Then the second angel blew his trumpet, and something that looked like a big mountain, burning with fire, was thrown into the sea. And a third of the sea became blood, [9]a third of the living things in the sea died, and a third of the ships were destroyed.

[10]Then the third angel blew his trumpet, and a large star, burning like a torch, fell from the sky. It fell on a third of the rivers and on the springs of water. [11]The name of the star is Wormwood.[n] And a third of all the water became bitter, and many people died from drinking the water that was bitter.

[12]Then the fourth angel blew his trumpet, and a third of the sun, and a third of the moon, and a third of the stars were struck. So a third of them became dark, and a third of the day was without light, and also the night.

## Shine Your Light

There are millions of children around the world who have no parents, no home, no school to go to, and even no food. Carissa's fifth and sixth grade Sunday school class in Absarokee, Montana, wanted to show that they cared about poor children in other countries. So they sponsored a child! They chose a Christian organization that collects money and then sends orphans and other needy children the things they need.

Every Sunday, Carissa's classmates brought a quarter (or two) to help with the project. At the end of each month, they raised enough money to sponsor their child! The class did a presentation in front of the church to encourage other people to get involved. They did such a good job that the organization asked the class if they could have a video tape of their presentation. In fact, they were the youngest group of kids to have ever done something like that!

Why not see if your Sunday school class (or your class at school) can sponsor a child together? Maybe you could do it with your family . . . or a couple of families in your neighborhood. Ask God to show you ways that *you* can help a poor child.

[13]While I watched, I heard an eagle that was flying high in the air cry out in a loud voice, "Trouble! Trouble! Trouble for those who live on the earth because of the remaining sounds of the trumpets that the other three angels are about to blow!"

9 Then the fifth angel blew his trumpet, and I saw a star fall from the sky to the earth. The star was given the key to the deep hole that leads to the bottomless pit. [2]Then it opened up the hole that leads to the bottomless pit, and smoke came up from the hole like smoke from a big furnace. Then the sun and sky became dark because of the smoke from the hole. [3]Then locusts came down to the earth out of the smoke, and they were given the power to sting like scorpions.[n] [4]They were told not to harm the grass on the earth or any plant or tree. They could harm only the people who did not have the sign of God on their foreheads. [5]These locusts were not given the power to kill anyone, but to cause pain to the people for five months. And the pain they felt was like the pain a scorpion gives when it stings someone. [6]During those days people will look for a way to die, but they will not find it. They will want to die, but death will run away from them.

[7]The locusts looked like horses prepared for battle. On their heads they wore what looked like crowns of gold, and their faces looked like human faces. [8]Their hair was like women's hair, and their teeth were like lions' teeth. [9]Their chests looked like

---

**8:11 Wormwood** *Name of a very bitter plant; used here to give the idea of bitter sorrow.* **9:3 scorpions** *A scorpion is an insect that stings with a bad poison.*

# Q & A

**Q** My parents still give me a bedtime! I think I'm responsible enough to stay up as late as I want. What should I do?

**A** There's nothing wrong with having a bedtime. You might not always realize the best time for you to get into bed. You think, "I'm not tired!" Your body wants rest, but you want to keep playing. Talk with your parents. Maybe you can agree to go to bed at a certain time but keep your lamp on for a while to read. Remember: do whatever they decide. God wants you to obey your parents, even if you think they're unfair!

iron breastplates, and the sound of their wings was like the noise of many horses and chariots hurrying into battle. ¹⁰The locusts had tails with stingers like scorpions, and in their tails was their power to hurt people for five months. ¹¹The locusts had a king who was the angel of the bottomless pit. His name in the Hebrew language is Abaddon and in the Greek language is Apollyon.ⁿ

¹²The first trouble is past; there are still two other troubles that will come.

¹³Then the sixth angel blew his trumpet, and I heard a voice coming from the horns on the golden altar that is before God. ¹⁴The voice said to the sixth angel who had the trumpet, "Free the four angels who are tied at the great river Euphrates." ¹⁵And they let loose the four angels who had been kept ready for this hour and day and month and year so they could kill a third of all people on the earth. ¹⁶I heard how many troops on horses were in their army—two hundred million.

¹⁷The horses and their riders I saw in the vision looked like this: They had breastplates that were fiery red, dark blue, and yellow like sulfur. The heads of the horses looked like heads of lions, with fire, smoke, and sulfur coming out of their mouths. ¹⁸A third of all the people on earth were killed by these three terrible disasters coming out of the horses' mouths: the fire, the smoke, and the sulfur. ¹⁹The horses' power was in their mouths and in their tails; their tails were like snakes with heads, and with them they hurt people.

²⁰The other people who were not killed by these terrible disasters still did not change their hearts and turn away from what they had made with their own hands. They did not stop worshiping demons and idols made of gold, silver, bronze, stone, and wood—things that cannot see or hear or walk. ²¹These people did not change their hearts and turn away from murder or evil magic, from their sexual sins or stealing.

## The Angel and the Small Scroll

**10** Then I saw another powerful angel coming down from heaven dressed in a cloud with a rainbow over his head. His face was like the sun, and his legs were like pillars of fire. ²The angel was holding a small scroll open in his hand. He put his right foot on the sea and his left foot on the land. ³Then he shouted loudly like the roaring of a lion. And when he shouted, the voices of seven thunders spoke. ⁴When the seven thunders spoke, I started to write. But I heard a voice from heaven say, "Keep hidden what the seven thunders said, and do not write them down."

⁵Then the angel I saw standing on the sea and on the land raised his right hand to heaven, ⁶and he made a promise by the power of the One who lives forever and ever. He is the One who made the skies and all that is in them, the earth and all that is in it, and the sea and all that is in it. The angel promised, "There will be no more waiting! ⁷In the days when the seventh angel is ready to blow his trumpet, God's secret will be finished. This secret is the Good News God told to his servants, the prophets."

⁸Then I heard the same voice from heaven again, saying to me: "Go and take the open scroll that is in the hand of the angel that is standing on the sea and on the land."

⁹So I went to the angel and told him to give me the small scroll. And he said to me, "Take the scroll and eat it. It will be sour in your stomach, but in your mouth it will be sweet as honey." ¹⁰So I took the small scroll from the angel's hand and ate it. In my mouth it tasted sweet as honey, but after I ate it, it was sour in my stomach. ¹¹Then I was told, "You must prophesy again about many peoples, nations, languages, and kings."

## The Two Witnesses

**11** I was given a measuring stick like a rod, and I was told, "Go and measure the temple of God and the altar, and count the people worshiping there. ²But do not measure the

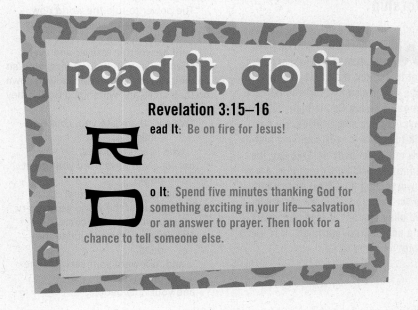

# read it, do it

### Revelation 3:15–16

**R**ead It: Be on fire for Jesus!

**D**o It: Spend five minutes thanking God for something exciting in your life—salvation or an answer to prayer. Then look for a chance to tell someone else.

9:11 **Abaddon, Apollyon** *Both names mean "Destroyer."*

yard outside the temple. Leave it alone, because it has been given to those who are not God's people. And they will trample on the holy city for forty-two months. [3]And I will give power to my two witnesses to prophesy for one thousand two hundred sixty days, and they will be dressed in rough cloth to show their sadness."

[4]These two witnesses are the two olive trees and the two lampstands that stand before the Lord of the earth. [5]And if anyone tries to hurt them, fire comes from their mouths and kills their enemies. And if anyone tries to hurt them in whatever way, in that same way that person will die. [6]These witnesses have the power to stop the sky from raining during the time they are prophesying. And they have power to make the waters become blood, and they have power to send every kind of trouble to the earth as many times as they want.

[7]When the two witnesses have finished telling their message, the beast that comes up from the bottomless pit will fight a war against them. He will defeat them and kill them. [8]The bodies of the two witnesses will lie in the street of the great city where the Lord was killed. This city is named Sodom[n] and Egypt, which has a spiritual meaning. [9]Those from every race of people, tribe, language, and nation will look at the bodies of the two witnesses for three and one-half days, and they will refuse to bury them. [10]People who live on the earth will rejoice and be happy because these two are dead. They will send each other gifts, because these two prophets brought much suffering to those who live on the earth.

[11]But after three and one-half days, God put the breath of life into the two prophets again. They stood on their feet, and everyone who saw them became very afraid. [12]Then the two prophets heard a loud voice from heaven saying, "Come up here!" And they went up into heaven in a cloud as their enemies watched.

[13]In the same hour there was a great earthquake, and a tenth of the city was destroyed. Seven thousand people were killed in the earthquake, and those who did not die were very afraid and gave glory to the God of heaven.

[14]The second trouble is finished. Pay attention: The third trouble is coming soon.

## The Seventh Trumpet

[15]Then the seventh angel blew his trumpet. And there were loud voices in heaven, saying:

"The power to rule the world now
        belongs to our Lord and his
        Christ,
    and he will rule forever and ever."

[16]Then the twenty-four elders, who sit on their thrones before God, bowed down on their faces and worshiped God. [17]They said:

"We give thanks to you, Lord God
        Almighty,
    who is and who was,
    because you have used your great
        power
    and have begun to rule!
[18]The people of the world were angry,
    but your anger has come.
The time has come to judge the
        dead,
    and to reward your servants the
        prophets
and your holy people,
    all who respect you, great and
        small.
The time has come to destroy those
        who destroy the earth!"

[19]Then God's temple in heaven was opened. The Ark that holds the agreement God gave to his people could be seen in his temple. Then there were flashes of lightning, noises, thunder, an earthquake, and a great hailstorm.

## The Woman and the Dragon

**12** And then a great wonder appeared in heaven: A woman was clothed with the sun, and the moon was under her feet, and a crown of twelve stars was on her head. [2]She was pregnant and cried out with pain, because she was about to give birth. [3]Then another wonder appeared in heaven: There was a giant red dragon with seven heads and seven crowns on each head. He also had ten horns. [4]His tail swept a third of the stars out of the sky and threw them down to the earth. He stood in front of the woman who was ready to give birth so he could eat her baby as soon as it was born. [5]Then the woman gave birth to a son who will rule all the nations with an iron rod.

---

## Worship

**W**orship means telling God how wonderful he is! At church, we often sing worship songs that talk about the great things God does and praise him for who he is. We can worship God in many different ways. We can sing praises. We can talk to him in prayer, thanking him for how much he loves us. Enjoying the beautiful world he's created is a way of worshiping him. Most importantly, we worship God when we serve him and obey him out of love. When worship comes from our heart, it is like a sweet perfume to God!

---

# Q&A

**Q** I'm taller and more developed than other girls my age. I'm uncomfortable sometimes and get teased. What should I do?

**A** Remind yourself God has designed you just right, and ask him to help you when kids are mean. You can't hide being tall (and most kids probably *admire* your height), but you can be careful of how you dress so that you're not drawing extra attention to your breasts or hips. Act confident about your looks! If you seem uncomfortable, kids will take advantage of that.

And her child was taken up to God and to his throne. [6]The woman ran away into the desert to a place God prepared for her where she would be taken care of for one thousand two hundred sixty days.

[7]Then there was a war in heaven. Michael[n] and his angels fought against the dragon, and the dragon and his angels fought back. [8]But the dragon was not strong enough, and he and his angels lost their place in heaven. [9]The giant dragon was thrown down out of heaven. (He is that old snake called the devil or Satan, who tricks the whole world.) The dragon with his angels was thrown down to the earth.

[10]Then I heard a loud voice in heaven saying:

"The salvation and the power and
     the kingdom of our God
and the authority of his Christ have
     now come.
The accuser of our brothers and
     sisters,
     who accused them day and night
          before our God,
     has been thrown down.
[11]And our brothers and sisters
          defeated him
     by the blood of the Lamb's death
     and by the message they
          preached.
They did not love their lives so much
     that they were afraid of death.
[12]So rejoice, you heavens
     and all who live there!
But it will be terrible for the earth
     and the sea,
     because the devil has come down
          to you!
He is filled with anger,
     because he knows he does not
          have much time."

[13]When the dragon saw he had been thrown down to the earth, he hunted for the woman who had given birth to the son. [14]But the woman was given the two wings of a great eagle so she could fly to the place prepared for her in the desert. There she would be taken care of for three and one-half years, away from the snake. [15]Then the snake poured water out of its mouth like a river toward the woman so the flood would carry her away. [16]But the earth helped the woman by opening its mouth and swallowing the river that came from the mouth of the

dragon. [17]Then the dragon was very angry at the woman, and he went off to make war against all her other children—those who obey God's commands and who have the message Jesus taught. [18]And the dragon[n] stood on the seashore.

## The Two Beasts

**13** Then I saw a beast coming up out of the sea. It had ten horns and seven heads, and there was a crown on each horn. A name against God was written on each head. [2]This beast looked like a leopard, with feet like a bear's feet and a mouth like a lion's mouth. And the dragon gave the beast all of his power and his throne and great authority. [3]One of the heads of the beast looked as if it had been killed by a wound, but this death wound was healed. Then the whole world was amazed and followed the beast. [4]People worshiped the dragon because he had given his power to the beast. And they also worshiped the beast, asking, "Who is like the beast? Who can make war against it?"

[5]The beast was allowed to say proud words and words against God, and it was allowed to use its power for forty-two months. [6]It used its mouth to speak against God, against God's name, against the place where God lives, and against all those who live in heaven. [7]It was given power to make war against God's holy people and to defeat them. It was given power over every tribe, people, language, and nation. [8]And all who live on earth will worship the beast—all the people since the beginning of the world whose names are not written in the Lamb's book of life. The Lamb is the One who was killed.

[9]Anyone who has ears should listen:
[10]If you are to be a prisoner,
     then you will be a prisoner.
If you are to be killed with the sword,
     then you will be killed with the
          sword.
This means that God's holy people must have patience and faith.

[11]Then I saw another beast coming up out of the earth. It had two horns like a lamb, but it spoke like a dragon. [12]This beast stands before the first beast and uses the same power the first beast has. By this power it makes everyone living on earth worship the first beast, who had the death wound that was healed. [13]And the second beast does great miracles so

# BibLe BaSicS

**D**id you know the Bible was first translated from its original languages into English only about six hundred years ago? Today most people can read the Bible in their own language. For those who still don't have the Bible in a language they understand, there are missionaries who spend most of their lives trying to make the Bible available to everyone! These missionaries often take years to translate the Bible and make sure every word is just right. Even if someone can't read the Bible in his or her own language, God provides other ways to hear about him and be saved. God wants every person to hear his Good News!

---

**12:7 Michael** *The archangel—leader among God's angels or messengers (Jude 9).*   **12:18 the dragon** *Some Greek copies read "I."*

ber, which is the number of a person. Its number is 666.*n*

## The Song of the Saved

**14** Then I looked, and there before me was the Lamb standing on Mount Zion.*n* With him were one hundred forty-four thousand people who had his name and his Father's name written on their foreheads. [2]And I heard a sound from heaven like the noise of flooding water and like the sound of loud thunder. The sound I heard was like people playing harps. [3]And they sang a new song before the throne and before the four living creatures and the elders. No one could learn the new song except the one hundred forty-four thousand who had been bought from the earth. [4]These are the ones who did not do sinful things with women, because they kept themselves pure. They follow the Lamb every place he goes. These one hundred forty-four thousand were bought from among the people of the earth as people to be offered to God and the Lamb. [5]They were not guilty of telling lies; they are without fault.

## The Three Angels

[6]Then I saw another angel flying high in the air. He had the eternal Good News to preach to those who live on earth—to every nation, tribe, language, and peo-

## god's promises

### Revelation 15:3—4

When something exciting happens in your life, you probably like to call your friends or family to share the good news. It feels great to tell others about our happiness, especially if it makes them glad, too!

The apostle John had the awesome privilege of getting a sneak preview of heaven and what would happen there. Guess what? People were still singing and shouting about how God had kept all of his great promises. Thousands of years before, God had said that he would be king of the nations and that all people would come and worship him. God had guaranteed that, someday, *everyone* would know of all the good and right things he had done. John saw that it had come true! God's Good News had been shared with everyone all over the world.

We are the ones who get to share the exciting news with others. What is that Good News? More than anything, God desires for all people to experience his grace and salvation through Jesus Christ. When we take the Good News to our neighbors, friends, and family, they can be a part of that future celebration of God's victory. This exciting news is too awesome to keep quiet about!

*God desires for all people to experience his grace and salvation.*

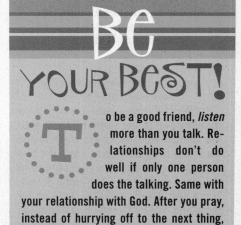

## Be YOUR BEST!

**T**o be a good friend, *listen* more than you talk. Relationships don't do well if only one person does the talking. Same with your relationship with God. After you pray, instead of hurrying off to the next thing, take time to sit quietly and "listen." He might send a message to your heart!

that it even makes fire come down from heaven to earth while people are watching. [14]It fools those who live on earth by the miracles it has been given the power to do. It does these miracles to serve the first beast. The second beast orders people to make an idol to honor the first beast, the one that was wounded by the deadly sword but sprang to life again. [15]The second beast was given power to give life to the idol of the first one so that

the idol could speak. And the second beast was given power to command all who will not worship the image of the beast to be killed. [16]The second beast also forced all people, small and great, rich and poor, free and slave, to have a mark on their right hand or on their forehead. [17]No one could buy or sell without this mark, which is the name of the beast or the number of its name. [18]This takes wisdom. Let the one who has understanding find the meaning of the num-

**13:18 666** *Some Greek copies read "616."* **14:1 Mount Zion** *Another name for Jerusalem; here meaning the spiritual city of God's people.*

WORSHIP GOD WHO MADE THE HEAVENS, AND THE EARTH, AND THE SEA, AND THE SPRINGS OF WATER.

ple. [7]He preached in a loud voice, "Fear God and give him praise, because the time has come for God to judge all people. So worship God who made the heavens, and the earth, and the sea, and the springs of water."

[8]Then the second angel followed the first angel and said, "Ruined, ruined is the great city of Babylon! She made all the nations drink the wine of the anger of her adultery."

[9]Then a third angel followed the first two angels, saying in a loud voice: "If anyone worships the beast and his idol and gets the beast's mark on the forehead or on the hand, [10]that one also will drink the wine of God's anger, which is prepared with all its strength in the cup of his anger. And that person will be put in pain with burning sulfur before the holy angels and the Lamb. [11]And the smoke from their burning pain will rise forever and ever. There will be no rest, day or night, for those who worship the beast and his idol or who get the mark of his name." [12]This means God's holy people must be patient. They must obey God's commands and keep their faith in Jesus.

[13]Then I heard a voice from heaven saying, "Write this: Blessed are the dead who die from now on in the Lord."

The Spirit says, "Yes, they will rest from their hard work, and the reward of all they have done stays with them."

## The Earth Is Harvested

[14]Then I looked, and there before me was a white cloud, and sitting on the white cloud was One who looked like a Son of Man.[n] He had a gold crown on his head and a sharp sickle[n] in his hand. [15]Then another angel came out of the temple and called out in a loud voice to the One who was sitting on the cloud, "Take your sickle and harvest from the earth, because the time to harvest has come, and the fruit of the earth is ripe." [16]So the One who was sitting on the cloud swung his sickle over the earth, and the earth was harvested.

[17]Then another angel came out of the temple in heaven, and he also had a sharp sickle. [18]And then another angel, who has power over the fire, came from the altar. This angel called to the angel with the sharp sickle, saying, "Take your sharp sickle and gather the bunches of grapes from the earth's vine, because its grapes are ripe." [19]Then the angel swung his sickle over the earth. He gathered the earth's grapes and threw them into the

# Christian Girls Around the World

## Kiki: Zimbabwe

Nontokozo (which means joy) lived in the Midlands province of Zimbabwe, Africa, before moving away a few years ago. Now she is called Kiki. The winters in Zimbabwe are not very cold, and there's no snow. Summers are hot, but not humid. Sadly, most parts of the country have not had enough rain for long periods of time.

Preteens in Zimbabwe go through certain customs as they prepare to become teenagers. Girls learn how to knit, make pottery, cook, and fetch water (if they live out in the country). Kiki says she and her friends grew up differently from North American girls. In Zimbabwe, they have a calmer lifestyle and are taught never to talk back to any adult. In fact, to show respect, they kneel down when an adult speaks to them.

The games the girls play in Zimbabwe usually don't cost a penny! They play-act being parents and having tea parties (called *mahumbwe*). They also cook small meals like they see their parents do, build little homes, and make dolls from scrap pieces of cloth and grocery bags.

Most of the preteens go to church. Kiki grew up in a Christian home and participated in different church activities, especially MV, which stands for "Missionary Volunteers." At MV, Kiki enjoyed knitting, cooking, and being a "Brownie"—she and other kids would go out and help people in the neighborhood and then ask them to sign their little book. Each time she helped five people, Kiki got another badge. She also competed in memorizing verses; when she was ten years old, she already knew fifty verses by heart! Kiki asked Jesus into her heart when she was only eight. She had seen how much God had done for her family, and she knew she could trust him with her whole life.

In most parts of Zimbabwe, young Christian people aren't made fun of for their beliefs because a lot of their friends are also Christians. But these days, many people are finding it hard to live as a Christian because of poverty. When it doesn't rain for a long time, sometimes there is absolutely no food to cook for the next day. Some families start to lose faith because of these conditions. Though others didn't always trust God, Kiki believed he would always take care of her—and he has!

14:14 **Son of Man** *"Son of Man" is a name Jesus called himself.*    14:14 **sickle** *A farming tool with a curved blade. It was used to harvest grain.*

great winepress of God's anger. [20]They were trampled in the winepress outside the city, and blood flowed out of the winepress as high as horses' bridles for a distance of about one hundred eighty miles.

## The Last Troubles

**15** Then I saw another wonder in heaven that was great and amazing. There were seven angels bringing seven disasters. These are the last disasters, because after them, God's anger is finished.

[2]I saw what looked like a sea of glass mixed with fire. All of those who had won the victory over the beast and his idol and over the number of his name were standing by the sea of glass. They had harps that God had given them. [3]They sang the song of Moses, the servant of God, and the song of the Lamb:

"You do great and wonderful things,
                              *Psalm 111:2*
    Lord God Almighty.        *Amos 3:13*
Everything the Lord does is right and
        true,                 *Psalm 145:17*
    King of the nations."[n]
[4]Everyone will respect you, Lord,
                              *Jeremiah 10:7*
    and will honor you.
Only you are holy.
All the nations will come
    and worship you,    *Psalm 86:9–10*
because the right things you have
        done
    are now made known."
                          *Deuteronomy 32:4*

[5]After this I saw that the temple (the Tent of the Agreement) in heaven was opened. [6]And the seven angels bringing the seven disasters came out of the temple. They were dressed in clean, shining linen and wore golden bands tied around their chests. [7]Then one of the four living creatures gave to the seven angels seven golden bowls filled with the anger of God, who lives forever and ever. [8]The temple was filled with smoke from the glory and the power of God, and no one could enter the temple until the seven disasters of the seven angels were finished.

## ALL THE NATIONS WILL COME AND WORSHIP YOU, . . .

## The Bowls of God's Anger

**16** Then I heard a loud voice from the temple saying to the seven angels, "Go and pour out the seven bowls of God's anger on the earth."

[2]The first angel left and poured out his bowl on the land. Then ugly and painful sores came upon all those who had the mark of the beast and who worshiped his idol.

[3]The second angel poured out his bowl on the sea, and it became blood like that of a dead man, and every living thing in the sea died.

[4]The third angel poured out his bowl on the rivers and the springs of water, and they became blood. [5]Then I heard the angel of the waters saying:

"Holy One, you are the One who is
        and who was.
    You are right to decide to punish
        these evil people.
[6]They have poured out the blood of
    your holy people and your
        prophets.
    So now you have given them blood
        to drink as they deserve."

[7]And I heard a voice coming from the altar saying:

"Yes, Lord God Almighty,
    the way you punish evil people is
        right and fair."

[8]The fourth angel poured out his bowl on the sun, and he was given power to burn the people with fire. [9]They were burned by the great heat, and they cursed the name of God, who had control over these disasters. But the people refused to change their hearts and lives and give glory to God.

[10]The fifth angel poured out his bowl on the throne of the beast, and darkness covered its kingdom. People gnawed their tongues because of the pain. [11]They also cursed the God of heaven because of their pain and the sores they had, but they refused to change their hearts and turn away from the evil things they did.

[12]The sixth angel poured out his bowl on the great river Euphrates so that the water in the river was dried up to prepare the way for the kings from the east to come. [13]Then I saw three evil spirits that looked like frogs coming out of the mouth of the dragon, out of the mouth of the beast, and out of the mouth of the false

## Looking Ahead

### CHANGING BODY

Your body is always changing and growing—and over the next several years you'll notice it more! Growing up is nothing to worry about. Your body will develop at just the right pace; you just need good food, rest, and exercise. As your body changes, you might feel uncomfortable by the attention it causes or how you begin to look. You can't prevent your body from changing, and it's nothing to feel awkward about. It's actually exciting! If you have questions about your changing body, talk to your mom or a trusted adult woman. And remember what 1 Peter 3:3–4 says: real beauty comes from within!

prophet. [14]These evil spirits are the spirits of demons, which have power to do miracles. They go out to the kings of the whole world to gather them together for the battle on the great day of God Almighty.

[15]"Listen! I will come as a thief comes! Blessed are those who stay awake and keep their clothes on so that they will not walk around naked and have people see their shame."

[16]Then the evil spirits gathered the kings together to the place that is called Armageddon in the Hebrew language.

[17]The seventh angel poured out his bowl into the air. Then a loud voice came out of the temple from the throne, saying, "It is finished!" [18]Then there were flashes of lightning, noises, thunder, and a big earthquake—the worst earthquake that has ever happened since people have been on earth. [19]The great city split into three parts, and the cities of the nations were destroyed. And God remembered the sins of Babylon the Great, so he gave that city the cup filled with the

**15:3 King . . . nations** Some Greek copies read "King of the ages."

## god's promises

### Revelation 21:4

When you cry for a long time, you might get a headache, a runny nose, hiccups, or even a sore tummy. Not only does your heart hurt, but even your body ends up hurting. Sometimes, if you're really upset, it might feel like you'll never stop crying. The only thing that makes it worse is crying when you're all alone. If you have a parent or friend holding you and wiping away your tears, it sometimes helps.

Can you imagine never crying? There is a place where people won't cry out of sadness! It's not because they don't have feelings, but because, in this place, no one dies. No one has sad things happen to them. No one experiences any pain. It's not at all like the world we live in now and nowhere *near* it either. But you can go there one day!

God has promised that anyone who accepts his free gift of salvation—by believing in Jesus and confessing her sins—will one day live in this special place. When you become a Christian, *you* can look forward to living forever in heaven—where you will never cry again! And God himself will "wipe away every tear" from your eyes when you get there (Revelation 21:4)!

**There is a place where people won't cry!**

wine of his terrible anger. ²⁰Then every island ran away, and mountains disappeared. ²¹Giant hailstones, each weighing about a hundred pounds, fell from the sky upon people. People cursed God for the disaster of the hail, because this disaster was so terrible.

### The Woman on the Animal

**17** Then one of the seven angels who had the seven bowls came and spoke to me. He said, "Come, and I will show you the punishment that will be given to the great prostitute, the one sitting over many waters. ²The kings of the earth sinned sexually with her, and the people of the earth became drunk from the wine of her sexual sin."

³Then the angel carried me away by the Spirit to the desert. There I saw a woman sitting on a red beast. It was covered with names against God written on it, and it had seven heads and ten horns. ⁴The woman was dressed in purple and red and was shining with the gold, precious jewels, and pearls she was wearing. She had a golden cup in her hand, a cup filled with evil things and the uncleanness of her sexual sin. ⁵On her forehead a title was written that was secret. This is what was written:

THE GREAT BABYLON
MOTHER OF PROSTITUTES
AND OF THE EVIL THINGS OF THE EARTH

⁶Then I saw that the woman was drunk with the blood of God's holy people and with the blood of those who were killed because of their faith in Jesus.

When I saw the woman, I was very amazed. ⁷Then the angel said to me, "Why are you amazed? I will tell you the secret of this woman and the beast she rides—the one with seven heads and ten horns. ⁸The beast you saw was once alive but is not alive now. But soon it will come up out of the bottomless pit and go away to be destroyed. There are people who live on earth whose names have not been written in the book of life since the beginning of the world. They will be amazed when they see the beast, because he was once alive, is not alive now, but will come again.

⁹"You need a wise mind to understand this. The seven heads on the beast are seven mountains where the woman sits. ¹⁰And they are seven kings. Five of the kings have already been destroyed, one of the kings lives now, and another has not yet come. When he comes, he must stay a short time. ¹¹The beast that was once alive, but is not alive now, is also an eighth king. He belongs to the first seven kings, and he will go away to be destroyed.

¹²"The ten horns you saw are ten kings who have not yet begun to rule, but they will receive power to rule with the beast for one hour. ¹³All ten of these kings have the same purpose, and they will give their power and authority to the beast. ¹⁴They will make war against the Lamb, but the Lamb will defeat them, because he is Lord of lords and King of kings. He will defeat them with his called, chosen, and faithful followers."

¹⁵Then the angel said to me, "The waters that you saw, where the prostitute sits, are peoples, races, nations, and languages. ¹⁶The ten horns and the beast you saw will hate the prostitute. They will

# December

← start here

**1**

**2** Pray for a person of influence: Today is singer Britney Spears's birthday.

**3** Design your own Christmas wrapping paper.

**4**

**5** Pray for a person of influence: Today is actor Frankie Muniz's birthday.

**6**

**7** Pray for a person of influence: Today is singer Aaron Carter's birthday.

**8** Wear something red or green.

**9**

**10** Pray for a person of influence: Today is actress Raven Symoné's birthday.

**11** Give your body a break today! Go to bed half an hour early.

**12**

**13**

**14** Write down 5 ideas for great Christmas gifts that can't be bought with money.

**15** Read Galatians 6:2. Then find a special way to help someone today.

**16** Use your secret code to write your friends' Christmas cards!

**17**

**18** Pray for a person of influence: Today is singer Christina Aguilera's birthday.

**19**

**20**

**21** Make hot chocolate for your whole family tonight.

**22** Put on some Christmas music and sing along!

**23**

**24**

**25** Christmas Day—Before opening presents, talk to Jesus and thank him for all he's done for you.

**26**

**27**

**28** Clean up the kitchen after dinner so your family can relax.

**29**

**30** Look up the word "blossom." Ask God to help you blossom into who he wants you to be next year!

Ticker says, "Make a list!"

take everything she has and leave her naked. They will eat her body and burn her with fire. [17]God made the ten horns want to carry out his purpose by agreeing to give the beast their power to rule, until what God has said comes about. [18]The woman you saw is the great city that rules over the kings of the earth."

## Babylon Is Destroyed

**18** After the vision of these things, I saw another angel coming down from heaven. This angel had great power, and his glory made the earth bright. [2]He shouted in a powerful voice:

"Ruined, ruined is the great city of
   Babylon!
She has become a home for
   demons
and a prison for every evil spirit,
   and a prison for every unclean bird
      and unclean beast.
[3]She has been ruined, because all the
      peoples of the earth
   have drunk the wine of the desire
      of her sexual sin.
She has been ruined also because
      the kings of the earth
   have sinned sexually with her,
and the merchants of the earth
   have grown rich from the great
      wealth of her luxury."
[4]Then I heard another voice from
   heaven saying:

"Come out of that city, my people,
   so that you will not share in her
      sins,
   so that you will not receive the
      disasters that will come to her.
[5]Her sins have piled up as high as the
      sky,
   and God has not forgotten the
      wrongs she has done.
[6]Give that city the same as she gave to
      others.
   Pay her back twice as much as she
      did.
Prepare wine for her that is twice as
      strong
   as the wine she prepared for
      others.
[7]She gave herself much glory and rich
      living.
   Give her that much suffering and
      sadness.
She says to herself, 'I am a queen
      sitting on my throne.
   I am not a widow; I will never be
      sad.'
[8]So these disasters will come to her in
      one day:
   death, and crying, and great
      hunger,
and she will be destroyed by fire,
   because the Lord God who judges
      her is powerful."
[9]The kings of the earth who sinned sexually with her and shared her wealth will see the smoke from her burning. Then they will cry and be sad because of her

death. [10]They will be afraid of her suffering and stand far away and say:

"Terrible! How terrible for you, great
      city,
   powerful city of Babylon,
because your punishment has come in
      one hour!"
[11]And the merchants of the earth will cry and be sad about her, because now there is no one to buy their cargoes— [12]cargoes of gold, silver, jewels, pearls, fine linen, purple cloth, silk, red cloth; all kinds of citron wood and all kinds of things made from ivory, expensive wood, bronze, iron, and marble; [13]cinnamon, spice, incense, myrrh, frankincense, wine, olive oil, fine flour, wheat, cattle, sheep, horses, carriages, slaves, and human lives.

[14]The merchants will say,
"Babylon, the good things you wanted
      are gone from you.
All your rich and fancy things have
      disappeared.
   You will never have them again."
[15]The merchants who became rich from selling to her will be afraid of her suffering and will stand far away. They will cry and be sad [16]and say:

"Terrible! How terrible for the great
      city!
   She was dressed in fine linen,
      purple and red cloth,
   and she was shining with gold,
      precious jewels, and pearls!
[17]All these riches have been destroyed
      in one hour!"

# Relationships

**D**id you know that Jesus' own brothers didn't believe in him until after his death and resurrection? They gave him a hard time about doing God's work and even told him they thought he was crazy! If you have family members who don't share your faith in Jesus, you might know how that feels. Like Jesus, don't let your family keep you from serving God—and don't give up on them either. Keep praying and showing them God's love. Be yourself and let Jesus shine through you. You can also count on your church family for spiritual help.

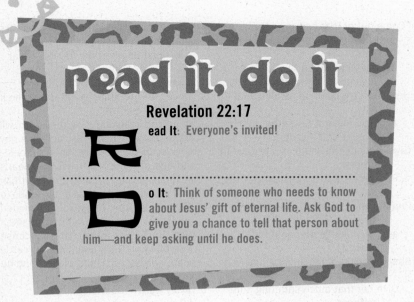

**read it, do it**

**Revelation 22:17**

**R**ead It: Everyone's invited!

**D**o It: Think of someone who needs to know about Jesus' gift of eternal life. Ask God to give you a chance to tell that person about him—and keep asking until he does.

Every sea captain, every passenger, the sailors, and all those who earn their living from the sea stood far away from Babylon. [18]As they saw the smoke from her burning, they cried out loudly, "There was never a city like this great city!" [19]And they threw dust on their heads and cried out, weeping and being sad. They said:

"Terrible! How terrible for the great city!

All the people who had ships on the sea
    became rich because of her wealth!
But she has been destroyed in one hour!"

[20]Be happy because of this, heaven!
    Be happy, God's holy people and apostles and prophets!
God has punished her because of what she did to you."

[21]Then a powerful angel picked up a large stone, like one used for grinding grain, and threw it into the sea. He said:

"In the same way, the great city of Babylon will be thrown down,
    and it will never be found again.
[22]The music of people playing harps
    and other instruments, flutes, and trumpets,
    will never be heard in you again.
No workman doing any job
    will ever be found in you again.
The sound of grinding grain
    will never be heard in you again.
[23]The light of a lamp
    will never shine in you again,

and the voices of a bridegroom and bride
    will never be heard in you again.
Your merchants were the world's great people,
    and all the nations were tricked by your magic.
[24]You are guilty of the death of the prophets and God's holy people
    and all who have been killed on earth."

## People in Heaven Praise God

**19** After this vision and announcement I heard what sounded like a great many people in heaven saying:

"Hallelujah![n]
Salvation, glory, and power belong to our God,
[2]    because his judgments are true and right.
He has punished the prostitute
    who made the earth evil with her sexual sin.
He has paid her back for the death of his servants."

[3]Again they said:

"Hallelujah!
She is burning, and her smoke will rise forever and ever."

[4]Then the twenty-four elders and the four living creatures bowed down and worshiped God, who sits on the throne. They said:

"Amen, Hallelujah!"

[5]Then a voice came from the throne, saying:

"Praise our God, all you who serve him
    and all you who honor him, both small and great!"

[6]Then I heard what sounded like a great many people, like the noise of flooding water, and like the noise of loud thunder. The people were saying:

"Hallelujah!
    Our Lord God, the Almighty, rules.
[7]Let us rejoice and be happy
    and give God glory,
because the wedding of the Lamb has come,
    and the Lamb's bride has made herself ready.
[8]Fine linen, bright and clean, was given to her to wear."

(The fine linen means the good things done by God's holy people.)

[9]And the angel said to me, "Write this: Blessed are those who have been invited to the wedding meal of the Lamb!" And the angel said, "These are the true words of God."

[10]Then I bowed down at the angel's feet to worship him, but he said to me, "Do not worship me! I am a servant like you and your brothers and sisters who have the message of Jesus. Worship God, because the message about Jesus is the spirit that gives all prophecy."

## The Rider on the White Horse

[11]Then I saw heaven opened, and there before me was a white horse. The rider on the horse is called Faithful and True, and he is right when he judges and makes war. [12]His eyes are like burning fire, and on his head are many crowns. He has a name written on him, which no one but himself knows. [13]He is dressed in a robe dipped in blood, and his name is the Word of God. [14]The armies of heaven, dressed in fine linen, white and clean, were following him on white horses. [15]Out of the rider's mouth comes a sharp sword that he will use to defeat the nations, and he will rule them with a rod of iron. He will crush out the wine in the winepress of the terrible anger of God the Almighty. [16]On his robe and on his upper leg was written this name: KING OF KINGS AND LORD OF LORDS.

[17]Then I saw an angel standing in the sun, and he called with a loud voice to all

---

**19:1 Hallelujah** This means "praise God!"

# Q&A

**Q** The Bible is a really old book. Is it still useful for me today?

**A** As you study the Bible more and more, you will be surprised to see how many verses sound like they were written just a few months ago! And even the stories in the Old Testament show us that people haven't changed very much since thousands of years ago. We can learn lessons from their mistakes and also from their dedication to God (2 Timothy 3:16–17; 1 Corinthians 10:6). Ask God to help you as you read the Bible. He will show you things that fit perfectly in your life today!

the birds flying in the sky: "Come and gather together for the great feast of God [18]so that you can eat the bodies of kings, generals, mighty people, horses and their riders, and the bodies of all people—free, slave, small, and great."

[19]Then I saw the beast and the kings of the earth. Their armies were gathered together to make war against the rider on the horse and his army. [20]But the beast was captured and with him the false prophet who did the miracles for the beast. The false prophet had used these miracles to trick those who had the mark of the beast and worshiped his idol. The false prophet and the beast were thrown alive into the lake of fire that burns with sulfur. [21]And their armies were killed with the sword that came out of the mouth of the rider on the horse, and all the birds ate the bodies until they were full.

## The Thousand Years

**20** I saw an angel coming down from heaven. He had the key to the bottomless pit and a large chain in his hand. [2]The angel grabbed the dragon, that old snake who is the devil and Satan, and tied him up for a thousand years. [3]Then he threw him into the bottomless pit, closed it, and locked it over him. The angel did this so he could not trick the people of the earth anymore until the thousand years were ended. After a thousand years he must be set free for a short time.

[4]Then I saw some thrones and people sitting on them who had been given the power to judge. And I saw the souls of those who had been killed because they were faithful to the message of Jesus and the message from God. They had not worshiped the beast or his idol, and they had not received the mark of the beast on their foreheads or on their hands. They came back to life and ruled with Christ for a thousand years. [5](The others that were dead did not live again until the thousand years were ended.) This is the first raising of the dead. [6]Blessed and holy are those who share in this first raising of the dead. The second death has no power over them. They will be priests for God and for Christ and will rule with him for a thousand years.

[7]When the thousand years are over, Satan will be set free from his prison. [8]Then he will go out to trick the nations in all the earth—Gog and Magog—to gather them for battle. There are so many people they will be like sand on the seashore. [9]And Satan's army marched across the earth and gathered around the camp of God's people and the city God loves. But fire came down from heaven and burned them up. [10]And Satan, who tricked them, was thrown into the lake of burning sulfur with the beast and the false prophet. There they will be punished day and night forever and ever.

## People of the World Are Judged

[11]Then I saw a great white throne and the One who was sitting on it. Earth and sky ran away from him and disappeared. [12]And I saw the dead, great and small, standing before the throne. Then books were opened, and the book of life was opened. The dead were judged by what they had done, which was written in the books. [13]The sea gave up the dead who were in it, and Death and Hades[n] gave up the dead who were in them. Each person was judged by what he had done. [14]And Death and Hades were thrown into the lake of fire. The lake of fire is the second death. [15]And anyone whose name was not found written in the book of life was thrown into the lake of fire.

## The New Jerusalem

**21** Then I saw a new heaven and a new earth. The first heaven and the first earth had disappeared, and there was no sea anymore. [2]And I saw the holy city, the new Jerusalem,[n] coming down out of heaven from God. It was prepared like a bride dressed for her husband. [3]And I heard a loud voice from the throne, saying, "Now God's presence is with people, and he will live with them, and they will be his people. God himself will be with them and will be their God.[n] [4]He will wipe away every tear from their eyes, and there will be no more death, sadness, crying, or pain, because all the old ways are gone."

[5]The One who was sitting on the throne said, "Look! I am making everything new!" Then he said, "Write this, because these words are true and can be trusted."

[6]The One on the throne said to me, "It is finished. I am the Alpha and the Omega,[n] the Beginning and the End. I will give free water from the spring of the water of life to anyone who is thirsty. [7]Those who win the victory will receive this, and I will be their God, and they will be my children. [8]But cowards, those who refuse to believe, who do evil things, who kill, who sin sexually, who do evil magic, who worship idols, and who tell lies—all these will have a place in

## speakout!

**Q** If you could change one thing in this world, what would it be?

**A** I would get rid of the devil so nothing bad will happen again. —Alisha, 12

---

**20:13 Hades** *The place of the dead.* **21:2 new Jerusalem** *The spiritual city where God's people live with him.* **21:3 and . . . God** *Some Greek copies do not have this phrase.* **21:6 Alpha and the Omega** *The first and last letters of the Greek alphabet. This means "the beginning and the end."*

the lake of burning sulfur. This is the second death."

[9]Then one of the seven angels who had the seven bowls full of the seven last troubles came to me, saying, "Come with me, and I will show you the bride, the wife of the Lamb." [10]And the angel carried me away by the Spirit to a very large and high mountain. He showed me the holy city, Jerusalem, coming down out of heaven from God. [11]It was shining with the glory of God and was bright like a very expensive jewel, like a jasper, clear as crystal. [12]The city had a great high wall with twelve gates with twelve angels at the gates, and on each gate was written the name of one of the twelve tribes of Israel. [13]There were three gates on the east, three on the north, three on the south, and three on the west. [14]The walls of the city were built on twelve foundation stones, and on the stones were written the names of the twelve apostles of the Lamb.

[15]The angel who talked with me had a measuring rod made of gold to measure the city, its gates, and its wall. [16]The city was built in a square, and its length was equal to its width. The angel measured the city with the rod. The city was 1,500 miles long, 1,500 miles wide, and 1,500 miles high. [17]The angel also measured the wall. It was 216 feet high, by human measurements, which the angel was using. [18]The wall was made of jasper, and the city was made of pure gold, as pure as glass. [19]The foundation stones of the city walls were decorated with every kind of jewel. The first foundation was jasper, the second was sapphire, the third was chalcedony, the fourth was emerald, [20]the fifth was onyx, the sixth was carnelian, the seventh was chrysolite, the eighth was beryl, the ninth was topaz, the tenth was chrysoprase, the eleventh was jacinth, and the twelfth was amethyst. [21]The twelve gates were twelve pearls, each gate having been made from a single pearl. And the street of the city was made of pure gold as clear as glass.

[22]I did not see a temple in the city, because the Lord God Almighty and the Lamb are the city's temple. [23]The city does not need the sun or the moon to shine on it, because the glory of God is its light, and the Lamb is the city's lamp. [24]By its light the people of the world will walk, and the kings of the earth will bring their glory into it. [25]The city's gates will never be shut on any day, because there is no night there. [26]The glory and the honor of the nations will be brought into it. [27]Nothing unclean and no one who does shameful things or tells lies will ever go into it. Only those whose names are written in the Lamb's book of life will enter the city.

## 22

Then the angel showed me the river of the water of life. It was shining like crystal and was flowing from the throne of God and of the Lamb [2]down the middle of the street of the city. The tree of life was on each side of the river. It produces fruit twelve times a year, once each month. The leaves of the tree are for the healing of all the nations. [3]Nothing that God judges guilty will be in that city. The throne of God and of the Lamb will be there, and God's servants will worship him. [4]They will see his face, and his name will be written on their foreheads. [5]There will never be night again. They will not need the light of a lamp or the light of the sun, because the Lord God will give them light. And they will rule as kings forever and ever.

[6]The angel said to me, "These words can be trusted and are true." The Lord, the God of the spirits of the prophets, sent his angel to show his servants the things that must happen soon.

[7]"Listen! I am coming soon! Blessed is the one who obeys the words of prophecy in this book."

[8]I, John, am the one who heard and saw these things. When I heard and saw them, I bowed down to worship at the feet of the angel who showed these things to me. [9]But the angel said to me, "Do not worship me! I am a servant like you, your brothers the prophets, and all those who obey the words in this book. Worship God!"

[10]Then the angel told me, "Do not keep secret the words of prophecy in this book, because the time is near for all this to happen. [11]Let whoever is doing evil continue to do evil. Let whoever is unclean continue to be unclean. Let whoever is doing right continue to do right. Let whoever is holy continue to be holy."

[12]"Listen! I am coming soon! I will bring my reward with me, and I will repay each one of you for what you have done. [13]I am

# Q & A

**Q** What is heaven like?

**A** No one can give you a perfect description of heaven because it is greater than the most amazing thing you can imagine! In Revelation 21, we read about the apostle John's vision of heaven, but it's still hard to imagine what it will really look like. What we *can* be sure of is that there's no sin, death, pain or crying there. Best of all, God is in heaven!

the Alpha and the Omega,[n] the First and the Last, the Beginning and the End.

[14]"Blessed are those who wash their robes[n] so that they will receive the right to eat the fruit from the tree of life and may go through the gates into the city. [15]Outside the city are the evil people, those who do evil magic, who sin sexually, who murder, who worship idols, and who love lies and tell lies.

[16]"I, Jesus, have sent my angel to tell you these things for the churches. I am the descendant from the family of David, and I am the bright morning star."

[17]The Spirit and the bride say, "Come!" Let the one who hears this say, "Come!" Let whoever is thirsty come; whoever wishes may have the water of life as a free gift.

[18]I warn everyone who hears the words of the prophecy of this book: If anyone adds anything to these words, God will add to that person the disasters written about in this book. [19]And if anyone takes away from the words of this book of prophecy, God will take away that one's share of the tree of life and of the holy city, which are written about in this book.

[20]Jesus, the One who says these things are true, says, "Yes, I am coming soon."

Amen. Come, Lord Jesus!

[21]The grace of the Lord Jesus be with all. Amen.

**22:13 Alpha and the Omega** *The first and last letters of the Greek alphabet. This means "the beginning and the end."* **22:14 wash their robes** *This means they believed and obeyed Jesus so that their sins could be forgiven by Christ's blood. The "washing" may refer to baptism (Acts 22:16).*

# 30 Days with Jesus

1. John 1:1–51
2. Luke 2:1–52
3. Mark 1:1–11
4. Luke 4:1–44
5. John 3:1–36
6. Luke 5:1–39
7. John 4:1–54
8. Luke 6:1–49
9. Luke 7:1–50
10. Luke 8:1–56
11. Mark 8:1–38
12. Luke 10:1–42
13. Matthew 5:1–48
14. Matthew 6:1–34
15. Matthew 7:1–29
16. Luke 14:1–35
17. Luke 15:1–32
18. Luke 16:1–31
19. John 8:1–59
20. Luke 17:1–37
21. Luke 18:1–43
22. John 9:1–41
23. Luke 19:1–48
24. Luke 20:1–47
25. John 10:1–42
26. John 11:1–57
27. Mark 13:1–37
28. Luke 22:1–71
29. Matthew 27:1–66
30. Luke 24:1–53

# The Miracles of Christ

| Miracle | Matthew | Mark | Luke | John |
|---|---|---|---|---|
| 1. Healing a Man with Skin Disease | 8:2 | 1:40 | 5:12 | |
| 2. Healing an Army Officer's Servant (of paralysis) | 8:5 | | | 7:1 |
| 3. Healing Peter's Mother-in-law | 8:14 | 1:30 | 4:38 | |
| 4. Healing the Sick at Evening | 8:16 | 1:32 | 4:40 | |
| 5. Calming the Storm | 8:23 | 4:35 | 8:22 | |
| 6. Demons Entering a Herd of Pigs | 8:28 | 5:1 | 8:26 | |
| 7. Healing a Paralyzed Man | 9:2 | 2:3 | 5:18 | |
| 8. Raising the Synagogue Leader's Daughter | 9:18, 23 | 5:22, 35 | 8:40, 49 | |
| 9. Healing the Hemorrhaging Woman | 9:20 | 5:25 | 8:43 | |
| 10. Healing Two Blind Men | 9:27 | | | |
| 11. Curing a Demon-possessed, Mute Man | 9:32 | | | |
| 12. Healing a Man's Crippled Hand | 12:9 | 3:1 | 6:6 | |
| 13. Curing a Demon-possessed, Blind, and Mute Man | 12:22 | | 11:14 | |
| 14. Feeding the Five Thousand | 14:13 | 6:30 | 9:10 | 6:1 |
| 15. Walking on the Lake | 14:25 | 6:48 | | 6:19 |
| 16. Healing the Non-Jewish Woman's Daughter | 15:21 | 7:24 | | |
| 17. Feeding the Four Thousand | 15:32 | 8:1 | | |
| 18. Healing the Epileptic Boy | 17:14 | 9:17 | 9:38 | |
| 19. Temple Tax in the Fish's Mouth | 17:24 | | | |
| 20. Healing Two Blind Men | 20:30 | 10:46 | 18:35 | |
| 21. Drying Up the Fig Tree | 21:18 | 11:12 | | |
| 22. Casting Out an Evil Spirit | | 1:23 | 4:33 | |
| 23. Healing a Deaf and Dumb Man | | 7:31 | | |
| 24. Healing a Blind Man at Bethsaida | | 8:22 | | |
| 25. Escape from the Hostile Multitude | | | 4:30 | |
| 26. Catch of Fish | | | 5:1 | |
| 27. Raising of a Widow's Son at Nain | | | 7:11 | |
| 28. Healing the Infirm, Crippled Woman | | | 13:11 | |
| 29. Healing the Man with Dropsy | | | 14:1 | |
| 30. Cleansing the Ten Men with Skin Disease | | | 17:11 | |
| 31. Restoring a Servant's Ear | | | 22:51 | |
| 32. Turning Water into Wine | | | | 2:1 |
| 33. Healing the Officer's Son | | | | 4:46 |
| 34. Healing a Sick Man at Bethzatha | | | | 5:1 |
| 35. Healing a Man Born Blind | | | | 9:1 |
| 36. Raising of Lazarus | | | | 11:43 |
| 37. Second Catch of Fish | | | | 21:1 |

# Bible
## Memory Cards

Cut along the lines below to create your own Bible flashcards. Then tuck them in your backpack or purse and read over them any time you get a few minutes of down time. Once you memorize them, you'll find God's words coming to your mind just when you need them!

**Luke 6:31**

Do to others what you would want them to do to you.

**John 3:16**

God loved the world so much that he gave his one and only Son so that whoever believes in him may not be lost, but have eternal life.

**Romans 5:8**

But God shows his great love for us in this way: Christ died for us while we were still sinners.

**1 Corinthians 15:33**

Do not be fooled: "Bad friends will ruin good habits."

**Ephesians 4:2**

Always be humble, gentle, and patient, accepting each other in love.

**Ephesians 6:1**

Children, obey your parents as the Lord wants, because this is the right thing to do.

**Philippians 2:14**

Do everything without complaining or arguing.

**Colossians 3:23**

In all the work you are doing, work the best you can. Work as if you were doing it for the Lord, not for people.

**1 Thessalonians 5:16–18**

Always be joyful. Pray continually, and give thanks whatever happens. That is what God wants for you in Christ Jesus.

**1 Peter 3:4**

Your beauty should come from within you— the beauty of a gentle and quiet spirit that will never be destroyed and is very precious to God.